Introduction

Welcome to the second edition of *Tourist Attractions & Events of the World*, which has been fully revised and updated since last year. It is the only reference work of its kind to cover the world's most important tourist attractions. This book contains practical and descriptive information on 400 tourist attractions, covering well-known landmarks like the *Sydney Opera House* and *Universal Studios Hollywood*, alongside lesser-known, though equally dramatic, attractions such as the ancient city of *Bagan* in Myanmar. The title is designed to complement other travel guides produced by Columbus, such as the *World Travel Guide*, *Columbus City Guide – Europe*, the *World Travel Atlas* and the *World Airport Guide*.

This year, the guide is organised by country and its respective individual attractions are arranged alphabetically within. Each entry contains: a detailed description of the attraction, describing its history and highlights; a contact address; transportation information; opening times; the price of admission; UNESCO listing; facilities including car parks, shops, restaurants and disabled access.

Individual attraction entries can be found either by locating the country in which the attraction is found, or by consulting the alphabetical index at the back of the book. Attractions are listed in the native language, with the English translation in brackets. Thus, *Prague Castle* in the Czech Republic is listed as Prazsky Hrad (Prague Castle), and *Angel Falls* in Venezuela are listed as Salto Ángel (Angel Falls).

It must be stressed that the attraction entries included in this book are only a selection of the thousands of tourist attractions around the world. Entries have been chosen to reflect a number of different criteria, and those that appear are not necessarily the most popular attractions in their respective countries. This year, the selection has been expanded to include natural attractions such as *Copacabana Beach* and theme parks such as *Alton Towers*. Columbus Travel Guides believes that the attractions listed are representative of many of the world's unique places and thus demonstrate some of the motivating factors encouraging today's generation of travellers.

Top cultural and sporting events in major cities around the world are also included in this edition of the guide. We have listed 150 top events and festivals, such as New Orleans' *Mardi Gras* and Edinburgh's *Hogmanay*. The list is by no means inclusive of all annual events which take place around the world; it is nonetheless a comprehensive list of major events which take place on an annual basis in some of today's most important tourist destinations.

Columbus Travel Guides would like to thank the many tourist offices, embassies, high commissions, consulates, chambers of commerce and public relations departments that assisted in the preparation of this edition. If there is anything that you would like to see expanded, clarified or included for the first time, or if you come across any information that is no longer accurate, please write to:

The Editors
Tourist Attractions & Events of the World
Columbus Travel Guides
Jordan House
47 Brunswick Place
London N1 6EB, UK
Tel: +44 (020) 7608 6684 *or* 7608 6559.
Fax: +44 (020) 7608 6593.
E-mail: rblakeborough@columbus-group.co.uk *or*
khenders@columbus-group.co.uk

TOURIST ATTRACTIONS & EVENTS of the WORLD

ISBN: 1-902221-55-9

Columbus Publishing Limited
Jordan House
47 Brunswick Place
London N1 6EB, UK
Tel: (020) 7608 6666
Fax: (020) 7608 6569
E-mail: booksales@columbus-group.co.uk

Editorial Director:	Kate Meere
Deputy to the Editorial Director:	Charlotte Evans
Editors:	Ruth Blakeborough, Karen Henderson
Picture Researcher:	Victoria Jennison
Researcher:	Alexandra Müller
Cartographer:	David Burles
Indexer:	Angie Hipkin
Publisher:	Pete Korniczky

Designed & produced by Space Design and Production Services, London EC2A.
Reprographics by Kingswood Steele, London EC2A.
Printed & bound by Stephens & George, Wales.

The publishers would like to thank all the organisations and individuals who have assisted in the preparation of this publication. Whilst every effort is made by the publishers to ensure the accuracy of the information contained in this edition of Tourist Attractions & Events of the World, the publishers can accept no responsibility for any loss occasioned to any person acting or refraining from acting as a result of the material contained in this publication, nor liability for any financial or other agreements which may be entered into with any organisations or individuals listed in the text.

CONTENTS

Argentina

1	Cataratas del Iguazú (Iguazú Falls)
2	Parque Nacional Los Glaciares (Los Glaciares National Park)
3	Parque Nacional Nahuel Huapi (Nahuel Huapi National Park)

Tourist Information

Secretaría de Turismo de la Nación (National Tourist Board)
Calle Suipacha 1111, 20°, 1368 Buenos Aires, Argentina
Tel: (011) 4312 5621. Fax: (011) 4313 6834.
Website: www.sectur.gov.ar/homepage.htm

Embassy of the Argentine Republic
65 Brooke Street, London W1Y 4AH, UK
Tel: (020) 7318 1200. Fax: (020) 7318 1301.
E-mail: seruni@mrecic.gov.ar
Website: www.argentine-embassy-uk.org

Cataratas del Iguazú (Iguazú Falls)

The *Iguazú Falls* fittingly receive their name from the Guarani Indian word meaning 'great waters'. Surrounded by the virgin jungle of *Iguazú National Park*, home to 2000 species of flora and 400 species of bird (including parrots and toucans), the *Paraná River* divides into 275 separate falls. The highest, the *Garganta del Diabolo* (Devil's Throat) reaches 70m (230ft), which is one and a half times the height of the Niagara Falls. Besides taking in the stunning view from a series of catwalks, visitors may enjoy kayaking, canoeing and other watersports. Nearby historic Jesuit Mission ruins, such as those at *San Ignacio Miní*, are also popular.

Contact Address

Iguazú National Park, Victoria Aguirre Street 66, 3379 Puerto Iguazú, Province Misiones, Argentina
Tel: (037) 5742 0722. Fax: (037) 5742 0382.
E-mail: bniguacu@entreguacu.com

Transportation

Air: Ministro Pistarini Airport (Buenos Aires). **Road:** Coach: Services from Buenos Aires.

Opening Times

Daily 0800-1900.

Admission Fees

US$5 (adult), US$2.50 (child under 12).

Parque Nacional Los Glaciares (Los Glaciares National Park)

Los Glaciares National Park is the second largest in Argentina and runs for 170km (106 miles) along the border with Chile; it is characterised by rugged mountains and clear lakes. Some 40 per cent of the Park's 6600 sq kilometres (2548 sq miles) is covered by vast ice fields that hold 47 major glaciers. The largest glacier is *Upsala*, but the most popular is the mighty *Moreno* glacier, where massive chunks of ice shear off and fall into *Lago Argentino*, the largest lake in Argentina, to form icebergs. Visitors can view the advancing *Moreno* glacier from catwalks and platforms.

Contact Address

Parque Nacional Los Glaciares, Avenida Libertador 1302, 9405 Calafate, Santa Cruz, Argentina
Tel: (02) 491 005 *or* 491 755 *or* 491 026.
E-mail: apnglaciares@cotecal.com.ar
Website: www.parquesnacionales.gov.ar

Transportation

Air: Ministro Pistarini Airport (Buenos Aires) or Calafate International Airport. **Road:** Coach: Services to the bus terminal on Avenida Julia Roca (from El Calafate). Car: Route 40 (from Río Gallegos).

Opening Times

Daily 0800-2000.

Admission Fees

US$5 (per person), US$3 (per car).

Parque Nacional Nahuel Huapi (Nahuel Huapi National Park)

Occupying 710,000 hectares (1,754,386 acres), *Nahuel Huapi National Park* is something like the Yosemite of South America. Dr Francisco P Moreno donated the land on 6 November 1903 and it was originally called *Parque Nacional del Sur* (Southern National Park), but was renamed Nahuel Huapi in 1934. The name comes from the Mapuche language, Nahuel meaning tiger and Huapi meaning island. The largest town in the area, San Carlos de Bariloche, is renowned in Argentina as a resort destination, providing such alpine activities as skiing, trout fishing, and golf. The park, however, offers trekkers and sightseers many areas of natural beauty, including an extinct volcano called *Tronador*, alpine meadows and amazing fauna. The sprawling glacial lake, Lake Nahuel Huapi, stretches over 100km (63 miles) to the border with Chile; the lake contains a nature reserve, the Isla Victoria, which can be reached by private or organised boat trips.

Contact Address

Parque Nacional Nahuel Huapi, Administrative Offices, Avenida San Martin 24, 8400 San Carlos de Bariloche, Rio Negro Province, Argentina
Tel/Fax: (029) 4443 0476.

Transportation

Air: Ministro Pistarini Airport (Buenos Aires). **Road:** Coach: Services from San Carlos de Bariloche.

Opening Times

Daily 24 hours.

Admission Fees

US$5.

Iguazú Falls

Secretaría de Turismo de la Nación, Argentina

Australia

Capital Territory

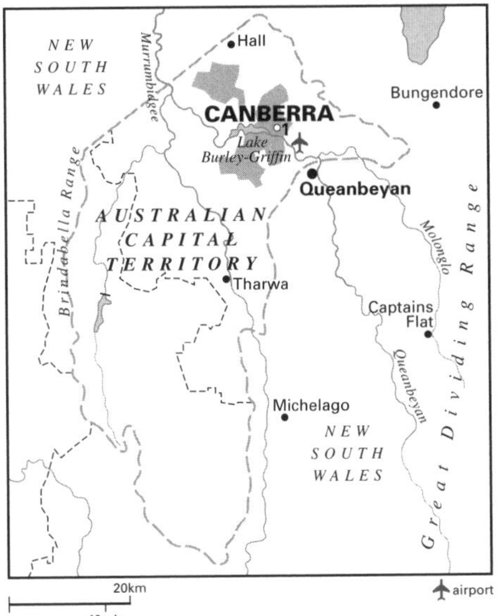

1 National Gallery of Australia

Tourist Information

Australian Tourist Commission
PO Box 2721, Sydney, NSW 1006, Australia
Tel: (02) 9360 1111. Fax: (02) 9331 2538.
Website: www.atc.net.au *or* www.australia.com

Australian Tourist Commission
Gemini House, 10-18 Putney Hill, London SW15 6AA, UK
Tel: (020) 8780 2229 *or* (0906) 863 3235 (Aussie Helpline; calls cost 60p per minute). Fax: (020) 8780 1496.

National Gallery of Australia

The *National Gallery of Australia* houses many of Australia's finest art collections, including a selection of indigenous works, such as the permanent feature *The Aboriginal Memorial* (1987/88). The gallery, which opened in the early 1980s, has a permanent art collection which boasts more than 10,000 works and is also home to regular international art and photography exhibitions. Collections housed in the gallery cover 5000 years and include works from many contemporary artists, including Jackson Pollock and Andy Warhol. There is also a beautiful landscaped garden located in the grounds between the gallery and the banks of Lake Burley Griffin, where many sculptures are on permanent display.

Contact Address

National Gallery of Australia, Parkes Place, Canberra, ACT 2601, Australia
Tel: (02) 6240 6502. Fax: (02) 6240 6561.
E-mail: webmanager@nga.gov.au
Website: www.nga.gov.au

Transportation

Air: Canberra International Airport. **Rail:** Train: Canberra Station. **Road:** Car: The gallery is situated in central Canberra, on the banks of Lake Burley Griffin.

Opening Times

Daily 1000-1700. Closed 25 Dec.

Admission Fees

Free.

National Gallery of Australia

Canberra Tourism & Events Corporation

New South Wales

1 AMP Tower Centrepoint
2 Sydney Harbour Bridge and The Rocks
3 Sydney Opera House

Tourist Information

Australian Tourist Commission

PO Box 2721, Sydney, NSW 1006, Australia

Tel: (02) 9360 1111. Fax: (02) 9331 2538.

Website: www.atc.net.au *or* www.australia.com

Australian Tourist Commission

Gemini House, 10-18 Putney Hill, London SW15 6AA, UK

Tel: (020) 8780 2229 *or* (0906) 863 3235 (Aussie Helpline; calls cost 60p per minute). Fax: (020) 8780 1496.

AMP Tower Centrepoint

Standing at 305 metres (1001ft) high, *AMP Tower Centrepoint* is the tallest building in Sydney. Located in the Central Business District in the heart of the city, visitors can experience amazing views across Sydney Harbour from the newly refurbished Observation Deck, which is the highest of its kind in the Southern Hemisphere. The tower, which was completed in 1981, also has a revolving restaurant which slowly rotates through 360˚ degrees. Visitors can also experience the Skytour attraction on the podium level of the Centrepoint building, which takes them on a 40-minute visual journey through the Rainforest, the Outback, the Urban and the Seashore to experience a simulated expedition around Australia. The AMP Tower itself forms part of the Centrepoint complex which is home to around 140 shops, as well as the Centrepoint Convention and Exhibition Centre.

Contact Address

AMP Tower Centrepoint, Suite 6, Level 1, 100 Market Street, Sydney NSW 2000, Australia
Tel: (02) 9231 1000. Fax: (02) 9231 1200.
E-mail: skytour@vitascope.com.au
Website: www.centrepoint.com.au

Transportation

Air: Sydney (Kingsford Smith) Airport. **Rail:** Monorail: City Centre Station.

Opening Times

Sun-Fri 0900-2230, Sat 0900-2330.

Admission Fees

A$19.80 (adult), A$13.20 (child).

Sydney Harbour Bridge and The Rocks

Sydney Harbour Bridge is one of the most famous man-made structures in the world, and is undoubtedly one of Sydney's most famous icons. The bridge, which is a feat of engineering genius and affectionately known as 'the Coathanger', took 1400 workers (16 of whom were killed in the process) eight years to complete. It was started at the end of 1926 and offically opened on 19 March 1932. If the views from the *Pylon Lookout* across *Sydney Harbour* and over the *Opera House* are not spectacular enough, thrill-seekers can take part in the *BRIDGECLIMB*. This gives them the chance to walk to the top of the 50-storey-high bridge, over the cars and trains rumbling across the deck below, and down the other side. Crocodile Dundee actor Paul Hogan, a former bridge-painter, was one of the first to climb the bridge. Situated at the foot of the bridge, is the area known as *The Rocks*. Recognised as Sydney's historical birthplace, *The Rocks* is made up of winding streets, sandstone cottages and some of Sydney's oldest pubs. The area was also the site of the first landing from Plymouth, England in 1788; today *The Rocks* is a busy area consisting of cafés, restaurants, galleries, museums and countless souvenir shops. Among the district's most significant historic buildings are the *Hero of Waterloo Inn*, the *Sydney Observatory*, *Cadman's Cottage*, the *Museum of Contemporary Art, Merchants' House, Garrison Church* and *Susannah Place*.

Contact Address

Bridgeclimb: 5 Cumberland Street, The Rocks, Sydney NSW 2000, Australia
Tel: (02) 8274 7777. Fax: (02) 9240 1122.
E-mail: admin@BRIDGECLIMB.com
Website: www.bridgeclimb.com
The Rocks: The Rocks Visitor Centre, 18 Argyle Street, Sydney, Australia
Tel: (02) 9251 5500.

Transportation

Air: Sydney (Kingsford Smith) Airport. **Rail:** Train: Circular Quay Station.

Opening Times

Sydney Harbour Bridge: Daily 24 hours. *BRIDGECLIMB*: Mon-Fri 0745-1855, Sat and Sun 0805-1855. *The Rocks*: Daily 0900-1800.

Admission Fees

Sydney Harbour Bridge: Free. *BRIDGECLIMB*: A$117 (adult), A$96 (child 12-16) (Mon-Fri during the day); A$142 (adult), A$118 (child 12-16) (Mon-Fri at night); A$142 (adult), A$118 (child 12-16) (Sat and Sun during the day); A$164 (adult), A$140 (child 12-16) (Sat and Sun at night). Free to cross bridge on foot or by car. *The Rocks*: Free.

Sydney Opera House

Opened in 1973, *Sydney Opera House* is not only the most recognisable symbol of both the city of Sydney and the country of Australia but is also considered one of the 20th century's great buildings. Revolutionary in concept, the building's Danish architect, Jørn Utzon designed the building to resemble a ship at sea with its roof appearing as a billowing white sail. It is also one of the busiest performing arts centres in the world, housing a large complex of theatres and halls that play host to a wide range of performing arts such as classical and contemporary music, dance, ballet, drama, events for children and outdoor activities as well, of course, as opera. Located on Bennelong Point, the Opera House, which offers spectacular views of Sydney Harbour, is visited by more than 4.5 million tourists every year. Various tours – including the Front of House and Backstage areas – can be taken.

Contact Address

Sydney Opera House, PO Box R239, Royal Exchange, NSW 1225, Australia
Tel: (02) 9250 7250.
E-mail: tservice@soh.nsw.gov.au
Website: www.soh.nsw.gov.au

Transportation

Air: Sydney (Kingsford Smith) Airport. **Rail:** Train: Circular Quay Station.

Opening Times

Sydney Opera House: Daily 0830-2400. *Front of House tour*: Daily 0915-1700. Closed Good Friday and 25 Dec.

Admission Fees

Front of House tour: A$14.80 (adult), A$10.60 (child).

Sydney Opera House by night

Tourism New South Wales

Northern Territory

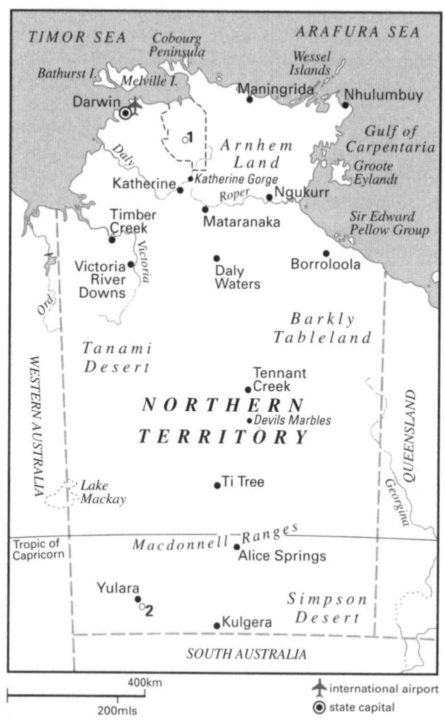

1 Kakadu National Park
2 Uluru-Kata Tjuta National Park

Kakadu National Park

Located in Australia's tropical Northern Territory and stretching from Arnhem Land in the east to Katherine Gorge in the south, *Kakadu National Park* is one of the few UNESCO World Heritage Sites to be listed for both natural and cultural reasons. Many believe the park has been continuously inhabited for up to 40,000 years, and cave paintings and other archaeological sites, such as the famous *Ubirr* and *Nourlangie* rocks, testify to the Aboriginal history of the region. Kakadu is also home to approximately 900 species of plant, 300 types of birds, 50 native mammals and 75 reptiles, including the giant and very dangerous saltwater crocodile. Covering an area of 1.3 million hectares (3.2 million acres), the park is still home to around 300 Aboriginals today and encompasses river floodplains, savannah woodlands and rich tidal wetlands.

Contact Address

Kakadu National Park, PO Box 71, Jabiru, NT 0886, Australia
Tel: (08) 8938 1100. Fax: (08) 8938 1115.
E-mail: kakadunationalpark@ea.gov.au
Website:www.biodiversity.environment.gov.au/kakadu

Transportation

Air: Darwin International Airport. **Road:** Coach: Coach tours operate between Darwin, Jabiru and Cooinda. Car: The Arnhem Highway off the Stuart Highway leads from Darwin to the park headquarters near Jabiru. Kakadu Highway leads into the park (from Jabiru).

Opening Times

Park: Daily 24 hours. *Entry Stations*: Daily 0700-1900.

Admission Fees

A$16.25 (adult), free (child).

Uluru-Kata Tjuta National Park

Uluru-Kata Tjuta National Park is home to one of Australia's most popular tourist attractions and best-known national symbols: *Uluru*, which means 'great pebble' in the Aboriginal language. Formerly known as *Ayers Rock*, Uluru is a 3.6km-long (2.2-mile), 348m-high (1142ft) smooth chunk of

Tourist Information

Australian Tourist Commission
PO Box 2721, Sydney, NSW 1006, Australia
Tel: (02) 9360 1111. Fax: (02) 9331 2538.
Website: www.atc.net.au *or* www.australia.com
Australian Tourist Commission
Gemini House, 10-18 Putney Hill, London SW15 6AA, UK
Tel: (020) 8780 2229 *or* (0906) 863 3235 (Aussie Helpline; calls cost 60p per minute). Fax: (020) 8780 1496.

sandstone that rises abruptly and unexpectedly out of the sandy scrubland. It is the world's largest rock monolith and the most famous natural landmark in Australia. The rock, which is also of deep significance to the local Aboriginal people, who believe it was formed during the creation period, changes its colour from red to grey to black, depending on the weather and the time of day. The nearby *Kata Tjuta*, meaning 'many heads' and formerly known as *The Olgas*, is a series of 36 massive rock domes and a system of gorges and valleys. Visitors can walk through the *Valley of the Winds* and the *Olga Gorge*, and also visit the *Uluru-Kata Tijuta Cultural Centre*, which has exhibitions on local history and geology.

Contact Address
Uluru-Kata Tjuta National Park, NT 0872, Australia
Tel: (08) 8956 3138. Fax: (08) 8953 0295.

Transportation
Air: Darwin International Airport. **Rail:** Train: Alice Springs Station. **Road:** Bus: Services from Uluru. Car: Stuart Highway from either Darwin (in the north) or Alice Springs (in the south), then signs to Uluru-Kata Tjuta.

Opening Times
Cultural Centre (gateway): 0700-1730 (winter); 0700-1800 (summer).

Admission Fees
A$15 (adult), free (child under 16).

Uluru (Ayers Rock)

NTTC Visual Library

Queensland

1 Great Barrier Reef

Tourist Information

Australian Tourist Commission
PO Box 2721, Sydney, NSW 1006, Australia
Tel: (02) 9360 1111. Fax: (02) 9331 2538.
Website: www.atc.net.au *or* www.australia.com

Australian Tourist Commission
Gemini House, 10-18 Putney Hill, London SW15 6AA, UK
Tel: (020) 8780 2229 *or* (0906) 863 3235 (Aussie Helpline; calls cost 60p per minute). Fax: (020) 8780 1496.

Great Barrier Reef

The *Great Barrier Reef* is undoubtedly the most famous marine-protected area in the world and the largest World Heritage area according to UNESCO. Covering a geographical area of 35 million hectares (86 million acres) and stretching approximately 2000km (1243 miles) along the coast of northeastern Australia from Budaberg to Cape York, the Reef is bigger in size than the states of Victoria and Tasmania combined; it is, however, not a continuous barrier, but a maze of small islands and coral reefs ranging in size from one to 100,000 hectares (247,104 acres). The *Great Barrier Reef* is the largest coral reef system in the world and home to approximately 400 different types of coral. It is also an area of outstanding natural beauty and home to around 1500 different species of fish, 4000 types of mollusc and many endangered species, such as the dugong, as well as other rare animals and birds, including marine worms and reef herons. There are also more than 30 historic shipwrecks in the area and a number of archaeological sites which are of Aboriginal origin.

Contact Address

Great Barrier Reef Marine Park Authority, PO Box 1379, Townsville, Queensland 4810, Australia
Tel: (07) 4772 6093. Fax: (07) 4750 0700.
E-mail: registry@gbrmpa.gov.au
Website: www.gbrmpa.gov.au

Transportation

Air: Brisbane or Cairns Airport. Many domestic airlines fly to national airports located closer to the Reef on the Australian mainland. **Water:** Catamaran: The Great Barrier Reef can only be reached by boat; tour operators can arrange transfer from mainland Australia to resort islands via catamaran.

Opening Times

Daily 24 hours.

Admission Fees

AS$4 per day into the Great Barrier Reef Marine Park.

Heron Island, Great Barrier Reef

Tourism Queensland

Tasmania

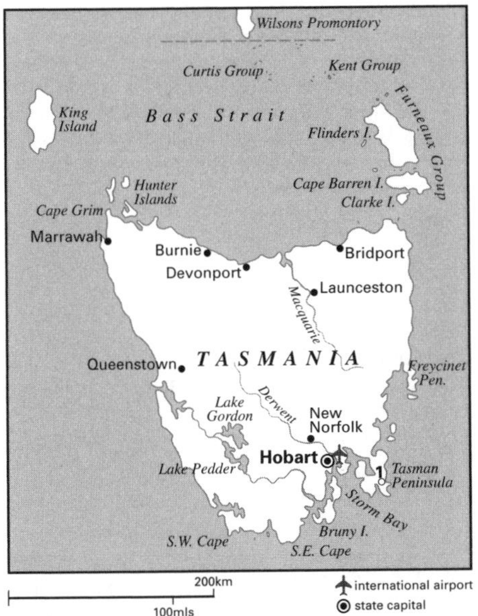

1 Port Arthur

Tourist Information

Australian Tourist Commission
PO Box 2721, Sydney, NSW 1006, Australia
Tel: (02) 9360 1111. Fax: (02) 9331 2538.
Website: www.atc.net.au *or* www.australia.com

Australian Tourist Commission
Gemini House, 10-18 Putney Hill, London SW15 6AA, UK
Tel: (020) 8780 2229 *or* (0906) 863 3235 (Aussie Helpline; calls cost 60p per minute). Fax: (020) 8780 1496.

Port Arthur

Located in Tasmania, *Port Arthur* is a former penal colony which originally opened as a timber station in 1830. It became a prison settlement for male convicts in 1833 and quickly gained a reputation for being 'hell-on-earth.' Convicts ranged from young boys aged between 9 and 18 through to hardened criminals who had to work in chain gangs and wear leg irons. The prison closed in 1877 and was renamed *Carnarvon* in an attempt to lose its former associations; it was however reinstated as *Port Arthur* in 1927. Today, the prison is open to the public and visitors can walk around the site imagining how life would have been for the convicts who served there. There are around 30 ruins and restored buildings at the site, as well as 40 hectares (99 acres) of English Oaks. Visitors can take part in guided tours, as well as ghost tours after dark.

Contact Address

Visitor Centre, Port Arthur Historic Site, Port Arthur, Tasmania 7182, Australia
Tel: (03) 6251 2300. Fax: (03) 6251 2322.
E-mail: lesley.kirby@portarthur.org.au
Website: www.portarthur.org.au

Transportation

Air: Hobart International Airport. **Road:** Car: Reached by scenic drive, which takes approximately 1.5 hours along the Tasman and Arthur highways.

Opening Times

Grounds and *ruins*: Daily 0830-dusk. *Tours*: 0900-1700 at regular intervals during the day. *Visitor Centre*: 0830-close of Historic Ghost tours at night.

Admission Fees

Grounds and *ruins*: A$19.80 (adult), A$9.90 (child). Tickets are valid for two days, allowing visitors a chance to stay overnight.

Port Arthur Church

Corel

Austria

1 Hofburg (Hofburg Palace)
2 Kunsthistorisches Museum (Museum of Fine Art)
3 Mozarts Geburtshaus und Mozarts Wohnhaus (Mozart's Birthplace and Residence)
4 Österreichische Galerie Belvedere (Belvedere Palace)
5 Riesenrad (Giant Ferris Wheel)
6 Schloss Schönbrunn (Schönbrunn Palace)

Tourist Information

Österreich Werbung (Austrian National Tourist Office - ANTO)
Margaretenstrasse 1, 1040 Vienna, Austria
Tel: (01) 58866 *or* 587 2000. Fax: (01) 588 6620.
E-mail: oeinfo@oewwien.via.at
Website: www.austria-tourism.at

Austrian National Tourist Office (ANTO)
PO Box 2363, London W1A 2QB, UK
Tel: (020) 7629 0461. Fax: (020) 7499 6038.
E-mail: info@anto.co.uk
Website: www.austria-tourism.at

Hofburg (Hofburg Palace)

The *Hofburg Palace* was home to the Austrian Hapsburg emperors until 1918. The palace buildings have been constantly added to for over 800 years, with the first fortifications being erected by King Ottakar Premysl in the 13th century. Today, the palace serves as a repository of Austrian culture and history, embracing 22 separate museums, a 14th-century Augustinian church, the famous *Spanische Hofreitschule* (Spanish Riding School), the *Österreichische Nationalbibliothek* (National Library), as well as the president's offices. The most popular of the museums is the *Kaiserappartements*, which takes visitors on a tour of the Kaiser's Imperial apartments. The *Vienna Boys' Choir* sings Sunday mass at the Royal Chapel.

Contact Address

Hofburg, Innerer Burghof, Kaisertor, 1010 Vienna, Austria
Tel: (01) 533 7570. Fax: (01) 5337 57033.
E-mail: hofburg@schoenbrunn.at

Transportation

Air: Vienna International Airport. **Rail:** Underground: Herrengasse. Tram: B-line to Burgtor. **Road:** Bus: 2A to Michaelerplatz. Car: A1 Westautobahn or A2 Südautobahn to the city centre.

Statuary and Dome, Hofburg Palace

Corel

Opening Times

Daily 0900-1630.

Admission Fees

Hofburg (combined ticket for Kaiserappartements and Silberkammer): öS95 (adult), öS75 (student under 25 and OAP), öS50 (child). *Spanische Hofreitschule*: öS160 (adult), öS120 (OAP), öS70 (student under 25 and child). *Österreichische Nationalbibliotek*: öS60 (adult), öS40 (student), free (child under 10).

Kunsthistorisches Museum (Museum of Fine Art)

Opened in 1891 to house the imperial family's vast art collection, Vienna's *Museum of Fine Art* was designed by Gottfreid von Semper and Karl Hasenauer. It was built in the style of the Italian Renaissance to firmly establish the building's link with one of history's great artistic periods. Today, the museum, which is located in Marie-Theresien-Platz, holds one of the most important art collections in the world. The magnificent central staircase is home to a Theseus group by the Italian neoclassical sculptor Antonio Canova (1757-1822), whilst the museum's ceiling painting is by Mihály von Munkácsy. The *Gemäldegalerie* (picture gallery) contains works by Rubens, Rembrandt, Vermeer, Dürer and Titian, and the largest collection of work by Brueghel in the world.

Contact Address

Kunsthistorisches Museum, Marie-Theresien-Platz, 1010 Vienna, Austria
Tel: (01) 5252 4401. Fax: (01) 523 2770.
E-mail: info@khm.at
Website: www.khm.at

Transportation

Air: Vienna International Airport. **Rail:** Underground: Volkstheater. Tram: Tram D to Burging/Kunsthistorisches Museum. **Road:** Bus: 2A or 57A. Car: A1 Westautobahn or the A2 Sudautobahn to the city centre.

Opening Times

Tues-Sun 1000-1800, except Thurs 1000-2100. Open Mondays only during exhibitions.

Admission Fees

öS100 (adult), öS70 (concessions).

Mozarts Geburtshaus und Mozarts Wohnhaus (Mozart's Birthplace and Residence)

Born Joannes Christosomos Wolfgang Theopolis Mozart to Leopold and Anna Maria Mozart on 27 January 1756, Mozart is one of the most famous musicians of all times. The musical genius was born in *Getreidegasse 9* in Salzburg, known today as *Mozarts Geburtshaus* (Mozart's Birthplace), where the family lived from 1747 to 1773. Under his father's teaching, Mozart quickly became a child prodigy, playing in front of kings and emperors across Europe. In 1773, the family moved to a house in *Makartplatz* which is known today as *Mozarts Wohnhaus* (Mozart's Residence), where they remained until 1787. Every year, thousands of visitors come to Salzburg to see these two houses, which are both now popular museums. Music lovers from around the world come to see artefacts, such as Mozart's childhood violin, his concert violin, his clavichord and portraits of his family. Most of Mozart's Residence was destroyed by a bomb in 1944; the building has however been restored to its original glory by the Mozarteum Foundation.

Contact Address

Mozarts Geburtshaus, Getreidegasse 9, 5020 Salzburg, Austria
Tel: (06) 6284 4313. Fax: (06) 6284 0693.
Mozarts Wohnhaus, Makartplatz 8, 5020 Salzburg, Austria
Tel: (06) 62874 22740. Fax: (06) 6287 2924.

Transportation

Air: Salzburg Airport. **Rail:** Train: Salzburg Central Station.

Opening Times

Daily 0900-1730 (Sep-Jun); daily 0900-1830 (Jul-Aug).

Admission Fees

öS230 for a Salzburg Card (adult) allowing free entry to Mozart's Birthplace, Mozart's Residence and numerous other attractions in Salzburg; öS115 for a Salzburg Card (child). The card is valid for 24 hours.

Österreichische Galerie Belvedere (Belvedere Palace)

Belvedere Palace, situated right in the heart of Vienna, is Austria's most famous art gallery and home to *der Kuss* (The Kiss) which was painted by Gustav Klimt. There are two permanent collections – *Oberes Belvedere* (Upper Belvedere) and *Unteres Belvedere* (Lower Belvedere) – in the Palace, which is one of the most exquisite Baroque buildings in the world. The palace was built by Lukas von Hildebrandt between 1714 and 1723 as a summer residence for Prince Eugene of Savoy. The Upper Belvedere offers fine views across the palace's gardens to the Lower Belvedere and across Vienna itself. The two museums house an impressive collection of Austrian art from the Middle Ages through to the 20th century. Today, the Upper Belvedere is home to the Austrian Gallery and works by Renoir, Monet, Klimt, Kokoschka and Schiele, whilst the Lower Belvedere houses Medieval and Baroque works in the Baroque Museum and the Museum of Medieval Austrian Art.

Contact Address

Österreichische Galerie Belvedere, Prinz Engen-Strasse 27, 1037 Vienna, Austria
Tel: (01) 795 570. Fax: (01) 798 4337.
E-mail: belvedere@belvedere.at
Website: www.belvedere.at

Transportation

Air: Vienna International Airport. **Rail:** Underground: Südbahnhof. Tram: D.

Opening Times

Tues-Sun 1000-1700 (winter); Tues-Sun 1000-2000 (summer). Closed Mondays.

Admission Fees

öS100 (adult), free (infant), öS40 (schoolchild), öS70 (OAP and student).

Riesenrad (Giant Ferris Wheel)

Located in the giant wooded park and fairground known as the *Prater*, Vienna's *Giant Ferris Wheel* is one of Austria's best-known and best-loved landmarks. The Ferris Wheel was completed in 1897 at a time when other such ferris wheels stood in cities like London, Paris and Blackpool, but it is the only one of its era still surviving. The wheel is famous for featuring in many films including *The Third Man, The Living Daylights* and *Before Sunrise*.

Contact Address

Riesenrad, Prater 90, 1020 Vienna, Austria
Tel: (01) 729 5430. Fax: (01) 7295 43020.
E-mail: wr.riesenrad@aon.at
Website: www.wienerriesenrad.com

Transportation

Air: Vienna International Airport. **Rail:** Train: S-Bahn to Wien Nord (Praterstern) from Wien Mitte. Underground: Praterstern. Tram: 21. **Road:** Bus: Wien Prater. Car: Signs for Vienna city centre, then take Praterstrasse.

Opening Times

Daily 1000-2300 (Apr); daily 0900-2400 (May-Sep); daily 1000-2200 (Oct); daily 1000-1800 (Nov-Dec).

Admission Fees

öS55 (adult), öS20 (child). Concessions available.

Schloss Schönbrunn (Schönbrunn Palace)

One of the most renowned Baroque structures in Europe, *Schönbrunn Palace* began life as a hunting lodge during the 16th century, but was turned into a lavish palace by the Empress Maria Theresa in 1750. Home to the Hapsburg emperors from the 18th century to 1918, the palace was built by the architects Johann Bernhard Fischer von Erlach and Nicolaus Pacassi. A tour offers visitors the chance to admire the site's opulent elegance, including the famous ceiling frescoes of the *Great Gallery*, and the *Hall of Mirrors* where Mozart played. The Baroque grounds of the palace include a *Flower Garden*, *Tiergarten* (a zoo dating from 1752), the *Neptune Fountain*, and a reproduction of a maze that was created at the beginning of the 18th century.

Contact Address

Schloss Schönbrunn Kultur und Betriebs GmbH, Schloss Schönbrunn, 1130 Vienna, Austria
Tel: (01) 8111 3239. Fax: (01) 8111 3333.
E-mail: info@schoenbrunn.at
Website: www.schoenbrunn.at

Transportation

Air: Vienna International Airport. **Rail:** Train: Schönbrunn Station. Underground: Schönbrunn. **Road:** Bus: 10A to Schönbrunn. Car: Ostautobahn from the airport towards Vienna, then the A23 (Sudosttangente) towards Graz (Altmannsdorf exit).

Opening Times

Daily 0830-1700 (1 Apr-30 Jun); daily 0830-1900 (1 Jul-31 Aug); daily 0830-1700 (1 Sep-31 Oct); daily 0830-1630 (1 Nov-31 Mar).

Admission Fees

Grand Tour: öS135 (adult), öS70 (child). *Imperial Tour*: öS105 (adult), öS55 (child). Concessions available.

Bangladesh

1 Chittagong

Tourist Information

Bangladesh Parjatan Corporation (National Tourism Organisation)
233 Airport Road, Tejgaon, Dhaka-1215, Bangladesh
Tel: (02) 811 7855-9. Fax: (02) 811 7235.
E-mail: bpcho@bangla.net
Website: www.parjatan.org

High Commission for the People's Republic of Bangladesh
28 Queen's Gate, London SW7 5JA, UK
Tel: (020) 7584 0081. Fax: (020) 7581 7477.
E-mail: bdesh.lon@dial.pipex.com

Chittagong

Chittagong, the second largest city in Bangladesh, is a port city, set against the blue waters of the Bay of Bengal and surrounded by green forests, coconut groves and sandy beaches. The *Ethnological Museum* houses objects from 12 different Bangladeshi tribes, and items from tribes in Australia, India and Pakistan. Places of interest in the Old City include the 17th-century *Shahi Jama-e-Masjid Mosque* and the colourful multi-domed *Chandanpura Mosque*. The *Tomb of Sultan Bayazid Bostami* is a sacred shrine situated on a hilltop 6km (4 miles) outside the town where visitors can see a large tank filled with hundreds of tortoises, said to be the descendants of evil spirits. *Foy's Lake*, an artificial lake named after the Englishman responsible for its design, is located 8km (5 miles) from Chittagong, and is a popular picnic site. Chittagong is also a good base from which to explore the *Rangamati Hill District*, famous for its beautiful flora and lakes and the predominantly Buddhist tribal culture.

Contact Address

Tourist Information Centre, Motel Shaikat, Station Road, Chittagong, Bangladesh
Tel: (031) 619 845.

Transportation

Air: Chittagong MA Hannan International Airport.
Rail: Train: Chittagong Station.

Opening Times

Chandanpura Mosque: Daily 0600-dusk. *Ethnological Museum*: Mon-Thurs, Sat and Sun 0900-1700. *Foy's Lake*: Daily 24 hours. *Shahi Jama-e-Masjid Mosque*: Daily 0600-dusk. *Tomb of Sultan Bayazid Bostami*: Daily 0600-dusk.

Admission Fees

Chandanpura Mosque: Free. *Ethnological Museum*: Tk1 (adult), Tk0.50 (child). *Foy's Lake*: Free. *Shahi Jama-e-Masjid Mosque*: Free. *Tomb of Sultan Bayazid Bostami*: Free.

Belgium

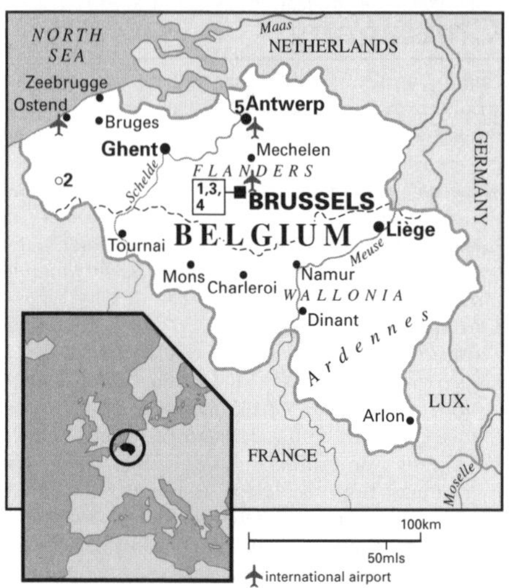

1 Atomium
2 Flanders Fields
3 Grand' Place (Central Square)
4 Manneken Pis (Statue of the Pissing Boy)
5 Onze Lieve Vrouwe-Kathedraal (Cathedral of Our Lady)

Tourist Information

Office de Promotion du Tourisme Wallonie-Bruxelles (Belgian Tourist Office – Brussels & Ardennes)
61-63 rue du Marché-aux-Herbes, B-1000 Brussels, Belgium
Tel: (02) 504 0390. Fax: (02) 504 0270.
E-mail: info@belgium-tourism.org
Website: www.belgique-tourisme.net

Toerisme Vlaanderen (Tourism Flanders-Brussels)
Grasmarkt 61-63, B-1000, Brussels, Belgium
Tel: (02) 504 0300 *or* 504 0390. Fax: (02) 513 8803.
E-mail: info@toerismevlaanderen.be
Website: www.visitflanders.com

Belgian Tourist Office – Brussels & Ardennes
225 Marsh Wall, London E14 9FW, UK
Tel: 0906 302 0245 (calls cost 50p per minute) *or* (0800) 954 5245 (brochure request line; toll free UK only) *or* (020) 7531 0391 (trade enquiries only). Fax: (020) 7531 0393.
E-mail: info@belgium-tourism.org
Website: www.belgium-tourism.net

Tourism Flanders-Brussels
31 Pepper Street, London E14 9RW, UK
Tel: (09001) 887 799 (brochure request line; calls cost 60p per minute). Fax: (020) 7458 0045.
E-mail: office@flanders-tourism.org
Website: www.visitflanders.com

Atomium

The *Atomium* was designed by engineer André Waterkeyn as a celebration of scientific progress for the 1958 World Fair. The structure stands 102 metres (334 feet) high, weighs 2400 metric tonnes (2439 tons), and represents an iron crystalline molecule enlarged 165 billion times. Inside the nine spheres visitors can see an exhibition showing how the Atomium has been depicted in comic strips through the years and an audiovisual presentation on the construction of the Atomium. There are splendid views across Brussels and the surrounding countryside from the top of the structure.

Contact Address

Atomium, Boulevard du Centenaire, 1020 Brussels, Belgium
Tel: (02) 474 8977. Fax: (02) 474 8398.
E-mail: info@atomium.be
Website: www.atomium.be

Transportation

Air: Brussels Airport. **Rail:** Train: Bruxelles Centrale Station. Underground: Heysel. Tram: 23 or 81. **Road:** Bus: 84 or 89. Car: Ring road West (exit 8 Wemmel-Heizel).

Opening Times

Daily 1000-1730 (1 Sep-31 Mar); daily 0900-1930 (1 Apr-31 Aug). Closed one week at the end of January.

Admission Fees

BFr220 (adult), BFr160 (child).

Flanders Fields

Flanders Fields was the site of around half a million deaths in the horrific trenches of World War I. There are numerous military cemeteries and 'Missing Memorials' in the region commemorating those of all nationalities who fell in battle, as well as the playing of the 'Last Post' every evening at 2000, under the arch of the *Menin Gate*. Most of the soldiers who perished were the victims of poison gas attacks: the deadly gas *Yperite* was invented in the nearby city of Ypres, which was a renowned commercial centre during the Middle Ages but was almost completely destroyed during World War I. At the *In Flanders Fields* museum in Ypres, visitors can discover what it was like to be a soldier in the trenches and learn about major events and aspects of the war such as the first gas attack, the Christmas Truces of 1914, and No Man's Land.

Contact Address

In Flanders Fields Museum, Lakenhallen – Grote Markt 34, 8900 Ieper, Belgium
Tel: (057) 228 584. Fax: (057) 228 589.
E-mail: toerisme@ieper.be
Website: www.inflandersfields.be/english/eng-index.html

Transportation

Air: Brussels Airport. **Rail:** Train: Ieper/Ypres Station. **Road:** Car: N369 (from Ostend).

Opening Times

In Flanders Fields Museum: Daily 1000-1800 (Apr-Sep); Tues-Sun 1000-1700 (Oct-Mar). Closed first three weeks after Christmas holiday.

Admission Fees

In Flanders Fields Museum: BFr250 (adult), BFr125 (child 7-15), free (child under 7).

Grand' Place (Central Square)

The *Grand' Place* has been at the heart of Brussels' life since the 11th century. Having been almost totally destroyed by the French bombardment ordered by Louis XIV in 1695, it was later rebuilt in its original architectural style by various workers' guilds. The splendid neo-Gothic and Baroque houses that surround the cobbled square (which is about the size of a football pitch) once housed the headquarters of corporations of artists, merchants

Grand' Place

OPT/Potigny

and tailors; the *City of Brussels Museum* (tel: (02) 279 4355) in the former *Maison du Roi* (King's Residence) allows visitors to explore the city's illustrious trading history. Other buildings in the Grand' Place which provide insights into Brussels' traditions are the *Town Hall* (tel: (02) 279 4365), the *Museum of Cocoa and Chocolate* (tel: (02) 514 2048) and the *Museum of Brewing* (tel: (02) 511 4987). Many of the houses were given names – for example numbers 26 and 27 are called *Le Pigeon* (The Pigeon), and were once the residence of French novelist Victor Hugo during his exile in Brussels.

Contact Address

Office de Tourisme et d'Information de Bruxelles, Hôtel de Ville, Grand-Place, 1000 Brussels, Belgium
Tel: (02) 513 8940. Fax: (02) 513 8320.

Transportation

Air: Brussels Airport. **Rail:** Train: Bruxelles Centrale Station. Underground: Bourse, De Brouckère, Gare Centrale. Tram: 23, 52, 55, 56 or 81. **Road:** Bus: 29, 34, 47, 48, 60, 63, 65, 66, 71, 95 or 96.

Opening Times

Brussels Town Hall: Guided tours Tues and Wed at 1130 and 1315 only (Apr-Sep); Tues, Wed and Sun at various times between 1130-1515 (Oct-Mar). *City of Brussels Museum*: Tues-Fri 1000-1700 (Apr-Sep); Tues-Fri 1000-1600 (Oct-Mar). *Museum of Brewing*: Daily 1000-1700. *Museum of Cocoa and Chocolate*: Tues-Sun 1000-1700.

Admission Fees

Brussels Town Hall: BFr100. *City of Brussels Museum*: BFr100. *Museum of Cocoa and Chocolate*: BFr200 (adult), free (child under 12). *Museum of Brewing*: BFr100.

Manneken-Pis (Statue of the Pissing Boy)

The *Manneken-Pis*, situated in Rue de l'Etuve, is as funny as it is well known. Crowds of tourists patrol the meandering cobbled streets near Brussels' Grand' Place hoping to find this small statuette of a little boy in the midst of a never-ending pee. Sometimes known as 'Little Julian', the statue is, in its own way, a typically Belgian symbol of cultural self-mockery. Since its creation by J Duquesnoy in the 17th century, the *Manneken-Pis* has attracted a great deal of attention, having been stolen (by the English in 1745 and the French in 1747), vandalised and dressed in over 600 costumes, which are on display at the *City of Brussels Museum*.

Contact Address

Office de Tourisme et d'Information de Bruxelles, Hôtel de Ville, Grand-Place, 1000 Brussels, Belgium
Tel: (02) 513 8940. Fax: (02) 513 8320.
E-mail: tourism.brussels@tib.be
Website: www.belgium-tourism.org

Transportation

Air: Brussels Airport. **Rail:** Train: Bruxelles Centrale Station. Underground: Bourse. Tram: 52, 55, 58 or 62. **Road:** Bus: 29, 34, 48, 63 or 71.

Opening Times

City of Brussels Museum: Tues-Fri 1000-1700 (Apr-Sep); Tues-Fri 1000-1600 (Oct-Mar).

Admission Fees

City of Brussels Museum: BFr100.

Onze Lieve Vrouwe-Kathedraal (Cathedral of Our Lady)

Onze Lieve Vrouwe-Kathedraal is the largest Gothic church in the Low Countries and rises to a height of 123m (404ft), piercing the skyline of historic Antwerp. Although construction began in 1352, it was not completed until 1521; the roof and Gothic furniture were then destroyed by fire in 1533. The interior of the cathedral is Baroque in style, the original Gothic features having been destroyed by religious idealists in the late 16th century. There are many fine works of art in the nave, the most famous being Ruben's 'Descent from the Cross' (1611-14).

Contact Address

Onze Lieve Vrouwe-Kathedraal, Groenplaats 21, 2000 Antwerp, Belgium
Tel: (03) 3213 9940. Fax: (03) 231 8617.
E-mail: kathinfo@mail.dma.be
Website: www.dma.be/cultuur/kathedraal

Transportation

Air: Brussels Airport. **Rail:** Train: Antwerp Central Station. Tram: 2 or 15. **Road:** Car: N1.

Opening Times

Mon-Fri 1000-1700, Sat 1000-1500, Sun 1300-1600.

Admission Fees

BFr70.

Bolivia

1 Lago Titicaca (Lake Titicaca)

Tourist Information

Viceministerio de Turismo (Bolivian Tourist Office)
Avenida Mariscal Santa Cruz, Palacio de las Comunicaciones, Piso 16, La Paz, Bolivia
Tel: (02) 367 441. Fax: (02) 374 630.
E-mail: turismo@mcei-bolivia.com
Website: www.mcei-bolivia.com

Embassy and Consulate of the Republic of Bolivia
106 Eaton Square, London SW1W 9AD, UK
Tel: (020) 7235 4248. Fax: (020) 7235 12868.

Lago Titicaca (Lake Titicaca)

At an elevation of 3810m (12,492ft), *Lake Titicaca* is one of the world's highest navigable lakes. It is named after the native word for 'puma of stone' and its shape bears a strong resemblance to this animal when viewed from above. Measuring 194km (121 miles) long and 65km (45 miles) wide, it has been revered in history, featuring prominently in Inca creation myths. There are daily tours to the *Uros* and *Taquile Islands*; the *Uros* people live on floating islands made out of reeds that grow in the lake, whilst the inhabitants of *Taquile Island* are renowned for maintaining ancient traditions and for their remarkable weaving skills.

Contact Address

For more information on Lake Titicaca, contact the Viceministerio de Turismo (see **Tourist Information** above).

Transportation

Air: El Alto Airport (La Paz). **Road:** Bus: Daily services leave La Paz every 30 minutes. Car: From La Paz (journey time: 2.5 hours).

Opening Times

Daily 24 hours.

Admission Fees

Free.

Isla del Sol, Lake Titicaca

Jonathan Carr

Botswana

1 Moremi Wildlife Reserve

Tourist Information

Department of Tourism
Ministry of Commerce and Industry, Private Bag 0047, Gaborone, Botswana
Tel: (267) 353 024 *or* 313 314. Fax: (267) 308 675.
E-mail: botswanatourism@gov.bw
Website: www.gov.bw/tourism *or* www.botswana-tourism.gov.bw

Department of Tourism UK Representation Office
Southern Skies Marketing, 10 Barley Mow Passage, London W4 4PH, UK
Tel: (020) 8400 6113. Fax: (020) 8987 0488.
E-mail: botswanatourism@aol.com

Moremi Wildlife Reserve

Botswana's *Moremi Wildlife Reserve* lies in the centre of the Okavango Delta, the largest inland delta in the world. Named after the chief of the Batawana tribe who declared the reserve in 1963, it consists of permanently swamped areas, seasonally swamped areas and dry land, and covers an area of 3000 sq kilometres (1170 sq miles). The reserve encompasses a wide range of habitats – from wetland, floodplain and reed beds to forest and savannah woodland. The fauna inhabiting the park is abundant and equally diverse, ranging from exotic birds, zebras, buffalo, wildebeest and giraffes to hippos and lions; the only large African mammals not found here are rhino. Boats take visitors to various lagoons, such as Xakanaxa, Gcobega and Gcodikwe, to view game and birdlife. There are many campsites and lodges in the reserve, each with its own viewing possibilities and activities.

Contact Address

For more information on the Moremi Wildlife Reserve, contact the Botswana Department of Tourism (see **Tourist Information** above).

Transportation

Air: Maun Airport (internal) or Gaborone Sir Seretse Khama International Airport. **Rail:** Train: Francistown Station. **Road:** Car: Main road to Maun (visitors must have a 4x4 vehicle to enter the reserve).

Opening Times

Daily 0600-1800.

Admission Fees

P120 (adult), P60 (child 8-18), free (child under 8).

Mokora Ride, Moremi Wildlife Reserve

Chris McIntyre

Brazil

1 Cristo Redentor (Statue of Christ the Redeemer)
2 Foz do Iguaçú (Iguaçú Falls)
3 Pão de Açúcar (Sugar Loaf Mountain)
4 Praia de Copacabana (Copacabana Beach)

Tourist Information

Instituto Brasileiro do Turismo – EMBRATUR (Brazilian Tourist Board)
SCN, Quadra 02, BLG 2/A, CEP 70710-500 Brasília, DF, Brazil
Tel: (061) 429 7753. Fax: (061) 273 9290 *or* 328 9889. E-mail: webm@embratur.gov.br
Website: www.embratur.gov.br

Brazilian Embassy and Tourist Office
32 Green Street, London W1Y 4AT, UK
Tel: (020) 7399 9000. Fax: (020) 7399 9100 *or* 7399 9102 (tourist office and commercial section).
E-mail: tourism@infolondres.org.uk
Website: www.brazil.org.uk

Cristo Redentor (Statue of Christ the Redeemer)

The *Statue of Christ the Redeemer*, standing 30 metres (98ft) tall and overlooking the city of Rio de Janeiro, is one of the tallest statues in the world. The statue represents Jesus standing with outstretched, welcoming arms and is one of the most famous symbols of this lively city. Developed by the engineer Heitor da Silva Costa and originally conceived in 1921, the project took almost five years to complete. The statue sits on top of *Corcovado Mountain* (Hunchback Mountain) and is located in *Tijuca National Park*, a lush spot for picnics and walking. Visitors can access the base of the statue, which, at 709m (2326ft) high, affords superb views of Sugar Loaf Mountain, downtown Rio de Janeiro and Rio's beaches. Visitors can take a train to the top of the mountain to see the statue up-close and to make the most of the stunning views.

Contact Address

Embratur Tourist Office, Rua Uruguaiana 174, Rio de Janeiro, CEP 20.050-090, Brazil
Tel: (021) 509 6017. Fax: (021) 509 7381.
E-mail: rio@embratur.gov.br
Website: www.embratur.gov.br

Transportation

Air: Rio de Janeiro International Airport. **Rail:** Train: Rua Cosmevehlo Station. **Road:** Coach: Novo Rio Coach Station. Car: Routes to Corcovado.

Opening Times

Train: Daily 0900-1800.

Admission Fees

By train: US$9. By car: US$2.50 per car, plus US$2.50 per passenger.

Foz do Iguaçú (Iguaçú Falls)

The *Iguaçú Falls* fittingly receive their name from the Guarani Indian word meaning 'great waters'. The falls are formed by the *Paraná River* dividing into 275 separate falls; they are surrounded by the virgin jungle of *Iguaçú National Park* which is home to 2000 species of flora and 400 species of bird (including parrots and toucans). The highest fall, the *'Garganta del Diabolo'* (Devil's Throat) reaches 70m (230ft), which is one and a half times the height of *Niagara Falls*. Besides taking in the stunning view from a series of catwalks, visitors may participate in kayaking, canoeing and other watersports. Nearby historic Jesuit Mission ruins, such as those at *San Ignacio Mini*, are also popular.

Embratur

Iguaçú Falls, Brazil

Contact Address

Iguaçú National Park, Catarata's Road, BR369, Brazil
Tel: (045) 523 8383. Website: www.iguassu.com.br

Transportation

Air: Foz de Iguaçú International Airport. **Road:** Coach: Services from Curitiba. Car: BR-277; then BR-469 (from Curitiba).

Opening Times

Mon 1300-1800, Tues-Sun 0800-1800.

Admission Fees

US$4 (adult), US$1 (child). Concessions available.

Pão de Açúcar (Sugar Loaf Mountain)

Shaped like a Victorian sugar loaf and 396 metres (1299ft) tall, *Sugar Loaf Mountain* stands high above the city of Rio de Janeiro and *Baía de Guanabara* (Guanabara Bay). The mountain is one of the most famous in the world and is a spectacular backdrop to Brazil's most lively city. Visitors can see excellent views of Rio de Janeiro (which literally translates as January River) from the top of the mountain and sunsets are said to be particularly spectacular. Cable cars, which were introduced by the engineer Augusto Ferreira Ramos in 1912, take visitors to the top of the mountain, although more adventurous travellers may choose to make the steep climb on foot.

Contact Address

Embratur Tourist Office, Rua Uruguaiana 174, Rio de Janeiro, CEP 20.050-090, Brazil
Tel: (021) 509 6017. Fax: (021) 509 7381.
E-mail: rio@embratur.gov.br
Website: www.embratur.gov.br

Transportation

Air: Rio de Janeiro International Airport. **Rail:** Cable Car: Cable cars take visitors to the top (from Praça General Tibúrcio at Praia Vermelha in Urca). **Road:** Bus: Bus marked 'Urca' from Centro and Flamengo or 500, 511 or 512 from the zona sul. The open airbus that runs along the Ipanema and Copacabana beaches also goes to Sugar Loaf. Coach: Novo Rio Coach Station. Car: Road towards city centre, then coastal road past Ipanema and Copacabana beaches to Urca (from the south); south towards Ipanema and Copacabana beaches, then the exit marked Urca (from the city centre).

Opening Times

Cable Car: Daily 0800-2200.

Admission Fees

Cable Car: US$9.

Praia de Copacabana (Copacabana Beach)

Copacabana Beach is one of the world's most famous beaches. Located right in the heart of Rio de Janeiro, it is also one of the most lively beaches in the world with thousands of visitors flocking to this 3km (1.9 miles) beach every year. Located in front of the black and white wavy mosaics on *Avenida Atlântica* which were designed by Burle Max, the area is busy both day and night and lined with shops, bars, restaurants and luxury hotels. There are also fine examples of *Art Deco* architecture in the area, such as the *Copacabana Palace Hotel* which was built in 1923. *Copacabana Fort*, which was built in 1914 to defend Guanabara Bay, is situated at the end of the beach and offers panoramic views of the surrounding area.

Contact Address

Embratur Tourist Office, Rua Uruguaiana 174, Rio de Janeiro, CEP 20.050-090, Brazil
Tel: (021) 509 6017. Fax: (021) 509 7381.
E-mail: rio@embratur.gov.br
Website: www.embratur.gov.br

Transportation

Air: Rio de Janeiro International Airport. **Road:** Coach: Novo Rio Coach Station.

Opening Times

Not applicable.

Admission Fees

Free.

Brunei Darussalam

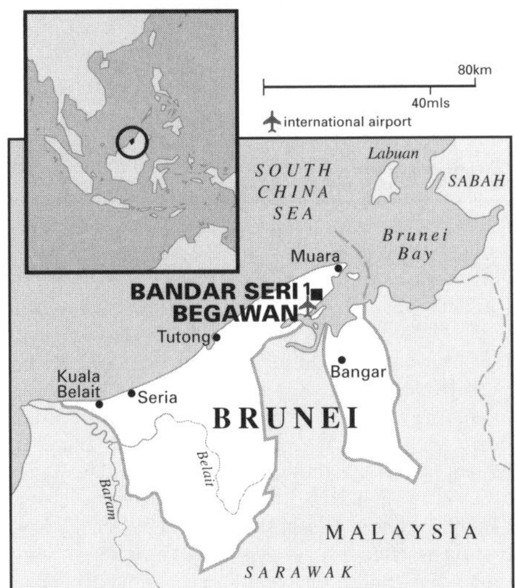

1 Di Masjid Omar Ali Saifuddin (Omar Ali Saifuddin Mosque)

Tourist Information

Brunei Tourism
Ministry of Industry and Primary Resources, Jalan Menteri Besar, Bandar Seri Bagawan BB3910, Brunei Darussalam
Tel: (02) 382 822. Fax: (02) 383 811.
E-mail: bruneitourism@brunet.bn
Website: www.visitbrunei.com
High Commission of Brunei Darussalam
20 Belgrave Square, London, SW1X 8PG, UK
Tel: (020) 7581 0521. Fax: (020) 7235 9717.

Di Masjid Omar Ali Saifuddin (Omar Ali Saifuddin Mosque)

Omar Ali Saifuddin Mosque is one of the most spectacular mosques in Asia Pacific and is a magnificent sight, whether viewed in the bright sunlight or illumunated at night. Named after the 28th Sultan of Brunei, the mosque, which is seen as a symbol of the Islamic faith in Brunei, dominates the skyline in the capital city, Bandar Seri Begawan. The golden dome of the mosque stands at 52m (171ft) high and can be seen from virtually anywhere in the city. The building was completed in 1958 and is an impressive example of Islamic architecture, with magnificent mosaic stained glass, as well as many arches, domes and columns. Marble from Italy, granite from Shanghai and chandeliers from England were all used in the construction of Brunei's most ornate building.

Contact Address

For more information on Omar Ali Saifuddin Mosque, contact Brunei Tourism (see **Tourist Information** above).

Transportation

Air: Bandar Seri Begawan International Airport. **Road:** Taxi: Taxis can be hailed in the city centre to take visitors to the mosque.

Opening Times

Sun-Wed 0800-1200, 1300-1530 and 1630-1730, Fri 1630-1730. Closed to non-muslims on Thurs.

Admission Fees

Free.

Omar Ali Saifuddin Mosque

Royal Brunei Airlines

Bulgaria

1 Hram-pametnik Aleksander Nevski (St Alexander Nevski Cathedral)
2 Rilski Manastir (Rila Monastery)

Tourist Information

National Information and Advertising Center to the Ministry of Economy
1 St Sophia Street, Sofia 1040, Bulgaria
Tel: (02) 987 9778 *or* 987 1152. Fax: (02) 987 9778 *or* 989 6939.
E-mail: info@bulgariatravel.org
Website: www.bulgariatravel.org

Embassy of the Republic of Bulgaria
186-188 Queen's Gate, London SW7 5HL, UK
Tel: (020) 7584 9400. Fax: (020) 7584 4948 *or* 7589 4875 (commercial department).
E-mail: bgembassy@globalnet.co.uk

Hram-pametnik Aleksander Nevski (St Alexander Nevski Cathedral)

St Alexander Nevski Cathedral is one of Sofia's most famous monuments. This neo-Byzantine structure, which is surmounted by copper and golden domes, was built between 1882 and 1912 in honour of the Russian soldiers who died trying to liberate Bulgaria from Ottoman rule during the War of Liberation in 1878. The cathedral, which is also one of the finest buildings in the Balkan States, takes its name from Alexander Nevski, the patron saint of the family of the Russian Tsar at the time, Alexander II. There are three altars inside the cathedral, dedicated to St Alexander Nevski, St Boris, who brought Christianity to Bulgaria and Saints Cyril and Methodius, who created the Cyrillic alphabet. Visitors can also see the *Icon Museum*, located in the Crypt, which houses around 300 exhibits following the development of Bulgarian icon-painting from the ninth to 19th centuries. Sofia also has many other fine attractions, including the *Rotunda of St George, St Sofia Church,* the *Church of St Nedely, Vassil Levski Monument* and the *Dragalevtsi* and *Boyana Churches.*

Contact Address

For more information on St Alexander Nevski Cathedral, contact the National Information and Advertising Center to the Ministry of Economy (see **Tourist Information** above).

Transportation

Air: Sofia Airport. **Rail:** Train: Sofia Station. Tram: 2, 12, 14, 20, 21 or 22. Trolley: 1, 2, 4, 7, 9 or 11. **Road:** Bus: 280 or 306 run past the university, which is located close to the church. Minibus: Shuttle services run from all residential areas of Sofia. Car: Signs for Sofia city centre, then over Orlov Most (Eagle Bridge). The cathedral overlooks Alexander Nevski Ploshtad, which can be reached from Tsurkva Sveta Nikolai (St Nicholas Russian Church).

Opening Times

Daily 0900-1800.

Admission Fees

Cathedral: Free. *Icon Museum*: Lv10.

Rilski Manastir (Rila Monastery)

Rila Monastery, the largest monastery in Bulgaria, is situated in the spectacular *Rhodope Mountains* in *Rila National Park* and is included on the UNESCO list of World Cultural Heritage Sites. Rila was the first Christian monastery to be built in Bulgaria and was founded by followers of John of Rila (the patron saint of Bulgaria) during the 10th century. Rila was damaged by fire several times over the years and was not fully restored to its current state until 1816. The monastery is ornately decorated with murals which were painted by famous artists, including Kosta Valyov and Zahari Zograph, between 1840 and 1848. It is also an ideal starting point for hiking in Rila National Park, with its dense pine forests and many mountain paths.

Contact Address

For more information on Rila Monastery, contact the National Information and Advertising Center to the Ministry of Economy (see **Tourist Information** above).

Transportation

Air: Sofia Airport. **Road:** Bus: There is no direct shuttle bus to the Rila Monastery, and visitors are advised to travel via Dupnitsa or Blagoevgrad. Visitors can then connect to a bus that will take them to the monastery. Car: E79 south of Sofia for 100km (62 miles), then a further 21km (13 miles) to arrive at Rila Monastery.

Opening Times

Daily 0900-1700.

Admission Fees

Free.

Mural in the Rila Monastery

National Information & Advertising Center to the Ministry of Economy

Cambodia

1 Angkor (Angkor Temple Complex)

Tourist Information

Krâsuong Peschor (Ministry of Tourism)
3 Boulevard Monivong, Phnom Penh, Cambodia
Tel: (023) 213 911. Fax: (023) 426 364 *or* 426 107.
E-mail: somara@cambodia-web.net
Website: www.cambodia-web.net
Royal Embassy of Cambodia
4 rue Adolphe Yvon, 75116 Paris, France
Tel: (01) 4503 4720. Fax: (01) 4503 4740.

Angkor (Angkor Temple Complex)

Angkor, the former capital of the ancient Khmer Empire, is one of the greatest and most spectacular Hindu religious sites in the world. Construction of this elaborate temple complex – built in honour of the god Vishnu – began in AD 879 during the reign of King Suryavarman II and was completed in 1191. It lay concealed for many years, however, until the site was discovered by Frenchman Henri Mahout in 1860. The central complex, *Angkor Wat* (Angkor Temple), features an elaborate, unmortared 66-metre (215-foot) central tower surrounded by four smaller towers. Stretching around the outside of the temple complex is an 800m-long (2625ft) bas-relief, the longest in the world, best known for the scene of the *Churning of the Ocean of Milk*. This depicts a central event in Hindu mythology when gods and demons joined forces to recover the elixir of immortality from below the cosmic ocean.

Contact Address

Ministry of Tourism, Boulevard Preah Monivong, Corner Rue 232, Phnom Penh
Tel: (023) 362 085) *or* 880 623 (Phnom Penh office) *or* (063) 380 069 (Siem Reap office). Fax: (023) 426 364 *or* 880 159 (Phnom Penh office) *or* (063) 380 070 (Siam Reap office). E-mail: tourism@camnet.com.kh
Website: www.cambodia-web.net

Transportation

Air: Siem Reap Airport. **Road:** Car: Route 6 (from Phnom Penh to Siem Reap).

Opening Times

Daily 0500-1900.

Admission Fees

US$20 (one day), US$40 (two days), US$60 (one week).

Monks at Angkor Wat

Corel

Canada

Alberta

1	Banff National Park	3	West Edmonton Mall
2	Jasper National Park		

Banff National Park

Canada's first national park, *Banff National Park* was created by the Canadian government in 1885 in recognition of the area's natural beauty and wildlife. Visitors continue to be awestruck by the stunning vistas of the *Rocky Mountains* and the opportunity to see elk grazing only metres away from them. The park has 6641 sq kilometres (2564 sq miles) of mountains, rivers, forests, lakes, glaciers and hot springs, and is home to wolves, mountain goats, eagles and grizzly bears, along with the notorious – and sometimes dangerous – elk. The most famous man-made addition to the area is the *Banff Springs Hotel*, completed in 1888. It was built to resemble a baronial Scottish castle and accommodates more than 800 guests. *Lake Louise*, named in honour of Queen Victoria's daughter, Princess Louise Caroline Alberta, is one of the most popular sites in the *Rocky Mountains*. Thousands of people, from film stars to local people come to its shores to ski, hike and relax in the many cafés and hotels.

Contact Address

Banff Lake Louise Tourism Bureau, Box 1298, Banff, Alberta, T0L 0C0, Canada
Tel: (403) 762 8421. Fax: (403) 762 8163.
E-mail: info@banfflakelouise.com
Website: www.banfflakelouise.com

Transportation

Air: Calgary International Airport. **Road:** Coach: Services from Calgary. Car: Trans-Canada Hwy-1.

Opening Times

Daily 24 hours.

Tourist Information

Canadian Tourism Commission
8th Floor West, 235 Queen Street, Ottawa, Ontario K1A 0H6, Canada
Tel: (613) 946 1000. Fax: (613) 954 3964.
E-mail: ctc_feedback@businteractive.com
Website: www.canadatourism.com

Travel Alberta
178-11 116th Avenue, Edmonton, Alberta T5J 2J2, Canada
Tel: (780) 427 4321. Fax: (780) 427 0867.
E-mail: info@travelalberta.com
Website: www.travelalberta.com

Visit Canada Centre
PO Box 5396, Northampton NN1 2FA, UK
Tel: (0906) 871 5000. Fax: (0870) 165 5665.
E-mail: visitcanada@dial.pipex.com
Website: www.canadatourism.com

Travel Alberta UK
24A Friday Street, Warnham, West Sussex RH12 3QX, UK
Tel: (01403) 754 424. Fax: (01403) 754 423.
E-mail: amandanewby@btinternet.com

Admission Fees

C$5 (adult), C$2.50 (child 6-16), free (child under 6); campers require extra permits. Concessions available.

Jasper National Park

Jasper National Park was originally called Jasper Forest Park when it was established in 1907 and is the largest of Canada's *Rocky Mountains* parks, spanning 10,878 sq kilometres (4200 sq miles). The spectacular scenery is characterised by glaciers, rugged mountains, forests and meadows carpeted with alpine flowers. The park protects a huge ecosystem – elk, moose, bear, bighorn sheep and mule deer are regular sights – and contains the last fully protected range of caribou in the *Rocky Mountains*. The best places to view wildlife are the Maligne Valley Road, Highway 16 and Highway 93A to Athabasca Falls. *Maligne Lake*, 48km (30 miles) southeast of Jasper is surrounded by snow-capped mountains and its crystal clear waters are popular for boating and fishing.

Contact Address

Jasper National Park Visitor Information Centre, 500 Connaught Drive, Jasper, Alberta, Canada
Tel: (780) 852 6176.
Website: www.worldweb.com/ParksCanada-Jasper

Transportation

Air: Calgary International Airport. **Rail:** Train: Jasper Station. **Road:** Bus: Jasper Bus Station. Car: Hwy-16 (from Edmonton); Hwy-1 (Trans-Canada Highway); Hwy-93 (from Calgary).

Opening Times

Daily 0800-1700 (16 May-13 Jun); daily 0800-1900 (14 Jun-1 Sep); daily 0900-1200 and 1300-1700 (2 Sep-15 May).

Admission Fees

C$5 (adult), C$2.50 (child). Concessions available.

West Edmonton Mall

West Edmonton Mall is the largest shopping and entertainment centre in the world, encompassing over 800 retail outlets (including ten restaurants), 19 cinemas and seven theme parks. Located in the west end of Alberta's capital, Edmonton, this huge complex is 48 times the size of a city block and attracts 55,000 visitors a day. The mall has the world's only indoor bungee jump for the more daring, and other activities on offer include dolphin watching, ice skating and golf. At the *Galaxyland* theme park visitors can experience the 14-storey 'Mindbender' – a triple-loop rollercoaster and the *World Waterpark* provides fun in the form of waterslides and wavepools. The *Deep Sea Adventure* takes visitors in a submarine 122m (335ft) under water to view shipwrecks, coral reef and over 200 species of marine life.

Contact Address

West Edmonton Mall, 2472, 8882-170 Street, Edmonton, Alberta T5T 4M2, Canada
Tel: (780) 444 5200. Fax: (780) 444 5223.
E-mail: tourism@westedmontonmall.com
Website: www.westedmontonmall.com

Transportation

Air: Edmonton International Airport (a shuttle service runs between the airport and the mall). **Road:** Bus: 100 Express, 1 or 2. Car: Hwy-16; Calgary Trail.

Opening Times

Retail shopping: Mon-Fri 1000-2100, Sat 1000-1800, Sun 1200-1800; some shops closed 25 Dec and 1 Jan. *Theme parks*: Daily 0930-2200 (however hours vary greatly depending on the season and park – visitors are advised to check in advance).

Admission Fees

Deep Sea Adventure: C$9.95 (adult), C$5 (child 3-10), free (child under 2). Concessions and family pass available. *Dolphin Shows*: C$3. *Galaxyland Amusement Park*: C$24.95 (adult), C$18.95 (child under 4), free (child under 1). Concessions and family pass available. *Ice Palace*: C$4.50 (adult), C$2.50 (child 3-10), free (child under 2), skate hire C$3. Concessions and family pass available. *Professor Wem's Adventure Golf*: C$7.50 (adult), C$5 (child 3-10), free (child under 2). Concessions and family pass available. *Sea Life Caverns*: C$6. Family pass available. *World Waterpark*: C$24.95 (adult), C$18.95 (child 3-10), free (child under 2). Concessions and family pass available.

Jasper National Park

Travel Alberta

Ontario

1	Algonquin Provincial Park
2	CN Tower
3	National Gallery of Canada
4	Niagara Falls

Tourist Information

Canadian Tourism Commission

8th Floor West, 235 Queen Street, Ottawa, Ontario K1A 0H6, Canada

Tel: (613) 946 1000. Fax: (613) 954 3964.

E-mail: ctc_feedback@businteractive.com

Website: www.canadatourism.com

Ontario Tourism Marketing Partnership

9th Floor, Hearst Block, 900 Bay Street, Toronto, Ontario M7A 2E1, Canada

Tel: (416) 314 0944. Fax: (416) 326 3133.

Website: www.ontariotravel.net

Visit Canada Centre

PO Box 5396, Northampton NN1 2FA, UK

Tel: (0906) 871 5000. Fax: (0870) 165 5665.

E-mail: visitcanada@dial.pipex.com

Website: www.canadatourism.com

Ontario Tourism Marketing Partnership

c/o CIB, 1 Battersea Church Road, London SW11 3LY, UK

Tel: (020) 7771 7004 (trade enquiries only).

Fax: (020) 7771 7059.

E-mail: ontario@cibgroup.co.uk

Algonquin Provincial Park

Spanning 7725 sq kilometres (4800 sq miles), *Algonquin Provincial Park* was established in 1893 to develop a wildlife sanctuary in a rugged, beautiful part of southern Ontario. It soon became popular with outdoors enthusiasts and canoeists because of its beautiful lakes, forests, bogs, rivers, cliffs and beaches. For campers and day visitors, *Highway 60* is the centre of the park, offering campgrounds, walking trails, conducted hikes and access to public wolf-howling sessions. In winter, cross-country skiing trails are a popular way to enjoy the scenery and catch glimpses of the animals that inhabit the park, including otter, moose, Ruffed Grouse and marten. Visitors can also soak up the history of the park in the *Logging Museum*, or in the *Algonquin Gallery*, which focuses on the Canadian artist Tom Thomson's (1877-1917) famous group of painters, the *Group of Seven*, who were inspired to paint the landscape of Northern Ontario.

Contact Address

Algonquin Provincial Park, PO Box 219, Whitney, Ontario, K0J 2M0, Canada

Tel: (705) 633 5572 (information) *or* (1888) 668 7275 (reservations).

E-mail: info@algonquinpark.on.ca

Website: www.algonquinpark.on.ca

Transportation

Air: Lester B Pearson International Airport (Toronto). **Rail:** Train: Huntsville Station. **Road:** Coach: Services to Huntsville (from Toronto). Car: Hwy-11, Hwy-17 or Hwy-60.

Opening Times

Daily 0800-2100. Opening times may vary seasonally.

Admission Fees

C$10 per vehicle per day (Parkway Corridor); C$8.50 per vehicle per day (East Side); campers require extra permits. Concessions available.

P ✕ 🧺 ♿

CN Tower

As the world's tallest free-standing structure, the *CN Tower* is the defining feature of Toronto's lakefront skyline. Completed in 1976, the 550m (1804ft) tower offers stunning views of Toronto and Lake Ontario. It takes only 58 seconds to reach the LookOut level in a glass-fronted lift which travels at 22km (15 miles) per hour. Once there, visitors can enjoy a meal at the revolving *360 Restaurant* (each rotation takes 72 minutes), walk across a glass floor on the 113th storey or get an even better view from the *Sky Pod* that is 447 metres (1465ft) high. There is also a collection of entertainment attractions at the base of the tower, including two motion simulator rides, and a short documentary film describing the feat of engineering undertaken to build this colossal structure.

Contact Address

CN Tower, 301 Front Street West, Toronto, Ontario, M5V 2T6, Canada
Tel: (416) 360 8500. Fax: (416) 601 4713.
E-mail: web_cntower@cntower.ca
Website: www.cntower.ca

Transportation

Air: Lester B Pearson International Airport (Toronto). **Rail:** Train: Union Station. Underground: Union Station. **Road:** Car: Hwy-427 (from the north).

Opening Times

CN Tower: Sun-Thurs 0900-2200, Fri and Sat 0900-2300. *Entertainment Centre*: Daily 1100-1900.

Admission Fees

C$15.99 (adult), C$10.99 (child 4-12), plus C$4.75 (Sky Pod) and C$7.50 (entertainment centre). Concessions available.

National Gallery of Canada

The National Gallery of Canada was founded in 1880 by the Governor General, the Marquess of Lorne and since then has grown to become an internationally-renowned art museum. The permanent collections reflect Canada's diverse history, and include works by European masters such as Monet, Turner and Di Cosimo, as well as avant-garde Canadian paintings from the 1960s and religious sculptures from Québec. The museum also contains a large collection of Inuit art, including prints, drawings and whale bone sculptures, many of which portray the cultural and social issues that have affected Canada's indigenous population since World War II. The Media Arts collection holds films by Fernand Léger and Man Ray amongst others and includes interactive displays; there is also an extensive photography collection. The National Gallery also plays host to a wide variety of temporary exhibitions, which have in the past ranged from Mexican Modern Art (1900-1950) to an exhibition of paintings depicting World War I through Canadian and foreign eyes.

Contact Address

National Gallery of Canada, 380 Sussex Drive, Box 427, Station A, Ottawa, Ontario K1N 9N4, Canada
Tel: (613) 990 1985. Fax: (613) 993 4385.
E-mail: info@gallery.ca
Website: www.national.gallery.ca

Transportation

Air: Ottawa Macdonald-Cartier International Airport. **Rail:** Train: Ottawa VIA Rail Station. **Road:** Bus: 3. Car: Hwy-7 or Hwy-417.

Opening Times

Wed and Fri-Sun 1000-1700, Thurs 1000-2000.

Admission Fees

Free.

Niagara Falls

Niagara Falls is one of the most popular tourist destinations in North America, made up of two separate parts, *Horseshoe Falls*, on the Canadian side and *American Falls* on the USA side. Although not the highest waterfall in the world (that record goes to the *Angel Falls* in Venezuela), they move a staggering volume of 168,000 cubic metres (219,600 cubic yards) of water per minute over a drop of 51m (167ft), making them one of the natural wonders of the world. In the past, people have attempted a number of daring stunts here, including walking a tightrope across the falls and dropping over the edge in a barrel. The surrounding town, a celebrated North American honeymoon destination, offers a wealth of visitor activities including a casino, as well as land and boat tours of the falls.

Contact Address

Niagara Falls Tourism, 5515 Stanley Avenue, Niagara Falls, Ontario L2G 3X4, Canada
Tel: (905) 356 6061. Fax: (905) 356 5567.
E-mail: info@niagarafallstourism.com
Website: www.discoverniagara.com

Transportation

Air: Buffalo Niagara Airport or Lester B Pearson International Airport (Toronto). **Rail:** Train: Niagara Falls VIA Rail Station. **Road:** Coach: Niagara Falls Coach Station. Car: Queen Elizabeth Way (QEW) towards Niagara, then Hwy-420 to Niagara Falls (from Toronto).

Opening Times

Daily 24 hours.

Admission Fees

Free.

Yukon Territory

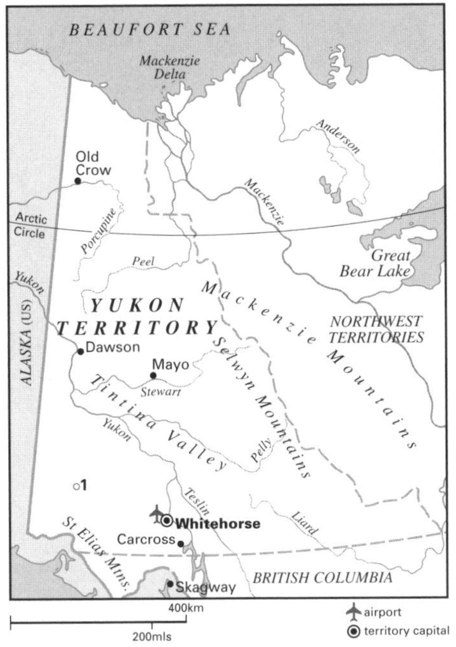

1 Kluane National Park and Reserve

Tourist Information

Canadian Tourism Commission
8th Floor West, 235 Queen Street, Ottawa, Ontario K1A 0H6, Canada
Tel: (613) 946 1000. Fax: (613) 954 3964.
E-mail: ctc_feedback@businteractive.com
Website: www.canadatourism.com

Tourism Yukon
PO Box 2703, Whitehorse, Yukon Territory Y1A 2C6, Canada
Tel: (867) 667 5340. Fax: (867) 667 3546.
E-mail: info@touryukon.com
Website: www.touryukon.com

Yukon First Nations Tourism Association
1109 First Avenue, PO Box 4581, Whitehorse, Yukon Y1A 2R8, Canada
Tel: (867) 667 7698. Fax: (867) 667 7527.
E-mail: yfnta@yknet.yk.ca
Website: www.yfnta.org

Visit Canada Centre
PO Box 5396, Northampton NN1 2FA, UK
Tel: (0906) 871 5000. Fax: (0870) 165 5665.
E-mail: visitcanada@dial.pipex.com
Website: www.canadatourism.com

Kluane National Park and Reserve

Kluane National Park and Reserve, established in 1972, has for thousands of years been the home of the Southern Tutchone First Nations people; the name Kluane (pronounced Kloo-wah-nee) is derived from a Southern Tutchone word meaning 'lake with many fish' (Kluane is Yukon Territory's largest lake). The park is a vast expanse of mountains and ice and encompasses the *Icefield Ranges*; the highest mountain in this range, *Mount Logan*, rises to 5959 metres (19,545 ft) and is the highest peak in Canada. *Kluane National Park and Reserve* also contains the most extensive icefields outside the polar region and visitors can fly over the icefields by helicopter – some trips include landings to allow the more adventurous to hike across sections of the icefields with a guide. Other popular activities on offer in the park include cross-country skiing, boating, fishing, snowmobiling, cycling, mountainbiking and horseriding. A rafting trip down the *Alsek River* allows visitors to view the wildlife (including grizzly bears, Dall sheep and golden eagles) and glaciers along the way; however, permits for rafting on this Canadian Heritage river are strictly limited to one departure per day and visitors are advised to arrange their trip well in advance.

Contact Address

Kluane National Park and Reserve, Box 5495 Haines Junction, Yukon Y0B 1L0, Canada
Tel: (867) 634 7250. Fax: (867) 634 7208.
Website: parkscan.harbour.com/kluane

Transportation

Air: Vancouver International Airport, then Whitehorse Airport (domestic flight). **Road:** Car: Alaska Highway or Haines Highway.

Opening Times

Daily 24 hours.

Admission Fees

C$5 per day (adult), free (child under 16).

Québec

1 Vieux Port de Montréal (Old Port of Montréal)
2 Vieux Québec (Old Québec)

Tourist Information

Canadian Tourism Commission
8th Floor West, 235 Queen Street, Ottawa, Ontario K1A 0H6, Canada
Tel: (613) 946 1000. Fax: (613) 954 3964.
E-mail: ctc_feedback@businteractive.com
Website: www.canadatourism.com

Tourisme Québec
Centre Infotouriste Montréal, 1001 Square Dorchester, Bureau 100, Montréal, Québec H3B 4V4, Canada
Tel: (514) 873 2015. Fax: (514) 864 3838.
E-mail: info@tourisme.gouv.qc.ca
Website: www.bonjour-quebec.com

Visit Canada Centre
PO Box 5396, Northampton NN1 2FA, UK
Tel: (0906) 871 5000. Fax: (0870) 165 5665.
E-mail: visitcanada@dial.pipex.com
Website: www.canadatourism.com

Destination Québec
Suite 154, 4th Floor, 35-37 Grosvenor Gardens, London SW1W 0BS, UK
Tel: (020) 7233 8011 (trade enquiries only).
Fax: (020) 7233 7203 (trade enquiries only).
E-mail: destquebec@aol.com (trade enquiries only).

Vieux Port de Montréal (Old Port of Montréal)

The *Old Port* is located in the historic heart of the cosmopolitan, francophone city of Montréal. It was once the sea-trading hub of North America and in the first half of the 20th century was the second largest port in North America after New York. After port operations declined in the late 1950s, the Canadian government decided to redevelop the area, and it is now a thriving arts and entertainment venue, visited by five million people each year. The port is surrounded by the city's original 17th-century walled fortifications and the activities on offer reflect both the area's illustrious past and its modern, forward-looking philosophy. The *Clock Tower* offers excellent views across the city and houses an exhibition tracing the city's history, whilst the new *iSci Centre* allows visitors of all ages to explore the world of science and technology through activities and interactive displays. Another popular option is to see an *IMAX* film in the city where IMAX technology was born. In winter, there is a huge open-air skating rink at *Bonsecours Basin*, as well as horse-drawn sleigh rides, and the Old Port has a bustling café culture all year round.

Contact Address

The Old Port of Montréal Corporation Inc., 333 rue de la Commune Ouest, Montréal, Québec H2Y 2E2, Canada
Tel: (877) 496 4724.
Website: www.oldportofmontreal.com

Transportation

Air: Montréal Dorval International Airport or Montréal Mirabel International Airport. **Rail:** Train: Montréal Station (Gare Centrale). Underground: Square-Victoria, Champ-de-Mars or Place d'armes. **Road:** Car: Ville-Marie Expressway (Hwy-720).

Opening Times

IMAX: Shows every hour Sun-Thurs 1015-2115 and Fri-Sat 1015-2215. *iSci*: Daily 1000-1800. *Ice-skating*:

Daily 1000-2200 (early Dec-early Mar); daily 1000-1800 (24 Dec and 31 Dec).

Admission Fees

IMAX: C$9.95 (adult), C$7.95 (child 4-12). Concessions and family pass available. *iSci exhibitions*: C$9.95 (adult), C$8.95 (child 13-17), C$7.95 (child 4-12). *iSci IMMERSION cinema*: C$5.50 (adult), C$4.95 (child 4-17). Concessions and family pass available; combination *IMAX* and *IMMERSION* passes available. *Ice-skating*: C$2 (adult), free (child under 6). Concessions and family pass available. *Skate hire*: C$6.

Vieux Québec (Old Québec)

The only walled city north of Mexico, *Québec* was settled in 1608 as a fur trading post. Its fortified exterior and strategic position high above the St Lawrence River is a testament to the territorial tensions between the French and English that culminated in the Battle of the Plains of Abraham (1759). Divided into two sections, *Haute* and *Basse*, the old town seems more like an island of old Europe, with winding cobblestone streets, 17th- and 18th-century buildings and churches, squares, parks and numerous monuments. The *Château Frontenac*, a Canadian landmark, is its most prominent building – built in 1893, it is now a luxury hotel with views over the St Lawrence River and Old Québec.

Contact Address

Tourisme Québec, PO Box 979, Montréal, Quebec H3C 2W3, Canada
Tel: (514) 873 2015 *or* (877) 266 5687. Fax: (514) 864 3838. E-mail: info@bonjourquebec.com
Website: www.vieux-quebec.com

Transportation

Air: Jean-Lesage International Airport. **Rail:** Train: Québec Station (Gare du Palais). **Road:** Bus: Gare du Palais Station. Car: Hwy-20 or Hwy-40.

Opening Times

Daily 24 hours.

Admission Fees

Not applicable.

Château Frontenac, Québec

Denis Trudel, Tourisme Québec

Chile

1 Rapa Nui (Easter Island)

Tourist Information

Servicio Nacional de Turismo (SERNATUR)
Avenida Providencia 1550, PO Box 14802, Santiago, Chile
Tel: (02) 236 1416. Fax: (02) 251 8469.
E-mail: info@sernatur.cl
Website: www.segegob.cl/sernatur/inicio.html

Embassy and Consulate of the Republic of Chile
12 Devonshire Street, London W1N 2DS, UK
Tel: (020) 7580 6392. Fax: (020) 7436 5204.
Website: www.echileuk.demon.co.uk

Need more information on Chile?
Consult the *World Travel Guide*

Rapa Nui (Easter Island)

A lonely volcanic island in the middle of the Pacific Ocean, as far away from Chile as from Tahiti, *Easter Island* is famous for its mysterious stone statues, or *moais*, that form an almost unbroken ring around the coast. Three hundred statues and related items of stonework, which were built during the tenth to 16th centuries, grace the island. Scientists are fascinated to learn how native inhabitants designed and forged the massive sculptures from hard volcanic rock, and how they transported them to the coast from inland quarries. Today, about 2000 people inhabit *Easter Island*, most of them living in the town of Hanga Roa.

Contact Address

SERNATUR, Tourist Information, Tuu Maheke s/n, esquina Apina, Easter Island, Chile
Tel: (032) 100 255. Fax: (032) 100 255.
E-mail: sernatur-rapanui@entelchile.net
Website: www.sernatur.cl

Transportation

Air: Mataveri Airport (Easter Island).

Opening Times

Daily 24 hours.

Admission Fees

Free.

Statues on Easter Island

Mark Sullivan

People's Republic of China

1 Beijing Dongwu Yuan (Beijing Zoo)
2 Bingma Yong (Terracotta Army)
3 Kukhar Potrang (Potala Palace)
4 Sanxia (Three Gorges of the Yangtze River)
5 Tai Ping Shan (Victoria Peak)
6 Wanli Changcheng (Great Wall of China)
7 Xijin Cheng (Forbidden City)
8 Yi He Yuan (Summer Palace)

Tourist Information

China National Tourism Administration (CNTA)
Department of Marketing and Communications, 9A Jianguomennei Avenue, Beijing 100740, People's Republic of China
Tel: (010) 6520 1411 *or* 6512 2905. Fax: (010) 6512 2851.
Website: www.cnta.com

China National Tourist Office (CNTO)
4 Glentworth Street, London NW1 5PG, UK
Tel: (020) 7935 9787 *or* (09001) 600 188 (brochure request and general information; calls cost 60p per minute). Fax: (020) 7487 5842.

Tibet Tourism Administration
Yuanlin Road, Lhasa, Tibet 850001, People's Republic of China
Tel: (0891) 683 4313. Fax: (0891) 683 4632.

Beijing Dongwu Yuan (Beijing Zoo)

Beijing Zoo is the oldest and largest zoo in Asia Pacific and the world-famous home of the giant pandas. Located in the northwest area of the city, the zoo is home to more than 7000 animals, including golden monkeys from Sichuan, yaks from Tibet, sea turtles from the Chinese sea, Manchurian tigers and snow leopards. The zoo is also famous for being the home of zoological research and for housing many rare birds and animals. During the Ming Dynasty (1368-mid 17th century), the zoo was an imperial park, whilst during the Qing Dynasty (1644-early 20th century), it became an experimental farm and small menagerie. It was first opened to the public in 1908, but was destroyed during the Japanese occupation of Beijing (1937-1945), only to reopen in 1950.

Contact Address

Beijing Dongwu Yuan, 137 Xizhimenwai, Xicheng District, Beijing, People's Republic of China
Tel: (010) 6831 4411.
E-mail: bjzoo@public3.bta.net.cn
Website: www.beijingzoo.com

Transportation

Air: Beijing Capital Airport. **Rail:** Train: Beijing Station.

Opening Times

Daily 0800-1700 (winter); daily 0700-1800 (summer).

Admission Fees

RMBY10 (adult), RMBY3 (child). Admission fees include entrance to several shows.

Bingma Yong (Terracotta Army)

The *Terracotta Army* is an enormous collection of Chinese warriors made out of hardened clay, 40km (25 miles) east of the town of Xi'an. The army, which is set out in rigid columns, was created in the second century BC by the emperor Shih Huang-Ti, the first emperor of a unified China, and was entombed with him upon his death. It was discovered in 1974 during an attempt to dig a well, and since then three separate chambers have revealed over 10,000 figures. The clay figures are all individual, and are made to represent actual members of the imperial army, including both soldiers and officers. Some are armed with real weapons, standing in battle formation next to real wooden chariots. The collection also includes clay horses and is often referred to as 'the eighth wonder of the world'.

Contact Address

For more information on the Terracotta Army, contact China National Tourism Administration (CNTA) (see **Tourist Information** above).

Transportation

Air: Beijing Capital Airport or Xi'an Airport (domestic flights). **Rail:** Train: Xi'an Station. **Road:** Taxi: Services from Xi'an.

Opening Times

Daily 0930-1700.

Admission Fees

RMBY80.

Kukhar Potrang (Potala Palace)

The *Potala Palace* is the largest structure in Tibet. It stands 130m (427ft) above the Lhasa Valley and was built in the seventh century as a retreat for the local lord, Songsten Gampo, and his bride Princess Wen Cheng. At 13 storeys high, and standing on top of a 3700m (12,139ft) cliff, it is the world's highest palace. The palace complex is made up of two sections, the *Red Palace* and the *White Palace*. The upper Red Palace includes the living quarters and tombs of most of the Dalai Lamas, and many temples containing a myriad of gilded statues of Buddha. Visitors can see the *Hall of the Buddha*, the *Scripture Hall* and the *Memorial Hall*, housing gold-traced portraits of Sakyamuni and the late Dalai Lamas, copies of Buddhist sutras and stupas of deceased Dalai Lamas. The White Palace below once housed a printing press, two small chapels, more temples and the administrative offices of the Tibetan government. Today, the palace boasts many treasures from Tibet's rich history, including many religious and cultural artefacts.

Contact Address

Tibet Tourism Administration, Yualin Road, Lhasa, Tibet 85001, People's Republic of China
Tel: (0891) 633 5472. Fax: (0891) 683 4632.

Transportation

Air: Gonggar International Airport. **Road:** Taxi: From various locations in Lhasa (the palace is located in the centre of Lhasa). Car: Chengdu-Lhasa Highway (from Chengdu); Lhasa-Zham Friendship Bridge-Kathmandu Highway (from Kathmandu).

Opening Times

Mon-Thurs 0930-1200. (Palace opening hours change frequently and travellers are advised to check with the tourist office before their visit.)

Admission Fees

RMBY45.

Sanxia (Three Gorges of the Yangtze River)

The *Three Gorges of the Yangtze River* are a system of breathtaking gorges on China's longest river, which is also the third longest river in the world (after the Amazon and the Nile), stretching for 6300km (3915 miles). The *Qü-tang Gorge*, the shortest of the three gorges, is best known for its steep precipices that form an enormous gateway over the river. At 45km (28 miles), the *Wu Gorge* is the longest gorge, and is home to the famous 12 peaks of *Mount Wushan*, the most beautiful of which is *Goddess Peak*. The *Xiling Gorge* is known for its hidden reefs, perilous cliffs and tumbling rapids, as well as the orange groves and tea plantations on its shores. The Yangtze River's watershed covers about 20 per cent of China's total land and is home to over 350 million people.

Contact Address

For more information on the Three Gorges of the Yangtze River, contact China National Tourism Administration (CNTA) (see **Tourist Information** above).

Transportation

Air: Beijing Capital Airport or Shanghai Hongqiao Airport. **Water:** Ferry: Services from Yichang. **Rail:** Train: Yichang Station.

Opening Times

Daily 24 hours.

Admission Fees

Free.

Tai Ping Shan (Victoria Peak)

At 552m (1514ft) above sea level, *Victoria Peak* is the most conspicuous landmark in Hong Kong. The peak was rarely visited until 1888, the year the *Peak Tramway* was opened, and its popularity has risen steadily since. Today, it is home to Hong Kong's wealthiest executives and bankers who favour the rarefied, natural surroundings. The view from the top is breathtaking – visitors who come here to look out over the awesome skyline of Hong Kong may even be able to see Macau and mainland China on a clear day. There are many restaurants and attractions, including a *Madame Tussaud's Wax Museum* in the *Peak Galleria* at the summit. Walking trails allow visitors to explore the peak's natural beauty, including forests of bamboo and fern, stunted Chinese pines and sightings of birds, such as magpies, goshawks and kites.

Contact Address

Hong Kong Tourism Board, 9-11th Floor, Citicorp Centre, 18 Whitefield Road, North Point, Hong Kong, People's Republic of China
Tel: (852) 2508 1234. Fax: (852) 2806 0303.
E-mail: info@hktourismboard.com
Website: www.discoverhongkong.com

Transportation

Air: Hong Kong International Airport. **Rail:** Train: Peak Tram (from Garden Road). Underground: Central Station (exit Exchange Square). **Road:** Bus: 15.

Opening Times

Peak Tower (all attractions): Daily 0900-2200.

Admission Fees

Peak Tower (all attractions): HK$65 (adult), HK$46 (child under 12). Concessions available.

Wanli Changcheng (Great Wall of China)

One of the only man-made structures visible from space, the *Great Wall of China* is the greatest symbol of China's history and grandeur. Begun in the third century BC, the Great Wall connected a number of earlier walls to create a defence against nomads invading from the north. Although the wall ultimately failed in this regard, it was effective in bringing stability and continuity to Chinese culture. Much of the wall that exists today was rebuilt between the 14th and 18th centuries by the Ming dynasty. The wall has an average height of 7.6 metres (25ft) and is between 4.6 metres (15ft) and 9.1 metres (30ft) at the base.

Contact Address

For more information on the Great Wall of China, contact China National Tourism Administration (see **Tourist Information** above).

Transportation

Air: Beijing Capital Airport. **Rail:** Train: Badaling Station. **Road:** Bus: Tourist bus (from Beijing city centre). Car: Motorway to Badaling (from Beijing) (journey time: approximately two hours).

Opening Times

Daily 0900-1600 (winter); daily 0900-1700 (summer).

Admission Fees

RMBY100.

Xijin Cheng (Forbidden City)

Built in the early 15th century during the Ming dynasty, the *Forbidden City* served as the home for 24 of China's Ming and Qing emperors. The palace drew its name from the fact that vast sections of it were off limits to virtually all save the emperor himself. Its 9000 rooms, filled with paintings, pottery and bronzes, are redolent of China's imperial past, an era of concubines, palace eunuchs and a rigid power structure. Among the Forbidden City's more notable landmarks are the *Meridian Gate*, the *Hall of Supreme Harmony* and the *Imperial Garden.*

Contact Address

For more information on the Forbidden City, contact China National Tourism Administration (see **Tourist Information** above).

Transportation

Air: Beijing Capital Airport. **Rail:** Train: Beijing Station. Underground: Qianmen. **Road:** Bus: 111, 103 or 109. Car: Towards Beijing city centre.

Opening Times

Daily 1000-1600 (winter); daily 0900-1800 (summer).

Admission Fees

RMBY100.

Yi He Yuan (Summer Palace)

Considered to be one of the finest classical gardens in China, the *Summer Palace* was first built in 1153 and served as a retreat for the royal court to escape the heat in the city. The imperial residences are built on the shores of Kunming Lake, which contains small islands, ornamental bridges and a marble boat that was once a teahouse. The palace was rebuilt in 1888 by the Empress Dowager Ci Xi, who spent large amounts of money, from a fund intended for building a Chinese navy, on bringing the garden to its present state of glory. Covering an area of 290 hectares (717 acres), the gardens consist of a large lake with halls, towers, galleries, pavilions and bridges dotting the surrounding hilly land.

Contact Address

For more information on the Summer Palace, contact China National Tourism Administration (see **Tourist Information** above).

Transportation

Air: Beijing Capital Airport. **Rail:** Train: Beijing Station. **Road:** Bus: 332, 320, 362 or 904.

Opening Times

Daily 0900-1600 (winter); daily 0900-1700 (summer).

Admission Fees

RMBY90.

Bridge at the Summer Palace

Corel

Costa Rica

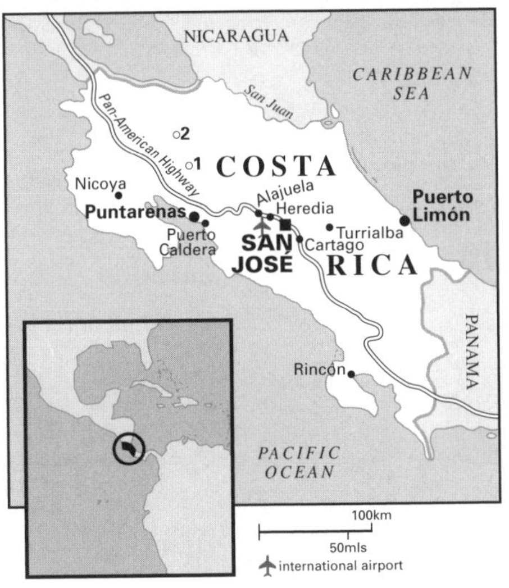

1 Bosque Nuboso de Monteverde (Monteverde Cloud Forest)
2 Volcán Arenal (Arenal Volcano)

Tourist Information

Instituto Costarricense de Turismo (Costa Rica Tourist Board)
PO Box 777, 1000 San José, Costa Rica
Tel: 223 1733. Fax: 223 5452.
E-mail: info@tourismcostarica.com
Website: www.tourism-costarica.com

Embassy and Consulate of the Republic of Costa Rica
Flat 1, 14 Lancaster Gate, London W2 3LH, UK
Tel: (020) 7706 8844. Fax: (020) 7706 8655.
E-mail: info@embcrlon.demon.co.uk
Website: www.embrclon.demon.co.uk

Bosque Nuboso de Monteverde (Monteverde Cloud Forest)

Straddling the Continental Divide and covering 170 sq kilometres (66 sq miles), this vast forest has its head – and its feet – in the clouds. The ever-present drizzle and mist provide a home to six different vegetation communities, over 100 mammal species (including howler monkeys, anteaters and 68 species of bat), 400 bird species (including Quetzals and Emerald Toucanets), 120 amphibian species and at least 2500 plant species. Access to the high level of biodiversity is through extensive trails, shelters deep within the forest for overnight camping, and a 91-metre (300-feet) suspension bridge that takes visitors from ground level high up into the canopy of the forest. There is also a *Visitor Centre, Butterfly Centre, Orchid Garden, Serpentarium* and *Hummingbird Gallery.*

Contact Address

Monteverde Cloud Forest Preserve, Apdo 55-5655, Monteverde, Puntarenas, Costa Rica
Tel: 645 5122. Fax: 645 5034.
E-mail: montever@sol.racsa.co.cr
Website: www.cct.or.cr *or* www.cloudforestalive.org

Transportation

Air: Juan Santamaria International Airport (San José).
Road: Coach: Services to Santa Elena (from Puntarenas); express service to Monteverde (from San José). Car: From San José, Pan-American Highway to Kilometre #149 (from San José).

Opening Times

Daily 0700-1600.

Admission Fees

US$10 (adult), US$5.50 (child 12-16), free (child under 12), US$15.25 (guided tours). Concessions available.

Volcán Arenal (Arenal Volcano)

One of the world's most active volcanoes, *Arenal,* with its classic cone-shaped crater, can be seen from anywhere in the surrounding area, even the cafés of the nearest town, La Fortuna. The volcano had lain dormant for over 400 years until 1968, when it erupted, forming a lava landscape around the base. Research centre *Arenal Observatory Lodge* provides excellent views and *Arenal Volcano National Park* offers trails around the slopes and views of the summit; there are also hot spring spas with views over the surrounding area. The volcano's intermittent daily eruptions create vast clouds of ash in the sky and huge booms. At night, the view is even more spectacular, as molten rocks and lava tumble down the slopes, creating a dramatic 'firework' display that is fortunately always at least five kilometres (three miles) away.

Contact Address

Arenal Observatory Lodge, PO Box 321-1007, Centro Colón, Costa Rica
Tel: 257 9489 *or* 695 5033. Fax: 257 4220.
E-mail: info@arenal-observatory.co.cr
Website: www.arenal-observatory.co.cr

Transportation

Air: Juan Santamaria International Airport (San José) or Daniel Oduber Airport. **Road:** Coach: Services to La Fortuna (from San José and Ciudad Quesada). Car: Pan-American Highway (from San José).

Opening Times

Arenal Volcano National Park: Daily 0800-1600; night tours depart from La Fortuna at 1800.

Admission Fees

Arenal Volcano National Park: US$6 (adult), free (child under 12).

Arenal Volcano

Costa Rica Tourist Board

Croatia

1	Dubrovnik
2	Nacionalni Park Plitvicka Jezera (Plitvice Lakes National Park)

Tourist Information

Hrvatska turistička zajedni (Croatian National Tourist Board)
Iblerov Trg 10/IV, 10000 Zagreb, Croatia
Tel: (01) 455 6455. Fax: (01) 455 7827.
E-mail: info@htz.hr
Website: www.htz.hr

Croatian National Tourist Office
2 The Lanchesters, 162-164 Fulham Palace Road, London W6 9ER, UK
Tel: (020) 8563 7979. Fax: (020) 8563 2616.
E-mail: info@cnto@freeserve.co.uk
Website: www.htz.hr

Dubrovnik

The writer George Bernard Shaw recommended that 'Those who seek paradise on earth should come to Dubrovnik and see Dubrovnik'. This small fortified city with a population of about 43,000, lies on the Dalmatian coast in southern Croatia and is often referred to as the 'Pearl of the Adriatic'. Founded in the seventh century, Dubrovnik reached its heyday as an important sea-trading port in the late Middle Ages, and the proliferation of Gothic, Renaissance and Baroque buildings are a legacy of its rich and glorious past. The most famous sights are the *Franjevačkog Samostana Mala Braca* (Franciscan Friars Minor Monastery) in the west, which houses one of the three oldest pharmacies in Europe, the 15th-century *Dominikanskog Samostana* (Dominican monastery), located in the east of the city, and the 17th-century *Katedrale* (cathedral). The *Dubrovački Muzej* (Dubrovnik Museum) housed in the splendid *Kneažev Dvor* (Rector's Palace) is also worth a visit. Many of Dubrovnik's monuments have been painstakingly restored after the great earthquake of 1667 and Croatia's struggle for independence in 1991; the city was listed as a UNESCO World Heritage Site in 1979. The city is surrounded by the deep blue waters of the Adriatic and has a distinctly laid-back, Mediterranean feel, with many cafés and fish restaurants lining the cobbled streets.

Contact Address

Dubrovnik Tourist Board, C Zuzoric 1/ 2, 20000 Dubrovnik, Croatia
Tel: (020) 426 303. Fax: (020) 426 480.
E-mail: tzgd@du.tel.hr
Website: www/dubrovnik.laus.hr

Transportation

Air: Dubrovnik International Airport or Zagreb International Airport. **Water:** Ferry: Services from Bari (Italy). **Road:** Bus: 1, 1A, 3 or 6 (from ferry terminal or bus station). Coach: Services from Split. Car: Adriatic Coastal Road from Split, Trieste and Zagreb (via Karlovec and Makarska).

Opening Times

Dominikanskog Samostana: Daily 0900-1800. *Dubrovački Muzej*: Daily 0900-1400. *Franjevačkog Samostana Mala Braca*: Daily 0900-1600. *Katedrale*: Daily 0900-1900.

Admission Fees

Dominikanskog Samostana: K10 (adult), K5 (child). *Dubrovački Muzej*: K10 (adult), K5 (child). Concessions available. *Franjevačkog Samostana Mala Braca*: K5 (adult), K3 (child). *Katedrale*: K5 (adult), K3 (child).

Nacionalni Park Plitvicka Jezera (Plitvice Lakes National Park)

Plitvice Lakes National Park, in the heart of Croatia, consists of 16 beautiful blue-green lakes, linked by a series of waterfalls and cascades to form a chain through a wooded valley. Over thousands of years, the waters that flow through this area have passed over limestone and chalk, creating deposits which form natural barriers between the lakes. The lakes range in height from *Proscansko Jezero* at 636.6m (1746ft) above sea level, to the lowest, *Kaludjerovac*, at 505.2m (1386ft), and in surface area from 81 hectares (33 acres) to one hectare (2.5 acres). Many species of rare bird inhabit the woods around the lakes, as do bears and wolves. Aside from the great beauty of the Plitvice Lakes, which afford many opportunities for hiking, boating and other activities, visitors come here to breathe in the pure mountain air and enjoy local hospitality in the traditional lodges and hotels that lie within the bounds of the park.

Contact Address

Plitvice Lakes National Park, 53231 Plitvička Jezera, Croatia
Tel: (053) 751 015. Fax: (053) 751 013.
E-mail: np-plitvice@np-plitvice.tel.hr
Website: www.np-plitvice.tel.hr

Transportation

Air: Zagreb International Airport. **Road:** Coach: All coaches on the Zagreb-Zadar route stop at Plitvice; it is also possible to visit Plitvice as a day trip from most coastal resorts between the Kvarner Riviera and mid-Dalmatia.

Opening Times

Daily 0800-1830.

Admission Fees

K60 (adult), K40 (child). Concessions available. Prices include a bus tour and a boat ride across the main lake.

Dubrovnik Old Town

Dubrovnik County Tourism Association

Cuba

1 Vieja Habana (Old Havana)

Tourist Information

Ministerio de Turismo (Ministry of Tourism)
Calle 19, No 710, Entre Paseo y A, Vedado, Havana, Cuba
Tel: (07) 330 545. Fax: (07) 334 086.
E-mail: promo@mintur.mit.cma.net

Cuba Tourist Board
154 Shaftesbury Avenue, London WC2 8DR, UK
Tel: (020) 7240 6655. Fax: (020) 7836 9265.
E-mail: cubatouristboard.london@virgin.net

Vieja Habana (Old Havana)

Old Havana, with its overhanging balconies and smart hotels, harks back to Cuba's days as a colonial outpost and its subsequent era as a glamorous, sophisticated Caribbean playground. Although some of the crumbling palaces look like they could do with a lick of paint, many of its colonial buildings, majestic boulevards, elegant plazas and tiny side streets have been restored, attracting more and more visitors each year. The *Plaza de la Catedral* (Cathedral Square), dominated by the towers of the 18th-century Baroque *Catedral de San Cristobal de La Habana*, perhaps best captures Old Havana's spirit. The oldest building in the square is the splendid *Museo de Arte Colonial* (Colonial Art Museum; tel: (07) 626 440), which dates from 1720 and houses a fine collection of colonial furniture in rooms grouped around shady courtyards filled with tropical plants.

Contact Address

Infotur, 5ta Avenida esq. 112, Miramar, La Habana, Cuba
Tel: (07) 247 036. Fax: (07) 243 977.

Transportation

Air: Havana Jose Marti International Airport. **Rail:** Train: Miramar Station. **Road:** Bus: 34, 232 or 264. Car: Carreterra Central (across Cuba via Havana); Autopista (from Pinar del Rio or Ciego de Avila to Havana).

Opening Times

Catedral de San Cristobal de la Habana: Officially open every day, but is often locked. *Museo de Arte Colonial*: Daily 0930-1900.

Admission Fees

Catedral de San Cristobal de la Habana: Free. *Museo de Arte Colonial*: US$2.

Old Havana

Cuba Tourist Board

Cyprus

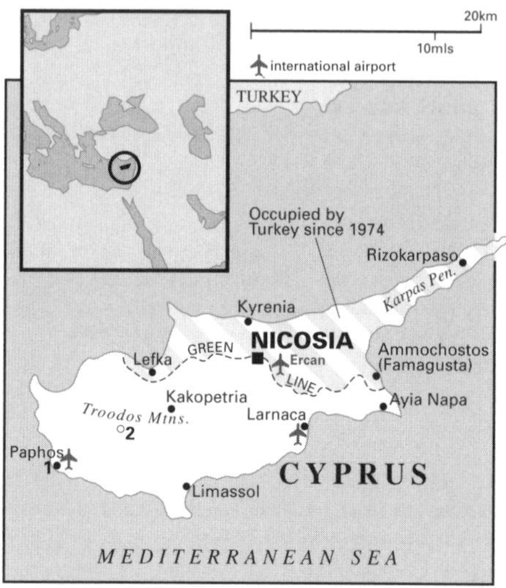

1 Pafos (Paphos)
2 Panagia tou Kykkou (Kykkos Monastery)

Tourist Information

Cyprus Tourism Organisation
Street address: 19 Limassol Avenue, Melkonian Building, Nicosia, 1390, Cyprus
Postal address: PO Box 24535, Nicosia 1390, Cyprus
Tel: (02) 337 715. Fax: (02) 331 644.
E-mail: cytour@cto.org.cy
Website: www.cyprustourism.org

Cyprus Tourism Organisation
17 Hanover Street, London W1S 1YP, UK
Tel: (020) 7569 8800. Fax: (020) 7499 4935.
E-mail: ctolon@ctolon.demon.co.uk
Website: www.cyprustourism.org

Pafos (Paphos)

The town of *Paphos*, which is listed as a World Heritage Site by UNESCO, is famed for being the birthplace of Aphrodite (the Goddess of Love) and home to *Aphrodite's Rock* (Petra Toy Romiou), which was erected by the Myceneans in the 12th century BC. The town also boasts numerous forts, palaces and churches, as well as the beautiful *Mosaics of Paphos*. These are located near the harbour in Kato Pafos and are considered to be the finest mosaics in the Eastern Mediterranean, depicting scenes from greek mythology and still in excellent condition. The *Tombs of the Kings*, a maze of underground tombs dating back to the fourth century BC which actually housed the remains of high officials rather than kings, can also be found in the Paphos area, along with the many relics in the *Medieval Fort*, the *Paphos District Archaelogical Museum*, the *Byzantine Museum* and the *Ethnographical Museum*. The impressive second century *Odeon*, which was rediscovered in 1973, the 12th-century *Saranta Kolones Castle*, the fifth-century *Panagia Limeniotissa Basilica* and the 13th-century *Panagia Chrysopolitissa Church* are also worth a visit for their architectural and historical importance.

Contact Address

Paphos Chamber of Commerce and Industry (PCCI), 7 Athinon Avenue and Alexandrou Papagou Corner, Tolmi Court, 1st Floor, Office 101-102, Paphos, Cyprus
Tel: (06) 235 115. Fax: (06) 244 602.
E-mail: evepafos@cytanet.com.cy

Transportation

Air: Paphos International Airport. **Road:** Car: Coastal road east to Paphos (from Limassol). Coastal road south to Paphos (from the Polis region). Road southwest, past Platres and Kedares (from Troodos). Then coast road east from Limassol, (from Troodos).

Opening Times

Aphrodite's Rock: Daily. *Byzantine Museum*: Mon-Fri 0900-1700 (Oct-May); Mon-Fri 0900-1900 (Jun-Sep); Sat 0900-1400. *Ethnographical Museum*: Mon-Fri 0900-1300 and 1400-1700 (Oct-Apr); Mon-Fri 0900-1300 and 1500-1900 (May-Sep); Sat 0900-1300; Sun 1000-1300. *Medieval Fort*: Daily 0900-1700 (winter); daily 0900-1930 (summer). *Mosaics of Paphos*: Daily 0800-1700 (winter); daily 0800-1930 (summer). *Pafos District Archaeological Museum*: Mon-Sat 0900-1700; Sun 1000-1300. *Tombs of the Kings*: Daily 0800-1700 (winter); daily 0830-1930 (summer). Opening times may vary for churches and other attractions.

Admission Fees

Aphrodite's Rock: Free. *Byzantine Museum*: C£0.50. *Ethnographical Museum*: C£0.50. *Medieval Fort*: C£0.50. *Mosaics of Paphos*: C£1.00. *Paphos District Archaelogical Museum*: C£0.50. *Tombs of the Kings*: C£0.50.

Panagia tou Kykkou (Kykkos Monastery)

Kykkos Monastery, which is located 20km (12 miles) west of Pedoulas village in the Kykkos Mountains, is the largest and most famous monastery in Cyprus. Founded in AD 1100 by the Byzantine emperor Alexios Komnenos, the monastery is dedicated to the Virgin Mary and is home to one of the three surviving icons painted by the Apostle Luke. According to legend, the hermit Esaias asked the Byzantine governor Doux Manuel Voutoumites to bring the icon of the Virgin Mary from Constantinople to Cyprus in return for curing his daughter of a mysterious illness. The Emperor Alexios Komnenos finally agreed to this, despite originally intending to send a copy of the icon, as the Virgin Mary supposedly appeared to him in a dream expressing her desire for the original to be brought to Cyprus. Kykkos Monastery is ornately decorated and covered in a silver gilt, enclosed in a tortoiseshell shrine. It is also famous for its museum, located within the monastery grounds, which houses an impressive collection of icons, woodcarvings and manuscripts, and other Cypriot antiquities. The nearby *Troodos Mountains*, with magnificent hills and valleys, should also be explored as they are home to nine Byzantine churches, included on UNESCO's World Heritage List, and richly decorated with murals and Byzantine paintings.

Contact Address

For more information on Kykkos Monastery, contact Cyprus Tourism Organisation (see **Tourist Information** above).

Transportation

Air: Paphos International Airport. **Road:** Car: Road to Pedoulas which leads to Kykkos (from Troodos). Road north towards Platres, past Pedoulas to Kykkos (from Limassol). Towards Limassol, then northeast past Kedares to Platres (from Paphos). The monastery is well-signposted.

Opening Times

Monastery: Daily dawn-dusk. *Museum*: Daily 1000-1700 (Oct-Mar); daily 1000-1800 (Apr-Sep).

Admission Fees

Monastery: Free. *Museum*: C£1.25.

Golden artwork above the entrance to Kykkos Monastery

Cyprus Tourism Organisation

Czech Republic

1 Karluv most (Charles Bridge)
2 Kutná Hora
3 Prazsky Hrad and Katedrála sv Víta (Prague Castle and St Vitus Cathedral)
4 Staroměstské náměstí (Old Town Square)

Tourist Information

Ceská centrála cestovního ruchu (Czech Tourist Authority)
Vinohradská 46, PO Box 32, 12041 Prague 2, Czech Republic
Tel: (02) 2158 0111. Fax: (02) 242 570 *or* 2424 7516. E-mail: cccr@cccr-cta.cz
Website: www.visitczech.cz

Czech Tourist Authority
95 Great Portland Street, London W1N 5RA, UK
Tel: (020) 7291 9925. Fax: (020) 7436 8300.
E-mail: CTAinfo@czechcentre.org.uk
Website: www.antour.com

Karluv most (Charles Bridge)

The *Charles Bridge* is Prague's most familiar monument. Built in 1357, this 520m-long bridge (1770ft) was the only connection between the two halves of Prague for four hundred years. Originally, the bridge was bare of ornamentation except for one solitary cross; however, as the Counter Reformation took hold in Bohemia, the bridge eventually gained over 30 Baroque statues. The earliest, erected in 1683, is a bronze statue of martyr St John of Nepomuk who was thrown off the bridge. Many have been damaged by pollution and have been replaced, although the originals can still be seen in the *Lapidarium* (rock garden) in Letná Park. Craft stalls and buskers along the bridge add to the atmosphere and make it a popular meeting place.

Contact Address

Prague Information Service, Betlémské námesti 2, 11 698 Prague 1, Czech Republic
Tel: (02) 12444.
E-mail: info@pis.cz *or* tourinfo@pis.cz
Website: www.pis.cz

Transportation

Air: Praha Ruzyně International Airport. **Rail:** Train: Hlavní nádraží Station (Prague Station). Underground: Staromestská. Tram: 17 or 18 (Karlovy Lazne). **Road:** Bus: 207 (Starometská). Car: E48, E50, E55 or E67 towards Prague.

Opening Times

Daily 24 hours.

Admission Fees

Free.

Kutná Hora

It may now be a sleepy provincial town, but *Kutná Hora*, located 60km (37 miles) east of Prague, once rivalled Prague and even London in terms of size and importance. The discovery of silver ore here in the 14th century led to the creation of the Royal Mint and the town became the political, cultural and economic centre of Bohemia. The legacy of this glorious epoch can be seen in the fine Gothic and Italianate buildings that line the cobbled streets. The most famous of all is the magnificent *St Barbara's Cathedral*, built between 1388-1565 by the town's miners (St Barbara is the patron saint of miners) to rival St Vitus' Cathedral in Prague; the oldest, however, is the church of St James (Sv Jakub), which dates back to 1330-1420. The *Italian Court (Vlassky dvyr)* was once the Mint of the Czech State and the residence of the king of Bohemia; nowadays it houses an exhibition of Czech coins and medals. Other popular sights in Kutná Hora include the Gothic *Stone House* and *Stone Fountain*. Visitors with a taste for the macabre should pay a visit to the monastic church at nearby *Sedlec*, the interior of which is made entirely of human bones.

Contact Address

Information Centre – Kutná Hora, Palackého nám 377, 284 01, Kutná Hora, Czech Republic
Tel: (0327) 515 556. Fax: (0327) 512 378.
Website: www.kutnahora.cz

Transportation

Air: Praha Ruzyně International Airport. **Rail:** Train: Kutná Hora Mesto Station. (From Prague, change at Kolin and Kutná Hora Hln Stations). **Road:** Coach: Kutná Hora Lorecka Bus Station (from Praha-Florenc Coach Station) (journey time: 90 minutes). Car: Hwy-38.

Opening Times

St Barbara's Cathedral: Tues-Sun 0900-1730 (May-Sep); Tues-Sun 0900-1130 and 1400-1530 (Oct-Mar); Tues-Sun 0900-1130 and 1300-1600 (Apr and Oct). *Italian Court*: Daily 0900-1800 (Apr-Sep); daily 1000-1600 (Nov-Feb); daily 1000-1700 (Mar and Oct). *St James' Church* (visits only before or after mass): Mon, Wed and Fri 1800, Tues, Thurs and Sat 0645, Sun 0900.

Admission Fees

St Barbara's Cathedral: Kč30 (adult), Kč15 (child). Concessions available. *Italian Court*: Kč30 (adult), Kč15 (child 6-16), free (child under 6). *St James' Church*: Free.

Prazsky Hrad and Katedrála sv Vita (Prague Castle and St Vitus Cathedral)

The reaching spires of *Prague Castle*, the seat of Bohemian government for a thousand years, can be seen from virtually anywhere in Prague. It is actually more of a complex than a castle, covering 45 hectares (110 acres) and comprising three courtyards, fortifications and gardens. Its most famous attraction is the Gothic *St Vitus Cathedral*, the country's largest church, which was begun in 1344 under Charles IV but not completed until 1929,

Kutná Hora

Czech Tourist Authority

and is much loved for its stained glass. From *St Wenceslas' Chapel*, which contains the tomb of the country's most famous patron saint and a cycle of paintings depicting scenes from his life, visitors can enter the *Crown Chamber* to see the Bohemian coronation jewels. Another interesting place to visit is the *Royal Palace*, which has housed generations of Bohemian kings; the huge *Vladislav Hall* is now used for the swearing-in ceremony of the president of the Czech Republic. Directly behind the cathedral is the *National Gallery of Bohemian Art*.

Contact Address

Prazsky Hrad, 11908 Prague 1, Czech Republic
Tel: (02) 2437 3368. Fax: (02) 2437 2357.
E-mail: emil.sedoc@hrad.cz
Website: www.hrad.cz

Transportation

Air: Praha Ruzyně International Airport. **Rail:** Train: Hlavní nádraží Station (Prague Station) or Praha-Holesovice Station (for some international express trains). Tram: 22 to Prazsky hrad. **Road:** Coach: Praha-Florenc Coach Station.

Opening Times

Castle grounds: Daily 0500-2400 (1 Apr-31 Oct); daily 0600-2300 (1 Nov-31 Mar). *Interiors*: Daily 0900-1700 (1 Apr-31 Oct); daily 0900-1600 (1 Nov-31 Mar). *Gardens*: Daily 1000-1800.

Admission Fees

Kč120 (adult), Kč60 (child 6-16), free (child under 6).

Staromestké námestí (Old Town Square)

Prague's picture-book *Old Town Square*, with its colourful facades and cobbled surface, is perhaps one of the most familiar tourist scenes of Central Europe. Although many of the facades are Baroque in style, the houses actually date from Medieval times when the square was the centre of the Bohemian world, and a meeting place for merchants and traders from across Europe. The *Astronomical Clock* on the *Town Hall (Staromětská radnice)* chimes every hour between 0900-2100; its ornate face is a complex work of art and shows three sets of time: Central European Time, Old Bohemian Time and Babylonian Time. The *Town Hall* dates from the 14th century, although much of the original structure was destroyed when the Nazis set fire to it in May 1945 during the Prague Uprising. Another monument of particular interest is the rather incongruous *Jan Hus Monument* which was commissioned in 1900, hence its Art Nouveau style. It took sculptor Ladislav Šaloun 15 years to complete and is an important national symbol for the Czech people. The *House at the Stone Bell (Dům U kamenného zvonu)* was restored in the 1970s and now houses avant-garde art exhibitions.

Contact Address

Prague Information Service, Betlémské námesti 2, 11 698 Prague 1, Czech Republic
Tel: (02) 12444.
E-mail: info@pis.cz or tourinfo@pis.cz
Website: www.pis.cz

Transportation

Air: Prague Ruzyně International Airport. **Rail:** Train: Hlavní nádraží Station (Prague Station). Underground: Staromestká. **Road:** Coach: Praha-Florenc Coach Station; Želivského coach park. Car: E55 (from Dresden/Berlin); E67 (from Warsaw/Wroclaw); E50 (from Paris). Visitors should note that the historic centre of Prague is pedestrianised.

Opening Times

Town Hall (Staromestská radnice): Mon 1100-1700, Tues-Sun 0900-1800.

Admission Fees

Town Hall (Staromestská radnice): Kč30. Concessions available.

Astronomical Clock, Old Town Square

Corel

Denmark

1 Kronborg Slot (Kronborg Castle)
2 Legoland®
3 Lille Havrue (Little Mermaid)
4 Tivoli

Tourist Information

Danmarks Turistråd (Danish Tourist Board)
Vesterbrogade 6 D, DK-1606 Copenhagen V, Denmark
Tel: 3311 1415. Fax: 3393 1416. E-mail: dt@dt.dk
Website: www.dt.dk *or* www.visitdenmark.com
Danish Tourist Board
55 Sloane Street, London SW1X 9SY, UK
Tel: (020) 7259 5959. Fax: (020) 7259 5955.
E-mail: dtb.london@dt.dk

Kronborg Slot (Kronborg Castle)

Strategically located on a site overlooking the Sound, the stretch of water between Denmark and Sweden, *Kronborg Castle* at Helsingør (Elsinore) is of great historical importance to the people of Denmark, playing a key role in the history of Northern Europe during the 16th to 18th centuries. Work began on the castle in 1574, with its defences being reinforced in the late 17th century. Kronborg, which is one of the most important Renaissance castle's in Northern Europe, is also famous for being the setting for William Shakespeare's play Hamlet (the Prince of Denmark) and has staged many performances of the play over the centuries. The famous statue of *Holger Danske* is also housed at Kronborg. Built in 1906, according to legend, the statue stands guard over Denmark to defend it against enemy attack.

Contact Address

Kronborg Slot, DK 3000 Helsingør, Denmark
Tel: 4921 3078. Fax: 4921 3052.
E-mail: kronborg@ses.dk
or info@kronborgcastle.com
Website: www.kronborgcastle.com

Transportation

Air: Copenhagen Airport. **Rail:** Train: Elsinore Station or Grønnehave Station. The castle is approximately 15 minute's walk from Elsinore Station. **Road:** Bus: 340, 347, 801, 802 or 803.

Opening Times

Daily 1100-1500 (Nov-Mar, closed Mon); daily 1100-1600 (Apr, closed Mon); daily 1030-1700 (Easter); daily 1030-1600 (May-Sep); daily 1100-1600 (Oct, closed Mon).

Admission Fees

DKr60 (adult), DKr25 (child), DKr60 (OAP). Includes admission into the main halls, the chapel, casements and the *Danish Maritime Museum.*

Legoland®

With Lego as Denmark's most famous gift to children, it's not surprising that the country has built (literally) an amusement park from it. The renowned ten-hectare (25-acre) amusement park, which is located north of Billund, features attractions and rides built from no less than 40 million plastic Lego blocks. Shows are performed daily by the Children's Theatre, and there are also circus acts in high season. Adults and children can marvel at the detailed Lego reconstructions of famous sights from around the world in Miniland; Duplo Land, with its chunkier bricks, is particularly popular with younger children. Visitors can meet Captain Roger and his parrot in Pirateland whilst the dragon train in Castleland takes visitors on a whirlwind adventure into the Medieval Castle to meet kings and princesses. The sophisticated *Port of Copenhagen* exhibit, featuring electronically controlled trains, cranes and ships, is also a favourite for many.

Contact Address

Legoland A/S, Nordmarksvej 9, 7190 Billund, Denmark
Tel: 7533 1333. Fax: 7535 3179.
E-mail: danmark@legoland.dk
Website: www.legoland.dk

Transportation

Air: Billund International Airport. **Rail:** Train: Vejle Station, Kolding Station, or Fredericia Station. **Road:** Bus: 44/912, 406, 117, 79 or 76. Car: A7/E-45 (exit 63).

Opening Times

Daily 1000-2000 (23 Jun-8 Jul); daily 1000-2100 (9 Jul-12 Aug); daily 1000-2000 (13 Aug-2 Sep); Mon-Fri 1000-1800; Sat, Sun and school holidays 1000-2000 (3 Sep-28 Oct); Mon-Fri 1000-1800; Sat, Sun and school holidays 1000-2000 (31 Mar-22 Jun).

Admission Fees

DKr150 (adult), DKr140 (child 3-13), free (child under 2) (31 Mar-28 Oct); two-day passes are available. Admission fees include all rides, attractions and shows in the park.

Lille Havrue (Little Mermaid)

Denmark's most famous cultural symbol comes from a tale told by its most renowned poet, Hans Christian Andersen. In his story the youngest daughter of the Sea King rescues a drowning prince and falls in love, but in the end gets turned into sea foam. The idea for the statue originated in 1909 when brewer Carl Jacobsen saw the ballet version of the *Little Mermaid* and was so impressed that he commissioned sculptor Edvard Eriksen to create a bronze statue on Copenhagen's waterfront. Eriksen modelled the mermaid on his wife and she is now Copenhagen's most famous symbol as she stares dreamily across the water from *Langelinie*. The fairytale image has, however, been somewhat marred by vandalism: in 1963 she had her hair painted red, and the latest scandal occurred in 1998 when she was decapitated for the second time.

Contact Address

Wonderful Copenhagen Tourist Information, GL Kongevej 1, 1610 Copenhagen V, Denmark
Tel: 7022 2442. Fax: 7022 2452.
E-mail: touristinfo@woco.dk
Website: www.visitcopenhagen.dk

Transportation

Air: Copenhagen Airport. **Rail:** Train: Copenhagen Central Station or S-Bahn to Østerport. **Road:** Bus: 29. Car: Signs to København harbour and Langelinie waterfront, then Lille Havrue.

Opening Times

Daily 24 hours.

Admission Fees

Free.

Tivoli

Opened in 1843 as a theme park and public garden, *Tivoli Gardens* has outlasted the great parks of Europe that were its inspiration – the Tivoli in Paris and Vauxhall Gardens in London. Tivoli Gardens still retains a flavour of that era, seeming more like an open-air garden than it does a theme park. Visitors can stroll, listen to symphonies and eat sausages; there are also plenty of rides, however, including the new *Golden Tower*, *Valhalla Castle*, a *Ferris Wheel* and a roller coaster that zooms through the treetops. *The Monsoon* is a new ride which opened in May 2001 – visitors are taken 12m (33ft) into the air with their legs dangling below before being dropped towards the water. The less daring can enjoy the many concerts, circus acts, and theatrical performances that also find a home at Tivoli. The famous *Copenhagen Christmas Market* is held here in November and December, making this a particularly atmospheric time to visit.

Contact Address

Tivoli, Vesterbrogade 3, 1630 Copenhagen V, Denmark
Tel: 3315 1001. Fax: 3375 0381. E-mail: info@tivoli.dk
Website: www.tivoligardens.com

Transportation

Air: Copenhagen Airport. **Rail:** Train: Copenhagen Central Station or S-Bahn to København H. **Road:** Bus: Services to Town Hall Square. Car: Signs to the city centre and the Town Hall.

Opening Times

Sun-Thurs 1100-2100, Fri and Sat 1100-2200 (20 Nov-23 Dec); Sun-Tues 1100-2300, Wed and Thurs 1100-2400, Fri and Sat 1100-0100 (11 Apr-14 Jun); Sun-Thurs 1100-2400, Fri and Sat 1100-0100 (15 June-19 Aug); Sun-Tues 1100-2300, Wed and Thurs 1100-2400, Fri and Sat 1100-0100 (20 Aug-23 Sep).

Admission Fees

DKr50 (adult), DKr25 (child) (15 Jun-19 Aug); DKr45 (adult, Sun-Thurs), DKr50 (adult, Fri and Sat), DKr20 (child) (20 Aug-23 Sep, 11 Apr-14 Jun and 20 Nov-23 Dec). Concessions and family pass available.

Commonwealth of Dominica

1 Morne Trois Pitons National Park

Tourist Information

National Development Corporation (NDC)
Division of Tourism, PO Box 293, Valley Road, Roseau, Commonwealth of Dominica
Tel: 448 2045. Fax: 448 5840.
E-mail: ndc@cwdom.dm
Website: www.dominica.dm

Dominica Tourist Office
Morris-Kevan International, Mitre House, 66 Abbey Road, Bush Hill Park, Enfield, Middlesex EN1 2QE, UK
Tel: (020) 8350 1009. Fax: (020) 8350 1011.
E-mail: cto@carib-tourism.com
Website: www.caribtourism.com

Morne Trois Pitons National Park

The *Morne Trois Pitons National Park* encompasses 69 sq kilometres (27 sq miles) of varied landscape – lush tropicana and rainforests contrast starkly with volcanic terrain characterised by deep valleys and bubbling pools. The park was created in 1975 and is centred around the *Morne Trois Pitons* (meaning 'mountain of three peaks'), a triple-spiked mountain formed from volcanic remains, which rises to 1342m (3681ft) above sea level. The *Valley of Desolation* is a barren area of volcanic rock which contains over 50 fumaroles (geysers) emitting sulphurous gases and steam, where visitors can see multicoloured mineral streams and pools of boiling grey mud. One of the most beautiful sites in the park is the *Emerald Pool*, a waterfall grotto located against a backdrop of tropical plants and flowers. The *Boiling Lake* is the largest of its kind in the world and lies in a volcanic crater. Many of the sites in the park can be visited via the many trails, although some of the trails, such as the one which runs to the *Boiling Lake*, are difficult and are best undertaken with a local guide.

Contact Address

Morne Trois Pitons National Park, Forestry, Wildlife and Parks Division, Botanical Gardens, Roseau, Commonwealth of Dominica
Tel: 448 2401. Fax: 448 7999.
E-mail: forestry@cwdom.dm

Transportation

Air: Melville Hall Airport. **Road:** Bus: Laudat services (from Kings Judge V Street, Roseau to *Valley of Desolation* and *Boiling Lake*) or Castle Bruce services (from Kings Judge V Street, Roseau to *Emerald Pool*). Taxi: Services from Roseau or Trafalgar. Car: Imperial Road (to *Emerald Pool* from Roseau), Trafalgar Road, then Laudat Road (from Roseau to Trafalgar Falls); Valley Road (to *Freshwater Lake* or *Boiling Lake* from Roseau).

Opening Times

Emerald Pool Visitor Centre: Daily 0900-1700. *Morne Trois Pitons National Park*: Daily 24 hours. *Trafalgar Falls Visitor Centre*: Daily 0900-1700.

Admission Fees

Single Site Ticket: US$2. Day Pass: US$5.

Ecuador

1 Islas Galapagos (Galapagos Islands)

Tourist Information

Ministerio de Turismo (Ministry of Tourism)
Avenida Eloy Alfaro N32-300 y Carlos Tobar, Quito, Ecuador
Tel: (02) 507 562 *or* 228 303. Fax: (02) 229 330.
E-mail: subtur@ec-gov.net
Website: wwwpub4.ecua.net.ec/mintur

Embassy of the Republic of Ecuador
Flat 3B, 3 Hans Crescent, London SW1X 0LS, UK
Tel: (020) 7584 1367. Fax: (020) 7823 9701.

Islas Galapagos (Galapagos Islands)

Straddling the Equator 1000km (622 miles) off the coast of Ecuador, the *Galapagos Islands* are famous for being the inspiration for Charles Darwin's theory of evolution. There are 13 large islands and six small, which were formed by oceanic volcanoes some three to five million years ago. Visitors come to the islands to see the unparalleled variety of wildlife that flourishes due to the remote location and temperate climate. The most famous residents are the giant tortoises after whom the islands are named, although other regular sightings include iguana, dolphins, boobies and cormorants. The animals are used to human company – visitors can even swim with penguins and sea lions – and snorkelling and sailing are also popular.

Contact Address

Galapagos National Park Service, Puerto Ayora, Santa Cruz, Galapagos, Ecuador
Tel: (05) 526 189. Fax: (05) 526 190.
E-mail: infopng@fcdarwin.org.ec
Website: www.parquegalapagos.org.ec

Transportation

Air: Isla Baltra Airport.

Opening Times

Daily 24 hours.

Admission Fees

Galapagos National Park and Galapagos Marine Reserve: US$100 (adult), US$50 (child under 12). Concessions available.

Giant Tortoise on the Galapagos Islands

Corel

Egypt

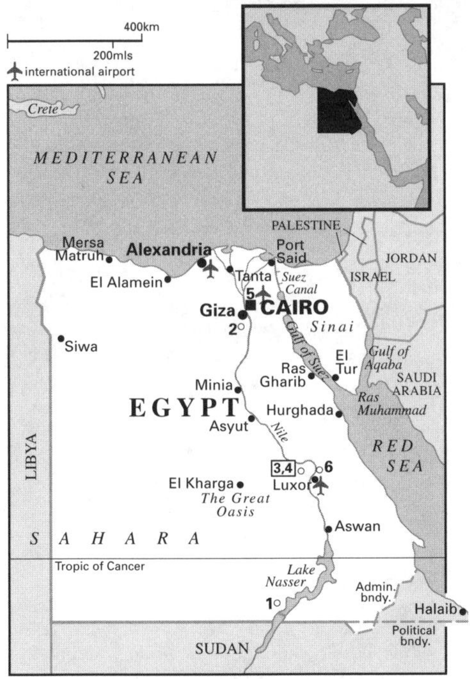

1 Abu Simbel
2 Ahramat Al-Jizah and Abu el-Hol (Pyramids at Giza and the Sphinx)
3 Biban el-Melouk and Biban el-Harem (Valley of the Kings and Valley of the Queens)
4 Deir el-Bahri (Hatshepsut's Temple)
5 El Mathas El Massry (Egyptian Antiquities Museum)
6 Ipet-Isut (Karnak Temple)

Tourist Information

Wezarit El Suaha (Ministry of Tourism)
Misr Travel Tower, Abassia Square, Cairo, Egypt
Tel: (02) 684 1707 *or* 682 8439. Fax: (02) 859 551.
Website: www.touregypt.net

Egyptian State Tourist Office
Egyptian House, Third Floor, 170 Piccadilly, London W1V 9DD, UK
Tel: (020) 7493 5283 *or* (09001) 600 299 (24-hour brochure service: calls cost 60p per minute) *or* (09001) 887 777 (visa information). Fax: (020) 7408 0295.
E-mail: egypt@freenetname.co.uk
Website: www.touregypt.net

Abu Simbel

One of the most famous ancient Egyptian sites, the two temples of *Abu Simbel* were carved out of sandstone cliffs high above the River Nile in 1257 BC, under the orders of Pharaoh Ramses II (1304-1237 BC). The most famous of the two features four colossal 20m-high (65ft) statues of Ramses II flanking the entrance, although they are actually dedicated to the sun god Re-Herakhte. The temples, which were rediscovered by the Swiss explorer Burckhardt in 1813, withstood the passage of time until the construction of the Nasser Dam in 1970, which caused the waters of Lake Nasser to rise significantly. With the support of UNESCO, an international appeal was launched and the temples were gradually relocated to a higher elevation over a four-year period between 1964 and 1968.

Contact Address

For more information on Abu Simbel, contact the Ministry of Tourism (see **Tourist Information** above).

Transportation

Air: Luxor International Airport. Internal flights are available to Aswan International Airport and Abu Simbel Airport. **Water:** Boat: Cruise boats and feluccas take visitors to the site. **Road:** Bus: Public buses also leave from Aswan, although they depart very early in the morning. Minibus: Hotels in Aswan organise tours to the site. Taxi: Taxis can be hired in Aswan.

Opening Times

Daily 0600-1600 (winter); daily 0600-1700 (summer).

Admission Fees

E£36 (adult), E£18 (student).

Ahramat Al-Jizah and Abu el-Hol (Pyramids at Giza and the Sphinx)

The *Pyramids* at Giza are among the best-known ancient monuments in the world and the only one of the Seven Wonders of the ancient world still standing. Of the three pyramids, the *Great Pyramid of Cheops*, which consists of two million blocks of stone, is the oldest and largest; it was built between 2589 and 2566 BC by the IV Dynasty pharaoh Khufu

Egyptian State Tourist Office

Giza, Cairo

and is 140m (482ft) high. Of the other two pyramids, the *Pyramid of Chephren*, which is sometimes known as the *Second Pyramid*, is the more famous due to its imposing size, with its base once covering an area of 216 sq metres (2325 sq ft). It was discovered in 1818 and is situated to the southwest of Cheops. Although it appears to be taller than the Great Pyramid, as it stands on higher ground, this pyramid, which was built by Khufu's son Khafre, is actually smaller than Cheops. The third pyramid, the *Pyramid of Mycerinus*, which stands some 67m (220ft) high, was started by Khafre's successor, Menkaure, although he died before it was completed. The famous *Sphinx*, which is called *Abu al-Hol* in Arabic, stands in front of the Great Pyramid, with the body of a lion joined to the head of a man. The Sphinx, which is 60m (200ft) long and 20m (65ft) high, was carved over 4500 years ago out of a single block of sandstone left over from building the Great Pyramid. The sights at Giza are among the most famous in the world and continue to fascinate hordes of visitors every year. There is a Sound and Light show every night at Giza which adds to the atmosphere surrounding these mysterious ancient sights.

Contact Address

For more information on the Pyramids at Giza and the Sphinx, contact the Ministry of Tourism (see **Tourist Information** above).

Transportation

Air: Cairo International Airport. **Rail:** Train: Ramses Station. **Road:** Bus: 8 from Midan Tahrir. Public buses also run from Ahmed Helmi Bus Station. Taxi: Many visitors take a taxi from Cairo city centre. Car: Sharia al-Ahram (Pyramids Road) (from Cairo city centre).

Opening Times

Daily 0700-1600.

Admission Fees

Site: E£40 (adult), E£20 (student). *Great Pyramid*: E£40 (adult), E£20 (student).

Biban el-Melouk and Biban el-Harem (Valley of the Kings and Valley of the Queens)

The *Valley of the Kings* is a limestone valley situated in the Theban Hills where the mummified bodies of many Egyptian pharaohs were interred. The area marks a period in ancient Egyptian history in which the pharaohs abandoned the pyramid style and chose instead tombs dug within limestone in order to preserve the mummies for eternity and prevent grave robbing. The secretive tombs were decorated with murals depicting hunting and banqueting scenes and all aspects of daily life, as well as scenes representing the pharaoh's journey into the Underworld. The pharaohs were buried along with their daily possessions in order to recreate their mortal life and keep their belongings in prime condition for the afterlife. The tombs, although stripped of many of their contents centuries ago, still display fantastic wall paintings depicting the lives of the pharaohs in ancient Egypt, down to the minutest detail. The most famous tomb, that of the young pharaoh Tutankhamun, was discovered in pristine condition by Howard Carter in 1922. The many treasures found in the tomb are now exhibited in the *Egyptian Antiquities Museum* in Cairo. Nearby, the wall paintings in the tombs of the *Valley of the Queens* and the *Valley of the Nobles* are equally fascinating, depicting ancient Egyptian scenes from the perspective of these 'lesser mortals'. The most famous tomb in the Valley of the Queens is the *Tomb of Queen Nefertari*, the principal wife of Ramses II, which was only opened to the public in 1995.

Contact Address

Luxor Tourist Office, Nile St, Luxor, Egypt
Tel: (095) 382 215. Website: www.luxorguide.com

Transportation

Air: Luxor International Airport. **Water:** Ferry: A tourist ferry leaves from the East Bank to take passengers across the River Nile. Motor boats can also be hired. **Road:** Coach: The majority of tourists visit the temple as part of an organised coach tour. Taxi: Taxis are available to take visitors to the temple and can be hired on arrival on the West Bank. Bicycle: Bicycles can be hired in Luxor.

Opening Times

Valley of the Kings and *Valley of the Queens*: Daily 0700-1700.

Admission Fees

Any three tombs in the *Valley of the Kings*: E£20 (adult), E£10 (student). *Valley of the Queens*: E£12 (adult), E£6 (student). Additional tickets are required for extra tombs, including entry to the Tomb of Tutankhamun and the Tomb of Queen Nefertari.

Deir el-Bahri (Hatshepsut's Temple)

Hatshepsut's Temple is the mortuary temple of Queen Hatshepsut. Located on the West Bank in Luxor, this spectacular temple was built by the Queen's architect, Senenmut, in honour of the only woman ever to reign over Egypt as pharoah. Set against towering cliffs in the *Theban Hills*, this unique temple attracts bus loads of tourists every day to see one of the most impressive sites in the *Necropolis*. The temple, with its many monumental ramps, fine terraces, elegant columns and hieroglyphic paintings, also tells the story of Hatshepsut's journey to the *Land of Punt* (which is believed to be modern-day Somalia) to bring back treasures such as ebony, ivory, gold, perfumes and myrrh trees.

Contact Address

Luxor Tourist Office, Nile Sreet, Luxor, Egypt
Tel: (095) 382 215. Website: www.luxorguide.com

Transportation

Air: Luxor International Airport. **Water:** Ferry: A tourist ferry leaves from the East Bank to take passengers across the River Nile. Motor boats can also be hired. **Road:** Coach: The majority of tourists visit the temple as part of an organised coach tour. Taxi: Taxis are available to take visitors to the temple and can be hired on arrival on the West Bank.

Opening Times

Daily 0600-1700.

Admission Fees

E£12 (adult), E£6 (student).

El Mathas El Massry (Egyptian Antiquities Museum)

The 107 halls of the *Egyptian Antiquities Museum* in Cairo were built in 1900 by the French architect Marcel Dourgnon and opened in 1902. The collection itself dates back to 1835, however, when the *Service des Antiques de l'Egypte* (Egyptian Antiquities Service) was set up to protect government-owned artefacts and put a halt to the raiding of archaeological sites. Today, the museum houses a number of ancient Egypt's greatest artefacts, including mummified pharaohs from the 18th-20th Dynasties which were discovered in Thebes, as well as mummies found in the tomb of

Amenhotep II. By far the most popular attractions at the museum are the treasures from Tutankhamun's tomb, which include the boy-king's famous golden facemask, as well as approximately 1700 other objects. The museum exhibits around 120,000 objects in total, including artefacts from the tombs of the Middle Kingdom found at Dahshur in 1894, the contents of the Royal tombs of Tuthmosis III, Tuthmosis IV, Amenhotep III and Horemheb, and artefacts from the Amarna period found in Tell el Amarna, Hermopolis, Thebes and Memphis between 1912 and 1933.

Contact Address

El Mathas El Massry, Maydan El Tahrir, Cairo, Egypt
Tel: (02) 760 390. Fax: (02) 579 4596.
E-mail: eldamaty@email.com
Website: www.egyptianmuseum.gov.eg

Transportation

Air: Cairo International Airport. **Train:** Rail: Ramses Station. Underground: Sadat (Tahrir) Station. **Road:** Bus: Abdel Mouneem Riyad Bus Terminal. Car: Delta Road or Alexandria Desert Road to Cairo (from Alexandria).

Opening Times

Daily 0900-1700.

Admission Fees

E£20 (adult), E£10 (student).

Ipet-Isut (Karnak Temple)

Karnak Temple, which is situated 1.6km (one mile) east of Luxor, is a vast complex consisting of three main temples, several smaller enclosed temples, and a number of outer temples. The most spectacular of these is the *Temple of Amun* (*Amun's Precinct*). This is entered via the *Avenue of the Sphinxes* that once connected Karnak and *Luxor Temples,* and led through the ancient city of Thebes, the capital of Egypt during the period of the Middle and New Kingdoms. The whole complex was built over a period of 1300 years and includes several of the finest examples of ancient Egyptian design and architecture. Among them are the *Hypostyle Hall,* considered one of the world's great architectural achievements with around 130 enormous carved columns covering an area of 6000 sq metres (64,586 sq ft), and the *Obelisk of Thutmose I,* a 22m (71ft) monument, the only one of four original obelisks that is still standing. Other highlights at Karnak include the *Sacred Lake,* which is the centrepiece for the spectacular Sound and Light Show, and the *Open Air Museum,* found at the northern end of Amun's Precinct.

Contact Address

Luxor Tourist Office, Nile St, Luxor, Egypt
Tel: (095) 382 215. Website: www.luxorguide.com

Transportation

Air: Luxor International Airport. **Rail:** Train: Luxor Station. **Road:** Coach: The vast majority of tourists visit the temple as part of an organised coach tour. Bus: Luxor Bus Station. Taxis: Taxis can be hired from the centre of Luxor; alternatively visitors can travel by *caleche* (horse and cart).

Opening Times

Daily 0700-1700.

Admission Fees

E£20 (adult), E£10 (student).

Amon-Ra Temple with Statue of Taharka, Karnak

Egyptian State Tourist Office

Estonia

1 Raekoja plats (Tallinn Town Hall Square)

Tourist Information

Eesti Turismiamet (Estonian Tourist Board)
Mündi 2, 10146 Tallinn, Estonia
Tel: (06) 990 420. Fax: (06) 990 432.
E-mail: info@tourism.ee
Website: www.visitestonia.com
or www.tourism.ee

Embassy of the Republic of Estonia
16 Hyde Park Gate, London SW7 5DG, UK
Tel: (020) 7589 3428. Fax: (020) 7589 3430.
E-mail: Embassy.London@estonia.gov.uk
Website: www.estonia.gov.uk

Raekoja plats (Tallinn Town Hall Square)

Tallinn's old town was classified as a World Heritage Site by UNESCO in 1997. With its colourful buildings, turreted walls and gabled roofs it is one of the best-preserved historic centres in Europe. All the winding cobbled streets lead on to the *Raekoja plats* (Town Hall Square), which is dominated by the imposing façade of the *Raetoda*, or Town Hall (tel: (06) 440 819; e-mail: raetoda@tallinnlv.ee). The building was constructed in the 14th and 15th centuries at a time when Tallinn was an important member of the German-dominated Hanseatic League, an association of Baltic trading ports, and is the only surviving late Gothic town hall in Northern Europe. Its soaring steeple bears a 16th-century weather vane portraying the medieval warrior, 'Old Thomas', guardian of the city. The *Raeapteek* (Town Council Pharmacy) lies on the northern side of the square; although the present façade dates from the 17th century, there has been a pharmacy here since 1422 – fortunately the remedies it sells have improved from those available in Medieval times. Open-air concerts are held here in summer and its many cafés and eating places make it a bustling meeting place for both tourists and Tallinners alike.

Contact Address

Tallinn City Tourist Office, Mündi 2, 10146 Tallinn, Estonia
Tel: (06) 457 777. Fax: (06) 457 778.
E-mail: turismiinfo@tallinnlv.ee
Website: www.tallinn.ee

Transportation

Air: Tallinn Airport. **Water:** Ferry: Reisisadam Sea Port (Tallinn). **Rail:** Train: Balti jaam Station. **Road:** Coach: Autobussijaam (Tallinn Bus Station).

Opening Times

Town Hall: Mon-Fri 1000-1600 (by guided tour only – visitors must book in advance). *Town Council Pharmacy*: Mon-Sat 0900-1700.

Admission Fees

Town Hall: ekr30 (adult), ekr10 (child). *Town Council Pharmacy*: Free.

Raekoja plats

Tallinn City Tourist Office

Finland

1 Linnanmäki
2 Suomenlinna Sveaborg (Suomenlinna Sea Fortress)

Tourist Information

Matkailun Edistämiskeskus (Finnish Tourist Board)

Head Office: Töölönkatu 11, PO Box 625, 00101 Helsinki, Finland
Tel: (09) 417 6911. Fax: (09) 4176 9333.
E-mail: mek@mek.fi
Website: www.mek.fi
Tourist Information: Eteläesplanadi 4, 00131 Helsinki, Finland
Tel (09) 4176 9300 *or* 4176 9211.
Fax: (09) 4176 9301.

Finnish Tourist Board

30-35 Pall Mall, London SW1Y 5LP, UK
Tel: (020) 7365 2512 *or* 7930 5871 (trade and press only). Fax: (020) 7321 0696.
E-mail: mek.lon@mek.fi
Website: www.finland-tourism.com *or* www.mek.fi

Linnanmäki

Founded in 1950, *Linnanmäki* amusement park is one of the most popular tourist attractions in Finland and has attracted around 43 million visitors since it opened its doors to the public. This giant theme park was opened by six Finnish child welfare organisations to promote children's events in the country. The *Children's Day Foundation* was set up by these six charities with responsibility for managing the park in 1956. This is still the case today and all profits are donated to charity. The most popular ride at the park is the *Big Dipper*, which was built in 1951. Other rides include the *Space Express* roller coaster and *Space Shot* adventure ride. The *Toy and Play Museum* opened in 1996 and its collection features examples of toys and games past and present. Additionally, the *Journey in Time* exhibition takes the visitor through the history of children's toys.

Contact Address

Linnanmäki, Tivolikuja 1, 00510 Helsinki, Finland
Tel: (09) 7739 9400. Fax: (09) 768 152.
Website: www.linnanmaki.fi

Transportation

Air: Helsinki-Vantaa Airport. **Rail:** Tram: 3T (from Mannerheimintie). **Road:** Bus: 23 or 23N (from Helsinki city centre).

Opening Times

Daily 1200-2200 (28 Apr-Sep). Times may vary according to the day of the week or the season.

Admission Fees

Entry to park: Fmk20 (adult), free (child under 6). Wrist band allowing access to all rides: Fmk95 (adult), Fmk65 (child under 120cm/47.3 inches).

Suomenlinna Sveaborg (Suomenlinna Sea Fortress)

Suomenlinna Sea Fortress, which was built more than 250 years ago, once had a population of 4600, larger than the population of Helsinki at the time, which totalled just 4200. Construction began off the coast of Helsinki in 1748, when Finland was part of the Swedish Empire and the Swedes built a fortress on the islands as a counter to the increasing Russian naval strength in Kronstadt. In 1808, the fortress surrendered to the Russians, with Finland becoming part of the Russian empire. The fortress was originally called *Sveaborg* (literally, Sweden's Fortress), but was renamed *Suomelinna* (Finland's Fortress) in 1918, one year after Finland finally gained independence from Russia. Today, the fortress which was transferred to civil administration in 1973 is one of the most important monuments in Helsinki and is included on the UNESCO World Heritage List. Thousands of visitors travel to the islands every year to see the impressive fortifications, as well as to enjoy an area of natural beauty. There are a variety of attractions on the islands, including the *Suomenlinna Museum,* the *Ehrensuärd Museum*, the *Doll and Toy Museum* and *Submarine Vesikko*, which is displayed in the *Coast Artillery Museum*.

Contact Address

Suomenlinna Tourist Information, Suomenlinna C74, 00190 Helsinki, Finland
Tel: (09) 684 1880. Fax: (09) 668 348.
E-mail: matkailu@suomenlinna.fi
Website: www.suomenlinna.fi

Transportation

Air: Helsinki-Vantaa Airport. **Water:** Ferry: Ferries leave from the eastern edge of the main market square, Kauppatori. Tickets are available on the ferry (journey time: 15 minutes). Waterbuses also operate in summer and leave from their own jetty at Market Square. Tickets are sold on the waterbus (journey time: 20 minutes).

Opening Times

Suomenlinna Sea Fortress: Daily 24 hours. *Coast Artillery Museum*: Sat-Sun 1100-1500 (Mar-May); daily 1000-1700 (May-Aug); daily 1100-1500 (Sep); Sat-Sun 1100-1500 (Oct). *Doll and Toy Museum*: Sat-Sun 1100-1600 (May); daily 1100-1700 (May-Aug); Sat-Sun 1100-1600 (Sep). *Ehrensuärd Museum*: Sat-Sun 1100-1630 (Mar-Apr); daily 1000-1700 (May-Aug); daily 1100-1700 (Sep); Sat-Sun 1100-1630 (Oct). *Suomenlinna Museum*: Sat-Sun 1100-1700 (Mar-Apr); daily 1000-1800 (May-Aug); daily 1000-1700 (Sep); Sat-Sun 1100-1700 (Oct).

Admission Fees

Suomenlinna Sea Fortress: Free. *Coast Artillery Museum*: Fmk20 (adult), Fmk5 (child). *Doll and Toy Museum*: Fmk20 (adult), Fmk10 (child). *Ehrensuärd Museum*: Fmk15 (adult), Fmk7 (child). *Suomenlinna Museum*: Fmk20 (adult), Fmk15 (child).

Suomenlinna Sea Fortress

Finnish Tourist Board

France

1 Abbaye du Mont Saint-Michel (Mont Saint-Michel Abbey)
2 Arc de Triomphe (Triumphal Arch)
3 Arènes d'Arles (Roman Amphitheatre in Arles)
4 Basilique du Sacré Coeur de Montmartre (Sacré Coeur Basilica, Montmartre)
5 Cathédrale de Chartres (Chartres Cathedral)
6 Cathédrale de Notre Dame (Notre Dame Cathedral)
7 Château de Chenonceau (Chenonceau Castle)
8 Château de Versailles (Palace of Versailles)
9 Cimitière du Père Lachaise (Père Lachaise Cemetery)
10 Cité de Carcassonne (The Walled Town of Carcassonne)
11 Cité des Sciences et de l'Industrie (Science and Technology Park)
12 Disneyland® Paris
13 Grotte de Lascaux (Cave of Lascaux)
14 Maison de Claude Monet et Jardin d'Eau (Claude Monet's House and Water Garden)
15 Musée d'Orsay (Museum of Fine Arts)
16 Musée du Louvre (Louvre)
17 Palais des Papes (Popes' Palace)
18 Parc Astérix
19 Parc du Futuroscope (Futuroscope Park)
20 Parc Naturel Régional des Volcans d'Auvergne (Regional Nature Park of the Volcanoes of Auvergne)
21 Plages du débarquement de la Bataille de Normandie (D-Day Beaches)
22 Pont du Gard (Gard Aqueduct)
23 Pont St-Bénézet (St Bénezet Bridge)
24 Rocamadour
25 Tapisserie de la Reine Mathilde (Bayeux Tapestry)
26 Tour Eiffel (Eiffel Tower)

Tourist Information

Maison de la France (French Tourist Office)
20 avenue de l'Opéra, 75041 Paris, Cedex 01, France
Tel: (01) 4296 7000. Fax: (01) 4296 7011.
E-mail: admin@france.com
Website: www.franceguide.com

French Tourist Office
178 Piccadilly, London W1V 0AL, UK
Tel: (09068) 244 123 (information line; calls cost 60p per minute). Fax: (020) 7493 6594.
E-mail: info@mdlf.co.uk
Website: www.franceguide.com

Abbaye du Mont Saint-Michel (Mont Saint-Michel Abbey)

Mont Saint-Michel (Saint Michael's Mount) is a rocky island surrounded by perilous waters one kilometre (0.6 miles) off the coast of Normandy. It was founded in 708 by the Bishop of Avranches who built a chapel there after the Archangel Michael appeared to him in a dream. Construction of the spectacular *Abbaye du Mont Saint-Michel* (Mont Saint-Michel Abbey) started in 1023 and finished some 400 years later. Fashioned from granite, its delicate contours are an extension of the shape of the island and encompass a range of architectural styles, from Norman to Gothic. For centuries, the Abbey was a place of pilgrimage but it has also variously served as a prison, a fortress against the English and a monastery. There is still a Benedictine monastery in the Abbey, which can be visited on a guided tour. In the maze of cobbled streets on the rest of the island there are other attractions, including a waxwork museum, a maritime museum and the Archéoscope, a multimedia museum which tells the story of the island up to the present day.

Contact Address

Abbaye du Mont Saint-Michel, 50116 Le Mont Saint-Michel, France
Tel: (02) 3389 8000. Fax: (03) 3370 8308.
E-mail: hochet@monuments-france.fr
Website: www.monuments-france.fr

Transportation

Air: Caen-Carpiquet Airport, Paris Roissy-Charles de Gaulle Airport or Paris Orly Airport. **Water:** Sea:

Ferry services from the UK and Ireland to Cherbourg, Caen, Le Havre and Dieppe. **Rail:** Train: Pontorson Railway Station; high-speed TGV services from Pariş Gare Montparnasse via Rennes. **Road:** Car: N176 (from St Malo and Avranches) or N175 (from Rennes).

Opening Times

Abbaye du Mont Saint-Michel: Daily 0900-1730 (2 May-30 Sep); daily 0930-1630 (1 Oct-30 Apr). Closed 1 Jan, 1 May, 1 Nov, 11 Nov and 25 Dec.

Admission Fees

Abbaye du Mont Saint-Michel: FFr40 (adult), FFr25 (child). Concessions available.

Arc de Triomphe (Triumphal Arch)

Commissioned by Napoleon to commemorate the victorious French Army, the *Arc de Triomphe* has been a defining symbol of Paris ever since its completion in 1836. Engraved on the arch are numerous names of important and not-so-important victories and beneath it lies the *Tomb of the Unknown Soldier*. Visitors can reach the 50m-tall (164ft) top of the arch for stunning views of Paris, including the *Louvre* and the *Champs Elysées*, or tour the museum inside which charts the history and construction of the arch. The Champs-Elysées is considered to be one of the most elegant boulevards in the world, despite being nothing but fields and marshland until it was first developed in 1667. It used to be a showground for Parisian high society who would take walks down the tree-lined pavements, and although it now has its fair share of car showrooms and cinemas, it still retains an air of exclusivity, with luxury boutiques and expensive cafés.

Contact Address

Arc de Triomphe, Rond Point Place Charles de Gaulle, 75008 Paris, France
Tel: (01) 5537 7377. Fax: (01) 4380 6412.

Transportation

Air: Paris Roissy-Charles de Gaulle Airport or Paris Orly Airport. **Rail:** Train: Paris Gare du Nord (Eurostar) Station. Underground: Charles-de-Gaulle-Étoile. RER: Charles-de-Gaulle-Etoile. **Road:** Bus: 22, 30, 31, 52, 73, 92 or Balabus. Car: A1 (from Lille); A16 (from Boulogne); E60 (from Brussels); A62, then A20, A71 and A10 (from Toulouse); A3 (from Paris Roissy-Charles de Gaulle Airport); A4 (from Strasbourg); A6 (from Lyon and Marseille) or A13 (from Caen).

Opening Times

Daily 1000-2230 (Oct-Mar); daily 0930-2300 (Apr-Sep).

Admission Fees

FFr40 (adult), FFr25 (child 12-25), free (child under 12). Concessions available. Free the first Sunday of each month.

Arènes d'Arles (Roman Amphitheatre in Arles)

The two-tiered *Roman Amphitheatre* is probably the most prominent tourist attraction in the charming city of Arles, which thrived in Roman times. Measuring 136m (446 ft) in length and 109m (358 ft) wide, the 120 Romanesque arches date back to the first century BC. The amphitheatre was capable of seating over 20,000 spectators, and was built to provide entertainment in the form of chariot races and bloody hand-to-hand battles. Today, it draws large crowds for a sport only slightly less brutal – bullfighting – as well as plays and concerts. When it is not being used, visitors can explore the labyrinthine maze of corridors and enjoy views of Arles and the surrounding Provençal landscape from the upper level.

Contact Address

Arènes d'Arles, Rond-Point des Arènes, 13200 Arles, France
Tel: (04) 9049 3686.

Transportation

Air: Marseille-Provence Airport. **Rail:** Train: Arles Station. **Road:** Bus: La Starlette shuttle bus runs from the railway station to the town centre. Car: A54 (exit Arles-Centre).

Arles Ampitheatre

Office de Tourisme d'Arles

Opening Times

Daily 0900-1730 (1 Mar-30 Apr); daily 0900-1830 (2 May-30 Sep); daily 0900-1730 (1-31 Oct); daily 1000-1630 (1 Nov-28 Dec). Times are for last ticket sales; the amphitheatre closes 30 minutes later.

Admission Fees

FFr20 (adult), FFr15 (child under 18). Concessions available.

Basilique du Sacré Coeur de Montmartre (Sacré Coeur Basilica, Montmartre)

Designed by the Architect, Abadie, who was also responsible for the restoration of *St Front Cathedral* in Périgueux, work began on the construction of *Sacré Coeur* in 1875. Abadie, however, died in 1884 and work was not completed until 1914. The white-domed church, which is built in a Roman-Byzantine style houses one of the world's largest mosaics, designed by the French architect Luc Olivier Merson, depicting Christ with outstretched arms. The domed bell tower contains the *Savoyarde*, which was cast in Annecy in 1895 and is one of the heaviest bells in the world, weighing in at 19 tons. Today, thousands of visitors climb up the steep steps or take the funicular railway to the top of the *Butte de Montmartre* (the Hill of Martyrs) every day for the spectacular views across Paris. On a clear day, it is possible to see for 40km (25 miles) from the top of the 112m (367ft) bell tower, which is the highest point in Paris.

Contact Address

Basilique du Sacré Coeur de Montmartre, 35 rue de Chevallier, 75018 Paris, France
Tel: (01) 5341 8900. Fax: (01) 5341 8910.

Transportation

Air: Paris Roissy-Charles de Gaulle Airport. **Rail:** Funicular: Trains run from the base of the Butte de Montmartre to the church at the summit. Underground: Anvers or Abbesses. **Road:** Bus: 30, 31, 54, 80 or 85.

Opening Times

Basilica: Daily 0645-2230. *Dome* and *Crypt*: Daily 0900-1800 (Oct-Mar); daily 0900-1900 (Apr-Sep).

Admission Fees

Basilica: Free. *Dome*: FFr15. *Crypt*: FFr15. Concessions available.

Cathédrale de Chartres (Chartres Cathedral)

Chartres Cathedral is considered by many to be the finest Gothic cathedral in France, if not in Europe. The *Sancta Camisia*, the cloth that the Virgin Mary was wearing when she gave birth to Christ, was once housed in the town of Chartres. The cathedral itself was first built in 1145, but was destroyed by fire in 1194. The Sancta Camisia remained intact, which was seen as a sign of Mary's love and led a papal representative to convince the spiritually devastated people of Chartres to build a new cathedral on the same foundations. The result, which took until about 1260 to complete, was a spectacular combination of early Gothic and high Gothic, attracting hordes of visitors every year. Built of limestone, the cathedral, which set the standard for 13th-century architecture, stands 34m high (112ft) and 130m long (427ft). The cathedral is particularly well known for its asymmetrical spires, its 176 stained glass windows and its numerous religious sculptures depicting scenes from both the Old and New Testaments.

Contact Address

Office du Tourisme, Place de la Cathédrale, BP289, 28005 Chartres, France
Tel: (02) 3718 2626. Fax: (02) 3721 5191.
E-mail: chartres.tourism@wanadoo.fr

Transportation

Air: Paris Roissy-Charles de Gaulle Airport or Paris Orly Airport. **Rail:** Train: Chartres Station from Paris Montparnasse Station. **Road:** Bus: Chartres Station. Car: A6 to A10 and A11, N10 and D39 (from Paris).

Opening Times

Daily 0800-1915 (Jan-Apr and Oct-Dec); daily 0800-2000 (Apr-Oct).

Admission Fees

Free.

Cathédrale de Notre Dame (Notre Dame Cathedral)

Begun in 1163 by the architect Maurice de Sully and completed in about 1345, *Notre Dame* ranks as one of France's finest examples of Gothic architecture. During its long life, besides being a resplendent medieval cathedral, Notre Dame was reportedly set on fire during the Commune of 1871, when the Communards rose against the French government in the wake of their defeat during the Franco-Prussian war, and was also used to house livestock. It has also been the site of many historical events, including the crowning of Henry VI of England in 1430 and the marriage of the Catholic Marguerite de Valois to the Huguenot (Protestant) Henri of Navarre in 1572, which sparked the St Bartholomew's Day Massacre during the French Wars of Religion. Today, the cathedral still awes visitors with its massive rose windows, its 7800-pipe organ, towering spire and splayed flying buttresses.

Contact Address

Cathédrale de Notre Dame, Place du Parvis de Notre Dame, 75004 Paris, France
Tel: (01) 4234 5610 *or* 4432 1670 (towers). Fax: (01) 4051 7098.
E-mail: ecrire@catholique-paris.com
Website: www.catholique-paris.com

Transportation

Air: Paris Roissy-Charles de Gaulle Airport or Paris Orly Airport. **Rail:** RER: Châtelet-Les Halles or St-Michel-Notre-Dame. Underground: Cité. **Road:** Bus: 21, 24, 27, 38, 47, 85 or 96. Car: A1 (from Lille); A4 (from Strasbourg); A16 (from Dunkirk); A13 (from Caen) or A6 (from Lyon). In Paris, from either bank of the River Seine, signs are marked to Ile de la Cité.

Opening Times

Daily 0800-1845 (cathedral); daily 0930-1700 (towers).

Admission Fees

FFr36 (adult), FFr23 (adult 18-23), free (child under 18).

Château de Chenonceau (Chenonceau Castle)

Standing on the River Cher, the *Château de Chenonceau* is probably the most celebrated of the many châteaux that are situated in the Loire Valley. Used as a working mill in the early Middle Ages, the château, which was built by Thomas Bohier in 1513, spans the whole width of the river, seeming to float on water. Often referred to as the *Château des Femmes* and owned by a succession of powerful noblewomen – including Henri II's mistress Diane de Poitiers, the Queen Regent Catherine de Medici and her daughter-in-law Louise de Lorraine – its developing style and décor benefited from their grace and charm. The interior is well known for its elegant 59m-long (194ft) gallery, for the library used by Catherine de Medici, and for the famous guard room. Visitors can also see Francois I's bedroom, Louis XIV's living room and Diane de Poitiers's bedroom. The castle was purchased by Henri Menier in 1913 and is still owned by his descendants to this day.

Contact Address

Château de Chenonceau, 37150 Chenonceaux, France
Tel: (02) 4723 9007. Fax: (02) 4723 8088.
E-mail: chateau.de.chenonceau@wanadoo.fr
Website: www.chenonceau.com

Transportation

Air: Paris Roissy-Charles de Gaulle Airport. **Rail:** St-Pierre-des-Corps Station (Tours). **Road:** Car: A10 motorway (exits Blois or Amboise).

Opening Times

Daily 0900-1630 (mid Nov-Jan); daily 0900-1700 (Feb-mid Feb); daily 0900-1730 (mid Feb-end Feb); daily 0900-1800 (Mar-mid Mar); daily 0900-1900 (mid Mar-mid Sep); daily 0900-1830 (mid Sep-end Sep); daily 0900-1800 (Oct-mid Oct); daily 0900-1730 (mid Oct-end Oct); daily 0900-1700 (Nov-mid Nov).

Admission Fees

FFr50 (adult), FFr40 (child). Concessions available.

Château de Versailles (Palace of Versailles)

Situated 23km (15 miles) southwest of Paris, the *Palace of Versailles* is one of the most visited sites in France and famous for its immense size. The palace began as a 'modest' hunting lodge, built by Louis XIII in 1623, and was transformed by the architect Jules Hardouin Mansart under the guidance of Louis XIII's son, Louis XIV, into a grand palace complex surrounded by lavish French and English gardens designed by André Le Nôtre. Louis XIV, who was also known as the Sun King, was so taken with the palace that by 1682 it had become the official residence of the court of France and a lavish and potent statement of monarchical power. The palace became a symbol of monarchical folly and excess prior to the start of the French Revolution in 1789. Today, visitors are still able to view much of the palace, including the renowned 75m (250ft) *Galerie des Glaces* (Hall of Mirrors), where the Treaty of Versailles was signed in 1919, signifying the end of World War I. Visitors can also see the former Royal bedchambers, the grand staircase and the spectacular gardens, with their extraordinarily ornate fountains and elaborate pools.

Contact Address

Château de Versailles, RP 834, 78008 Versailles, France
Tel: (01) 3083 7800. Fax: (01) 3083 7890.
Website: www.chateauversailles.fr

Transportation

Air: Paris Roissy-Charles de Gaulle Airport or Paris Orly Airport. **Rail:** Train: Versailles-Chantiers Station or Versailles-Rive-Gauche Station. RER: Versailles-Rive-Gauche Station on line C. **Road:** Bus: 71 to Versailles-Place d'Armes. Car: A13 towards Rouen, first exit signposted Versailles-Château.

Opening Times

Château: Daily 0900-1730 (Oct-Apr); daily Tues-Sun 0900-1830 (May-Sep). *Gardens*: Daily from 0800 (Nov-Mar); daily from 0700 (May-Sep). Closing times may vary during the season.

Admission Fees

Château: FFr46 (adult), FFr35 (adult after 1530), free (child). *Gardens*: Free.

Cimitière du Père Lachaise (Père Lachaise Cemetery)

The *Cimitière du Père Lachaise*, which occupies 109 hectares (44 acres) on the eastern edge of Paris, is one of the city's less obvious tourist attractions, yet features on many a visitor's itinerary. It is named after Père François de la Chaise, who was confessor to Louis XIV, and quickly became the most prestigious burial ground in the whole of the city, due to its location and royal connections. This fact is reflected in the many famous names whose graves adorn the site, including singers Edith Piaf and Maria Callas, composer Frédéric Chopin, impressionist painter Camille Pissarro, and writers Honoré de Balzac and Oscar Wilde. Jim Morrison's grave, decorated with graffiti and littered with burning incense and candles, invariably attracts the most attention. Père Lachaise is the largest green space in Paris and its peaceful atmosphere makes it a popular place to bring a picnic. Guided tours are also available by prior arrangement.

Contact Address

Cimitière du Père Lachaise, 16 rue du Repos, 75020 Paris, France
Tel: (01) 5525 8210. Fax: (01) 4370 4216.
Website: www.paris-france.org

Transportation

Air: Paris Roissy-Charles de Gaulle Airport or Paris Orly Airport. **Rail:** Train: Paris Gare du Nord (Eurostar) Station. Underground: Philippe Auguste or Père Lachaise. **Road:** Bus: 61. Car: A1 (from Lille); A16 (from Boulogne); E60 (from Brussels); A62, then A20, A71 and A10 (from Toulouse); A3 (from Roissy-Charles de Gaulle Airport); A4 (from Strasbourg); A6 (from Lyon and Marseille) or A13 (from Caen).

Opening Times

Mon-Fri 0800-1800, Sat 0830-1730, Sun and public holidays 0900-1730 (16 Mar-4 Nov); Mon-Fri 0800-1730, Sat 0830-1730, Sun and public holidays 0900-1730 (5 Nov-15 Mar).

Admission Fees

Free.

Cité de Carcassonne (The Walled Town of Carcassonne)

Set on a hillside allowing extensive views over the *Pyrénées* mountains and the surrounding countryside, the medieval town of *Carcassonne*, which is the largest former fortress in Europe, dates back to the Roman Empire. The ramparts were built during the fourth century, whilst the château was built during the 12th century by Vicomte Trencavel. The town was invaded by Charlemagne during the eighth century, and is named after the Grand Dame of Carcas, the town's widowed Moorish Queen, who rushed to its defence, ringing the town's bell (*Carcas a sonné les cloches*) to indicate her victory over the invader. Carcassonne was captured by Simon de Montfort during the Crusade against the Albigenses in the 11th century and an outer wall was constructed, along with an inner rampart, to strengthen the fortress's position. Carcassonne quickly became one of the most important symbols of royal power in France due to its geographical location, although it lost its strategic importance in 1659 when the Treaty of the Pyrenees was drawn up, ending France's war with Spain. The town was renovated and restored during the 19th century by the architects Eugène Viollet-le-Duc and Paul Boeswillwald, giving it back some of its former glory and importance. Today, the town, which is beautifully illuminated at night, remains an impressive site despite its heavy tourist presence; the main attractions within the city's walls are the *Château Domtal,* which was transformed into a citadel in around 1226, the *Cour du Midi* remains of a Gallo-Roman villa, and the torture chamber at the *Exposition Internationale*. Visitors can also see the *Musée International de Dessin Animé* and the *Basilique St Nazaire*.

Contact Address

Cité de Carcassonne, Château Vicomtal, Monument National, 11000 Carcassonne, France
Tel: (04) 6811 7077. Fax: (04) 6811 7071.
E-mail: colin@monuments-france.fr
Website: www.carcassonne.culture.fr

Transportation

Air: Carcassonne Salvaza Airport. **Water:** Boat: Cruise and leisure boats have moorings along the Canal du Midi just after Carcassonne lock. **Rail:** Train: Carcassonne Station. **Road:** Car: N9, D213, A9, A61 and N113 (from Narbonne) or A620, A61, N161, D118 and N113 (from Toulouse).

Opening Times

Daily 0930-1700 (Nov-Mar); 0930-1800 (Apr, May and Oct); 0930-1930 (Jun-Sep). Closed 1 Jan, 1 May, 11 Nov and 25 Dec.

Admission Fees

Free entry onto city walls.

Cité des Sciences et de l'Industrie (Science and Technology Park)

Located on a large urban renewal site devoted to culture and leisure, *Cité des Sciences et de l'Industrie* was completed in 1986 with a mandate to educate visitors about science and technology. Designed by the architect Adrien Fainsilber and based on three themes, water, plant life and light, the Cité has welcomed approximately 40 million visitors since it first opened its doors to the public on 13 March 1986, coinciding with the arrival of Halley's Comet. Located in the Parc de la Vilette, which was formerly a giant abattoir and covers an area of 55 hectares (136 acres), this highly innovative complex is one of the biggest scientific and cultural centres in the world and is made up of several individual sites. *Explora* offers visitors activities such as piloting an aeroplane or travelling through the human body; the *Géode* is a large geodesic dome containing a 1000 sq metre (10,764 sq ft) screen and *Cinaxe* is a simulator fitted with equipment used to train airline

Aeriel View of the Walled Town of Carcassonne

Patrice Cartier, Office Municipal de Tourisme de Carcassonne

pilots. For children, the *Cité des Enfants* offers a chance to learn how electricity is supplied, whilst in *Techno Cité* they can take control of a helicopter or attempt to crack a safe. There is also a 400-tonne submarine in the *Submarine Argonaute* area, which was the pride of the French Navy during the 1950s and was installed at the Cité in 1989.

Contact Address

Cité des Sciences et de l'Industrie, 30 avenue Corentin-Cariou, 75930 Paris, France
Tel: (01) 4005 1212. Fax: (01) 4005 8190.
Website: www.cite-sciences.fr

Transportation

Air: Paris Roissy-Charles de Gaulle Airport or Paris Orly Airport. **Rail:** Underground: Porte de La Villette. **Road:** Bus: 75, 139, 150, 152 or PC. Car: Towards central Paris, off the Boulevard Périphérique (N2) (Porte de la Villette exit).

Opening Times

Tues-Sat 1000-1800, Sun 1000-1900.

Admission Fees

Cinaxe: FFr34 (adult). *Cité des Enfants*: FFr25 (adult and child). *Explora*: 50FFr (adult), free (child under 7). *Submarine Argonaute*: 25FFr (adult). *Techno Cité*: FFr25 (adult and child).

Disneyland® Paris

Opened in 1992, *Disneyland Paris* is the Walt Disney Company's first attempt to win the hearts of the Europeans. Although locals have taken some time to warm to it, the resort's success means that Disney intends to open a second theme park, *Disney Studios*, in 2002. The original park is very much like its American cousin, featuring sections like *Mainstreet USA, Discoveryland, Adventureland, Frontierland* and *Fantasyland*, however, enthusiasts rave that the more modern engineering of the French Parks can make for a superior experience.

Contact Address

Disneyland Paris, Guest Relations, BP100, 77777 Marne la Vallée, France
Tel: (08705) 030 303 in the UK.
Website: www.2000.disneylandparis.com

Transportation

Air: Paris Roissy-Charles de Gaulle Airport or Paris Orly Airport. Shuttle services are available from both airports to the park. **Rail:** Train: Eurostar or RER line A to Marne-la-Vallée/Chessy Station (from Paris). **Road:** Car: A4, 32km (20 miles) east of Paris (exit 14) (signposted Val d'Europe, Parc Disneyland).

Opening Times

Daily 0900-2000 (low season), 0900-2300 (high season). Times may vary according to the day of the week or the season.

Admission Fees

Low season: FFr170 (adult one-day pass), FFr140 (child one-day pass). High Season: FFr236 (adult one-day pass), FFr184 (child one-day pass).

Grotte de Lascaux (Cave of Lascaux)

Discovered by chance in 1940 by a group of teenagers, the cave paintings at Lascaux are considered to be among the world's best examples of prehistoric art. The area around Périgueux features many such cave paintings, although the 15,000-year-old images of bulls, horses and reindeer are believed to be some of the best. After the discovery of the cave, the increasing levels of carbon dioxide emitted by visitors were found to be damaging the paintings and, as a result, the caves were sealed in 1963, following an order from the French Ministry of Cultural Affairs. In order to compensate for the closure, a precise cement replica of the original caves, known as Lascaux II, was opened to the public in 1983; these caves feature the two most important parts of the original caves, the *Great Hall of the Bulls* and the *Painted Gallery*. Visitors can also see a replica of *the Shaft of the Dead Man*, the *Chamber of Felines* and the *Chamber of Engravings*.

Contact Address

Grotte de Lascaux, Semitour Périgord, 25 rue du Président Wilson, BP 1024, 24001 Périgueux Cedex, France
Tel: (05) 5335 5010. Fax: (05) 5306 3094.
E-mail: semitour@perigord.tm.fr
Website: www.culture.fr/culture/arcnat/lascaux/en

Transportation

Air: Périgueux-Basillac Airport. **Rail:** Train: Condat-Le-Lardin Station. **Road:** Bus: Services to Périgueux (from Montignac). Car: D901, D31 and D86 (from Brive-La-Gaillarde) or N21, D705, D4, D75, D7, D31 and D86 (from Périgueux).

Opening Times

Tues-Sun 0930-1830 (Sep-Jun); daily 0900-2000 (Jul-Aug).

Admission Fees

FFr50 (adult), FFr25 (child 6-12), free (child under 6).

Maison de Claude Monet et Jardin d'Eau (Claude Monet's House and Water Garden)

The Impressionist painter Claude Monet, who was born in Paris in 1840, spent the latter part of his life in Giverny in Northern France. Monet purchased a house in the village in 1883 and remained there until his death in 1926. Today, visitors can see the renovated house and wander around the beautiful gardens at Giverny. Inside the house, the walls are filled with a collection of Monet's Japanese prints, whilst the gardens, which were one of the painter's great joys, feature the French-style *Clos Normand* garden, and the Japanese-style *Jardin d'Eau*, home to the famous Japanese bridge. Visitors can also see a beautiful display of waterlilies in the Jardin d'Eau, which greatly inspired the painter and featured in some of his most famous works.

Contact Address

Maison de Claude Monet et Jardin d'Eau, Fondation Claude Monet, 27620, Giverny, France
Tel: (02) 3251 2821.
E-mail: contact@fondation-monet.com
Website: www.fondation-monet.com

Transportation

Air: Paris Roissy-Charles de Gaulle Airport. **Rail:** Train: Vernon Station (from St Lazare Station in Paris). **Road:** Bus: Buses leave every 15 minutes from Vernon Station.

Opening Times

Tues-Sun 1000-1800 (1 Apr-1 Nov).

Admission Fees

FFr35 (adult), FFr20 (child under 12), free (child under 7). Concessions available.

Musée d'Orsay (Orsay Museum)

This magnificently restored railway station houses the French national collection of art from 1848 to 1914. Since opening in 1986, the museum has attracted pilgrims from far and wide who come to take in the stunning collection of Impressionist and Post Impressionist art. Paintings include five Monet canvases of Rouen Cathedral, ballet scenes by Dégas, Courbet's shocking *L'Origine du Monde* (the Origins of the World), a hyperrealistic painting depicting a naked woman lying on her back, and works by Cézanne, Van Gogh, Renoir and Toulouse-Lautrec. The museum's collection also contains several fine sculptures as well as examples from the Art Nouveau movement. The museum works upwards in chronological order, and there is a café on the sky-lit upper level, where views of Paris can be enjoyed from behind the original station clock.

Contact Address

Musée d'Orsay, 62 rue de Lille, 75343 Paris, France
Tel: (01) 4049 4872. Fax: (01) 4222 1184.
E-mail: spa@musee-orsay.fr
Website: www.musee-orsay.fr

Transportation

Air: Paris Roissy-Charles de Gaulle Airport or Paris Orly Airport. **Rail:** Paris Gare du Nord (Eurostar) Station. RER: Musée d'Orsay. Underground: Solférino. **Road:** Bus: 24, 63, 68, 73, 83, 84 or 94. Car: A1 (from Lille); A16 (from Boulogne); E60 (from Brussels); A62, then A20, A71 and A10 (from Toulouse); A3 (from Roissy-Charles de Gaulle Airport); A4 (from Strasbourg); A6 (from Lyon and Marseille) or A13 (from Caen).

Opening Times

Tues-Wed 1000-1800, Thurs 1000-2145, Fri-Sat 1000-1800, Sun 0900-1800.

Admission Fees

FFr40 (adult), FFr30 (adult 18-25), free (child under 18).

Musée du Louvre (Louvre)

Constructed as a fortress in the Middle Ages and rebuilt in the mid-sixteenth century as a royal palace, it wasn't until 1793 that the *Louvre* became a museum. Today, it is the home of some of the world's most famous works of art, including the *Mona Lisa* and *Venus de Milo*. The rest of the permanent collection includes Greek, Etruscan, Roman, Egyptian and oriental antiquities, as well as sculptures, *objets d'art* and prints and drawings. Entrance to the museum is through the largest of the three glass pyramids that dominate the courtyard. Considered by many to be a work of art in themselves, despite controversy at their unveiling in 1985, they were commissioned by former President, the late François Mittérand, and designed by Chinese architect I M Pei.

Contact Address

Musée du Louvre, 75058 Paris Cedex 01, France
Tel: (01) 4020 5050. Fax: (01) 4020 5442.
E-mail: info@louvre.fr
Website: www.louvre.fr

Transportation

Air: Paris Roissy-Charles de Gaulle Airport or Paris Orly Airport. **Rail:** Train: Paris Gare du Nord (Eurostar). Underground: Palais Royal-Musée du Louvre. **Road:** Bus: 21, 27, 39, 48, 68, 69, 72, 81 or 95. Car: A1 (from Lille); A16 (from Boulogne); E60 (from Brussels); A62, then A20, A71 and A10 (from Toulouse); A3 (from Paris Roissy-Charles de Gaulle Airport); A4 (from Strasbourg); A6 (from Lyon and Marseille) or A13 (from Caen).

Opening Times

Mon and Wed 0900-2145, Thurs-Sun 0900-1800.

Admission Fees

FFr46 (adult until 1500), FFr30 (adult after 1500 and all day Sun), free (child under 18). Free first Sunday each month.

Palais des Papes (Popes' Palace)

The imposing *Palais des Papes* towers over Avignon, a symbol of the time when the Provençal city was the centre of the Christian world, after the papacy was moved here from Rome in 1309, due to a schism within the Church. The palace was commissioned by Pope Clement VI, who decided that the existing building was unworthy of his prestige. Although the papacy moved back to Rome in 1377, Avignon remained the property of the Holy See and the palace was used to house papal legates and Italian vice-legates, and also to house Avignon's two rival popes during the Great Schism between 1378-1417. Various popes added to the buildings during the Middle Ages, creating the largest Gothic palace in Europe, and today visitors can enter 25 of the rooms. Although the ransacking of the palace by the French National Assembly in 1791 left many of the rooms rather empty, some of the original frescoes remain, including those painted by Italian

Popes' Palace, Avignon

Palais des Papes

artist Matteo Giovanetti in the *Great Audience Room*. One part of the palace not to be missed is the *Great Chapel*, also built by Clement VI, which is more like a cathedral than a chapel in terms of size. The palace also gave its name to the famous *Châteauneuf-du-Pape* wine, and regular tastings are held in the cellars.

Contact Address

Palais des Papes, RMG – 6 rue Pente Rapide Charles Ansidéi, BP 149, 84008 Avignon, Cedex 1, France
Tel: (04) 9027 5000. Fax: (04) 9086 3612.
E-mail: monument@palais-des-papes.com
Website: www.palais-des-papes.com

Transportation

Air: Marseille-Provence Airport. **Rail:** Train: High-speed TGV services to Avignon (from Paris Gare de Lyon, Montpellier, Barcelona and Lyon). **Road:** Car: A7 or A9 (from Lyon, Marseille and Nîmes).

Opening Times

Daily 0930-1745 (2 Nov-31 Mar); daily 0900-1900 (1 Apr-31 May); daily 0900-2100 (1-31 July); daily 0900-2000 (1 Aug-30 Sep). Last tickets sold one hour before closing.

Admission Fees

FFr46 (adult), FFr36 (child). Concessions available.

Parc Astérix

Opened in 1989, *Parc Astérix* is a giant theme park based on the adventures of the popular cartoon character, Astérix. Located in the heart of protected forest, 35km (22 miles) north of Paris, the park takes visitors on a humorous journey through ancient Gaul, the Roman Empire and the Middle Ages to the 21st century. Visitors can meet the Gauls of prehistoric times, step back in time to Le Moyen-Âge (the Middle Ages), travel through Rome and Ancient Greece, and shake hands with the Three Musketeers. There are around 30 permanent rides at the park, as well as regular shows to entertain visitors. Highlights include the *Tonnere de Zeus* rollercoaster, the *Main Basse sur la Joconde* suspense show to steal the Mona Lisa and the *Théâtre de Poséidon* sea lion and dolphin display. New for 2001 is the *La Trace du Hourra* giant slide which is 850m (2789ft) long and 31m (102ft) high.

Contact Address

Parc Astérix, BP8, 60128, Plailly, France
Tel: (03) 4462 3404 *or* (08) 3668 3010.
Fax: (03) 4462 3294.
E-mail: contact@parcasterix.com
Website: www.parcasterix.fr *or* www.parcasterix.com

Transportation

Air: Paris Roissy-Charles de Gaulle Airport. There is a free ADP shuttle bus between Roissy-Charles de Gaulle 1 and Roissy-Charles de Gaulle 2. **Rail:** Train: Roissy Charles de Gaulle 2 TGV Station. Underground: Roissy-Charles de Gaulle (line B3). **Road:** Bus: Regular bus to Parc Asterix via Courriers Ile-de-France (from Roissy-Charles de Gaulle 1). Car: A1 Paris–Lille motorway, 30km (19 miles) north of Paris (exit 7-8) (signposted Parc Astérix).

Opening Times

Daily 0930/1000-1800/1930 (31 Mar-14 Oct). Opening times vary according to season. Closed 4, 11, 14, 18, 21 and 28 May, as well as 1, 8, 11 and 15 June.

Admission Fees

FFr185 (adult), FFr135 (child), free (child under 3).

Parc du Futuroscope (Futuroscope Park)

Located just outside Poitiers in western France, *Futuroscope* is a giant 53 hectare-theme park (131 acres) with a difference. With 3-D cinemas, giant screens and interactive attractions, the park offers visitors numerous exhibits and shows using the latest audio-visual technologies. Opened in 1987, this space-age park, which features futuristic architecture including silver spheres and crystal cubes, has more than 20 high-tech attractions. These include *Le Solido* cinema and *Le Tapis Magique* (flying carpet) which is located in a cathedral-like structure, allowing visitors to watch natural delights pass before their eyes in a giant audiovisual display; a particular highlight is a chance to watch the 3000km (1364 mile) journey undertaken by Monarch butterflies migrating from Canada to Mexico. The park is at the cutting edge of information technology and is an educational day out for adults and children alike where they can discover the wonders of earth and space through innovative interactive displays. The park is one of Europe's biggest moving image parks, offering sophisticated entertainment including the nightly *Lac aux Images* (Lake of Images) *Son et Lumière* laser and light show and the *Kinémax* attraction which, at 35m-high (115ft) and enclosing a 450-seat cinema, is the largest rock-crystal structure in the world. The park recently opened the *Cyber Avenue* attraction where the latest in multimedia and virtual technology are on display in the *Cyber Video* and *Cyber Média* exhibits.

Contact Address

Parc Européen de l'Image, 86130 Jaunay Clan, France

Tel: (020) 7499 8049 (from the UK) *or* (05) 4949 3080 (from France). Fax: (05) 4949 3025.
E-mail: webmaster@futuroscope.fr
Website: www.futuroscope.org

Transportation

Air: Poitiers-Biard Airport. **Rail:** Train: TGV Futuroscope Station (journey time: 1 hour 20 minutes from Paris). **Road:** Car: Autoroute A10 (exit 28).

Opening Times

Daily 0900-1900 (low season); daily 0900-2400 (high season). Closed 7 Jan-1 Feb 2002. Times may vary according to the day of the week or the season.

Admission Fees

Low season: FFr145 (adult), FFr100 (child). High season: FFr210 (adult), FFr145 (child 5-12).

Parc Naturel Régional des Volcans d'Auvergne (Regional Nature Park of the Volcanoes of Auvergne)

Covering an area of more than 395,000 hectares (976,085 acres), the *Parc Naturel Régional des Volcans d'Auvergne* is the largest national park in France. The park, which was created in 1977, is home to four volcanic massifs: the *Chaîne des Puys* (*Puy de Dôme*, 1465m/4792ft high), *Monts Dore* (*Puy de Sancy*, 1886m/6188ft high), *Monts du Cézalier* (*Signal du Luguet*, 1551m/5089ft high) and *Monts du Cantal* (*Plomb du Cantal*, 1855m/6086 ft high). There are glaciers, lakes and peatland throughout the park, as well as numerous exhibitions of flora, fauna and traditional architecture. Visitors to the park can, amongst other activities, taste local cheeses at the *Maison des Fromages* and the *Maison de Buronnier* or spot many thousands of birds. For the more active, sporting activities include hiking, riding, cycling, hand-gliding and hot-air ballooning. Those interested in geology and history can visit the *Maison de la Pierre de Volvic* where an explanation is given as to how volcanic rock was once cut and extracted. There are numerous other educational centres located within the park, including the *Maison de l'Eau et de la Pêche*, *Maison de la Faune*, *Maison des Fleurs d'Auvergne*, *Maison des Tourbières et du Cézalier* and *La Chaumière de Granièr*.

Contact Address

Regional Nature Park of the Volcanoes of Auvergne Information Centre, Montlosier 63970 Aydat, France
Tel: (04) 7365 6400. Fax: (04) 7365 6678.
E-mail: Parc.Volcans@wanadoo.fr
Website: www.parcs-naturels-regionaux.tm.fr

Transportation

Air: Clermont Ferrand Airport. **Rail:** Train: Clermont Ferrand Station. **Road:** Car: A71 (from Paris) or A72 (from Lyon).

Opening Times

La Chaumière de Granièr (Granièr Cottage): Daily 1400-1800 (15 Jun-15 Sep). *Maison de Buronnier* (Buron Centre): Daily 1400-1800 (15-30 Jun and 1-15 Sep); daily 1000-1230 and 1430-1900 (Jul-Aug). *Maison de l'Eau et de la Pêche* (Water and Angling Centre): Daily 1000-1200 and 1400-1600 (1 May-30 Sep). *Maison des Fromages d'Auvergne* (Auvergne Cheese Centre): Daily 1400-1800 (15-30 Jun and 1-15 Sep); daily 1000-1230 and 1430-1900 (Jul-Aug). *Maison de la Faune* (Fauna Centre): Daily 1000-1200 and 1500-1900 (Jul-Aug). *Maison des Fleurs d'Auvergne* (Auvergne Flower Centre): Daily 1000-1900 (1 May-15 Sep). *Maison de la Pierre de Volvic* (Volvic Stone Centre): Daily 1000-1200 and 1400-1700 (Mar-Apr and 1 Oct-15 Nov); daily 1000-1200 and 1400-1800 (2 May-30 Sep). *Maison des Tourbières et du Cézalier* (Peat Bogs and Cézalier Centre): Daily 1000-1200 and 1400-1900 (1 May-30 Sep).

Admission Fees

Park: Free. *Various Centres*: Between FFr18-25.

Plages du Débarquement de la Bataille de Normandie (D-Day Beaches)

The Allied Landings that took place at dawn on D-Day, 6 June 1944, signalled the beginning of the end of World War II. Some 83,000 British and Canadian and 73,000 US troops landed by sea and air along a 64-kilometre (40-mile) stretch of the Normandy coast in northern France. The horrific conditions, with many of the floating tanks sunk before they even reached the beaches, meant that thousands of soldiers never returned. The war cemeteries where many of the soldiers were laid to rest are open to the public, and some contain chapels and memorials. One of the most famous beaches is Omaha Beach, portrayed in Steven Spielberg's film 'Saving Private Ryan', where there is a large American cemetery overlooking the beach at *Colleville-sur-Mer*; the largest British cemetery is at *Bayeux*, where there is also the *Musée Memorial de la Bataille de Normandie 1944* (Battle of Normandy Museum; tel: (02) 3151 4690). The most significant beaches for the British are *Sword Beach* and *Gold Beach*. The *Mémorial de Caen* (Caen Memorial) museum (tel: (02) 3106 0644) tells the story of the two World Wars and shows an impressive film entitled *D-Day* in its twin-screened cinema. There are also various memorials to Allied soldiers from each country along the coastal road. Visitors should contact the *Comité Régionale de Tourisme de Normandie* (tel: (02) 3233 7900) for leaflets detailing specific itineraries, each of which focuses on a different D-Day campaign.

Contact Address

Comité Régionale de Tourisme de Normandie, 14 rue Charles Corbeau, 27000 Evreux, France
Tel: (02) 3233 7900. Fax: (02) 3231 1904.
E-mail: normandy@imaginet.fr
Website: www.normandy-tourism.org

Transportation

Air: Caen-Carpiquet Airport, Paris Roissy-Charles de Gaulle Airport or Paris Orly Airport. **Water:** Ferry: Services to Cherbourg, Caen and Le Havre (from Ireland and the UK). **Rail:** Train: Caen Station or Bayeux Station (services from Paris St Lazare). **Road:** Car: D514 (coastal road) or D513, N158, N13 (to Caen).

Opening Times

Mémorial de Caen (Caen Memorial): Daily 0900-1900. *Musée de la Bataille de Normandie* (Battle of Normandy Museum): Daily 0930-1730 (1 May-mid-Sep); daily 1000-1230 and 1400-1700 (16 Sep-30 Apr). Times shown are for last admission – the museum closes approximately one hour later.

Admission Fees

Mémorial de Caen (Caen Memorial): FFr76 (adult), FFr66 (child 10-18), free (child under 10). Concessions available. *Musée de la Bataille de Normandie* (Battle of Normandy Museum): FFr34 (adult), FFr16 (child 10-18), free (child under 10).

Pont du Gard (Gard Aqueduct)

Constructed by the son-in-law of Emperor Augustus, the stunning *Pont du Gard* is the largest surviving piece of a Roman aqueduct that spanned the *River Gardon*, northeast of Nîmes. At a height of 49m (161ft) and with a length of 273m (896ft), it consists of three tiered levels of arches. At one time, it was part of a greater engineering marvel that transported water over a distance of more than 50km (35 miles). The aqueduct took over a century to complete and was constructed without mortar. There is now a new *Centre Culturel* (Cultural Centre) at the aqueduct, which contains exhibitions on Roman civilisation and the building of the aqueduct. Every night in summer the aqueduct is illuminated in a *son et lumière* show. Many people come to the Pont du Gard to swim or go canoeing on the river, which is particularly picturesque at this point, and there are also several campsites and hiking trails.

Contact Address

Concession Pont du Gard, BP 7, Route de Pont du Gard, 30210 Vers Pont du Gard, France
Tel: (04) 6637 5112. Fax: (04) 6637 5150.
E-mail: accueil-pontgard@nimes.cci.fr

Transportation

Air: Marseille-Provence Airport or Garons Airport. **Rail:** Train: Avignon Station or Nîmes Station. **Road:** Bus: Roemonlins. Car: A9, N100 or N86.

Opening Times

Pont du Gard: Daily 0700-0100. *Centre Culturel*: Daily 1000-1800 (1 Nov-30 Mar); daily 0930-1900 (2 Apr-14 Jun); daily 0930-2130 (16 Jun-31 Aug); daily 0930-1900 (1 Sep-31 Oct).

Admission Fees

Pont du Gard: Free. *Centre Culturel*: FFr85 (adult), FFr75 (child 5-21), free (child under 5).

Pont St-Bénézet (St Benezet Bridge)

'Sur le pont d'Avignon, on y danse, on y danse ...' – this 19th-century children's song continues to draw visitors to the famed bridge every year. Officially called *Pont St-Bénézet* after the shepherd Bénézet whose heavenly vision and determination caused the bridge to be built, this 900m-structure (2953ft) once spanned the two channels of the River Rhône and the island in between (*Ile de la Barthelasse*). Built between 1177 and January 1185, and originally made of wood, it was the only bridge linking the important trade hub, the Mediterranean and Lyons, during the Middle Ages. The bridge had to be continuously rebuilt over the centuries, but was finally washed away by the river in the mid-

1600s. Today, only four of its original 22 arches and the tiny *Chapelle St-Nicholas* remain. The small *Musée des Images* offers pictures of the bridge in its former glory.

Contact Address

Office du Tourism d'Avignon, 41 cours Jean Jaurès, 84000 Avignon, France
Tel: (04) 3274 3274. Fax: (04) 9082 9503.
E-mail: information@ot-avignon.fr
Website: www.avignon-tourisme.com

Transportation

Air: Marseilles-Provence Airport. **Rail:** Train: Avignon Station. **Road:** Bus: Porte de L'Oulle. Car: A7, N107 and D225 to Avignon (from Lyon).

Opening Times

Daily 0930-1745 (Nov-Mar); daily 0900-1900 (Apr-Jun and Oct-Nov); daily 0900-2100 (Jul); daily 0900-200 (Aug-Sep).

Admission Fees

FFr19 (adult), FFr15 (child), free (child under 7).

Rocamadour

Built into limestone cliffs, with its medieval houses clinging precariously over the gorge of the River Alzou, *Rocamadour* is a major pilgrimage site, home to an ancient oratory which was dedicated to the Virgin Mary some time before the tenth century. The town is famed for being the site where the body of St Amadour, who is believed to actually be Zacchaeus of the gospel, was discovered near the town's chapel in 1166, an event which led to a succession of miracles in the town. Dedicated to the Virgin Mary, the town ranks behind only Rome, Jerusalem and Santiago de Compostela as a pilgrimage site. Visitors to the town can climb the *Grand Escalier* (Great Ladder) to the 12th-century *Cité Religeuse* (Religious City) at the top, which consists of seven chapels; the most important of these is the *Chapelle Notre-Dame*, which sits on top of the *Crypte St Amadour*. Other highlights include the *Musée d'Art Sacrée* (Museum of Sacred Art), which houses many relics, paintings and statues, the *Chapelle St Michel* and the *Basilique St Sauveur*. Visitors can also climb the *Chemin de Croix* (Way of the Cross) and see exceptional views of the Dordogne countryside from the ramparts of the 14th-century château at the top. Other attractions nearby include the *Rocher des Aigles* birds of prey conservation centre, the *Forêt des Singes* monkey sanctuary and the *Grottes de Lacave* underground caves.

Contact Address

Office de Tourisme de Rocamadour, 46500 Rocamadour, France
Tel: (05) 6533 2200. Fax: (05) 6533 2201.
E-mail: rocamadour@wanadoo.fr
Website: www.rocamadour.com

Transportation

Air: Bordeaux Airport or Toulouse International Airport. **Rail:** Train: The four levels of the city are connected by a small train and a lift. **Road:** Bus: Buses to St Denis Près Martel (from Brive and Sarlat). Taxis: Available to take visitors from Rocamadour-Padirac Station. Car: N140, N89, D32 and D36 (from the west); N20, D23 and D36 (from the south); N20, A20, N140, D32 and D36 (from the north) or A75, N89, N20, A20, N140, D32 and D36 (from the east). A winding road leads from the village at the base of the hill to the top.

Opening Times

Rocamadour: Daily 24 hours. *Cité Religeuse*: Mon-Fri 0830-1200 and 1400-1700 (Apr-Jun and Sep); Mon-Sat 0830-1700 (Jul-Aug). *Forêt des Singes*: Tues-Sun 0930-1830 (Sep-Jun); daily 0900-2000 (Jul-Aug). *Grottes de Lacave*: Daily 1000-1200 and 1300-1800 (Apr-Jun and Sep); daily 1000-1900 (Jul-Aug); Mon-Sat 1300-1700, 1000-1200 and Sun 1300-1700 (Oct-Nov). *Musée d'Art Sacrée*: Daily 1000-1200 and 1400-1700 (Mar-Jun and Oct); daily 0930-1830 (Jul-Aug); daily 0930-1200 and 1400-1730 (Oct). *Rocher des Aigles*: Mon-Sat 1400-1600, Sun 1400-1700 (Apr-Jun and Sep); daily 1400-1700 (Jul-Aug); Mon-Sat 1500 only, Sun 1500-1600 (Oct-Nov). Opening times vary for other attractions in Rocamadour according to the day of the week and season; visitors are advised to check with the Office du Tourisme de Rocamadour for further details.

Admission Fees

Rocamadour: Free. *Cité Religeuse*: FFr22 (adult), FFr15 (child). *Forêt des Singes*: FFr40 (adult), FFr25 (child). *Grottes de Lacave*: FFr43 (adult), FFr32 (child). *Musée d'Art Sacrée*: FFr30 (adult), FFr17 (child). *Rocher des Aigles*: FFr40 (adult), FFr25 (child).

Tapisserie de la Reine Mathilde (Bayeux Tapestry)

The *Bayeux Tapestry*, which is one of the most historically important, and unusual, chronicles of its day, is now located in the town of Bayeux in Normandy. The 70m-long (231ft) tapestry offers a splendidly vivid depiction of the events leading up to the Norman Conquest of England in 1066. It begins with Harold of Wessex's visit to Normandy and his meeting with Duke William in 1064, and culminates with the flight of the English army at Hastings. All the main intervening events, including the death of King Edward the Confessor in January 1066, Harold's coronation, William's elaborate invasion preparations, his landing at Pevensey, the Battle of Hastings and Harold's death, are covered in painstaking detail. Along the top and bottom of the tapestry run decorated borders illustrating scenes of contemporary warfare, hunting and husbandry and also some episodes from the fables of Aesop and Phaedrus. The tapestry is known in French as *La Tapisserie de la Reine Mathilde* (Queen Mathilda's Tapestry) after William's wife. Although it was almost destroyed in 1792 when French revolutionaries used it as a wagon cover, the whole tapestry (with the exception of the final section, thought to have depicted William's coronation in Westminster Abbey on Christmas Day 1066) has survived to this day and can still be viewed by visitors to the town of Bayeux.

Contact Address

Tapisserie de la Reine Mathilde, Centre Guillaume le Conquérant, Rue de Nesmond, 14400 Bayeux, France
Tel: (02) 3151 2550. Fax: (02) 3151 2559.

Transportation

Air: Caen-Carpiquet Airport. **Rail:** Train: Bayeux Station. **Road:** Bus: Bybus Station. Car: N13, A14, A13, N413, N175, E46, N13 and D6 (from Paris).

Opening Times

Daily 0930-1230 and 1400-1800 (Oct-Mar); daily 0900-1830 (Mar-Apr and Sep-Oct); daily 0900-1900 (May-Aug). Closed 1 Jan and 25 Dec.

Admission Fees

FFr41 (adult), FFr16 (child over 10), free (child under 10). Concessions available.

Tour Eiffel (Eiffel Tower)

Originally created as the centrepiece of Paris' *Exposition Universelle* in 1889, in commemoration of the centenary of the French Revolution, the *Eiffel Tower* went on to become the centrepiece of the city itself. The tower that has become symbolic of Paris the world over weighs 10,100 tonnes and contains 18,000 pieces of iron, held together by 2,500,000 rivets. At 324m (888ft) high, it was, until 1929, the tallest structure in the world; although that record was broken many years ago, there are still superb views over Paris from the first floor, which can be reached by a stairway, and even better views from the third floor, which is accessible by lift.

Contact Address

Tour Eiffel, Champ de Mars, 7500 Paris, France
Tel: (01) 4411 2323. Fax: (01) 4411 2322.
E-mail: courrier@tour-eiffel.fr
Website: www.tour-eiffel.fr

Transportation

Air: Paris Roissy-Charles de Gaulle Airport or Paris Orly Airport. **Rail:** Train: Paris Gare du Nord (Eurostar). Underground: Bir-Hakeim, Trocadéro or Ecole Militaire. RER: Champ de Mars-Tour Eiffel. **Road:** Bus: 42, 69, 72, 82 or 87. Car: A1 (from Lille); A16 (from Boulogne); E60 (from Brussels); A62, then A20, A71 and A10 (from Toulouse); A3 (from Roissy-Charles de Gaulle Airport); A4 (from Strasbourg); A6 (from Lyon and Marseille) or A13 (from Caen).

Opening Times

Lift: Daily 0930-2300 (1 Sep-9 Jun); daily 0900-2400 (10 Jun-31 Aug). *Stairs*: Daily 0930-1830 (1 Sep-9 Jun); daily 0900-2400 (10 Jun-31 Aug).

Admission Fees

Lift: FFr24 (First floor), FFr45 (Second floor), FFr65 (Third floor) (adult); FFr14 (First floor), FFr25 (Second floor), FFr35 (Third floor) (child 3-12); free (child under 3). *Stairs*: FFr20 (First and Second floors only).

Bayeux Tapestry: Harold's Coronation and (top right) Halley's Comet

Society of Antiquaries, London

Germany

1	Brandenburger Tor (Brandenburg Gate)
2	Englischer Garten (English Garden)
3	Freiburg Münster (Freiburg Cathedral)
4	Haus am Checkpoint Charlie (Checkpoint Charlie Museum)
5	Kölner Dom (Cologne Cathedral)
6	Münchener Residenz (Munich Residence)
7	Pergamonmuseum (Pergamon Museum)
8	Reichstag (Town Hall)
9	Schloss Heidelberg (Heidelberg Castle)
10	Schloss Neuschwanstein (Neuschwanstein Castle)
11	Schloss Sanssouci (Sanssouci Palace)

Tourist Information

Deutsche Zentrale für Tourismus e.V. (German National Tourist Office)
Beethovenstraße 69, 60325 Frankfurt/M, Germany
Tel: (069) 974 640. Fax: (069) 751 903.
E-mail: gntofra@d-z-t.com
Website: www.germany-tourism.de

German National Tourist Office
PO Box 2695, London W1A 3TN, UK
Tel: (09001) 600 100 (recorded information and brochure request line; calls cost 60p per minute) *or* (020) 7317 0908 (general enquiries).
Fax: (020) 7495 6129.
E-mail: gntolon@d-z-t.com
Website: www.germany-tourism.de

Brandenburger Tor (Brandenburg Gate)

Built in 1791 as a triumphal arch, the *Brandenburg Gate*, the only remaining town gate in the country, is an enduring symbol of Berlin and Germany. The design, by architect Carl Gotthard Langhans, is modelled on the entrance to the Acropolis in Athens, and is crowned by a statue of a horse-drawn chariot, which symbolises Victory; the overall effect was intended to testify to the might and power of the Prussian Empire. It has survived multiple wars, including the long Cold War, during which it was sealed off in no-man's land by the *Berlin Wall*, and became a symbol of division between east and west. In 1989, it was reopened to the public following the destruction of the Berlin Wall, and has become a central focus for tourists who flock to the many stalls that claim to sell genuine pieces of the wall.

Contact Address

Berlin Tourist Office, Am Karlsbad 11, 10785 Berlin, Germany
Tel: (0180) 575 4040. Fax: (030) 2500 2424.
E-mail: information@btm.de
Website: www.berlin-tourism.de

Transportation

Air: Berlin Tegel Airport. **Rail:** Train: S-Bahn to Unter den Linden. Underground: Friedrichstrasse, Französische Strasse or Mohrenstrasse. **Road:** Bus: 100 (to Pariser Platz).

Opening Times

Daily 24 hours.

Admission Fees

Free.

Englischer Garten (English Garden)

The *Englischer Garten*, measuring 3.7 square kilometres (1.4 square miles), is one of Europe's oldest urban landscaped parks, originally laid out in 1789 by American Benjamin Thomson as a garden for the military. It was soon opened to the public, however, and has been popular with locals and visitors ever since, due to the natural landscapes and wide open spaces which make it an oasis in the centre of the city. Popular activities include boating on the *Kleinhesselhoher Lake*, and sunbathing (there is even a special area for naturists) and visitors can also watch Japanese tea ceremonies in the *Japanisches Teehaus* (Japanese Teahouse). The beer garden at the *Chinesischer Turm* (Chinese Tower) is popular with all age groups for beer, coffee and cakes. In winter, the garden hosts a Christmas market and in summer there are open-air concerts and plays performed in the amphitheatre.

Contact Address

Verwaltung des Englischen Gartens München, Englischer Garten 2, 80538 Munich, Germany
Tel: (089) 341 986. Fax: (089) 335 169.

Transportation

Air: Munich International Airport. **Rail:** Tram: 17 (Tivolistrasse). Underground: Universität, Giselastrasse or Münchener Freiheit. **Road:** Bus: 54, 154 (Chinesischer Turm). Car: A9 to Schwabing, signs then marked Englischer Garten.

Opening Times

Daily 24 hours.

Admission Fees

Free.

Freiburg Münster (Freiburg Cathedral)

Consecrated in 1513, having taken over 300 years to build, *Freiburg Cathedral* is a masterpiece of Gothic architecture. The 116-metre (318-ft) high west tower, which soars above the jumbled rooftops of the Black Forest city, was described by Swiss historian Jacob Burckhardt as 'the most beautiful spire in Christendom' and contains the 'Hosanna' bell which dates from 1258; the bell is still rung

Brandenburg Gate

Presse- und Informationsamt des Landes Berlin

every Friday at 1100. Visitors can climb the tower for excellent views over Freiburg and the *Black Forest*. The interior of the cathedral is just as beautiful, the highlight being Hans Baldung Grien's Renaissance *High Altar*, depicting the life of the Virgin Mary. *Münsterplatz*, the cathedral square, is a lively venue all year round, but is particularly atmospheric during the Christmas market each winter, and on long summer evenings, when people sit outside cafés enjoying the wine that is produced in local vineyards.

Contact Address

Freiburg Wirtschaft und Touristik GmbH & Co KG, Rotteckring 14, 79098 Freiburg, Germany
Tel: (0761) 388 101. Fax: (0761) 37003.
E-mail: touristik@fwt-online.de
Website: www.freiburg-online.com

Transportation

Air: Euro-Airport Basel-Mulhouse-Freiburg. **Rail:** Train: ICE (InterCity Express) trains to Freiburg Hauptbahnhof (from Hamburg, Frankfurt and Basel) and IC/EC (InterCity and regional) trains to Freiburg Hauptbahnhof (from Hamburg, Frankfurt and Cologne). Tram: Bertoldsbrunnen, Oberlinden. **Road:** Car: A5 Frankfurt-Basel (exit Freiburg-Mitte).

Opening Times

Tues-Sat 1000-1700, Sun 1300-1700.

Admission Fees

DM2.50 (adult), DM0.50 (child under 12). Concessions available.

Haus am Checkpoint Charlie (Checkpoint Charlie Museum)

Checkpoint Charlie was the monitoring tower used to control the area around the *Berlin Wall* that divided the city during the Cold War. It was demolished soon after the 1989 revolution, but the *Haus am Checkpoint Charlie* museum that stands in its place is well worth a visit to discover the historic significance of this apparently unremarkable site. There were many brave, if foolhardy, attempts by civilians to escape from the east – 80 were shot after being detected from Checkpoint Charlie – and the ingenious methods used are described alongside photos from the Cold War era. A cinema shows films on the Third Reich and the Cold War era, and the museum also details the history of the Berlin Wall, a piece of which still stands a short distance from the museum, complete with decorations on the western side.

Contact Address

Haus am Checkpoint Charlie, Friedrichstrasse 43-45, 10969 Berlin–Kreuzberg, Germany
Tel: (030) 253 7250. Fax: (030) 251 2075.
E-mail: info@mauer-museum.com
Website: www.mauer-museum.com

Transportation

Air: Berlin Tegel Airport or Berlin Schönefeld Airport. **Rail:** Train: Bahnhof Berlin Zoologischer Garten Station or Lehrter Bahnhof Station. Underground: Kochstrasse or Stadtmitte. **Road:** Coach: Zentraler Omnibusbahnhof (ZOB) am Funkturm. Car: A10 (orbital); A111 or A115 (from western Berlin); A24 (from Hamburg); A2 (from Hanover); A9 (from Leipzig and Munich); A13 (from Dresden) or A12 (from Polish border).

Opening Times

Daily 0900-2200.

Admission Fees

DM12 (adult), DM6 (child under 18). Concessions available.

Kölner Dom (Cologne Cathedral)

Begun in 1248 and completed in 1880, *Cologne Cathedral* is a celebration of the finest aspects of Gothic architecture, with its intricate detail and elaborate decoration. Although Romanesque architecture was more in vogue in the rest of Germany at the time, the Gothic style was chosen to reflect the importance of Cologne's status as a major centre of the Holy Roman Empire. Its twin towers stand 157m (515ft) above the city, on the left bank of the Rhine, and made the cathedral the tallest structure in the world until the *Eiffel Tower* was built in 1889. The interior is equally impressive, with 14th-century stained glass, a resplendent choir, and a large gold shrine, considered a masterpiece of medieval goldwork. Remarkably the cathedral survived a total of 14 bomb raids during World War II and today visitors can climb the tower for superb views over Cologne and the *Rhineland*.

Contact Address

Kölner Dom, Domforum, Domkloster 2, 50667 Cologne, Germany
Tel: (0221) 9258 4720. Fax: (0221) 9258 4731.
Website: www.koelner-dom.de

Transportation

Air: Cologne/Bonn Airport. **Rail:** Train: Cologne Station. Tram: Dom or Hbf (Hauptbahnhof). **Road:**

Car: A1, A3, A4, A57 or A555; signs are marked either 'Hauptbahnhof' or 'Dom'.

Opening Times

Daily 0600-1930.

Admission Fees

Cathedral: Free. *Treasury*: DM3. *Tower*: DM3 (adult), DM1.50 (child).

Münchener Residenz (Munich Residence)

The *Munich Residence*, located in the centre of the city is a magnificent complex of buildings constructed by the powerful Wittelsbach family who ruled Bavaria for 800 years. Although originally dating from the 14th century, subsequent additions and alterations gave the Residence a variety of architectural styles, right up until the fall of the Wittelsbach dynasty in 1918. Renaissance features predominate but one of the most impressive rooms in the complex is the Baroque *Golden Hall*. The *Antiquarium*, built in 1571, is the oldest part of the palace and houses the family's collection of antiquities, whilst the *Schatzkammer* (treasury) holds an exquisite array of diamonds, rubies and other precious stones. Other rooms display porcelain, Italian portraits and vistas, and even Egyptian art. The Rococo *Cuvilliés Theatre* was once the private theatre of the Wittelbach court. Both the theatre and the Residence were destroyed during World War II but have been rebuilt in their original style.

Contact Address

Münchener Residenz, Residenzstrasse 1, 80333 Munich, Germany
Tel: (089) 290 671. Fax: (089) 2906 7225.
E-mail: info@bsv.bayern.de

Transportation

Air: Munich International Airport. **Rail:** Train: München Hauptbahnhof (Munich Station); daily ICE (InterCity Express) services (from Dortmund via Düsseldorf, Cologne and Mannheim); (from Hamburg via Hanover and Kassel) or (from Berlin via Frankfurt and Stuttgart or Nuremberg). International services (from Salzburg, Lindau and Venice via Innsbruck). Underground: Odeonsplatz or Marienplatz. Tram: 19 (Nationaltheater). **Road:** Coach: München Hauptbahnhof (Munich Station) or Starnberger Station. Bus: 52 (Marienplatz) or 53 (Odeonplatz). Car: A9 (from Berlin and Nuremberg); A92 (from Passau); A95 (from the Alps); A8 (from Salzburg).

Fremdenverkehrsamt München/Wilfred Hoesl

Munich Residence

Opening Times

Museum and treasury: Daily 1000-1600, guided tours at 1000 and 1230 (16 Oct-31 Mar); Mon-Wed and Fri-Sun 0900-1800, Thurs 0900-2000 (1 Apr-15 Oct). *Cuvilliés-Theater*: Mon-Sat 1400-1700 and Sun 1000-1700.

Admission Fees

Museum or *treasury*: DM8 (adult), free (child under 18 accompanied by adult). Concessions available. *Combined ticket*: DM14 (adult), free (child under 18 accompanied by adult). Concessions available. *Cuvilliés-Theatre*: DM4 (adult), free (child under 18 accompanied by adult).

Pergamonmuseum (Pergamon Museum)

One of the world's great museums, the *Pergamon Museum* lies on Berlin's *Museumsinsel* (Museum Island) complex, which is situated between the River Spree and Kupfergraben. Five museums were built here between 1824 and 1930 to house archaeological treasures and art collections. The last of the five to be built was the Pergamon Museum which was designed by Alfred Messel and houses spectacular works of architectural antiquities, including collections of Greek, Assyrian, Islamic and Far Eastern art. Many objects are of a magnitude rarely found indoors, such as the *Pergamon Altar*, with a 120 metre (394ft) frieze, the *Market Gate of Miletus* and the *Ishtar Gate* from Babylon. The building also houses the *Museum of Islamic Art* and the *Near Eastern Museum*. Other attractions on Museum Island, which has been listed as a UNESCO World Heritage Site since 1999, include the *Museum of Applied Art*, the *Museum of European Cultures* and the *Museum of East Asian Art*.

Contact Address

Pergamonmuseum, Bodestrasse 1-3, 10178 Berlin, Germany
Tel: (030) 2090 5577. Fax: (030) 2090 5502.
E-mail: ant@smb.spk-berlin.de *or*
isl@smb.spk-berlin.de *or*
vam@smb.spk-berlin.de
Website: www.pergamonmuseum.de

Transportation

Air: Berlin Tegel Airport. **Rail:** Train: S-Bahn to Friedrichstrasse or Hackescher Markt. Tram: 1, 2, 3, 4, 5, 6, 50 or 53. Underground: Friedrichstrasse. **Road:** Bus: 100, 157, 200 or 348 (Lustgarten stop) or 147 (Universitätsstrasse stop). Car: Am Lustgarten and Bodestrasse (from Berliner Dom in Berlin city centre).

Opening Times

Tues-Sun 1000-1800 (Thurs until 2200).

Admission Fees

DM8 (adult), DM4 (child). Concessions available.

Reichstag (Town Hall)

The imposing neo-Renaissance *Reichstag*, located in the heart of Berlin's city centre near the River Spree and the *Brandenburg Gate*, was completed in 1894. It was home to the German parliament until 1933, when a huge fire destroyed the building – an event that coincided with Adolph Hitler assuming dictatorial control of the country. In 1990, following the fall of the Berlin Wall in 1989 and German re-unification, the parliament (which is known as the *Bundestag*) moved from Bonn to meet again in the historic Reichstag. In 1999, the parliament moved permanently to a renovated and renewed Reichstag. A new glass dome symbolises the transparency of the democratic process, and visitors can walk along the different levels of the dome to watch the government in session below.

Contact Address

Reichstag, Platz der Republik 1, 11011 Berlin, Germany
Tel: (030) 2273 2152 *or* 2272 2152. Fax: (030) 2273 0027 *or* 2272 0027.
E-mail: DBT-Besucherdienst@t-online.de
Website: www.bundestag.de

Transportation

Air: Berlin Tegel Airport. **Rail:** Train: S-Bahn to Unter den Linden. **Road:** Bus: 100 to Reichstag/ Bundestag. Car: Signs are marked for the Reichstag in Berlin city centre.

Opening Times

Roof Terrace and *Dome*: Daily 0800-2400. *Plenary Chamber*: Mon-Fri 0900-1600, Sat, Sun and public holidays 1000-1600.

Admission Fees

Free.

Schloss Heidelberg (Heidelberg Castle)

Situated high above the *River Neckar*, *Heidelberg Castle* is one of Germany's most romantic locations. It has had a long and turbulent history since it was first constructed in the early 15th century as a residence for the Palatine princes, the powerful secular rulers who presided over this part of southern Germany during the Holy Roman Empire. Having been totally destroyed during the Thirty Years War, and later by the French in 1689 and 1693, the red sandstone building was struck by lightning in 1764 and even its stones were taken for use in other building projects. Subsequent rebuilding has led to a variety of architectural styles, from Gothic to Baroque, and yet the castle's somewhat delapidated air adds to its charm. The best way to reach the site is by cable car, and there are excellent views over the university city of Heidelberg and the *Neckar Valley* from the summit. Balls and concerts are held in the *King's Hall*, and the courtyard hosts a musical version of the 1950s film *The Student Prince* in summer; there are firework displays in July and September. Visitors can also tour the *Pharmacy Museum* and see a huge wine barrel which can hold 185,500 litres (49,000 gallons) in the cellar of the Renaissance *Friedrichsbau Wing*. There is wheelchair access to the courtyard but not inside the castle itself.

Contact Address

Schloss Heidelberg, Schlossverwaltung, Im Schlosshof 1, 69117 Heidelberg, Germany

Tel: (06221) 538 414. Fax: (06221) 167 732.
E-mail: info@schloss-heidelberg.de

Transportation

Air: Frankfurt Airport (a coach service runs directly from the airport to Heidelberg). **Rail:** Train: Direct services from across Europe or via Mannheim to Heidelberg Hauptbahnhof. Funicular: From Kornmarkt. **Road:** Coach: Heidelberg Busbahnhof. Bus: 11 or 33 (to Rathaus/Bergbahn). Car: A5 (from Frankfurt), then A656 (exit Autobahnintersection Heidelberg or Heidelberg/Schwetzingen).

Opening Times

Castle: Daily 0800-1800. *Pharmacy Museum*: Daily 0800-1700.

Admission Fees

DM6 (adult), DM3 (child). Concessions available. Admission is by guided tour only (tel: (06221) 538 431).

Schloss Neuschwanstein (Neuschwanstein Castle)

Neuschwanstein Castle is one of three castles built by 'mad' Ludwig II of Bavaria, who was born in 1845 and died in 1886. This fairytale castle sits perched among the natural splendour of the Alps. Its Neo-Romanesque architecture imitates that of a medieval castle and, in turn, Neuschwanstein was the inspiration for Disney's Magic Kingdom. Built between 1869 and 1886, only about a third of the castle was actually completed as Ludwig II was found to be mentally unfit by a government commission. Visitors can take guided tours of the interior of the castle and see the 17 rooms that were finished, including the opulent *Singer's Hall* and the majestic throne room. Nearby *Marienbrüecke* (Mary's Bridge), which spans a deep gorge, provides magnificent views of the castle.

Contact Address

Schlossverwaltung Neuschwanstein, Neuschwansteinstrasse 20, 87645 Schwangau, Germany
Tel: (08362) 81035. Fax: (08362) 8990.

Transportation

Air: Munich International Airport. **Rail:** Füssen Station. **Road:** Coach: Services from Füssen to Hohenschwangau. Car: A9 (from Berlin and Nuremberg); A92 (from Passau); A95 (from the Alps); A8 (from Salzburg) or B17 (from Munich).

Opening Times

Daily 1000-1600 (Oct-Mar); Mon-Wed and Fri-Sun 0900-1800, Thurs 0900-2000 (Apr-Sep).

Admission Fees

DM14 (adult), DM12 (child). Concessions available.

Schloss Sanssouci (Sanssouci Palace)

Sanssouci Palace was built for Prussian emperor Frederick II as his summer retreat, and its name, which literally means 'no worries' in French, reflects the fact that he intended this as an escape from the pressures of Berlin and married life. The elegant Baroque design of the palace contains 12 richly-decorated Rococo rooms, such as the *Marmorhalle* (Marble Hall), where Frederick entertained his guests. The real showpiece of Sanssouci, however, is the park. Visitors can wander through a series of beautifully landscaped gardens, including the *Sizilianischer Garten* (Sicilian Garden), which is filled with subtropical plants. A series of fountains and terraces leads to other structures within the park, such as the *Neue Orangerie* (New Orangery) and the *Bildergalerie* (Picture Gallery), which holds paintings by Renaissance artists, including Caravaggio, Rubens and Van Dyck.

Contact Address

Stiftung Preussische Schlösser und Gärten, Berlin-Brandenburg, Postfach 60 14 62, 14414 Potsdam, Germany
Tel: (0331) 969 4202. Fax: (0331) 969 4107.
Website: www.spsg.de

Transportation

Air: Berlin Tegel Airport or Berlin Schönefeld Airport. **Rail:** Train: S-Bahn to Potsdam-Hauptbahnhof Bahn (from Berlin-Zoo). **Road:** Bus: 695 (Schloss Sanssouci). Car: B1 over the Glienicke Bridge, then signs for Schloss Sanssouci.

Opening Times

Tues-Sun 0900-1600 (Nov-Mar); Tues-Sun 1300-1600 (1 Jan); Tues-Sun 0900-1700 (Apr-Oct). Closed 24, 25 and 31 Dec.

Admission Fees

DM16 (adult), DM10 (child).

Gibraltar

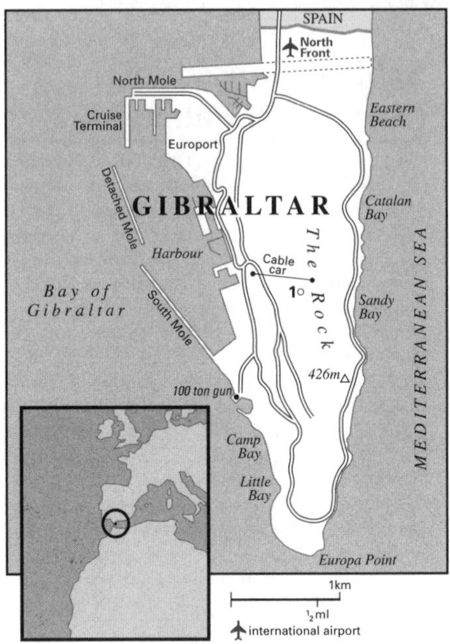

1	Upper Rock Nature Reserve

Tourist Information

Gibraltar Tourist Board
Duke of Kent House, Cathedral Square, Gibraltar
Tel: 74950. Fax: 74943.
E-mail: tourism@gibraltar.gi
Website: www.gibraltar.gi

Gibraltar Tourist Board
Arundel Great Court, 178/9 The Strand, London, WC2R 1EH, UK
Tel: (020) 7836 0777. Fax: (020) 7240 6612.
E-mail: giblondon@aol.com
Website: www.gibraltar.gov.gil

Upper Rock Nature Reserve

The *Upper Rock Nature Reserve* is a protected area of great natural beauty perched about 1380ft (421m) above sea level on the limestone peninsula of Gibraltar. Its most famous residents are the *Barbary Apes*, which have lived on the Rock for hundreds of years as Europe's only free-roaming monkeys. According to legend, when the apes leave, Gibraltar will cease to be British. The Reserve is also home to many species of bird, such as buzzards and Barbary partridges, and flora, including honeysuckle, jasmine and Gibraltar Sea Lavender. Visitors also come to see *St Michael's Cave*, one of a vast warren of caves containing stalagmites and stalactites, and the *Siege Tunnels*, which were used as a defence system by the British in the Great Siege (1779-1783) against the French and Spanish. The *Military Heritage Centre* displays weapons used by the British Army in Gibraltar and houses a *Memorial Chamber* of remembrance to those who served in the Armed Forces. Another popular site in the Reserve is the 14th-century *Moorish Castle*, which testifies to the diverse history of the peninsula.

Contact Address

For more information on the Upper Rock Nature Reserve, contact the Gibraltar Tourist Board (see **Tourist Information** above).

Transportation

Air: Gibraltar Airport. **Rail:** Cable Car: From Grand Parade. **Road:** Bus: 3. Car: Access from the border with Spain at La Linea.

Opening Times

Upper Rock Nature Reserve, including all attractions: Daily 0930-1900. *Cable car*: Daily 0930-1715 (up), daily 0930-1745 (down).

Admission Fees

Upper Rock Nature Reserve, including all attractions: £7 (adult), £4 (child 5-12), free (child under 4), £1.50 per vehicle. Concessions available. *Upper Rock Nature Reserve*, excluding attractions: £2. Concessions available. *Cable car* (return journey): £5.90 (adult), £3.95 (child).

Greece

1 Akrópoli (Acropolis)
2 Delfí (Delphi)
3 Epídavros (Epidaurus)
4 Ethnikó Archaiologikó Mouseio (National Archaeological Museum)
5 Knossos
6 Mycenae
7 Olimbía (Olympia)
8 Samaria (Samarian Gorge)

Tourist Information

Ellinikos Organismos Tourismou (Greek/Hellenic National Tourism Organisation)
Odos Amerikis 2b, 105 64 Athens, Greece
Tel: (01) 327 1300. Fax: (01) 322 4148.
E-mail: infoxenios@areianet.gr
Website: www.areianet.gr/infoxenios/GNTO

Greek/Hellenic National Tourism Organisation (GNTO)
4 Conduit Street, London W1S 2DJ, UK
Tel: (020) 7734 5997 *or* 7499 8161.
Fax: (020) 7287 1369.
E-mail: eot-greektouristoffice@btinternet.com
Website: www.antor.com/greece

Akrópoli (Acropolis)

The *Acropolis* is one of the most famous sites of the ancient world and a symbol of Greek civilization. Often referred to as the 'Sacred Rock' and rising over 60 metres (200ft) above Athens, the Acropolis reached its apogee during the golden age of Pericles (461-429 BC). It is the site of three different temples dedicated to Athena Parthenos, the patron goddess of Athens, the most famous of which is the internationally-renowned *Parthenon*. Completed in 438 BC, its broad flank of Doric columns is synonymous with ancient culture throughout the world. Built entirely of marble that glows at sunset, the Parthenon once housed a statue of Athena. Much of the monument was destroyed by a Venetian bomb in 1687, and during the 19th century, parts of the structure were stolen by Lord Elgin, the British Ambassador in Constantinople, who sold them to the British Museum in London, where they are still on display today. Visitors can also see the *Propylaea,* which is the main gateway into the Acropolis, designed by the architect Mnesikles and constructed in 437-432 BC, the *Temple of Athena Nike* (the Goddess of Victory), designed by Callicrates, the *Erechtheion Temple* which is named after Erechtheus who was a local hero and legendary king of Athens, and the *Acropolis Museum,* which houses many treasures from the Acropolis.

Contact Address

Acropolis Museum, 1st Ephorate of Prehistoric and Classical Antiquities, 2-4 Makrygianni Street, 11742 Athens, Greece
Tel: (01) 321 0219 (Acropolis) *or* 323 6665 (Acropolis Museum). Fax: (01) 321 4172.
E-mail: protocol@aepka.culture.gr
Website: www.culture.gr

Transportation

Air: Athens International Airport. **Rail:** Underground: Syntagma Station. **Road:** Bus: Plaka Station. Car: B8A towards Athens and signs for the Acropolis.

Opening Times

Acropolis and *Museum*: Daily 0830-1500 (winter); daily 0800-1830 (summer).

Admission Fees

Acropolis and *Museum*: Dr2000 (adult), free (child). Concessions available.

Delfí (Delphi)

According to Greek mythology, Delphi stands at the point where two doves, released to the east and west by the god Zeus, met, thus marking the centre of the world. Soaring high above the Gulf of Corinth, on Mount Parnassos, it has long been home to the sanctuary of Apollo and the seat of his oracle. Perhaps the best known of Delphi's ancient inhabitants, dating from the second millennium BC, his predictions affected matters as grand as those of warfare. Today, the ancient site lies in ruins, although visitors still come in their thousands to see the remains, as well as the Doric *Temple of Apollo* and the *Sacred Way*, all of which were excavated between 1892-1935. The *Delphi Museum*, which was built in 1903, exhibits various statues and treasures from ancient Greece.

Contact Address

Delphi Museum, 33054 Delphi, Greece
Tel: (0265) 82313. Fax: (0265) 82966.
Website: www.culture.gr

Transportation

Air: Athens International Airport. **Road:** Bus: Arahova Bus Stop. Car: Road to Galaxidi, then road to Arahova Acropolis (from Athens).

Opening Times

Delphi Museum and *site*: Mon-Fri 0900-1530, Sat and Sun 0830-1445 (winter); Mon-Fri 0700-2100, Sat and Sun 0830-1500 (summer).

Admission Fees

Delphi Museum or *site*: Dr1200 (adult), free (child). Concessions available. *Delphi Museum* and *site*: Dr2000 (adult), free (child).

Epídavros (Epidaurus)

The *Sanctuary of Asclepius* at *Epidaurus* was once an important healing centre, as well as a religious centre and spa. Built in the fourth century BC, the sanctuary was dedicated to the healer god, Asclepius, and boasts a well-preserved 1400-seat theatre, which was designed by Polycleitus, who built similar buildings at Olympia and Delphi. The theatre is the most famous of all the ancient theatres in Greece and comes alive every summer with theatrical performances. The site was not actually discovered until the 19th century, and little actually remains of it today. Apart from the theatre itself, there are also ruins of hospitals, guest houses, large bath houses, a gymnasium and a stadium, as well as several shrines. There is also a small excavation museum near Epidaurus, which was built between 1902 and 1909, and contains many remains from the sanctuary.

Contact Address

Epídavros, Lygourio 21052, Argolis, Peloponnesos, Greece
Tel: (0753) 22009.

The Tholos, Delphi

Ruth Blakeborough

Transportation

Air: Athens International Airport. **Road:** Bus: Buses leave from the Peloponnesian Bus Station in Athens and from Náfplion Bus Station. Car: Left after the Corinth Canal, then coast road to Theatro (from Athens or Corinth). Epidaurus is signposted (from Náfplion).

Opening Times

Daily 0800-1700 (1 Nov-31 Mar); Tues-Sun 0800-1500 (1 Jul-31 Oct).

Admission Fees

Dr1500 (adult), free (child). Concessions available.

Ethnikó Archaiologikó Mouseio (National Archaeological Museum of Athens)

The most important museum in Athens, the *National Archaeological Museum* houses one of the richest collections of Ancient Greek art in the world. Completed in 1899, the collection includes artefacts from all periods of Ancient Greek civilisation. It is particularly well known for objects found at the ancient city of *Mycenae*, including the *Mask of Agamemnon*, ornate vessels and gold dishes. The museum also has a large collection of Cycladic art on display, as well as the *Statue of Poseidon*, the *Helène Stathatos Collection* of gold jewellery which dates from the ancient and Byzantine worlds, and the *Numismatic Collection* of around 400,000 coins.

Contact Address

Ethnikó Archaiologikó Mouseio, Patission 44, Athens 10682, Greece
Tel: (01) 821 7717. Fax: (01) 821 3573.
E-mail: protocol@eam.culture.gr

Transportation

Air: Athens International Airport. **Rail:** Underground: Omonia. **Road:** Bus: Museum Bus Stop. Car: B8A towards Athens, then signs for the city centre.

Opening Times

Mon 1030-1700, Tues-Sun 0830-1500 (winter); Mon 1030-1900, Tues-Sun 0800-1900 (summer).

Admission Fees

Dr2000 (adult), free (child). Concessions available for students.

Knossos

Located on the island of Crete, *Knossos* is the site of the most important palace of the ancient Minoans, the earliest of the Aegean civilisations. It was home to King Minos and, as tradition has it, the Minotaur, a giant bull, who inhabited the perilous Labyrinth. The Minoan civilisation spread to mainland Greece to form the Mycenaean civilisation, a precursor to the Ancient Greeks. The site was first discovered by Minos Kalokairinos in 1878 and was excavated further by Arthur Evans between 1900 and 1931, who was also responsible for restoring the palace to its present day state. Today, Knossos offers the modern-day visitor an abundance of ancient sites, including the *Palace of Knossos*, the *Little Palace*, the *Royal Villa*, the *House of Frescoes* and the *Temple Tomb*.

Contact Address

Knossos Palace, Crete, Greece
Tel: (081) 231 940.

Transportation

Air: Heraklion Airport. **Road:** Bus: Services to Knossos (from Heraklion Airport). Car: E75 to Knossos (from Heraklion).

Opening Times

Daily 0800-1800 (winter); daily 0800-1900 (summer).

Admission Fees

Dr1500 (adult), free (child). Concessions available.

Mycenae

Mycenae was first inhabited during Neolithic times and is located between Corinth and Argos, on top of a hill halfway up the Euboea Mountain. It was a citadel palace that included extensive fortifications, shrines and private dwellings. The site continued to be inhabited until the end of the third century AD. Mycenae was first discovered in 1874 by the German archaeologist Heinrich Schliemann, who began excavation in search of gold and believed the site he had found to be the home of Agamemnon, the leader of the Greek assault on Troy. Highlights at Mycenae, which is one of the most popular attractions in Greece, include the *Citadel*, the *Treasury of Atreus*, the *Lion Gate* and the *Royal Cemetery*.

Contact Address

Mycenae 21200, Argolis, Peloponnesos, Greece
Tel: (0751) 76585.

Transportation

Air: Athens International Airport. **Road:** Bus: Buses

depart from the Peloponnesian Bus Station in Athens for Corinth, Árgos and Náfplion, where visitors can connect to buses for Mycenae. Car: South on the old Corinth–Árgos road, then after about 50km (31 miles), left to Mycenae (from Corinth). Towards Árgos, then Corinth–Árgos road; after about 16km (10 miles), right on the road to Mycenae (from Náfplion).

Opening Times

Daily 0800-1700 (winter); daily 0830-1500 (summer).

Admission Fees

Dr1500 (adult), free (child). Concessions available.

Olimbía (Olympia)

Dedicated to the father of the gods, Olympian Zeus, *Olympia* is the birthplace of the Olympic Games, which were first held here in 776 BC. Situated in a Peloponnesus Valley in Southern Greece, the site has been inhabited since prehistoric times and boasts many ancient buildings, including the *Heraeum*, which was dedicated to Hera (the wife of Zeus), the *Stadium* which dates from the early fifth century BC and was once the site of sporting events watched by 45,000 spectators, and the *Hippodrome* where ancient horse races were held. There was also a *Palaestra*, or wrestling school, and a *Gymnasium*, at the site, where competitors were obliged to train for at least a month. Today, visitors to Olympia come to see the *Temple of Zeus*, which once contained a gold and ivory statue of Zeus, and the nearby *Archaelogical Museum*, which contains many artefacts from Olympia, including a collection of terracottas, statues and bronzes.

Contact Address

Olimbía, 7th Ephorate of Prehistoric and Classical Antiquities, 27065, Ancient Olympia, Greece
Tel: (0624) 22517. Fax: (0624) 22529.
E-mail: protocol@zepka.culture.gr

Transportation

Air: Athens International Airport. **Rail:** Train: Train to Pirgos, then change for Olympia (from Athens). **Road:** Bus: Services to Olympia (from the Peloponnese Bus Station in Athens) or (from Pátras via Pirgos). Car: Coast road, which connects Athens with Corinth and Pátras, or the inland route via Tripolis (from Athens).

Opening Times

Olympia and *Museum*: Mon-Fri 0800-1700, Sat-Sun 0830-1500 (winter); daily 0830-1500 (summer).

Admission Fees

Olympia or *Museum*: Dr1200 (adult), free (child). Concessions available. *Olympia* and *Museum*: Dr200 (adult), free (child). Concessions available. Admission is free on Sundays (Nov-Mar) and on public holidays.

Samaria (Samarian Gorge)

Regarded as one of Europe's greatest natural wonders, the *Samarian Gorge* is a beautiful 18km- (11 mile) hike through the Samaria National Park in Crete's White Mountains. The gorge is believed to be the longest in Europe and is home to beautiful flora and fauna and dramatic rock formations. There are several churches and chapels, including the church dedicated to Saint Maria of Egypt, found in the village of Samaria and dating back to 1379, where the name Sa(int)maria comes from. According to legend, one of the Titans living on Crete slashed the land with his knife to create the gorge, which today is home to Cretian wild goats, known as Kri-Kri, and rare birds, such as griffon vultures and golden eagles. The gorge's narrowest point, *Portes* (Gates), is supposedly the most photographed place in Crete, with thousands of visitors passing through it every year to marvel at the rocky narrows. After a long day's hike, visitors can relax on beaches at the end of the gorge before taking a boat back along the coast to embark on their return journey to Chania.

Contact Address

Samaria, Forest Directorate of Chania, Chania GR 73100, Greece
Tel: (0821) 92287. Fax: (0821) 91295.

Transportation

Air: Chania International Airport. **Water:** Boat: Services to Soúyia or Hóra Sfakíon (from Ayía Roúmeli), then bus service back to Chania. **Road:** Coach: Many visitors book through tour operators who organise day trips to the gorge, including transportation from Chania by coach. Bus: Local buses to Omalos (from Chania Bus Station). Car: It is not advisable to travel by car to the entrance of the gorge, as visitors must return to their starting point to pick up their car.

Opening Times

Daily 0600-1500 (1 May-31 Oct).

Admission Fees

Dr1200 (adult), free (child). Concessions available.

Guatemala

1 Tikal

Tourist Information

Instituto Guatemalteco de Turismo (INGUAT) (Guatemala Tourist Commission)
7a Avenida 1-17, zona 4, Centro Cívico, Guatemala City, Guatemala
Tel: 331 1333. Fax: 331 4416.
E-mail: inguat@guate.net
Website: www.guatemala.travel.com.gt
Embassy of the Republic of Guatemala
13 Fawcett Street, London SW10 9HN, UK
Tel: (020) 7349 0346 (tourism section). Fax: (020) 7349 0331 (tourism section).
E-mail: inguat@guate.net
Website: www.guatemala.travel.com.gt

Tikal

Located 300km (190 miles) north of Guatemala City, the ancient site of *Tikal* was once home to an estimated 100,000 Maya. Unlike many other ancient Mayan sites, the wonders of Tikal are hidden deep within the rainforest. Every year, visitors come to gaze at its towering 44m- (144ft) high pyramid and ancient plazas to the accompaniment of jungle sounds from monkeys, tree frogs, parrots and whatever else happens to be lurking in the treetop canopy. The site has more than 3000 structures including temples and palaces and is located in *Tikal National Park*, which is listed as a UNESCO World Heritage Site and is home to many species of wildlife. There is also an on-site museum, which contains a collection of objects found during excavations at the site.

Contact Address

For more information on Tikal, contact Guatemala Tourist Commission (see **Tourist Information** above).

Transportation

Air: Guatemala City La Aurora International Airport. **Road:** Coach: Services to Tikal (from Guatemala City). Car: CA9 to junction Ruidosa, then the main CA11 road from Flores (from Guatemala City).

Opening Times

Site: Daily 0600-1800.

Admission Fees

Site: Q50 for foreigners.

Tikal

INGUAT

Hungary

1 Budavári Palota (Buda Castle Palace)
2 Halászbástya (Fisherman's Bastion)
3 Nagy Zsinagóga (Budapest Central Synagogue)

Tourist Information

Magyar Turizmus Rt (Hungarian National Tourist Office – HNTO)
Margit Körút 85, 1024 Budapest, Hungary
Tel: (01) 355 1133. Fax: (01) 375 3819.
E-mail: htbudapest@hungarytourism.hu
Website: www.hungarytourism.hu

Hungarian National Tourist Office (HNTO)
46 Eaton Place, London SW1X 8AL, UK
Tel: (020) 7823 1032 *or* 7823 1055 *or* (0891) 171 200 (recorded information; calls cost 60p per minute). Fax: (020) 7823 1459.
E-mail: htlondon@btinternet.com
Website: www.hungarytourism.hu

Budavári Palota (Buda Castle Palace)

Located in Budapest's picturesque Old Town, *Buda Castle Palace* was first inhabited by King Béla of Hungary during the 13th century. The king, who fled to the Adriatic Sea in 1241 following the Mongol invasion, returned to live in the palace, building a stronghold to protect the palace from further attack. Over a period of 700 years, the palace was home to many royal residents, including King Lajos the Great, King Matthias I and King Charles III. The palace was also damaged by numerous invasions and fires over the centuries, with the subsequent rebuilding resulting in a mixture of architectural styles, ranging from Gothic to Baroque. Today, the palace is home to a number of museums, including the *Ludwig Museum*, the *Hungarian National Gallery* and the *Budapest History Museum*. The Ludwig Museum is named after its patron Peter Ludwig, whose donations included works by Picasso, Warhol and Lichenstein, and contains mostly Eastern European paintings and sculpture. The Hungarian National Gallery contains an encyclopaedic collection of Hungarian art from the tenth century to the present day, whilst the Budapest History Museum houses Gothic sculptures from the former palace, as well as exhibitions explaining the history of the city.

Contact Address

I Budvári Palota, Dísz tér 17, Budapest, Hungary
Tel: (01) 375 7533. Fax: (01) 212 2534.

Transportation

Air: Budapest Ferihegy Airport. **Rail:** Tram: 18 to Dózsa tér. **Road:** Bus: 16. Car: M1 to Budapest (from Vienna or Graz). Road signs are then marked for the 'centrum' and the 'citadella'.

Opening Times

Ludwig Museum and *Hungarian National Gallery*: Tues-Sun 1000-1800, closed Mon. *Budapest History Museum*: Mon and Wed-Sun 1000-1800, closed Tues.

Admission Fees

Ludwig Museum: Ft400 (adult), Ft200 (child over 6), free (child under 6). *Hungarian National Gallery*: Ft500 (adult), Ft250 (child over 6), free (child under 6). *Budapest History Museum*: Ft500 (adult), Ft200 (child over 6), free (child under 6).

Halászbástya (Fisherman's Bastion)

The *Fisherman's Bastion* was built in 1905 and named after the guild of fishermen responsible for defending this stretch of wall from enemy attack during the Middle Ages. An almost Disney-like tower dominates this stone wall with seven turrets representing the Magyar tribes who once populated the country. Excellent views can be had from the top of the tower across the River Danube to *Margaret Island*, *Parliament*, *St Stephen's Basilica* and the *Chain Bridge*. Visitors can also see the *nearby Nagyboldogasszony Templom* (Church of Our Lady), which was built at the beginning of the 14th century and is more commonly called *Matthias Church* (1443-1490AD) after King Matthias who held both his wedding ceremonies here.

Contact Address

Tourism Office of Budapest, 1364 Budapest, PF 215, 1052 Budapest, Hungary
Tel: (01) 266 0479. Fax: (01) 266 7477.
E-mail: info@budapestinfo.hu
Website: www.hungarytourism.hu

Transportation

Air: Budapest Ferihegy Airport. **Rail:** Underground: Moszka tér. Tram: 18. **Road:** Bus: 16 or Castle bus. Car: No access.

Opening Times

Daily 24 hours.

Admission Fees

Fisherman's Bastion: Free. *Matthias Church*: Ft600.

Nagy Zsinagóga (Budapest Central Synagogue)

Budapest Central Synagogue is the largest synagogue in Europe and the second largest in the world after the *Emanuel Synagogue* in New York. Completed in 1859, it was built in a Moorish-Byzantine style by the Austrian architect Ludwig Förster. The building was partly destroyed by bombing campaigns during World War II, but has been the subject of much renovation to restore its two shining Moorish domes to their former brilliance. The *Jewish Museum* next door recounts the horrors of the Holocaust and displays exhibits dating as far back as the Middle Ages. The museum, which was built between 1931 and 1936, stands on the former home of Theodor Herzl, who was the founding father of Zionism and responsible for developing the idea of a modern Jewish state.

Contact Address

Nagy Zsinagóga, VII. Dohány utca 2, Budapest, Hungary
Tel: (01) 342 2353.

Transportation

Air: Budapest Ferighegy Airport. **Rail:** Train: Keleti Station (East). Underground: Astoria. Tram: Astoria. **Road:** Bus: 7 or 9. Car: M1, M5, M7 or main roads 5, 6, 7, 51 to M0 (circular road around Budapest) or M3 towards Budapest. Follow signs to Astoria (city centre).

Opening Times

Mon-Fri 1000-1500, Sun 1000-1300.

Admission Fees

Ft600 (adult), Ft200 (child). Also includes admission to the *Jewish Museum*.

Buda Castle Palace

Hungarian National Tourist Office

Iceland

1 Geysir (Geyser)
2 Gullfoss (Golden Waterfall)
3 Perlan (The Pearl)

Tourist Information

Islenska Tourist Board (Icelandic Tourist Board)
Laekjargata 3, 101 Reykjavik, Iceland
Tel: 535 5500. Fax: 535 5001.
E-mail: info@icetourist.is
Website: www.icetourist.is *or* www.geysircenter.is *or* www.south.is/geysir.html

Icelandic Tourist Information Office/ Icelandair
3rd Floor, 172 Tottenham Court Road, London W1P 0LY, UK
Tel: (020) 7874 1019. Fax: (020) 7387 5711.
E-mail: london@icelandair.is
Website: www.icelandair.co.uk

Geysir (Geyser)

Until 1916, *Geysir*, located 125km (78 miles) northeast of Reykjavik, was one of the world's great geysers, spouting boiling water and steam 60-80m (165-220ft) into the air at three-hourly intervals. Mysteriously, though, it fell dormant (some say due to hundreds of tourists filling its chamber with objects) and has come to life only once since then, in 1935. The smaller *Strokkur* geyser nearby makes up for its big brother's silence by erupting every five to ten minutes. The entire area is a geothermal park, with belching mud pits, hissing steam vents, hot and cold springs, warm streams and even primitive plants.

Contact Address

For more information on Geysir, contact the Iceland Tourist Board (see **Tourist Information** above).

Transportation

Air: Reykjavik Keflavik Airport. **Road:** Bus: 2 (Geysir). Car: Ring road 1, then left near Selfoss to Road 35.

Opening Times

Daily 24 hours.

Admission Fees

Free.

Gullfoss (Golden Waterfall)

Located just a few kilometres from Geysir, *Gullfoss* (Golden Waterfall) is the most dramatic section of the Hvita River (White River) in southern Iceland. In the midst of lush vegetation, white water thunders down a 32-metre (105-feet) drop into a narrow canyon 70m (192ft) deep and 2.5km (1.5 miles) long. On a sunny day, visitors can see a rainbow through the drizzle, and in winter, the scene is even more spectacular as Gullfoss is covered in ice and snow. The site was bought by the Icelandic government to prevent foreign investors from turning it into a commercial site, and the footpath is opened each morning by a local farmer to allow visitors to see the waterfall from a viewing platform.

Contact Address

For more information on Gullfoss, contact the Icelandic Tourist Board (see **Tourist Information** above).

Transportation

Air: Reykjavik Keflavik Airport. **Road:** Bus: Austurleid run services 2 or 2A to Gullfoss. Car: Hwy-1, then Road 35 (from Reykjavik).

Opening Times

Daily 0800-1800.

Admission Fees

Free.

Perlan (The Pearl)

Perlan (The Pearl) is as much an architectural masterpiece as it is a feat of engineering. Designed by architect Ingimundur Sveinsson, this awesome ten-storey building, opened to the public in 1991, is geothermally heated by water forced through steel supports, and provides a means of water storage and power for the greater Reykjavik region. There are a total of six storage tanks, each with a capacity for holding four million litres (879,875 gallons) of water heated to 85ºC (185ºF). Excellent views of Reykjavik can be had from the *Viewing Deck* on level four. There is a revolving restaurant in the glass dome at the top of the building, where diners can enjoy Icelandic specialities, such as reindeer carpaccio and herring tartar, or more conventional dishes such as fresh fish and grilled meats. Cocktails are the speciality in the Perlan bar, and art exhibitions and concerts are held regularly.

Contact Address

Perlan, Post 5252, 125 Reykjavik, Iceland
Tel: 562 0200. Fax: 562 0207.
E-mail: perlan@perlan.is
Website: www.perlan.is

Transportation

Air: Reykjavik Keflavik Airport. **Road:** Bus: 7 (Perlan). Car: Bustrdrvegur Road towards Perlan (from Reykjavik).

Opening Times

Daily 1000-2200.

Admission Fees

Free.

Gullfoss

South Iceland Tourist Information Centre

India

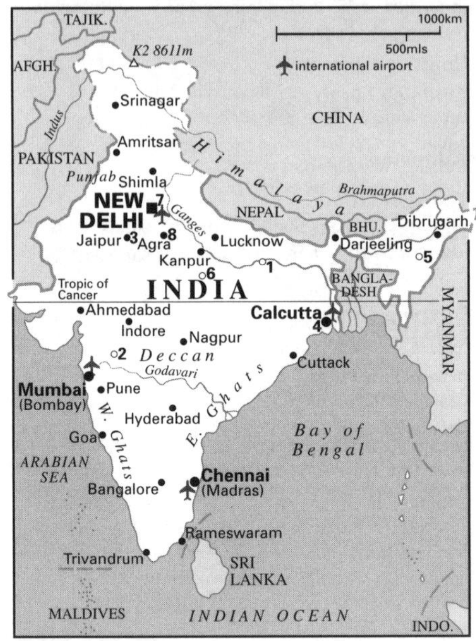

1 Banaras Ghats (Ghats at Varanasi)
2 Ellora Temple Caves
3 Hawa Mahal (Palace of the Winds)
4 Indian Museum, Calcutta
5 Kaziranga National Park
6 Khajuraho
7 Lal Quila (Red Fort)
8 Taj Mahal (Crown Palace)

Tourist Information

Government of India Tourist Office (GITO)
88 Janpath, New Delhi 110 001, India
Tel: (011) 332 0342. Fax: (011) 332 0109.
Government of India Tourist Office (GITO)
7 Cork Street, London W1X 2LN, UK
Tel: (020) 7437 3677. Fax: (020) 7494 1048.
E-mail: info@indiatouristoffice.com
Website: www.indiatouristoffice.org

Banaras Ghats (Ghats at Varanasi)

Varanasi, which was created by Lord Shiva, is one of the oldest and holiest cities in India and home to the most famous *ghats* (steps leading down to the river) in the country. Worshippers flock to the *ghats* every day to bathe in the holy River Ganges and then worship at the many temples lining the riverbank. Huge crowds of pilgrims gather to take part in this ancient ritual which involves making offerings (puja) to the rising sun; they are watched every morning by large numbers of tourists who come to take photographs of this unusual spectacle. There are more than 100 ghats in Varanasi, originally known as *Kashi* or the City of Light, the most famous of which are *Dasaswamedh Ghat* (ghat of ten sacrificed horses), *Asi Ghat, Man Mandir Ghat,* built by the Maharaja of Jaipur, *Manikarnika Ghat* and *Lalita Ghat.*

Contact Address

Government of India Tourist Office, 15B The Mall, Cantt, Varanasi 221002, Uttar Pradesh, India
Tel: (0542) 343744.
E-mail: varanasi@tourismindia.com *or*
goitovns@satyam.net.in
Website: www.tourismindia.com

Transportation

Air: Indira Gandhi International Airport or Babatpur Airport. **Rail:** Train: Varanasi Station. **Road:** Bus: Main bus stop in Varanasi City Centre. Car: NH2 to Delhi, then NH7 to Kanya and NH29 to Gorakhpur (from Calcutta).

Opening Times

Daily dawn–dusk.

Admission Fees

Free.

Ellora Temple Caves

The *Ellora Temple Caves* consist of 34 separate religious shrines carved into the actual rock of a basaltic hill and containing a wealth of sculptural and architectural treasures. Carved between AD 200 and 1000, the caves represent three separate faiths: Buddhism, Jainism and Hinduism. The 16 *Buddhist Caves* are the oldest in the group and consist of graceful angles, intricate detail and a 4.6m-high (15ft) statue of a preaching buddha. The *Jain Caves* illustrate the non-violent, ascetic beliefs of this religion, depicting scenes of pastoral beauty and images such as lotus flowers. In terms of stylistic ambition, the *Hindu Caves* outdo their neighbours – one cave alone, the *Temple of Kailasa* covers twice the area of the *Parthenon* in Athens and took 100 years to complete. Dedicated to Lord Shiva, this temple is the largest monolith in the world and is undoubtedly the most visited site at Ellora.

Contact Address

Government of India Tourist Office, Krishna Villas, Station Road, Aurangabad, 431005, Maharastra, India
Tel: (02) 408 1217. Fax: (02) 338 577.
E-mail: gitoaur@vsnl.com
Website: www.tourismindia.com

Transportation

Air: Mumbai Chhaprati Shivaji International Airport, then Aurangabad Airport. **Rail:** Train: Aurangabad Station. **Road:** Bus: MRSTC Services to Ellora Temple Caves (from Aurangabad). Car: NH50 towards Nashik and major roads to Ellora (from Pune).

Opening Times

Tues-Sun 0900-1700.

Admission Fees

Rs450 (adult), Rs225 (child 5-12), free (child under 5).

Hawa Mahal (Palace of the Winds)

Built in 1799, *Hawa Mahal* is the most stunning sight in the city of Jaipur. The palace, part of a huge complex, overlooks one of Jaipur's main streets and was originally constructed to offer women of the court a vantage point, behind stone-carved screens, from which to watch the activities taking place in the bazaar and the surrounding streets. For this purpose, it was designed with over 900 niches, and the entire building is shaped like a crown adorning Lord Krishna's head. The site offers superb views of the city, including the many old palaces and houses which were painted ochre-pink, the colour of hospitality, by the Rajputs, for the 1853 visit of Prince Albert.

Contact Address

Rajasthan Tourism, Department of Tourism, Arts and Culture, Government of Rajasthan, Government Hostel Campus, M I Road, Jaipur, India
Tel: (0141) 376 362. Fax: (0141) 376 362.
E-mail: mail@rajasthan-tourism.com
Website: www.rajasthan-tourism.com

Transportation

Air: Indira Gandhi International Airport or Jaipur Airport (domestic flights). **Rail:** Train: Jaipur Station. **Road:** Bus: Services to central bus stand at Sindi Camp (from Delhi, Bhopal or Agra). Car: NH8 (from Delhi); NH11 (from Agra); or NH12 (from Bhopal).

Opening Times

Daily 0900-1630.

Admission Fees

Rs5. Photography permit: Rs30. Videocamera permit: Rs70.

Indian Museum, Calcutta

Originally established in 1814, and moved to its present site in 1878, Calcutta's *Indian Museum* is the largest and best museum in the country. Founded by Dr Nathaniel Wallich and housed in a magnificent Italian-style building, designed by W L Granvil, the museum has over 60 galleries and is divided into six different sections: archaeology, art, anthropology, geology, zoology and industry. The art section contains a picture gallery, with Persian- and Indian-style drawings and paintings, and also contains other artefacts and textiles, including silk-woven Tibetan temple banners. Other sections of the museum contain diverse treasures, such as an Egyptian mummy, the skeleton of a whale, rare statues and a collection of meteorites.

Contact Address

Indian Museum, 27 Jawaharlal Nehru Road, Calcutta 700016, India
Tel: (033) 249 9902 *or* 249 9979 *or* 249 8948.
Fax: (033) 249 5699 *or* 249 5696.
E-mail: imbot@cal2.vsnl.net.in *or* director@indianmuseum-calcutta.org
Website: www.indianmuseum-calcutta.org

Transportation

Air: Calcutta International Airport. **Rail:** Train: Howrah Station or Sealdah Station. Underground: Park Street Station. **Road:** Bus: Jawaharlal Nehru Road. Car: NH2 (from Delhi); NH28A, NH28, NH31 and NH34 (from Kathmandu) or NH5 and NH6 (from Bhubaneswar).

Opening Times

Tues-Sun 1000-1630 (Dec-Feb); Tues-Sun 1000-1700 (Mar-Nov).

Admission Fees

Rs150 (Non-resident visitor), Rs10 (Resident visitor).

Kaziranga National Park

Kaziranga National Park was set aside as a game sanctuary in 1926 and became a national park in 1974. It is made up of 688 sq km (266 sq miles) of breathtaking land, containing rainforests, mighty rivers, sprawling grasslands and herds of wild elephant. It is best known for its thriving population of one-horned Indian rhino, which is the largest in the world. The rhino's natural enemy, the tiger, is also found in abundance, along with many other typical species of Indian wildlife, including king cobras, monitor lizards, leopards, swamp deer, hoolock gibbon and a variety of bird life. Visitors can either view the park using a traditional mode of transport – the elephant; or the more prosaic method – by jeep or car. The park has been included on the UNESCO World Heritage List since 1985.

Contact Address

Kaziranga National Park, PO Bokakhat, District Jorhat, Assam 785612, India
Tel: (03776) 68007.
Website: www.indiatouristoffice.org/East/kaziranga.htm

Transportation

Air: Indira Gandhi International Airport, Calcutta International Airport, Gawahati Airport or Jorhat Airport. **Rail:** Train: Furkating Station. **Road:** Bus: Services to Kohara (from Guwahiti, Jorhat and Furkating). Car: NH37.

Opening Times

On Elephant Back: Daily 0500-0600, 0630-0730 and 1530-1630 (mid-Oct-mid-Apr). *By Road*: Daily 0800-1100 and 1400-1630 (mid-Oct-mid-Apr).

Admission Fees

On Elephant Back: Rs75 (adult), Rs50 (child). *Vehicle Charges*: Rs75 (jeep or car), plus Rs10 (per person); Rs100 (minibus), plus Rs10 (per person); Rs125 (bus), plus RS10 (per person).

Khajuraho

The famous erotic temples of *Khajuraho* form one of the most popular tourist attractions in India. Built between AD 950 and 1050 by the kings of the Chandela, the site originally possessed 85 temples, of which 20 are still reasonably preserved. Lost for centuries after the decline of the Chandela, the small village of Khajuraho was rediscovered in 1838 by a British army captain. The temples, of Brahman and Jain origin, are best known for the erotic friezes on their walls. Celebrating life and love, these friezes in fact only make up a fraction of the total ornamental carvings, which depict gods, goddesses and celestial maidens. The name Khajuraho is derived from Khajur, the local word for the date trees which grow in abundance in the region. A *son et lumière* show every evening tells the story of the Chandela Kings and the history of the temples.

Contact Address

Regional Office, Madhya Pradesh State Tourism Development Corporation Ltd, Chandela Cultural Centre, Khajuraho, India
Tel: (0768) 644 051. Fax: (0768) 642 330.
Website:
www.indiatouristoffice.co.uk/West/khajuraho.htm *or* www.mptourism.com/dest/khajuraho.html

Transportation

Air: Indira Gandhi International Airport or Khajuraho Airport (domestic flights). **Rail:** Train: Mahoba or Jhansi stations. **Road:** Coach: Services from Satna, Harpalpur, Jhansi and Mahoba.

Opening Times

Daily dawn–dusk.

Admission Fees

Entrance: Rs450. *Son et lumière show*: Rs200 (adult), Rs100 (child). Free entrance Fri.

Lal Quila (Red Fort)

Completed in 1648, the *Red Fort* is the largest of Old Delhi's monuments. Its red sandstone walls dominate Old Delhi's Muslim district, rising above a wide dry moat to a height of up to 33m (108ft), and are lined with turrets and bastions. Today, rather than repel enemy invaders, they keep out the noise of the surrounding city, and the serene gardens and pavilions within the fort hark back to the power and majesty of the Mughal emperors. The main entrance of the Red Fort opens onto a bazaar that was at one time home to the city's most skilled goldsmiths, carpet makers and jewellers. Further within lies the *Hall of Public Audiences*, where the emperor would listen to the complaints of the common people, and the *Royal Baths*, three large domed rooms with a fountain in the centre.

Contact Address

Government of India Tourist Office (GITO), 88 Janpath, New Delhi 110 001, India
Tel: (011) 332 0005 *or* 332 0342. Fax: (011) 332 0109.
E-mail: newdelhi@tourisminindia.com
Website: www.tourisminindia.com

Transportation

Air: Indira Gandhi International Airport. **Rail:** Train: Main Delhi Station (Old Delhi). **Road:** Bus: Services to Lal Quila entrance. Car: Grand Trunk Road NH1 (from Amritsar and north); Mathura Road (from Agra and south); NH2 (from Calcutta and east); Gurgaon Road (from Jaipur and west).

Opening Times

Daily dawn-dusk.

Admission Fees

Rs150 (adult), free (child under 10).

Taj Mahal (Crown Palace)

The *Taj Mahal* has been described as the most extravagant monument ever built for love. It is also India's most emblematic and famous tourist attraction. Renowned for its tree-lined reflective pond leading up to the fabulous domed roof, few know that the Taj Mahal is, in fact, a mausoleum not a mosque. Completed in 1653, it was built by the Emperor Shah Jahan in memory of his second wife, Mumtaz Mahal, who died in childbirth. Revered for its grace and detailed beauty, the Taj Mahal is considered to be the zenith of Indo-Persian architecture and the elaborate marble designs are inlaid with semi-precious stones such as jade, crystal, turquoise and coral. Many people choose to spend at least several hours here as the changing light and shadows affect the colour and patterns of the Taj Mahal, and it is also possible to picnic in the tranquil gardens.

Contact Address

Government of India Tourist Office, 191 The Mall, Agra 282001, India
Tel: (0562) 363 959. Fax: (0562) 363 377.
E-mail: agra@tourisminindia.com
Web site: www.tourisminindia.com

Transportation

Air: Indira Gandhi International Airport or Agra Airport (domestic flights). **Rail:** Train: Agra Cantt Station. **Road:** Bus: Services to Indian Tourist Office bus stop. Car: NH24, then NH2 (from Delhi); NH11 (from Jaipur) or NH25, then NH2 (from Lucknow).

Opening Times

Tues-Sun 0600-1900.

Admission Fees

Rs970 (adult), free (child under 14).

Khajuraho

Government of India Tourist Office

Indonesia

1 Loro Jongrang (Prambanan Temple Compounds)

Tourist Information

Directorat Jenderal Parewisata (Directorate General of Tourism)
PO Box 1409, Jalan Medan, Merdeka Barat, Jakarta 10110, Indonesia
Tel: (021) 383 823 *or* 383 8211.
Fax: (021) 386 7589.
Website: www.tourismindonesia.com

Embassy of the Republic of Indonesia and Indonesia Tourist Promotion Office (ITPO)
38 Grosvenor Square, London W1X 9AD, UK
Tel: (020) 7499 7661. Fax: (020) 7491 4993.
E-mail: kbri@indolondon.freeserve.co.uk

Loro Jongrang (Prambanan Temple Compounds)

The *Prambanan Temples* form the largest temple complex on the Indonesian island of Java. Constructed around AD 900, the compound was deserted soon after it was completed, possibly due to the eruption of nearby Mount Merapi. The temples were restored, however, in 1953 and now form one of the world's great Hindu shrines. There are 224 temples in total, but the site is dominated by the imposing figures of the three main temples: the *Brahma Temple*, the *Vishnu Temple* and the *Shiva Temple*. Each temple is dedicated to one of the principal Hindu gods (Brahma, Vishnu and Shiva) and decorated with reliefs depicting the *Ramayana*, a famous Hindu epic. The Shiva Temple is the largest at 47m (154ft) high and dates back to the eighth-century Sanjaya Dynasty. From May to October, the *Ramayana Ballet*, a traditional Indonesian dance based on the same Hindu epic, is performed at Prambanan on nights when there is a full moon.

Contact Address

Yogyakarta Tourist Information Centre, Maioboro 16, Yogyakarta, Indonesia
Tel: (027) 458 6809. Fax: (027) 456 4402.
Website: www.vocal.net/twc/prambanan.html

Transportation

Air: Adi Sucipto Airport or Jakarta Soekarno-Hatta Airport. **Road:** Coach: Services from Yogyakarta. Car: Signposted Central Java, Yogyakarta, then Prambanan (from Jakarta).

Opening Times

Daily 0800-1630.

Admission Fees

Rp45,000.

Iran

1 Naghsh-é Jahan (Imam Square)
2 Takht-é Jamshid (Persepolis)

Need more information on Iran?
Consult the *World Travel Guide*

Tourist Information

Iran Touring and Tourism Organisation (ITTO)
Hajj and Pilgrimage Building, Roudaki Avenue, Azadi Street, Tehran, Iran
Tel: (021) 643 2098 *or* 643 2099.
Fax: (021) 694 2039.
E-mail: moezi@sr.co.ir
Website: www.irantourism.org

Embassy of the Islamic Republic of Iran
16 Prince's Gate, London SW7 1PT, UK
Tel: (020) 7225 3000. Fax: (020) 7589 4440.
E-mail: info@iran-embassy.org.uk
Website: www.iran-embassy.org.uk

Naghsh-é Jahan (Imam Square)

With its tiled mosques and exotic palaces, the city of Isfahan is considered by many to be the jewel in the Iranian crown. The central square, *Naghsh-é Jahan*, cannot fail to impress – seven times the size of *St Mark's Square* in Venice, and framed by a series of elegant archways, it contains several of the city's most important monuments. *Masjid-é Imam*, the Imam Mosque, is a near-perfect example of Islamic architecture and was built by Shah Abbas the Great during the city's Golden Age in the early 17th century. The women's mosque, the *Sheikh Lotfollah*, is decorated with exquisite Persian tilework and is the highlight of the square for many visitors. In the 17th and 18th centuries, the Safavid rulers used to watch polo tournaments from the balcony of the *Ali Qapu Palace*, which stands opposite. The central area consists of a formal park and a lake with a central fountain, and the covered bazaar, which leads out of the square to the enormous *Masjid-é Jamé* (Friday Mosque), provides ample opportunity for admiring brasswork in the workshops, or haggling over beautifully-woven carpets.

Contact Address

Isfahan Tourist Office, Naghsh-é Jahan, Isfahan, Iran
Tel: (031) 228 491.

Transportation

Air: Tehran Mehrabad International Airport or Isfahan Airport (domestic flights). **Road:** Coach: Services from Tehran.

Opening Times

Masjid-é Imam: Mon-Thurs, Sat and Sun 0900-2100 (opening times vary, visitors are advised to avoid prayer times). *Sheikh Lotfollah*: Mon-Thurs, Sat and Sun 0900-2100 (opening times vary, visitors are advised to avoid prayer times). *Ali Qapu Palace*: Daily 0900-1800. *Masjid-é Jamé*: Daily 0900-2100 (opening times vary, visitors are advised to avoid prayer times).

Admission Fees

Masjid-é Imam: IR20,000. *Sheikh Lotfollah*: IR20,000. *Ali Qapu Palace*: IR20,000. *Masjid-é Jamé*: Free.

Takht-é Jamshid (Persepolis)

Persepolis is thought to have been founded by Darius I in 518 BC as the capital city of the vast and powerful Achaemenid Empire. The name Persepolis translates from Greek as 'Persian City', and it was built over a period of 120 years, complete with running water and its own sewer system. Despite its having been set on fire and looted by Alexander the Great in 330 BC, it is still possible to gain an impression of the former glory of the city. The palace complex is astounding in its size and splendour – constructed on a large terrace 10m (27ft) high, access is up a staircase wide enough to accommodate five horses abreast, and the huge pillars of the *Audience Hall* dwarf the visitors who come to see the impressive ruins. Ornate bas relief carvings of warriors, kings and religious figures have survived remarkably intact; it is also possible to see the decorated tombs of the Achaemenid kings which are hewn out of the mountainside and modelled on those of the Egyptian pharaohs.

Contact Address

For more information on Persepolis, contact Iran Touring and Tourism Organisation (see **Tourist Information** above).

Transportation

Air: Tehran Mehrabad International Airport or Shiraz Airport (domestic flights). **Road:** Taxi: Services from Shiraz.

Opening Times

Daily 0900-1730.

Admission Fees

IR50,000.

P ♿ UNESCO

Animal Capital, Persepolis

Ali Rahimpoor

Ireland

1	Blarney Castle
2	Bunratty Castle and Folk Park
3	Cliffs of Moher
4	Dublin Zoo
5	Glendalough
6	Guinness Storehouse
7	Killarney National Park
8	National Gallery of Ireland
9	Trinity College Dublin
10	Waterford Crystal Visitor Centre

Tourist Information

Bord Fáilte Eireann (Irish Tourist Board)
Baggot Street Bridge, Dublin 2, Ireland
Tel: (01) 602 4000. Fax: (01) 602 4100.
E-mail: fdowney@irishtouristboard.ie
Website: www.ireland.travel.ie

Irish Tourist Board
150 New Bond Street, London W1S 2AQ, UK
Tel: (020) 7518 0800. Fax: (020) 7493 9065.
E-mail: info@irishtouristboard.co.uk
Website: www.irishtravel.co.uk

Blarney Castle

Set in idyllic Irish countryside, *Blarney Castle* is home to the famous *Blarney Stone*. Situated high in the battlements of the castle, the stone is thought to be half of the Stone of Scone, an ancient Scottish stone believed to have special powers. Kissing the stone can only be achieved by leaning back over a rather intimidating drop whilst holding onto an iron railing. Those who make the effort, however, are said to inherit the gift of eloquent speech; in fact, the word 'Blarney' was introduced into the English language by Elizabeth I of England and means 'pleasant talk, intending to deceive without offending'. The castle itself began life as a tenth-century hunting lodge and was rebuilt in stone in 1210, only to be demolished and reconstructed in its original form by Dermot McCarthy, King of Munster, in 1446. Today, much of it lies in ruins.

Contact Address

Blarney Castle, Blarney, County Cork, Ireland
Tel: (021) 438 5252. Fax: (021) 438 1518.
E-mail: info@blarneyc.ie
Website: www.blarneycastle.ie

Transportation

Air: Cork Airport. **Rail:** Train: Cork Station. **Road:** Bus: Regular bus services to Blarney (from Cork Station). Car: N20 (from Cork).

Opening Times

Mon-Sat 0900-1800, Sun 0930-sunset (Oct-Apr); Mon-Sat 0900-1830, Sun 0930-1730 (May); Mon-Sat 0900-1900, Sun 0930-1730 (Jun-Aug); Mon-Sat 0900-1830, Sun 0930-1730 (Sep).

Admission Fees

Ir£3.50 (adult), Ir£1 (child 4-18), free (child under 8). Concessions and family pass available.

Bunratty Castle and Folk Park

Built in 1425 by the McNamara family on the site of an earlier Viking settlement, and later acquired by the Anglo-Irish Studdart family who lived there until the 19th century, *Bunratty Castle* is one of the finest existing examples of an Irish tower house. Tower houses were based on Norman 'motte and bailey' stone castles and Bunratty has a rectangular tower with three floors and four turrets. Inside is a

Irish Tourist Board

Bunratty Castle

beautifully preserved collection of Medieval furniture, a reminder of Ireland's Celtic heritage. A Medieval banquet is served every night on demand to enable guests to experience what it was like to be entertained in the castle's heyday. The adjacent *Folk Park* recreates daily life as it was in rural Ireland a century ago – farmhouses, shops and cottages have all been reconstructed in detail to provide visitors with an authentic experience. The park staff even bake bread, churn milk and demonstrate crafts such as weaving and forging. A particular highlight for younger children is a trip to the adjoining farm.

Contact Address

Central Reservations, Bunratty Castle and Folk Park, Bunratty, County Clare, Ireland
Tel: (061) 360 788. Fax: (061) 361 020.
E-mail: reservations@shannon-dev.ie
Website: www.shannonheritagetrade.com

Transportation

Air: Shannon Airport. **Rail:** Train: Limerick Station. **Road:** Bus: Services from Limerick or Ennis. Car: N18 (from Limerick, Ennis or Galway City).

Opening Times

Daily 0930-1730 (Sep-May); daily 0900-1830 (Jun-Aug).

Admission Fees

Ir£6.50 (adult), Ir£2.60 (child). Reduced admission fees apply outside peak season.

Cliffs of Moher

The majestic *Cliffs of Moher* are one of Ireland's most spectacular and most visited tourist attractions. The cliffs rise out of the Atlantic Ocean, reaching a maximum height of 230m (755ft), and border the region called the *Burren*, home to interesting rock formations, rare plants and wildlife. The Burren is named after the Irish, Bhoireann, which means stony place, and is considered by experts to be the largest karstic limestone area in Western Europe, where limestone rock has been heavily eroded to form underground streams. The area is also home to many historical tombs and monuments, including the famous *Poulnabrone* megalithic dolmen, which literally means 'The Hole of the Sorrows'. Poulnabrone was excavated in 1968 and found to contain the remains of around 20 adults and six children. There are over 70 megalithic tombs in the area, along with ringforts, holy wells, cairns and stone forts, indicating that man inhabited the area during the Stone Age. The cliffs themselves are best seen from *O'Briens Tower*, which provides superb views across the rolling, blue Atlantic to the Aran Islands in Galway Bay and the hills of Connemara.

Contact Address

Shannon Heritage Visitor Centre, Liscannor, County Clare, Ireland
Tel: (065) 708 1171 *or* 708 1565.

Transportation

Air: Shannon Airport. **Rail:** Train: Ennis Station or Galway Station. **Road:** Car: N-18, N-85 and N-67 (from Ennis).

Opening Times

O'Brien's Tower: Daily 0930-1900 (winter); daily 0900-2000 (summer). *Visitor Centre*: Daily 0930-1530 (winter); daily 0900-2000 (summer).

Admission Fees

O'Brien's Tower: Ir£1 (adult), Ir£0.60 (child).

Dublin Zoo

First opened in 1831 with animals supplied by London Zoo, *Dublin Zoo* is one of the city's most popular attractions. It covers a 173-hectare (70-acre) site at *Phoenix Park* in the west of Dublin and houses a wide variety of animals, including red panda, South American birds, Arctic fox, otter, elephants, and even a pack of grey wolves. A recent addition to the exhibits is *African Plains* where visitors can see larger species of animal such as giraffe and zebra. Other activities include the city farm, which has a special children's corner and a flock of Galway sheep, and the Californian sea lion pool where audiences watch the animals train at regular intervals throughout the day.

Contact Address

Dublin Zoo, Phoenix Park, Dublin 8, Ireland
Tel: (01) 677 1425. Fax: (01) 677 1660.
E-mail: info@dublinzoo.ie
Website: www.dublinzoo.ie

Transportation

Air: Dublin Airport. **Water:** Ferry: Services from Holyhead (Wales) and Stranraer (Scotland) to Dun Laoghaire Port and Dublin Port. **Rail:** Train: Heuston Station. **Road:** Bus: 10 (from top of O'Connell Street). Car: N1 (from Dublin Airport); M11, then N11 (from Wicklow); N7 (from Kildare); N11 (from Dun Laoghaire port), then signs to Dublin city centre and to Dublin Zoo.

Opening Times

Mon-Fri 0930-1600, Sat 0930-1700, Sun 1030-1700 (Oct-Mar); Mon-Sat 0930-1800, Sun 1030-1800 (Apr-Sep).

Admission Fees

Ir£7.20 (adult), Ir£4.50 (child 3-16), free (child under 3). Concessions and family pass available.

Glendalough

Known in Irish as 'glenn of the two lakes', *Glendalough* is a glacially sculpted green valley of characteristic Irish beauty. During Ireland's 'Golden Age' (AD 500-900), the country, which was known as the 'Island of Saints and Scholars', flourished as the poetry, music and writing of its missionaries and teachers influenced scholars across Europe. During this time, Glendalough was home to a monastic settlement established by St Kevin, a reclusive monk, who for seven years enjoyed a simple and solitary existence, with animals and birds as his only companions. St Kevin came to the area during the sixth century and founded his monastery in AD 498, remaining there until his death at the grand old age of 120. During his lifetime, thousands of people flocked to Glendalough, which became an important centre for piety and learning for both Irish and European disciples. Today, visitors can find well-preserved ruins 24km (15 miles) west of Wicklow, including the famous *Round Tower*, many stone crosses and several cathedrals and churches.

Contact Address

Glendalough Visitors Centre, Glendalough, Ireland
Tel: (0404) 45352. Fax: (0404) 45626.

Transportation

Air: Dublin Airport. **Rail:** Train: Rathdrum Station. **Road:** Coach: St Kevin's bus to Glendalough (from St Stevens Green in Dublin). Car: N11 (exit Kilmacanogue), then R755 and R756 to Glendalough (from Dublin).

Opening Times

Daily 0930-1800 (mid-Mar-May and Sep-mid-Oct); daily 0900-1830 (Jun-Aug); daily 0930-1700 (mid-Oct-mid-Mar).

Admission Fees

Ir£2 (adult), Ir£1 (child). Concessions available.

Guinness Storehouse

The *Guinness Storehouse* is a whole museum dedicated to Ireland's most famous export, Guinness stout. Arthur Guinness first began brewing the 'black gold' on the site in 1759. Today, through a series of interactive displays, visitors can find out all about the brewing process, from the combining of ingredients and the fermentation stage, through to international distribution and the successful advertising campaigns. Entry to The Guinness Storehouse is through a pint glass-shaped atrium capable of holding 10,000 pints of stout, and there is a free pint of the magic brew for every visitor at the end of the tour.

Contact Address

Guinness Storehouse, St James Gate, Dublin 8, Ireland
Tel: (01) 453 8364.
E-mail: guinness-storehouse@guinness.com
Website: www.guinness.com

Transportation

Air: Dublin Airport. **Water:** Ferry: Services from Holyhead (Wales) and Stranraer (Scotland) to Dun Laoghaire Port and Dublin Port. **Rail:** Train: Connolly Station or Heuston Station. **Road:** Coach: Busaras (central bus station). Bus: 747 (from the airport to O'Connell Street); 78A (from Aston Quay); 123 (from Aston Quay or Dame Street). Car: M1, then M50, then signs for City Centre/Galway at junction with N4 (from Dublin Airport); N11, then M50, then signs for City Centre/Galway at junction with N4 (from Dun Laoghaire Port).

Opening Times

Daily 0930-1700 (1 Oct-31 Mar); daily 0930-1800 (1 Apr-30 Sep). Closed 25-26 Dec and Good Friday.

Admission Fees

Ir£9 (adult), Ir£4 (child). Concessions and family pass available.

Killarney National Park

Killarney National Park covers over 10,000 hectares (25,000 acres) of woodland, lakes, mountains, parks and gardens in the far southwest of Ireland. It was Ireland's first national park and was founded in 1932 when the Muckross estate was given to the Irish people by Senator Arthur Vincent. The remote geography of the park makes it home to some unusual species of flora, such as Yew woodland and Oakwoods, and fauna, including red deer, Northern Emerald dragonfly and Greenland white-fronted geese. Popular sports include trout fishing in the three lakes, boating at *Ross Castle*, walking and cycling. *Muckross House*, a Victorian mansion completed in 1843, was once the home of Lord Ardilaun, a member of the famous Guinness family, and is open to the public, as is its working farm and the beautiful landscaped gardens. Other attractions within the grounds of the park include the 15th-century *Muckross Abbey* and the ruined seventh-century monastery at *Inisfallen Island* on *Lough Leane*, where the 'Annals of Inisfallen', detailing Ireland's early history, were written by the monks.

Contact Address

Muckross House, Muckross, Killarney, Ireland
Tel: (064) 31440. Fax: (064) 33926.
E-mail: killarneynationalpark@ealga.ie
Website: http://homepage.tinet.ie/~knp

Transportation

Air: Cork Airport. **Road:** Car: Killarney National Park is located 6.5km (4 miles) from Killarney on the N71 (Kenmare Road).

Opening Times

Visitor Centre: Daily on request (1 Nov-mid-Mar); daily 0900-1800 (mid-Mar-mid-Jun); daily 0900-1900 (1 Jul-31 Aug); daily 0900-1800 (1 Sep-31 Oct). Pedestrian access to the park all year round.

Admission Fees

Free.

National Gallery of Ireland

The *National Gallery of Ireland* was founded in 1854 and houses the national collection of Irish art, as well as the national collection of European Old Masters, such as works by Caravaggio and Rubens, the *National Portrait Collection* and the *Yeats Collection*. The latter features many works by Jack B Yeats, Ireland's most important 20th-century artist. The Italian School is represented by elaborate early Renaissance altarpieces and paintings by Fra Angelico, Mantegna and Titian, whilst treasures in the *Baroque Gallery* include works by Maratta. Other painters featured include Monet, Sisley, Picasso, Goya and Gainsborough and there are sculptures by Rodin and Moore. Scattered throughout the rooms are various *objets d'art*, such as Irish furniture, silverware, fans and examples of stained glass by Evie Hone, a 20th-century Dublin artist and Harry Clarke, also from the city, who won awards for his designs in the 1920s. The National Gallery also hosts regular exhibitions and events in which the public can participate, such as talks and workshops on artistic themes. The National Gallery building, with its colonnaded façade, stands in the south of the city and dominates Merrion Square, one of Dublin's finest Georgian squares.

Contact Address

National Gallery of Ireland, Merrion Square West, Dublin 2, Ireland
Tel: (01) 661 5133. Fax: (01) 661 5372.
E-mail: artgall@eircom.net
Website: www.nationalgallery.ie

Transportation

Air: Dublin Airport. **Water:** Ferry: Services from Holyhead (Wales) and Stranraer (Scotland) to Dun Laoghaire Port and Dublin Port. **Rail:** Train: Heuston Station, Connolly Station or Tara Street Station. DART (electric rail): Pearse Station. **Road:** Bus: 10 (to Merrion Row and Pembroke Street), 5, 6, 7, 7A or 8 (to Merrion Square North and Clare Street), 44, 47, 47B, 48A or 62 (to Merrion Square West). Car: N1 (from Dublin Airport); M11, then N11 (from Wicklow); N7 (from Kildare); N11 (from Dun Laoghaire port), then signs to Dublin city centre.

Opening Times

Mon-Wed 0930-1730, Fri-Sat 0930-1730, Thurs 0930-2030, Sun 1200-1730. Closed 24-26 Dec and Good Friday (and Sep-Oct 2001 for refurbishment).

Admission Fees

Free.

Trinity College Dublin

Founded in 1592 by a small group of Dublin citizens who obtained a royal charter from Queen Elizabeth I of England, *Trinity College* is Ireland's most prominent university, with a list of alumni that includes Samuel Beckett, Jonathan Swift and Oscar Wilde. It has played a somewhat controversial role in Irish politics and religion, since, until 1873, only Anglicans could enrol as full members of the university to obtain degrees and scholarships; Catholics were not even permitted to use the library. In the 17th century Trinity College survived the upheavals of two civil wars and the temporary expulsion of its students to make way for King James II's soldiers' barracks, to gain a reputation as a serious and industrious seat of learning. Today, as well as strolling through the campus' lush grounds, visitors flock to the *Old Library*. Built in 1732, the

Old Library is the largest in Ireland and holds four million volumes and an extensive collection of manuscripts. Its main chamber, the *Long Room,* is 65m (213ft) long and has a barrel-vaulted ceiling. The gallery bookcases are interspersed with marble busts of alumni, including one of Jonathan Swift. The most famous work in the collection is the *Book of Kells,* one of the finest examples of medieval decorated manuscripts, which was written in about AD 800 and contains the four gospels with prefaces, summaries and concordances. Visitors to the library can see two pages of intricate Latin script and a whole illustrated page. In the Long Room are displayed various items of interest belonging to the college, including a copy of the 1916 Proclamation of the Irish Republic, which led to the Easter Rising, an annotated copy of Samuel Beckett's play 'Waiting for Godot', and a collection of 18th-century political cartoons. The *Dublin Experience* is a multimedia presentation of Dublin, featuring photographs and music, and provides an excellent introduction to the city.

Contact Address

Trinity College Library, College Street, Dublin 2, Ireland
Tel: (01) 608 2320. Fax: (01) 608 2690.
E-mail: adiffley@tcd.ie
Website: www.tcd.ie

Transportation

Air: Dublin Airport. **Water:** Ferry: Services from Holyhead (Wales) and Stranraer (Scotland) to Dun Laoghaire Port and Dublin Port. **Rail:** Train: Heuston Station, Connolly Station or Tara Street Station. DART (electric rail): Pearse Station. **Road:** Bus: Trinity Bus Stop. Car: N1 (from Dublin Airport); M11, then N11 (from Wicklow); N7 (from Kildare); N11 (from Dun Laoghaire port), then signs to Dublin city centre.

Trinity College Dublin

Irish Tourist Board

Opening Times

Dublin Experience: Daily presentations every hour 1000-1700 (mid-May-30 Sep). *Old Library* and *Book of Kells*: Mon-Sat 0930-1700, Sun 1200-1630 (Oct-Mar); Mon-Sat 0930-1700, Sun 0930-1630 (Jun-Sep).

Admission Fees

Dublin Experience: Ir£2.50. *Old Library* and *Book of Kells*: Ir£4.50 (adult), free (child under 12). Concessions available.

Waterford Crystal Visitor Centre

Waterford is famous the world over as the home of beautiful crystal designs. The *Waterford Factory* was opened in 1783 by George and William Penrose, and bowls, vases and ornaments continue to be made on the site. The crystal mix is transformed into glass in a 1200ºC (2192ºF) furnace before being blown and decorated with deep engravings by a team of skilled workers. Visitors to the centre can watch the glass being formed into decanters, bowls and wine glasses and learn about the unique production techniques used at Waterford, through audiovisual displays and chatting to the craftsmen in their workshops. Many of the most prestigious pieces of Waterford Crystal, which have been presented to celebrities and politicians, are on display in the *Gallery.*

Contact Address

Waterford Crystal Visitor Centre, Kilbarry, Cork Road, Waterford, Ireland
Tel: (051) 373 311. Fax: (051) 332 716.
E-mail: visitorreception@waterford.ie
Website: www.waterfordvisitorcentre.com

Transportation

Air: Shannon Airport or Dublin Airport, then Waterford Airport (domestic flights). **Rail:** Train: Plunkett Station (Waterford). **Road:** Bus: City Imp services run from Plunkett Station in Waterford to the Waterford Factory every 10 minutes. Car: N25 (from Cork).

Opening Times

Daily 0900-1515 (1 Nov-31 Mar); daily 0830-1600 (1 Apr-31 Oct).

Admission Fees

Ir£4.50 (adult), free (child under 12).

Israel

1 Al-Haram al-Sharif (Temple Mount)
2 HaKotel HaMaaravi (Western Wall)
3 Horvot Mezada (Masada)
4 Yam Ha-melah (Dead Sea)

Tourist Information

Misrad Hatayarut (Ministry of Tourism)
PO Box 1018, King George Street 24, Jerusalem, Israel
Tel: (02) 675 4811. Fax: (02) 625 7955.
Website: www.infotour.co.il

Israel Government Tourist Office
UK House, 180 Oxford Street, London W1D 1NN, UK
Tel: (020) 7299 1111. Fax: (020) 7299 1112.
E-mail: information@igto.co.uk
Website: www.infotour.co.il

Al-Haram al-Sharif (Temple Mount)

Temple Mount, a walled section of the Old City of Jerusalem, is a site of tremendous religious significance to Jews, Muslims and Christians. The area, which is one of Jerusalem's most famous landmarks, is believed to be the site of the holy rock where Abraham offered his son Isaac for sacrifice. It is also reputedly the site where Solomon erected the First Temple to house the Ark of the Covenant, which had been brought to Jerusalem by his father David, and also the area from where Mohammed ascended to heaven. The Babylonians captured Jerusalem in 587 BC and burned down the temple, exiling many of the people to Babylonia. A Second Temple was subsequently constructed in 515 BC, only to be destroyed by the Roman Emperor Titus in AD 70. Today, the site is dominated by the *Dome of the Rock* and is also home to the silver domed *Al Aqsa Mosque*, which is a Muslim place of worship, as well as the *Islamic Museum*, which houses a collection of Korans, as well as Islamic artefacts and relics.

Contact Address

For more information on Temple Mount, contact the Ministry of Tourism (see **Tourist Information** above).

Transportation

Air: Ben-Gurion International Airport. **Road:** Bus: 1 or 2 to Dung Gate. Car: Hwy-1 (from Tel Aviv).

Opening Times

Temple Mount complex and attractions: Sat-Thurs 0800-1130 and 1230-1400, closed Fri. Opening times may vary during religious holidays.

Admission Fees

Temple Mount: Free. *Dome of the Rock*, *Al Aqsa Mosque* and *Islamic Museum* (combined ticket): IS24.

HaKotel HaMaaravi (Western Wall)

The *Western Wall*, known to non-Jews as the Wailing Wall, is a 584m (1916ft) stretch of wall which is all that remains of the *Second Temple of Jerusalem*. The most sacred Jewish place in the world, it attracts thousands of devout Jews every year who come to pray, and push prayer notes and messages of goodwill into the cracks of the wall. It also attracts many hundreds of non-Jews who come to spectate. The wall was built more than two thousand years ago under King Herod, and has been under Israeli control since 1967. It is also sacred to Muslims who believe that the wall marks the place where the prophet Mohammed tied up his winged horse, al-Burak, before ascending to heaven. The wall is 20m (60ft) high and 50m (160ft) wide, and is made of chiselled stones. It has been divided into two sections of prayer, the left for men and the right for women, and forms part of a larger wall surrounding the *Dome of the Rock* and *Al Aqsa Mosque*.

Contact Address

For more information on the Western Wall, contact the Ministry of Tourism (see **Tourist Information** above).

Transportation

Air: Ben-Gurion International Airport. **Road:** Bus: 1 or 2 to Dung Gate. Car: Hwy-1 to central Jerusalem (from Tel Aviv).

Opening Times

Daily 24 hours.

Admission Fees

Free.

Horvot Mezada (Masada)

Perched high on a sheer-sided plateau, *Masada* is famous for being the site of a mass suicide by a group of Jewish people who put their religious and cultural pride before their own lives. Located in Negev, on the southern coast of Israel, the fortress was originally built around 35 BC as a luxurious refuge for King Herod, but was taken by the Jewish people, following a Jewish revolt. When the Romans were on the brink of recapturing the fort, however, all 967 men, women and children courageously took their own lives. The site was excavated between 1963-65 and is, today, one of the most visited in Israel, consisting of a national park, reconstructed buildings of the old walled town, a museum and a cable car.

Contact Address

Horvot Mezada, M P Yam Hamelach, Negev, Israel
Tel: (07) 658 4207. Fax: (07) 658 4464.
E-mail: gl.mezada@nature-parks.org.il

Transportation

Air: Ben-Gurion International Airport. **Rail:** Cable Car: A cable car runs from the Masada Cable Car Station at the bottom of the mountain to the summit. **Road:** Bus: Services run from Jerusalem and Bersheva. Car: Route 3199 (from Arad).

Opening Times

Sun-Thurs and Sat 0800-1600, Fri 0800-1500 (winter); Sun-Thurs and Sat 0800-1700, Fri 0800-1500 (summer).

Admission Fees

Entrance and cable car: IS56 (adult), IS31 (child). Entrance only: IS20 (adult), IS10 (child).

Yam Ha-melah (Dead Sea)

Lying 400m (1320ft) below sea level and spanning the border between Israel and Jordan, the *Dead Sea* is a natural wonder. It contains more minerals and salt than any other stretch of water in the world, and thus it really is possible to float on top of the water. Its natural properties make it a prime centre for spa treatments and relaxation therapies and there are a number of resorts in the area. The Dead Sea has strong Biblical connections: the salt mountain range of *Mount Sodom*, located on the southwestern shores of the sea is, according to the Bible, the site of the sinful city that perished alongside Gomorra. In turn, the *Dead Sea Scrolls*, the oldest Biblical documents known to be in existence, were discovered at *Qumran*, a restored archaeological site in the north. *Masada*, the magnificent mountaintop fortress of King Herod is also located on the Israeli shores of the Dead Sea. The *Ein Gedi Nature Reserve and Kibbutz* provides opportunities for spotting desert wildlife and offers trails to waterfalls, canyons, caves and shallow pools. *Metzoke Dragot*, located in a deep crater, is a popular site for more adventurous sports such as abseiling, climbing (with amazing desert views) and mountain biking.

Contact Address

Dead Sea Regional Tourist Organization, NP Dead Sea 86910, Israel
Tel: (07) 668 8808. Fax: (07) 658 4150.
E-mail: info@deadsea.co.il
Website: www.deadsea.co.il

Transportation

Air: Ben-Gurion International Airport. **Road:** Coach: 444, 486 or 487 (Egged services from Jerusalem). Taxi: Sheshir taxis (from Ben-Gurion International Airport).

Opening Times

Daily 24 hours.

Admission Fees

Free.

Italy

1 Basilica di San Marco (St Mark's Basilica)
2 Basilica di San Pietro (St Peter's Basilica)
3 Colosseo (Colosseum)
4 Duomo Santa Maria del Fiore (Florence Duomo)
5 Fontana di Trevi (Trevi Fountain)
6 Foro Romano (Roman Forum)
7 Galleria degli Uffizi (Uffizi Gallery)
8 Musei Vaticani e Capella Sistina (Vatican Museums and Sistine Chapel)
9 Palazzo Ducale (Doges' Palace)
10 Panteone (Pantheon)
11 Piazza del Campo (Siena Main Square)
12 Pompeii
13 Ponte Vecchio (Old Bridge)
14 Scalinata della Trinità dei Monti e Keats-Shelley Memorial House (Spanish Steps and Keats-Shelley Memorial House)
15 Torre Pendente di Pisa (Leaning Tower of Pisa)

Tourist Information

Ente Nazionale Italiano per il Turismo (Italian State Tourist Office – ENIT)
Via Marghera 2, 00185 Rome, Italy
Tel: (06) 49711. Fax: (06) 446 3379.
E-mail: sedecentrale.enit@interbusiness.it
Website: www.enit.it
Italian State Tourist Office (ENIT)
1 Princes Street, London W1R 8AY, UK
Tel: (020) 7408 1254 *or* 7355 1557 (trade enquiries only) *or* (09001) 600 280 (brochure line; calls are charged at 60p per minute). Fax: (020) 7493 6695.
E-mail: enitlond@globalnet.co.uk
Website: www.enit.it

Basilica di San Marco (St Mark's Basilica)

The glittering façade of *St Mark's Basilica* dominates the vast expanse of *St Marks' Square* and stands as a potent symbol of Venice's status as city state and maritime power in the late Medieval period. The basilica, which was consecrated in 1094, is the third church to be built on the site since the body of St Mark, the city's patron saint, was reputedly brought here to be buried in AD 828. The exotic Byzantine architecture of the basilica reflects the Venetian lagoon's strong trading links with the Orient and the exterior is decorated with marble brought back after the Venetian conquest of Constantinople in 1204; the five vaulted domes which form the roof are set in the shape of a Greek cross. The interior is just as magnificent, with gold mosaics covering the ceilings and walls, and marble floors. There are further displays of riches brought back from foreign crusades in the *Tesoro* (treasury), whilst the *Pala D'Oro* (Golden Altarpiece) is an ornate altar screen in a gilded frame with enamel panels made in Byzantium. It is possible to climb up to the *Loggia* (veranda) on the front of the basilica for views over the lagoon and the surrounding islands, or to ascend the nearby *Campanile* (bell tower) which, at 99m (272ft), is the tallest building in Venice.

Contact Address

Basilica di San Marco, Piazza San Marco, 30124 Venice, Italy
Tel: (041) 522 5205 *or* 522 5697. Fax: (041) 520 8289.

Transportation

Air: Venice Marco Polo Airport. **Water:** Ferry: Line 1, 51 or 82. Waterbus (Vaporetto): San Marco or San Zaccaria. **Rail:** Train: Venezia Santa Lucia Station (Venice Station). **Road:** Bus: 1, 82, 42 or 52 (to San Zaccaria). Car: A4 (from Turin); A13 (from Bologna); A1 (from Rome or Florence); A1, then A13, then A4 (from Naples); SS11 (from Padua).

Opening Times

Mon-Sat 0945-1700, Sun and public holidays 1400-1700.

Admission Fees

Basilica: Free. *Campanile*: L10,000. *Loggia*: L3000. *Pala d'Oro*: L3000. *Tesoro*: L4000.

Basilica di San Pietro (St Peter's Basilica)

St Peter's Basilica stands in the Vatican City above the supposed resting place of the remains of St Peter. A church was first built on the site in the fourth century by Constantine but the 16th-century popes decided to build a monument and place of worship that would better reflect the power of the Catholic church. Construction began in 1506 under Pope Julius II, but it was not completed until 120 years later, and the result is awe-inspiring. Until 1989, when it was superseded by the *Basilica of Our Lady of Peace* in Yamoussourkro in Ivory Coast, St Peter's was the largest church in Christendom. Michelangelo designed its graceful *cupola* (dome), and stunning views over Rome and the surrounding countryside can be seen from the top. The interior is an unbridled display of Renaissance and Baroque grandeur and features Bernini's *Throne of St Peter* made from bronze purloined from the *Pantheon*, as well as imposing statues of the popes and Michelangelo's *Pietà*.

Contact Address

Centro Servizi, Pellegrini e Turistiche Informazioni 00120 Vatican City, Italy
Tel: (06) 6988 1662. Website: www.christusrex.org

Transportation

Air: Rome Leonardo da Vinci Airport (Fiumicino) or Rome Ciampino Airport. **Water:** Ferry: Civitavecchia port, from where there are services to central Rome. **Rail:** Train: Roma Termini Station, Roma Tiburtina Station, Roma Ostiense Station or Roma Trastevere Station. Underground: Ottaviano. **Road:** Bus: Services to Piazza del Risorgimento. Car: A12 (from the west); A24 (from the east); SS7 (from Rome Ciampino Airport).

Opening Times

Daily 0700-1800 (1 Oct-31 Mar); daily 0700-1800 (1 Apr-30 Sep).

Admission Fees

Basilica: Free. *Cupola*: L7000 (without lift), L8000 (with lift).

Colosseo (Colosseum)

The *Colosseum* is arguably ancient Rome's most famous building. This massive structure, with arch upon arch reaching 48m (157ft) into the air and measuring 190m by 155m (620ft by 513ft), used to hold up to 50,000 boisterous Roman citizens. Opened in AD 80 by Emperor Titus in a ceremony that included 100 days of games, the Colosseum played host to Rome's favourite spectator sports – gladiatorial contests, combats between men and wild animals and even mock naval battles. Such sports were outlawed in the fifth century AD, and only the shell remains, along with a view down to the passages through which slaves and animals were led before entering into battle. Unlike other Roman amphitheatres that are dug into hillsides, the Colosseum is a free-standing structure of stone and concrete and has long served as a model for stadia around the world.

Contact Address

Il Colosseo, Piazza Colosseo, Formece 72, Rome, Italy
Tel: (06) 700 4261. Fax: (06) 700 4261.

Transportation

Air: Rome Leonardo da Vinci Airport (Fiumicino) or Rome Ciampino Airport. **Water:** Ferry: Civitavecchia port, from where there are services to central Rome. **Rail:** Train: Roma Termini Station, Roma Tiburtina Station, Roma Ostiense Station or Roma Trastevere Station. Underground: Colosseo. Tram: Piazza del Colosseo. **Road:** Bus: 60, 75, 85, 87, 110, 117, 175, 186 or 204. Car: A12 (from the west); A24 (from the east); SS7 (from Rome Ciampino Airport).

Opening Times

Daily 0900-1900.

Admission Fees

L10,000 (adult), free (child under 18 if EU citizen), L10,000 (child under 18 from any other country).

Colosseum

Azienda di Promozione Turistica di Roma

Duomo Santa Maria del Fiore (Florence Duomo)

Florence's *Duomo*, or cathedral, completed in 1327, is the fourth largest church in the world, and its domed roof is symbolic of the meeting of Renaissance craft and culture. Engineered by the architect and sculptor Filippo Brunelleschi (1377-1446), using specially invented machines, the *cupola* (dome) was one of the greatest achievements of the Italian Renaissance. Its octagonal form has a diameter of 46.5m (153ft) at the base, and was completed in 1436; it is possible to climb to the top of the dome for magnificent views over the city. The vast interior boasts sculptures by Renaissance masters such as Paolo Uccello, Andrea del Castagno, Giorgio Vasari and Federico Zuccari. The Duomo stands on the remains of an older cathedral, which can be seen in the archaeological area revealed beneath the floor. The bronze doors of the *battistero* (baptistry), the oldest building in Florence, were cast by Lorenzo Ghiberti in the early part of the 15th century and were described by Michelangelo as fit to be the gates to paradise. The nearby *campanile* (bell tower) is decorated inside with frescoes by Giotto and Donatello, amongst others.

Contact Address

Azienda di Promozione Turistica, Via A Manzoni 16, 50121 Florence, Italy
Tel: (055) 23320. Fax: (055) 234 6286.
Website: www.firenze.turismo.toscana.it

Transportation

Air: Amerigo Vespucci Airport (Florence) or Galileo Galilei Airport (Pisa). **Rail:** Train: Firenze Santa Maria Novella Station (Florence). Road: Bus: 14 or 23. Car: A1 (from Milan, Bologna, Rome or Naples); A11 (from Pisa, Lucca, Prato or Siena).

Opening Times

Battistero: Mon-Sat 1200-1900, Sun 0830-1400. *Campanile*: Daily 0900-1930. *Cupola*: Mon-Fri 0830-1900, Sat 0830-1740. *Duomo*: Mon-Wed and Fri 1000-1700, Thurs 1000-1730, Sat 1000-1645, Sun 1300-1645.

Admission Fees

Battistero: L5000 (adult), free (child under 6). *Campanile*: L10,000 (adult), free (child under 6). *Cupola*: L10,000 (adult), free (child under 6). *Duomo*: Free.

Fontana di Trevi (Trevi Fountain)

Located in the heart of Rome's *centro storico* (historic centre), the *Trevi Fountain* derives its name from its position at the intersection of three roads (*tre vie*). According to legend, anyone who throws a coin into the water is guaranteed to return to the Eternal City. There has been a source of water at this site for over a thousand years, although it was not until 1485 that Pope Nicholas V commissioned Gianlorenzo Bernini to create the actual fountain – and even then the project was abandoned after the death of Pope Urban VIII in 1644. In 1732, Pope Clement XII employed Niccolò Salvi to continue the work, and the result is a Baroque masterpiece that takes the visitor by surprise, filling, as it does, the cramped square that it occupies with its mass of allegorical figures and gushing water. The central niche depicts Neptune riding a chariot driven by sea horses and the water flows over rocks before collecting in a pool below. Although the water is no longer safe to drink, the fountain is still a popular place to enjoy an icecream from one of the *gelaterie* in the square.

Contact Address

For more information on the Trevi Fountain, contact Ente Nazionale Italiano per il Turismo (see **Tourist Information** above).

Transportation

Air: Rome Leonardo da Vinci Airport (Fiumicino) or Rome Ciampino Airport. **Water:** Ferry: Civitavecchia port, from where there are services to central Rome. **Rail:** Train: Roma Termini Station, Roma Tiburtina Station, Roma Ostiense Station or Roma Trastevere Station. Underground: Barberini. **Road:** Car: A12 (from the west); A24 (from the east); SS7 (from Rome Ciampino Airport).

Opening Times

Daily 24 hours.

Admission Fees

Free.

Foro Romano (Roman Forum)

The *Roman Forum*, located between the Capitoline and Palatine hills in the centre of Rome, was the main focus of the Roman Republic and later the symbolic heart of an empire that stretched from England to Carthage. The religious and political institutions, law courts, shops and markets would have bustled with life, and the temples and imperial monuments were architectural triumphs. Today, it requires a certain amount of imagination to picture the Forum in its former glory, as the ravages of history have not been kind. Fire, invasions and general decay have all played their part, and most recently, in 1932, the Italian fascist dictator Mussolini ordered a main road to be built straight through the site, bulldozing the narrow alleyways. Among the best-preserved monuments are the triumphal *Arch of Septimius*, eight columns of the *Temple of Saturn* and the rectangular *House of the Vestal Virgins* – where six virgin priestesses devoted thirty years of service to attending the sacred flame in the Temple of Vesta, the Roman goddess of the hearth.

Contact Address

Foro Romano, Via de Fori Imperiali, Piazza Santa Maria Nova 53, 00100 Rome, Italy
Tel: (06) 699 0110. Fax: (06) 678 7689.
Website: www.capitolium.org

Transportation

Air: Rome Leonardo da Vinci Airport (Fiumicino) or Rome Ciampino Airport. **Water:** Ferry: Civitavecchia port, from where there are services to central Rome. **Rail:** Train: Roma Termini Station, Roma Tiburtina Station, Roma Ostiense Station or Roma Trastevere Station. Underground: Colosseo. **Road:** Bus: 84 or 87 (to Piazza Venezia or Via dei Fori Imperiali). Car: A12 (from the west); A24 (from the east); SS7 (from Rome Ciampino Airport).

Opening Times

Daily 0900-one hour before sunset.

Admission Fees

L12,000 (adult), L5000 (child 8-18), free (child under 8).

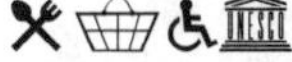

Galleria degli Uffizi (Uffizi Gallery)

The *Uffizi Gallery* in Florence houses the richest and most important art collection in the world. The building, located in the *Piazza della Signoria* close to the banks of the River Arno, was designed in the 16th century by the painter and architect Giorgio Vasari to house Florence's government offices (*uffizi*), and was bequeathed to the gallery as the Medici art collection in 1737, on the condition that it should never leave the city. The museum is a showcase for the Renaissance movement, one of the greatest periods in the history of art, and focuses more specifically on the Florentine School. Some of the extraordinary masterpieces exhibited in the 45 rooms and corridors include Botticelli's *Birth of Venus* and *Primavera* and Leonardo da Vinci's *Annunciation*, as well as frescoes by Giotto, Titian, Tintoretto and Raphael. Later periods in painting are represented by Caravaggio, Van Dyck and Rembrandt and there are also many antiques, sculptures, drawings and prints on display.

Contact Address

Galleria degli Uffizi, Via della Ninna 5, 50122 Florence, Italy
Tel: (055) 238 8651 *or* 238 8652. Fax: (055) 238 8699.
E-mail: info@uffizi.firenze.it
Website: www.uffizi.firenze.it

Transportation

Air: Amerigo Vespucci Airport (Florence) or Pisa Galileo Galilei Airport. **Rail:** Train: Santa Maria Novella Station. **Road:** Bus: Galleria degli Uffizi Castellani. Car: A1 (from Milan, Bologna, Rome or Naples); A11 (from Pisa, Lucca, Prato or Siena), then signs to Centro Storico.

Opening Times

Tues-Sun 0815-1900. Closed 25 Dec, 1 Jan and 1 May.

Admission Fees

L15,000 (adult), L7500 (adult 18-25), free (child under 18, EU citizens only).

Musei Vaticani e Capella Sistina (Vatican Museums and Sistine Chapel)

The *Vatican Museums* constitute the largest museum complex in the world. Founded in 1506 by Pope Julius II, the collections are staggeringly diverse and are essentially the legacy of the Popes who were not only fabulously rich, but also great patrons of the Arts. Egyptian antiquities, classical statues, Etruscan relics and Byzantine paintings all have their place, but two areas that should not be missed are the *Stanze di Raffaello* (Raphael Rooms) and the *Cappella Sistina* (Sistine Chapel). Renowned equally for the crowds that line up to see it as it is for its breathtaking beauty, the Sistine Chapel was constructed between 1475 and 1480 as a private chapel for the Popes. The painting of its ceiling was charged to a reluctant Michelangelo, whose subsequent depiction of the *Creation of Adam* ranks among the most famous painted images of all time and is considered to be one of the finest achievements of the Renaissance. The *Last Judgement*, also by Michelangelo, hangs behind the altar, while other famous Renaissance works by artists such as Botticelli and Ghirlandaio adorn the rest of the interior.

Contact Address

Musei Vaticani, Viale Vaticano, 00120 Vatican City, Italy
Tel: (06) 6988 3860. Fax: (06) 6988 5100 (information) *or* 6988 5961 (guided tours).
Website: www.vatican.va

Transportation

Air: Rome Leonardo da Vinci Airport (Fiumicino) or Rome Ciampino Airport. **Water:** Ferry: Civitavecchia port, from where there are services to central Rome. **Rail:** Underground: Ottaviano. **Road:** Bus: 49 (to Piazza Risorgimento or Via Leone IV).

Opening Times

Mon-Fri 0845-1645, Sat 0845-1345, first Sun of each month 0845-1345; last entry is 75 minutes before closure. The Vatican City observes many religious holidays, when the museums are closed.

Admission Fees

L18,000 (adult over 26), L12,000 (adult 18-26), L12,000 (child 6-18), free (child under 6); free last Sun of each month. Concessions available.

Palazzo Ducale (Doges' Palace)

Located in Venice's renowned *Piazza San Marco*, adjacent to the *Basilica di San Marco*, the *Doges' Palace* was home to the government of the former Venetian Republic from AD 697 to 1797. Although the palace was originally built in AD 814, the present structure was completed in the early 15th century. The palace was a showplace for artistry, craftsmanship and architecture, and still exemplifies the splendour of Venetian Gothic style, with graceful arcades and ornate portals. As well as ruling the city state, the doges (a Venetian word from the Latin *dux*, meaning leader) were great patrons of the arts and the palace is filled with works by Venetian Renaissance masters such as Veronese and Tintoretto. The *Ponte dei Sospiri*, or Bridge of Sighs, is an integral part of the palace and forms the link between the courts and the prisons across the canal. It is named after the noise prisoners used to make as they were led to confinement in the damp and gloomy cells, which can still be visited on a tour of the palace, and which provide a stark contrast to the opulent living conditions of the doges.

Contact Address

Palazzo Ducale, Piazza San Marco, Venice, Italy
Tel: (041) 522 4951. Fax: (041) 528 5028.

Transportation

Air: Venice Marco Polo Airport. **Water:** Ferry: Line 1, 51 or 82. Waterbus (Vaporetto): San Marco or San Zaccaria. **Rail:** Train: Venezia Santa Lucia Station (Venice Station). **Road:** Bus: 1, 82, 42 or 52 (to San Zaccaria). Car: A4 (from Turin); A13 (from Bologna); A1 (from Rome or Florence); A1, then A13, then A4 (from Naples); SS11 (from Padua). Cars must be left at the car park at Piazzale Roma directly outside the historic centre, from where it is possible to travel by water or foot to the Doges' Palace.

Opening Times

Daily 0900-1700 (winter); daily 0900-1900 (summer).

Admission Fees

L18,000 (adult over 29), L10,000 (adult 15-29), L6000 (child 6-15), free (child under 6).

Doges' Palace

Azienda di Promozione Turistica di Venezia

Panteone (Pantheon)

Considered by many to be the best preserved of all great classical monuments, the *Pantheon* was dedicated in 27 BC by Agrippa, the admiral who defeated Anthony and Cleopatra, and rebuilt by Hadrian in AD 125 after it had been struck by lightning and burnt down sometime between AD 98-117. Originally, the structure served as a temple for the seven Roman planetary deities, Apollo, Diana, Mars, Mercury, Jupiter, Venus, and Saturn, but was later consecrated as a Catholic church in AD 609. The Pantheon possesses a dome with a span of 43.2m (142ft), the largest of its kind until the Duomo in Florence was built in the 15th century. There is no obvious support mechanism for the dome, but the quality of the materials used and the fact that the diameter is exactly equal to the height have enabled it to survive more or less intact. The bronze and gold décor was stripped away to be used in other Roman monuments, such as St Peter's Basilica, but the sheer size and age of the building cannot fail to impress. Inside visitors can see the tomb of the Renaissance master Raphael.

Contact Address

Il Panteone, Piazza della Rotunda, Rome, Italy
Tel: (06) 6830 0230. Fax: (06) 588 3340.

Transportation

Air: Rome Leonardo da Vinci Airport (Fiumicino) or Rome Ciampino Airport. **Water:** Ferry: Civitavecchia port, from where there are services to central Rome. **Rail:** Train: Roma Termini Station, Roma Tiburtina Station, Roma Ostiense Station or Roma Trastevere Station. **Road:** Bus: 64 (to Largo Argentina or Via del Corso). Car: A12 (from the west); A24 (from the east); SS7 (from Rome Ciampino Airport).

Opening Times

Mon-Sat 0830-1930, Sun 0900-1800.

Admission Fees

Free.

Piazza del Campo (Siena Main Square)

The shell-shaped *Piazza del Campo* lies at the heart of Siena and has served as a focus for life in the city for centuries. It is widely regarded as the finest Medieval square in Europe and twice a year, in July and August, provides a splendid backdrop for the *Corsa del Palio*, a fast and furious bareback horse race dating back to the 15th century. The *Palazzo Pubblico* (Town Hall), which stands proudly at the top of the piazza, was constructed between 1297-and 1310 as the seat of the *Governo dei Nove*, or Government of Nine, who ruled Siena from 1287-1355, when the city enjoyed considerable economic and cultural prosperity. The interior of the building, which is now the *Museo Civico* (Civic Museum), contains many paintings by Sienese masters such as Simone Martini and Ambrogio Lorenzetti, as well as the remains of the *Gaia Fountain* decorated by renowned sculptor Jacopo della Quercia, who was also born in the city. Next to the Palazzo Pubblico stands the *Torre del Mangia* (Mangia Tower), a belltower which rises to 102m (334ft); visitors can climb to the top for views of the winding cobbled streets which fan out from the piazza, and timeless vistas of the Tuscan countryside.

Contact Address

Museo Civico, Palazzo Comunale, Piazza del Campo, 53100 Siena, Italy
Tel: (0577) 292 265. Fax: (0577) 292 296.

Transportation

Air: Pisa Galileo Galilei Airport. **Rail:** Train: Siena Station. **Road:** Car: A1 (from Rome, exit Valdichiana); Superstrada del Palio (from Florence); A12 (from Genoa). The historic centre of Siena is pedestrianised.

Opening Times

Museo Civico: Daily 1000-1830 (1 Nov-15 Mar); daily 1000-1900 (16 Mar-31 Oct). *Torre del Mangia*: Daily 1000-1600.

Admission Fees

Museo Civico: L12,000 (adult), L7000 (child 11-18), free (child under 11). Concessions available. *Torre del Mangia*: L10,000 (adult), free (child under 6).

Pompeii

Once a lavish resort town for wealthy Romans, *Pompeii*, situated 25km (16 miles) south of Naples, was literally buried alive under hot volcanic ash and mud during an eruption of nearby *Mount Vesuvius* in AD 79. The city was eventually forgotten, and it was not until the 16th century that it was rediscovered. Now excavated, it provides an enthralling insight into the everyday lives of the ancient Romans. Visitors can view restored villas complete with erotic and religious wall paintings, temples and the forum, as well as actual brothels and plaster casts of fallen volcano victims. Nearby *Ercolano* (Herculaneum) was also destroyed by Vesuvius, and is a smaller but better-preserved site consisting of villas and shops. From Ercolano, the modern town, it is possible to take a bus to the top of Mount Vesuvius.

Contact Address

Pompeii Visitors Centre, Via Satra 1, CAP 80045, Pompeii, Italy
Tel: (081) 850 7255. Fax: (081) 863 2401.

Transportation

Air: Naples International Airport. **Rail:** Train: Pompeii FS Station, Pompeii Santuario, Pompeii–Villa dei Misteri Station or Ercolano Station. Circumvesuviana (Bay of Naples rail system): Pompeii-Scavi-Villa dei Misteri Station. **Road:** Car: A3 to Pompeii (from Naples); S18 to Ercolano (from Naples).

Opening Times

Herculaneum: Daily 0830-1700 (last admission 1530) (1 Nov-31 Mar); daily 0830-1830 (last admission 1800) (1 Apr-31 Oct). Closed 25 Dec and 1 Jan. *Pompeii*: Daily 0900-one hour before sunset. Closed 25 Dec and 1 Jan.

Admission Fees

Pompeii: L15,000 (adult), L7500 (child 12-18), free (child under 12). *Herculaneum*: L16,000 (adult over 24), L8000 (adult 18-24, EU citizens only), free (child under 18, EU citizens only). Adult price applies to most non-EU citizens.

Ponte Vecchio (Old Bridge)

This famous 14th-century bridge, built by Taddeo Gaddi and home to medieval Florence's gold and silversmiths, is still paved with jewellers' shops today. The *Ponte Vecchio*'s genteel atmosphere dates back to the days of Cosimo de' Medici, a member of the city's ruling dynasty in Renaissance times, who threw out a group of butchers who set up shop on the bridge. Above the shops that line the bridge is a secret passageway known as the *Corridoio Vasariano*, linking the *Palazzo Vecchio*, *Uffizi Gallery* and the *Pitti Palace*, and originally built as a private passage for the Medici family. The Ponte Vecchio was the only bridge across the River Arno to be spared German bombing during World War II.

Contact Address

Azienda per il Turismo di Firenze, Via A Manzoni 16, 50121 Florence, Italy
Tel: (055) 23320. Fax: (055) 234 6286.
Website: www.firenze.turismo.toscana.it

Transportation

Air: Amerigo Vespucci Airport (Florence) or Pisa Galileo Galilei Airport. **Rail:** Train: Santa Maria Novella Station. **Road:** Bus: 6, 11, 23, 36 or 37. Car: A1 (from Milan, Bologna, Rome or Naples); A11 (from Pisa, Lucca, Prato or Siena).

Opening Times

Daily 24 hours.

Admission Fees

Free.

Scalinata della Trinità dei Monti e Keats-Shelley Memorial House (Spanish Steps and Keats-Shelley Memorial House)

Although they have been known as the *Spanish Steps*, after the nearby Spanish Embassy, ever since their construction between 1721-25, the steps that lead up to the rose-coloured *Trinità dei Monti* church, with its twin towers and fine views over Rome, were in fact constructed and funded after a financial gift from the French King, Charles VIII. At the bottom of the steps, which are covered in a riot of red azaleas in early summer, is the *Piazza di Spagna* (Spanish Square), and Pietro Bernini's *Fontana della Barcaccia* (Barcaccia Fountain). The steps have served as a meeting point for generations of travellers, from the English Grand Tourists of the 18th century, to the young people of all nationalities who flock here today, but one of the most famous residents was the English Romantic poet, John Keats. He spent the last few months of his life in the *Casina Rossa*, or Little Red House, nursed by his artist friend Joseph Severn, before he tragically died of tuberculosis in 1821. The house was left to go to ruin until it was bought by a group of British and Americans in 1903 and turned into a museum where visitors can learn about the lives of Keats, Shelley, Byron and other English poets who were inspired by Italy.

Contact Address

Keats-Shelley Memorial House, Piazza di Spagna 26, 00187 Rome, Italy
Tel: (06) 678 4235. Fax: (06) 678 4167.
E-mail: info@Keats-Shelley-House.org
Website: www.Keats-Shelley-House.org

Transportation

Air: Rome Leonardo da Vinci Airport (Fiumicino) or Rome Ciampino Airport. **Water:** Ferry: Civitavecchia port, from where there are services to central Rome. **Rail:** Train: Roma Termini Station, Roma Tiburtina Station, Roma Ostiense Station or Roma Trastevere Station. Underground: Spagna. **Road:** Bus: 116, 117 or 119. Car: A12 (from the west); A24 (from the east); SS7 (from Rome Ciampino Airport).

Opening Times

Mon-Fri 0900-1300 and 1500-1800, Sat 1100-1400 and 1500-1800.

Admission Fees

L5000 (adult), free (child under 6).

Torre Pendente di Pisa (Leaning Tower of Pisa)

Constructed in 1174, at a time when the Pisans were enjoying an era of military success, the *Leaning Tower of Pisa,* located in Pisa's *Campo dei Miracoli* (Field of Miracles) is famous not only because of its striking beauty but also because of its awkward geometry. It served as the bell tower of the equally impressive *Duomo* (Cathedral) and *Battistero* (Baptistry), and as a result of the poor swampy soil beneath has leaned almost since construction first started. Under normal circumstances, the tower would have fallen long ago. Due, however, to the fact that its construction was often interrupted by war and its limestone is unusually flexible, the tower still stands today, with one side five metres (16ft) closer to the ground than it ought to be. Galileo used the tower for experiments to prove his theory of motion whilst he was chair of mathematics at the *Università di Pisa* (Pisa University) in 1589. The tower itself has for many years been closed to visitors as engineers sought to to stabilise its foundations. Considerable progress has been made, and the tower should be open to visitors by late 2001.

Contact Address

Azienda di Promozione Turistica, Via B Croce 26, 56125 Pisa, Italy
Tel: (050) 561 820 *or* 560 547. Fax: (050) 560 505.
Website: www.torre.duomo.pisa.it

Transportation

Air: Pisa Galileo Galilei Airport. **Rail:** Train: Pisa Centrale Station. Road: Car: A12 (from Genoa and the north); A11 (from Florence).

Opening Times

Battistero: Daily 0900-1640 (winter); daily 0900-1740 (spring); daily 0800-1940 (summer); daily 0900-1740 (autumn). *Duomo*: Mon-Fri 1000-1245, Sat and Sun 1500-1645 (winter and spring); Mon-Fri 1000-1940, Sat and Sun 1300-1940 (summer); Mon-Fri 1000-1940, Sat and Sun 1300-1940 (autumn). *Torre Pendente*: Daily 24 hours.

Admission Fees

Battistero: L9000. *Duomo*: L3000. *Torre Pendente*: Free.

Piazza di Spagna and the Keats-Shelley Memorial House

Azienda di Promozione Turistica di Roma

Jamaica

1 Dunn's River Falls

Tourist Information

Jamaica Tourist Board (JTB)
64 Knutsford Boulevard, Kingston 5, Jamaica
Tel: 929 9200. Fax: 929 9375.
E-mail: projamaicatrv@aol.com
Website: www.jamaicatravel.com

Jamaica Tourist Board
1-2 Prince Consort Road, London SW7 2BZ, UK
Tel: (020) 7224 0505. Fax: (020) 7224 0551.
E-mail: jtb_uk@compuserve.com
Website: www.jamaicatravel.com

Dunn's River Falls

Located in a dense tropical forest, *Dunn's River Falls* is Jamaica's most famous attraction. This Caribbean paradise consists of a number of waterfalls, which cascade over rock terraces down to the Caribbean Sea below, and beautiful natural pools that have formed in the rockface. The falls are shallow enough to enable visitors to climb the 183m (600ft) limestone tiers to reach a tropical shower, from where they can enjoy panoramic views of the surrounding area. There are beautiful beaches at the bottom of these magnificent falls that are also famous for featuring in the first James Bond film, 'Dr No'. They are considered by many to be the Niagara Falls of the Caribbean and are set in the luscious surroundings of the Dunn's River Falls Park with its many tree ferns and orchids.

Contact Address

Dunn's River Falls and Park, Ocho Rios, St Ann, Jamaica
Tel: 974 2857 *or* 974 4767.

Transportation

Air: Norman Manley International Airport. **Road:** Car: A3 North Coast Highway (from Kingston).

Opening Times

Daily 0900-1700.

Admission Fees

US$6 (adult), US$3 (child).

Dunn's River Falls

Corel

Japan

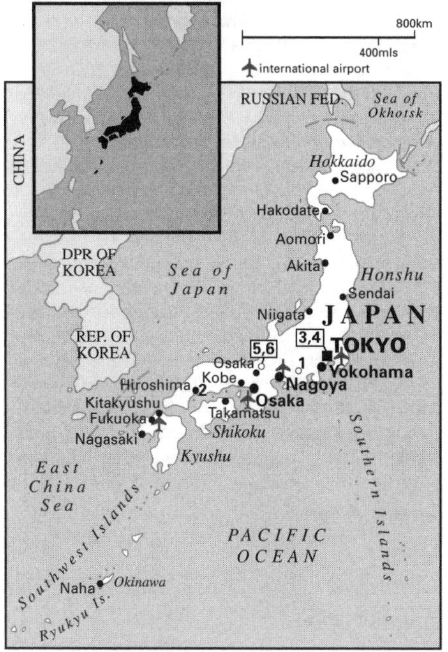

1 Fuji-yama (Mount Fuji)
2 Heiwa Kinen Shiryôkan (Hiroshima Peace Memorial Museum)
3 Kinryuzan Senso-ji (Senso-ji Temple)
4 Meiji Jingu (Meiji Shrine)
5 Nijo-jo (Nijo Castle)
6 Sanjusangen-do Temple

Tourist Information

Kokusai Kanko Shinkokai (Japan National Tourist Organisation – JNTO)

Overseas Promotion Department, 2-10-1, Yurakucho, Chiyoda-ku, Tokyo 100-0006, Japan
Tel: (03) 3216 1902. Fax: (03) 3216 1846.
E-mail: jnto@jnto.go.jp
Website: www.jnto.go.jp

Japan National Tourist Organisation (JNTO)

Heathcoat House, 20 Saville Row, London W1S 3PR, UK
Tel: (020) 7734 9638. Fax: (020) 7734 4290.
E-mail: jntolon@dircon.co.uk

Fuji-yama (Mount Fuji)

This perfectly symmetrical, 3776m (12,389ft) volcanic cone is one of the most famous volcanoes in the world and the highest peak in Japan. Of extreme historical and religious importance to the Japanese, *Mount Fuji* is also one of the nation's most significant emblems. Although it has erupted 16 times since AD 781, the mountain is safe and popular for climbing, and has not erupted since 1707 when it last covered the streets of Tokyo in volcanic lava. Most excursions take place in July and August, although the mountain can be climbed at any time of year. The top offers overnight huts, a volcanic crater and unparalleled views of Japan. The *Fuji Five Lakes* located on the northern side of the mountain, namely Lake Yamanaka, Lake Kawaguchi, Lake Nishi, Lake Shojin and Lake Motosu, were created by volcanic eruptions and are fantastic sites from which to see excellent views of Mount Fuji itself.

Contact Address

Fuji-yama, Japan National Trust, 810 Shin-Kokusai Bldg 4-1, Marunouchi 3-chome, Chiyoda-ku, Tokyo 100, Japan
Tel: (03) 3214 2631. Fax: (03) 3214 2633.
E-mail: hdqrt@ntrust.or.jp
Website: www.mt-fuji.com

Transportation

Air: New Tokyo Narita International Airport, then Haneda Airport (domestic flights). **Rail:** Train: Shinjuku (Tokyo) Station to Kawaguchi-ko Station. **Road:** Coach: Services to Fuji Gogome (from Kawaguchi-ko). Car: Fuji-Subaru Line to Gogome (from Chuo expressway, Kawaguchiko interchange); Fuji-Skyline to ShinGogome (from Tomei expressway, Gotenba interchange); NishiFuji Road,

Mount Fuji

Japan National Tourist Organisation

then Fuji-Skyline to ShinGogome (from Tomei expressway, Fuji interchange).

Opening Times

Daily 24 hours.

Admission Fees

Free.

Heiwa Kinen Shiryôkan (Hiroshima Peace Memorial Museum)

Hiroshima in Western Honshu is known around the world as the city which was destroyed by the world's first atomic bomb on August 6, 1945. Every year, millions of visitors come to the city to pay their respects in the *Hiroshima Peace Memorial Park* and the *Peace Memorial Museum*. The park, which was reconstructed in 1949, is home to many famous monuments and buildings, including the *Children's Peace Monument* and the *A-Bomb Dome*, which was built in 1915 and designed by the Czech architect Jan Letzel. The ruins of the dome, which are included on the UNESCO World Heritage List, have become the symbol of an international desire for peace. Inside the Peace Memorial Museum's East and West buildings, visitors can learn about the history of Hiroshima before and after the bombing and see a collection of artefacts, such as a charred lunch box, which remained after the explosion.

Contact Address

Hiroshima Peace Memorial Museum, 1-2 Nakajima-cho, Naka-ku, Hiroshima, 730-0811, Japan
Tel: (082) 241 4004. Fax: (082) 542 7941.
E-mail: hpcf@pcf.city.hiroshima.jp
Website: www.tourism.city.hiroshima.jp

Transportation

Air: Hiroshima Airport. **Road:** Bus: Heiwa-Kinen-Koen stop from JR Hiroshima Station (South Exit). Streetcar: Direction Ujina via Kamiya-cho, stop marked Chuden-mae. Alternatively direction Koi/Eba/Miyajima, stop marked Genbaku-Dome-mae.

Opening Times

Peace Memorial Museum: Daily 0900-1800 (1 Apr-31 Jul and 16 Aug-30 Nov); daily 0900-1900 (1 Aug-15 Aug); daily 0900-1700 (1 Dec-31 Mar). Closed 29 Dec-2 Jan.

Admission Fees

Peace Memorial Museum: ¥50 (adult), ¥30 (child). Concessions available for groups and school-children.

Kinryuzan Senso-ji (Senso-ji Temple)

Tokyo's most revered temple, the *Senso-ji Temple*, has attracted visitors and pilgrims for over one thousand years. It was founded in AD 628 to enshrine a gold statuette of the *Kannon Bodhisattva* (the Goddess of Mercy) which, according to legend, was found by two local fishermen. Also known as *Asakusa Kannon* in Japan, the temple and its five-storey pagoda may today be a post-war concrete reconstruction, but nonetheless its precincts are always bustling with worshippers. A huge incense burner at the front of the temple is said to have curative healing powers, whilst the *Kaminarimon* (Thunder Gate), which guards the entrance to the temple, is one of Tokyo's most recognised sites and is famous for its enormous red paper lantern and guardian statues. There are also many Shinto shrines within the temple's grounds. The most celebrated of which is *Asakusa-jinja* (Asakusa Shrine), founded during the 17th century and dedicated to the two fishermen who originally discovered the Kannon statuette, whilst fishing in the Sumida River.

Contact Address

Kinryuzan Senso-ji, 2-3-1 Asakusa, Taito-ku, Tokyo 111-0032, Japan
Tel: (03) 3842 0181. Fax: (03) 3845 6933.

Transportation

Air: New Tokyo Narita International Airport, Haneda Airport (domestic flights). **Rail:** Train: Tokyo Station. Underground: Asakusa. **Road:** Bus: Asakusa Bus Stop. Car: Tomei-Meishin Expressway (from Kobe); Chuo Expressway (from Nagano and Nagoya).

Opening Times

Daily 24 hours.

Admission Fees

Free.

Meiji Jingu (Meiji Shrine)

Tokyo's *Meiji Shrine* is one of the holiest and most visited temples in the country. This Shinto shrine is dedicated to the Emperor Meiji, who was credited with opening Japan up to the outside world, and to his wife Empress Shoken. Built in 1920 following their deaths in 1912 and 1914 respectively, the original shrine burnt down during World War II, only to be rebuilt by 1958. Today, as well as the *Naihaiden* (Inner Shrine), which is home to the main shrine, visitors can also see the *Gehaiden*

(Outer Shrine), which was completed in 1926. Other highlights are the *Shinko* (Treasure Museum), which was built in 1921 and houses photos and personal belongings of the emperor and empress, and the large gates to the shrine, which are made from the Japanese Cypress, and said to be over 1700 years old. The *Jingu Neien* (Iris Garden), which is dedicated to the Empress, is considered to be one of the best in Japan, and is home to around 365 different species of trees, as well as around 100 varieties of irises.

Contact Address

Meiji Jingu, 1-1 Joyogi Kamizonocho, Shibuya-ku, Tokyo 151-8557, Japan
Tel: (03) 3379 5511. Website: www.meijijingu.or.jp

Transportation

Air: New Tokyo International Narita Airport, then Haneda Airport (domestic flights). **Rail:** Train: Harajku Station. Underground: Meiji-jingu-mae. **Road:** Bus: Meiji-jingu Station. Car: Tomei-Meishin expressway from Kobe (via Nagoya, Kyoto and Osaka); Tohoku expressway (from northern Japan); Chuo expressway (from Nagano and Nagoya).

Opening Times

Shrine: Daily dawn-dusk. *Treasure Museum*: Daily 0900-1630. Closed every third Friday of the month.

Admission Fees

Shrine: Free. *Treasure Museum*: ¥500 (adult), ¥250 (child).

Nijo-jo (Nijo Castle)

Nijo Castle was built in 1603 by Tokugawa Ieyasu, one of Japan's most powerful shoguns and founder of the Tokugawa Shogunate. The shoguns ruled Japan for a total of 700 years between the 13th and 19th centuries, with Tokugawa Ieyasu founding his dynasty in 1600. Built as a symbol of his power, the castle is filled with many fine works of art, including beautiful paintings of trees and animals by some of Japan's most famous artists of the period. The castle, set in stunning gardens in the old capital of Japan, Kyoto, was built almost entirely of Hinoki wood (Japanese Cypress). Key elements are the *Honmaru* (the main area surrounding the inner moat), originally known as *Katsura-no-miya Palace*, and the immense *Ninomaru Palace*. The latter comprises five buildings and 33 rooms and is modelled on nearby *Momoyama Castle*, which was built in 1594 by Toyotomi Hideyoshi.

Contact Address

Kyoto Tourist Information Center (TIC), First Floor, Kyoto Tower Building, Shichijo-Karasuma sagaru, Shimogyo-ku, Kyoto 600-8216, Japan
Tel: (075) 371 5649.

Transportation

Air: Kansai International Airport, then Kyoto Airport (domestic flights). **Rail:** Underground: Oike. Train: Kyoto Station. **Road:** Bus: 9, 12, 50, 52, 61 or 67 to Nijo-jo-mae stop.

Opening Times

Daily 0845-1600 (last admission).

Admission Fees

¥600 (adult), ¥300 (child).

Sanjusangen-do Temple

Completed in 1266, the *Sanjusangen-do Temple* which is officially called Rengeo-in Temple, is a faithful copy of an original that was built in 1164, but burned down in 1249. Originally built by Taira no Kiyomori for the emperor Go-Shirakawa, the temple is today a national treasure. It is best known for its wooden image of the *Thousand-Armed Kannon* (the Buddhist Goddess of Mercy), a masterpiece of the Kamakura period, which stands surrounded by 1000 smaller statues of the same goddess. The *hondo* (main building) is split into 33 *sanjusan* (bays) that exist between its many pillars to symbolise the 33 incarnations of Kannon, hence the name Sanjusangen-do Temple, which literally means '33 Bay Hall'.

Contact Address

Department of Industry and Tourism, Tourist Section, Kyoto City Government, Kyoto Kaikan, Okazaki, Sayo-ku, Kyoto, Japan
Tel: (075) 752 0215 (administration) *or* 525 0033 (Temple). Fax: (075) 561 6698 (Temple).
Website: raku.city.kyoto.jp/sight_e.phtml

Transportation

Air: Kansai International Airport, then Kyoto Airport (domestic flights). **Rail:** Train: Shichijo Station. **Road:** Bus: Sanjusangen-do stop. Car: Hiezan Driveway (from Imazu-cho); Meishin Expressway (from Osaka); Tomei Expressway or Meishin Expressway (from Nagoya).

Opening Times

Daily 0900-1600 (Nov-Mar); daily 0800-1700 (Mar-Oct).

Admission Fees

¥500 (adult), ¥250 (child). Concessions available.

Jordan

1 Al-bahr Al-mayyit (Dead Sea)
2 Petra

Tourist Information

Jordan Tourism Board
PO Box 830688, Amman 11183, Jordan
Tel: (06) 464 2311 *or* 464 2314. Fax: (06) 464 8465.
E-mail: jtb@nets.com.jo
Website: www.see-jordan.com

Jordan Tourism Board
Brighter PR, Lee House, Second Floor, 109 Hammersmith Road, London W14 0QH, UK
Tel: (020) 7371 6496. Fax: (020) 7603 2424.
E-mail: info@jordantourismboard.co.uk
Website: www.see-jordan.com

Al-bahr Al-mayyit (Dead Sea)

Lying 400m (1320ft) below sea level and spanning the border between Israel and Jordan, the *Dead Sea* is a natural wonder. It contains more minerals and salt than any other stretch of water in the world, and thus it really is possible to float on top of the water. Its natural properties make it a prime centre for spa treatments and relaxation therapies and there are four resorts in the area: the *Movenpick Dead Sea*, the *Movenpick Zara Spa*, the *Dead Sea Spa Hotel* and the *Dead Sea Rest House*. There are also several interesting sites around the Dead Sea, including *Bethany*, where it is believed Jesus was baptized, and *Lot's Cave*, where the prophet Lot lived after his village was destroyed by two angels sent by God. Although the Dead Sea itself is true to its name and sustains no life, the *Wadi Mujib Nature Reserve* on the eastern shores is a beautifully preserved area of mountains and rivers, providing a natural habitat for eagles, vultures, wolves and the endangered Nubian ibex, a large mountain goat. There are many hiking trails within the reserve.

Contact Address

For more information on the Dead Sea, contact the Jordan Tourism Board (see **Tourist Information** above).

Transportation

Air: Queen Alia International Airport. **Road:** Taxi: There are many taxi services covering the 55-kilometre (34-mile) route from Amman to the Dead Sea. Car: Desert Highway (from Amman).

Opening Times

Daily 24 hours.

Admission Fees

Free.

Petra

Jordan's best-known tourist attraction, *Petra*, is one of the great wonders of the Middle Eastern world – a city that was carved straight into solid rock. That it unfolds grandly after a two kilometre (1.2 mile) walk through a very narrow chasm only adds to its mystery and grandeur. Built during the fifth and sixth centuries BC, Petra is the ruined capital of the Nabatean Arabs. Its immense façades were lost for almost 1000 years, however, until rediscovered by the Swiss traveller Johan Ludwig Burckhardt in 1812. Today, there are still many sites to see including the *el Khazneh* (The Treasury) monument, which is a giant tomb carved out of rock, the *Temple of the Winged Lions,* the *al-Deir* (Monastery) and the small *Archaeological Museum*, which displays artefacts found at Petra during the 19th and 20th centuries.

Contact Address

For more information on Petra, contact the Jordan Tourism Board (see **Tourist Information** above).

Transportation

Air: Queen Alia International Airport. **Road:** Coach: Abdali Bus Station or Wahdat Bus Station. Car: Desert Highway or King's Highway (from Amman).

Opening Times

Petra: Daily 0600-1800. *Visitors' Centre*: Daily 0700-1600 (winter); daily 0700-1700 (summer). *Archaeological Museum*: Daily 0800-1600.

Admission Fees

Petra: JD20 (one-day pass, including entry to all sites). *Visitors' Centre*: Free. *Archaeological Museum*: Free.

Petra

Jordan Tourism Board

Kenya

1 Amboseli National Park
2 Maasai Mara National Reserve
3 Mount Kenya National Park

Tourist Information

Kenya Tourist Board
PO Box 30630, Nairobi, Kenya
Tel: (02) 724 042/4. Fax: (02) 724 169.
E-mail: ktb@form-net.com
Website: www.kenyatourism.org

Kenya National Tourist Office
25 Brook's Mews, Davies Street, Mayfair, London W1K 4DD, UK
Tel: (020) 7355 3144. Fax: (020) 7495 8656.

Amboseli National Park

Amboseli National Park extends across 392 sq kilometres (151 sq miles) of grassland and swamps at the foot of *Mount Kilimanjaro*, Africa's highest peak. It was designated a national park in 1974 and, despite suffering floods in 1993 which caused many of the animals to retreat, it remains one of Africa's best known game spotting locations, with viewing possibilities including baboons, lions, cheetah, black rhino, wildebeest, hippos and gazelles. The predominant animals in Amboseli, however, are the 1000 elephants, each of which are known to the park wardens by name, age and gender. As well as game-viewing, hiking and camping, bird-watching and camel safaris are also popular and visitors can learn about the culture and way of life of the indigenous Masai population, through homestead visits and lectures. More adventurous travellers can arrange to climb Mount Kilimanjaro with a local guide.

Contact Address

Senior Warden, Amboseli National Park, PO Box 18 Namanga, Amboseli, Kenya
Tel: (0302) 22251. Fax: (0302) 22250.
E-mail: kws@kws.org
Website: www.kws.org/amboseli

Transportation

Air: Jomo Kenyatta International Airport. **Road:** Coach: Many tour operators provide transport to Amboseli. Car: Via the towns of Namanga and Emali (from Nairobi); via Emali (from Mombasa).

Opening Times

Daily 0630-1830.

Admission Fees

US$27 (adult), US$10 (child 3-18).

Maasai Mara National Reserve

Opened in 1974, the *Maasai Mara National Reserve* is the most popular game park in Kenya. Managed by the Maasai tribe, the area is named after this group of people who first migrated to South Kenya from the Nile Valley in the mid-17th century. The Maasai herdsmen are nomadic people who do not believe in the concept of land ownership and choose instead to live in harmony with the wildlife grazing in the area. The reserve, which occupies a 320-sq-km

(124-sq-mile) chunk of the famous Serengeti plains, is inhabited by many of Africa's most popular wild animals, including lions, cheetahs, elephants, leopards, black rhinos and hippos. There are also over 500 resident birds in the park including ostrich, lark and sunbird. The area is famous for rolling grassland and for the Mara River, which runs through the reserve from North to South. It is also the place for one of Nature's best spectacles – the annual migration from the dry plains of Tanzania of thousands of wildebeest crossing crocodile-infested waters in order to reach more fertile grazing.

Contact Address

Maasai Mara National Reserve, PO Box 19, Narok, Kenya
Tel: (0305) 2220 *or* 2246. Fax: (0305) 2260.

Transportation

Air: Jomo Kenyatta International Airport. **Rail:** Train: Naivasha Station (from Nairobi Station); visitors must then travel by road into the Maasai Mara. **Road:** Bus: Private tour operators run safaris into the Maasai Mara National Reserve (from Nairobi and Lake Nakura). Car: Road to Mai Mahiu, Narok and Ewaso Nyiro (from Nairobi).

Opening Times

Daily 0600-1800 (last entry at 1800).

Admission Fees

KSh1751 (adult), KSh649 (child 3-18), free (child under 3).

Mount Kenya National Park

Mount Kenya, which is an extinct volcano sitting on the Equator, is Africa's second highest mountain and stands at a height of 5199m (17,058ft). Opened as the *Mount Kenya National Park* in 1949, the mountain, with its gleaming snowy-white peaks, has been revered by local inhabitants for generations. It was first sighted by an outsider in 1849 – the missionary Johann Ludwig Krapf – although the idea that there could be snow on the Equator was not believed until the British geographer Halford John Mackinder reached the summit in 1899. The park itself, which covers an area of 600 sq km (232 sq miles), offers exotic mountain scenery, starting with upland forest near the bottom and progressing to mountain forest, bamboo forests and glacier peaks. A wide variety of wildlife inhabits the park, some unique to it, including Sykes and Colobus monkeys, buffaloes, elephants, black rhinos, leopards, Bongo antelopes and giant forest hogs. It is also home to many species of birds such as the giant kingfisher, olive pigeons and red-fronted parrots.

Contact Address

Kenya Wildlife Service, PO Box 40241, Nairobi, Kenya
Tel: (02) 501 081 *or* 501 082. Fax: (02) 505 866.
E-mail: kws@africaonline.co.ke
Website: www.mountkenya.com

Transportation

Air: Jomo Kenyatta International Airport or Wilson Airport. **Rail:** Train: Thika Station. **Road:** Bus: Services to Nanyuki (from Nairobi). Car: A2 heads northwest from Nairobi, by-passing Murunga, before heading west around the base of Mount Kenya to Nanyuki.

Opening Times

Daily 0600-1830.

Admission Fees

Non-residents of Kenya: KSh973 (adult), KSh324 (child aged 3-18), free (child under 3). Residents of Kenya: KSh100 (adult), KSh50 (child aged 3-18), free (child under 3).

Giraffe in Maasai Mara

Kenyan Tourist Board

Republic of Korea

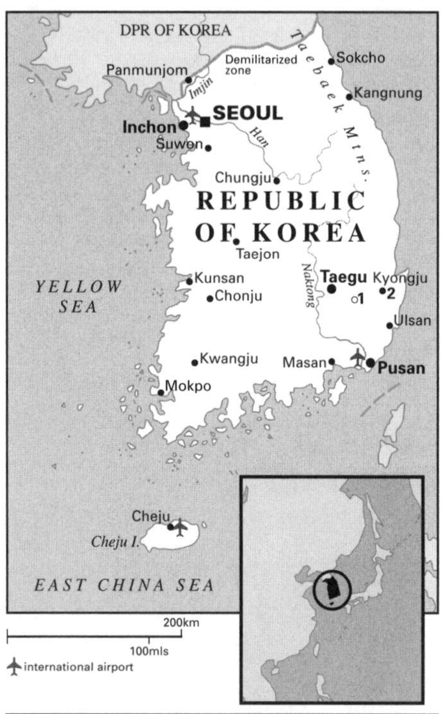

1	Haeinsa Temple
2	Kyongju

Need more information on Korea?
Consult the *World Travel Guide*

Tourist Information

Hangook Kwankwong Kongsa (Korea National Tourism Organisation – KNTO)
10 Ta-dong, Chung-gu, Seoul 100-180, Republic of Korea
Tel: (02) 729 9600. Fax: (02) 757 5997.
E-mail: webmaster@www.knto.or.kr
Website: www.visitkorea.or.kr

Korea National Tourism Organisation (KNTO)
8th Floor, New Zealand House, Haymarket, London SW1Y 4TE, UK
Tel: (020) 7321 2535. Fax: (020) 7321 0876.
E-mail: koreatb@dircon.co.uk
Website: www.visitkorea.co.uk

Haeinsa Temple

Haeinsa Temple was originally built in AD 802 by two monks, Sunung and Ijong, during King Aejang of the Silla Kingdom's reign. Despite many fires and subsequent reconstructions, the temple remains one of the most beautiful in Korea, due to its idyllic location deep in Gayasan National Park. It eventually reached its present-day size during the mid-tenth century. The temple is famous for housing the *Tripitaka Koreana* – 80,000 wooden printing blocks carved during the Koryo Dynasty (AD 918-1392), which, together, make up the oldest and best-preserved collection of Buddhist scriptures in the world. The first set of blocks were completed in 1087, although this set was lost in a fire during the Mongol invasion of Korea in 1232. The blocks on display today were carved in the 13th century to replace the earlier set and were moved from Chich'on-sa in Seoul to the remote temple at Haeinsa in 1398, due to fears that they might be stolen by Japanese sea robbers. As well as Tripitaka Koreana, the temple houses a great number of artefacts that have been designated national treasures including the *Seated Stone Buddha*, found at *Cheongyangsa Temple*, and the *Stone Pagoda* at *Wolgwang Temple*.

Contact Address

Haeinsa Temple, Information Office, Republic of Korea
Tel: (055) 933 8637.

Transportation

Air: Seoul Kimpo International Airport. **Road:** Bus: Local buses to Haeinsa Temple (from Daego Seobu Bus Terminal) (journey time: 70 minutes); (from Hapcheon Bus Terminal) (journey time: 60 minutes); (from Jinju Bus Terminal) (journey time: 2 hours 30 minutes). Car: 88 Expressway to Haeinsa Temple (from Seoul).

Opening Times

Daily 0800-1730 (winter); daily 0800-1800 (summer). Opening hours may vary. Admission to the Tripitaka Koreana is generally upon request only.

Admission Fees

W2800 (adult), W900 (child).

Kyongju

The city of *Kyongju* was once one of the six largest cities in the world and the capital of the Shilla

Kingdom, which existed between 57 BC and AD 935. Known today as the 'museum without walls' and often spelt *Gyeongju*, the city houses numerous historical sites and relics, and is one of the most important ancient cities in the world, attracting around eight million visitors every year. The city has many royal tombs, museums, temples and monuments and houses an impressive collection of relics from the Shilla period in the *Kyongju National Museum*. Highlights include artefacts found in the *Kumgwanchiong* and *Ch'onmach'ong* tombs, which are considered to be among the finest in the world, as well as the *Sokkuram Grotto* and *Pulguska Temple*, which both feature on the UNESCO World Heritage List. *Sokkuram Grotto's* main feature is an enormous granite Buddha, whilst *Pulguska Temple* is one of the most impressive Buddhist temples in Korea.

Contact Address

For more information on Kyongju, contact the Korea National Tourism Organisation (see **Tourist Information** above).

Transportation

Air: Seoul Kimpo International Airport. Internal flights are available to Pusan, Ulsan and Taegu airports. Shuttle buses operate from these airports to Kyongju. **Rail:** Train: Kyongju (Gyeongju) Station. **Road:** Bus: Services to Kyongju Express Bus Terminal (from Seoul, Taejon, Taegu, Pusan and Kwangju). Once in Kyongju, there are regular buses and coaches which serve most areas of the city. Taxis: Taxis can be hailed in the street.

Opening Times

Daily 0900-1800, although some sites are open longer. Opening times vary according to the time of year and attraction visited.

Admission Fees

Pulguska Temple: W3000 (adult), W1500 (child). *Sokkuram Grotto*: W3000 (adult), W1500 (child). *Bunhwangsa Temple*: W1000 (adult), W600 (child). *Girimsa Temple*: W2000 (adult), W1000 (child). *Kyongju National Museum*: W400 (adult), free (child).

Kyongju Pulguska Temple

Korea National Tourism Organisation

Lebanon

1 Jeita Grotto
2 Tyre

Tourist Information

Wzart al Siaha (Ministry of Tourism)
PO Box 11-5344, Beirut, Lebanon
Tel: (01) 340 9404. Fax: (01) 343 279.
E-mail: mot@Lebanon-Tourism.gov.lb
Website: www.lebanon-tourism.gov.lb
Embassy of the Republic of Lebanon
15 Palace Gardens Mews, London W8 4RA, UK
Tel: (020) 7727 6696 *or* 7229 7265 (consular section). Fax: (020) 7243 1699.
E-mail: emb.leb@btinternet.com

Jeita Grotto

Jeita Grotto is one of the most impressive underground caverns in the world. Situated under Mount Lebanon in the *Nahr el Kalb (Dog River) Valley*, these caves, which have been known to man since Paleolithic times, consist of a lower and upper gallery. The caves were discovered by the American missionary Reverend William Thomson in 1836, who ventured 50 metres (164ft) underground; in 1873, engineers working for the Beirut Water Company explored a further 1000 metres (3281ft) into the caves. Between 1873 and 1940, there were further excavations by English, American and French explorers to discover the full extent of the caves. Today, visitors can explore the 6200-metre deep (20,341ft) lower gallery by boat, whilst the upper gallery, which was not discovered until 1958, can be visited on foot by travelling down a 120-metre (394ft) tunnel to see this 650-metre (2133ft) long cavern. There are numerous multicoloured stalactites and stalagmites, and a huge underground lake in what is one of the world's most impressive natural wonders.

Contact Address

For more information on Jeita Grotto, contact the Ministry of Tourism (see **Tourist Information** above).

Transportation

Air: Beirut International Airport. **Road:** Coach: Many tourists visit the sites as part of an organised tour. Taxi: Taxis can be hired in Beirut to take visitors to the site.

Opening Times

Tues-Thurs 0900-1800, Fri-Sun 0900-1900. Closed Mon, unless a public holiday.

Admission Fees

L£16,500 (adult), L£9,250 (student), free (child).

Tyre

Often referred to in the Bible's New Testament, *Tyre* was founded at the start of the third millennium BC and originally consisted of a city on the mainland, as well as a settlement offshore on a small island. The city experienced a golden age during the first millennium BC when Hiram, King of Tyre, joined the two areas and extended the city. It was also an important port, primarily trading in purple dye, which was extracted from the Murex marine snail, as well as glass and cedar wood, which brought much prosperity and power to the ancient city. Tyre later suffered at the hands of its jealous enemies, with Nebuchadnezzar, King of Babylon, laying seige to the city during the 6th century BC, and Alexander the Great partly destroying the city in 332 BC, and either butchering or selling into slavery the city's 30,000 residents. Tyre eventually fell under Roman rule in 64 BC and during Roman Occupation, an acqueduct, triumphal arch and hippodrome were built; the hippodrome, which was only excavated in 1967, was the largest of its kind in ancient antiquity. Still standing today are: the impressive 480 metre (131ft) hippodrome, which once seated up to 20,000 spectators, the remains of a cathedral built during the Crusades and the necropolis, which was built between the second and sixth centuries AD. Other highlights found at Tyre today include the first Phoenician cemetery to be discovered in the Lebanon, which was unearthed in 1991, as well as many fine colonnades and mosaics, and excavations from Hellenic, Roman and Byzantine periods. Tyre was declared a UNESCO World Heritage Site in 1979 and is one of finest examples of architecture from the ancient world.

Contact Address

For more information on Tyre, contact the Ministry of Tourism (**see Tourist Information** above).

Transportation

Air: Beirut International Airport. **Road:** Coach: Many tourists visit the sites as part of an organised tour. Taxi: Taxis can be hired in Beirut to take visitors to the site.

Opening Times

Daily 0900-1800.

Admission Fees

L£6000 (adult), L£1000 (student), free (child).

Marble sarcaphogus, Tyre

Ministry of Tourism of Lebanon

Malawi

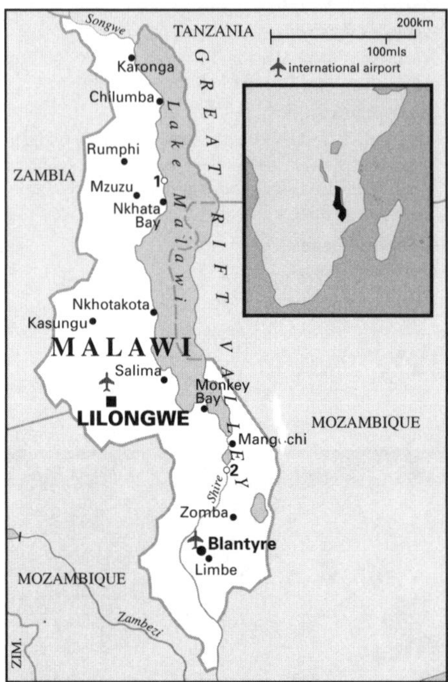

1 Lake Malawi National Park
2 Liwonde National Park

Tourist Information

Malawi Department of Tourism
PO Box 402, Downs House, Blantyre, Malawi
Tel: 620 300. Fax: 620 947 *or* 621 923.
E-mail: enquiries@malawitourism.com
Website: www.malawitourism.com

Ministry of Tourism, Parks and Wildlife
P/Bag 326, Lilongwe 3, Malawi
Tel: 771 073 *or* 771 295. Fax: 770 650.

Malawi Tourist Office
33 Grosvenor Street, London W1X 0DE, UK
Tel: (020) 7491 4172. Fax: 7491 9916. E-mail: tourism@malawihighcomm.prestel.co.uk

Lake Malawi National Park

Lake Malawi National Park was created in 1980 as the world's first freshwater national park. It is centred around *Lake Malawi*, Africa's third largest lake, which stretches for 600km (373 miles) and forms a natural border between Malawi, Tanzania and Mozambique. The park encompasses a wide variety of scenery, ranging from the wooded rocky mountains sloping down to the shores of the lake, to sandy coves and beaches. The lush vegetation is home to baboons, monkeys and antelope, although the park is primarily known for the many species of bird and fish it contains. Birds found in the park include terns, fish eagles, black eagles, and kingfishers. The lake itself protects an extraordinarily high diversity of fish species, most of which are brightly-coloured cichlids – freshwater fish found in tropical climates – and the clear blue waters of the lake are popular for snorkelling and scuba diving, as well as sailing, kayaking and swimming. Within the park, visitors can stay at lodges to enjoy traditional Malawian hospitality and fresh fish from the lake.

Contact Address

Malawi Tourism Information Service, c/o Geo Group & Associates, 4 Christian Fields, London SW16 3JZ, UK
Tel: (0115) 982 1903. Fax: (0115) 981 9418.
E-mail: enquiries@malawitourism.com
Website: www.malawitourism.com

Transportation

Air: Lilongwe Airport. **Road:** Car: Direct from Lilongwe. Many tour operators provide transport to Lake Malawi National Park.

Opening Times

Daily 0600-1800.

Admission Fees

US$5.

Liwonde National Park

Liwonde National Park is generally regarded as the best game reserve in Malawi, due to its unspoilt environment. It covers 550 sq kilometres (212 sq miles) of mopane and savanna woodland on the floodplains of the *River Shire* and *Lake Malombe* in the south of the country. The park provides a natural habitat for a wide variety of wildlife. Large herds of elephant and hippopotamus bathe in the waters of the river; the most promising viewing times are early in the morning or at dusk. Other animals include crocodile, antelope, zebra, warthogs, bushbuck and sable, solitary fox-like creatures that feed on small animals and eggs. Leopard can be seen on night-viewing game safaris, and lucky visitors may even spot one of the few lions that come into the eastern areas of the park from Mozambique. The river plains are home to many species of bird, including white-breasted cormorant, palmnut vulture, paradise flycatcher and Malawi's only population of Lilian's lovebird. Plants and trees found in Liwonde National Park include the baobab, a large native African tree bearing a gourd-like fruit with a delicious pulp, and the impala lily which has star-shaped flowers. There has been great emphasis in recent years on reintroducing many species of mammal, such as black rhino, to the park and although the number of visitors has steadily increased as a result, the park is still relatively peaceful and uncommercialised. Activities on offer in Liwonde include game watching (from boats, four-wheel drive vehicles or by foot), birdwatching tours or simply relaxing by the River Shire.

Contact Address

Central African Wilderness Safaris, PO Box 489, Lilongwe, Malawi
Tel: 771 153. Fax: 771 397.
E-mail: info@wilderness.malawi.net
Website: www.wilderness-safarismalawi.com

Transportation

Air: Lilongwe Airport. **Road:** Car: Direct from Lilongwe. Many tour operators provide transport to Liwonde National Park.

Opening Times

Daily 0600-1800.

Admission Fees

US$5.

Lake Malawi Beach, Cape Maclear

Geoslides Photography

Malaysia

1 Gua Batu (Batu Caves)
2 Menara Kembar Petronas (Petronas Towers)

Tourist Information

Tourism Malaysia

17th floor, Menara Dato' Onn, Putra World Trade Centre, 45 Jalan Tun Ismail, 50480 Kuala Lumpur, Malaysia

Tel: (03) 293 5188.

Fax: (03) 293 5884 *or* 2693 0207.

E-mail: tourism@tourism.gov.my

Website: www.tourism.gov.my

Tourism Malaysia

Malaysia House, 57 Trafalgar Square, London WC2N 5DU, UK

Tel: (020) 7930 7932. Fax: (020) 7930 9015.

E-mail: mpb.london@tourism.gov.my

Website: www.tourism.gov.my

Gua Batu (Batu Caves)

Since their discovery just over 100 years ago, the *Batu Caves* have consistently attracted visitors and are now considered one of Kuala Lumpur's most visited sites. Located in an area of outstanding beauty, the caves contain stalactites and stalagmites, and impressive fauna and flora. There are three main caves and numerous smaller ones, the most famous of all being the *Temple Cave*. Accessible only by a climb of 272 steps, the Temple Cave is a large cavern with a vaulted 100m-high (328ft) ceiling. Below it is the *Dark Cave*, a vast network of untouched caverns inhabited by several indigenous species of animals. Discovered by the American explorer William Hornaby in 1878, the Batu Caves are also an important Hindu shrine, attracting as many as 80,000 devotees during the holy festival of Thaipusam which takes place in January or February every year.

Contact Address

For more information on Batu Caves, contact Tourism Malaysia (see **Tourist Information** above).

Transportation

Air: Kuala Lumpur International Airport, then Sultan Abdul Aziz Shah Airport (domestic flights). **Rail:** Train: Kuala Lumpur Station. **Road:** Coach: Pudu Raya Bus Terminal. Bus: 11 or 11D (from Bangkok Bank bus stand in Kuala Lumpur.) Car: Kuching Road towards Selayang (Batu Caves are signposted just before the Selayang interchange, if driving from the south); North-South Highway, exit at Rawang Interchange, then after the Selayang wet market, left turn towards Karak Highway, where the Batu Caves can be found on the left (from Ipoh).

Opening Times

Daily 0600-2100.

Admission Fees

Free.

Menara Kembar Petronas (Petronas Towers)

Standing 452m (1483ft) tall, the 88-storey *Petronas Towers* in Kuala Lumpur is the tallest building in the world, taller than the second-placed Sears Tower in Chicago (USA) which measures 442m (1450ft). The towers are owned by Midciti Resources Sdn Bhd and are located on the northeast corner of the 100 acre (40 hectare) Kuala Lumpur City Centre development which also includes a 29 acre (20 hectare) park designed by the architect Roberto Burle Marx, a retail complex and an entertainment centre. Completed in 1997 and designed by Cesar Pelli & Associates, the building consists of two similarly shaped towers joined by a 58m (192ft) *Skybridge* on the 41st and 42nd floors. The building's design is based on geometric principles typical of Islamic architecture, with each floor plan based on an eight-point star. The historically referential design and sheer size of the towers are symbolic of Malaysia's emerging importance as a commercial and cultural centre.

Contact Address

For more information on Petronas Towers, contact

Tourism Malaysia (see **Tourist Information** above).

Transportation

Air: Kuala Lumpur International Airport, then Sultan Abdul Aziz Shah Airport (domestic flights). **Rail:** Train: Kuala Lumpur Central Station or PUTRA light rail transit to KLCC. **Road:** Bus: 176, 178, 183 or 185 (from Jalan Hang Lekiu bus stop). Car: North–South Expressway Central Link (NSCEL), Federal Highway, Shal Alam Expressway and Klang Valley Expressway Highway all lead into Kuala Lumpur (from the surrounding area). Visitors should follow signs for KLCC (Kuala Lumpur City Centre).

Opening Times

Mon-Sat 1000-1600.

Admission Fees

Free.

Petronas Towers

Tourism Malaysia

Malta

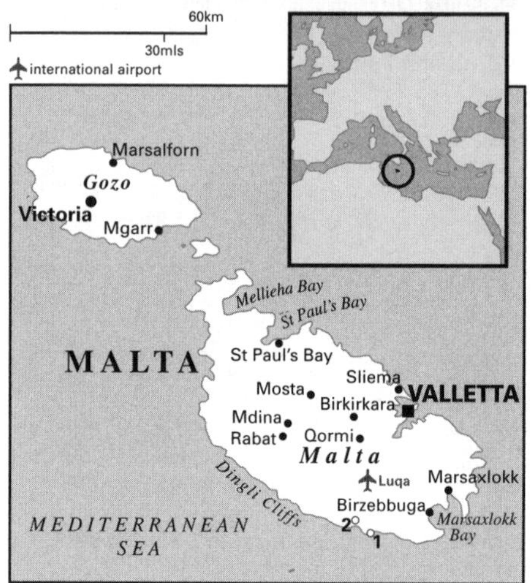

1	Hagar Qim
2	Il-Hnejja (Blue Grotto)

Tourist Information

Malta Tourism Authority
280 Republic Street, Valletta CMR 02, Malta
Tel: 224 444/5. Fax: 220 401.
E-mail: info@visitmalta.com
Website: www.visitmalta.com

Malta Tourism Authority
Malta House, 36-38 Piccadilly, London W1J 0LD, UK
Tel: (020) 7292 4900. Fax: (020) 7734 1880.
E-mail: office.uk@visitmalta.com
Website: www.visitmalta.com

Hagar Qim

Discovered under a mound of rubble in 1839, the Neolithic temples of *Hagar Qim*, which date from 300 BC, are some of the oldest human structures in the world. Reminiscent of England's Stonehenge, the temples are built of limestone rock, some towering six metres (20ft) high, and weighing several tonnes. The complex is an impressive maze of corridors, chambers, niches and altars, all carved out of stone using flint. On the morning of the summer solstice, sunlight passes through a hole known as the 'oracle hole' and fills the apse of the temple. The nearby *Mnajdra* temples are also breathtaking and are included, along with the Hagar Qim, the *Tarxien*, *Ta'Hagrat*, *Skorba* and *Ggantija* temple complexes, on the UNESCO World Heritage List.

Contact Address

Hagar Qim, Director, Museum of Archaeology, Auberge de Provence, Valetta, Malta
Tel: 221 623 *or* 239 545. Fax: 243 628.

Transportation

Air: Malta International Airport. **Road:** Bus: 32, 34 or 38 (from Valletta). Car: Road towards Wied Zurreieq (from Valletta).

Opening Times

Mon-Sat 0815-1700, Sun 0815-1615 (Oct-15 Jun); daily 0745-1400 (16 Jun-Sep).

Admission Fees

Lm1.00 (adult), Lm0.25 (child). Free admission on Sunday.

Il-Hnejja (Blue Grotto)

The *Blue Grotto* is the most famous cave in Malta, with its deep waters displaying magnificent dazzling colours, ranging from turquoise to deep blue. Situated near the village of Zurreiq in southwestern Malta, which is famous for its rocky coastline, the waters around the limestone caves and archways are said to be at their most impressive in the early morning when the sun's rays glimmer through the opening to the grotto. The cave, which is known as *Il-Hnejja*, meaning 'The Arch', in Maltese, was given its English name by British soldiers who thought that its blue waters resembled the *Grotta Azzurra* (Blue Grotto) in Capri. To get to the grotto, visitors travel by boat, passing under a massive arch, deep into the 43m-high (140ft) cave which is hollowed out of the cliff rockface.

Contact Address

For more information on the Blue Grotto, contact Malta Tourism Authority (see **Tourist Information** above).

Transportation

Air: Malta International Airport. **Water:** Boat: Boats depart from Wied iz-Zurrieq for the Blue Grotto. **Road:** Bus: 38 (from Valletta). Car: Road to Zurrieq (from Valletta). The Blue Grotto is situated off the southern coast, near Wied iz-Zurrieq and 2.5km (1.6 miles) from Zurrieq.

Opening Times

Daily 24 hours.

Admission Fees

Free.

Mexico

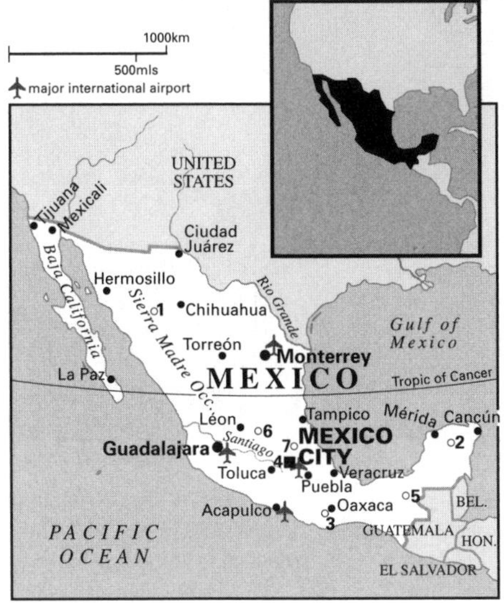

1 Barrancas del Cobre (Copper Canyon)
2 Chichén Itzá
3 Monte Alban (White Mountain)
4 Museo Nacional de Antropologia (National Museum of Anthropology)
5 Palenque
6 Parroquia (San Miguel de Allende Parish Church)
7 Teotihuacán

Tourist Information

Secretaria de Turismo (Ministry of Tourism — SECTUR)
Presidente Mazaryck 172, Colonia Polanco, 11570 México DF, Mexico
Tel: (05) 254 8920 (marketing).
Fax: (05) 254 0942 (marketing).
Website: www.mexico-travel.com

Mexican Tourism Promotion Board
Wakefield House, 41 Trinity Square, London EC3N 4DT, UK
Tel: (020) 7488 9392. Fax: (020) 7265 0704.
E-mail: info@mexicotravel.co.uk
Website: www.mexicotravel.co.uk

Barrancas del Cobre (Copper Canyon)

One of the largest canyon systems in the world, *Copper Canyon* is a land of mountains, rivers, waterfalls, desert and forest. Four of the canyons are deeper than Arizona's famous *Grand Canyon*, although none of them are as wide. Perhaps the most famous attraction for visitors is the *Chihuahua al Pacífico Railway*, a scenic journey that crosses 36 major bridges, travels through 87 tunnels and climbs to a height of 2438m (8000ft) before descending back down to sea level. The *Sierra Tarahumara* mountains are inhabited by Tarahumara Indians, who live in isolated communities along the railway line.

Contact Address

For more information on the Copper Canyon, contact the Secretaria de Turismo (see **Tourist Information** above).

Transportation

Air: Mexico City International Airport, then Los Mochis Airport or Chihuahua Airport. **Rail:** Train: Copper Canyon Railway to Creel (from Los Mochis or Chihuahua City). **Road:** Coach: Services to Creel (from Chihuahua City). Car: Hwy-16 to Creel (from Chihuahua City).

Opening Times

Daily 24 hours.

Admission Fees

Free.

Chichén Itzá

Located deep within the jungles of Yucatán, 193km (120 miles) west of Cancún, lies *Chichén Itzá*, one of the most impressive sites of the mysterious Mayan civilisation. Meaning 'Mouth of the Itzas's well' in the Mayan language, Chichén Itzá is believed to have reached its peak in around 600 to 900 BC. It was the site of countless human sacrifices and flourished until about the year 1200, when it was suddenly abandoned. Today, the old road between Cancún and Mérida cuts through the middle of the site, creating two separate ruins, *Chichén Viejo* and *Chichén Nuevo*, which together form the most intact ruins from the Mayan period. Highlights at the complex, which covers an area of approximately 15

Toltec Pyramid of Quetzalcoatl, Chichén Itzá

sq km (6 sq miles), include the *Kukulcán Pyramid* (also known as the Castle), the *Ball Court* (the largest Mayan ball court ever discovered), the *Thousand Columns* and the *Tzompantli*.

Contact Address

For more information on Chichén Itzá, contact the Secretaria de Turismo (see **Tourist Information** above).

Transportation

Air: Mexico City International Airport, then Mérida Airport. **Road:** Coach: Services from Cancún or Mérida. Car: Highway (Autopista) from Cancún or Mérida.

Opening Times

Site: Daily 0800-1700. *Sound and Light Show*: Daily 2000.

Admission Fees

Site and *Sound and Light Show*: US$8. Free Sun and public holidays. *Sound and Light Show* only: US$4.

Monte Alban (White Mountain)

Another of Mexico's famous ancient ruins, *Monte Alban* was at one time home to 50,000 Zapotec people. The builders of Monte Alban artificially levelled the top of the mountain, which overshadows the three surrounding valleys of Oaxaca. The site emerged as a political centre in around 400 BC, and later developed as an important cultural centre between 500 BC to AD 700. The site was abandoned by the Zapotecs when they began to lose political power, which resulted in conflict between them and the Mixtecs, who moved into the Valley and used it as a burial ground. It was later invaded by the Aztecs and then by the Spanish who gave the site the name Monte Alban, meaning White Mountain, due to the white flowering trees that grow in the area. Key features include a *Zapotec Ball Court*, a *Palace*, the *Monumento de los Danzantes* (The Dancers) monument – which depicts naked human figures believed to be dancers – and the *Observatory*; it is also home to a labyrinth of tunnels and tombs, and a prominent central plaza.

Contact Address

Monte Alban, Office of Administration, Archaeological Site, Pino Suarez 715, Centro, CP 68000, Mexico
Tel: (09) 516 1215.
E-mail: montealban@spersaoaxaca.com.mx
Website: www.montealban.org.mx

Transportation

Air: Mexico City International Airport. **Road:** Coach: Shuttle services from Oaxaca. Car: Access from Oaxaca.

Opening Times

Daily 0800-1800.

Admission Fees

peso35 (adult), free (child under 13 and on Sun), peso30 (charge for videocamera).

Museo Nacional de Antropología (National Museum of Anthropology)

Mexico's *National Museum of Anthropology* is one of the world's great museums, known not only for its vast and rich collection, but also for its simplicity of design. Opened in 1964, the exhibition halls surround a shallow pond shaded by a square concrete umbrella, which is in turn supported by a single pillar. The halls themselves house Mexico's greatest archaeological collection, celebrating the country's pre-Columbian inhabitants and its existing indigenous peoples. As it is impossible to cover the whole museum at once, it is more rewarding to limit a visit to a few areas of particular interest. Some of the most fascinating rooms are the *Mexica*, which showcases Aztec culture, the *Maya* hall, and the *Teotihuacán* hall. The *Sala de Orientación* provides an overall view of the main Mexican cultures through an audiovisual presentation, and there are also rooms devoted to recent archaeological discoveries.

Contact Address

Museo Nacional de Antropología, Paseo de la Reforma, Chapultepec Park, Mexico City, Mexico Tel: (05) 553 1902. Fax: (05) 5286 1791.

Transportation

Air: Mexico City International Airport. **Rail:** Underground: Auditorio. **Road:** Car: 57/57D (from the north); 95D (from the south); 150D (from the east); 45D (from the west).

Opening Times

Tues-Sun 0900-1700.

Admission Fees

US$3 (adult), US$1.50 (child 12-18), free (child under 12); free Sun and public holidays.

Palenque

Located in *Palenque National Park* in the northern Chiapas highlands, *Palenque* is one of the grandest of all classical Mayan sites. Situated on a ledge picturesquely overlooking swampy plains to the north, and set against a backdrop of lush, green mountains, Palenque was in its prime between AD 500-700. Visitors can wander from one structure to another amongst waterfalls and jungle, taking in the marvels of this ancient settlement, which is all the more remarkable for having been constructed without the aid of metal tools, the wheel or pack animals. The most notable structures are the *Palace* and the *Temple of Inscriptions* pyramid crypt, which are decorated with reliefs detailing scenes from Mayan mythology. The site has yielded countless archaeological finds, and its broad, angular design has influenced various periods of architecture.

Contact Address

For more information on Palenque, contact the Secretaria de Turismo (see **Tourist Information** above).

Transportation

Air: Mexico City International Airport, then Villa Hermosa Airport (domestic flights). **Road:** Coach: Services from Palenque. Car: Main road (from Villa Hermosa or Tuxtla Gutierriz).

Opening Times

Tues-Sun 0800-1730.

Admission Fees

peso30 (adult), peso15 (child). Free Sun.

Parroquia (San Miguel de Allende Parish Church)

La Parroquia, a pink, Gothic parish church, is one of San Miguel de Allende's most famous landmarks as well as one of the finest examples of colonial architecture in Mexico. Standing in the city's main square *(El Jardin)*, the church was originally built in 1683 by the architect Marco Anotinio Sobrarias, but was given a facelift in 1880 by the local artisan, Zeferino Guitierrez. He modelled the church on French cathedrals he had seen on postcards and built a striking, parish church, with tall spires dominating the central plaza and soaring high above the city's skyline. The crypt underneath the main altar contains the remains of Felipe Gonzalez and General Anastasio Bustamante, both of whom were heroes of the Mexican War of Independence (1810-1821) against Spain. There is also a sculpture of Ignacio Allende, who is the city's namesake, displayed on the main altar; he was born in San Miguel in 1779 and became a leader and martyr during the Mexican independence movement, prior to his execution in 1811. San Miguel de Allende, which was declared a national monument in 1926, boasts many other fine buildings and colonial mansions; these include *Iglesia de San Francisco* (San Francisco Church), *El Oratorio de San Felipe Neri* (Oratorio of St Philip Neri) and *Iglesia de Nuestra Señora de la Salud* (Church of Our Lady of Health).

Corel

National Museum of Anthropology

Contact Address

Secretaria de Turismo (SECTUR), San Miguel de Allende, Guanajuato, Mexico
Tel: (0415) 20900. E-mail: turisma@mpsnet.com.mx
Website: www.sanmigueldeallende.gob.mx

Transportation

Air: Mexico City International Airport or Leon/Guanajuato International Airport. **Road:** Bus: Transfers are available to San Miguel de Allende (from Mexico City International Airport). Buses also run from Mexico City (journey time: 4 hours), Querétaro (journey time: 3 hours) and Guanajuato (journey time: 1.5 hours). Car: Federal Hwy-57 (from Querétaro); Hwy-49 and Hwy-45D (from Irapuato). San Miguel de Allende is 274km (171 miles) northwest of Mexico City.

Opening Times

Church: Daily 0900-1400 and 1600-1900. *Crypt*: Only open 2 Nov (Day of the Dead).

Admission Fees

Free.

Teotihuacán

Located 50km (31 miles) northeast of Mexico City, *Teotihuacán* grew to be the largest of Mexico's pre-Hispanic cities, with an estimated population of 200,000 during its zenith in the sixth century AD. Known for the geometric and symbolic arrangement of its monuments, its greatest building is the *Pyramid of the Sun*, standing at a height of 63m (207ft). It is joined on the Avenue of the Dead, Teotihuacán's main street, by another enormous building, the *Moon Pyramid*, which was originally part of a 'Moon Plaza'. The site was first excavated in 1884. Visitors can also see the various palaces once inhabited by the priests who ruled the city; research has brought to light many of the rituals of this ancient civilisation, including ceremonial human sacrifice and elaborate festivals.

Contact Address

For more information on Teotihuacán, contact the Secretaria de Turismo (see **Tourist Information** above).

Transportation

Air: Mexico City International Airport. **Road:** Coach: Services from Mexico City. Car: Main road to Hidalgo (from Mexico City).

Opening Times

Tues-Sun 0800-1800.

Admission Fees

peso30. Free Sun.

Morocco

1	Djemaa el Fna (Place of the Dead)
2	Fès el Bali (Fès Medina)
3	Tour Hassan (Hassan Tower)

Tourist Information

Office National Marocain de Tourisme (Moroccan National Tourist Office)
Angle 31 rue Oued Fès et avenue Abtal, Agdal, Rabat, Morocco
Tel: (037) 681 531 *or* 681 532. Fax: (037) 777 437.
Website: www.tourism-in-morocco.com
Moroccan National Tourist Office
Second Floor, 205 Regent Street, London W1R 7DE, UK
Tel: (020) 7437 0073. Fax: (020) 7734 8172.
E-mail: mnto@btconnect.com
Website: www.tourism-in-morocco.com

Djemaa el Fna (Place of the Dead)

Djemaa el Fna is the hub of daily life in Marrakesh, and this town square is as much a focus for the local people as it is for the tourists who flock here to find their bearings and watch the daily spectacle unfold. During the day it serves as little more than a thoroughfare for the cars, mopeds and donkeys that trundle past the countless fresh orange juice stalls on their way in and out of the *medina*, or old quarter, where the famous *souks*, or bazaars, can be found. At night, the square comes alive and turns into an open-air stage filled with acrobats, storytellers, snakecharmers and musicians, lit by lanterns and enveloped in a haze of smoke from barbecues and tagine pots. There are literally hundreds of food stalls to choose from, selling anything from hearty *harira* soup and couscous to grilled meats and french fries. All this is not merely a show for the tourists either – the entertainers who perform here do so to earn a living, and are carrying on a centuries-old tradition that remains a fundamental part of Marrakesh life.

Contact Address

Marrakesh Tourist Office, Abdelmoumen Ben Ali Square, Marrakesh, Morocco
Tel: (04) 443 6131. Fax: (04) 443 6057.

Transportation

Air: Marrakesh Ménara Airport. **Rail:** Train: Marrakesh Station. **Road:** Coach: Bab Doukkala Bus Station. Bus: 3 or 8.

Opening Times

Daily 24 hours.

Admission Fees

Free.

Fès el Bali (Fès Medina)

Fès is the oldest of Morocco's imperial cities, founded shortly after the Arabs first entered North Africa in the eighth century AD. Its *medina*, the ancient quarter or the old city, is also the largest medina in Morocco, an enchanting, winding, medieval maze of mosques, food markets and covered bazaars filled with crafts, such as metalwork objects and rugs. The *Souk Dabbaghin* houses the tanneries where leather has been dyed for hundreds of years. Today, this traditional craft is still practised and visitors can see the huge vats of dye and the coloured leather that is laid out to dry in the sun. The medina is also home to the *Al-Qarawiyin Theological University*, founded in AD 857, which is the oldest university in the western world; unfortunately non-Muslim visitors are not permitted to enter. The *Medersa Bou Inania* was founded in 1350 as a rival to the Al-Qarawiyin University and is a splendid example of Andalusian architecture. Visitors can enter the courtyard around which the students used to live, to admire the patterned tilework decorated with extracts from the Koran.

Contact Address

For more information on the Medina in Fès, contact the Moroccan National Tourist Office in London (see **Tourist Information** above).

Transportation

Air: Casablanca Mohammed V Airport or Saïss Airport. **Rail:** Train: Fès Station. **Road:** Car: Route de Immouzel (from Saïss Airport).

Opening Times

Daily 24 hours.

Admission Fees

Free.

Tour Hassan (Hassan Tower)

The *Tour Hassan*, the grandiose minaret of a vast yet incomplete mosque, is Rabat's most famous landmark. Begun in 1195, the minaret was intended to be the largest in the Muslim world, soaring some 86m (260ft) into the sky. Construction was abandoned, however, upon the death of the sultan, Yacoub al-Mansour, in 1199 and the tower instead rises to just 44m (140ft). The shortfall in height does not, however, detract from the beauty of its design, with every façade displaying a different pattern. Two hundred columns mark out the area where the mosque was to stand. Today, the site also houses the *Mosque and Mausoleum of Mohammed V*, the grandfather of the present king of Morocco, which is one of the few sacred sites in the country that non-Muslims are allowed to enter.

Contact Address

For more information on Tour Hassan, contact the Moroccan National Tourist Office in London (see **Tourist Information** above).

Transportation

Air: Casablanca Mohammed V Airport or Rabat Salé Airport. **Rail:** Train: Rabat Agdal Station or Rabat-Ville Station. **Road:** Car: Casablanca-Rabat Highway.

Opening Times

Daily 24 hours.

Admission Fees

Free.

Tilework in Fès Medina

Ruth Blakeborough

Myanmar

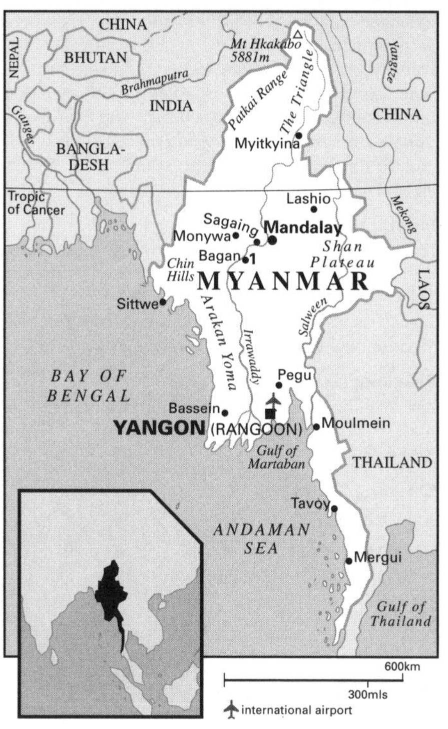

1 Bagan

Tourist Information

Myanmar Tourism Promotion Board
5 Signal Pagoda Road, Dagon Township, Yangon, Myanmar
Tel: (01) 243 63943. Fax: (01) 245 001.
Website: www.myanmar-tourism.com

Embassy of the Union of Myanmar
19A Charles Street, London W1J 5DX, UK
Tel: (020) 7499 8841 *or* (0906) 550 8924 (recorded visa and tourism information; calls cost 60p per minute). Fax: (020) 7629 4169.

Bagan

The ancient city of *Bagan* was founded in AD 849 by the Myanmar, or Burmans, as the capital of their empire. It is one of the most amazing archaeological sites in the world – 5000 temples, stupas (Buddhist dome-shaped monuments believed to contain relics of the Buddha himself) and pagodas lie scattered across an area of 42 sq km (16.2 sq miles) on the eastern bank of the Ayeyarwaddy River, testifying to the power and status of Bagan in bygone times. The most significant pagoda is the golden *Shwezigon Pagoda*, constructed in 1057 by King Anawrahta, the founder of the Myanmar dynasty, as a place of prayer and meditation. The small but informative *Archaeological Museum* displays murals, plaster carvings and other artefacts from the empire. Many visitors take a river excursion to take in large stretches of the site, which is particularly beautiful at sunset.

Contact Address

Myanmar Travel and Tours, c/o Ministry of Hotels and Tourism, 77-91 Sule Pagoda Road, Yangon, Myanmar. Tel: (01) 283 997 *or* 282 310. Fax: (01) 289 588 *or* 254 417. E-mail: mtt.mht@mptmail.net.mn

Transportation

Air: Yangon International Airport, then Nyaung-U Airport (located 11km (7 miles) from Bagan). **Rail:** Train: Bagan Station has services to/from Yangon via Pyay or Thazi and from Mandalay direct. Further services arrive at Nyaung-U Station. **Road:** Bus: Nyaung-U Bus Station is located 6.5km (4 miles) from Bagan; there are regular buses to/from Yangon, Mandalay, and Chiang Mai (Thailand). Car: There are road connections to Bagan from Yangon (via Pyay or Meikhtila), Mandalay (via Meikhtila or Myingyan), Taunggyi (via Thazi); from Nyaung-U, the Anawratha Road connects with the site.

Opening Times

Daily 0600-1900.

Admission Fees

Bagan Zone: US$10. *Archaeological Museum*: US$5.

Bagan

Ministry of Hotels and Tourism

Namibia

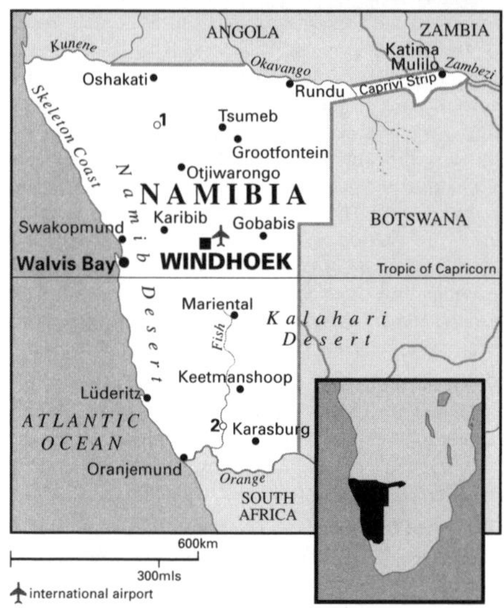

1 Etosha National Park
2 Fish River Canyon

Tourist Information

Namibia Tourism
Private Bag 13306, Windhoek, Namibia
Tel: (061) 284 2111. Fax: (061) 221 930 *or* 284 2364.
E-mail: tourism@iwwn.com.na
Website: www.iwwn.com.na

Namibia Tourism
6 Chandos Street, London W1G 9LU, UK
Tel: (020) 7636 2924. Fax: (020) 7636 2969.
E-mail: info@namibiatourism.co.uk
Website: www.namibiatourism.co.uk

Etosha National Park

Etosha National Park is located 500km (311 miles) north of Namibia's capital city, Windhoek. It is one of the largest game reserves in the world and famous for its many species of wildlife. Until the 1960s, it was the largest game reserve in the world, when its surface area was reduced due to political reasons. Today, Etosha has three restcamps – *Okaukejo, Namutoni* and *Halali*. Okaukejo is famous for its floodlit waterholes, which are frequented by elephants, giraffes, black rhino and lions; Namutoni is centred around a historic fort and Halali is situated halfway between the two and is the quietest of the three camps. The park, which has an estimated 300 lions, 2000 giraffes and 1500 elephants, owes its unique landscape to the *Etosha Pan*, a giant clay salt pan forming a shallow depression which allows amazing views of the game.

Contact Address

Namibia Wildlife Resorts Ltd, Private Bag 13378, Windhoek, Namibia
Tel: (061) 256 446. Fax: (061) 256 715.
E-mail: nwr@mweb.com.na
Website: www.namibiawildliferesorts.com

Transportation

Air: Windhoek International Airport. **Road:** Car: C38 road (from Outjo); C39 and C40 roads (from Khorixas).

Opening Times

Daily sunrise-sunset.

Admission Fees

NAD30 (adult), NAD2 (child).

Fish River Canyon

Fish River Canyon, located near Namibia's border with South Africa, is the largest canyon in the Southern Hemisphere, second only in the world to the *Grand Canyon*. The whole gorge measures 160km (99 miles) in length and is 127km (79 miles) wide, whilst its impressive inner canyon is an amazing 550m (1804ft) deep. The gorge which has formed over hundreds of millions of years winds through the arrid desert landscape, cutting through the great plateau and surrounded by imposing cliffs and large boulders. The site is the main tourist attraction in the far south of Namibia, popular with hikers who set out on the testing trail through the canyon, which begins with a steep descent from the main viewpoint near Hobas. The view from Hobas is said to be unequalled anywhere else in the world, offering visitors a spectacular view over the winding river and the rugged landscape below. At the southern end of the canyon, after a long hike through the desert terrain, weary walkers arrive at *Ai-Ais* (meaning Burning Water in the local Nama language), a hot water spring which wells from the earth and is believed to cure rheumatism. Fish River meets Orange River 76km (47 miles) south of the canyon and has been flowing out of the narrow gorge for centuries.

Contact Address

Namibia Wildlife Resorts Ltd, Private Bag 13378, Windhoek, Namibia
Tel: (061) 256 446. Fax: (061) 256 715.
E-mail: nwr@mweb.com.na
Website: www.namibiawildliferesorts.com

Transportation

Air: Windhoek International Airport. **Road:** Car: B4 southwest for around 44km, then left onto the C12 (from Keetmanshoop). After 77km (48 miles) a right turn is signposted for Fish River Canyon.

Opening Times

Canyon: Daily sunset-sunrise. *Hiking Trail*: Open 15 Apr-15 Sep.

Admission Fees

NAD20 (adult), NAD2 (child).

Elephant in the Etosha National Park

Namibia Tourism

Nepal

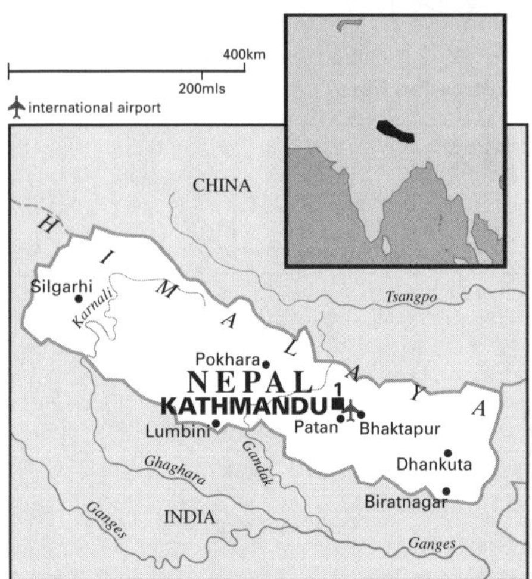

1	Kathmandu Durbar Square

Tourist Information

Nepal Paryatan Board (Nepal Tourism Board)
Bhrikuti Mandap, Kathmandu, Nepal
Tel: (01) 256 909 *or* 256 229. Fax: (01) 256 910.
E-mail: info@ntb.wlink.com.np
Website: www.welcomenepal.com

Royal Nepalese Embassy
12A Kensington Palace Gardens, London W8 4QU, UK
Tel: (020) 7229 1594 *or* 7229 5352.
Fax: (020) 7792 9861.
E-mail: rnelondon@compuserve.com
Website: www.welcomenepal.com

Kathmandu Durbar Square

Kathmandu's *Durbar Square* is one of three *durbar* (royal palace) squares in the Kathmandu Valley. It is the site of the *Hanuman Dhoka Palace Complex*, which was the royal Nepalese residence until the 19th century and where important ceremonies, such as the coronation of the Nepalese monarch, still take place today. The two-hectare (five-acre) palace complex is divided into two main chowks, or courtyards and was initially constructed in the 16th century, although subsequent additions were made in the Shah (Gurkha) dynasty in the 18th century and by the Rana rulers in the19th century. The palace is decorated with elaborately-carved wooden windows and panels and houses the *King Tribhuwan Memorial Museum*, dedicated to the monarch who opened up Nepal to the outside world, and the *Mahendra Museum*, dedicated to his son, King Mahendra. It is also possible to visit the *State Rooms* inside the palace. At the southern end of Durbar Square is one of the most curious attractions in Nepal, the *Kumari Chowk*. This gilded cage contains the Raj Kumari, a young girl chosen through an ancient and mystical selection process to become the human incarnation of the Hindu mother goddess, Durba. She is worshipped during religious festivals and makes public appearances at other times for a fee paid to her guards.

Contact Address

Department of Archaeology, Hanumandhoka Section, Ramshah Path, Kathmandu, Nepal
Tel: (01) 250 683 *or* 250 685. Fax: (01) 263 856.

Transportation

Air: Kathmandu International Airport. **Road:** Coach: Services from Darjeeling, Calcutta and Varanasi (India). Car: Prithvi Highway (from Pokhara).

Opening Times

King Tribhuwan Memorial Museum: Tues-Sat 0930-1500 (16 Nov-12 Feb); Tues-Sat 0930-1630 (13 Feb-12 Nov). *Mahendra Museum*: Tues-Sat 0930-1500 (16 Nov-12 Feb); Tues-Sat 0930-1630 (13 Feb-12 Nov).

Admission Fees

King Tribhuwan Memorial Museum: Rs250. *Mahendra Museum*: Rs250.

Carved detail in Durbar Square

Corel

The Netherlands

1	Anne Frankhuis (Anne Frank House)
2	Keukenhof (Keukenhof Gardens)
3	Koninklijk Paleis (Royal Palace)
4	Rijksmuseum (State Museum)
5	Van Gogh Museum

Tourist Information

Nederlands Bureau voor Toerisme (Netherlands Board of Tourism)
PO Box 458, 2260 MG Leidschendam, The Netherlands
Tel: (070) 370 5705. Fax: (070) 320 1654.
E-mail: info@nbt.nl
Website: www.holland.com

Netherlands Board of Tourism
18 Buckingham Gate, London SW1E 6LB, UK
Tel: (020) 7931 0661 *or* (0891) 717 777 (recorded information; calls cost 60p per minute).
Fax: (020) 7828 7941.
E-mail: information@nbt.org.uk
Website: www.holland.com/uk

Anne Frankhuis (Anne Frank House)

Anne Frank House is the historic house where Jewish teenager Anne Frank, her family and four other Jews hid from the Nazis during World War II. Anne herself shared a tiny room with family friend Fritz Pfeffer (known to Anne as Albert Dussel). In August 1944, after more than two years living in a cramped secret annex of the canalside townhouse on Prinsengracht in the centre of Amsterdam, they were betrayed to the Germans. Anne died at the Bergen-Belsen concentration camp; however, her father survived and published her diary, which became world famous as testament to one person's courage in the face of persecution. Today, the house is a permanent exhibition dedicated to the memory of Anne Frank, and the place where the original diary is on display. Visitors can see the room where Anne wrote most of her diary and, although the house was stripped by the Nazis after the Franks' arrest, audiovisual presentations document how the rooms would have looked.

Contact Address

Anne Frankhuis, PO Box 730, 1000 AS Amsterdam, The Netherlands
Tel: (020) 556 7100. Fax: (020) 620 7999.
Website: www.annefrank.nl

Transportation

Air: Amsterdam Airport Schiphol. **Rail:** Train: Amsterdam Centraal Station. Tram: 13, 17 or 20 (to Westermarkt). **Road:** Bus: 20, 170,171 or 172 (to Westermarkt). Car: Hwy-A10 (exit Centrum S105).

Opening Times

Daily 0900-1900 (Sep-Mar); daily 0900-2100 (Apr-Aug); daily 1200-1900 (25 Dec and 1 Jan); daily 0900-1900 (4 May). Closed 27 Sep.

Admission Fees

Dfl12.50 (adult), Dfl5 (child 10-17), free (child under 10). Concessions available.

Keukenhof (Keukenhof Gardens)

Located in the town of Lisse, *Keukenhof Gardens* are named after the kitchen gardens where Countess Jacoba of Bavaria grew fruit, vegetables and herbs in the grounds of her estate between 1401-1436 (hence the name Keukenhof which literally means kitchen garden). Keukenhof was designed as a park by two horticultural architects called Zochter in 1840, with the flower garden opening in 1949 when a bulb-growing consortium acquired the site and decided to develop an open-air flower exhibition. Today, Keukenhof Gardens, which is the largest flower attraction in the Netherlands and the largest display of bulbs in the world, is an impressive and flamboyant example of the Dutch population's love of tulips. Although open daily, the best time of year to visit is between the last week in March and the last week in May when the beautiful bulb flowers are in full bloom. These 28-hectare (69-acre) gardens are filled with over five million bulbs, planted in layers of three, of narcissi, hyacinths, and, of course, tulips. The gardens claim to be among the top three photographed sites in the world and have been visited by many prominent figures including Queen Elizabeth II (UK), Hilary Clinton (USA) and President Eisenhower (USA).

Contact Address

Keukenhof, PO Box 66, 2160 AB Lisse, The Netherlands
Tel: (0252) 465 564. Fax: (0252) 465 565.
E-mail: info@keukenhof.nl
Website: www.keukenhof.nl

Transportation

Air: Amsterdam Airport Schiphol. **Rail:** Train: Leiden Central Station or Haarlem Station. **Road:** Bus: 50, 51, 52 or 54. Car: A4 towards the Hague, then N207 towards Lisse and signs for Keukenhof (from Amsterdam); A44 towards Amsterdam, then N208 towards Lisse (from The Hague).

Opening Times

Daily 0800-1930.

Admission Fees

Dfl20 (adult), Dfl10 (child). Concessions available.

Koninklijk Paleis (Royal Palace)

The *Royal Palace*, which dates from 1648 and was designed by Jacob van Campen, was originally Amsterdam's town hall and is regarded today as the most important cultural and historical building from 17th-century Amsterdam. The building's exterior was originally made of white stone, although none of the white is actually visible today, whilst famous painters including Rembrandt and Ferdinand Bol were brought in to contribute to the interior. Located in Dam Square in the heart of the city, the building was converted into a palace on King Louis Napoleon's orders after he made Amsterdam his home in 1808. France invaded the Netherlands in 1794, capturing Amsterdam and setting up the Batavian Republic (1795-1806); this republic was brought to an end in 1806 however when Napoleon Bonaparte named his brother, Louis, as King of Holland. Louis originally set up home in The Hague, but moved to Amsterdam in 1808 as it was of greater economic importance. The palace was returned to the city of Amsterdam in 1813, following the fall of Napoleon. Today, the palace, which has been state property since 1936, houses an impressive collection of furniture left behind by Napoleon, as well as chandeliers and clocks from this period. Other highlights include the magnificent domed bell tower which is crowned by a weather vane and the *Burgerzaal* (Citizens Hall), with its marble floor, enormous pillars and impressive sculptures above the east and west entrances. The palace is the official residence of the Dutch Royal Family, and although they actually live in *Huis ten Bosch Palace* in The Hague, which was also built during the 17th century, the present Queen, Beatrix, still uses the Royal Palace to host official functions such as the Queen's New Year reception and various state visits.

Contact Address

Koninklijk Paleis, Nieuwezijds Voorburgwal 147, The Netherlands
Tel: (045) 4921 0515. Fax: (045) 4921 7299.
E-mail: info@kon-paleisamsterdam.nl
Website: www.kon-paleisamsterdam.nl

Keukenhof Gardens

Corel

Transportation

Air: Amsterdam Airport Schiphol. **Rail:** Train: Amsterdam Centraal Station. Tram: 1, 2, 4, 5, 9, 13, 14, 16, 17, 20, 24 or 25. **Road:** Signs are marked for Dam Square (from Amsterdam Centraal Station).

Opening Times

Daily 1100-1700 (30 Jun-9 Sep). Opening times vary during the winter season.

Admission Fees

Dfl9.50 (adult), Dfl7.50 (child). Concessions available.

Rijksmuseum (State Museum)

The largest and most popular museum in the Netherlands, the *Rijksmuseum* was first opened as the *Nationale Konstgallerij* (National Art Gallery) in 1800 in *Huis ten Bosch* in The Hague. It moved to Amsterdam in 1808 under the orders of Louis Napoleon, King of Holland, first to the *Koninklijk Paleis* (Royal Palace) in Dam Square, and then to the *Trippenhuis*, a mansion on Kloveniersburgwal, in 1817. The collection was moved to its present building, a mix of Gothic and Renaissance styles, designed by the Dutch architect Cuypers, in 1885. A new wing was added between 1906-1909 and 1913-1916 to house the growing number of 19th-century paintings. Today, the museum houses an impressive collection of 15th to 19th-century paintings, including work by the Dutch masters Rembrandt, Frans Hals, Jan Steen and Vermeer, and a fine collection of sculpture, furniture and historical items from the Low Countries. Highlights include the museum's most famous piece, Rembrandt's *The Night Watch*, painted in 1642, and *The Kitchen Maid* by Vermeer, dating from 1658. The *Print Room* is also worth visiting and regularly exhibits famous prints, drawings and photos, whilst the *Asiatic Art* rooms contain an impressive collection of Oriental objets d'arts.

Contact Address

Rijksmuseum, PO Box 74888, 1070 DN Amsterdam, The Netherlands
Tel: (020) 674 7000 *or* 674 7047. Fax: (020) 674 7001.
E-mail: info@rijksmuseum.nl
Website: www.rijksmuseum.nl

Transportation

Air: Amsterdam Airport Schiphol. **Rail:** Train: Amsterdam Centraal Station. Tram: 2, 5, 6, 7, 10, 12 or 20. **Road:** Car: A10 towards Amsterdam (RAI exit). Signs are marked for the Rijksmuseum (from the city centre).

Opening Times

Daily 1000-1700.

Admission Fees

Dfl17.50 (adult), free (child). Concessions available.

Van Gogh Museum

Opened in 1973, the *Van Gogh Museum* houses the collection of paintings bequeathed from the Dutch painter Vincent Van Gogh to his brother Theo. The paintings were transferred to the Vincent Van Gogh Foundation in 1962 by Vincent's nephew Vincent Willem Van Gogh, on the initiative of the Dutch government, and they have been on permanent loan to the museum ever since. Located in the Museumplein in the centre of Amsterdam, between the Rijksmuseum and the Stedelijk Museum, the modern glass building was designed by the Dutch architect Gerrit Rietveld. It contains the world's largest collection of works by Van Gogh, including some 200 paintings, 500 drawings, 700 letters and the artist's own collection of Japanese prints. Highlights of the Van Gogh collection include his first large-scale painting, *The Potato Eaters* which was painted in 1885 and *The Sunflowers*, one of his most famous pieces, painted in 1889. The museum also houses a large collection of work by Van Gogh's contemporaries, including paintings by Henri de Toulouse-Lautrec and Paul Gauguin.

Contact Address

Van Gogh Museum, PO Box 75366, 1070 AJ Amsterdam, The Netherlands
Tel: (020) 570 5200 *or* 570 5252. Fax: (020) 673 5053.
E-mail: info@vangoghmuseum.nl
Website: www.vangoghmuseum.nl

Transportation

Air: Amsterdam Airport Schiphol. **Rail:** Train: Amsterdam Centraal Station. Tram: 2 or 20 (to Museum Square). **Road:** Bus: 170 (to Museum Square). Car: A10 towards Amsterdam (exit S106). Signs are marked for Museum Square (from the city centre).

Opening Times

Daily 1000-1800.

Admission Fees

Dfl15.50 (adult), Dfl5 (child). Concessions available.

New Zealand

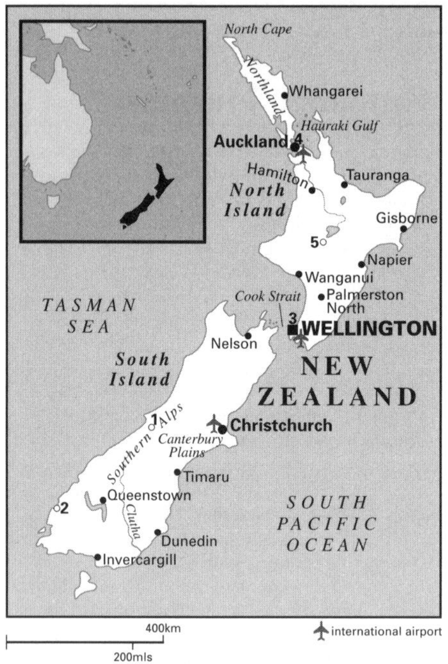

1 Aoraki Mount Cook
2 Fiordland National Park
3 Museum of New Zealand Te Papa Tongarewa
4 Sky City Tower
5 Tongariro National Park

Tourist Information

Tourism New Zealand
Fletcher Challenge House, 89 The Terrace, Wellington, New Zealand
Tel: (04) 472 8860. Fax: (04) 478 1736.
E-mail: enquiries@nztb.govt.nz
Website: www.purenz.com (trade information) *or* www.nztb.govt.nz (consumer information).

Tourism New Zealand
New Zealand House, Haymarket, London SW1Y 4TQ, UK
Tel: (020) 7930 1662 *or* (09069) 101 010 (recorded information line; calls cost 60p per minute).
Fax: (020) 7839 8929.
E-mail: enquiries@nztb.govt.nz
Website: www.purenz.com (trade information) *or* www.nztb.govt.nz (consumer information).

Aoraki Mount Cook

Aoraki Mount Cook is the highest mountain in New Zealand, standing 3754m (12,316ft) high. The mountain, which attracts climbers from all over the world to its snow-covered peaks, stands in *Aoraki/Mount Cook National Park*, on New Zealand's South Island. Aoraki means 'Cloud Piercer' in Maori and the mountain is so called due to its breathtaking peaks which tower high above the clouds. The first recorded attempt to climb the peak was made by the Swiss guide Ulrich Kaufmann with his client Reverend W S Green in 1882, although the first known climbers to actually reach the summit were three New Zealanders, Tom Fyfe, Jack Clarke and George Graham, who reached the top in 1894. The national park, which was formally gazetted in 1953, covers an area of 70,111 hectares (173,251 acres). There are regular guided tours from Mount Cook to the *Tasman Glacier*, which, at 27km (17 miles) long, 3km (1.9 miles) wide and 600m (1968ft) deep, is New Zealand's largest glacier. Other highlights include the smaller *Hooker Glacier*, *Murchison Glacier Mount Tasman* and *Mount Dampier*. Outdoor activities include helicopter rides, alpine flights, horse trekking, hunting and fishing, mountain biking and hiking through the mountains. The park is also home to around 750 different species of flowering plants, including the Mount Cook Lily and the world's largest buttercup, as well as hundreds of different species of insects, moths, butterflies and birds, such as the Kea, the only mountain parrot in the world.

Contact Address

Mackenzie Tourism and Development Board, Lake Pukaki V̂isitor Centre, State Highway 8, PO Box 68, Twizel, New Zealand
Tel: (03) 435 3280. Fax: (03) 435 3283.
E-mail: lake.pukaki@xtra.co.nz
Website: www.mtcook.org.nz

Transportation

Air: Christchurch International Airport, Aoraki/Mount Cook Airport (domestic flights); there are regular shuttle buses from Aoraki/Mount Cook Airport throughout the Mackenzie region. **Road:** Bus: Greatsights or Intercity buses from Christchurch and Queenstown. The Cook Connection also runs from Timaru and Oamaru, as do shuttles from Twizel. Car: Aoraki/Mount Cook National Park is approximately 3 hours 45 mins southwest of Christchurch and 3 hours north of Queenstown. State Hwys-1, -79 and -8 (from Christchurch); State Hwy-8 (Mount Cook – Queenstown Highway) (from Queenstown). Then State Hwy-80 to

Mount Cook and Tasman Glacier (from Lake Pukaki); a gravel road (just before Mount Cook village) leads to the Tasman Glacier.

Opening Times

Aoraki Mount Cook: Daily 24 hours. *Visitor Centre*: Daily 0830-1830 (Nov-Mar); daily 0830-1700 (Mar-Nov).

Admission Fees

Free.

Fiordland National Park

At nearly 1.2 million hectares (3 million acres), *Fiordland National Park* is New Zealand's largest national park – a breathtaking stretch of coastal landscape that typifies the country's natural splendour. Created in 1952, it is a land of ice, beech forests, mountains and waterfalls that tumble into the ocean below. It is home to around 700 plants not found anywhere outside the park, including varieties of tussock, tree daisies, speargrasses and buttercups. It is also the residence of some of the strangest varieties of birds and insects in the country, including the takahe, a large flightless moorhen which was once believed to be extinct, the brown kiwi bird and over 20 species of giants weevils. One of the park's most famous sights is *Milford Sound*, which is the largest glacier-carved fiord on New Zealand's coastline and attracts large numbers of sightseers and cruise ships every year. The park is immensely popular amongst visitors wishing to take part in outdoor pursuits, including hiking, sea kayaking, diving, cycling, golf, fishing and sailing. The *Milford Track*, which stretches some 56km (35 miles) from Glade Wharf to Sandfly Point, has been described as the finest walk in the world, taking visitors on a rugged, alpine journey through the park's most breathtaking scenery. Visitors should, however, note that a permit is required for the track and these must be booked through the Visitor Centre in Te Anau.

Contact Address

Fiordland National Park Visitor Centre, c/o Department of Conservation, Lakefront Drive, PO Box 29, Te Anau, New Zealand
Tel: (03) 249 7924. Fax: (03) 249 7613.
E-mail: fiordlandvc@doc.govt.nz
Website: www.doc.govt.nz

Transportation

Air: Christchurch International Airport, Te Anau Airstrip (domestic flights). **Road:** Bus: Services to Milford Sound and Queenstown (from Te Anau). Car: Hwy-94 to Te Anau (off the main Invercargill – Queenstown Road); Milford Road to Milford Sound (from Te Anau).

Opening Times

Daily 0830-1630 (winter); daily 0830-1700 (summer excluding Jan); daily 0830-2000 (Jan).

Admission Fees

Free.

Museum of New Zealand Te Papa Tongarewa

Te Papa (meaning 'Our Place' in Maori), the national museum of New Zealand, is located on Wellington's waterfront, from where it enjoys magnificent views across the harbour. Its origins can be traced back to the Colonial Museum which opened near the Parliament Buildings in Wellington in 1865. It moved to a site in Buckle Street in 1936 to house the National Art Gallery and the Dominion Museum, with its name changing to the National Museum in 1972. By 1987, it had become apparent that the Buckle Street site had become too small and there was a great need for a new museum to house the treasures from the National Musuem and the National Art Gallery under one roof. The new Te Papa museum, which opened in 1998, has attracted international acclaim with its ultra-modern and interactive displays. It was opened to enable the people of New Zealand to learn more about their cultural identity and their country's geography. Constructed by a team from JASMAX, headed by the architect Ivan Mercep, who won a national competition to design the building, the museum took almost four years to complete. It occupies a floor space measuring 36,000 sq m (387,513 sq ft) and houses many national artefacts, enabling visitors to learn about the art, history and natural environment of New Zealand. It also has several permanent exhibitions, including the *Time Warp* display, which allows visitors to travel back in time to New Zealand's prehistoric age, and the *Rima* exhibit, which is a journey into how Wellington will look in the future. As well as Maori treasures and contemporary works of art, visitors can also take part in interactive exhibitions about New Zealand's plants and animals in the *Mountains to Sea* exhibition, and see rocks and fossils in the *Bush City* display.

Contact Address

Museum of New Zealand Te Papa Tongarewa, Cable Street, PO Box 467, Wellington, New Zealand
Tel: (04) 381 7000. Fax: (04) 381 7070.
E-mail: mail@tepapa.govt.nz
Website: www.tepapa.govt.nz

Transportation

Air: Wellington International Airport. **Road:** Bus: City Circular Bus from the railway station to Te Papa. Taxi: There is a rank outside the museum. Car: Wellington motorway (Aotea Quay exit), then along Waterloo, Customhouse and Jervois Quay, which leads directly to Cable Street.

Opening Times

Mon-Wed and Fri-Sun 1000-1800, Thurs 1000-2100.

Admission Fees

Free.

Sky City Tower

Standing at 328m (1076ft) high, *Sky City Tower* is the tallest tower in the Southern Hemisphere and the 12th tallest in the world, towering above the *Eiffel Tower* in Paris which is 324m (888ft) high and *AMP Centrepoint Tower* in Sydney which is 305 metres (1001ft) high. Completed over a two year, nine-month period, the tower is situated in the *Sky City* entertainment complex, which also houses *Sky City Casino, Sky City Theatre, Sky City Hotel and Conference Centre* and *Sky City Restaurants*. The postmodern Sky City Tower was designed by the architects Craig Craig Moller and completed in 1997; it is illuminated at night when it is said to resemble a giant hypodermic needle towering high into the night's sky. The tower has four circular observation levels, the highest of which is the *Sky Deck*, which gives a 360-degree view across Aukland and Waitemata Harbour, over the top of Rangitoto Island to the other islands in the Hauraki Gulf, allowing visitors to see up to 82km (51 miles) on a clear day. Visitors can also eat in the *Orbit* rotating restaurant and travel to the top of the tower in one of six high-tech glass-fronted lifts.

Contact Address

Sky Tower, Sky City, PO Box 90643, Auckland, New Zealand
Tel: (09) 912 6400. Fax: (09) 912 6032.
E-mail: skytower@skycity.co.nz
Website: www.skycity.co.nz

Transportation

Air: Auckland International Airport. **Road:** Bus: Intercity Bus Terminal. Car: State Hwy-1 to Auckland (from Hamilton and Warkworth); State Hwy-22 to Auckland (from Raglan). Then from the city centre, signs along Hobson Street (from Quay Street) or Federal Street (from Customs Street).

Opening Times

Daily 0830-late.

Admission Fees

NZ$15 (adult), NZ$13.50 (senior citizen), NZ$7.50 (child 5-15), free (child under 5). NZ$3.50 extra to climb to the *Sky Deck* (top public level).

Tongariro National Park

Originally a gift to Queen Victoria by the Tuwharetoa Maori chief Te Heuheu Tukino IV in 1887, *Tongariro National Park* was the first national park in New Zealand and the fourth oldest in the world. Since its inception, the park has grown to a size of nearly 80,000 hectares (197,688 acres). The area is of religious and cultural importance to the Maoris who first occupied the area in the ninth century when they arrived from Polynesia. In particular, they believed the region's mountains had god-like ancestors, and the core of the park centres around three active volcanoes, *Tongariro, Ruapehu* and *Ngauruhoe.* Areas resemble a lunar landscape, which has been carved by flowing lava, alongside forests and tussock lands. It is home to many creatures native to New Zealand, including the short- and long-tailed bat, kereru (New Zealand's native pigeon), fantails and parakeets. Visitors to the area can ski on an active volcano, as well as hike through alpine herb fields, passing by waterfalls and emerald-coloured lakes, before reaching spectacular lookout points. The *Tongariro Crossing*, completed by about 70,000 hikers every summer, is considered to be one of the best one-day walks in the country, offering magnificent volcanic scenery and fine views of *Lake Taupo* and *Mount Taranaki.*

Contact Address

Tongariro National Park, c/o Tongariro/Taupo Conservancy, Private Bag, Turangi, New Zealand
Tel: (07) 386 8607. Fax: (07) 386 7086.
Website: www.doc.govt.nz

Transportation

Air: Wellington International Airport, then Taupo Airport. **Rail:** Train: The main trunk railway runs through the towns of National Park and Ohakune (from Auckland and Wellington). **Road:** Bus: Services to Ohakune, National Park and Turangi (from Taupo, Auckland and Wellington). Shuttle services also run to Whakapapa, which is located inside the park. Car: State Hwy-1 (from Auckland in the north or from Wellington in the south).

Opening Times

Daily 24 hours.

Admission Fees

Free.

Norway

1 Bryggen (Wharfside)
2 Hardanger Fjord
3 Nidarosdomen (Trondheim Cathedral)

Tourist Information

Norges Turistrad (Norwegian Tourist Board)
Drammensveien 40, PO Box 2893 Solli, NO-0230 Oslo, Norway
Tel: 2292 5200. Fax: 2256 0505.
E-mail: norway@ntr.no
Website: www.ntr.no *or* www.visitnorway.com

Norwegian Tourist Board
Charles House, 5 Lower Regent Street, London SW1Y 4LR, UK
Tel: (020) 7839 6255. Fax: (020) 7839 6014.
E-mail: infouk@ntr.no
Website: www.visitnorway.com

Bryggen (Wharfside)

Considered by UNESCO to be one of the world's foremost showcases of the Middle Ages, *Bryggen* consists of a series of gabled buildings situated on the old wharf of Bergen. It stands as a reminder of Bergen's prominent role in the days of the Hanseatic League, an organisation founded by a group of northern German towns to protect their mutual trading interests in the 13th to 15th centuries. The buildings were mainly used as warehouses for the dried fish trade, but also contained offices and simple living quarters for merchants, journeymen and apprentices. They have survived countless threats over the last 60 years, including fires and Nazi bombings, and many of the houses have now been restored to their original state. Today, Bryggen is alive with restaurants, cafés and artists' workshops, and a colourful attraction at the eastern end is *Torget*, a weekday market selling fruit and vegetables, handicrafts and souvenirs.

Contact Address

Bergen Tourist Office, Vågsallmenningen, 5014 Bergen, Norway
Tel: 5532 1480. Fax: 5532 1464.
E-mail: info@bergen-travel.com
Website: www.bergen-travel.com

Transportation

Air: Bergen Flesland Airport. **Rail:** Train: Bergen Central Station. **Road:** Bus: 70 or 71. Car: E16 (from Oslo); E39 (from Stavanger, Ålesund or Kristiansand, then signs are marked for the city centre).

Opening Times

Daily 24 hours.

Admission Fees

Free.

Hardanger Fjord

Hardanger Fjord, which is located 75km (47 miles) east of Bergen, is one of the most popular tourist destinations in Norway. This scenic area offers virtually every kind of natural landscape available in the country, from scenic waterways, apple and cherry orchards, and hiking trails, to mountain plateaux. The area also contains *Hardangervidda*, Norway's largest national park, two of Norway's largest glaciers, *Folgefonna* and *Hardangerjøkulen*, and some of Norway's most popular waterfalls, including *Vøringfossen, Steinsdalsfossen* and *Låtefossen*. There are also various museums in the area, including *Hardanger folkemuseum* (Hardanger Folk Museum) and *Hardanger Fartøyvernsenter* (Hardanger Ships Preservation Centre) treeboat museum. The area is also famous for its connections with the classical Norwegian composer Edvard Grieg (1843-1907) who built a cabin in Lofthus in 1875 where he lived for several years. Here, inspired by the tranquillity of the magnificent surrounding countryside, he wrote many of his finest pieces.

Contact Address

Destination Hardanger Fjord, PO Box 66, 5601 Norheimsund, Norway
Tel: 5655 3870. Fax: 5655 3871.
E-mail: info@hardangerfjord.com
Website: www.hardangerfjord.com

Transportation

Air: Bergen Flesland Airport. **Rail:** Train: Voss Station. **Road:** Bus: Services to Norheimsund (from Bergen). Car: Route 7 towards Norheimsund (from Bergen); E-16 and Route 7 (from Oslo).

Opening Times

Hardanger Fjord: Daily 24 hours. *Hardanger Folk Museum*: Mon-Sat 1000-1500 (Sep-Apr); Mon-Sat 1000-1600, Sun 1200-1600 (May-Jun); Mon-Sat 1000-1800, Sun 1200-1800 (Jul-Aug). *Hardanger Ships Preservation Centre*: Daily 1000-1700 (May-Sep).

Admission Fees

Hardanger Fjord: Free. *Hardanger Folk Museum*: NOK40 (adult), free (child). *Hardanger Ships Preservation Centre*: NOK50 (adult), NOK25 (child). Concessions available.

Nidarosdomen (Trondheim Cathedral)

According to Norwegian history, King Olav Haraldsson, who was killed in the battle of Stiklestad in 1030 and who subsequently became Norway's patron saint several days later, was buried on the exact spot where *Trondheim Cathedral* now stands. Construction of the church began in 1070 after pilgrims began to flock to St Olav's grave, but it was not completed until 1300, when it was widely reputed to be the most beautiful church in Norway. Now restored after fire damage and years of decay and pillage endured during the Reformation, it is particularly renowned for its fine stone statues on the exterior and the quality and quantity of stained glass in the Gothic interior. Norway's monarchs are still crowned and buried in Trondheim Cathedral and there are regular music recitals under the high-vaulted arches. Visitors can admire the *Crown Jewels* on display and also climb the tower for fine views over Trondheim.

Contact Address

Nidarosdomen, Postboks 4447, Hospitalsløkkan, 7418 Trondheim, Norway
Tel: 7353 9160. E-mail: nidarosdomen@kirken.no
Website: www.nidarosdomen.no

Transportation

Air: Bergen Flesland Airport, Oslo Gardermoen International Airport, Trondheim Værnes Airport. **Water:** Ferry: Hurtigruten coastal steamer (from Bergen). **Rail:** Train: Trondheim Station (direct services from Oslo, Bergen and Stockholm, services from Stavanger via Oslo, services from Copenhagen via Oslo). **Road:** Coach: NOR-WAY express buses (from Bergen, Ålesund, Røros, Aure and Namsos). Bus: 2, 41, 48 or 49 (from Pier Terminal). Car: E6 (from Oslo, Gothenburg or Copenhagen).

Opening Times

Cathedral: Mon-Fri 1200-1430, Sat 1130-1400, Sun 1300-1500 (15 Sep-30 Apr); Mon-Fri 0900-1500, Sat 0900-1400, Sun 1300-1600 (1 May-19 Jun); Mon-Fri 0900-1800, Sat 0900-1400, Sun 1300-1600 (20 Jun-20 Aug); Mon-Fri 0900-1500, Sat 0900-1400, Sun 1300-1600 (21 Aug-14 Sep); the cathedral may close periodically between 27 Jul-5 Aug for preparations for St Olav's Festival. *Tower*: Daily every 30 mins (20 Jun-20 Aug). *Crown Jewels*: Sat 1200-1400 (1 Apr-31 May); Mon-Fri 0900-1230, Sat 0900-1230, Sun 1300-1600 (1 Jun-20 Aug); Sat 1200-1400 (21 Aug-31 Oct). *Cathedral guided tours*: Mon-Fri 1100, 1400, 1600 (20 Jun-20 Aug).

Admission Fees

NOK35 (adult), NOK20 (child). Family pass available.

Hardanger Fjord

Norwegian Tourist Board

Panama

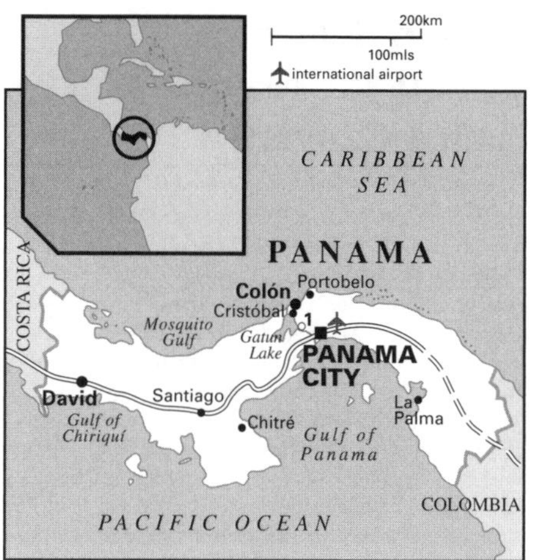

1 Canal de Panamá (Panama Canal)

Tourist Information

Instituto Panameño de Turismo/IPAT (Institute of Tourism)
Apartado 4421, Centro de Convenciones ATLAPA, Vía Israel, Panama 5, Panama
Tel: 226 7000. Fax: 226 3483.
Website: www.ipat.gob.pa

Embassy of Panama
40 Hertford Street, London W1Y 7TG, UK
Tel: (020) 7493 4646. Fax: (020) 7493 4333.
E-mail: emb.pan@lineone.net

Canal de Panamá (Panama Canal)

The idea of building a canal across the Isthmus of Panama was first raised by the Holy Roman Emperor Charles V (who was also King Charles I of Spain) during the 16th century. Even during the 1600s, people saw the great potential of building a canal, which would avoid having to sail around Cape Horn in South America. It was not until 1880, however, that the French made an attempt to build a canal across this stretch of water under the command of the French businessman, Ferdinand de Lessups.

Alfredo Maikez

Panama Canal

Unfortunately the attempt failed miserably due to high costs, with over 22,000 workers dying from malaria and yellow fever. The United States began construction work in 1904, employing nearly 75,000 men and women to build the canal, which opened to traffic ten years later on 15 August 1915. Today, the 80km (50 mile) stretch of water is one of the most important and fantastic engineering feats in the world, providing passage for over 12,000 ships every year. An open-air balcony at *Miraflores Locks* offers visitors good views of the electrical locomotives or 'mules' pulling giant ships through as the water levels are balanced.

Contact Address

Panama Canal Authority, PO Box 5413, Miami, FL 33102, USA
Tel: 272 3165 *or* 272 3202 (in Panama). Fax: 272 1657 (in Panama).
E-mail: info@pancanal.com
Website: www.pancanal.com

Transportation

Air: Tocument International Airport. **Road:** Coach: Many private companies operate coach tours to the canal (from Panama City). Taxi: Taxis operate from the airport to the canal. Car: Corredor Sur Highway to central Panama City, then through the Albrook Residential and Commercial Area, and right to Miraflores Locks (from Tocument International Airport).

Opening Times

Canal: Daily 24 hours. *Visitor Centre*: Daily 0900-1700.

Admission Fees

Canal and *Visitor Centre*: Free.

Peru

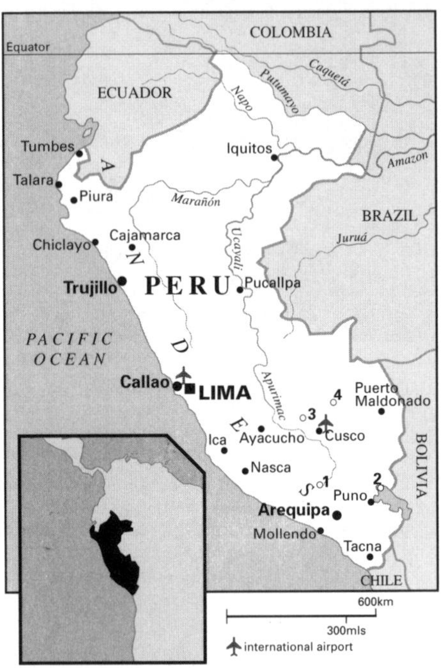

1 Cañon del Colca-Arequipa (Arequipa-Colca Canyon)
2 Lago Titicaca (Lake Titicaca)
3 Machu Picchu
4 Parque Nacional del Manu (Manu National Park)

Tourist Information

PromPerú (Commission for the Promotion of Peru)
Calle 1 Oeste 50, Edificio Mitinci, 14th Floor, Urb. Córpac, San Isidro, Lima 27, Peru
Tel: (01) 224 3279. Fax: (01) 224 3323.
E-mail: postmaster@promperu.gob.pe
Website: www.peruonline.net

Embassy of the Republic of Peru
52 Sloane Street, London SW1X 9SP, UK
Tel: (020) 7235 1917. Fax: (020) 7235 4463.
E-mail: consulate@peruembassy-uk.com
Website: www.peruembassy-uk.com

Cañon del Colca-Arequipa (Arequipa-Colca Canyon)

At a depth of more than 3400m (11,333ft), the *Arequipa-Colca Canyon* is one of the deepest in the world and almost twice the depth of the Grand Canyon (1829m/6000ft). The Rio Colca winds its way through the gorge, with the impressive Sabancaya and Ampato volcanoes looming high in the background. The canyon, which is named after the *Colcas* (warehouses) where the Incas used to store grain in sealed vaults in the canyon walls, is dotted with flora and fauna such as the nopal cactus and ichu (high altitude grass), which is eaten by llamas and alpacas. Visitors to the region can still see Colcas today in the Pumunuta Caves; these warehouses, which are part of an ancient Inca tradition dating back to around 1800 BC, measure 1m (3.3ft) in diameter and are made of straw and mud. A highlight of any trip to the region is a chance to see the giant Andean Condor that inhabits the canyon; visitors can view these great birds soaring into the wind from the *Cruz del Condor* observation point. The valley towns, such as Yanque and Chivay, which have maintained their original appearance for almost 400 years, and the many pre-Inca tombs and ruins in the area, are also of interest.

Contact Address

Dirección Regional de Industria y Turismo, Jacinto Ibanez 456, Parque Industrial, Arequipa, Peru
Tel: (054) 232 957. Fax: (054) 235 660.
E-mail: arequipa@mitinci.gob.pe

Transportation

Air: Lima Jorge Chavez International Airport, Arequipa Airport (domestic flights). **Rail:** Train: Services from Arequipa to Sumbay three times a week (journey time: 3.5 hours). **Road:** Car: Arequipa–Yura–Chivay road (journey time: 4 hours); Arequipa–Charcani–Chivay road (journey time: 5 hours).

Opening Times

Daily 24 hours.

Admission Fees

S/.6 (payable to see the view at *Cruz del Condor*).

Lago Titicaca (Lake Titicaca)

At an elevation of 3810m (12,492ft), *Lake Titicaca* is one of the world's highest navigable lakes. It is named after the native word for 'puma of stone' and its shape bears a strong resemblance to this animal when viewed from above. Measuring 194km (121 miles) long and 65km (45 miles) wide, it has been revered in history, featuring prominently in Inca creation myths. There are daily tours to the *Uros* and *Taquile Islands*; the *Uros* people live on floating islands made out of reeds that grow in the lake, whilst the inhabitants of *Taquile Island* are renowned for maintaining ancient traditions and for their remarkable weaving skills.

Contact Address

Dirección Regional de Turismo, Jr Ayacucho 682, Puno, Peru
Tel: (054) 351 261. Fax: (054) 351 261.
E-mail: dritpuno@terra.com.pe

Transportation

Air: Lima Jorge Chavez International Airport, Puno Airport (domestic flights). **Rail:** Train: Uuliaca Station. **Road:** Coach: Services from Main Square in Puno. Car: Hwy-3 (from Lima).

Opening Times

Daily 24 hours.

Admission Fees

Free.

Machu Picchu

This Inca site, located 112km (70 miles) northwest of Cusco and constructed as a refuge against the Spanish in the 16th century, is the most mysterious, most spectacular and best known in South America. Although it is now of great spiritual and cultural significance to millions of Peruvians, its existence was known only to a few locals until American explorer Hiram Bingham happened upon it on 24 July 1911. Numerous archaeological visits and explorations have been made since; however, much of the purpose of the site remains a mystery, even though it is virtually intact, right down to the high quality of its stonework. Visitors to the site can see the remains of the two areas, urban and agricultural, including priests' houses, royal mausoleums, temples, farmers' lodgings and irrigated terraces. *Machu Picchu* also possesses the last *Inihuatana* (sundial) remaining in South America. Located within incredible cloud forest, the site marks a fitting and dramatic conclusion to the end of the Inca Trail.

Contact Address

Oficina de Información, Avenida de la Cultura 734, Cusco, Peru
Tel: (084) 223 701. Fax: (084) 223 761.
E-mail: turismo@tourcusco.com
Website: www.machupicchuperu.com

Transportation

Air: Lima Jorge Chavez International Airport. **Rail:** Train: Aguas Calientes Station or Puente Ruinas Station (from Cusco). **Road:** Coach: Shuttle service to citadel (from Aguas Calientes Station or Puente Ruinas Station). Car: Hwy-101 (from Lima).

Opening Times

Daily 0630-1730.

Admission Fees

Entrance fee: S/.14. Two-day trail: S/.42. Four-day trail: S/.60. Arrival by shuttle: S/.35. Concessions available.

Parque Nacional del Manu (Manu National Park)

Manu National Park covers a staggering 1.5 million hectares (3.7 million acres) of terrain, consisting of successive tiers of vegetation. It is protected by UNESCO as a World Biosphere Reserve, can only be entered as part of a licensed tour, and is so remote that some of the indigenous tribes that live there have had no contact with the outside world. Its unspoiled atmosphere means that it is home to species that are unknown elsewhere in the world; the tropical Amazon jungle in the lower section is home to over literally thousands of species of plant, butterfly and bird and countless reptiles and insects. Two hundred types of mammal, including jaguars and rare species such as the giant otter and the giant armadillo, have also been sighted. Further up, the *Andean High Plateau* rises to 4300m (14,100ft) and the *Tres Cruces* lookout on the road from Manu to Cusco offers far-reaching views across the Amazon. The park also contains a vast network of rivers and lakes, and many tours enter by boat along the *Manu River*.

Contact Address

Instituto de Recursos Naturales, Calle 17, No 355, San Isidro, Peru
Tel: (01) 255 1053. Fax: (01) 224 3298.

Transportation

Air: Lima Jorge Chavez International Airport, Boca Manu Airstrip (domestic flights). **Water:** Motorised launch: Services from Atalaya to Boca Manu (journey time: 16 hours). **Road:** Coach: Services from Cusco to Atalaya (journey time: 8 hours); access is then by river. Car: Cusco–Atalaya road to Atalaya (journey time: 8 hours); access is then by river from Atalaya to Manu.

Opening Times

Entrance days: Mon, Wed, Fri and Sun 0800-1000. Exit days: Tues, Thurs, Sat and Sun from 0700.

Admission Fees

S/.92 (adult), free (child under 12).

Machu Picchu

PromPeru

Philippines

1 Banaue Rice Terraces

Banaue Rice Terraces

Nestled deep in the heartlands of the *Cordilleras* mountains and rising to an altitude of 1525m (5000ft) are the *Banaue Rice Terraces*. The terraces were carved out of the mountain range over 3000 years ago by the *Ifugaos*, the oldest mountain tribe in the area, using only the most primitive tools. The irrigation system uses gravity to harness water from the forests 1800m (2185ft) above thus ensuring a continuous supply of crops. Measured from end to end, the terraces would stretch a total length of 22,400km (13,919 miles), enough to encircle half the globe. They are often dubbed the eighth wonder of the ancient world as their age and scale is comparable to that of the official seven wonders, of which only the Pyramids of Giza remain.

Contact Address

Tourism Office, Cordillera Administrative Region, Department of Tourism, DOT Complex, Government Pack Road, 2600 Baguio City, Philippines
Tel: (074) 442 6708 *or* 442 7014. Fax: (074) 442 8848.
E-mail: dotcar@mozcom.com
Website: www.tourism.gov.ph

Transportation

Air: Manila Ninoy Aquino International Airport, Baguio Airport (domestic flights) or Bagabag Airport (domestic flights). **Rail:** Train: Manila Station. **Road:** Bus: Services from Baguio and Manila. Car: Halsema Highway (from Baguio); main road (from Lagawe).

Opening Times

Daily 24 hours.

Admission Fees

Free.

Banaue Rice Terraces

Philippine Department of Tourism

Tourist Information

Philippine Department of Tourism
Department of Tourism Building, T M Kalaw Street, Rizal Park, Manila 1000, Philippines
Tel: (02) 52384 1129. Fax: (02) 521 7374 *or* 522 2194.
E-mail: dotgca@info.com.ph
Website: www.tourism.gov.ph

Philippine Cultural and Tourism Office
146 Cromwell Road, London SW7 4EF, UK
Tel: (020) 7835 1100. Fax: (020) 7835 1926.
E-mail: tourism@pdot.co.uk
Website: www.tourism.gov.ph

Poland

1 Auschwitz-Birkenau
2 Rynek Glowny, Krakow (Main Market Square, Krakow)
3 Zamek Krolewski w Warsawie (Warsaw Royal Castle)
4 Zamek Krolewski na Wawelu (Wawel Royal Castle)

Tourist Information

Polska Organizacja Turystyczna (Polish Tourism Organisation)
4-6 Chalubinskiejo Street, 00-928 Warsaw, Poland
Tel: (022) 630 1747. Fax: (022) 630 1762.
Website: www.infolinia.pl

Polish National Tourist Office
First Floor, Remo House, 310-312 Regent Street, London W1B 3AX, UK
Tel: (020) 7580 8811 (brochure request line) *or* 7580 6688 (tourist enquiries) *or* 7580 4488 (trade and press only). Fax: (020) 7580 8866.
E-mail: info@visitpoland.org
Website: www.visitpoland.org

Auschwitz-Birkenau

Auschwitz-Birkenau, situated 70km (46 miles) west of Krakow, is the most infamous and the largest of the Nazi death camps. It saw the cruel death of an estimated four million people. Today, the camp is a museum dedicated to the memory of those who suffered and perished there. The forbidding entrance gate, surrounded by barbed wire, still bears the words *Arbeit Macht Frei* (Work Brings Freedom) and the railway and gas chambers remain as they were when the camp was liberated by Soviet troops in May 1945. The *Museum of Martyrdom* shows a film depicting the nature of the atrocities, and there are further displays of photos and personal articles, such as children's shoes, women's hair and toothbrushes, that were taken from the victims.

Contact Address

State Museum of Auschwitz-Birkenau, ulica Wiezniow Oswiecimia 20, 32-620 Oswiecim, Poland
Tel: (033) 843 2022. Fax: (033) 843 1934.
E-mail: muzeum@auschwitz-muzeum.oswiecim.pl
Website: www.auschwitz-muzeum.oswiecim.pl

Transportation

Air: Krakow-Balice John Paul II International Airport. **Rail:** Train: Oswiecim Station. **Road:** Bus: Services to the museum (from Oswiecim). Car: A4, then Road 933 (from Krakow); E75, then Road 950 (from Katowice).

Opening Times

Daily 0800-1500 (16 Dec-28 Feb); daily 0800-1600 (1-31 Mar); daily 0800-1700 (1 Apr-31 May); daily 0800-1900 (1 Jun-31 Aug); daily 0800-1700 (1-30 Sep); daily 0800-1800 (1-31 Oct); daily 0800-1600 (1 Nov-15 Dec).

Admission Fees

Entry to site: Free. Film: Z2. Guided tour: Z10.

Rynek Glowny, Krakow (Main Market Square, Krakow)

Krakow's magnificent *Rynek Glowny* is one of the largest Medieval squares in Europe and dates from 1257. It is dominated by the *Sukiennice*, the arcaded Renaissance cloth hall that stands in the centre, crowned by an elaborate attic construction known as a Polish parapet, and decorated with carved masks. The lower part of the building still serves as a market, selling traditional Polish crafts and food, and the upper floor is devoted to an exhibition of 19th-century Polish painting. On the southern side is the copper-domed *Kosciol sw Wojchiecha* (St Adalbert's Church), Krakow's first church, which dates from the tenth century and is the oldest building in the square. The *Ratusz* tower, with its Baroque spire, is all that remains of the 14th-century town hall after it was demolished in 1820 as part of a city development project. There are fine views over Krakow from the top. Other important buildings include the Medieval *Kosciol Mariacki* (St Mary's Church), fronted by two towers, and several mansions which, although originally Gothic in style, have been embellished with Renaissance and Baroque features by the writers, artists and wealthy families who have inhabited them over the years.

Contact Address

Krakowskie Centrum Informacji Turystycznej (Krakow Tourist Information Centre), ulica Pawia 8, Cracow, Poland

Tel: (012) 422 6091. Fax: (012) 422 0471.

Transportation

Air: Krakow-Balice John Paul II International Airport. **Rail:** Train: Krakow Station. Road: Coach: Services from Lviv (Ukraine), Prague (Czech Republic) and Vienna (Austria) to Dworzec PKS (Central Bus Station). Car: E77 (from Warsaw and Gdansk); E40 (from Lviv in the Ukraine and Dresden in Germany).

Opening Times

Daily 24 hours.

Admission Fees

Free.

Zamek Królewski w Warsawie (Warsaw Royal Castle)

Set on a plateau over looking the River Vistula, Warsaw's *Royal Castle* was built in the 14th century as a wooden fortress for the Dukes of Mazovia. It became a royal residence when King Zygmunt III made plans to move the Polish capital to Warsaw from Krakow in 1569 (although the final move to Warsaw was not made until the early 17th century). The castle then remained the seat of the monarchy and the *Sejm* (Polish parliament) for almost 250 years. During this period substantial improvements were made, most notably the restyling of the building into a polygonal shape by Italian architects in the late 16th century, and the addition of many Baroque features throughout the 1700s. In 1918, the castle became the official residence of the Polish president but was completely destroyed by the Nazis during World War II. The building that visitors enter today is thus a remarkable reconstruction, carried out in the 1970s, with only a few parts of the interior salvaged from the ruins. The neo-Baroque rooms are filled with museum pieces, including period furniture, porcelain, tapestries, and Oriental rugs; paintings on display include views of Warsaw by Canaletto. There are plans to re-landscape the castle gardens that lead down to the river.

Contact Address

Zamek Królewski, Plac Zamkowy 4, 00277 Warsaw, Poland

Tel: (022) 657 2170. Fax: (022) 635 7260.

E-mail: zamek@zamek-krolewski.art.pl

Website: www.zamek-krolewski.art.pl

Transportation

Air: Warsaw-Okecie Airport. **Rail:** Train: Warszawa Centralna (Warsaw Central Station). Tram: 4, 13, 26 or 32. **Road:** Bus: 125, 170 or 190. Car: E30 (from Berlin and Lodz); E67 (from Wroclaw); E77 (from Gdansk and Krakow).

Opening Times

Tues-Sat 1000-1600, Sun 1100-1600 (1 Oct-15 Apr); Tues-Sat 1000-1800, Sun and Mon 1100-1800 (16 Apr-30 Sep). Closed 1 Nov, 24-25 Dec, 31 Jan, 30-31 Mar and 1 May.

Admission Fees

Z14 (adult), Z8 (child under 16), free Sun. Concessions available.

Warsaw Royal Castle

Polish National Tourist Office

Zamek Krolewski na Wawelu (Wawel Royal Castle)

Wawel Royal Castle was the seat of Polish royalty from the 11th century until the early 17th century when King Zygmunt III moved the Polish capital to Warsaw. The majority of the castle is in the Renaissance style, although significant Romanesque and Gothic elements remain. Today, it functions as a museum, with some of the original Renaissance decoration, including Flemish tapestries, Italian furniture and various Italian and Dutch paintings, still existing. Among its many treasures are the *Crown Treasury and Armoury*, where visitors can see the *Szczerbiec*, a weapon once used to crown Polish monarchs. The *Lost Wawel* exhibition is centred around excavations of the Wawel hill's oldest ruins, including the oldest church known to exist in Poland, the Rotunda of St Felix and St Adauctus, which dates from the 11th century. The *Oriental Art* exhibition features displays of Turkish and Persian tents, carpets and weapons and Chinese and Japanese ceramics. Visitors can also enter the *Dragon's Den*, a cave with karstic limestone features, where, according to Polish legend, a child-eating creature called the Wawel Dragon once lived.

Contact Address

Zamek Krolewski, Wawel 5, 31-001 Krakow, Poland
Tel: (012) 422 5155. Fax: (012) 429 3336.
Website: www.cyfronet.krakow.pl/wawel

Transportation

Air: Krakow-Balice John Paul II International Airport. **Rail:** Train: Dwolzec Station. **Road:** Bus: 501 or 502. Car: A77 (from Warsaw), then signs to the city centre.

Opening Times

State Rooms, Crown Treasury, Armoury and *Oriental Art Room*: Tues-Thurs 0930-1500, Fri 0930-1600, Sat 0930-1500, Sun 1000-1500. *Lost Wawel*: Mon 0930-1500, Wed-Thurs 0930-1500, Fri 0930-1600, Sat 0930-1500, Sun 1000-1500. *Dragon's Den*: Daily 1000-1700.

Admission Fees

State Rooms or *Crown Treasury* and *Armoury*: Z12 (adult), Z7 (child or adult under 25). *Lost Wawel*: Z6 (adult), Z4 (child or adult under 25), free Sun. *Oriental Art*: Z6 (adult), Z4 (child or adult under 25), free Sun. *Dragon's Den*: Z3.

Wawel Royal Castle

Polish National Tourist Office

Portugal

1 Castelo de São Jorge (Castle of St George)
2 Mosteiro dos Jerónimos (Jeronimos Monastery)
3 Torre de Belém (Tower of Belém)

Tourist Information

Investimentos, Comércio e Turismo de Portugal/ ICEP (Portuguese Trade and Tourism Office)
Avenida 5 de Outubro 101, 1050-051
Lisbon, Portugal
Tel: (021) 790 9500.
Fax: (021) 793 5028 *or* 795 0961.
E-mail: dinf@icep.pt
Website: www.portugal.org *or* www.icep.pt *or* www.portugalinsite.pt

ICEP/Portuguese Trade and Tourism Office
Second Floor, 22-25A Sackville Street, London W1S 3LY, UK
Tel: (09063) 640 610. Fax: (020) 7494 1868.
E-mail: iceplondt@aol.com

Castelo de São Jorge (Castle of St George)

Perched on the highest of Lisbon's seven hills, above the old Moorish quarter, the *Castle of St George* was the royal residence until the late 15th century. Originally built by the Visigoths and later named after King Joao I, the castle, along with much of Lisbon, was severely damaged by a devastating earthquake in 1755. The castle was declared a National Monument in 1910, with rebuilding work starting in 1940 to restore the site to its former state of luxury. Today the castle offers spectacular views of Lisbon from the well-preserved ramparts, as well as beautiful gardens full of olive, cork and pine trees, and flamingo, peacock and swans. There is also a giant periscope in the *Torre de Ulisses* (Tower of Ulysses-Camera Obscura), from where visitors can see spectacular, live images of Lisbon below, reflected onto a large screen.

Contact Address

Castelo de São Jorge, Edificio das Antigas Prisões, 1100-129 Lisbon, Portugal
Tel: (021) 887 7244. Fax: (021) 887 5695.
E-mail: mareagoaosousa@abahl.pt

Transportation

Air: Lisbon International Airport. **Rail:** Tram: 12 or 28. **Road:** Bus: 37 to Pracafegueyra Square. Car: A1 to Lisbon (from Porto); A2 (from the Algarve via Almada); A8 (from Caldas da Rainha in the north).

Opening Times

Castle and *Gardens*: Daily 0900-1800 (Nov-Feb); daily 0900-2100 (Mar-Oct). *Tower of Ulysses*: Mon and Wed-Sun 1000-1300 and 1400-1730 (15 Mar-15 Sep).

Admission Fees

Castle and *Gardens*: Free. *Tower of Ulysses*: Esc300 (adult), free (child under 14).

✗ 🧺 ♿

Mosteiro dos Jerónimos (Jeronimos Monastery)

This 16th-century monastery is one of the few surviving examples of medieval, Manueline architecture. Commissioned by Manuel I (after whom the style of architecture is named), work began on the monastery in 1502. The original design was the work of the architect Diogo de Boytac, although other Masters, namely João de Castilho and Diogo de Torralva, were involved in the actual construction. It is listed (along with the *Torre de Belém*) as a UNESCO World Heritage

Site and is a spectacular building with high arches, impressive columns and ornate spires. It is also the resting place of Vasco da Gama, who set sail from Bélem in 1497 to discover India, and of Portugal's most famous poet, Luís de Camões, who wrote *Os Lusiadas* (the Lusiads). Visitors can see various monastic rooms, including a refectory and chapter house, as well as a church hall designed by João de Castilho. Other places of interest are the chapels, with the tombs of royal descendants of Manuel I, and the cloister, which has many impressive galleries.

Contact Address

Mosteiro dos Jerónimos, Praca do Emperio, 1400-206 Lisbon, Portugal
Tel: (021) 362 0034. Fax: (021) 363 9145.
E-mail: mosteirojeronimos@mosteirojeronimos.pt
Website: www.mosteirojeronimos.pt

Transportation

Air: Lisbon International Airport. **Water:** Boat: Bélem River Station (from Trafaria and Porto Brandão). **Rail:** Train: Bélem Station. Tram: 15, 16 or 17. **Road:** Bus: 27, 28, 29, 43, 49, 51 or 112. Car: A1 to Lisbon (from Porto); A2 (from the Algarve via Almada); A8 (from Caldas da Rainha in the north). Then, Ponte 25 de Abril and Avenida da India to Belém (from Lisbon).

Opening Times

Daily 1000-1700 (Oct-Apr); daily 1000-1800 (May-Sep).

Admission Fees

Esc600 (adult), Esc300 (child).

Torre de Belém (Tower of Belém)

Completed in 1515, the *Tower of Belém* is one of Lisbon's most famous sights. Built under the instruction of Francisco de Arruda, who was influenced by the style of fortifications in Morocco, it was intended to provide strategic defence to the River Tagus. Symbolically, it was also the last sight seen by seafarers leaving the city. The tower has a famous 18th-century statue of Virgin and Child, Our Lady of Safe Homecoming, built into the terrace of the bastion, as well as sentry posts on each corner. Highlights of this unique site that is sharply outlined against Lisbon's skyline include the Manueline exterieur with its intricate stone carvings and Moorish-style domes, as well as beautiful balconies and arches adorned with detailed sculpture. Today, a gangway leads visitors to the museum; there is also a drawbridge and bulwark, and a terrace offering superb views across the river and of the western part of Lisbon.

Contact Address

Torre de Belém, Praca do Emperio, 1400-206 Lisbon
Tel: (021) 362 0034. Fax: (021) 363 9145.
E-mail: mosteirojeronimos@mosteirojeronimos.pt
Website: www.mosteirojeronimos.pt

Transportation

Air: Lisbon International Airport. **Rail:** Train: Belém Station. Tram: 15, 16 or 17. **Road:** Bus: 27, 28, 29, 43, 49 or 51. Car: A1 to Lisbon (from Porto); A2 (from the Algarve via Almada); A8 (from Caldas da Rainha in the north). Then, Ponte 25 de Abril and Avenida da India to Belém (from Lisbon).

Opening Times

Tues-Sun 1000-1700 (winter); daily 1000-1800 (summer).

Admission Fees

Esc500 (adult), Esc300 (child). Concessions available.

Jeronimos Monastery

Turismo de Lisboa

Romania

1 Castelul Bran (Bran Castle)

Tourist Information

Oficiul Nationl Roman De Turism (Romanian National Tourist Office)
Strada Apolodor 17, Bucharest 570633, Romania
Tel: (01) 410 0491. Fax: (01) 336 6784.
E-mail: turism@kappa.ro
Website: www.romaniatravel.com *or* www.romtourprom.ro

Romanian National Tourist Office
22 New Cavendish Street, London W1M 7LH, UK
Tel: (020) 7224 3692. Fax: (020) 7935 6435.
E-mail: uktouroff@romania.freeserve.co.uk
Website: www.romaniatravel.com

Castelul Bran (Bran Castle)

Perched high on a rock in the midst of Transylvanian forest, *Bran Castle*, named after the nearby town, is one of Romania's most famous attractions, thanks to its connections with Bram Stoker's novel, 'Dracula'. In fact, Stoker cites his further north than Bran Castle, but its Gothic towers, winding corridors and labyrinth of secret passages fit the image of the vampire's home so perfectly that it has been dubbed *Dracula's Castle*. Built between 1377 and 1382 as a palace and military fortress, it was once the residence of Queen Maria of Romania, the granddaughter of Queen Victoria, whose heart is reputed to have been found hidden in the castle in a silver box. Nowadays, visitors who dare enter the eerie chambers can see collections of furniture, weaponry and armour, and admire the well-preserved Gothic architecture.

Contact Address

Castelul Bran, 498 Traian Mosoiu Street, Bran, Romania
Tel: (068) 238 335. Fax: (068) 475 607.

Transportation

Air: Bucharest Otopeni Airport. **Rail:** Zarnesti Station. **Road:** Coach: Services to Bran (from Brasov). Car: E60, then National Road 67 (from Bucharest).

Opening Times

Tues-Sun 0900-1700.

Admission Fees

Lei50,000 (adult), Lei12,500 (child 7-18), free (child under 7).

Bran Castle

Romanian National Tourist Office

Russian Federation

1	Gosudarstvenny Ermitazh (State Hermitage Museum)
2	Krasnaya ploshchad (Red Square)
3	Moskovsky Kreml' (Kremlin)
4	Pokrovsky Sobor (St Basil's Cathedral)

Tourist Information

Ministerstvo Turisma (Ministry of Tourism)
18 ul. Kazakova, 103064 Moscow, Russian Federation
Tel: (095) 263 0840. Fax: (095) 263 0761.

Embassy of the Russian Federation
13 Kensington Palace Gardens, London W8 4QX, UK
Tel: (020) 7229 2666. Fax: (020) 7727 8625.

Gosudarstvenny Ermitazh (State Hermitage Museum)

The *State Hermitage Museum* in St Petersburg is one of the largest museums in the world, housing over three million works of art and tracing the development of culture from prehistoric times to the present day. Highlights include Italian Renaissance art, in particular works by Michelangelo and Raphael, Flemish and Dutch painting, French Impressionist painting, and collections of Russian and Oriental art. The foundation of the collection stems from a purchase, in 1764 by Catherine the Great, of a considerable group of Western European paintings. First opened to the public in 1852, the State Hermitage Museum has belonged to the Russian people since the October Revolution in 1917; one of the five buildings in which it is housed is the magnificent *Winter Palace*, the former residence of the Russian Tsars.

Contact Address

Gosudarstvenny Ermitazh, Dvortzovaya nab. 34-36, St Petersburg 191186, Russian Federation
Tel: (0812) 110 9625 (recorded information) *or* 110 3420 (central information desk).
Fax: (0812) 311 9009.
E-mail: info@hermitage.ru
Website: www.hermitagemuseum.org

Transportation

Air: Pulkovo II International Airport (St Petersburg).

Rail: Train: Moscow Station. Tram: Ermitazh. Underground: Nevskiy Prospect or Gostiny Dvor. **Road:** Bus: 7, 10 or 47. Trolleybus: 1, 5, 7, 10 or 22. Car: M10 (from Moscow or Helsinki, Finland); M11 (from Berlin, Germany via Poland).

Opening Times

Tues-Sat 1030-1800, Sun 1030-1700.

Admission Fees

Rb300 (adult), free (child under 17). Concessions available. Museum photography charge: Rb75. Museum videorecording charge: Rb250.

Krasnaya ploshchad (Red Square)

Moscow's *Red Square* has seen centuries of Russian history played out across its vast 700-metre (2300-foot) expanse. Laid out during the reign of Ivan III in the 15th century and originally serving as a market place, it has born the name *Krasnaya*, from the old Russian for 'beautiful', since the late 17th century. Nowadays, it is framed by three structures of world renown – the *Kremlin, St Basil's Cathedral* and the *Lenin Mausoleum*, which contains the embalmed body of the founder of the Russian Communist Party and leader of the 1917 Russian Revolution. It has been the scene of numerous executions, riots, parades and demonstrations, including, until 1991, the May Day and October Revolution military parades celebrating the power of the Soviet State. The square also contains various monuments commemorating Bolsheviks who fell during the 1917 Revolution and past Soviet leaders such as Stalin and Brezhnev; the ashes of Russian writer, Maxim Gorky and Yuri Gagarin, the first man in space, are interred in the Kremlin wall behind the Lenin Mausoleum. The *GUM* department store on the east side was once state owned but was privatised after the fall of the USSR.

Contact Address

For more information on Red Square, contact the Ministry of Tourism (see **Tourist Information** above).

Transportation

Air: Moscow Sheremetyevo International Airport. **Rail:** Train: Kiev Station. Underground: Kitay-Gorod. **Road:** Bus: 2 or 33 to Okhotny ryad. Car: M1

St Basil's Cathedral, Red Square

Corel

(from Minsk); M2 (from Kiev); M7 (from Nizhny Novgorod); M9 (from Riga); M10 (from St Petersburg). Then, Moskovskaya Koltsevaya Avtomobilnaya Doroga (Moscow ring road) to the city centre.

Opening Times

GUM: Mon-Sat 1000-2000, Sun 1100-1800. *Kremlin*: Fri-Wed 1000-1700. *St Basil's Cathedral*: Wed-Mon 1100-1800. *Lenin Mausoleum*: Tues-Thurs and Sat 1000-1300.

Admission Fees

GUM: Free. *Kremlin*: Rb200 (adult), Rb110 (child). *St Basil's Cathedral*: Rb90 (adult), Rb45 (child). *Lenin Mausoleum*: Free.

Moskowksy Kreml' (Kremlin)

The *Kremlin* (literally 'fortified town') is a walled fortress dating back to the founding of Moscow in 1147, when it was erected above the Neglina and Moskva rivers. The white-stone walls and towers were added between 1367 and 1368 under the Prince of Moscow and the Grand Prince of Vladimir, Dmitry Donskoy (1350-1389). The building was totally rebuilt between 1485 and 1495, when it assumed its present-day appearance. From 1276 to 1712, it was the seat of government for the grand princes and tsars of Russia, and from 1917 onwards it has been the seat of power for the Communist government. The heart of the Kremlin centres around *Cathedral Square*, which is surrounded by several important churches, including the *Cathedral of the Assumption*, the *Cathedral of the Archangel* and the *Cathedral of the Annunciation*. The redbrick walls and towers house many other historic sights, including the *Armoury Museum*, the *State Diamond Fund*, the *Patriarch's Palace*, the *Tsar Cannon* and the *Tsar Bell*.

Contact Address

The State Historical-cultural Museum-preserve, Moscow Kremlin, Moscow 103073, Russian Federation
Tel: (095) 202 6649 *or* 202 3832. Fax: (095) 202 0052.
E-mail: press@kremlin.museum.ru
Website: www.kremlin.museum.ru

Transportation

Air: Moscow Sheremetyevo International Airport. **Rail:** Train: Kiev Station. Underground: Biblioteka imeni Lenina or Aleksandrovski Sad. **Road:** Trolleybus: 2 or 33. Car: M1 (from Minsk); M2 (from Kiev); M7 (from Nizhny Novgorod); M9 (from Riga); M10 (from St Petersburg). Then, Moskovskaya Koltsevaya Avtomobilnaya Doroga (Moscow ring road surrounding the city).

Opening Times

Mon-Wed and Fri-Sun 1000-1700.

Admission Fees

All buildings surrounding the *Kremlin* (with the exception of the *Armoury Museum*): Rb200 (adult), Rb110 (child). *Armoury Museum*: Rb400 (adult), Rb155 (child).

Pokrovsky Sobor (St Basil's Cathedral)

The wildly coloured, onion-shaped domes of *St Basil's Cathedral* are undoubtedly one of Russia's most famous images. Situated in Moscow's Red Square, each dome has a distinctive patterning and colour scheme, creating a stunning, fantastical effect, reminiscent of whipped meringue. The cathedral was commissioned by Ivan the Terrible and built during the 1550s to commemorate Russia's military victory over the Khanates of Kazan in 1552. It is called *Pokrovsky Sobor* in Russian, which literally means the Cathedral of the Intercession of the Virgin. Designed by the architects Postnik and Barma, it has been a branch of the State Historical Museum since 1929. A chapel was added in 1588 to house the tomb of the holy fool Basil (Vasily) the Blessed, after whom the cathedral is now known. Basil, who died in 1552, was a well-known prophet who wandered the streets of Moscow and predicted, correctly, that there would be a fire in the city in 1547.

Contact Address

Pokrovsky Sobor, Krasnaya ploshchad 4, Moscow, Russian Federation
Tel: (095) 298 3304.

Transportation

Air: Moscow Sheremetyevo International Airport. **Rail:** Train: Kiev Station. Underground: Kitay-Gorod. **Road:** Trolleybus: 2 or 33 to Okhotny ryad stop. Car: M1 (from Minsk); M2 (from Kiev); M7 (from Nizhny Novgorod); M9 (from Riga, Latvia); M10 (from St Petersburg). Then, Moskovskaya Koltsevaya Avtomobilnaya Doroga (Moscow ring road surrounding the city).

Opening Times

Mon-Tues and Wed-Sun 1100-1800.

Admission Fees

Rb90 (adult), Rb45 (child).

Singapore

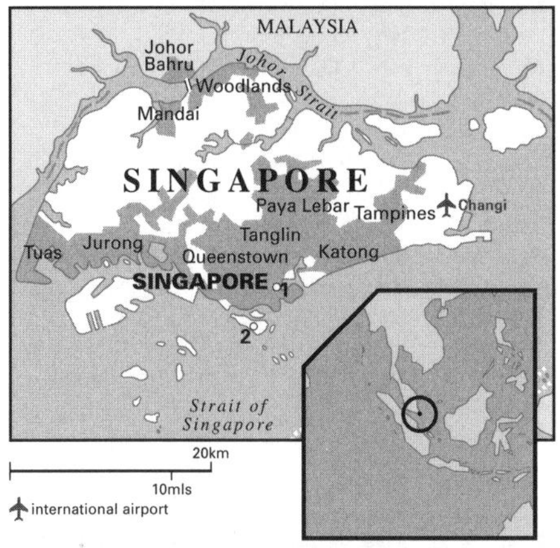

1	Raffles Hotel
2	Sentosa

Tourist Information

Singapore Tourism Board
Tourism Court, 1 Orchard Spring Lane, Singapore 247729
Tel: 736 6622. Fax: 736 9423.
E-mail: stb_sog@stb.gov.sg
Website: www.stb.com.sg *or* www.newasia-singapore.com

Singapore Tourism Board
First Floor, Carrington House, 126-130 Regent Street, London W1R 5FE, UK
Tel: (020) 7437 0033 *or* (08080) 656 565 (toll free UK only). Fax: (020) 7734 2191.
E-mail: info@stb.org.uk

Raffles Hotel

Opened in 1887 by four Armenian brothers, Martin, Tigran, Aviet and Arshak Sarkies, the *Raffles Hotel* is one of the few remaining original grand hotels of the East. This world-famous hotel, which was named after Sir Stamford Raffles, the founder of modern Singapore, began life as a modest bungalow. Over the years, it has welcomed many famous guests, including Somerset Maugham, Rudyard Kipling, Joseph Conrad and Charlie Chaplin, all of whom were attracted by the hotel's luxury and elegance. Today, the hotel continues to attract the rich and famous, and its recent S$160-million facelift has ensured that it has the trappings of modern luxury yet retains the unique charm of the colonial era. Tourists regularly flock to drink afternoon tea in the *Tiffin Room* and enjoy a famous Singapore Sling in the *Long Bar*. The hotel was declared a National Monument in 1987 and houses 70 boutiques, as well as several restaurants, a museum and the Victorian-style playhouse, *Jubilee Hall*.

Contact Address

Raffles Hotel, 1 Beach Road, Singapore 189673
Tel: 337 1886. Fax: 339 7650.
E-mail: raffles@raffles.com
Website: www.raffleshotel.com

Transportation

Air: Singapore Changi Airport. **Rail:** Train: MRT City Hall Station. **Road:** Bus: 56, 80, 82, 100, 107, 107X or 961. Car: The hotel is located just off Nicoll Highway and can be reached from Bras Basah Road and then Beach Road.

Opening Times

Daily 24 hours.

Admission Fees

Free.

Sentosa

A purpose-built island theme park, *Sentosa* (which means 'peace and tranquility' in Malay) offers history, golf and gastronomy, as well as a host of themed attractions, including *VolcanoLand*, the *Asian Village*, *Fantasy Island* water ride and *Underwater World*, which is one of Asia's largest tropical fish aquariums. Opened in 1968, the island was originally known as *Pulau Blakang Mati* (which means 'island behind which lies death' in Malay), taking its name from an outbreak of malaria which wiped out the population of Bugis pirates who inhabited the island during the 18th century. It served as a British military fortress during the mid-20th century, before it was given back to the Singapore government in 1967. Owned and managed by Sentosa Development Corporation, today, Sentosa is Singapore's largest offshore island and home to beautiful beaches and gardens. The island's highlights include the *Butterfly Park*, which houses more than 2500 butterflies, *Fort Siloso* preserved fortification, which was built in the 1880s, and the *Images of Singapore Museum*, which exhibits artefacts from the history of Singapore.

Contact Address

Sentosa Development Corporation, 33 Allanbrooke Road, Sentosa, Singapore 099981
Tel: 275 0388. Fax: 275 0161.
Website: www.sentosa.com.sg

Transportation

Air: Changi Airport. **Sea:** Ferry: Services depart from the World Trade Centre in Singapore City. **Rail:** Cable Car: Services to Sentosa (from Mount Faber). **Road:** Bus: Orchard Bus E (from Orchard Road); Sentosa Bus Service A (from the World Trade Centre (WTC) Bus Terminal); Sentosa Bus Service C (from Tiong Bahru MRT (W3) Stop).

Opening Times

Sentosa: Daily 24 hours. *Images of Singapore*: Daily 0900-2100. *Fort Siloso*: Daily 0900-1900. *Asian Village*: Daily 1000-2100. *Butterfly Park* and *Insect Kingdom Museum*: Daily 0900-1830. *VolcanoLand*: Daily 1000-1900. *Fantasy Island*: Daily 1030-1900. *Underwater World*: Daily 0900-2100. Times vary for other attractions.

Admission Fees

Sentosa: S$6 (adult), S$4 (child). *Images of Singapore*: S$5 (adult), S$3 (child). *Fort Siloso*: S$3 (adult), S$2 (child). *Asian Village*: Free. *Butterfly Park* and *Insect Kingdom Museum*: S$6 (adult), S$3 (child). *VolcanoLand*: S$12 (adult), S$6 (child). *Fantasy Island*: S420 (adult), S$12.50 (child). *Underwater World*: S$17 (adult), S$11 (child). Additional charges apply for other attractions.

Raffles Hotel by Night

Singapore Tourism Board

Slovak Republic

1 Spissky Hrad (Spiš Castle)
2 Tatranský národný park (Tatra National Park)

Tourist Information

Slovenskej agentúry pre cestovný ruch (Slovak Tourist Board)

Nám. L Stura 1, PO Box 35, 974 05 Banská Bystrica, Slovak Republic

Tel: (088) 4136 1468. Fax: (088) 413 6149.

E-mail: sacr@sacr.sk

Website: www.slovakiatourism.sk

Embassy of the Slovak Republic

25 Kensington Palace Gardens, London W8 4QY, UK

Tel: (020) 7243 0803 *or* 7243 8935 (consular section) *or* (090) 6550 8956 (recorded visa information; calls cost £1 per minute).

Fax: (020) 7727 5824.

E-mail: mail@slovakembassy.co.uk

Website: www.slovakembassy.co.uk

Spissky Hrad (Spiš Castle)

Spiš Castle is one of the largest medieval castles in central Europe, alongside Prague Castle in the Czech Republic and Malbork Castle in Poland. Dating from the early 13th century and noted for its fine Romanesque and Gothic features, this imposing fortification stands 634 metres (2080ft) above sea level on cliffs dominating the Spiš region in eastern Slovak Republic. It was once one of the most important Gothic castles in Europe and was owned by the Royal Family until 1465. Thereafter it was purchased by a succession of noble families: first the Zapolsky family (until 1531); then the Thurzo family (until 1638); and finally the Csaky family, who owned it until 1945. The castle was almost entirely destroyed by fire in 1780 and the remains were subsequently allowed to slide into decay. It was declared a national monument in 1961 and attempts were made to restore it in order to make it accessible to the public. The castle has a small museum which is open to the public and documents the history of the castle during its apogee in the late Middle Ages. Although many parts of the castle's Gothic tower, chapel ramparts and dungeons still stand in ruins, there are fine views of the surrounding countryside from the summit of the hill.

Contact Address

Spissky Hrad, 05304 Spišské Podhradie, Slovak Republic

Tel: (0966) 454 1336.

Transportation

Air: Bratislava Airport. **Road:** Car: The castle can be reached from the Šibenik Pass (from the east and from Levoča). Foot: Visitors should approach the castle from the town of Spišské Podhradie.

Opening Times

Castle and *Museum*: Mon-Fri 0900-1800 (Nov-Sep); Mon-Fri 0900-1700 (Oct).

Admission Fees

Castle and *Museum*: Sk50 (adult), Sk30 (child).

Tatranský národný park (Tatras National Park)

Tatras National Park is the oldest national park in the Slovak Republic and home to the famous *Vysoké Tatry* (High Tatras Mountains). Founded in 1949 and covering an area of 741 sq km (286 sq miles), Tatras National Park is a hiker's paradise. The landscape incorporates dense forest on the mountains' lower slopes, as well as glacial lakes and mountain streams. Many footpaths pick their way through the valleys and up to the rocky peaks. The High Tatras is the only alpine mountain range in Eastern Europe and one of the smallest in the world. The mountains are also famous for their plant and wildlife, with *chamois* (mountain goat), bear and marmot roaming free on the slopes, and over 1300 different plant species blossoming each year. Also of interest are the *TANAP Museum*, which was founded in 1957 and describes the natural history and ethnography of the region through geology, flora and fauna displays and exhibits; and the *Tatras Nature Exposition*, a unique three hectare (seven acre) botanical garden, with over 250 species of plant life found in the mountains.

Contact Address

Tatranský národný park, Tatranska Lomnica, Slovak Republic
Tel: (0969) 446 7195.
E-mail: sprava@tanap.sk
Website: www.tanap.sk

Transportation

Air: Bratislava Airport. Special charter flights and private airplanes land at Poprad-Tary Airport. **Rail:** Cable car: Peaks reached by aerial tram include Skalnate Pleso, Lomnicky Stit, Solisko and col Lomnicke sedlo. **Road:** Bus: Buses depart from Štrbské Pleso, Starý Smokovec and Tatranská Lomnica. Car: The park can be approached from the Slovak – Polish border (from the north); from the Zdiar–Tatranska Kotlina road (from the east); from the Ticha dolina Valley (via Oravice and Biela skala and through the Sucha dolina Valley from the west).

Opening Times

Tatras National Park: Daily 24 hours. Visitors are recommended to visit during Jul-Sep. Some of the high mountain trails are closed Nov-Apr. *TANAP Museum*: Mon-Fri 0800-1200 and 1300-1630, Sat-Sun 0800-1200. *Tatras Nature Exposition*: Daily 0900-1500 (12 May-1 Jul and 1 Sep-16 Sep); daily 0830-1700 (2 Jul-31 Aug).

Admission Fees

Tatras National Park: Free. *TANAP Museum*: SKK20 (adult), SKK5 (child). *Tatras Nature Exposition*: SKK20 (adult) (16 May-15 Jul), SKK10 (adult) (16 Jul-15 Sep); SKK10 (child) (16 May-15 Jul), SKK5 (child) (16 Jul-15 Sep).

Spiš Castle

Slovak Tourist Board

Slovenia

1 Kobilarna Lipica (Lipica Stud Farm)
2 Postojnska jama (Postojna Cave)

Tourist Information

Slovenska Turisticna Organizacija (Slovenian Tourist Organisation)
WTC, Dunajska 156, 1000 Ljubljana, Slovenia
Tel: (01) 589 1840. Fax: (01) 589 1841.
E-mail: info@slovenia-tourism.si
Website: www.slovenia-tourism.si

Slovenian Tourist Office
49 Conduit Street, London W1R 9FB, UK
Tel: (020) 7287 7133. Fax: (020) 7287 5476.
E-mail: slovenia@cpts.fsbusiness.co.uk
Website: www.slovenia-tourism.si

Kobilarna Lipica (Lipica Stud Farm)

Lipica Stud Farm is the home of one of the world's most famous breed of horses, the Lippizaner. Founded by Archduke Charles of Austria in 1580, the farm has continuously bred the sturdy white horses for over four centuries, and some of the best perform at the *Spanish Riding School* in Vienna. As well as watching the horses perform at the *Classical Riding School* at Lipica, visitors can take the reins of a thoroughbred Lippizaner themselves and there are pony rides for children. Other activities on offer include horse-drawn carriage rides, tennis, cycling, and walking among the lime groves and oak-tree forests. It is also possible to spend an entire holiday on and around the stud farm; the two on-site hotels provide swimming pools, a fitness centre, sauna, casino and nightclub.

Contact Address

Kobilarna Lipica, 6210 Sežana, Lipica 5, Slovenia
Tel: (067) 31580. Fax: (067) 72818.
E-mail: lipica@siol.net
Website: www.k-lipica.si

Transportation

Air: Ljubljana Brnik Airport. **Rail:** Train: Divaca Station or Sežana Station. **Road:** Taxi: Services from Divaca Station or Sežana Station. Car: A10 (from Ljubljana); A1 (from Klagenfurt, Austria); S14 (from Trieste, Italy).

Opening Times

Daily 1100-1500 (1 Nov-28 Feb); Mon-Fri 1100-1600, Sat and Sun 1000-1600 (1-31 Mar); Mon-Fri 1000-1700, Sat and Sun 0900-1700 (1 Apr-30 Jun); Mon-Fri 0900-1800 (1 Jul-31 Aug); Mon-Fri 1000-1700, Sat and Sun 0900-1700 (1 Sep-31 Oct).

Admission Fees

Stud Farm Tour: SIT900 (adult), SIT450 (child 7-14), free (child under 7) (1 Nov-31 Mar); SIT1100 (adult), SIT550 (child 7-14), free (child under 7) (1 Apr-31 Oct). *Stud Farm Tour and Classical Riding School Presentation*: SIT2200 (adult), SIT1100 (child 7-14), free (child under 7). *Stud Farm Tour and Classical Riding School Training*: SIT1600 (adult), SIT800 (child 7-14). Concessions available.

Postojnska jama (Postojna Cave)

Postojna Cave in western Slovenia is a 15-kilometre (nine-mile) labyrinth of subterranean passages, filled with fantastical stalagmites, stalactites and other weird and wonderful rock formations. It is considered by experts to be one of the finest examples of karst landscape, where limestone rock has been heavily eroded to form underground streams, a phenomenon that has created several other caves in this area of Slovenia. Postojna Cave is also home to the Proteus Anguinus, a unique creature with no eyes, which can grow up to 30cm (1ft) in length and feeds on snails and worms. Visitors need not fear coming into contact with the Proteus Anguinus, however, as transport through the caves is by electric train. Speleological equipment can be provided at the cave for caving enthusiasts, and special interest tours can also be arranged.

Contact Address

Postojna jama – turizem, Jamska c30, 6230 Postojna, Slovenia
Tel: (05) 700 0100. Fax: (05) 700 0130.
E-mail: postojnska.jama@siol.net
Website: www.postojnska-jama.si

Transportation

Air: Ljubljana Brnik Airport. **Rail:** Train: Postojna Station. **Road:** Car: E61 or E70 (from Ljubljana); E751 (from Trieste, Italy).

Opening Times

Guided tours: Mon-Fri 1000 and 1400, Sat and Sun 1000, 1200, 1400, 1600 (1 Nov-28 Feb); daily 1000, 1200, 1400, 1600 (1-31 Mar); daily 1000, 1200, 1400, 1600, 1700 (1-30 Apr); daily 0900, 1000, 1100, 1200, 1300, 1400, 1500, 1600, 1700, 1800 (1 May-30 Sep); Mon-Fri 1000, 1200, 1400 and 1600, Sat and Sun 1000, 1100, 1200, 1300, 1400, 1500, 1600, 1700 (1-31 Oct).

Admission Fees

SIT2200 (adult), SIT1100 (child 6-14), free (child under 6).

Lipica Stud Farm

Slovenian Tourist Organisation

South Africa

1 Anglo-Boer War Battlefields
2 Blyde River Canyon Nature Reserve
3 Cape Point
4 Kruger National Park
5 Robben Island
6 Table Mountain

Tourist Information

South African Tourism Board (SATOUR)
Private Bag X10012, Sandton 2146, South Africa
Tel: (011) 778 8000. Fax: (011) 778 8001.
E-mail: jhb@southafricantourism.com
Website: www.southafrica.net

South African Tourism Board (SATOUR)
5-6 Alt Grove, London SW19 4DZ, UK
Tel: (0870) 155 0044 (tourism enquiry and brochure request line). Fax: (020) 8944 6705.
E-mail: info@south-african-tourism.org
Website: www.south-african-tourism.org

Anglo-Boer War Battlefields

The Anglo-Boer War began in 1899 with the British retaliation against President Paul Kruger's refusal to grant political rights to the mainly English outsiders in the gold- and diamond-rich Transvaal. In 1902, after three years of bitter fighting, the British claimed victory, having destroyed Boer farms and sent their occupants to concentration camps where 20,000 people perished. Today, various museums and memorial sites dedicated to the war are scattered in and around 15 towns, mostly located in the province of KwaZulu-Natal, but also further west and north, around Bloemfontein and Pretoria. The main museum is the *Anglo-Boer War Museum* in Bloemfontein (tel: (051) 447 3447), which displays artwork and artefacts and provides an insight into the horrors of the concentration camps. *Talana Museum* (tel: (034) 212 2654), is located at Talana Hill, near Dundee, the site of the first battle of the Anglo-Boer War on 20 October 1899; it is now an eight-hectare (20-acre) heritage park with a cemetery dedicated to those who fought and lost their lives there, and also features displays on local bush traditions. At *Melrose House* in Pretoria (tel: (012) 322 0420), visitors can see a photographic exhibition and the table at which the Vereeniging peace treaty was signed. Many of the blockhouses, two-storey stone fortifications which were used by the British to guard railway bridges and stop the movement of Boer troops, can also be seen along a 5900-kilometre (3700-mile) route at places such as *Tulbagh*, *Ketting* and *Victoria West* in West Cape Province.

Contact Address

KwaZulu Natal Tourism Authority, PO Box 2516, Durban 4000, South Africa
Tel: (031) 304 7144. Fax: (031) 305 6693.
E-mail: tkzn@iafrica.com
Website: www.zulukingdom.org

Transportation

Air: Johannesburg International Airport, Durban International Airport, Cape Town International Airport or Pretoria Airport. **Rail:** Train: Johannesburg Park Station, Durban Station, Cape Town Station, Dundee Station or Pretoria Station. **Road:** Car: N1 (Johannesburg-Bloemfontein-Cape Town); N3 (Johannesburg-Durban). There are various battlefield itineraries; for more information contact the South African Tourism Board (see **Tourist Information** above).

Opening Times

Anglo-Boer War Museum: Mon-Fri 0800-1630, Sat 1000-1630, Sun 1400-1630. *Blockhouses*: Daily 24 hours. *Melrose House*: Tues-Sun 1000-1700. *Talana Museum*: Mon-Fri 0800-1630, Sat, Sun and public holidays 1000-1630. Closed 29 Mar and 25 Dec.

Admission Fees

Anglo-Boer War Museum: R5 (adult), R2 (child 5-18), free (child under 5). *Blockhouses*: Free. *Melrose House*: R12. *Talana Museum*: R8 (adult), R1 (child under 18).

Blyde River Canyon Nature Reserve

Blyde River Canyon, located close to the border with Mozambique, provides some of South Africa's most breathtaking scenery and is the third largest gorge in the world, after the Grand Canyon (USA) and Fish River Canyon (Namibia). The 29,000-hectare (71,662-acre) reserve is home to a rich variety of wildlife including rare birds and lichens. At the heart of the nature reserve is the *Blyde Dam*, which provides a natural habitat for hippo and crocodile, whilst further afield, in the Lowveld plain at the entrance to the canyon, blue wildebeest, waterbuck and zebra can be seen. Popular activities in the reserve include fishing and hiking to beauty spots such as *God's Window*, which offers unparalleled views across the canyon and the Lowveld. At *Bourke's Luck*, visitors can explore the unusual pothole formations via a series of footbridges and paths. The town of *Pilgrim's Rest* is of particular interest as a former gold-mining town between 1873 and 1972; visitors can see a row of historic 19th-century houses that once belonged to gold prospectors, as well as several shops and the *Royal Hotel* from the same era.

Contact Address

For more information on Blyde River Canyon, contact the South African Tourism Board (see **Tourist Information** above).

Transportation

Air: Johannesburg International Airport. **Rail:** Train: Johannesburg Park Station or Pretoria Station. **Road:** Car: N4 (from Pretoria); N12 (from Johannesburg), then R36, then R532 (to Blyde River Canyon), then R533 (to Pilgrim's Rest).

Opening Times

Daily 24 hours.

Admission Fees

Free.

Blyde River Canyon Nature Reserve

SATOUR

Cape Point

Part of the *Cape Peninsula National Park*, *Cape Point* is an 8000-hectare (19,770-acre) narrow promontory of land jutting into a stretch of open sea popularly believed to be the meeting point of the Atlantic and Indian oceans. The peninsula, situated 60km (37 miles) southwest of Cape Town, is characterised by towering sea cliffs, the highest in South Africa, which reach a height of 249m (817ft). Criss-crossed by spectacular walks and trails, the area also features whale and penguin watching, tidal pools, over a thousand species of indigenous plants and a variety of mammals, such as baboon and buck. Popular activities around Cape Point also include abseiling, parasailing, horseriding and surfing.

Contact Address

Cape Peninsula National Park, PO Box 37, Constantia, 7848 Cape Town, South Africa
Tel: (021) 701 8692. Fax: (021) 701 8773.
E-mail: capepeninsula@parks-sa.co.za
Website: www.cpnp.co.za

Transportation

Air: Cape Town International Airport. **Rail:** Train: Simon's Town Station. **Road:** Bus: Services to Simon's Town (from Cape Town). Car: M3 towards Muizenberg (from Cape Town); M4 towards Cape Point (via Simon's Town).

Opening Times

Daily 0700-1800 (Sep-Apr); daily 0700-1700 (May-Aug).

Admission Fees

Until 11 Nov 2001: R20 (adult), R10 (child 5-16), free (child under 5). From 11 Nov 2001: R25 (adult), R15 (child 5-16), free (child under 5). Concessions available.

Kruger National Park

At 20,000 sq kilometres (7722 sq miles), *Kruger National Park* is the largest game reserve in South Africa and boasts the world's highest concentration of species. Created in 1898 to protect the flora and fauna of the *South African Lowveld*, the park is named after its original proponent, President Paul Kruger. Today, it is home to a wealth of wildlife, including cheetahs, leopards, lions, rhinos, wildebeest, buffaloes, elephants, giraffes, antelope and impala. The park is also renowned for its cultural heritage sites, including many native rock art sites. At *Thulamela Hill*, visitors can see the excavated remains of a late Iron Age settlement, whilst the village of *Masorini* provides an excellent example of the way of life of the Stone Age hunter-gatherers who inhabited South Africa long before the first white settlers arrived.

Contact Address

South African National Parks, PO Box 787, Pretoria 0001, South Africa
Tel: (012) 343 1991. Fax: (012) 343 0905.
E-mail: reservations@parks-sa.co.za
Website: www.parks-sa.co.za

Transportation

Air: Johannesburg International Airport, Skukuza Airport (domestic flights). **Road:** Coach: Services from Mpumalanga. Car: Mpumalanga Highway.

Opening Times

Daily 0630-1730/1800 (1 Sep-31 May); daily 0530-1830 (1 Jun-31 Aug).

Admission Fees

R30 (adult), R15 (child 2-15), free (child under 2); plus R24 (per private vehicle). Concessions available.

Robben Island

Situated 11km (seven miles) north of Cape Town harbour, *Robben Island* was the notorious island prison where thousands of political prisoners were incarcerated between 1961 and 1991 for campaigning against apartheid. Its most famous resident was Nelson Mandela, who referred to it as a 'harsh, iron-fisted outpost'. Used as a prison as far back as 1525, it has also housed the mentally ill and lepers; its long history as a place of cruelty and isolation has turned it into a worldwide symbol of the triumph of the human spirit over oppression. Since 1996, there has been a *National Museum* and cultural centre on Robben Island, where visitors can see, among other things, the cell where Nelson Mandela was imprisoned. Tours of the island are available; some of the tour guides are former political prisoners, able to provide a personal testimony of the terrible conditions suffered by the inmates.

Contact Address

Robben Island Museum, Robben Island 7400, South Africa
Tel: (021) 419 1300. Fax: (021) 419 1057.
E-mail: info@ robben-island.org.za
Website: www.robben-island.org.za

Transportation

Air: Cape Town International Airport. **Water:** Ferry: From Jetty 1 at the V&A Waterfront (Cape Town) to Autfhumato, Makana.

Opening Times

Daily 0900-1500.

Admission Fees

Robben Island Tour (includes ferry ride to Robben Island): R100 (adult), R50 (child 4-17), free (child under 4). Concessions available.

Table Mountain

Like Cape Point, *Table Mountain* is part of the strip of land forming *Cape Peninsula National Park*. Table Mountain, however, stands in the middle of Cape Town and defines the downtown area, with the forested ravines of its eastern buttresses flanking the southern suburbs. So named for its flat top, the mountain rises to a height of 1086m (3562ft). Maclear's Beacon was erected on the top in 1843 by astronomer Sir Thomas Maclear, who used it to obtain a more accurate measurement of the earth's circumference. Since 1929, a cable car has carried visitors up to the summit, which offers spectacular views of the city and its beaches. The mountain is also home to an indigenous rodent-like creature called the Rock Hyrax or 'dassie', the closest living relative to modern elephants.

Contact Address

Cape Peninsula National Park, PO Box 37, Constantia, 7848 Cape Town, South Africa
Tel: (021) 701 8692. Fax: (021) 701 8773.
E-mail: capepeninsula@parks-sa.co.za
Website: www.cpnp.co.za *or* www.tablemountain.co.za

Transportation

Air: Cape Town International Airport. **Rail:** Train: Cape Town Station. **Road:** Bus: Services from Cape Town Bus Terminus in Strand Street. Car: N1 (from Johannesburg); N2 (from Overberg and Garden Route); N7 (from West Coast or Namibia).

Opening Times

First cable car up: 0800 (1 Jan-30 Apr); 0830 (1 May-30 Nov); 0730 (1-31 Dec). Last cable car up: 2000 (1 Jan-30 Apr); 1700 (1 May-15 Sep); 1830 (16 Sep-30 Oct); 2000 (1-30 Nov); 2100 (1-31 Dec). Last cable car down: 2100 (1 Jan-30 Apr); 1800 (1 May-15 Sep); after sunset (16 Sep-30 Oct); 2100 (1-30 Nov); 2200 (1-31 Dec).

Admission Fees

Single ticket: R40 (adult), R28 (child 4-18), free (child under 4) (1 Dec-30 Apr); R35 (adult), R20 (child 4-18), free (child under 4) (1 May-10 Sep); R40 (adult), R28 (child 4-18), free (child under 4) (16 Sep-30 Oct); R45 (adult), R23 (child 4-18), free (child under 4) (1-30 Nov). Return ticket: R75 (adult), R40 (child 4-18), free (child under 4) (1 Dec-30 Apr); R68 (adult), R35 (child 4-18), free (child under 4) (1 May-10 Sep); R75 (adult), R40 (child 4-18), free (child under 4) (16 Sep-30 Oct); R85 (adult), R45 (child 4-18), free (child under 4) (1-30 Nov). Concessions and family pass available.

Impala at Kruger National Park

SATOUR

Spain

1 Acueducto de Segovia (Roman Aqueduct at Segovia)
2 Alhambra
3 Catedral de Santiago de Compostela (Santiago de Compostela Cathedral)
4 Catedral de Sevilla (Seville Cathedral)
5 Cuevas del Drach (Caves of Drach)
6 Monasterio de San Lorenzo de El Escorial (Monastery of San Lorenzo de El Escorial)
7 Museo del Prado (Prado Museum)
8 Museo Guggenheim Bilbao (Guggenheim Museum Bilbao)
9 Parc Güell (Güell Park)
10 Temple Expiatiori de la Sagrada Familia (Expiatory Temple of the Sagrada Familia)
11 Terra Mitíca
12 Universal Studios Port Aventura

Tourist Information

Dirección General de Turespaña (Spanish National Tourist Office)
Jose Lázaro Galdiano 6, 28036 Madrid, Spain
Tel: (091) 343 3500. Fax: (091) 343 3446.
E-mail: info@tourspain.es
Website: www.tourspain.es

Spanish National Tourist Office
22-23 Manchester Square, London W1M 5AP, UK
Tel: (020) 7486 8077 *or* (0906) 364 0630 (brochure request line; calls cost 60p per minute). Fax: (020) 7486 8034. Website: www.tourspain.es

Acueducto de Segovia (Roman Aqueduct at Segovia)

One of the best preserved Roman constructions, the *Roman Aqueduct at Segovia* was still in use as recently as 50 years ago. Constructed around AD 50 during the reign of the Roman Emperor Trajan out of some 200,400 granite blocks, the aqueduct was made without concrete and stands due to an equilibrium of forces. When in use, it carried water from the River Frio to the city of Segovia over a distance of 16km (ten miles). The portion of the aqueduct that is above ground is 728m (2388ft) in length and consists of 165 arches, each over 9m (30ft) high, which are spectacularly illuminated at night. It is possible to climb a staircase next to the aqueduct to get views over the structure itself as well as the city.

Contact Address

Spanish National Tourist Office, Plaza Mayor 10, 40001 Segovia, Spain
Tel: (0921) 460 334. Fax: (0921) 460 330.
E-mail: ciudas-patrimonio@cyberspain.com
Website: www.cyberspain.com/ciudades-patrimonio

Transportation

Air: Madrid Barajas Airport. **Rail:** Train: Segovia Station. **Road:** Bus: Services from central bus station in Segovia. Car: A6, then N603 (from Madrid).

Opening Times

Daily 24 hours.

Admission Fees

Free.

Alhambra

Overlooking the city of Granada, the *Alhambra* is the most important and most spectacular piece of Moorish architecture in Spain. The name means 'the red' in Arabic, and the building is so called because of the colour of the bricks forming the outer walls. It was begun in 1238 as both a palace and a fortress by Ibn Ahmar, founder of the Nasrid dynasty (who made Granada the capital of his Moorish kingdom), and it was subsequently elaborated upon by his successors until its completion in 1358. Spanish emperor Charles I rebuilt parts of the Alhambra in Renaissance style in the 16th century, and some of the towers were destroyed by the French in the War of Independence in 1812. The Alhambra has now been restored to its former glory. Visitors can explore the *Alcazaba*, or citadel, which is the oldest remaining part of the complex, as well as the *Alhambra Palace*, containing the fabled *Patio de los Leones* (Court of the Lions), an alabaster basin supported by 12 white marble lions. The *Generalife* gardens, dotted with pools and fountains, are located on the neighbouring hill and were laid out in the 14th century.

Contact Address

Patronato de la Alhambra y Generalife, Real de la Alhambra s/n, 18009 Granada, Spain
Tel: (0958) 220 912 *or* (091) 346 5936 (ticket sales).
Fax: (0958) 210 584.
Website: www.alhambratickets.com

Transportation

Air: Malaga Airport. **Rail:** Train: Granada Station. **Road:** Bus: 30. Car: N-IV, then E5, then N323 (from Madrid); N334, then N342 (from Seville).

Opening Times

Alcazaba, Alhambra Palace and *Generalife*: Mon 0730-1800, Tues-Sat 0730-2030, Sun 0730-1800 (winter); Mon 0730-2000, Tues-Sat 0730-2230, Sun 0730-2000 (summer).

Admission Fees

Alcazaba, Alhambra Palace and *Generalife*: Pta1125 (adult), Pta125 (child under 9). Concessions available (EU citizens only).

Catedral de Santiago de Compostela (Santiago de Compostela Cathedral)

According to legend, the *Catedral de Santiago de Compostela* holds the remains of one of Christ's apostles, St James (Santiago in Spanish), who was martyred in Jerusalem around AD 44. King Alfonso II of Asturias built a church over the tomb in the ninth century and this was expanded in later years, making the town the most important place of Christian pilgrimage after Jerusalem and Rome. The whole of Santiago de Compostela, apart from the tomb, was destroyed by the invading Moors in AD 997, and it was not until 1078 that King Alfonso VI of Leon and Castile ordered the building of the present cathedral, which was consecrated in 1211. Although it is predominantly Romanesque in style, significant

Santiago de Compostela Cathedral

additions have been made over the centuries, including a 15th-century dome and a Baroque façade called the *Obradoiro*. Within the Obradoiro is the *Pórtico de Gloria* (Gate of Glory), a porch featuring sculptured scenes of the Last Judgement by Maestro Mateo, considered to be Spain's finest piece of Romanesque sculpture. Pilgrims used to complete their journey to Santiago by praying as they touched the roots of the Tree of Jesse, depicting Christ's ancestors, which is carved into the Gate of Glory. One of the best, but also most crowded, times to visit the cathedral is during one of the special masses, where priests swing a huge incense-burner on a rope-and-pulley system from one end of the transept ceiling to the other. Santiago is still a place of pilgrimage for Christians, although nowadays many travellers walk the *Camino de Santiago* (Way of St James) simply to enjoy the mountainous green landscape that characterises northern Spain.

Contact Address

Comisión de Cultura, Praza Platerías s/n, 15704 Santiago de Compostela, Spain
Tel: (0981) 560 527. Fax: (0981) 563 366.

Transportation

Air: Madrid Barajas Airport, Santiago de Compostela Lavacolla Airport. **Rail:** Train: Hórreo Station, Santiago de Compostela. **Road:** Coach: Services to Santiago de Compostela Bus Station (from Madrid, Gijón, Bilbao and the rest of Europe). Car: A9 (from La Coruña or Ferrol); N-VI, then A9 (from Madrid).

Opening Times

Daily 0700-2100.

Admission Fees

Free.

Catedral de Sevilla (Seville Cathedral)

Seville Cathedral, which dates from the 14th century, is located in the city's *Plaza Virgen de los Reyes*, on the site of the *Gran Mezquita* (Great Mosque) originally used by the retreating Moors, who had invaded Spain from North Africa in the eighth century AD. Originally, the mosque was simply converted into a cathedral, but in 1402 the chapter, or ruling body of the cathedral, began plans to construct 'a church so large that everyone who sees it will think we are mad'. Builders retained the minaret and patio from the former mosque, and the cathedral they constructed remains the largest Gothic structure in the world. The main altarpiece, *Retablo Mayor*, is the largest altar in the world and features 45 scenes from the life of Christ, carved from wood by Pierre Dancart. The cathedral also houses the remains of the world-famous explorer, Christopher Columbus.

Contact Address

Centro de Información de Sevilla, Carrer Arjona 28, 41001 Seville, Spain
Tel: (0954) 505 600. Fax: (0954) 505 605.
E-mail: cis@sevilla.org
Website: www.sevilla.org

Transportation

Air: Seville Airport. **Rail:** Train: Santa Justa Station. **Road:** Bus: 25 or 26. Car: N-IV (from Madrid).

Opening Times

Mon-Sat 1100-1700, Sun 1400-1800.

Admission Fees

Pta800 (adult), Pta200 (child 12-18), free (child under 12), free Sun. Concessions available.

Cuevas del Drach (Caves of Drach)

The *Caves of Drach* are the most famous tourist attraction on the island of Mallorca. They are also known as *Dragon Caves* due to the fact that the dragon features in many Mallorcan fairytales and is believed to be a symbol of strength and a defence against intruders. There are three chambers inside the caves, *Cueva Negra* (Black Cave), *Cueva Blanca* (White Cave) and *Cueva Luis Salvator* (Luis Salvator Cave). The latter is named after the Archduke Ludwig Salvator of Austria who invited Édouard-Alfred Martel to explore the caves in 1896; the caves are also home to *Lago Martel* (Lake Martel), one of the largest subterranean lakes in the world. The former French lawyer and famous speleologist Édouard-Alfred Martel (1859-1938), who discoverd the *Gouffre de Padirac* (Padirac Cave) in the Lot region in France, entered the Caves of Drach for the first time in 1896. Here, he discovered a natural niche in the rock known as *La ventana* (the window), which allowed him a spectacular view of *Lago Martel* (Lake Martel), and the new part of the cave beyond, which is known as *Cueva de los Franceses* (Cave of the French). Today, visitors can take a boat ride on the lake and see the beautiful limestone formations, including stalactites protuding from the rockface and stalagmites hanging down from the roof of the cave. As part of their journey underground, they are accompanied by the sound of musicians performing classical music every hour on a boat, including compositions by Chopin.

Contact Address

Cuevas del Drach, E-07680, Porto Cristo, Mallorca, Spain
Tel: (0971) 820 753.

Transportation

Air: Palma de Mallorca Airport. **Road:** Car: The caves are located 1.5km (0.9 miles) south of Porto Cristo.

Opening Times

Daily 1045-1200 and 1400-1530 (Nov-Mar); 1000-1700 (Apr-Oct).

Admission Fees

Pta1100 (adult), free (child under 7).

Monasterio de San Lorenzo de El Escorial (Monastery of San Lorenzo de El Escorial)

The *Monastery of San Lorenzo de El Escorial* was built in the latter half of the 16th century by King Philip II of Spain, to commemorate his victory over the French at the battle of San Quentin. The battle was won on the 10th August 1557, which is actually San Lorenzo's (Saint Lawrence) Day, after whom the monastery is named. Saint Lawrence was a deacon who gave to the poor and became a martyr after he was burnt to death for disagreeing with the Prefect of Rome. Juan Bautista de Toledo was originally commissioned by the king to construct the monastery and began work on it in April 1563. He died in 1567, however, leaving the work to be completed by Juan de Herrera in September 1584. Housing a monastery, two palaces and a library, the complex was intended to serve all the functions of church and state. Although the exterior is somewhat austere, the magnificent interior houses numerous works of art, including paintings by Titian, Tintoretto, Dürer, Ribera and Velasquez, as well as 40,000 volumes in the library that was founded by Philip II himself. The monastery is famous for its symmetrical design, with four towers marking each of the monastery's four corners, and for being the resting place of the remains of many Spanish kings and queens in the *Baroque Royal Pantheon*.

Contact Address

Monasterio de San Lorenzo de El Escorial, San Lorenzo de El Escorial, Spain
Tel: (091) 890 5902/3/4. Fax: (091) 890 7818.

Transportation

Air: Madrid Barajas Airport. **Rail:** Train: El Escorial Station. **Road:** Bus: 661 to San Lorenzo de El Escorial (from Madrid). Car: M505 (from Las Rozas); Nacional VI Highway (from Madrid).

Opening Times

Tues-Sun 1000-1700 (Oct-Apr); Tues-Sun 1000-1800 (May-Sep).

Admission Fees

Pta1000 (adult), Pta500 (child 5-16), free (child under 5).

Museo del Prado (Prado Museum)

The *Prado Museum,* which opened to the public in 1819 to house the Royal art collection, is one of Europe's great museums. It houses a collection of 4000 paintings, emphasising Spanish, Flemish and Italian art from the 15th to 19th century, and including masterpieces by Titian, Bosch, Botticelli, Rembrandt and Fra Angelico. The museum also possesses a renowned collection of paintings by Francisco de Goya, ranging from his sun-soaked, festive early paintings to the grim madness of his black period. The museum was originally designed by the architect Juan de Villanueva, with work starting on it in 1785. It was first intended to be a science museum, but was opened as the *Royal Museum of Painting and Sculpture* under instruction from King Ferdinand VII. Today, there are two buildings at the museum, the *Villanueva* and the *Casón del Buen Retiro,* which also house many coins, drawings, etchings and medals.

Contact Address

Museo del Prado, Villanueva Building, Paseo del Prado s/n, 28014 Madrid, Spain
Tel: (091) 330 2800 *or* 330 2900 (information).
Fax: (091) 330 2856.
E-mail: museo.nacional@prado.mcu.es
Website: museoprado.mcu.es

Transportation

Air: Madrid Barajas Airport. **Rail:** Train: Atocha Station. Underground: Atocha or Banco de España. **Road:** Bus: 9, 10, 14, 19, 27, 34, 37 or 45. Car: N-1 (from Santander); N-2 (from Zaragoza); N-3 (from Valencia); N-4 (from Seville); N-5 (from Badajoz); A6 (from Tordesilos).

Opening Times

Tues-Sat 0900-1900, Sun 0900-1400. Closed 1 Jan, 13 Apr, 1 May and 25 Dec.

Admission Fees

Pta500 (adult), free (child) (Tues-Fri 0900-1900 and Sat 0900-1430); free (Sat 1430-1900 and Sun 0900-1400). Concessions available.

Museo Guggenheim Bilbao (Guggenheim Museum Bilbao)

The *Guggenheim Museum Bilbao*, which opened in 1997, has quickly become one of the most famous museums in the world. The museum's collection focuses primarily on American and European art from the 20th century, featuring styles such as Pop Art, Minimalism, Arte Povera, Conceptual Art and Abstract Expressionism, as well as artwork that contemporary European and American artists created specifically for the museum. The building itself was designed by renowned American architect Frank O Gehry and is as well known for its striking architecture as for its collection. Other Guggenheim museums around the world include the *Solomon R Guggenheim* and *Guggenheim Museum SoHo* in New York, the *Peggy Guggenheim Collection* in Venice and the *Deutsche Guggenheim Berlin* in Germany.

Contact Address

Museo Guggenheim Bilbao, Abandoibarra Etorbidea 2, 48001 Bilbao, Spain
Tel: (094) 435 9080 (information) *or* 435 9023 (brochure request). Fax: (094) 435 9039 (information) *or* 435 9040 (reservations).
E-mail: atelleria@guggenheim-bilbao.es
Website: www.guggenheim-bilbao.es

Transportation

Air: Bilbao Airport. **Rail:** Train: Bilbao-Abando Station. Underground: Moyua Station. **Road:** Bus: 1, 10, 11, 13, 18, 27, 38, 46, 48 or 71. Car: A3 (from San Sebastian).

Opening Times

Tues-Sun 1000-2000 (Jan-Jun and Sep-Dec); daily 0900-2100 (Jul-Aug).

Admission Fees

Pta1000 (adult), Pta500 (student and OAPs), free (child under 12) (Jan-Apr and Oct-Dec); Pta1200 (adult), Pta600 (student and OAPs), free (child under 12) (May-Sep).

Prado Museum

Spanish National Tourist Office

Parc Güell (Güell Park)

Created by the renowned Spanish architect Antonio Gaudí between 1900 and 1914, *Parc Güell* is a fantasy land that combines the natural and the man-made. The park was originally conceived as a residential garden city and built for Gaudí's patron, Eusebi Güell Bacigalupi, a textile manufacturer who had a keen interest in the arts and helped develop the architect's career. The project was not a great commercial success, however, and the park became municipal property in 1923. Covering a hill to the north of Barcelona and offering excellent views of the city, the park has fantastic pavilions, stairways and columned halls. Highlights include the organic plaza, decorated with stunning broken-mosaic work (*trencadís*), designed by Gaudí's assistant, Josep Maria Jujol, and the giant lizard that divides the grand stairway and is the most photographed symbol of the park. *Casa-Museu Gaudí*, which houses a collection of Gaudí's furnishings and other memorabilia, stands at the bottom of the hill. Designed by Francesc Berenguer in 1905, the building is Gaudí's former residence in the park, where he lived for the last 20 years of his life.

Contact Address

Parc Güell, Carrer D'Olot, Barcelona, Spain
Tel: (093) 424 3809.

Transportation

Air: Barcelona International Airport. **Rail:** Underground: Vallcarca/Lesseps. **Road:** Bus: 24 or 25.

Opening Times

Park and *Museum*: Daily 1000-1800 (Nov-Feb); daily 1000-1900 (Mar and Oct); daily 1000-1900 (Apr-Sep); daily 1000-2100 (May-Aug).

Admission Fees

Park: Free. *Museum*: Pta300. *Guided tours around the park*: Pta200.

Temple Expiatiori de la Sagrada Familia (Expiatory Temple of the Sagrada Familia)

The *Expiatory Temple of the Sagrada Familia* is the unfinished masterpiece of Barcelona's most celebrated architect, Antonio Gaudí, who began work on it in 1882. Known around the world simply as *La Sagrada Familia*, Gaudí worked on this towering example of Barcelona's modernist architecture for more than 40 years, right up until his death in 1926. Its eerie, snaking lines and omnipresent detail make it unique among Europe's many cathedrals, and its eight spires, which stand 100m (328ft) high, were intended, with the addition of another four, to represent Christ's Twelve Apostles. Despite the fact that work still continues on the cathedral to this day, it lies in a perpetual state of incompleteness, with only one of its three façades actually finished. There is a small Gaudí museum inside the temple, which details Gaudí's life and provides information on the history of the building.

Contact Address

Temple Expiatiori de la Sagrada Familia, Calle Mallorca 401, 08013 Barcelona, Spain
Tel: (093) 207 3031. Fax: (093) 476 1010.
E-mail: informa@sagradafamilia.org
Website: http://sagfam.deakin.edu.au

Transportation

Air: Barcelona International Airport. **Rail:** Train: Passeig de Gràcia Station. Underground: Sagrada Familia. **Road:** Bus: 19, 33, 34, 43, 44, 50 or 51. Car: A7 (from France in the north); A2 from (Zaragoza in the south).

Opening Times

Daily 0900-1800 (Nov-Feb); daily 0900-1900 (Mar and Sep-Oct); daily 0900-2000 (Apr-Aug).

Admission Fees

Pta850 (adult), Pta650 (student), free (child under 10).

Terra Mítica

Opened in 2000, Terra Mítica is a giant amusement park located just outside the popular Spanish resort of Benidorm. As well as regular live shows, there are five different areas at the park, all of which are associated with the Mediterranean Sea: *Egypt, Iberia, Greece, Rome* and *The Islands*. At the park, visitors can travel through ancient civilisations and go on the many themed rides, which include *El tren Bravo* (Bravo Train), *El vuelo del Fenix* (Phoenix' Flight) and *El Misterio de Keops* (Cheop's Mystery). En route, visitors will encounter characters and creatures from many myths and legends, including coming face-to-face with the Minotaur on the *El Laberinto del Minotauro* (Minotaur's Labyrinth) and attempting to rescue Ulysses on the *El Rescate de Ulises* (Ulysses' Rescue) ride.

Contact Address

Terra Mitica, Ctra: Benidorm a Finestrat, Camino de Moralet s/n, 3500 Benidorm, Alicante, Spain
Tel: (0902) 020 220.
E-mail: callcenter@terramiticapark.com
Website: www.terramiticapark.com

Transportation

Air: Alicante Airport. **Rail:** Train: Terra Mítica Station. **Road:** Car: A-7 to Terra Mítica's exit which is signposted between Benidorm and Villajoyosa (from Valencia or Alicante).

Opening Times

Sat-Sun 1000-1800 (weekends in Jan, Mar, Nov and Dec); daily 1000-2000 (15 Mar-15 Jun and 17 Sep-4 Nov); daily 1000-2400 (16 Jun-16 Sep). Opening times may vary and visitors are advised to check with the park owners before their visit.

Admission Fees

Pta3600 (adult), Pta2600 (child) (one-day pass, weekends in Jan, Mar, Nov and Dec); Pta4800 (adult), Pta3500 (child) (one-day pass, 15 Mar-4 Nov). Concessions available, as well as two- and three-day passes.

Universal Studios Port Aventura

This giant theme park, which opened in 1994, attracts thousands of holidaymakers every year who journey through its five worlds (*Mediterránia, Far West, Mexico, Polynesia* and *China*) on its many rides and attractions. Enjoying an enviable coastal location, between Salou and Vila-seca on Spain's Costa Dorada, this 117 hectare-site (289 acre) boasts entertainment aimed at all age groups. There are nightly shows, including *Fiestaventura* in the Mediterranean world, as well as many other attractions, including the *Sea Odyssey* underwater adventure, the *Stampida* roller coaster ride, and the *Grand Canyon Rapids* and *Tutuki Splash* water rides. New for 2001 is *Templo del Fuego*, which has the greatest number of fire and water effects ever used on any attraction. The park is owned by the Universal Studios Recreation Group, responsible for other theme parks around the world, including *Universal Orlando Resort* and *Universal Studios Hollywood*.

Contact Address

Universal Studios Port Aventura, Avenue Alcalde Pere Molas, Km 2, 43480 Vila-seca, Tarragona, Spain
Tel: (0977) 779 090. Fax: (0977) 779 082.
E-mail: amigos@portaventura.es
Website: www.portaventura.es

Transportation

Air: Barcelona International Airport, Reus Airport. **Rail:** Train: Port Aventura Station. **Road:** Car: Hwy-A7 or Hwy-N340 (from Valencia or Barcelona).

Opening Times

Daily 1000-1900 (Dec-Jan); Mon-Fri 1000-2000, Sat-Sun 1000-2230 (Mar-Jun); daily 1000-2400 (Jun-Sep); Mon-Fri 1000-2000, Sat-Sun 1000-2230 (Sep-Nov); Thurs-Sun 1000-1900 (Nov-Dec). Closed Jan-Mar.

Admission Fees

Pta4800 (adult one-day pass), Pta3600 (child one-day pass). Concessions available, as well as evening, two- and three-day passes.

Universal Studios Port Aventura

Spanish National Tourist Office

Sri Lanka

1 Dalada Maligawa (Temple of the Sacred Tooth)
2 Sigiriya

Tourist Information

Srilanka Sancharaka Mandeleye (Sri Lanka Tourist Board)
PO Box 1504, Colombo 3, Sri Lanka
Tel: (01) 437 059 *or* 437 060. Fax: (01) 437 953.
E-mail: tourinfo@sri.lanka.net
Website: www.srilankatourism.org

Sri Lanka Tourist Board
22 Lower Regent Street, London W2 2LU, UK
Tel: (020) 7930 2627. Fax: (020) 7930 9070.
E-mail: srilanka@cerbernet.co.uk

Dalada Maligawa (Temple of the Sacred Tooth)

Located in Kandy, an ancient religious centre for Buddhism, the octagonal, golden-roofed *Temple of the Sacred Tooth*, built between 1687 and 1707, is a stunning sacred temple, which is believed to house the left upper canine of the Lord Buddha himself. According to legend, the tooth was taken from the Buddha as he lay on his funeral pyre and smuggled to Sri Lanka hidden in Princess Hemamali's hair, where it survived numerous attempts to capture and destroy it. The tooth was brought from Kalninga in India during the fourth century by Princess Hemamali and Prince Danta on the orders of the princess's father, King Guhasiva; he was worried that the relic might fall into the hands of his enemies and so, in order to safeguard it, he gave it to King Kirti Sri Meghavarna (301-328) of Anuradhapura. Today, this famous religious relic attracts white-clad pilgrims every day bearing lotus blossoms and frangipani. The temple is joined to the *Pattiripuwa* (Octagon), built in 1803, which was originally used as a prison, but now houses a collection of palm-leaf manuscripts. There are many other attractions in this ancient city, including *Natha Devale*, a stone sanctuary and the oldest building in Kandy, and *Mahavishnu Devale*, a temple which is dedicated to Vishnu, the protector of Buddhism in Sri Lanka.

Contact Address

For more information on the Temple of the Sacred Tooth, contact Sri Lanka Tourist Board (see **Tourist Information** above).

Transportation

Air: Colombo Bandaranayake International Airport. **Rail:** Train: Kandy Station (from Colombo). **Road:** Bus: Services to Kandy which stop in front of the temple (from Colombo). Car: Colombo – Kandy road (from Colombo).

Opening Times

Daily 0700-2000.

Admission Fees

SLRs100. No concessions available.

Sigiriya

Taking its name from *giriya* ('jaws and throat') and *sinha* ('lion'), *Sigiriya* is a Buddhist site in central Sri Lanka. It contains the ruins of an ancient royal fortress and city founded in the fifth century AD by King Kasyapa. Three kilometres (1.8 miles) wide and one kilometre (0.6 miles) long, it stands on a remarkably steep, large rock, known as *Lion Mountain*, that rises 180m (600ft) above the surrounding plain. It was constructed in AD 477 as a safeguard against attack from Mogallana, Kasyapa's brother from whom he had usurped the throne after killing their father, and visitors were obliged then, as now, to enter through the jaws of a massive monumental lion. The magnificent site also features a series of water gardens, trees and pathways, laid out according to an 'echo plan', with the two sides reflecting one another in a symmetrical design. It is considered one of the best preserved, first-millennium city centres in Asia and is also renowned for its fifth-century rock paintings.

Contact Address

For more information on Sigiriya, contact the Sri Lanka Tourist Board (see **Tourist Information** above).

Transportation

Air: Colombo Bandaranayake International Airport. **Rail:** Train: Habarane Station. **Road:** Coach: Services from Dambulla. Car: Main road from Colombo.

Opening Times

Daily 0830-1800.

Admission Fees

SLRs1200 (adult), SLRs600 (child 5-12), free (child under 5).

Sigiriya

Ceylon Tourist Board

Sweden

1 Drottningholms Slott (Drottningholm Palace)
2 Kungliga Slottet (Royal Palace)
3 Statens Historiska Museet (Museum of National Antiquities)
4 Vasa Museet (Vasa Museum)

Tourist Information

Sveriges Rese – och Turistråd AB (Swedish Travel & Tourism Council)
PO Box 3030, 103 61 Stockholm, Sweden
Tel: (08) 725 5500. Fax: (08) 725 5531.
E-mail: info@swetourism.se
Website: www.swetourism.se (travel trade) *or* www.visit-sweden.com (public).

Swedish Travel & Tourism Council
11 Montagu Place, London W1H 2AL, UK
Tel: (020) 7870 5600 *or* (01476) 578 811 (24-hour brochure request line).
Fax: (020) 7724 5872.
E-mail: info@swetourism.org.uk
Website: www.visit-sweden.com

Drottningholms Slott (Drottningholm Palace)

Home to the Swedish Royal Family since 1981, when they moved from the *Kungliga Slottet* (Royal Palace) in Stockholm, *Drottningholm Palace* is one of the most magnificent legacies of Sweden's imperial age. King Johan III first built a palace on the site during the late 16th century; this building was destroyed, however, by fire in 1661 and work began on building a new palace in 1662. Designed by the architect Nikodemus Tessin the Elder, highlights inside the palace include the *Ehrenstrahl Drawing Room* and *Hedvig Eleonora's State Bedchamber*. Over the years, the interior has been embellished and improved upon by successive residents and it is now renowned for its

Drottningholm Palace

R Ryan/Stockholm Information Service

Argentina National Tourist Board

Guanajuato State Tourism

Corel

Corel

Clockwise from top left: Isla Victoria, Nahuel Huapi National Park, Argentina • La Parroquia, San Miguel de Allende, Mexico • Machu Picchu, Peru • Statue of Christ the Redeemer, Brazil

Corel

Corel

Corel

Travel Alberta

© Disney Enterprises, Inc.

Clockwise from top left: Statue of Liberty, USA • Golden Gate Bridge, USA • Toronto Skyline and CN Tower, Canada • Spaceship Earth, Epcot®, USA • Moraine Lake and the Valley of the Ten Peaks, Banff National Park, Canada

Corel

Corel

Corel

Corel

© Disney Enterprises, Inc.

Clockwise from top left: Universal Studios, USA • White House, USA • Mirror Lake, Yosemite National Park, USA • WALT DISNEY WORLD® Resort, USA • Crocodile Park in Everglades National Park, USA

The Flat Earth Collection

Corel

Corel

Clockwise from top left: Big Ben and British Airways London Eye, UK • Sacré Coeur Basilica, France • Alhambra, Spain

The Royal Pavilion, Libraries & Museum

Corel

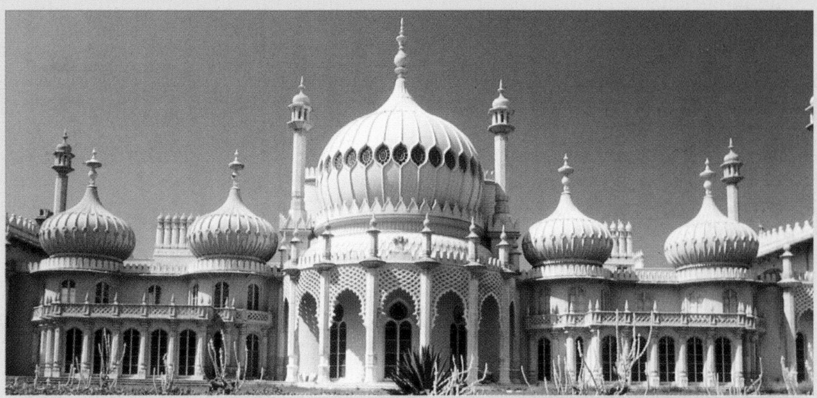

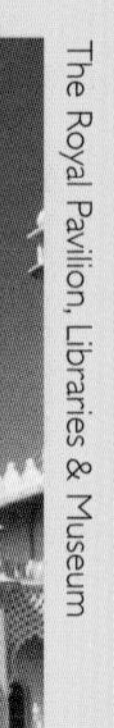

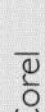

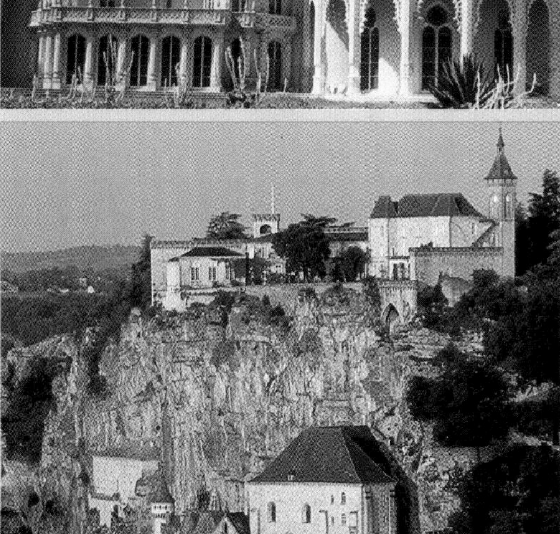

Corel

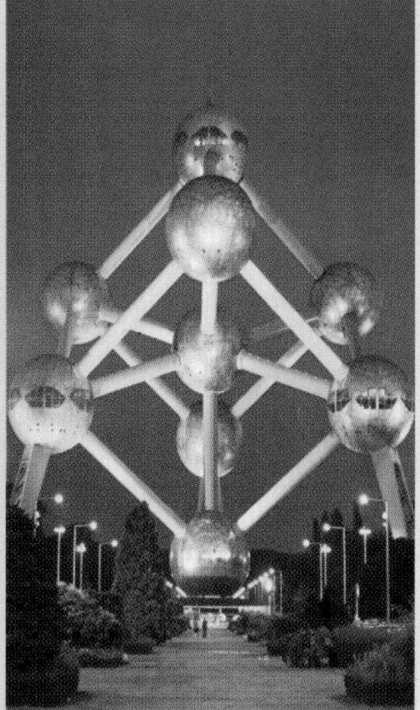

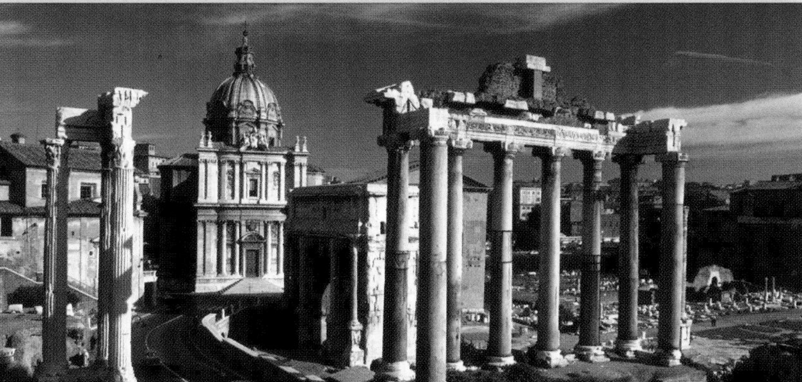

Corel

Clockwise from top left: Royal Pavilion, UK • Atomium, Belgium • Roman Forum, Italy • Rocamadour, France

Corel

Ruth Blakeborough

Corel

Hungarian National Tourist Office

Clockwise from top left: Kremlin and St Basil's Cathedral after dark, Russia • Blue Mosque, Turkey • Buda Castle Palace and Chain Bridge by night, Hungary • Charles Bridge, Czech Republic

Tunisian National Tourist Office

Egyptian State Tourist Office

South African Tourism Board (SATOUR)

Chris McIntyre

Corel

Clockwise from top left: Matmata, Tunisia • Valley of the Queens, Egypt • Blyde River Canyon, South Africa • Tour Hassan, Morocco • Moremi Game Reserve, Botswana

Corel

Australian Tourist Commission

Corel

Corel

Clockwise from top left: Taj Mahal, India • Sydney Harbour, Australia • Great Wall, China • Damnoen Saduak Floating Market, Thailand

Rococo decorations. The palace was handed over to Princess Lovisa Ulrika of Prussia in 1744 on her marriage to Adolf Fredrik of Sweden. Drottningholm is surrounded by splendid Baroque gardens, including the great English Park and the French formal garden, and is home to many fine buildings such as the *Chinese Pavilion*, the *Court Theatre* and the *Castle Church*.

Contact Address

Drottningholms Slott, 17802 Drottningholm, Sweden
Tel: (08) 402 6280. Fax: (08) 402 6281.
E-mail: info.drottningholms-slott@royalcourt.se
Website: www.royalcourt.se/drottningholm/eng

Transportation

Air: Stockholm Arlanda Airport. **Water:** Boat: Services to Drottningholm (from Stadshuskajen). **Rail:** Underground: Brommaplan. **Road:** Bus: 177, 178, 310 or 323. Car: The palace is located in central Stockholm. Car drivers should follow signs for Drottningholmsvägen (from Fridhemsplan to Brommaplan).

Opening Times

Sat and Sun 1200-1530 (Oct-Apr); daily 1000-1630 (May-Aug); daily 1200-1530 (Sep).

Admission Fees

SKr50 (adult), SKr25 (child), free (child under 7).

Kungliga Slottet (Royal Palace)

The *Royal Palace* is the official residence of Sweden's monarch, currently King Carl XVI Gustaf, and houses the offices of the King and Queen and the Duchess of Halland; the latter is the most senior member of the royal family after the King and Queen and their children. A fortress was first built on the site in the 13th century and, as Sweden increased in status, so did the castle, finally becoming the official royal residence in 1521 under Gustav Vasa. The Vasa family developed the palace on a grand scale, adding Renaissance and Baroque features. After fire struck in 1697, much of the interior of the palace was reconstructed over the next 60 years, resulting in a variety of architectural styles. Perhaps the most interesting feature is the difference in the façades of the four wings, each designed at the time to reflect a particular aspect of the Royal Family – the King, the Queen, their private interests and the Swedish nation. The palace also used to house the library, debating chamber and offices of the Swedish government. Visitors can view some of the magnificent rooms within the palace, such as the *Royal Apartments*, the *Treasury* and the *Apartments of the Orders of Chivalry* and watch the changing of the guard, which takes place every day.

Contact Address

Kungliga Slottet, 111 30 Stockholm, Sweden
Tel: (08) 402 6130. Fax: (08) 402 6167.
Website: www.royalcourt.se/kungliga_slottet

Transportation

Air: Stockholm Arlanda Airport. **Rail:** Train: Stockholm Central Station. Underground: Gamla Stan. **Road:** Bus: 43, 46, 55, 59 or 76. Car: E4 (from Malmö); E18 (from Oslo, Norway); E20 or E6 (from Gothenburg).

Opening Times

Apartments of the Orders of Chivalry: Tues-Sun 1200-1500 (1 Sep-14 May); daily 1000-1600 (15 May-31 Aug). *Royal Apartments*: Tues-Sun 1200-1500 (1 Sep-14 May); daily 1000-1600 (15 May-31 Aug). *Treasury*: Tues-Sun 1200-1500 (1 Sep-14 May); daily 1000-1600 (15 May-31 Aug).

Admission Fees

Apartments of the Orders of Chivalry: SKr60 (adult), SKr30 (child 7-18), free (child under 7). *Royal Apartments*: SKr60 (adult), SKr30 (child 7-18), free (child under 7). *Treasury*: SKr60 (adult), SKr30 (child 7-18), free (child under 7). *Guided tour of Apartments of the Orders of Chivalry and Royal Apartments*: Daily 1315. *Guided tour of Treasury*: Daily 1215.

Statens Historiska Museet (Museum of National Antiquities)

Sweden's *Museum of National Antiquities* traces more than 12,000 years of the nation's history from the Stone Age to the 16th century. Its most famous attraction is the Viking exhibition in the Gold Room, which houses the gold of the Viking chiefs, recovered from tombs and various hiding places. The museum also houses a fine collection of European painted medieval wooden religious sculpture and textiles. Artefacts from the Stone Age to the Viking Age are kept on the ground floor, whilst Swedish treasures from the Middle Ages are kept on the first floor, in the *Barrock Hall*, *Textile Chamber*, *Gothic Hall* and *Country Church*.

Contact Address

Statens Historiska Museet, Box 5428, S-114 84 Stockholm, Sweden

Tel: (08) 5195 5600. Fax: (08) 667 6578.
E-mail: info@historiska.se
Website: www.historiska.se

Transportation

Air: Stockholm Arlanda Airport. **Rail:** Underground: Karlaplan or Östermalmstorg. **Road:** Bus: 44 or 56 to Nistoriska Museet; 47, 69 or 76 to Djurgårdsbron/ Historiska Museet.

Opening Times

Tues-Wed and Fri-Sun 1000-1700, Thurs 1000-2000.

Admission Fees

SKr60 (adult), SKr50 (child 13-16), free (child under 12). Concessions available.

Vasa Museet (Vasa Museum)

The mighty Swedish warship, the Vasa, was the most powerful vessel of her day. Commissioned by King Gustavus Adolphus in 1625 as one of a fleet of battleships in the war against Poland, she was constructed by experienced Dutch shipbuilder Henrik Hybertsson who died one year before her completion. The Vasa's 1275 square metre- (1525 foot-) bulk was capable of holding 445 crew and weighed 1210 tonnes (1191 tons). Tragically, the ship keeled over on her maiden voyage on 10 August 1628, probably under the weight of the weapons on deck, and sank, killing around 40 of the 150 people on board. It was not until 1961 that the remarkably intact wreckage was salvaged by the Swedish Navy and preserved in a temporary museum until the opening of the *Vasa Museum* in 1990. Visitors to the Vasa Museum can see the remains of the ship as well as a 1:10 scale model of the Vasa, showing what she would have looked like in all her glory. Exhibitions, interactive displays and audiovisual presentations tell of the salvage operation, life on board ship and sea battles of the period.

Contact Address

Vasa Museet, Box 27 131, 102 52 Stockholm, Sweden
Tel: (08) 5195 4800. Fax: (08) 5195 4888.
E-mail: vasamuseet@sshm.se
Website: www.vasamuseet.se

Transportation

Air: Stockholm Arlanda Airport. **Water:** Ferry: Services from Slussen (all year) and Nybroplan (summer) to Djurgården Island. **Rail:** Train: Stockholm Central Station. **Road:** Bus: 44, 47 or 69. Car: E18 (from Oslo); E20 or E6 (from Gothenburg); E4 (from Malmö).

Opening Times

Mon and Tues 1000-1700, Wed 1000-2000, Thurs-Sun 1000-1700 (26 Aug-9 Jun); daily 0930-1900 (10 Jun-25 Aug).

Admission Fees

SKr70 (adult), SKr50 (adult, Wed 1700-2000), SKr10 (child 7-15), free (child under 7). Concessions available.

Royal Palace

Stockholm Information Service

Switzerland

1 Château de Chillon (Chillon Castle)
2 Jet d'Eau (Water Fountain)
3 Jungfraujoch
4 Musée Olympique Lausanne (Olympic Museum Lausanne)

Tourist Information

Schweiz Tourismus (Switzerland Tourism)
Tödistrasse 7, 8027 Zürich, Switzerland
Tel: (01) 288 1111. Fax: (01) 288 1205.
E-mail: info@switzerlandtourism.ch
Website: www.myswitzerland.com
Switzerland Tourism
Tenth Floor, Swiss Centre, 10 Wardour St, London, W1D 6QF, UK
Tel: (00800) 1002 0030 (toll-free Europe only) *or* (020) 7743 1921. Fax: (00800) 1002 0031 (toll-free Europe only) *or* (020) 7851 7437 4577.
E-mail: stc@stlondon.com
Website: www.myswitzerland.com

Château de Chillon (Chillon Castle)

Chillon Castle is the most famous castle in Switzerland. It enjoys a spectacular location on the eastern edge of Lake Geneva, near Montreux, with the *Dents du Midi* (literally meaning the Teeth of the South) mountains in the background. Built in the 13th century on Roman foundations by Thomas I Count of Savoy, the château was once visited by Lord Byron. Byron later wrote the poem 'Prisoner of Chillon' (1816) about the fate of François de Bonivard (1493-1570), the castle's most famous prisoner, who was incarcerated here between 1530 and 1536 after he was captured for trying to bring protestantism to Switzerland. The castle, which was once an important medieval fort, strategically located on an island to guard against invasion, has many impressive turrets, as well as a fort and keep, separating the castle from the mainland. Today, visitors can see the castle's famous prison, and also tour the the *Grand Hall*, the *Hall of Justice*, the

Chillon Castle

Château de Chillon

Armouries, the *Grand Hall of the Count*, the *Duke's Chamber* and *Saint George's Chapel*. Many of the rooms house antique weapons and a fine collection of furniture and paintings from the Middle Ages.

Contact Address

Association du Château de Chillon, 1820 Veytaux, Switzerland
Tel: (021) 966 8910. Fax: (021) 966 8912.
E-mail: chillon@worldcom.ch
Website: www.chillon.ch

Transportation

Air: Geneva International Airport. **Water:** Boat: Boats dock at the CGN jetty next to the castle. **Rail:** Train: Veytaux-Chillon Station. **Road:** Bus: Trolley bus VMCV serves the castle every day (from Montreux Station). Car: A1 and A9 towards Montreux (from Geneva); the castle is within walking distance of Montreux.

Opening Times

Daily 1000-1600 (Jan-Feb and Nov-Dec); daily 0930-1700 (Mar and Oct); daily 0900-1800 (Apr-Sep). Closed 1 Jan and 25 Dec.

Admission Fees

SFr7.50 (adult), SFr3.50 (child). Concessions available.

Jet d'Eau (Water Fountain)

Next to chocolates, watches, bankers and cowbells, a giant fountain seems an odd symbol to be associated with Switzerland, but Geneva's *Jet d'Eau* has been breaking the calm of this peaceful city for over a hundred years. The idea that a water fountain might be a tourist attraction came about purely by chance in 1886, when a solution was needed to relieve pressure at the *Forces Motrices* pumping and power station. The water initially reached a height of 30m (98ft), and quickly began to draw large crowds. This led to a more impressive fountain being introduced on Eaux-Vives jetty in 1891 to coincide with the 600th anniversary of the Swiss Confederation and the opening of the Federal Gymnastics Festival. The fountain, which reached a height of 90m (295ft) in 1891, has been technologically improved to spurt water 140m (460ft) into the air. At three times the height of the *Statue of Liberty*, it is now Europe's tallest fountain and today, two electric pumps are used to blast an estimated seven tonnes of water aloft at a speed of 200kmph (124mph).

Contact Address

Jet d'Eau, Services Industriéls de Genève, PO Box 2777, 1211 Geneva, Switzerland
Tel: (022) 420 7250 *or* 420 7091. Fax: (022) 420 9360.
E-mail: Charles.Drapel@sig-ge.ch
Website: www.sig-ge.ch

Transportation

Air: Geneva International Airport. **Rail:** Train: Cornavin Station. Tram: Cours de Rive Station. **Road:** Bus: Eaux-Vives Bus Stop. Car: A1 (from Lausanne).

Opening Times

Jet d'Eau: Mon-Thurs 1400-sunset, Fri-Sun 1000-sunset (Feb-Apr); Mon-Thurs 1000-sunset, Fri-Sun 1000-2230 (Apr-May); daily 0900-2315 (May-Sep); Mon-Thurs 1000-sunset, 1000-2230 (Sep-Oct). *Visits of the machinery*: Mon-Fri 0800-0900 (Mar-Oct).

Admission Fees

Free.

Jungfraujoch

The stereotypically Swiss hiking trails and snow-covered Alps of the *Jungfraujoch* have been attracting visitors for hundreds of years. The peak of the Jungfrau is 4158m (13,642ft) high, with the ridge or 'joch' lying below it. From this point, visitors can see the longest glacier in Europe, the 24km (15 miles) long *Aletsch Glacier*. Skiing and alpine activities are immensely popular with visitors here, however the best way to take in the region is by train. Completed in 1912, the *Jungfraujoch Railway* takes passengers to the mountain's summit where they can alight at the highest railway station in Europe, at an altitude of 3454m (11,333 ft). There is a *Sphinx* viewing platform at the top of the mountain, from where visitors can see as far as the Black Forest on a clear day and an *Ice Palace* inside the glacier, as well as a chance to go on dog sleigh rides through the snow.

Contact Address

Interlaken Tourism, Hoehweg 37, 3800 Interlaken, Switzerland
Tel: (033) 826 5300. Fax: (033) 826 5375.
E-mail: mail@interlakentourism.ch
Website: www.interlakentourism.ch

Transportation

Air: Geneva International Airport, Berne-Belp Airport. **Rail:** Train: Jungfrau Station. **Road:** Car: Via Bern to Interlaken, then Interlaken-Grindelwald Grund exit (from Zurich). Visitors must then take a train (from Grindelwald Grund).

Opening Times

Jungfraujoch: Daily dawn-dusk. *Train*: Daily dawn-1610 (winter); daily dawn-1700 (summer).

Admission Fees

Jungfraujoch: Free. *Train*: SFr103 (adult), SFr51.50 (first train of the day in summer or first two trains of the day in winter); SFr140 (adult), SFr70 (child) (all other trains).

Musée Olympique Lausanne (Olympic Museum Lausanne)

Inaugurated in June 1993, the *Olympic Museum* in Lausanne sits on the shores of Lake Geneva. Set in the beautiful *Olympic Park* gardens, which feature many striking sculptures by Botero, Folon and Calder, the museum displays sport, art and cultural collections from ancient Greece through to modern times. It is the centre of information on the Olympic Movement and preserves the heritage of the Olympic Games. There are both permanent and temporary exhibitions, an Olympic Studies Centre, a video library, meeting rooms and an auditorium. Permanent collections include *Modern Winter and Summer Olympic Games*, which features collectors' items such as Carl Lewis's shoe, and *Olympism in Classical Times*.

Contact Address

Musée Olympique Lausanne, 1 Quai d'Ouchy, 1001 Lausanne, Switzerland
Tel: (021) 621 6511. Fax: (021) 621 6512.
E-mail: info@museum.olympic.org
Website: www.museum.olympic.org

Transportation

Air: Geneva International Airport, Zurich International Airport. **Water:** Boat: Steamboats depart from Geneva, Vévey and Montreux and stop in Ouchy. **Rail:** Train: Lausanne Station. Cable Car: Cable train 'La Ficelle' to Ouchy (from Lausanne Station). **Road:** Car: Motorway signs for Lausanne Sud, then the first exit off the roundabout at the end of the motorway, then the road to Ouchy. Signs are then posted for the museum (from the east or west).

Opening Times

Tues-Sun 0900-1800 (Oct-Apr); daily 0900-1800 (May-Sep). The museum is open until 2000 on Thursdays. Closed 25 Dec and 1 Jan.

Admission Fees

SFr14 (adult), SFr7 (child 10-18). Concessions available.

Olympic Museum Lausanne

Jean-Jacques Strahm

Syrian Arab Republic

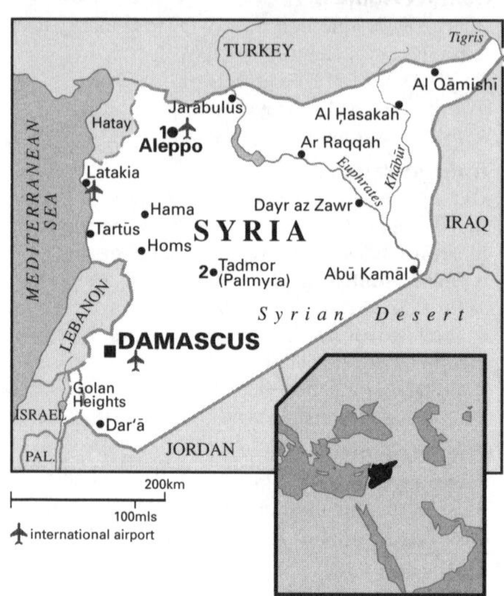

1	Halab (Aleppo)
2	Tadmor (Palmyra)

Tourist Information

Wazaretal Siyaha (Ministry of Tourism)
Shari Chukri, Quwatli, Damascus, Syrian Arab Republic
Tel: (011) 221 0122 *or* 224 2852.
Fax: (011) 224 2636.
E-mail: min-tourism@syriatel.net
Website: www.visitsyriatourism.org

Embassy of the Syrian Arab Republic
8 Belgrave Square, London SW1X 8PH, UK
Tel: (020) 7245 9012. Fax: (020) 7235 4621 *or* 7235 8976.

Halab (Aleppo)

Aleppo vies with Syria's capital Damascus for the record of the world's oldest continuously inhabited city. The city's name was first mentioned in texts as far back as the third millennium BC and it is therefore unsurprising that it has had a long and extremely rich history, having been under Hittite, Egyptian, Mitannian, Assyrian, Hellenic, Roman and Ottoman rule. The legacies that these empires left behind have provided Aleppo with numerous attractions, most famously the 12th-century *citadel*. Perched on a man-made mound 50m (165ft) above the old town, and surrounded by a 20-metre (66ft) deep moat and fortified by walls and towers, the citadel served first as a Greek acropolis and later as an Islamic fortress. Another draw for visitors is the 12 kilometres (8 miles) of covered bazaars, or *souks*, where visitors and locals alike come to haggle for anything from exotic silks and spices, beeswax candles and camel accessories to cleaning detergent and tinned fruit; it is also possible to see craftsmen at work. The *Great Mosque*, or *Zakariyah Mosque*, which was built in AD 715 and named after Zechariah, father of John the Baptist, is considered to be one of the best examples of Islamic architecture in Syria, with its spacious marble courtyard, elegant minaret and Kufic (early Islamic) inscriptions. Other attractions in Aleppo include the Ottoman *caravanserais*, or inns, where travelling merchants and pilgrims used to stay, the *Archaeological Museum* and the many 17th-century merchants' houses, a reminder of the city's importance, both past and present, as a commercial centre.

Contact Address

For more information on Aleppo, contact the Ministry of Tourism (see **Tourist Information** above).

Transportation

Air: Aleppo International Airport. **Rail:** Train: Aleppo Station. **Road:** Coach: Services from Damascus. Car: Route 5 (from Damascus).

Opening Times

Archaeological Museum: Wed-Mon 0900-1600 (winter); Wed-Mon 0900-1800 (summer). *Citadel*: Wed-Mon 0900-1600 (winter); Wed-Mon 0900-1800 (summer). All *mosques* and *souks*: Daily dawn-dusk.

Admission Fees

Archaeological Museum: S£300 (adult), S£15 (child 10-18), free (child under 10). Concessions available. *Citadel*: S£300 (adult), S£15 (child 10-18), free (child under 10). Concessions available. All *mosques* and *souks*: Free. Some mosques charge S£10 for a head covering for women.

P

Tadmor (Palmyra)

The ancient city of *Palmyra*, rises out of the Syrian desert 210km (130 miles) northeast of Damascus. It was originally known as *Tadmor*, meaning 'city of dates' and its existence was recorded on stone tablets dating from the 19th century BC. In the 3rd century BC, the city became one of the main trade routes linking east and west, and began to prosper. In the 1st century AD Tadmor came under Roman rule and was renamed Palmyra, meaning 'city of palm trees'. After a succession of rulers, both Roman and autonomous, Palmyra was captured by the Muslim leader Khalid ibn al-Walid in AD 634, and its status as a great trading city and cultural centre declined. Today visitors can explore the ruins, which include the *Temple of Bel*, the chief god of the Palmyrans, and the *Valley of the Tombs*, containing the *Hypogeum Tombs*, where several generations of families were buried over two centuries in layer upon layer of tombs. Some Aramaic inscriptions still remain and the architecture is predominantly Corinthian, with some Mesopotamian and Persian influences, reflecting the city's links with both the east and west. The *Palmyra Museum* contains a model of the Temple of Bel as it would once have looked, as well as exhibitions exploring life in the Syrian desert and local handicrafts. In the first week of May, the *Palmyra Festival* is held, featuring camel races, folk dancing, music, traditional costume and handicrafts.

Contact Address

For more information on Palmyra, contact the Ministry of Tourism (see **Tourist Information** above).

Transportation

Air: Damascus International Airport or Aleppo International Airport. **Road:** Car: Damascus – Palmyra Highway.

Opening Times

Hypogeum Tombs: Daily 0830-1000 and 1130-1400 (1 Oct-30 Apr); daily 0830-1000 and 1130-1630 (1 May-30 Sep). *Palmyra Museum* and *Temple of Bel*: Daily 0800-1300 and 1400-1600 (1 Oct-30 Apr); daily 0800-1300 and 1600-1800 (1 May-30 Sep).

Admission Fees

Whole site: S£300 (adult), S£15 (child 10-18), free (child under 10). Concessions available.

The Great Mosque, Aleppo

Syrian Ministry of Tourism, Archives of Tourist Relations Directorate

Tanzania

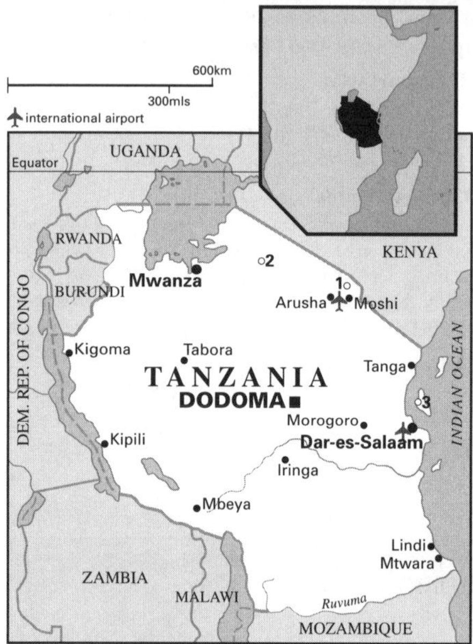

1 Kilimanjaro National Park
2 Serengeti National Park
3 Stonetown, Zanzibar

Tourist Information

Tanzania Tourist Board
PO Box 2485, Dar es Salaam, Tanzania
Tel: (022) 211 1244 *or* 213 6105.
Fax: (022) 211 6420.
E-mail: safari@ud.co.tz *or* ttb@ud.co.tz
Website: www.tanzania-web.com

Tanzanian Trade Centre
80 Borough High Street, London SE1 1LL, UK
Tel: (020) 7407 0566. Fax: (020) 7403 2003.
E-mail: director@tanzatrade.co.uk
Website: www.tanzania-online.gov.uk

Kilimanjaro National Park

Kilimanjaro National Park is the home of *Mount Kilimanjaro*'s equatorial snow-capped peaks, which form some of the most famous images of Africa. At 5896m (19,340ft), Mount Kilimanjaro, situated in northeast Tanzania, is the highest mountain in Africa and one of the largest free-standing mountains in the world. It is actually an active volcano and possesses the highest walkable summit in the world, Uhuru Peak, one of six glaciers and volcanic peaks at the top. Visitors climbing to the summit pass through hot savannah, alpine tropics and finally an arctic moonscape. The scenery is varied and at different stages includes coffee and banana fields, giant lobelia, mosses and lichens; particularly lucky visitors may even spot elephant wandering the higher slopes. A game reserve since 1921, the area was designated a national park in 1973.

Contact Address

Tanzania National Parks Authority, PO Box 3134, Arusha, Tanzania
Tel: (027) 250 3471 *or* 250 1931. Fax: (027) 254 8216.
E-mail: tanapa@habari.co.tz
Website: www.habari.co.tz/tanapa

Transportation

Air: Kilimanjaro International Airport, Dar-es-Salaam International Airport. **Rail:** Train: Moshi Station. **Road:** Bus: Services to Moshi Bus Station. Car: North–south route through Chalinze to Moshi (from Dar-es-Salaam).

Opening Times

Daily 0600-1830.

Serengeti National Park

David Woodward/Simon Jennison

Admission Fees

Non-Tanzanians: US$25 (adult), US$5 (child 6-16), free (child under 6). Tanzanian Residents: Tsh1500 (adult), Tsh500 (child 6-16), free (child under 6).

Serengeti National Park

Made a game reserve in 1921 and a national park since 1951, *Serengeti National Park* is the largest in Tanzania and one of the most famous in the world. Serengeti fittingly means 'endless plain' in the local Maasai tongue and at 14,763 sq km (5700 sq miles), it features a diversity of environments, ranging from savannah and grass plains to woodland and black clay plains. The glory of the Serengeti, however, is its wildlife, and the park is most famous for the annual migration of two million wildebeest, 200,000 zebra and 300,000 Thomson's gazelle. It also teems with lions, elephants and ostriches, and is home to around 500 different species of birds. The *Seronera Valley* is popular amongst visitors who come to see the resident prides of lions and photograph the many leopards that can be found in the branches of the acacia and sausage trees. The two saline lakes in the park, the *Lagaja* and the *Magadi*, are famous for attracting flamingos that feed on the lakes' animal and plant life.

Contact Address

Tanzania National Parks Authority, PO Box 3134, Arusha, Tanzania
Tel: (027) 250 3471 *or* 250 1931. Fax: (027) 254 8216.
E-mail: tanapa@habari.co.tz
Website: www.habari.co.tz/tanapa

Transportation

Air: Kilimanjaro International Airport. Charter flights are available from Arusha, Lake Manyara and Mwanza. **Rail:** Train: Moshi Station. **Road:** Bus: Aursha Bus Station. Car: North–South route through Chalinze and Moshi to Arusha (from Dar-es-Salaam), then through Lake Manyara National Park and Ngorongoro Conservation Area (from Arusha); through Ndaraka Gate (from Mwanza and Musoma).

Opening Times

Daily 0600-1830.

Admission Fees

Non-Tanzanians: US$25 (adult), US$5 (child 6-16), free (child under 6). Tanzanian Residents: Tsh1500 (adult), Tsh500 (child 6-16), free (child under 6).

Stone Town, Zanzibar

Zanzibar, which is known to the locals as *Unguja* (after an ancient settlement on the island called *Unguja Ukuu)*, is situated about 40km (25 miles) off the coast of Tanzania, and is 97km (60 miles) long and 32km (20 miles) wide. *Stone Town* is the old city and cultural centre of Zanzibar, which rose to prominence in the 17th century, and is said today to be the only functioning ancient town in East Africa. The town is made up of narrow streets and winding alleys, bazaars and mosques. It is also home to many grand Arab houses, which were built in the 19th century when Zanzibar was one of the most important trading centres in the Indian Ocean. Key attractions in Stone Town include the *Old Dispensary*, *Livingstone's House*, the *Peace Memorial Museum*, the *Palace Museum*, the *Arab Fort* and the *House of Wonders* (which translates from its local name, *Beit el Jaib*). The House of Wonders was built in 1883 for the Sultan Barghash and is one of the largest and most impressive buildings in Stone Town. Zanzibar itself has many breathtaking beaches and an abundance of coconut palm trees. It is also famed for the rare Kirk's Red Colobus monkey, which can be found in the *Jozani Forest*. As well as Zanzibar, Tanzania boasts many smaller islands which are just a short trip from Stone Town, including *Prison (Changu Island)*, *Chapwani*, *Chumbe* and *Bawe Islands*.

Contact Address

Zanzibar Commission for Tourism, PO Box 1410, Zanzibar, Tanzania
Tel: (024) 223 3485/6. Fax: (024) 223 3448.
Website: www.zanzibar.net/zautalii

Transportation

Air: Zanzibar Airport. **Water:** Ferry: Ferries operate to Zanzibar (from Dar-es-Salaam). **Road:** Car: Stone Town is located on the Western side of Zanzibar and can be reached via the main road (from the airport).

Opening Times

Stone Town: Daily 24 hours. *Old Dispensary*: Daily 0830-1800. *Arab Fort*: Daily 0830-1800. *House of Wonders*: Daily 0830-1800. *Palace Museum*: Daily 0830-1200 and 1400-1800. *Livingstone House*: Daily 0730-1530. *Peace Memorial Museum*: Daily 0830-1800.

Admission Fees

Stone Town: Free. *Old Dispensary*: Free. *Arab Fort*: Free. *House of Wonders*: Free. *Palace Museum*: Tsh2400 (adult), Tsh1600 (child). *Livingstone House*: Free. *Peace Memorial Museum*: Tsh800.

Thailand

1	Ao Phang-Nga (Phang Nga Bay)
2	Damnoen Saduak Talat Naam (Damnoen Saduak Floating Market)
3	Menam Kwai (Bridge Over the River Kwai)
4	Phra Barom Maha Rajcha Wang (Royal Grand Palace)
5	Piphit Thapan Sathan Hang Chart Ruer Pra Raj Pithee (Royal Barges National Museum)
6	Wat Pho (Temple of the Reclining Buddha)

Tourist Information

Kan Tong Teow Hang Prated Thai (Tourism Authority of Thailand)
Le Concorde Building, 202 Ratchadapisek Road, Bangkok 10310, Thailand
Tel: (02) 694 1222. Fax: (02) 694 1220.
E-mail: info1@tat.or.th
Website: www.tat.or.th *or* www.tourismthailand.org
Tourism Authority of Thailand
49 Albermarle Street, London W1Y 7RN, UK
Tel: (09063) 640 666 (consumer enquiries; calls cost 60p per minute).
Fax: (020) 7629 5519.
E-mail: info@tat-uk.demon.co.uk

Ao Phang-Nga (Phang Nga Bay)

Phang Nga Bay is one of the world's great scenic wonders. It covers an area of 400 sq km (154 sq miles) and consists of verdant limestone islands, some of which reach 300m (984ft) high. The bay is honeycombed with caves and aquatic grottoes, which are known as *hong* in Thai and lie beneath some of the islands, hiding unspoiled flora and fauna. Apart from the occasional village, few of the islands are densely populated. The most famous of the islands in the bay are *Ko Ping Kan* (more commonly known as *James Bond Island)* and *Koh Pannyi*. The former featured in the James Bond movie 'The Man with the Golden Gun', whilst the latter, which literally means 'Sea Gypsy Island', is a village built out over the water on stilts, guarded by a giant rock monolith. The area is also famous for its mountains that rise out of the sea, and is extremely popular for sailing and sea-kayaking as it is protected from the southwest and northeast monsoon seasons, making the waters calm all year round.

Contact Address

Tourism Authority of Thailand Southern Office, 73-75 Phuket Road, Amphoe Muang, Phuket 83000, Thailand
Tel: (076) 211 036 *or* 217 138 *or* 212 213.
Fax: (076) 213 582.
E-mail: tatphket@tat.or.th
Website: www.tat.or.th *or* www.tourismthailand.org

Transportation

Air: Phuket International Airport. **Water:** Boat: Many tourists visit Phang Nga Bay by boat; local companies operate day trips to the islands. **Rail:** Train: Surathani Station. **Road:** Bus: Phuket Bus Terminal in Phuket Town. Car: Route 4, then Hwy-402 (Tepkassatri Road, from Phuket).

Opening Times

Daily 24 hours.

Admission Fees

Free.

Damnoen Saduak Talat Naam (Damnoen Saduak Floating Market)

Located 80km (50 miles) southwest of Bangkok, *Damnoen Saduak Floating Market* is a daily riot of colour and noise. Farmers and smallholders from the surrounding hills turn up each morning to sell and exchange fruit and vegetables from their heavily-laden barges, as they sail up and down the canals amongst the orchards and vineyards. Trading starts early, at around 0600 and lasts only until 1100, with the main clients being other farmers and the residents of the stilt-houses that line the canals. Visitors can also take boat trips to see the way of life in the many villages up river.

Contact Address

For more information on Damnoen Saduak Floating Market, contact the Tourism Authority of Thailand (see **Tourist Information** above).

Transportation

Air: Bangkok International Airport. **Road:** Bus: 78 (from Bangkok Southern Bus Terminal to Damnoen Saduak Bus Terminal). Car: Hwy-4 (from Bangkok), then Bangpae-Damnoen Saduak Road.

Opening Times

Daily 0600-1100 (approximately).

Admission Fees

Free.

P ✕ 🧺 ♿

Menam Kwai (Bridge Over the River Kwai)

Internationally famous due to the eponymous 1957 film, the *Bridge Over the River Kwai* was constructed as part of the *Japanese Siam-Burma 'Death' Railway* during World War II. An estimated 16,000 Allied prisoners of war died, forced to endure back-breaking work under terrible conditions to complete the railway, and large numbers of troops perished during bombing raids on the iron structure by the Allies in 1945. The moving *JEATH War Museum* (JEATH representing the first letter of Japan, England, America, Australia, Thailand and Holland, the countries who lost soldiers in the region) is located in the provincial capital, Kanchanaburi and features photographs and various other memorabilia from World War II. There is also a war cemetery in the town, opposite the railway station, where the remains of 6982 Allied prisoners of war are buried. The peaceful *Chong-Kai War Cemetery* is located 2 km (1.2 miles) outside Kanchanapuri on the site of the Chong-Kai prisoner of war camp and contains the graves of 1750 soldiers from both sides of the campaign. There is a small *Railway Museum* of vintage locomotives to the east of the bridge.

Contact Address

Kanchanaburi Tourist Office: Tourism Authority of Thailand, Saeng Chuto Road, Amphoe Muang, Kanchanaburi 71000, Thailand
Tel: (034) 511 200 *or* 512 500. Fax: (034) 511 200.
JEATH War Museum: Wat Chaichumpol, Bantai, Muang, Thailand
Tel: (034) 515 203.

Transportation

Air: Bangkok International Airport. **Rail:** Train: Services to Kanchanaburi Station (from Bangkok Noi Station). **Road:** Bus: Services from Bangkok Southern Bus Terminal to Kanchanaburi Bus Terminal. Car: Hwy-4 (from Bangkok).

Opening Times

JEATH War Museum: Daily 0830-1800. *Railway Museum*: Daily 0700-1830.

Admission Fees

JEATH War Museum: B30 (adult), B10 (child). *Railway Museum*: B30 (adult), B10 (child under 18). Concessions available.

P ✕ 🧺 ♿

Phra Barom Maha Rajcha Wang (Royal Grand Palace)

The *Royal Grand Palace* is made up of a vast complex of intricate buildings, including the *Wat Mahathat* (the Palace Temple) and *Wat Phra Keow* (the Royal Chapel). Construction of the palace began in 1782 and was completed in time for the coronation of King Rama I, opening in 1785 to signify the end of the Burmese invasion of Thailand. The palace lies in the heart of the old town and covers an area of 160,000 sq metres (1,720,430 sq ft). The compound is surrounded by a moat and contains two sections, the former royal residence and the Buddhist temple. The Royal Chapel houses the famous *Emerald Buddha*, which is carved from a single piece of jade, and is the holiest and most revered religious object in Thailand. Although it is no longer used as the royal residence, the site is still used by the king for official ceremonies on special occasions.

Contact Address

Phra Barom Maha Rajcha Wang, Bureau of Royal Household, Na Phralan Road, Phra Nakhon, Bangkok 10200, Thailand

Tel: (02) 222 8181/3. Fax: (02) 226 4949.
Website: www.palaces.thai.net

Transportation

Air: Bangkok International Airport. **Rail:** Train: Hualamphong Station. **Road:** Bus: 1, 2, 3, 6, 9, 12, 15, 17, 30, 33, 39, 44, 53, 59, 60, 64, 65, 70, 80, 921, 201 or 203. Car: Hwy-4 (from Hua Hin); Hwy-3 (from Pattaya); Hwy-32 or Hwy-177 (from Phitsanulok). The entrance to the palace is on Na Phra Lan Road, near Sanam Luang in Bangkok.

Opening Times

Daily 0830-1530.

Admission Fees

B200 (adult), child (free).

Piphit Thapan Sathan Hang Chart Ruer Pra Raj Pithee (Royal Barges National Museum)

The *Royal Barges National Museum* houses several royal barges, which formerly served as war vessels and were subsequently used on royal and state occasions along the Chao Phraya River. The earliest evidence of the use of these decorative barges during royal processions dates back to 1357. One of the most well known of the barges is the *Suphanahong* (Golden Swan), which was built in 1911 and used by the king when celebrating the Buddhist *Royal Kathin Ceremony*, held during the months of October and November, at the end of Buddhist Lent. The king traditionally travelled along the river in this barge, visiting royal monasteries and offering robes to the monks as a reward for completing the three-month *Vassa Retreat*, during which time they are not permitted to travel. The barges are incredibly intricate in design, reflecting Thai religious beliefs and local history. The figure on the bow of each boat signifies whether it carries the King and Queen or other members of the royal family. Today, the royal barges, being so old, are rarely used by the royal family; they were last used at the end of 1999 to celebrate the king's 72nd birthday.

Contact Address

Royal Barges National Museum, Arun Amarin Road, Bangkok Noi, Bangkok 10700, Thailand
Tel/Fax: (02) 424 0004.

Transportation

Air: Bangkok International Airport. **Rail:** Train: Thonburi Station. **Road:** Bus: 83 runs to the site (from central Bangkok). Car: Hwy-4 (from Hua Hin); Hwy-3 (from Pattaya); Hwy-32 or Hwy-177 (from Phitsanulok). Taxi: Taxis can be hailed in the street to go to the museum.

Opening Times

Daily 0830-1630.

Admission Fees

B30.

Wat Pho (Temple of the Reclining Buddha)

Occupying a 20-hectare (20-acre) site next to the Royal Palace, *Wat Pho* is the oldest and largest temple in Bangkok. It was built in 1688 during the reign of King Petraja of Ayutthaya and contains one of Thailand's most spectacular sights, a 46-metre (150-ft) long and 15-metre (72-ft) high statue of a reclining Buddha. The statue itself, which is gold-plated and inlaid with mother-of-pearl on the soles of the feet, was not added until 1832 during the reign of King Rama III, and serves to illustrate the passing of Buddha into nirvana (the state of absolute blessedness). The grounds of Wat Pho house over 1000 Buddha statues, the largest such collection in Thailand, as well as 95 *stupas* – Buddhist religious monuments – and a series of marble slabs depicting part of the epic Thai poem, *Ramakian*, which depicts the struggle between good and evil. Visitors can also wander amongst the peaceful rock gardens and chapels. King Rama III also established Wat Pho as an important centre for Thai medicine and massage and thus founded Thailand's oldest seat of learning. It is still possible to have a massage or learn about the art of Thai massage and medicine at Wat Pho today.

Contact Address

Wat Pho, Thai Wang Rd, Bangkok, Thailand
Tel: (02) 222 0933.

Transportation

Air: Bangkok International Airport. **Rail:** Train: Hualamphong Station. **Road:** Bus: 1, 25, 44, 47, 53, 57, 62, 83 or 91 or Aircon buses 6, 8 or 12. Car: Hwy-4 (from Hua Hin); Hwy-3 (from Pattaya); Hwy-32 or Hwy-177 (from Phitsanulok).

Opening Times

Daily 0900-1700.

Admission Fees

B20.

Tunisia

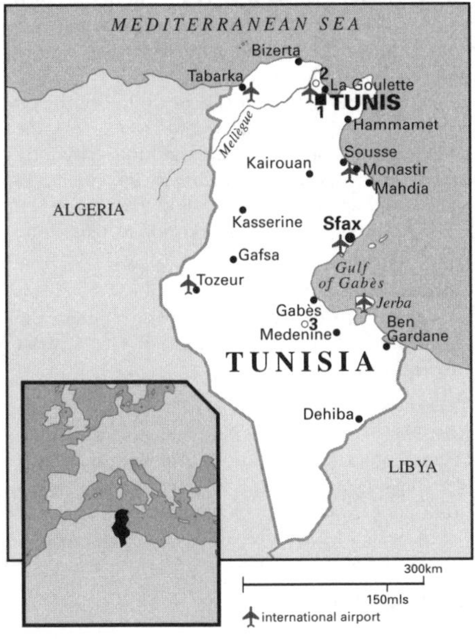

1 al-Madinah (Medina in Tunis)
2 Carthage
3 Matmata

Tourist Information

Office National du Tourisme Tunisien/ONTT (Tunisian National Tourist Office)
1 avenue Mohamed V, 1000 Tunis, Tunisia
Tel: (01) 341 077. Fax: (01) 342 997.
E-mail: info@tourismtunisia.com
Website: www.tourismtunisia.com
Tunisian National Tourist Office
77A Wigmore Street, London W1U 1QF, UK
Tel: (020) 7224 5561 (enquiries) *or* 7224 5598 (administration). Fax: (020) 7224 4053.
E-mail: tntolondon@aol.com

al-Madinah (Medina in Tunis)

The *medina*, or old quarter, of Tunis was built during the seventh century AD. From the 12th to the 16th centuries, Tunis was considered to be one of the greatest and wealthiest cities of the Islamic world and its medina is testimony to its former grandeur. Today, visitors can step back in time through the maze of narrow, winding streets and barter for souvenirs with the locals; goods on sale include colourful hand-made carpets, hand-crafted jewellery, copper and brassware, pottery and exotic spices. Among the more frequented attractions found within the walls of the medina are: the ninth-century *Ez-Zitouna Mosqu* (*Mosque of the Olive Tree*), which is the largest mosque in the city and is located at the centre of the medina; the perfume makers' *Souk el Attarine* and Tunis's first Ottoman-style mosque, *Sidi Yousef*, built in the 17th century. There are five entrances to the medina, the most commonly-used by tourist is the *Bab el-Bhar Gate* (Door to the Sea).

Contact Address

For more information on the Medina in Tunis, contact the Office National du Tourisme Tunisien (see **Tourist Information** above).

Transportation

Air: Tunis-Carthage International Airport. **Water:** Ferry: Services from Sardinia, Sicily, Genoa, Naples, Marseille and Malta. **Rail:** Train: Tunis Ville Station. Underground: Medina. **Road:** Taxi: Services operate from the airport. Car: Avenue Habib Bourguiba, Place de l'Independence and Avenue de France (from Carthage).

Opening Times

Medina: Daily 24 hours. *Ez-Zitouna Mosqu*: Sun-Thurs 0800-1200 (16 Sep-31 Mar); Sun-Thurs 0800-1300 (1 Apr-15 Sep). *Souk el Attarine*: Daily 0900-1800. *Sidi Yousef*: Daily dawn-dusk. Visitors to the mosque must wear modest dress.

Admission Fees

Medina: Free. *Ez-Zitouna Mosqu*: TD1.6. *Souk el Attarine*: Free. *Sidi Yousef*: Free.

Carthage

The city of *Carthage*, which is located on the outskirts of Tunisia's capital city, Tunis, was, for many years, the arch-enemy of the ancient Roman empire. Between 264 and 146 BC, the two great cities were embroiled in a series of wars that saw Hannibal's famous attack on Rome, and Rome's subsequent sacking of Carthage in 146 BC. The Romans eventually settled in the conquered city, which went on to become the administrative capital of Roman Africa. Today, it is mainly Roman sites, including theatres, temples, villas and baths, which can be seen by visiting tourists. Many of the sites now stand in ruins, however, including the *Roman Ampitheatre* and the thermal *Antoine Baths*, which were once the largest baths built by the Romans. The *National Museum* nearby has an impressive collection of Punic objects which date from the wars between Carthage and Rome. Visitors can gain a superb view of Carthage by climbing the nearby *Byrsa Hill*.

Contact Address

Site de Carthage, Carthage, Tunisia
Tel: (01) 730 036.

Transportation

Air: Tunis-Carthage International Airport. **Water:** Ferry: Services from Sardinia, Sicily, Genoa, Naples, Marseille and Malta. **Rail:** Train: TGM (light rail) to Carthage Byrsa Station. **Road:** Bus: 47. Car: Avenue Habib Bourguiba towards Sidi Bou Said (from Tunis city centre).

Opening Times

All sites at *Carthage*: Daily 0830-1730 (16 Sep-31 Mar); daily 0800-1900 (1 Apr-15 Sep). *National Museum*: Daily 0830-1730 (16 Sep-31 Mar); daily 0800-1900 (1 Apr-15 Sep).

Admission Fees

All sites at *Carthage*: TD5.2 (adult), free (child under 6). *National Museum*: TD5.2 (adult), free (child under 6).

Matmata

Matmata is one of the most famous villages in Tunisia as it was the setting for the opening scenes of the film 'Stars Wars'. The village's lunar-like landscape and subterranean cave dwellings attract hundreds of visitors every day. They come to see the home of the Star Wars characters Uncle Owen and Aunt Beru, which was located in the fictional town of Sidi Driss. The Berber people first dug homes out of the ground over 1000 years ago in order to escape the midday heat. These Troglodyte communities formed craters beneath the earth and constructed tunnels between some of the courtyards to build an underground labyrinth. Today, *Hotel Sidi Driss*, which was the cantina in Star Wars, still stands, and visitors can spend the night in Berber-style accommodation as part of the whole experience.

Contact Address

For more information on Matmata, contact the Office National du Tourisme Tunisien (see **Tourist Information** above).

Transportation

Air: Tunis-Carthage International Airport. **Road:** Coach: The majority of tourists visit Matmata as part of an organised coach tour. Bus: Services to Matmata (from Gabes and Tunis). Car: Road southwest out of Gabes, which leads to New Matmata. Camel: Many tourists prefer to hire camels.

Opening Times

Daily 24 hours.

Admission Fees

Admission is generally included in the price of excursions, which are organised by tour operators.

Roman Temple, Carthage

Corel

Turkey

1 Aqua Fantasy Resort
2 Aya Sofya (Hagia Sophia)
3 Efes (Ephesus)
4 Göreme Milli Parklar (Göreme National Park)
5 Sultan Ahmet Camii (Blue Mosque)
6 Topkapi Sarayi (Topkapi Palace)
7 Truva (Troy)

Tourist Information

Turizm Bakanligi (Ministry of Tourism)
Ismet Inönü Bulvar 5, Bahçelievler, Ankara, Turkey
Tel: (0312) 212 8300. Fax: (0312) 212 8391.
Website: www.turizm.gov.tr *or* www.turkey.org/turkey

Turkish Tourist Office
First Floor, 170-173 Piccadilly, London W1J EJ, UK
Tel: (020) 7629 7771 *or* (09001) 7887 755 (brochure request line; calls are charged at the rate of 60p per minute). Fax: (020) 7491 0773.
E-mail: tto@turkishtourism.demon.co.uk

Aqua Fantasy Resort

Aqua Fantasy Resort is Turkey's biggest water park, comprising 65,000 sq m (77,740 sq yards) of slides, wave pools, waterfalls and rides, near Selçuk on Turkey's Mediterranean coast. It is a mecca for water babies and thrill seekers – the wave pools feature 10 different kinds of waves and the slides have such evocative names as *Anaconda*, *Black Thunder* and *Screamer*. Watersports on offer include beach volleyball, water polo and water volleyball and there are boat rides on the lazy river that stretches for 300m (328 yards) through the park. On *Treasure Island*, younger visitors can slide through the 25m (82ft) *Pirate Tunnel* or test their balance on the *Lily-Pad Raft Walk*. Various competitions are organised on a daily basis, including football, dance contests and tug-of-war challenges. For the less energetic, tropical drinks bars and barbecue grills are located around the park, and there are also several restaurants and beach cafés.

Contact Address

Aqua Fantasy Resort, Ephesus Beach, Selçuk/Izmir, Turkey
Tel: (0232) 893 1111. Fax: (0232) 893 1110.
E-mail: info@aquafantasy.com
Website: www.aquafantasy.com

Transportation

Air: Istanbul Atatürk Airport, Istanbul Sabiha Gökçen International Airport, Dalaman Airport or Adnanmenderes Airport, Izmir (domestic flights). **Rail:** Train: Selçuk or Kusadasi Stations. **Road:** Car: Selçuk–Kusadasi Road.

Opening Times

Daily 1000-1800 (15 May-14 Jun); daily 1000-1900 (15 Jun-30 Sep).

Admission Fees

TL22,000,000 (adult), TL13,500,000 (child 4-9), free (child under 4).

Aya Sofya (Hagia Sophia)

When the Christian Byzantine Emperor Justinian inaugurated *Hagia Sophia*, meaning Church of Divine Wisdom, in AD 537, it was the most impressive building in the world and remained the crowning achievement of the Byzantine Empire for over a millennium. In the 15th century, Mehmet the Conqueror converted it from a Christian church to a mosque, adding the minarets, tombs and fountains. In 1937, when Turkey became a secular republic, it was established as a museum, with many of its Byzantine mosaics revealed from underneath layers of Ottoman plaster. Although the interior is somewhat dark and less elaborately decorated than many of Istanbul's other religious monuments, visitors cannot fail to be inspired by the huge dome – 56m (183ft) high. Designed to represent the heavens, it appears to be

Ruth Blakeborough

Mosaic in Hagia Sophia

suspended in space due to its ingenious design by Greek mathematicians.

Contact Address

Museum of Hagia Sophia, Sultan Ahmet Square, Sultan Ahmet, Istanbul
Tel: (0212) 522 0989 *or* 522 1750.

Transportation

Air: Istanbul Atatürk Airport, Istanbul Sabiha Gökçen International Airport. **Rail:** Train: Sirkeci Station. Tram: Sultan Ahmet. **Road:** Bus: Services to Sultan Ahmet (from across Istanbul). Car: E80 or D100 (from Ankara, Izmit and Greece).

Opening Times

Tues-Sun 0900-1600.

Admission Fees

TL7,000,000.

Efes (Ephesus)

Ephesus, located 600km (373 miles) southwest of Istanbul, is one of the grandest and best-preserved ruins of the ancient world. According to evidence dating from around 1400 BC, the Hittites were the first to settle the site, which they named Apasas. Ephesus first attained importance in the first century BC, due to its position as a sheltered harbour and the starting point of the royal road leading to Susa, the capital of the Persian Empire. To the ancient Greeks, it was the most important city in Ionian Asia Minor, and cult followers of the Anatolian mother goddess, Artemis (Diana), would come to worship at the temple dedicated to her. The temple was originally founded in the seventh century BC as a shrine to the Anatolian goddess, Cybele. It was destroyed and subsequently rebuilt seven times; the classical marble structure with Ionic columns built around 550 BC was one of the seven wonders of the ancient world. The cult of Artemis brought great wealth to the city, largely through the elaborate gifts, such as gold statues and precious stones, brought to the temple by rich pilgrims from as far afield as India and Persia, but also due to the accompanying increase in trade. The Romans captured the city in 189 BC and it continued to flourish, with fountains, pools and the second largest library outside of Alexandria. The city is important, too, in the Christian heritage. St Paul came to preach Christianity here from AD 51-53, a period recorded in the New Testament. Ephesus was sacked by the Goths in AD 262 and although it continued under Roman and, subsequently, Byzantine rule, it never recovered its former glory. The site was first excavated in 1869 by British archaeologist, J T Wood and visitors can now see many of the Roman remains. One of Ephesus' attractions is the fact that so much of it remains intact and little imagination is required to see what the Roman city would have looked like. Highlights include the stunning façade of the *Celsus Library*, built by Gaius Julius Aquila in the second century AD in memory of his father Celsus Polemaeanus, a row of Roman public toilets, the *Harbour Gymnasium* and the *Temple of Hadrian*.

Contact Address

Ephesus, Atatürk Mah, Agora CAR 35, Turkey
Tel: (0232) 892 6945. Fax: (0232) 892 6945.
E-mail: info@selcukephesus.gen.tr
Website: www.selcukephesus.gen.tr

Transportation

Air: Istanbul Atatürk Airport, Istanbul Sabiha Gökçen International Airport, Dalaman Airport or Adnanmenderes Airport, Izmir (domestic flights). **Rail:** Train: Selcuk Station. **Road:** Bus: Minibus services to Ephesus (from Selcuk). Car: Selcuk–Kusadasi Road (from Selcuk or Kusadasi).

Opening Times

Daily 0830-1830.

Admission Fees

TL7,000,000 (adult), TL3,000,000 (child 12-18), free (child under 12).

Göreme Milli Parklar (Göreme National Park)

Göreme National Park in *Cappadocia*, central Turkey, is home to one of nature's most intriguing phenomena. Commonly referred to as the *Valley of the Fairy Chimneys*, after the strange rock formations that proliferate in the region, this weird and wonderful landscape of 9572 hectares (23,653 acres) was formed when three volcanoes, *Erciyes, Hasan* and *Melendiz Dağlari* erupted around 30 million years ago. The deposits they created make up a material called tuff, a soft rock that is easily eroded to form extraordinary table mountains, fairy chimneys and undulating, sand-dune like cliff faces. The fact that tuff is easily carved has been exploited by the indigenous population, who have used the rocks as dwelling places for hundreds of years; many of these rock houses have been turned into comfortable *pansiyon* (guesthouses). St Paul introduced Christianity to the region in the first century AD, and one of Cappadocia's chief attractions is the array of rock churches and monasteries that were hewn out of the landscape, thus being hidden from the pursuing Arab invaders. The town of *Göreme* has an open-air museum where many of these preserved houses and churches, adorned with frescoes, can be seen. Visitors with a sense of adventure will enjoy exploring the labyrinthine passages and holes of the long-abandoned *Zelve Monastery*, carved into the rock in pre-Iconoclastic times near the town of *Avanos*. Avanos, itself, is famous for its pottery and there are many workshops where visitors can see the colourful earthenware pots being made with red clay from the Kızılırmak River (the longest river in Turkey). Other towns within the park include *Kaymaklı*, where there is a huge underground city thought to date from the Hittite era, and *Ürgüp*, with its many beautiful Ottoman and Greek houses.

Contact Address

Nevsehir Directorate of Tourism, Atatürk Bulvari 14, Devlet Hastanesi Önü, Nevsehir, Turkey
Tel: (0384) 213 3659. Fax: (0384) 213 1137.

Transportation

Air: Ankara Esenboga Airport, Istanbul Atatürk Airport, Istanbul Sabiha Gökçen International Airport, Nevsehir Airport (domestic flights) or Kayseri Airport (domestic flights). **Road:** Coach: Services to Nevsehir Otogar (Nevsehir Bus Station), Göreme Otogar (Göreme Bus Station) and Ürgüp Otogar (Ürgüp Bus Station) (from Pamukkale, Selçuk and Mediterranean resorts). Car: Göreme–Ortahisar/Ürgüp Highway (from Göreme or Ürgüp); Ankara–Adana Highway (from Ankara or Adana); Aksaray–Nevsehir Highway (from Aksaray); Kayseri–Ürgüp Highway (from Kayseri).

Opening Times

Zelve Monastery: Tues-Sun 0800-1700 (winter); Tues-Sun 0800-1900 (summer). *Kaymaklı Underground City*: Tues-Sun 0800-1700 (Oct-Feb); Tues-Sun 0800-1930 (Mar-Sep). *Göreme Open-Air Museum*: Tues-Sun 0800-1700 (winter); Tues-Sun 0800-1900 (summer).

Admission Fees

Zelve Monastery: TL4,000,000 (adult), TL1,500,000 (child under 18). *Kaymaklı Underground City*: TL4,000,000 (adult), TL1,500,000 (child under 18). *Göreme Open-Air Museum*: TL5,000,000 (adult), TL2,200,000 (child under 18). Admission to all sites is free to disabled visitors.

Sultan Ahmet Camii (Blue Mosque)

With its cascade of opulent domes and slender, balconied minarets soaring towards the sky, Istanbul's *Blue Mosque* is one of the city's most striking images. Construction was begun in 1609 under the Ottoman Sultan Ahmet I, who wished to create a place of Islamic worship to rival the *Aya Sofya*, or Hagia Sophia, constructed by Roman ruler Septimus Severus in AD 200 and located across the *Hippodrome*, the old city's central plaza. Completed in 1619, the Blue Mosque, so called due to the colour of the thousands of intricate Iznik tiles that line the interior, was regarded as sacrilegious since it featured six minarets instead of four, as is traditional. The only other mosque to have six minarets was the most holy mosque of all, the *al-Haram Mosque* in Mecca. The interior of the mosque features a massive dome supported by four grand columns, five metres (16ft) in diameter, as well as characteristic Ottoman tile patterns and brightly-coloured windows. Hundreds of Muslims still use the mosque for daily prayer and worship. In the main section of the vast interior is a carpet, each tile of which is decorated with a pattern that points towards Mecca, the most holy Islamic city, which Muslims must face to pray. Visitors of all faiths who are modestly dressed may also enter the Blue Mosque; special slippers and head and shoulder coverings are distributed at the entrance.

Contact Address

Sultan Ahmet Camii, Sultan Ahmet Meydani, Istanbul, Turkey
Tel: (0212) 518 1319. Fax: (0212) 458 0776.

Transportation

Air: Istanbul Atatürk Airport, Istanbul Sabiha Gökçen International Airport. **Rail:** Train: Sirkeci Station. Tram: Sultan Ahmet. **Road:** Bus: Sultan Ahmet. Car: E-80 or D-100 (from Edirne).

Opening Times

Daily 0900-1700.

Admission Fees

Free.

Topkapi Sarayi (Topkapi Palace)

Topkapi Palace was created on the orders of Mehmed II, the 23-year-old sultan who captured the Byzantine city of Constantinople in 1453 and made it the capital of his mighty Ottoman empire, under the new name of Istanbul. The palace was constructed between 1459 and 1465 on the site of an olive grove, and rapidly grew to become a jumbled complex of elaborate living quarters and administrative offices. The layout of the palace, which seems rather haphazard by European standards, conforms to the traditions of Islamic architecture, featuring a series of interconnected courtyards. These courtyards progressed inwards, from the first, which was open to all citizens, through two courtyards reserved for administrative and training purposes, to the fourth, where the sultans had their gardens and *harem*, or private living area. The harem consisted of over 400 rooms, including opulent reception rooms, bedchambers, a library and even a swimming pool. Topkapi Palace remained the home of the Ottoman sultans until Sultan Abdül Mecid I moved the imperial residence to Dolmabaçe, further up the Bosphorus, in 1853. Today visitors can enter the gardens and courtyards, and take a guided tour of the harem to gain an impression of the extravagant lifestyle of the rulers of one of the world's greatest empires. There are fine views over the Bosphorus Straits (which divide Europe and Asia) from the terraces, and visitors can see various artefacts, including a fine collection of Ottoman pottery, in the *Topkapi Palace Museum.*

Contact Address

Topkapi Palace Museum, 34400 Sarayii, Sultan Ahmet, Istanbul, Turkey
Tel: (0212) 512 0480 *or* 512 0484.
E-mail: topkapisarayi@atlas.net.tr
Website: www.ee.bilkent.edu.tr/~history/topkapi.html

Transportation

Air: Istanbul Atatürk Airport, Istanbul Sabiha Gökçen International Airport. **Rail:** Train: Sirkeci Station. Tram: Sultan Ahmet. **Road:** Bus: Services to Sultan Ahmet from across Istanbul. Car: E80 or D100 (from Ankara, Izmit or Greece).

Opening Times

Wed-Mon 0900-1800.

Admission Fees

TL7,000,000 (adult), TL1,500,000 (child 10-16), free (child under 10). Concessions available.

Truva (Troy)

Until 1871, classical scholars the world over had thought the city of *Troy* the stuff of legend. That changed when Austrian millionaire-cum-archaeologist, Heinrich Schliemann, discovered the city that was the site of the famous war between the Greeks and the Trojans in the 12th century BC. According to Homer, war broke out when Paris, the son of King Priam of Troy, eloped with Helen, the beautiful wife of Menelaus of Sparta. An army led by Menelaus' brother, Agamemnon, set out in revenge to attack the Trojans. The ensuing war lasted 10 years, until the Greeks made a pretence of retreating. Instead, they hid inside a specially-constructed horse, which the Trojans foolishly believed to be a peace offering and took inside their walls, whereupon the cunning Greeks emerged and ransacked the city. The dramatic tale of the Trojan War captured the minds of classical authors, in particular the Greek writer, Homer, who recorded it in his 'Iliad'. The Roman writer Virgil's epic, 'Aeneid', also records the story of the Trojan Horse and the aftermath of the war. Today, the ruins of nine levels of the city are still being excavated (dating back as far as 3000 BC), and the finds are now on general display.

Contact Address

Çanakkale Tourist Information Office, Regional Directorate, Valilik Binasi, Kat 1, Çanakkale, Turkey
Tel: (0286) 217 5012 *or* 217 3791.
Fax: (0286) 217 2534.

Transportation

Air: Istanbul Atatürk Airport, Istanbul Sabiha Gökçen International Airport. **Rail:** Train: Balekisir Station or Bandirma Station. **Road:** Bus: Local Dolmus (minibus) services (from Çanakkale).

Opening Times

Daily 0800-1700 (winter); daily 0800-1930 (summer).

Admission Fees

TL400,000.

Uganda

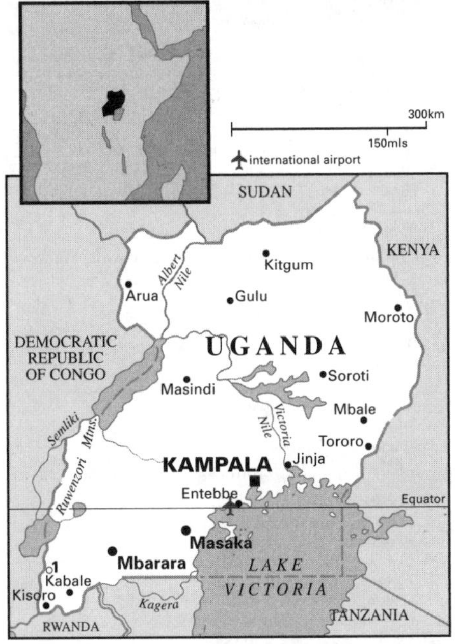

1 Bwindi Impenetrable Forest National Park

Tourist Information

Uganda Tourist Board
PO Box 7211, Impala House, Ground Floor, Kimathe Avenue, Kampala, Uganda
Tel: (041) 342 197. Fax: (041) 342 188.
E-mail: utb@starcom.co.ug
Website: www.visituganda.com

High Commission for the Republic of Uganda
Uganda House, 58-59 Trafalgar Square, London WC2N 5DX, UK
Tel: (020) 7839 5783. Fax: (020) 7839 8925.

Bwindi Impenetrable Forest National Park

Bwindi Impenetrable Forest National Park, located in southwestern Uganda, on the edge of the western Rift Valley, is a true jungle, with dense undergrowth, thick vines and much vegetation. Covering an area of 331 sq km (128 sq miles), the forest, which was designated a UNESCO World Heritage Site in 1994, is a sanctuary for around half the world's mountain gorillas, including the Mubare and the Habinyanja groups. It is also famed for being the home of the Colobus monkey, various species of chimpanzee, hundreds of species of birds and many other animals, including forest birds, snakes, lizards, chameleons and butterflies. As well as animals, the park is home to huge trees covered in creepers, a bamboo zone and rare plants, including mistletoe and orchids. Guides are available to take visitors on nature trails through the undergrowth to see the various tree species and the many jungle creatures.

Contact Address

Uganda Wildlife Authority, Plot 3 Kintu Road, Nakasero, PO Box 3530, Kampala, Uganda
Tel: (041) 346 287/8. Fax: (041) 346 291.

Transportation

Air: Entebbe International Airport. **Road:** Car: Kabale–Buhoma Road to the park headquarters at Buhoma (from Kabale). It is advisable to use four-wheel drive vehicles.

Opening Times

Daily 24 hours.

Admission Fees

USh10,000 (Resident adult), Ush5000 (Resident child), US$15 (Non-resident adult), US$8 (Non-resident child).

P ✗ 🏛

Gorilla in Bwindi Impenetrable Forest National Park

Uganda Tourist Board

United Kingdom

England

*Attractions marked * are in London.*

1 Albert Dock
2 Alton Towers
3 Big Ben and the Houses of Parliament*
4 Blackpool Pleasure Beach
5 British Airways London Eye*
6 British Museum*
7 Buckingham Palace*
8 Cambridge University
9 Camden Market*
10 Canterbury Cathedral
11 Chessington World of Adventures
12 Durham Castle and Cathedral
13 Eden Project
14 Greenwich*
15 Hadrian's Wall
16 Hampton Court Palace
17 Harrods*
18 Leeds Castle
19 Legoland® Windsor
20 London Dungeon*
21 London Zoo*
22 Madame Tussaud's and Tussaud's London Planetarium*
23 National Gallery*
24 National Museum of Photography, Film and Television
25 Natural History Museum*
26 Oxford University
27 Portsmouth Historic Dockyard
28 Roman Baths and Pumproom
29 Royal Armouries Leeds
30 Royal Botanic Gardens, Kew*
31 Royal Pavilion
32 Science Museum*
33 Shakespeare Houses
34 St Paul's Cathedral*
35 Stonehenge
36 Tate Britain*
37 Tate Modern*
38 Tintagel Castle
39 Tower of London*
40 Victoria & Albert Museum*
41 Warwick Castle
42 Westminster Abbey*
43 Windsor Castle
44 York Minster

Tourist Information

British Tourist Authority
Thames Tower, Black's Road, Hammersmith, London W6 9EL, UK
Tel: (020) 8846 9000. Fax: (020) 8563 0302.
E-mail: tradehelpdesk@bta.org.uk (trade enquiries only) *or* enquirydesk@bta.org.uk (consumer enquiries). Website: www.visitbritain.com

Albert Dock

In the 19th century, the city of Liverpool was a flourishing export and passenger port, employing thousands of workers from around Britain and Ireland. With the decline of the British Empire and the subsequent decrease in trade between Britain and its overseas markets after World War II, the area fell into disrepair until the city council embarked upon a major renewal project in the 1980s to restore the docks to their former glory and make them into a public recreation space. The centrepiece of this project is the *Albert Dock*, 3 hectares (7 acres) of water surrounded by renovated warehouses with iron colonnades. The warehouses have been converted into lively spaces for restaurants, shops and cafés, interspersed with museums chronicling the city's contribution to British history and culture. *The Beatles Story*, dedicated to the famous Fab Four, is one of Liverpool's top attractions, featuring a replica of the Cavern Club where the group performed in the early days, alongside posters, personal memorabilia, and other displays; visitors can tour the museum to the accompaniment of a

Beatles' soundtrack. The history of the docks is told in the nearby *Merseyside Maritime Museum*, where there are also exhibitions on emigration, shipbuilding, the transatlantic slave trade and smuggling on the *River Mersey*. Opposite is the *Museum of Liverpool Life*, which showcases all aspects of life in the city, from its famous footballers and pop music tradition to working life at the docks and political radicalism. Finally, there is the *Tate Gallery Liverpool*, Britain's largest gallery of contemporary art outside London, featuring displays of art from the Tate museums in London; collections include *Emotional Ties*, which examines human relationships, sculpture and prints by contemporary British artist William Tucker, and *Surrealism and British Art in the 1930s*.

Contact Address

Albert Dock Centre, Atlantic Pavilion, Albert Dock, Liverpool L3 4AE, UK
Tel: (0906) 680 6886 *or* (0151) 709 5111.
E-mail: askme@visitliverpool.com
Website: www.albertdock.com

Transportation

Air: Liverpool Airport, Manchester Airport. **Rail:** Train: Liverpool Lime Street Station. Underground: James Street. **Road:** Bus: 222 or Smartbuses 1 or 4. Car: M62 (from Leeds, Bradford or Manchester); A1, then M62 (from Newcastle and the north); M1, then M62 (from London), then signs to Liverpool city centre and Albert Dock.

Opening Times

The Beatles Story: Daily 1000-1700 (1 Nov-28 Feb); daily 1000-1800 (1 Mar-31 Oct). *Merseyside Maritime Museum*: Daily 1000-1700. *Museum of Liverpool Life*: Daily 1000-1700. *Tate Liverpool*: Tues-Sun 1000-1750. Closed Good Friday, 24-26 Dec and 1 Jan.

Admission Fees

The Beatles Story: £7.95 (adult), £5.45 (child under 16). Concessions and family pass available. *Merseyside Maritime Museum*: £3 (adult), free (child). *Museum of Liverpool Life*: £3 (adult), free (child under 16). *Tate Liverpool*: Free.

Alton Towers

Alton Towers is the most popular theme park in the UK. Set on an estate owned by the Earl of Shrewsbury, this giant amusement park has a wide range of rides and attractions aimed at young and old alike. The park, which opened in 1980, also includes 200 acres (81 hectares) of landscaped gardens, live entertainment and the historic towers building which was the residence of the Talbot family (the Earls of Shrewsbury) until 1923. The building was begun in 1814 by the 15th Earl of Shrewbury and completed by the architect Augustus Welby Northmore Pugin, who added large Gothic fireplaces and stained glass windows in the *Great Hall*. Today, visitors can explore different kingdoms in the grounds of the estate, such as *Ugland*, the *Forbidden Valley*, *Towers Street* and *Cred Street*. Popular rides include the *Black Hole*, which plunges participants into complete darkness, the famous *Corkscrew* rollercoaster, the *Log Flume* water slide and *Nemesis* rollercoaster. New for 2001 is the *Submission* white knuckle ride which subjects its victims to 90 seconds of continual spinning. The park's season comes to an end in late October with a giant firework display taking place in *The Gardens* area.

Contact Address

Alton Towers, Staffordshire, ST10 4DB, UK
Tel: (08705) 204 060.
Website: www.altontowers.com

Transportation

Air: Manchester Airport. **Rail:** Train: Alton Towers Station. Buses are available to take visitors to the park. **Road:** Coach: National Express operates coaches to Alton Towers (from major destinations in the UK). Car: M1 motorway, junction 23A (from London); M1 motorway, junction 28 (from Leeds); M6 motorway, junction 15 or 16 (from Manchester).

Opening Times

Daily 0930-1700/1900 (31 Mar-28 Oct).

Admission Fees

Off-Peak: £17 (adult), £14 (child). Peak: £22 (adult), £18 (child). Concessions available. Admission fees vary according to the day of the week and month; visitors are advised to check with the park operators before their visit.

Big Ben and the Houses of Parliament

The elaborate neo-Gothic *Palace of Westminster*, gracefully located beside the River Thames, is one of London's most timeless images. The adjoining clock tower, *St Stephen's*, is often mistakenly assumed to be called *Big Ben*, although this is actually the name of the bell inside. Big Ben rings every hour on the hour and is shown on British television at midnight on 31 December to count in the New Year. The original Palace of Westminster, constructed in the 12th century by Edward the Confessor and enlarged by William the Conqueror, was used as a royal palace until 1512 when it was damaged by fire. It only became the seat of the British government in the mid-16th century, and was rebuilt in its current style, to designs by architect Sir Charles Barry, after it was completely ravaged by fire in 1834. Since then, the building has housed the UK's bicameral parliament, consisting of the *House of Commons* and the *House of Lords*, as well as various parliamentary offices. For those who wish to watch a rowdy debate in one of the Houses, a guided tour can be arranged in advance (see details below). Alternatively, there are special guided tours of the building in July and August. There is no access to the clock tower for visitors.

Contact Address

House of Commons Information Office, London SW1A 0AA, UK
Tel: (020) 7219 4272. Fax: (020) 7219 5839.
E-mail: hcinfo@parliament.uk
Website: www.parliament.uk

Transportation

Air: London Heathrow Airport, London Gatwick Airport, London Stansted Airport, London Luton Airport. **Rail:** Train: London Victoria Station or London Waterloo Station. Underground: Westminster (Jubilee, Circle and District lines). **Road:** Car: M1 (from Leeds); A1 (M) (from Newcastle or Edinburgh); M4 (from Bristol, Reading or South Wales); M3 (from Southampton).

Opening Times

House of Commons Gallery: Mon-Wed 1430-2230, Thurs 1130-1930, Fri 0930-1500. Opening times apply only when the House is sitting. Advance booking required through local MP (UK residents) or UK Embassy or High Commission (all other visitors). *House of Lords Gallery*: Mon-Wed 1430-close, Thurs 1500-close, Fri 1100-close. Opening times vary and apply only when House is sitting. Advance booking required through local MP or peer (UK residents) or UK Embassy or High Commission (all other visitors). *Tour of Houses of Parliament*: Advance booking required (30 Sep-5 Aug); Mon-Sat 0915-1630 (6 Aug-29 Sep).

Admission Fees

House of Commons Gallery: Free. *House of Lords Gallery*: Free. *Tour of Houses of Parliament* (30 Sep-5 Aug): £3.50 (administration charge for telephone bookings).

Blackpool Pleasure Beach

The city of Blackpool has been attracting holiday visitors ever since 1735, when the first guest house

The Palace of Westminster and Big Ben

Corel

opened. In the 19th century, it became a popular working-class destination among the British and, in 1896, *Blackpool Pleasure Beach* was opened. Today, this American-style amusement park with a distinctly British feel has a variety of rides to suit all tastes and ages. Rides are classed according to their 'terror factor'. 'A' rides are white-knuckle rides and include the *Log Flume*, the classic wooden *Big Dipper* and the world-famous *Pepsi Max Big One*, a terrifying 1675.5-metre (5497-foot) long roller coaster that drops from heights of up to 63.7 m (209 ft) at a speed of 119.1 kmph (74 mph). The more sedate 'B' rides include a monorail ride around the pleasure beach, the *Ghost Train* and the *Black Hole*, which is a waltzer ride in the dark complete with flashing lights and disco music. 'C' rides are more suitable for children and feature two *Carousels*, a trip through a tilting reconstruction of *Noah's Ark* and the parks' oldest attraction, a centrifugal rocket ride called *Flying Machines. Valhalla*, which opened in 2000, is the world's biggest ride in the dark. There are also several shows to entertain visitors, such as *Eclipse at the Globe*, featuring acrobats, aerialists and dancers.

Contact Address

Blackpool Pleasure Beach, 525 Ocean Boulevard, Blackpool, Lancashire FY4 1EZ, UK
Tel: (0870) 444 5566. Fax: (01253) 407 609.
E-mail: marketing@bpbltd.com
Website: www.blackpoolpleasurebeach.co.uk

Transportation

Air: Manchester Airport, Blackpool Airport (domestic flights). **Rail:** Train: Blackpool North Station or Blackpool Pleasure Beach Station. **Road:** Bus: Services along the seafront to Blackpool Pleasure Beach. Car: M6 (to junction 32), then M55, then signs to Blackpool South Shore (via Blackpool Airport), then signs to Blackpool Pleasure Beach (from Manchester, Birmingham or London).

Opening Times

Daily 1000-2100 (these are general opening times which vary greatly depending upon the season; visitors are advised to call the park (tel: (0870) 444 5566) in advance to check specific opening times).

Admission Fees

Unlimited rides pass: £25 (1 day), £40 (2 days), £70 (1 day, family of 3), £85 (1 day, family of 4), £105 (1 day, family of 5), £10.95 (1 day Beaver Creek and all child rides). Concessions available. Pass includes show tickets. Sheet of 12-16 ride tickets: £24 (White Knuckle Rides), £24 (Pink Knuckle Rides), £10 (Beaver Creek and all child rides). Pass includes show tickets. Individual ride tickets: £2.25 (A rides), £1.75 (B rides), £1.25 (C rides).

British Airways London Eye

At 135m (443ft) tall, the *British Airways London Eye* is the world's largest observation wheel and the fourth tallest structure in London, after *One Canada Square* (more commonly known as Canary Wharf Tower), the *Nat West Tower* and *British Telecom Tower*. Designed by Marks Barfield Architects and managed by the Tussaud's Group, the wheel was finally erected in late 1999 after previous unsuccessful attempts to hoist it into its current position. It differs from a ferris wheel in that it has an A-frame support structure on only one side, while the pods are located on the exterior. These are stabilised by internal motors that keep them horizontal as the wheel slowly moves around. The structure has 32 separate capsules that rotate and can carry up to 25 people at any one time, taking passengers on a 30-minute trip high above London's skyline. Designed to be visually appealing from the exterior, the wheel carries passengers high into the air, providing staggering views of central London and further afield, to a distance as far away as 40km (25 miles).

Contact Address

British Airways London Eye, Riverside Building, County Hall, Westminster Bridge Road, London SE1 7PB, UK
Tel: (0870) 500 0600 *or* (020) 7654 0828.
Fax: (020) 7654 0806.
E-mail: capsules@ba-londoneye.com *or* customer.services@ba-londoneye.com
Website: www.ba-londoneye.com

Transportation

Air: London Heathrow Airport, London Gatwick Airport. **Rail:** Train: London Waterloo Station or London Charing Cross Station. Underground: Westminster (Jubilee, Circle or District lines), Waterloo (Bakerloo, Jubilee or Northern lines), Embankment (Bakerloo, Circle, District or Northern lines). **Road:** Bus: 11, 24 or 211. Coach: Belvedere Road. Car: Cross Westminster Bridge (from the Houses of Parliament). Lambeth Palace Road and York Road (from the South Bank).

Opening Times

Daily 1000-1900 (Jan-Mar and Oct-Dec); daily 1000-2000 (Mar-May and Sep); daily 1000-2200 (May-Sep).

Admission Fees

Adult: £8.50 (Jan-Apr), £9 (Apr-Jul and Oct-Dec), £9.50 (Jul-Sep). Child: £5 (Jan-Dec). Concessions available.

British Museum

The British Museum was founded in 1753 to promote a better public understanding of the arts, natural history and science. It contains one of the world's greatest displays of antiquities, documenting the rise and fall of civilisations from all over the world. The museum opened to the public in 1759, with the famous Rosetta Stone being presented to the museum in 1802, along with many other Egyptian antiquities. As well as the Rosetta Stone, the museum also houses many other famous objects, including the Parthenon sculptures, better known as the Elgin Marbles, and the Roman Portland Vase, which dates from the first century AD and is made of dark blue, cameo glass. Today, the museum's collection, which is in excess of six million objects, comprises art and antiquities from Egypt, Western Asia, Greece, Rome and Europe, amongst others, and includes many coins, medals, prints, drawings and ethnographical exhibits. The main building, which stands today, was designed by Sir Robert and Sidney Smirke and erected between the 1820s and 1850s. The spectacular Great Court, with its impressive glass roof, was opened in 2000, following the relocation of the British Library to St Pancras, and is the largest covered public square in Europe. This 0.8-hectare (two acre) courtyard was designed by Foster and Partners and built using funds raised from the Millennium Commission and the Heritage Lottery Fund. There are two huge stairwells leading down to the central Reading Room, as well as a new portico, built using 984 tons (1000 tonnes) of stone, and portals giving viewing access to the Great Court.

Contact Address

British Museum, Great Russell Street, London WC1B 3DG, UK
Tel: (020) 7323 8000 or 7323 8299.
Fax: (020) 7323 8616.
E-mail: information@thebritishmuseum.ac.uk
Website: www.thebritishmuseum.ac.uk

Transportation

Air: London Heathrow Airport. **Rail:** Train: London Kings Cross Station. Underground: Holborn (Central and Piccadilly lines), Tottenham Court Road (Central and Northern lines) or Russell Square (Piccadilly Line). **Road:** Bus: 7, 8, 10, 24, 25, 29, 38, 55, 68, 73, 91, 98, 134 or 188. Car: Right onto Bedford Avenue, then right onto Bloomsbury Street and first left onto Great Russell Street (from Tottenham Court Road).

Opening Times

Sat-Wed 1000-1730, Thu-Fri 1000-2030.

Admission Fees

Free; there are, however, admission fees for entry to temporary exhibitions.

Buckingham Palace

Work began on *Buckingham Palace*, the official London residence of the British Royal Family since 1837, in 1702 when it was built as 'Buckingham House' – the London home of the Duke of Buckingham. It was renamed 'Queen's House' in 1774 as it was the home of Queen Charlotte. In 1820, the palace passed to King George IV, who commissioned leading architect John Nash to refurbish the building, with work finishing in 1847. He increased the size of the building by adding new rooms in a French neo-classical style, making a total of 52 bedrooms, 78 bathrooms and 92 offices. The palace enjoys an imposing location in the centre of London, opposite *St James's Park*. Every year, millions of visitors come to see the *Changing of the Guard* ceremony, which takes place outside the palace at 1130 daily from April to July and on alternate days at other times of the year. They also come to see the famous *Royal Balcony* from where many members of the royal family have greeted the nation, including Prince Charles and Lady Diana on their wedding day, and the Queen Mother on her 100th birthday (4th August 2000). Visitors can also tour the inside of the palace during the summer months. The *Ball Room*, which is the largest room in the palace, opened to the public for the first time in 2000. The 19 *State Rooms* at the palace, which include the *Throne Room* and the *Picture Gallery*, house treasures including English and French furniture, paintings by Rembrandt and Rubens and sculpture by Canaletto. Visitors can also see inside the *Royal Mews*, which is one of the grandest working stables in the world.

Contact Address

Buckingham Palace, Buckingham Palace Road, London, Greater London, SW1A 1AA, UK
Tel: (020) 7839 1377. Fax: (020) 7930 9625.
E-mail: information@royalcollection.org.uk
Website: www.royalresidences.com

Transportation

Air: London Heathrow Airport. **Rail:** Train: London Victoria Station. Underground: St James's Park (District or Circle lines); Victoria (Victoria, District or Circle lines); Green Park (Piccadilly, Jubilee or Victoria lines). **Road:** Bus: 7, 11, 211, 139, C1 or C10 to stop on Buckingham Palace Road. Car: Buckingham Palace is situated at the end of The Mall in central London. Parking is difficult around this area and visitors are advised to use public transport.

Opening Times

Buckingham Palace: Daily 0930-1630 (4 Aug-30 Sep). *Royal Mews*: Daily 1200-1600 (Oct-Jul); daily 1030-1630 (Aug-Sep). Closed 25-26 Dec.

Admission Fees

Buckingham Palace: £11 (adult), £5.50 (child 5-16), free (child under 5). *Royal Mews*: £4.60 (adult), £2.60 (child 5-16), free (child under 5). Concessions available.

Cambridge University

Cambridge University is the second oldest university in England, with an unbroken educational tradition dating back to the late 12th century, and shares with Oxford University an unrivalled reputation for excellence and tradition. Its distinguished alumni include Sir Isaac Newton, John Milton and Steven Hawking. The university's various colleges, many of them architectural masterpieces, are scattered throughout the city. *St John's College* was founded by Lady Margaret Beaufort, mother of King Henry VII, in 1511 and contains the *New Bridge*, often referred to as the *Bridge of Sighs* due to its resemblance to the *Ponte dei Sospiri* in Venice. *Kings College* is perhaps the most famous of all the colleges due to its magnificent *chapel*, built between 1446 and 1515; the choir's Christmas Eve service of nine lessons and carols is internationally renowned, and constitutes an integral part of the festive season in Britain. *Trinity College*, founded in 1546 by King Henry VIII, who hoped it would produce the future leaders of the reformed Church of England, is the largest college; it is famous for the *Great Court* and the *Wren Library*, designed in 1695 by Sir Christopher Wren with limewood carvings by Grinling Gibbons. Another highlight, at *Queens' College*, is the *Mathematical Bridge*, designed by Sir Isaac Newton, that crosses the River Cam as it winds past the college buildings towards the *Backs*, the area of landscaped lawns and gardens that pass behind some of the main colleges.

Contact Address

Tourist Information Centre and Shop, The Old Library, Wheeler Street, Cambridge CB2 3QB, UK
Tel: (01223) 322 640. Fax: (01223) 457 588.
E-mail: tourism@cambridge.gov.uk
Website: www.cambridge.gov.uk/leisure/index.htm

Transportation

Air: London Heathrow Airport, London Gatwick Airport, London Stansted Airport, London Luton Airport. **Rail:** Train: Cambridge Station. **Road:** Bus: Services to Drummer Street. Car: M25, then M11 (from London); M11 (from London Stansted Airport); A14 (from the east and west); A1(M) (from the north and Midlands).

Opening Times

Kings College (including *Kings College Chapel*): Daily 0930-1530. Restricted opening times during chapel services and at certain other times; visitors are advised to contact the college (tel: (01223) 331 100) in advance. *Queens' College*: Daily 1345-1630 (1 Nov-24 Mar); Mon-Fri 1100-1500, Sat and Sun 1000-1630 (25 Mar-11 Apr); daily 1000-1630 (12-16 Apr); Mon-Fri 1100-1500, Sat and Sun 1000-1630 (Apr 17-20 May); daily 1000-1630 (24 June-30 Sep); Mon-Fri 1345-1630, Sat and Sun 1000-1630 (1-31 Oct). Closed 21 May-23 June. *St John's College*: Mon-Fri 1000-1700, Sat and Sun 0930-1700 (early Nov-Easter). Restricted opening times in winter. *Trinity College*: *Wren Library*: Mon-Fri 1200-1400, Sat 1030-1230 (full term-time only). Many colleges close during exam periods, particularly in May and June.

Admission Fees

Kings College: £3.50 (adult), £2.50 (child 12-17), free (child under 12). Concessions available. *Queens' College*: £1.20. *St John's College*: £2 (adult), £1.20 (child 12-17), free (child under 12). Concessions available. *Trinity College*: £2 (adult), £1 (child 12-17), free (child under 12). Concessions available. *Wren Library*: Free.

Camden Market

Thriving at the weekend, *Camden Market* is a popular place to spend an afternoon. It is the largest street market in the UK, attracting around 100,000 visitors every weekend. There are various markets located in *Camden Town*, which are collectively known as *Camden Market*; these are *Camden Lock Market, Camden Canal Market, Inverness Street Market, Camden (Bute Street) Market* and *Camden Stables Market*. The area around *Camden Lock* was first developed in around 1791 by the Earl of Camden, with the famous Regent's Canal opening in 1820. The first market to appear in Camden was *Camden Lock Market*, which opened in 1972. Today, there are hundreds of stalls selling a wide array of goods, including arts and crafts, vintage clothes, second-hand household items, records and CDs, jewellery and exotic food.

Contact Address

Camden Lock Limited, 56 Camden Lock Place, Chalk Farm Road, London NW1 8AF, UK
Tel: (020) 7284 2084. Fax: (020) 7485 2970.
E-mail: info@camdenlockmarket.com
Website: www.camdenlockmarket.com

Transportation

Air: London Heathrow Airport. **Rail:** Train: Camden Road Station and Kentish Town Station. Underground: Camden Town or Chalk Farm (Northern Line); exit only on Sunday afternoons at Camden Town. **Road:** Bus: 24, 29 or 134 (from

Tottenham Court Road); C2 (from Oxford Street); 27 (from High Street Kensington). Car: A400 northbound, then along Camden High Street on to Chalk Farm Road (from the A501 in central London).

Opening Times

Mon-Fri 1000-1800, Sat and Sun 0930-1830.

Admission Fees

Free.

Canterbury Cathedral

Canterbury Cathedral's history as a religious site dates back to AD 597 when Pope Gregory's missionary, St Augustine, was given a church in the town by King Ethelbert. The cathedral is a masterpiece of Romanesque and Gothic architecture. It was a noted place of pilgrimage for many centuries, as eloquently described by Geoffrey Chaucer in the 'Canterbury Tales'. Inside, visitors find, among many other curiosities, stained glass windows dating from the 12th century and the medieval tombs of King Henry IV and Edward the Black Prince, as well as those of numerous archbishops. The cathedral is also the former site of the shrine to the Archbishop Thomas Becket, who was murdered in the northwest transept in 1170. His shrine, which was desecrated in 1538 during the Reformation, became one of the most visited by pilgrims during the Middle Ages, many of whom travelled the famous Pilgrims' Way from Winchester to see it.

Contact Address

Canterbury Cathedral, Cathedral House, 11 The Precincts, Canterbury CT1 2EH, UK
Tel: (01227) 762 862. Fax: (01227) 865 222.
E-mail: visits@canterbury-cathedral.org
Website: www.canterbury-cathedral.org

Transportation

Air: London Gatwick Airport. **Rail:** Train: Canterbury East Station. **Road:** Bus: Canterbury Bus Station. Coach: National Express 020 (from London Victoria). Car: M26, M20 and A28 or A2 and M2 (from the M25). There are tourist signs to the Cathedral.

Opening Times

Mon-Sat 0900-1700, Sun 1230-1430 and 1630-1730 (Oct-Apr); Mon 0900-1730, Tues-Sat 0900-1830, Sun 1230-1430 and 1630-1730 (Apr-Sep). Opening hours may vary seasonally.

Admission Fees

£3.50 (adult), £2.50 (child over 6), free (child under 6). Concessions available.

Chessington World of Adventures

Chessington World of Adventures is the biggest theme park and zoo in the South of England. The park began life as a zoo, but was transformed into a theme park during the late 1980s, with the first rollercoaster ride opening in 1991. Attracting thousands of visitors every day, the park has many rides which include *Samurai, Rameses Revenge* and *Dragons Falls,* as well as a *Beanoland,* which is celebrating the 50th anniversary of Dennis the Menace in 2001. Today, visitors can also wander around the zoo, which has been combined with the park, and see one of the biggest families of gorillas in Europe and some of the world's rarest large cats. The *Trail of the Kings* animal enclosure opened in 2001, allowing visitors to see animals safely from behind viewing screens. The whole site is owned by the Tussaud's Group which also owns other major attractions in the UK, including *Madame Tussaud's London, The London Planetarium, Madame Tussaud's Rock Circus, Alton Towers, Warwick Castle* and *Thorpe Park.*

Contact Address

Chessington World of Adventures, Leatherhead Road, Chessington, Surrey, KT9 2NE, UK
Tel: (01372) 729 560 *or* (0870) 444 777. Fax: (01372) 725 050. Website: www.chessington.com

Transportation

Air: London Heathrow Airport. **Rail:** Train: Chessington South Station (from London Waterloo Station, Clapham Junction Station or Wimbledon Station). **Road:** Bus: 465 to Chessington (from Kingston); 467 to Chessington South (from Epsom). Car: M25, junction 9 and then the A243 towards central London.

Opening Times

Daily 1000-1700/1800 (30 Mar-15 Jul and 3 Sep-28 Oct); daily 1000-1930 (16 Jul-2 Sep). Closed 12-13, 19-20 and 26-27 Sep, and 1-4, 8-11 and 15-18 Oct.

Admission Fees

£19.95 (adult), £16.00 (child). Concessions available; tickets can be purchased in advance at a reduced rate.

Durham Castle and Cathedral

Durham Castle and *Cathedral,* seated high on a peninsula overlooking the River Wear, have been the first sight to greet visitors to this historic city for hundreds of years and were jointly designated a UNESCO World Heritage Site in 1986. Construction on the castle began in 1072, just after the Norman Conquest, under the orders of William the Conqueror, and it is a typical example of a motte and bailey fortification. It was initially used to control the rebellious Saxons who populated northern England. From the 11th century onwards it was used as the seat of power of the Prince Bishops, appointed by the British Crown to rule the Palatinate of Durham, the remote area of northern England vulnerable to attack from the Scots. In 1837, the last Prince Bishop, Bishop Van Mildert, helped found the *University of Durham* and donated the castle as its first home. It still houses students of *University College*, the oldest of the 14 university colleges, who live in the keep and dine in the wood-panelled Great Hall, containing portraits of the Prince Bishops. Across the lawned area, known as Palace Green, stands the *Cathedral Church of Christ and Blessed Mary the Virgin*, the best example of Norman-style architecture in England. It was built between 1093 and 1274, originally to house the relics of St Cuthbert, the Northumbrian evangelist who died in AD 687. Also interred in the cathedral is the Venerable Bede, who died in AD 735. Bede's work, '*The Ecclesiastical History of the English People*' is considered to be the first ever history of England. The cathedral's nave is one of the most complete examples of Romanesque architecture in Europe. At 61m (200ft) long and 22m (72ft) high, it features two rows of huge cylindrical and compound pillars supporting rounded arches. The twin *West Towers* overlook the River Wear and *Prebends Bridge*, which bears an inscription of a poem by Walter Scott in praise of the castle and cathedral. There are views of the cobbled streets of Durham and the surrounding countryside from the *Central Tower*.

Contact Address

Castle: University College, Palace Green, Durham DH1 3RW, UK
Tel: (0191) 374 3800.
E-mail: university-college.www@durham.ac.uk
Website: www.dur.ac.uk
Cathedral: The Dean and Chapter of Durham Cathedral, The Chapter Office, The College, Durham DH1 3EH, UK
Tel: (0191) 386 4266. Fax: (0191) 386 4267.
E-mail: enquiries@durhamcathedral.co.uk
Website: www.durhamcathedral.co.uk

Transportation

Air: Newcastle Airport. **Rail:** Train: Durham Station (frequent intercity services from London Kings Cross Station, Edinburgh, Newcastle or southwest England). **Road:** Coach: Durham Bus Station. Car: A1 (from London, the Midlands, Scotland or Newcastle). Visitors should avoid driving in the city centre where possible, as the streets are very narrow. The site is a short walk from the bus and train stations.

Opening Times

Guided tours of Castle: Mon, Wed, Sat at intervals during the afternoon (term-time 17 Apr-30 Sep); daily at intervals during the afternoon (other times 17 Apr-30 Sep). Other events may disrupt this schedule and visitors are therefore advised to check with the Castle Porter (tel: (0191) 374 3800) in advance. *Cathedral*: Mon-Sat 0730-1815, Sun 0745-1700.

Admission Fees

Castle: £3 (adult), £2 (child under 14). Family pass available. *Cathedral*: Free (requested donation of £3).

Eden Project

Opened in March 2001, the *Eden Project* consists of two enormous greenhouses built into a 50-metre-(164ft) deep claypit overlooking St Austell Bay in Cornwall. It was conceived by one man, former gardener and music producer Tim Smit, who raised millions of pounds in grants to create the world's largest greenhouse. His aim was to bring plants, grown from seeds and cuttings in nurseries, research stations and botanical gardens around the globe, to a central location, in order to promote environmental awareness and enable visitors to understand 'the vital relationship between plants, people and resources'. The most impressive of the two giant domes is the *Humid Tropics Biome*, which, at 200m (549ft) long, 100m (274ft) wide and 47m (129ft) high, could house the Tower of London. Its humid interior is filled with towering plants from the tropics, including balsa teak and mahogany, and there is also a Malaysian stilt house and garden as an example of how one culture

Eden Project

Ruth Blakeborough

uses its natural resources to survive. The second dome, the *Warm Temperate Biome*, contains plants from California, the Mediterranean and South Africa, such as lemon groves and olive trees. Visitors follow a path around the biomes, stopping to hear talks and sketches on the plants and learn about their uses from interactive displays; for those with a particular interest, there are themed trails, such as plants and medicine and plants and sport. Outside, 10 hectares (25 acres) of landscaped rockeries and gardens provide the setting for various events, including puppet shows and storytelling for children; visitors of all ages can discover more about natural products through chocolate days, tea-tasting and dyeing workshops.

Contact Address

Eden Project, Bodelva, St Austell, Cornwall PL24 2SG, UK
Tel: (01726) 811 911. Fax: (01726) 811 912.
Website: www.edenproject.com

Transportation

Air: Exeter International Airport, Southampton International Airport, Bristol International Airport or Plymouth City Airport (domestic flights). **Rail:** Train: St Austell Station. **Road:** Car: A390 (from Truro or St Austell); A38, then A390, then A391 (from Exeter); M5, then A38, then A390, then A391 (from Bristol, the Midlands and the north); M4, then M5, then A38, then A390, then A391 (from London and the southeast).

Opening Times

Daily 1000-1630 (1 Nov-28 Feb); daily 1000-1800 (1 Mar-31 Oct). Last admission 1-1.5 hours before closing. Closed 24 and 25 Dec.

Admission Fees

£9.50 (adult), £4 (child 5-15), free (child under 5). Concessions and family pass available.

Greenwich

The *London Borough of Greenwich*, which is situated on the South bank of the Thames, is home to a host of attractions, and recognised internationally both for its military and naval connections and as the home of Greenwich Mean Time. Famous sites in Greenwich include the *Cutty Sark Clipper Ship*, which was built in 1869 by the Scottish company Scott & Linton and is the finest tea clipper still surviving today, *Greenwich Market*, which sells an interesting array of craft, food and bric-a-brac, and the *Royal Observatory Greenwich*. The latter was designed by the famous architect, Sir Christopher Wren in the 17th century and is home to the *Greenwich Meridian*, the key meridian line in the world, responsible for setting the world clock on zero degrees latitude. The *National Maritime Museum*, the largest maritime museum in the world, and the Baroque-style *Old Royal Naval College*, which began life as Greenwich Hospital in 1694 to treat seamen, are also located in Greenwich. The borough has an historic past and was the birthplace of King Henry VIII and Queen Elizabeth I. It also boasts many green spaces including *Greenwich Park*, which forms one of eight royal parks in the capital and is the only royal park in East London; it is actually home to the Royal Observatory Greenwich, the National Maritime Museum and the Old Royal Naval College. The *Millennium Dome*, which closed on 31 December 2000, is also situated in Greenwich and is still visible high above London's skyline. The whole area was named a UNESCO World Heritage Site in 1997.

Contact Address

Greenwich Tourist Information Centre, 46 Greenwich Church High Street, Greenwich, London SE10 9BL, UK
Tel: (020) 8858 6376. Fax: (020) 8853 4607.

Transportation

Air: London City Airport, London Gatwick Airport, London Heathrow Airport. **Rail:** Train: Greenwich Station or Maze Hill Station. Docklands Light Railway: Cutty Sark Station or Greenwich Station. **Road:** Bus: 53, 177, 180, 188, 286 or 386. Car: M25, M11, A406 towards East London, A13 and then Blackwell Tunnel (from Cambridge); M25 and A2 to Greenwich (from Canterbury); A202, A2209, A200 and A2211 (from Victoria in central London).

Opening Times

Greenwich Market: Daily 0900-1730 (there are many more stalls at the weekend when there is a large flea market). *Cutty Sark Clipper Ship*: Daily 1000-1700. Closed 24-26 Dec. *National Maritime Museum*: Daily 1000-1700. *Royal Observatory Greenwich*: Daily 1000-1700. *Old Royal Naval College*: Mon-Sat 1000-1700, Sun 1230-1700. *Greenwich Park*: Daily dawn-dusk.

Admission Fees

Greenwich Market: Free. *Cutty Sark Clipper Ship*: £3.50 (adult), £2.50 (child). *National Maritime Museum*: £7.50 (adult), free (child). *Royal Observatory Greenwich*: £6.00 (adult), free (child). *Old Royal Naval College*: £3 (adult), £2 (child). *Greenwich Park*: Free.

Hadrian's Wall

Built by order of the Emperor Hadrian in AD 122, *Hadrian's Wall* is the best known and most important Roman monument in Britain, stretching

117km (73 miles) across the north of England, from Wallsend-on-Tyne to Bowness-on-Solway. The wall was built to mark the northern boundary of the Roman Empire in the British Isles and to keep out the pugilistic barbarians to the north. After the Empire receded in the fifth century AD, the wall was left to decay, and many of its stones were used in the construction of nearby buildings. Vast sections of the wall still remain, however, giving a genuine sense of its former importance. There are many different sites to be visited along the wall. *Housesteads Roman Fort and Museum*, known as *Vercovicium* to the Romans, is an excavated fort located amidst spectacular scenery, and contains the only visible example of a Roman hospital in Britain, and well-preserved Roman latrines. *Vindolanda Fort and Museum* is an open-air museum containing authentic reconstructions of the wall, as well as a Roman temple, house and shop; there are also displays of rare Roman writing tablets, textiles and leathers. The *Roman Army Museum* at Carvoran provides an insight into the life of a Roman soldier, through models, reconstructions and artefacts. *Chesters Roman Fort and Museum* is an extensively excavated cavalry fort with impressive Roman bathhouse remains.

Contact Address

Hadrian's Wall Tourism Partnership, Eastburn, South Park, Hexham, Northumberland NE46 1BS, UK
Tel: (01434) 602 505 *or* 605 555. Fax: (01434) 601 267 *or* 600 522. E-mail: info@hadrians-wall.org
Website: www.hadrians-wall.org

Transportation

Air: Newcastle Airport. **Rail:** Train: Haltwhistle Station or Hexham Station. **Road:** Bus: 93, 185, 685/85 or 880. Car: A1 then A74 (M) (from the west); A1(M) to Newcastle, then A68 towards Edinburgh (to central part of the wall from the east); A69 Newcastle – Carlisle runs parallel to Hadrian's Wall.

Opening Times

Chesters Roman Fort and Museum: Daily 1000-1600 (1 Nov-31 Mar); daily 0930-1800 (1 Apr-30 Sep); daily 1000-1700 (1-31 Oct). *Housesteads Roman Fort and Museum*: Daily 1000-1600 (1 Nov-31 Mar); daily 1000-1800 (1 Apr-30 Sep); daily 1000-1700 (1-31 Oct). Closed 24-26 Dec and 1 Jan. *Roman Army Museum*: Daily 1000-1600 (15-30 Nov); daily 1000-1600 (1-28 Feb); daily 1000-1700 (1 Mar-31 Oct). *Vindolanda Fort and Museum*: Daily 1000-1600 (15-30 Nov); daily 1000-1600 (1-28 Feb); daily 1000-1700 (1 Mar-31 Oct).

Hadrian's Wall

Corel

Admission Fees

Chesters Roman Fort and Museum: £2.90 (adult), £1.50 (child). Concessions available. *Housesteads Roman Fort and Museum*: £2.90 (adult), £1.50 (child), free to members of English Heritage and National Trust. Concessions available. *Roman Army Museum*: £3.10 (adult), £2.10 (child). Concessions available. *Vindolanda Fort and Museum*: £3.90 (adult), £2.80 (child). Concessions available. Many other sites along the wall are free.

Hampton Court Palace

Built by Cardinal Wolsey in the early 16th century and later owned by King Henry VIII (1491-1547), *Hampton Court Palace* occupies a beautiful riverside site 23km (14 miles) southwest of London. The palace was once the centre of royal and political life in England, with many famous monarchs residing there between 1525 and 1737, including King Henry VIII, King William III and Queen Mary during the 17th century, and King George II in the 18th century. The palace has been associated with many important events in history: King Henry VIII spent his honeymoon in the palace with Anne Boleyn in 1533 and married his sixth wife Catherine Parr there in 1543, whilst King Charles I was held prisoner in the palace in 1647 by Oliver Cromwell, who came to live there in 1653. The palace was opened to the public in 1838 by Queen Victoria and today, visitors can still see much of the grandeur of this impressive Tudor palace. Highlights of the former palace include Henry VIII's *Great Hall*, which is the biggest room in the palace, measuring 32m (106ft) long, 12m (40ft) wide and 18m (60ft) high, King William III's *State Apartments*, designed by Christopher Wren and completed in 1700, and the unmissable *Tudor Kitchens*, which are said to be the most impressive 16th-century kitchens in England. In the *Palace Gardens*, visitors can happily lose their way in the famous maze which was planted in the North Gardens in 1702.

Hampton Court Palace

Corel

Contact Address

Hampton Court Palace, Surrey, KT8 9AU, UK
Tel: (020) 8781 9500. Website: www.hrp.org.uk

Transportation

Air: London Heathrow Airport. **Water:** Boat: Services run along the River Thames in the summer (from Westminster, Richmond-upon-Thames and Kingston-upon-Thames). **Rail:** Train: Hampton Court Station (from London Waterloo Station). Underground: Wimbledon (District Line); Vauxhall (Victoria Line). **Road:** Bus: 111, 216, 411, 416, 451, 513, 727 or R68. Car: The Palace is located on the A308, close to the A3 and M3 (from Guildford).

Opening Times

Hampton Court Palace: Mon 1015-1630, Tues-Sun 0930-1630 (28 Oct-24 Mar); Mon 1015-1800, Tues-Sun 0930-1800 (25 Mar-27 Oct). Closed 24-26 Dec. *Gardens*: Daily 0700-dusk.

Admission Fees

£10.80 (adult), £7.20 (child under 16), free (child under 5). Concessions available.

Harrods

Harrods, perhaps London's most famous department store, is named after Charles Henry Harrod, who opened a family grocers shop on the site in 1849. The shop has grown to become a byword for expensive and glamourous shopping, priding itself on its motto *Omnia Omnibus Ubique*, meaning 'All things, for all people, everywhere'. Bought by Egyptian businessman Mohamed Al Fayed in 1985, the eye-catching seven-storey building, which is illuminated by 11,500 lightbulbs each night, contains over 300 departments selling luxury items, from furniture and ladies fashion to polo mallets and wax coats for dogs. For those on a tighter budget, there is a Harrods gift shop, selling assorted souvenirs such as pencils and teddybears. Two departments not to be missed are the *Food Halls*, each hall elaborately decorated according to the type of produce it sells, and the *Egyptian Halls*, where visitors can browse through the displays of handbags and accessories surrounded by statues of Queen Nefertiti and images of Luxor Temple. Harrods also provides banking and real estate services, currency exchange facilities and, for those who want to see the British capital in style, a luxury coach tour of London complete with tea and biscuits.

London Tourist Board

Harrods

Contact Address

Harrods Ltd, 87-135 Brompton Road, Knightbridge, London SW1X 7XL, UK
Tel: (020) 7730 1234. Website: www.harrods.com

Transportation

Air: London Heathrow Airport, London Gatwick Airport, London Stansted Airport, London Luton Airport. **Rail:** Train: London Paddington Station, London Victoria Station, London Euston Station, London Kings Cross Station, London Liverpool Street Station or London Waterloo Station. Underground: Knightsbridge (Piccadilly Line). **Road:** Bus: 14, 74, C1 or A1 (to Brompton Road); 19, 22 or 137 (to Sloane Street). Coach: London Victoria Coach Station. Car: M1 (from Leeds); A1 (M) (from Newcastle or Edinburgh); M4 (from Bristol, Reading or South Wales); M3 (from Southampton).

Opening Times

Mon-Sat 1000-1900.

Admission Fees

Free.

Leeds Castle

Leeds Castle in Kent is built on two islands in a lake. It was originally built as a royal manor in AD 857, but from 1278 onwards was used as a royal palace by King Edward I. Over the centuries, the castle has been home to several Queens of England, including Catherine de Valois (wife of Henry V), Eleanor and Margaret (Edward I's wives), Philippa of Hainhault (Edward III's wife), Catherine of Aragon (one of Henry VIII's six wives) and Elizabeth I. It was also home to Henry VIII and is full of many fine arts, furnishings and tapestries from its illustrious past. The castle was sold to Lady Baillie in 1926 who employed Armand-Albert Rateau amd Stéphane Boudin, two international interior designers, to transform the interior, filling it with fine furniture, tapestries and paintings. The castle is also famous for its *Aviary*, which is home to many birds including black swans and was built as a memorial to Lady Baillie, opening in 1988. The castle's grounds are also spectacular and include the *Maze, Wood Garden, Vineyard* and *Culpeper Garden*.

Contact Address

Leeds Castle, Leeds, Maidstone, Kent, ME17 1PL, UK
Tel: (01622) 765 400. Fax: (01622) 767 855.
E-mail: enquiries@leeds-castle.co.uk
Website: www.leeds-castle.co.uk

Transportation

Air: London Heathrow Airport or London Gatwick Airport. **Rail:** Train: Connex trains run to Bearsted Station (from London Victoria Station) and then connect with a coach service. **Road:** Coach: National Express runs coaches to the castle (from London Victoria Coach Station and from Dover, Folkestone, Hythe and Ashford). Car: M20 motorway (junction 8); the castle is signposted (from London).

Opening Times

Daily 1000-1500 (Nov-Feb); daily 1000-1700 (Mar-Oct). Closed 25 Dec.

Admission Fees

Admission to *Castle, Parks* and *Gardens*: £10 (adult), £6.50 (child). Concessions available.

Legoland® Windsor

Following on from the success of the original *Legoland* park in Billund, Denmark, *Legoland Windsor* welcomed its first visitors in 1996 and since then has become one of England's most popular theme parks. The park is split into seven different sections, each with its own theme. *Miniland* was the Danish counterpart's founding feature and remains one of the biggest attractions for visitors of all ages, consisting of miniature models of European sights, all created from a total of 20 million Lego bricks. *My Town* includes rides such as the *Lego® Adventures Wave Surfer*, a wet and wild tumble along rivers and down waterfalls, a *Carousel*, and *Explorers Institute*, an explorative trek through the jungle, the Arctic and the ancient Egyptian pyramids. The *Dragon Knights Castle*, in *Castleland*, takes visitors on a mysterious roller-coaster ride through the dragon's lair and into the wizard's workshop, before soaring up through the treetops. Children can create their own Lego and

Duplo inventions from the thousands of bricks in the *Imagination Centre* workshops, and visitors as young as three can learn to drive around a special lego driving track, complete with traffic lights. There are shows every day, including *Brickadilly's Circus* and an *Aqua Stunt Show* in *My Town*.

Contact Address

Legoland Windsor, Winkfield Road, Windsor, Berkshire SL4 4AY, UK
Tel: (0870) 504 0404.
Website: www.legoland.co.uk

Transportation

Air: London Heathrow Airport, London Gatwick Airport, London Stansted Airport, London Luton Airport. **Rail:** Train: Windsor Central Station (from London Paddington Station); Windsor & Eton Riverside Station (from London Waterloo Station). **Road:** Bus: Services to Legoland Windsor (from Windsor Central or Windsor & Eton Riverside Stations). Coach: Services from London Victoria Coach Station. Car: B3022 Windsor/Ascot Road, via M25 (from London); via M1, then M25 (from the north); via M3 (from Southampton); via M4 (from Bristol, southwest England or South Wales).

Opening Times

Daily 1000-1700/1800 (10 Mar-4 Nov); daily 1000-1900 (during school summer holidays). The park may open for Christmas; visitors are advised to check for details later in the year.

Admission Fees

£18.50 (adult), £15.50 (child 3-15), free (child under 3). Concessions and family pass available.

London Dungeon

This horror theme park situated on London's South Bank gives visitors the opportunity to explore the darker side of British and European history. The *London Dungeon*, which opened in 1975, is a creepy recreation of many of history's most gruesome events. Visitors can go on various themed rides, which are based around historical murders and executions; they can explore the streets of Victorian London that were home to the serial killer Jack the Ripper, relive the Great Fire of London and take a barge down the River Thames to Traitors Gate, where they are sentenced to death by an 18th-century judge. The London Dungeons are patrolled by scary characters, dressed in gruesome costumes, who wait in dark corners and jump out at unsuspecting tourists.

Contact Address

London Dungeon, 28/34 Tooley Street, London SE1 2SZ, UK
Tel: (09001) 600 066 *or* 7403 7221. Fax: (020) 7378 1529. Website: www.thedungeons.com

Transportation

Air: London Heathrow Airport, London Gatwick Airport. **Rail:** Train: London Bridge Station. Underground: London Bridge (Jubilee or Northern lines) or Monument/Bank (District, Circle, Central, Waterloo & City or Northern lines). **Road:** Bus: 17, 21, 22A, 35, 40, 43, 47, 48, 133, 313, 344, 501, 505, D1, D11 or P3. Car: London Dungeon is located just off London Bridge in central London, on the A200 and adjacent to London Bridge Station.

Opening Times

Daily 1030-1800 (1 Nov-31 Mar); daily 1000-1830 (1 Apr-14 Jul); daily 1000-2100 (15 Jul-3 Sep); daily 1000-1830 (4 Sep-31 Oct). Closed 25 Dec. Last admittance is one hour before closing time.

Admission Fees

£10.95 (adult), £6.95 (child). Concessions available. No unaccompanied children under 15 years of age.

London Zoo

London Zoo, which opened in 1828, is situated on the north side of Regent's Park. The zoo was the site of the world's first children's zoo, which opened in 1938, followed by the first reptile house in 1849, the first public aquarium in 1853 and the first insect house in 1881. Today, the Zoo is home to around 12,000 animals, including Asian lions, Sumatran tigers, Sloth bears, Leadbeater's possums and Death adders. In the *Reptile House*, visitors can see one of the largest collections of venomous snakes and reptiles in the UK; they can also see many nocturnal animals such as the Rodrigues fruit bat in the *Moonlight World*. The famous spiral-shaped *Penguin Pool*, which is Grade I listed, is the home of Black-footed penguins, whilst the *Aquarium* houses sharks, piranhas and other sea creatures. The zoo also has beautiful gardens, as well as innovative zoo buildings, designed by architects such as Decimus Burton who designed the *Giraffe House*, Berthold Lubetkin who was responsible for the Penguin Pool and Sir Hugh Casson, responsible for the *Elephant and Rhino Pavilion*. The zoo recently opened the Web of Life exhibition, which is an interactive display of animals around the world.

Contact Address

London Zoo, Outer Circle, Regent's Park London NW1 4RY, UK
Tel: (020) 7722 3333. Fax: (020) 7586 5743.
E-mail: marketing@zsl.org
Website: www.london zoo.co.uk

Transportation

Air: London Heathrow Airport. **Rail:** Train: London Kings Cross Station. Underground: Camden Town (Northern Line); the zoo is a short walk up Parkway from Camden Town Station. **Road:** Bus: 274 or C2. Car: A41, A5205 Prince Albert Road and Outer Circle (from the A501 in central London).

Opening Times

Daily 1000-1600 (Nov-Feb); daily 1000-1730 (Mar-Oct). Closed 25 Dec.

Admission Fees

£10 (adult), £7 (child 3-15), free (child under 3). Concessions available.

Madame Tussaud's and Tussaud's London Planetarium

Over 400 lifesize wax models of the rich and famous are exhibited in Madame Tussaud's. Lifesize replicas of stars of the stage and screen, musicians and monarchs are displayed alongside footballers and politicians. Madame Tussaud was born in Strasbourg in 1761 and after inheriting a wax museum from Philippe Curtius in 1794, moved to London to set up an exhibition on London's Baker Street. Following her death in 1850, her grandsons moved the display to its present location on Marylebone Road, where it has remained since 1884. Today, visitors can have their photo taken with the likes of filmstar Marilyn Monroe, Australian popstar Kylie Minogue, footballer David Beckham and even members of the British Royal Family. They can also descend into the *Chamber of Horrors* to see some of history's most notorious criminals and various torture instruments. *Tussaud's London Planetarium*, which is adjacent to Madame Tussaud's and opened in 1958, enables budding astronomers to see the stars and is one of the largest planetariums in the world.

Contact Address

Madame Tussaud's and Tussaud's London Planetarium, Marylebone Road, London NW1 5LR, UK
Tel: (0870) 400 3000 *or* (020) 7487 0200.
Fax: (020) 7465 0862.
Website: www.madame-tussauds.com *or* www.london-planetarium.com

Transportation

Air: London Heathrow Airport. **Rail:** Underground: Baker Street (Bakerloo, Circle, Jubilee, Metropolitan or Hammersmith & City lines). **Road:** Bus: 13, 18, 27, 30, 74, 82, 113, 139, 159 or 274. Car: Madame Tussaud's is situated just off the A501 in central London, which leads on from the M4 motorway (from Bristol and Reading).

Opening Times

Madame Tussaud's: Mon-Fri 1000-1730, Sat and Sun 0930-1730. Closed 25 Dec. *London Planetarium*: Mon-Fri 1230-1700, Sat and Sun 1000-1730. Opening times are subject to change during the summer season.

Admission Fees

Madame Tussaud's: £11.50 (adult), £8 (child). *London Planetarium*: £6.50 (adult), £4.35 (child). *Madame Tussaud's* and *London Planetarium* (combined ticket): £13.95 (adult), £8 (child). Concessions available.

National Gallery

With its Classical façade gracing the northern side of London's Trafalgar Square, the UK's *National Gallery* possesses one of the world's greatest collections of Western paintings. The collection was established in 1824 when the British government purchased the private collection of John Julius Angerstein, a philanthropist and collector, and was initially housed in Angerstein's former residence on Pall Mall, before being moved to its present home in 1838. On display are around 2300 pictures covering every European school of painting from the 13th to the 19th century. Highlights include the Wilton Diptych, an elaborate 14th-century devotional altarpiece crafted for King Richard II of England, and Renaissance masterpieces such as Piero della Francesca's 'Baptism of Christ' and Botticelli's 'Venus and Mars'. Other paintings by English masters include Constable's 'The Haywain' and Gainsborough's 'The Watering Place'. The Early Renaissance collection is housed in the Sainsbury Wing, which was designed by Philadelphian architects Venturi, Scott Brown & Associates and opened to the public in 1991. There are regular exhibitions at the National Gallery, ranging from displays of schoolchildren's artwork inspired by Hogarth's painting 'The Graham Children', to an exhibition of 19th-century German painting.

Contact Address

National Gallery, Trafalgar Square, London WC2N 5DN, UK
Tel: (020) 7747 2885. Fax: (020) 7747 2423.
Website: www.nationalgallery.org.uk

Transportation

Air: London Heathrow Airport, London Gatwick Airport, London Stansted Airport, London Luton Airport. **Rail:** Train: London Charing Cross Station.

Underground: Charing Cross (Northern or Bakerloo lines), Leicester Square (Northern or Piccadilly lines), Embankment (Northern, Bakerloo, Circle or District lines) or Piccadilly Circus (Piccadilly or Bakerloo lines). Road: Bus: 3, 12, 24, 29, 53, 88, 159 or 176. Car: M1 (from Leeds); A1 (M) (from Newcastle or Edinburgh); M4 (from Bristol, Reading or South Wales); M3 (from Southampton).

Opening Times

Mon and Tues 1000-1800, Wed 1000-2200, Thurs-Sun 1000-1800.

Admission Fees

Free.

National Museum of Photography, Film and Television

Founded in 1983 as part of the *National Museum of Science and Industry*, the decision to locate the *National Museum of Photography, Film and Television* outside the capital was based on Bradford's contribution to the development of UK cinema and the city's accessible location. This is an interactive museum and visitors have the opportunity to discover the media world through a variety of hands-on experiences, including reading the news to camera, discovering the workings of a television camera and creating their own animations. On display are the world's first negative, the world's first television footage and the world's first example of a moving picture. The museum has had to move with the times to reflect ever changing developments within the industry, and contains Europe's first gallery devoted to digital media, as well as Europe's first *IMAX* cinema showing 3-D films. On selected Saturdays, visitors also have the chance to relive cinema history by entering the world's only publicly-accessible *Cinerama* cinema, as mentioned in Bill Bryson's book 'Notes from a Small Island'. Here, audiences are treated to one of the earliest Cinerama films, the travelogue 'This is Cinerama', which was produced in 1952 using a then-revolutionary camera technique to create a wide-screen effect.

Contact Address

National Museum of Photography, Film and Television, Bradford, West Yorkshire BD1 1NQ, UK
Tel: (01274) 202 030. Fax: (01274) 723 155.
Website: www.nmpft.org.uk

Transportation

Air: Leeds/Bradford International Airport, Manchester Airport. **Rail:** Train: Bradford Forster Square Station or Bradford Interchange Station. **Road:** Bus: Bradford Interchange Station. Car: M1, then M62, then M606 (from London and the southeast); M5, then M62 (from Birmingham and the southwest); A1, then M62 (from the north).

Opening Times

Tues-Sun and public holidays 1000-1800. Closed Mon.

Admission Fees

Free.

Natural History Museum

The *Natural History Museum* in South Kensington began its life as the natural history section of the British Museum, featuring the collections of London physician and collector Sir Hans Sloane, who wished his collection to remain together to benefit as many people as possible after his death. Following a competition to choose the architect of the new building, Captain Robert Fowke drew up the original designs, seeing the museum as a cathedral of science, hence its church-like appearance. When he died in 1865, his work was continued by Alfred Waterhouse, who was responsible for the elaborate Romanesque carvings of animals and plants throughout the building. The Natural History Museum moved into its new home in 1883, since which time it has considerably increased the size of its collections, perhaps most famously to include the dinosaur gallery, where visitors can see huge dinosaur skeletons and even an animated T-Rex. The *Earth Galleries* explore the effects human life has on the planet around us and how scientists harness the resources we use in our everyday lives, as well as featuring displays of minerals and gemstones and an earthquake simulator. The *Life Galleries* allow visitors to explore human biology, Darwin's theory of natural selection and to see an enormous life-size model of a blue whale. There are also regular exhibitions, and outside the building, the wildlife garden provides an opportunity to discover British wildlife in the heart of London.

Contact Address

Natural History Museum, Cromwell Road, London SW7 5BD, UK
Tel: (020) 7942 5011 *or* 7942 5000.
Website: www.nhm.ac.uk

Transportation

Air: London Heathrow Airport, London Gatwick Airport, London Stansted Airport, London Luton Airport. **Rail:** Train: London Paddington Station,

London Victoria Station or London Waterloo Station. Underground: South Kensington (Circle, District or Piccadilly lines). **Road:** Bus: 14, 49, 70, 74, 345 or C1. Coach: Victoria Coach Station. Car: M1 (from Leeds); A1 (M) (from Newcastle or Edinburgh); M4 (from Bristol, Reading or South Wales); M3 (from Southampton).

Opening Times

Mon-Sat 1000-1750, Sun 1100-1750.

Admission Fees

£9 (adult), free (child under 16), free Mon-Fri after 1630 and Sat, Sun and public holidays after 1700. Last admission 1730. Concessions available.

Oxford University

As a centre of education dating back to the early 12th Century, *Oxford University* ranks as the oldest university in England and one of the most famous in the world. Its extensive list of important alumni includes John Locke, Christopher Wren, Lewis Carroll, Jonathan Swift, Oscar Wilde and, latterly, Tony Blair and Bill Clinton. The university itself is made up of a number of colleges, most displaying stunning architecture and trim lawns, situated throughout the city. Of particular interest to visitors are *Christ Church College*, founded in 1524 by Cardinal Wolsey, whose college chapel also serves as Oxford's cathedral; *Merton College*, one of the smaller colleges with only 250 undergraduates, which was founded in 1264 by Walter Merton, Bishop of Rochester, and has particularly beautiful gardens and courtyards; and the *Bodleian Library*, the central library of Oxford University, which is the oldest library in Europe and was originally founded in 1320 by Thomas Cobham, Bishop of Worcester. It contains the *Radcliffe Camera*, a round, domed building (*camera* being the Latin word for 'room') constructed by James Gibbs between 1737 and 1749 as a natural sciences library, and now a reading room for undergraduates.

Contact Address

Oxford Tourist Information Centre, The Old School, Gloucester Green, Oxford OX1 2DA, UK
Tel: (01865) 726 871. Fax: (01865) 240 261.
E-mail: tic@oxford.gov.uk
Website: www.oxford.gov.uk/tourism

Transportation

Air: London Heathrow Airport, London Gatwick Airport, London Stansted Airport, London Luton Airport. **Rail:** Train: Oxford City Station. **Road:** Bus: 2, 5 or 22. Coach: Oxford Tube or X90 Oxford Express (from London Victoria Coach Station); X70 Oxford Express (from London Heathrow Airport); X80 Oxford Express (from London Gatwick Airport); X50 Stagecoach (from Stratford-upon-Avon). Car: M40 (from London and the Midlands); A34 (from Southampton, Portsmouth and Bristol).

Opening Times

Christ Church College: Daily 0800-1800. Closed 25 Dec. *Merton College*: Mon-Fri 1400-1600, Sat and Sun 1000-1600. *Radcliffe Camera*: Mon-Fri 0900-2200, Sat and Sun 0900-1300 (term-time); Mon-Fri 0900-1900, Sat and Sun 0900-1300 (vacations). Some colleges close during exam periods.

Admission Fees

Christ Church College: £4 (adult), £3 (child under 18). Concessions available. *Merton College*: Free. *Radcliffe Camera*: Free.

Portsmouth Historic Dockyard

Portsmouth Historic Dockyard is home to three of the world's finest ships: the *Mary Rose, HMS Victory* and *HMS Warrior 1860*. The Mary Rose, which was Henry VIII's favourite warship, sank in 1545, but

HMS Victory

Flagship Portsmouth Trust

was raised from the sea in 1982. Today, visitors can enter the *Mary Rose Museum* and *Ship Hall*, where more than 1000 artefacts are on display. They can also see *HMS Victory*, which is the world's oldest commissioned warship, used by Nelson in the Battle of Trafalgar (1805) to defeat the Franco-Spanish fleet, and the *HMS Warrior 1860*, the world's first iron battleship, one of the largest and fastest warships at the time, and the pride of Queen Victoria's Black Battlefleet. The *Royal Naval Museum* can also be found in the buildings surrounding the Dockyard and there is an interactive *Dockyard Apprentice Exhibition*, where visitors can see how the great Dreadnought ships were built during the late-18th and early-19th centuries. *Flagship Portsmouth* opened *Action Stations* in May 2001, which tells the story of the Royal Navy, allowing visitors to experience how life in the navy would be for recruits today.

Contact Address

Flagship Portsmouth Trust, Building 1/7 College Road, HM Naval Base, Portsmouth, Hampshire PO1 3LJ, UK
Tel: (023) 9286 1512 (24-hour information line) *or* 9286 1533 *or* 9272 2562. Fax: (023) 9229 5252.
E-mail: enquiries@flagship.org.uk
Website: www.flagship.org.uk

Transportation

Air: Southampton International Airport. **Rail:** Train: Portsmouth Harbour Station. **Road:** Bus: 17 or 18. Coach: National Express Coaches terminate at the Hard, which is outside the Dockyard. Car: A27 (junction 12) and M275, then brown heritage signs to the Historic Waterfront and signs for the Historic Dockyard (from Brighton and Southampton).

Opening Times

Dockyard and all attractions except *HMS Victory*: Daily 1000-1700 (Nov-Mar); daily 1000-1730 (Apr-Oct). Opening times for the *HMS Victory* vary daily and visitors are advised to check with the Flagship Portsmouth Trust before their visit.

Admission Fees

Dockyard: Free. *Mary Rose Museum & Ship Hall*: £6 (adult), £4.50 (child). *HMS Victory & Royal Naval Museum*: £6.50 (adult), £4.80 (child). *HMS Warrior 1860*: £6 (adult), £4.50 (child). *Royal Naval Museum*: £3.50 (adult), £2 (adult). *Warships by Water Harbour Tour*: £3.50 (adult), £2 (child). *The Dockyard Apprentice*: £2.50 (adult), £1.50 (child). *Historic Dockyard Trail Acoustiguide*: £2 (adult), £1 (child). Concessions available.

Roman Baths and Pumproom

The ancient Romans were the first to capitalise on the only natural hot spring in Britain, building a temple and bathing complex more than 2000 years ago in the city of Bath. The city itself was originally called Aquae Sulis, after the baths and the temple which were dedicated to the goddess of wisdom and healing, Sulis Minerva. Its name was changed to Bath however during the Middle Ages. The healing spring, which is located within the bathing complex, produces approximately 2,273,050 litres (500,000 gallons) of water per day at a temperature of 46.5°C (116°F). The baths were once one of the finest in the Roman world, although the Roman structure gradually fell into disrepair. It was not until a visit by the ailing Prince George in 1702 that the baths once again became a popular healing destination. Over the course of the town's redevelopment, the Roman ruins were rediscovered (in 1879) and restored. Visitors can now view the Georgian grandeur of the Pump House and see the remains of the ancient Roman baths and temple. Today, highlights at what is one of the most celebrated Roman sites in the UK include the *Great Bath*, the adjacent *Circular Bath*, the remains of Sulis Minerva's temple and the *King's Bath*, which was built during the 12th century.

Contact Address

Roman Baths and Pumproom, Museum Enquiries, Stall Street, Bath BA1 1LZ, UK
Tel: (01225) 477 785. Fax: (01225) 477 743.
E-mail: museum_enquiries@bathnes.gov.uk
Website: www.romanbaths.co.uk

Transportation

Air: London Heathrow Airport, Bristol International Airport. **Rail:** Train: Bath Spa Station. **Road:** Bus: Bath Bus Station. Car: M4, then A46, junction 18 (from London); M5, M4 and A46, junction 18 (from Birmingham).

Opening Times

Daily 0930-1730 (Jan-Feb and Nov-Dec); daily 0900-1800 (Mar-Jun and Sep-Oct); daily 0900-2200 (Jul-Aug). Closed 25 and 26 Dec.

Admission Fees

Roman Baths: £7.50 (adult), £4.20 (child). *Pumproom*: Free. Concessions available.

Royal Armouries Leeds

The *Royal Armouries* is Britain's national collection of arms and armour, and was moved from its former home in the Tower of London to a specially-created

Board of the Trustees of the Armouries

Royal Armouries Leeds

building, designed by architect Derek Walker, in Leeds in 1996. Visitors can enter five galleries, each with its own theme covering self-defence, war, armour of the Orient, hunting and tournament. There is a wealth of different objects on display, including over 7500 swords, King Henry VIII's equestrian equipment, several longbows excavated from the sunken British battleship the Mary Rose, 50 instruments of torture, and arms and armour from as far afield as central Asia, India, Africa and Japan. The Armouries also hold a variety of events and exhibitions, the most popular of which have been the children's sleepovers, where children aged 6-12 and accompanied by an adult have the chance to stay the night in the galleries and be entertained, with face painting, bedtime snacks, sword-making and colouring activities on offer. Easter-egg trails and Hallowe'en stories are also available, depending on the time of year; those interested should check the website for details.

Contact Address

Royal Armouries Leeds, Armouries Drive, Leeds LS10 1LT, UK

Tel: (01274) 202 030. Fax: (01274) 723 155.

Website: www.armouries.org.uk/leeds

Transportation

Air: Leeds/Bradford International Airport. **Rail:** Train: Leeds Station. **Road:** Coach: Leeds Bus Station. Car: M1 (from London); A6110 (from Bradford); A64 (from York); A1 (from Newcastle); M62 (from Manchester).

Opening Times

Mon-Fri 1030-1630 (until 1730 during school holidays), Sat and Sun 1030-1730 (1 Nov-1 Apr); daily 1000-1730 (2 Apr-31 Oct).

Admission Fees

£4.90 (adult), £3.90 (child). Concessions and family pass available.

Royal Botanic Gardens, Kew

Kew Gardens comprise 132 hectares (326 acres) of herbaceous bedding, water features, botanical glasshouses, a large arboretum and historic buildings located on the banks of the River Thames in southwest London. Founded in 1759 by Augusta, the widow of Frederick, Prince of Wales, they initially featured botanical gardens, an orangery, pagoda and archway designed by the architect, Sir William Chambers. Augusta's son, King George III employed the celebrated landscape gardener Capability Brown to extend the gardens in 1766 and the gardens gained their first director, Sir William Hooker, in 1840 after the British Royal Family had donated various portions of land from the surrounding Richmond Estate and Kew Estate. Over the years, this vast oasis on the outskirts of the metropolis has become a favourite with visitors wishing to escape the pressures of the city, and has been extensively developed. Nowadays, its attractions include an aquatic garden, a bamboo garden, a woodland glade, a conservation area and a Japanese landscape. There are several glasshouses to explore, one of which, *Evolution House*, showcases 3500 million years of plant evolution. *Queen Charlotte's Cottage*, located within the grounds of *Richmond Lodge*, was a wedding gift to Queen Charlotte in 1861 and was also used by Queen Victoria until she presented it to the public upon her Diamond Jubilee in 1897; the building has now been restored to its original state. Visitors to Kew can either join in a guided tour, follow one of several themed trails, or wander around the attractions at their own pace.

Contact Address

Royal Botanic Gardens, Kew, Richmond, Surrey TW9 3AB, UK

Tel: (020) 8332 5000 *or* 8940 1171.

Fax: (020) 8332 5197.

E-mail: info@rbgkew.org.uk
Website: www.rbgkew.org.uk

Transportation

Air: London Heathrow Airport, London Gatwick Airport, London Stansted Airport, London Luton Airport. **Rail:** Train: Richmond Station (from north and south London); Kew Bridge Station (from London Waterloo Station). Underground: Kew Gardens (District Line). **Road:** Bus: 65, 237, 267, 391 or 419. Car: M1, then North Circular, then A205 or A307 (from the north); M4 then A205 or A307 (from the west); A3, then A205 or A307 (from the south).

Opening Times

Daily 0930-1615 (28 Oct-5 Feb); daily 0930-1730 (6 Feb-24 Mar); Mon-Fri 0930-1830, Sat and Sun 0930-1930 (25 Mar-2 Sep); daily 0930-1800 (3 Sep-27 Oct). Closed 25 Dec and 1 Jan.

Admission Fees

£6.50 (adult), free (children under 16). Concessions and family pass available.

Royal Pavilion

The *Royal Pavilion*, which is the former seaside home of King George IV, is one of the most exotic-looking buildings in the UK. It was originally a farmhouse, but was transformed into a neo-classical villa in 1787 by the architect Henry Holland. The building was further re-modelled by John Nash in 1820 in the style of an Indian palace. It was also used by George IV's brother, William IV and his niece Queen Victoria, but was sold to the town of Brighton by Victoria in 1850. Today, the exterior of this Regency building still has many domes and minarets, whilst the interior features a huge banqueting room with an impressive chandelier as its centrepiece, as well as a music room with lanterns hanging from a high-domed ceiling. The palace is ornately decorated with an array of Chinese and English furnishing and is set in lavish surrounding gardens.

Contact Address

Royal Pavilion, Pavilion Buildings, Brighton BN1 1EE, UK
Tel: (01273) 290 900. Fax: (01273) 292 871.
E-mail: visitor.services@brighton-hove.gov.uk
Website: www.royalpavilion.brighton.co.uk

Transportation

Air: London Gatwick Airport. **Rail:** Train: Brighton Station (from London Victoria Station or London Bridge Station). **Road:** Car: M23 and A23 (from London). The Royal Pavilion is located in Brighton city centre and is well-signposted.

Opening Times

Daily 1000-1700 (Oct-May); daily 1000-1600 (Jun-Sep). Closed 25 and 26 Dec.

Admission Fees

£5.20 (adult), £3.20 (child).

Science Museum

Together with the *National Railway Museum* and the *National Museum of Photography, Film & Television*, the *Science Museum* is part of the *National Museum of Science & Industry*. Located in central London, the museum owns an impressive collection of science exhibits, including the Apollo 10 Command Module, the V-2 rocket, which was the world's first long-range missile, and Stephensons' Rocket locomotive. The Science Museum, which originally opened along with the *Victoria and Albert Museum* in 1857 as the *South Kensington Museum*, now houses one of the largest collections of scientific, medical, industrial and technological exhibits in the world. There are numerous interactive displays and permanent exhibitions, as well as the new *Wellcome Wing*, which presents contemporary scientific and technological exhibits, and the *IMAX 3D* cinema.

Contact Address

Science Museum, Exhibition Road, South Kensington, London, SW7 2DD, UK
Tel: (0870) 870 4771. Fax: (020) 7942 4302.
E-mail: feedback@nmsi.ac.uk
Website: www.sciencemuseum.org.uk *or* www.nmsi.ac.uk

Transportation

Air: London Heathrow Airport. **Rail:** Train: London Victoria Station. Underground: South Kensington (Picadilly, Circle or District lines). **Road:** Bus: 9, 10, 14, 49, 52, 74, 345 or C1. Car: M4 and A4 (from Reading and west London). The Science Museum is located just off the A4, before the Victoria and Albert Museum.

Opening Times

Daily 1000-1800. Closed 24, 25 and 26 Dec.

Admission Fees

£7.95 (adult), £4.95 (student). Free after 1630.

Shakespeare Houses

William Shakespeare, considered by many to be the greatest dramatist and poet the world has ever known, was born in the market town of Stratford-upon-Avon in 1564 and maintained strong links with the town until his death in 1616. His legacy has turned Stratford into a major tourist destination crammed with historic houses relating to the writer's life and that of his family. *Shakespeare's Birthplace* is a half-timbered house in the centre of Stratford, which remained the property of his descendants until 1806, when it was bought by a board of trustees and restored as a museum. Visitors can tour the rooms where Shakespeare and his brothers and sisters grew up. The adjacent *Shakespeare's World Museum* guides visitors through the life and times of Shakespeare using drawings, maps, illustrations and audiovisual displays. In 1582, Shakespeare married Anne Hathaway, the daughter of a local farmer, and *Anne Hathaway's Cottage*, the picturesque thatched cottage where she was born and spent her early life, can be visited in the hamlet of Shottery, 1.6km (1 mile) from Stratford-upon-Avon. Shakespeare returned as a successful playwright to Stratford-upon-Avon from London in 1597 and bought *New Place*, the second largest house in the town, where he spent the last years of his life. New Place and its formal gardens can be entered by passing through the grounds of *Nash's House*, once owned by Thomas Nash, the first husband of Shakespeare's granddaughter, Elizabeth. Nash's House is now a museum on the history of Stratford-upon-Avon. *Hall's Croft*, a timber-framed house on the edge of the town centre is named after its former owner, John Croft, who was the husband of Shakespeare's daughter Susanna, and a physician famous for his publication of patient's case notes, which provide a fascinating insight into 17th-century medicine as well as biographical details of Shakespeare's family. Visitors can also tour the home of Shakespeare's mother, *Mary Arden's House* at *Glebe Farm*, which was fortunately rescued from demolition by the Shakespeare Trust in 1960.

Contact Address

The Shakespeare Centre, Henley Street, Stratford-upon-Avon CV37 6QW, UK
Tel: (01789) 204 016. Fax: (01789) 296 083.
E-mail: info@shakespeare.org.uk
Website: www.shakespeare.org.uk

Transportation

Shakespeare's Birthplace, Nash's House & New Place and *Hall's Croft*: **Air:** Birmingham International Airport. **Rail:** Train: Stratford-upon-Avon Station. **Road:** Car: A422 (from London or Oxford). *Anne Hathaway's Cottage*: **Air:** Birmingham International Airport. **Road:** Car: Alcester Road (A422/A46) out of Stratford, then left on Evesham Road, then right onto Hathaway Lane (from Stratford-upon-Avon). The house is located at the end of Cottage Lane and is clearly signposted. *Mary Arden's House*: **Air:** Birmingham International Airport. **Rail:** Train: Wilmcote Station. **Road:** Car: Birmingham Road (A3400), then turn left (from Stratford-upon-Avon); A3400 (from Birmingham). The house is clearly signposted.

Opening Times

Anne Hathaway's Cottage: Mon-Sat 0930-1600, Sun 1000-1600 (20 Oct-19 Mar); Mon-Sat 0900-1700, Sun 0930-1700 (20 Mar-19 Oct). *Hall's Croft*: Mon-Fri 1000-1600, Sun 1030-1600 (20 Oct-19 Mar); Mon-Sat 0930-1700, Sun 1000-1700 (20 Mar-19 Oct). *Mary Arden's House*: Mon-Sat 1000-1600, Sun 1030-1600 (20 Oct-19 Mar); Mon-Sat 0930-1700, Sun 1000-1700 (20 Mar-19 Oct). *Nash's House*: Mon-Sat 1000-1600, Sun 1030-1600 (20 Oct-19 Mar); Mon-Sat 0930-1700, Sun 1000-1700 (20 Mar-19 Oct). *New Place*: Mon-Sat 1000-1600, Sun 1030-1600 (20 Oct-19 Mar); Mon-Sat 0930-1700, Sun 1000-1700 (20 Mar-19 Oct). *Shakespeare's Birthplace*: Mon-Sat 0930-1600, Sun 1000-1600 (20 Oct-19 Mar); Mon-Sat 0900-1700, Sun 0930-1700 (20 Mar-19 Oct). *Shakespeare's World* and *Visitors Centre*: Daily 1000-1600 (20 Oct-19 Mar); Mon-Fri 0900-1700, Sun 0930-1700 (20 Mar-19 Oct).

Admission Fees

Anne Hathaway's Cottage: £4.50 (adult), £2 (child under 16). Concessions and family pass available. *Hall's Croft*: £3.50 (adult), £1.70 (child under 16). Concessions and family pass available. *Mary Arden's House*: £5.50 (adult), £2.50 (child under 16). Concessions and family pass available. *Nash's House*: £3.50 (adult), £1.70 (child under 16). Concessions and family pass available. *New Place*: £3.50 (adult), £1.70 (child under 16). Concessions and family pass available. *Shakespeare's Birthplace* (including *Shakespeare's World)*: £6.00 (adult), £2.50 (child under 16). Concessions and family pass available. Pass for *Shakespeare's Birthplace, Nash's House* and *New Place*: £8.50 (adult), £4.20 (child under 16). Concessions and family pass available. Pass for all houses: £12 (adult), £5 (child under 16). Concessions and family pass available.

St Paul's Cathedral

Built in 1673, *St Paul's Cathedral* is Sir Christopher Wren's most famous work. Its dome, one of the largest in Europe, stands out as one of the most distinctive features of London's skyline. There has been a cathedral dedicated to St Paul on the site for more than 1400 years, and the present Cathedral stands on the site of an even older medieval cathedral that burned down during the Great Fire of 1666. Decorating the interior of the dome is the *Whispering Gallery*, so named for its incredible acoustics. Higher up, there are magnificent views across London. Contained beneath the main cathedral floor is the *Crypt*, which is the largest in Europe, housing more than 200 tombs, including those of Admiral Nelson and the Duke of Wellington, and the tomb of Sir Christopher Wren himself. Over the years, the cathedral has been the setting for many historic events, including Sir Winston Churchill's funeral in 1965, and the wedding of Prince Charles and the late Princess of Wales in 1981.

Contact Address

St Paul's Cathedral, The Chapter House, St Paul's Churchyard, London EC4M 8AD, UK
Tel: (020) 7236 4128. Fax: (020) 7248 3104.
E-mail: reception@stpaulscathedral.org.uk
Website: www.stpauls.co.uk

Transportation

Air: London Heathrow Airport, London Gatwick Airport. **Rail:** Train: City Thameslink Station. Underground: St Paul's (Central Line). **Road:** Bus: 4, 11, 15, 23, 26 or 100. Car: New Bridge Street, then Ludgate Hill (from Blackfriars Bridge in central London).

Opening Times

Sightseeing: Mon-Sat 0830-1600. *Worship*: Mon-Fri 0730-1700 (last service), Sat 0800-1700 (last service), Sun 0800-1800 (last service).

Admission Fees

£5 (adult), £2.50 (child under 16). Price includes admission to the Crypt, Ambulatory and Galleries. Concessions available.

St Paul's Cathedral

The Flat Earth Collection

Stonehenge

Erected some time between 3000 and 1600 BC, *Stonehenge* is a giant stone circle that stands on Salisbury Plain and is considered today to be one of the most famous surviving sites from the ancient world. The stones, which are 6.7m (22ft) high, attract hundreds of visitors every day, who come to marvel at the ingenuity of those who engineered the construction of the site and the techniques used to move and position the stones. The first prehistoric structures appeared at the site in approximately 3100 BC. However, it was not until 2150 BC that the 3.9-ton (4-tonne) bluestones were brought to Stonehenge from the Preseli Hills in Pembrokeshire, southwest Wales, using manpower alone. The 30 sarsen stones, which form the Sarsen Circle with raised lintels around the edge, were brought 150 years later from the Marlborough Downs, 32km (20 miles) away, the largest weighing an astonishing 49.2 tons (50 tonnes). The term bluestone refers to igneous rocks, mainly dolerites and rhyolites, whilst sarsen stone is a type of sandstone. *Avebury*, which is located 37km (24 miles) from Stonehenge, is another ancient mystery to modern-day man, and one of the biggest stone circles ever built. There are also many burial mounds nearby, as well as long barrows from the Neolithic Age, the most famous of which is *West Kennet Long Barrow*.

Contact Address

Stonehenge, Abbey Buildings, Abbey Square, Amesbury, Wiltshire SP4 7ES, UK
Tel: (01980) 624 715. Fax: (01980) 623 465.
E-mail: clews.everard@english-heritage.org.uk
Website: www.stonehengemasterplan.org

Transportation

Air: London Heathrow Airport. **Rail:** Train: Salisbury Station. **Road:** Bus: Coach services run to Amesbury and Stonehenge (from Salisbury). Car: A30 and A303 (from Exeter); A360, A304 and A344 (from Salisbury).

Opening Times

Daily 0930-1600 (end Oct-mid Mar); daily 0930-1800 (mid-Mar-May); daily 0900-1900 (Jun-Aug); daily 0930-1800 (Sep-mid Oct); daily 0930-1700 (mid Oct-end Oct). Closed 1 Jan and 24-26 Dec.

Admission Fees

£4.20 (adult), £2.20 (child). Concessions available.

Tate Britain

Tate Britain, which was known as the *Tate Gallery* until *Tate Modern* was opened in 2000, houses the national collection of British art from 1500 to the present day, the largest and most comprehensive collection of British art in the world. The Neoclassical building, situated on the banks of the River Thames, was designed by Sidney Smith to house the art collection of the sugar tycoon Sir Henry Tate and was first opened to the public in 1897. Unusually, works from different periods are arranged together according to theme to provide more thought-provoking displays and to enable visitors to see well-known paintings in a new light; themes include *Literature and Fantasy, Home and Abroad* and *Public and Private.* The collection includes works by Blake, Constable, Gainsborough, Hogarth, Rosetti and Hockney. Thè *Clore Gallery,* opened in 1987, houses a magnificent collection of paintings by British Romantic landscape artist JMW Turner. Tate Britain also hosts special events such as themed talks, artists' talks, lectures and films.

Contact Address

Tate Britain, Millbank, London SW1P 4RG, UK
Tel: (020) 7887 8000.
Website: www.tate.org.uk/britain

Transportation

Air: London Heathrow Airport, London Gatwick Airport, London Stansted Airport, London Luton Airport. **Rail:** Train: London Paddington Station, London Victoria Station, London Waterloo Station or London Vauxhall Station. Underground: Pimlico (Victoria Line), Vauxhall (Victoria Line) or Westminster (Jubilee, Circle or District lines). **Road:** Bus: 2, 3, C10, 36, 77A, 88, 159, 185 or 507. Car: M1 (from Leeds); A1 (M) (from Newcastle or Edinburgh); M4 (from Bristol, Reading or South Wales); M3 (from Southampton). Entrance to car parks from John Islip Street.

Opening Times

Daily 1000-1750. Closed 24-26 Dec.

Admission Fees

Free.

Tate Modern

Tate Modern, housed in the former Bankside Power Station on the south bank of the River Thames, is Britain's new national museum of modern art, opened in 2000. It showcases international modern art from 1900 to the present day and, like its sister museum, Tate Britain, it presents visitors with a themed, rather than a chronological, tour of art. Each theme is set in its own set of galleries where a variety of media, including photography, film, sculpture and painting are displayed. The themes are *Nude/Action/Body, History/Memory/Society, Still Life/Object/Real Life* and *Landscape/Matter/Environment,* and feature works by artists such as Dalí, Picasso, Matisse, Warhol, Rothko and Gilbert & George. One of the most provocative displays is Tracey Emin's video booth, in which the avant-garde British artist provides a candid account of her personal life experiences as a metaphor for common humanity. More subtle and thought-provoking is an exhibition entitled '1985: Shape of a Year', which explores the similarities and differences in art from around the world in a single year, and the ways in which art reflected global fashions and events of the time. 'Ways of Seeing' uses paintings, photographs, sculpture and audiovisual art to look into the relationship between art and reality and how the advent of photography changed the way artists portrayed the world.

Contact Address

Tate Modern, Bankside, London SE1 9TG, UK
Tel: (020) 7887 8000. Minicom: (020) 7887 8687.
Website: www.tate.org.uk/modern

Transportation

Air: London Heathrow Airport, London Gatwick Airport, London Stansted Airport, London Luton Airport. **Rail:** Train: London Blackfriars Station or London Bridge Station. Underground: Southwark (Jubilee Line) or Blackfriars (Circle or District lines). **Road:** Bus: 45, 63, 100, 381 or 344. Car: M1 (from Leeds); A1 (M) (from Newcastle or Edinburgh); M4 (from Bristol, Reading or South Wales); M3 (from Southampton).

Opening Times

Sun-Thurs 1000-1800, Fri and Sat 1000-2200.

Admission Fees

Free.

Tintagel Castle

The ruins of the legendary 12th-century *Tintagel Castle* stand on windswept cliffs in North Cornwall on one of England's most dramatic coastlines. Believed to be the birthplace of King Arthur who was protected by his magical sword, Excaliber, from the evil wrought by the magician, Merlin, the medieval castle was built in around 1250 by Richard, Earl of Cornwall. The castle is surrounded in mystery and little is actually known about its history; according to legend, however, King Mark's nephew Tristan fell in love with Isolt here and Uther Pendragon seduced Queen Igraine with the help of Merlin. Today, the remains of the castle stand on rugged cliffs high above the sea. Over the years, the mainland has been eroded by the elements and the castle is now only accessible via a narrow bridge and steep steps. Many claim that Tintagel is one of the most romantic places in the UK, with beautiful walks along the Cornish Coastal Path.

Contact Address

Tintagel Castle, Tintagel, Cornwall, PL34 0HE, UK
Tel: (01840) 770328. Fax: (01840) 770328.
Website: www.english-heritage.org.uk

Transportation

Air: Exeter International Airport. **Road:** Bus: First Western National X10 to Boscastle (from Exeter St David's); Fry's Bus Service to Boscastle (from Wadebridge). Car: A392, A39 and B3263 to Tintagel (from Newquay); A30, A395, A39 and B3263 to Tintagel (from Exeter). Tintagel Castle is situated on Tintagel Head, 0.8km (0.5 miles) from the main road; it cannot be reached by car.

Opening Times

Daily 1000-1600 (1 Nov-31 Mar); daily 1000-1800 (1 Apr–8 Jul); daily 1000-1900 (9 Jul-26 Aug); daily 1000-1800 (27 Aug-30 Sep); daily 1000-1700 (1-31 Oct). Closed 24-26 Dec and 1 Jan.

Admission Fees

£3 (adult), £1.50 (child). Concessions available.

Tower of London

Work began on the infamous *Tower of London* in 1078 on the orders of William the Conqueror, 12 years after his Norman invasion of England. The tower, which is situated on the north bank of the River Thames and once dominated the city of London, is also known as the *White Tower*, after the Central Keep which is made of white Caen limestone. It remained a royal residence until the 16th century and was also a notorious prison where key historical figures, such as Catherine Howard, Sir Walter Raleigh, the two Royal Princes (Edward V and Richard Duke of York) and King Henry VI, lost their lives. Today, it houses the *Crown Jewels* and the *Royal Armouries*, and is also an important museum. The site is guarded by *Yeoman Warders* (or *Beefeaters*), so-called because they used to have to taste the king's food to see if it had been poisoned) and is apparently protected by ravens; according to legend if the ravens ever leave the tower a great disaster will take place in England.

Contact Address

Tower of London, Tower Hill, London EC3N 4AB, UK
Tel: (020) 7709 0765.
Website: www.tower-of-london.com *or* www.hrp.org.uk

Transportation

Air: London Heathrow Airport. **Rail:** Train: Fenchurch Street or London Bridge Stations. Underground: Tower Hill (District or Circle lines). Docklands Light Railway: Tower Gateway. **Road:** Bus: 15, 25, 42, 78, 100 or D1. Car: Tower Bridge and Tower Bridge Approach (from the South Bank); A10 (from the North Circular through Islington).

Opening Times

Tues-Sat 0900-1600, Sun and Mon 1000-1600 (Nov-Mar); Mon-Sat 0900-1700, Sun 1000-1700 (Apr-Oct).

Admission Fees

£11.30 (adult), £7.50 (child under 15), free (child under 5). Concessions available.

Victoria & Albert Museum

The *Victoria & Albert Museum* is Britain's national museum of art and design. It was first opened in 1852 at Marlborough House in central London as a Museum of Manufacturers, following the success of the Great Exhibition which had been held in London the previous year. In 1857 it was moved to Brompton in west London, where it was renamed the Victoria and South Kensington Museum. It acquired its current name in 1899 in honour of Queen Victoria (and her beloved husband, Albert) who had laid the foundation stone as her last public appearance. The V&A is the largest museum of decorative arts in the world and highlights include the largest collection of Italian Renaissance sculpture outside Italy, paintings and drawings by Constable, the *Glass Gallery* (which contains over 7000 glass articles, such as stained-glass windows, beads and vases), the *Fashion Court*, featuring displays of costumes through the centuries and the *Canon Photography Gallery*. Other items on display include ceramics, textiles, jewellery and furniture from Britain, Europe and Asia. The museum also holds regular exhibitions centred around various themes.

Contact Address

Victoria & Albert Museum, Cromwell Road, South Kensington, London SW7 2RL, UK
Tel: (020) 7942 2000. Fax: (020) 7492 2266.
E-mail: infodome@vam.ac.uk
Website: www.vam.ac.uk

Transportation

Air: London Heathrow Airport, London Gatwick Airport, London Stansted Airport, London Luton Airport. **Rail:** Train: London Paddington Station, London Victoria Station or London Waterloo Station.

Underground: South Kensington (District, Circle and Piccadilly lines). **Road:** Coach: Victoria Coach Station. Bus: 14, 49, 70, 74, 345 or C1. Car: M1 (from Leeds); A1 (M) (from Newcastle or Edinburgh); M4 (from Bristol, Reading or South Wales); M3 (from Southampton).

Opening Times

Mon and Tues, Thurs-Sun 1000-1745, Wed and selected Fri 1000-2200. Closed 24-26 Dec.

Admission Fees

£5 (adult), free (child). Concessions available. Free to all visitors after 22 Nov 2001.

Warwick Castle

Warwick Castle ranks amongst the most popular of all Britain's many historic attractions due to its size, picturesque location and turbulent history. The castle was created as a fortification in AD 914, to protect the small hilltop settlement from Danish invaders who posed a threat to the Anglo-Saxon kingdom of Mercia, and was later enlarged by William the Conqueror who turned it into a motte and bailey fort in 1068. Fortifications were added by King Richard III until his death at the Battle of Bosworth in 1485. The castle has witnessed some key events in English history. These include the capture of Piers Gaveston, favourite of King Edward II, before his murder by jealous barons in 1312, and, in 1469, the imprisonment of King Edward IV during the Wars of the Roses by Richard Neville, Earl of Warwick ('Warwick the Kingmaker'). Royal guests welcomed to the castle have included Queen Elizabeth I, King Charles I, King George III and Queen Elizabeth II. The castle was expanded by the Beauchamp family, who were Earls of Warwick from 1268 and later, in the 17th century, by Sir Fulke Grenville, poet and courtier to Queen Elizabeth I, who added the chapel with its beautiful stained-glass windows. Grenville was stabbed to death in the 14th-century ghost tower by a bitter manservant in 1628. The opulent *State Rooms* were added by Grenville's descendants in the 17th and 18th centuries, as were the gardens, laid out by the famous English landscape gardener, Capability Brown. Today, visitors can explore the varied history of the castle's dungeons, fortifications and living quarters, as well as the Rose Garden and the formal gardens. The *Private Apartments* contain a display of waxwork figures, showing how the rooms would have looked at the weekend parties hosted by the Countess of Warwick for some of the most prominent figures of Victorian society in the late 19th century. Across the River Avon is the

Warwick Castle

Warwick Castle

Island, where jesters, archers and craftsmen show off their skills in the summer months alongside re-enactments of battles and tournaments.

Contact Address

Warwick Castle, Warwick CV34 4QU, UK
Tel: (01926) 406 600. Fax: (01926) 406 611.
E-mail: customer.information@warwick-castle.co.uk
Website: www.warwick-castle.co.uk

Transportation

Air: Birmingham International Airport. **Rail:** Train: Warwick Station; from the station visitors should turn right onto Coventry Road, right onto Smith Street, left onto Castle Hill and right onto Castle Lane. **Road:** Car: M40 (from London, Birmingham, Manchester, Leeds, Bristol or Stratford-upon-Avon).

Opening Times

Daily 1000-1700 (1 Nov-31 Mar); daily 1000-1800 (1 Apr-31 Oct). Closed 25 Dec.

Admission Fees

£10.25 (adult), £6.25 (child) (10 Sep-28 Feb); £11.50 (adult), £6.75 (child) (12 May-9 Sep). Concessions and family pass available.

Westminster Abbey

England's most visited religious site, *Westminster Abbey* is a monument to British history. Inside there are buried kings, statesmen, warriors, scientists, musicians and poets, including Charles Darwin, Geoffrey Chaucer, Charles Dickens, Mary I, James I and Charles II. Initially the site of a Norman abbey, Henry III built the present building in the 13th century to compete with the

Corel

Windsor Castle

great European cathedrals of the time. The abbey has seen the coronation of every English monarch since William the Conqueror, with the exception of Edward V and Edward VIII (who were never crowned at all). The abbey has continued, over the centuries, to play a crucial role in royal state occasions and was the setting for the coronation of the present monarch, Queen Elizabeth II, on 2nd June 1953, as well as the funeral of the late Princess of Wales on 6th September 1997. Today, visitors to the abbey come to see the *Grave of the Unknown Warrior*, the *Royal Tombs* and Edward I's *Coronation Chair*, as well as the *Lady Chapel* and *Poets' Corner*, where there is a memorial statue of William Shakespeare.

Contact Address

The Chapter Office, Dean's Yard, Westminster Abbey, London SW1P 3PA, UK
Tel: (020) 7222 5152 *or* 7222 7110 (information desk). Fax: (020) 7233 2072.
E-mail: info@westminster-abbey.org
Website: www.westminster-abbey.org

Transportation

Air: London Heathrow Airport. **Rail:** Train: Waterloo Station or Victoria Station. Underground: Westminster (Jubilee, Circle or District lines) or St James Park (Circle or Distric lines). **Road:** Bus: 3, 11, 12, 24, 53, 77A, 88, 159, 211 or 721. Car: Parliament Square and Millbank (from Westminster Bridge).

Opening Times

Mon-Fri 0900-1645, Sat 0900-1445.

Admission Fees

£6 (adult), £3 (child under 16), free (child under 11). Concessions available.

Windsor Castle

Windsor Castle, overlooking the Berkshire town of Windsor, is one of the official homes of Queen Elizabeth II and is the largest and oldest occupied castle in the world. It was constructed under William the Conqueror (c. 1028-1087) as a means of guarding the western approaches to London, due to its position high above the River Thames on the edge of a Saxon hunting ground. Since then, it has been continuously inhabited by Britain's monarchs who have created both an impressive fortress and a regal residence. The castle was painstakingly restored after fire swept through more than 100 rooms and *St George's Chapel* in 1992. Visitors can now once again enter many parts of the castle. Highlights include the *Waterloo Chamber*, built to commemorate the British Army's victory over Napoleon in 1815, the grand *State Apartments* and *Queen Mary's Dolls House*, a miniature house, created in the 1920s to designs by Sir Edward Lutyens and containing tiny copies of books written by Rudyard Kipling and G K Chesterton. Many of the rooms contain drawings from the Royal Collection, including works by Rembrandt, Rubens, Holbein and Van Dyck. One of the highlights of a visit to the castle is St George's Chapel, founded in 1475 by King Edward IV and completed by King Henry VIII. It is one of the best examples of Perpendicular Gothic architecture in Britain, and contains the remains of numerous British sovereigns, including King Henry VIII, Jane Seymour, Charles I and George V. King George III is buried in the *Albert Memorial Chapel*, which was built by King Henry VII as a royal mausoleum and restored by Queen Victoria in memory of her husband, Prince Albert. The 200 hectares (500 acres) of *Home Park* surround the castle, containing the site of *Frogmore*, where Queen Victoria and Prince Albert were laid to rest. A popular place to go walking is in the sweeping 700-hectare (1800-acre) expanse of *Windsor Great Park*, which can be accessed by the *Long Walk*, a broad path lined with elm trees planted under the instructions of King Charles II in 1685.

Contact Address

The Visitor Office, Windsor Castle, Berkshire SL4 1NJ, UK
Tel: (01753) 869 898. Fax: (01753) 832 290.
E-mail: windsorcastle@royalcollection.org.uk
Website: www.the-royal-collection.org.uk

Transportation

Air: London Heathrow Airport, London Gatwick Airport, London Stansted Airport, London Luton Airport. **Rail:** Train: Windsor Central Station (from London Paddington); Windsor & Eton Riverside Station (from London Waterloo). **Road:** Coach: Services from London Victoria Coach Station. Car: B3022 Windsor/Ascot Road, via M25 (from London); via M1, then M25 (from the north); via M3 (from Southampton); via M4 (from Bristol, southwest England or South Wales).

Opening Times

Daily 0945-1615 (1 Nov-28 Feb); daily 0945-1715 (1 March-31 Oct). Last admission 75 minutes before closing. Closed 29 Mar, 31 Mar (morning of), 21 Apr (morning of), 9 Jun (afternoon of), 11 June, 17 June, 25-26 Dec. St George's Chapel has more restrictive opening hours.

Admission Fees

£11 (adult), £5.50 (child under 17). Concessions and family pass available.

York Minster

The largest Gothic cathedral in Northern Europe, the present *York Minster* was constructed in 1220. For hundreds of years before this, however, the site had been of religious and political significance, witnessing numerous battles between the English and the Vikings for control of the city and its cathedral, which had been specially constructed for the baptism of Edwin, King of Northumbria, in the seventh century. Today, half of the surviving medieval stained glass in England is in the minster, with the *Great East Window* displaying over 100 Biblical scenes. The *Chapterhouse*, built in Decorated Gothic style and completed in 1286, contains intricately carved walls and has been the meeting room of the Dean and Chapter, who govern the cathedral, for centuries. The *nave* is the widest Gothic nave in England and features a statue of St Peter, the minster's patron saint. The elaborate astronomical clock in the *North Transept* was designed and constructed at the Royal Greenwich Observatory to commemorate 18,000 airmen from Yorkshire and northeast England who lost their lives in World War II. A fire in the South Transept in 1984 led to a £2 million-pound restoration project, and the ceiling now features 62 new bosses decorated with natural and local scenes designed by schoolchildren. There are views of the winding cobbled streets of York and the surrounding Yorkshire countryside from the *Central Tower*.

Contact Address

York Minster Visitors Centre, St Williams College, 4-5 College Street, York YO1 2JF, UK
Tel: (01904) 557 216. Fax: (01904) 557 201.
E-mail: info@yorkminster.org
Website: www.yorkminster.org

Transportation

Air: Manchester Airport, Leeds/Bradford International Airport, Newcastle Airport. **Rail:** Train: York Station. **Road:** Bus: Services to Rougier Street. Car: M1, then M18, then A1(M), then A64 (from London); M6, then M42, then M1, then M18, then A1(M), then A64 (from Birmingham); M62, then M621, then A653, then A61, then A58(M), then A64 (from Manchester); A7, then A68, then A1, then A59 (from Edinburgh).

Opening Times

Daily 0700-1800 (winter); daily 0700-2030 (summer).

Admission Fees

Cathedral: Free. *Cathedral guided tour*: £3 (adult), £1 (child). *Chapterhouse*: £1 (adult), free (child). *Treasury* and *Chapterhouse*: £2.60 (adult), £0.70 (child under 16). Concessions available. *Tower*: £3 (adult), £1 (child).

Northern Ireland

1 Giant's Causeway

Tourist Information

Northern Ireland Tourist Board

St Anne's Court, 59 North Street, Belfast BT1 1NB, UK
Tel: (028) 9023 1221. Fax: (028) 902 4060.
E-mail: info@nitb.com
Website: www.discovernorthernireland.com

Northern Ireland Tourist Board

24 Haymarket, London SW1Y 4DG, UK
Tel: (0541) 555 250 (information) *or* (020) 7766 9920 (trade and marketing). Fax: (020) 7766 9929.
E-mail: infogb@nitb.com
Website: www.discovernorthernireland.com

Giant's Causeway

Situated on the northern coast of Ireland, the *Giant's Causeway* is a unique geological feature consisting of a protrusion of basalt hexagonal columns jutting into the sea. According to scientific facts, the Causeway was formed some 62-65 million years ago by the cooling of volcanic rock. Local legend leads us to believe, however, that the Causeway was built by two feuding giants, Finn MacCool in Ireland and Benandonner in Scotland, who needed to travel across the sea in order to do battle. The site was discovered in 1692 by the Bishop of Derry and attracts many visitors every year to see the estimated 40,000 columns. Antrim's coastline and the local scenery are both spectacular, including *Lacada Point* and *Bengore Head*. As well as being an area of outstanding natural beauty, Lacada Point is also famed for being the place where the *Girona*, a Neapolitan galleass which was part of the Spanish Armada, foundered in 1588, killing 1200 men, whilst sailing from Killebegs in County Donegal to Scotland. The Giant's Causeway was declared a UNESCO World Heritage Site in 1986 and was Northern Ireland's first and, as yet, only tourist attraction to be recognised by UNESCO.

Contact Address

Giant's Causeway Visitor Centre, 44 Causeway Road, Bushmills, County Antrim BT57 8SU, UK
Tel: (028) 2073 1855. Fax: (028) 2073 2537.
E-mail: causewaytic@hotmail.com
Website: www.northantrim.com/giantscauseway.htm

Transportation

Air: Belfast International Airport. **Rail:** Train: Port Rush Station. **Road:** Car: M2, A26 and A2 (from Belfast).

Opening Times

Giant's Causeway: Daily 24 hours. *Visitor Centre*: Daily 1000-1700.

Admission Fees

Free.

Giant's Causeway

Dan Boyd

Scotland

1 Edinburgh Castle
2 Edinburgh Zoo
3 Gallery of Modern Art (GOMA)
4 Kelvingrove Art Gallery and Museum
5 Royal Botanic Garden Edinburgh
6 Royal Museum and Museum of Scotland
7 Scotch Whisky Heritage Centre and Royal Mile
8 Stirling Castle

Tourist Information

Visit Scotland
23 Ravelston Terrace, Edinburgh EH4 3TP, UK
Tel: (0131) 332 2433. Fax: (0131) 315 4545 (information) *or* 343 1513 (general enquiries).
E-mail: info@stb.gov.uk
Website: www.visitscotland.com

Edinburgh Castle

Edinburgh Castle looks over the city of Edinburgh from its perch on top of an extinct volcano. The oldest building in Edinburgh and its most popular tourist attraction, the castle has served both as fortress and royal residence. Today, it houses the *Scottish Crown Jewels*, the *Stone of Destiny* and *Mons Meg* (a massive 15th-century bombard), as well as the headquarters of the British Army's Scottish Division and a permanent exhibition which depicts the history of Scotland. The site has been used as a fortification for around 2000 years, and was first used as a royal residence during the 11th century. The castle has had a rich and colourful history, withstanding numerous attacks from Oliver Cromwell's Roundheads in 1650, and William and Mary's army in 1689. It was also the birthplace of James VI of Scotland (who became James I of England in 1603), who was born to Mary Queen of Scots in a tiny room in the *Royal Residence* in 1566. Within the castle premises stands *St Margaret's Chapel*, a tiny Norman building that has stood for more than 900 years. Every day, except Sunday and Bank Holidays, the one o'clock gun is fired from the castle, and for three weeks in August, the annual *Military Tattoo* takes place in the *Castle Esplanade*.

Contact Address

Edinburgh Castle, Castle Hill, Edinburgh EH1 2NG, UK
Tel: (0131) 225 9846. Fax: (0131) 220 4733.
Website: www.historic-scotland.gov.uk

Transportation

Air: Edinburgh Airport. **Rail:** Train: Waverley Station. **Road:** Bus: 23, 27, 41 or 46. Car: M8 to Edinburgh (from Glasgow); A696 and A68 or A1 (from Newcastle-Upon-Tyne). The Royal Mile is located in Edinburgh city centre, just off the A7 North Bridge.

Opening Times

Daily 0930-1700 (Oct-Mar); daily 0930-1800 (Apr-Sep).

Admission Fees

£7.50 (adult), £2.00 (child 5-15), free (child under 5). Concessions available.

Edinburgh Zoo

Founded in 1913 by the Royal Zoological Society of Scotland, *Edinburgh Zoo* is one of the most significant zoos in Europe. It is Scotland's most popular wildlife attraction, with over 1500 animals, including meerkats, pygmy hippos, snow leopards and blue poison arrow frogs. Set in 32 hectares (80 acres) of beautiful parkland on the slopes of Corstorphine Hill, with stunning views of the surrounding countryside, the zoo is famous for having the world's biggest penguin pool, which is home to the largest colony of penguins in Europe. As well as animals, there are many other attractions, such as the *African Plains Experience*, the *Maze*, the

Magic Forest and the *Hilltop Safari Tour.*

Contact Address

Edinburgh Zoo, 134 Corstorphine Road, Murrayfield, Edinburgh EH12 6TS, UK
Tel: (0131) 334 9171. Fax: (0131) 316 4050.
E-mail: info@edinburghzoo.org.uk
Website: www.edinburghzoo.org.uk

Transportation

Air: Edinburgh Airport. **Rail:** Train: Waverley Station. **Road:** Bus: 2, 12, 26, 31, 36, 69 or 86 (from Princes Street). Car: M8 to Edinburgh (from Glasgow); A696 and A68 or A1 (from Newcastle-Upon-Tyne). The zoo is situtated just off the A8 in the Corstorphine area of Edinburgh.

Opening Times

Daily 0900-1630 (Nov-Feb); daily 0900-1700 (Oct and Mar); daily 0900-1800 (Apr-Sep).

Admission Fees

£7 (adult), £4 (child). Concessions available.

Gallery of Modern Art (GOMA)

The *Gallery of Modern Art*, which is situated near George Square and Buchanan Street in the centre of Glasgow, is home to the city's principal modern art collection. The gallery is located in a former Grecian-style mansion, which became a branch of the Royal Bank of Scotland in 1817, before being redesigned by the architect David Hamilton in 1827 when it opened as the *Royal Exchange.* Glasgow's most recent art gallery, which opened in 1996, houses an impressive selection of Glasgow's post-war art and design, including work by international artists, such as Andy Warhol and David Hockney, and by Scottish artists, such as Ken Curry and John Bellany. The collection is housed in the Stirling Library in the historic Royal Exchange Square and spread over four floors, encompassing work themed around the four elements: earth, fire, air and water. Highlights include the artist Beryl Cook's paintings 'By the Clyde' and 'Karaoke', and the Scottish artist Avril Paton's painting 'Windows in the West'.

Contact Address

Gallery of Modern Art, Queen Street, Glasgow, G1 3AH, UK
Tel: (0141) 229 1996. Fax: (0141) 204 5316.

Transportation

Air: Glasgow Airport. **Rail:** Underground: St Enoch Station or Buchanan Street Station. **Road:** Car: From the A814 (Clyde Street), Jamaica Street, and then right onto Argyle Street, then first left into Buchanan Street (from Glasgow city centre).

Opening Times

Mon-Sat 1000-1700, Sun 1100-1700.

Admission Fees

Free.

Kelvingrove Art Gallery and Museum

Kelvingrove Art Gallery and Museum, which is the principal art gallery and museum in the city of Glasgow, is one of Scotland's most popular free attractions. The imposing late-Victorian, red sandstone building, which opened in 1901, houses an impressive display of archaeology, natural history and ethnography, including European armour, prehistoric relics and military weapons. It also houses a wide range of European paintings by Botticelli, Rembrandt, Millet, Monet, Van Gogh, Derain and Picasso. On permanent show is the Glasgow 1900 exhibition which exhibits paintings, furniture and decorative art objects dating from Glasgow at the turn of the 20th century. The main attraction at Kelvingrove is a room dedicated to the works of the 19th-century architect Charles Rennie Mackintosh who studied at the famous Glasgow School of Art.

Contact Address

Kelvingrove Art Gallery and Museum, Kelvingrove, Glasgow G3 8AG, UK
Tel: (0141) 287 2699. Fax: (0141) 287 2690.

Transportation

Air: Glasgow Airport. **Rail:** Underground: Kelvinhall Station. **Road:** Car: From the A814 Pointhouse Road, B808 Beith Street which leads into Byres Road. Then right onto Argyle Road (from Glasgow).

Opening Times

Mon-Sat 1100-1700, Sun 1000-1700.

Admission Fees

Free.

Royal Botanic Garden Edinburgh

Regarded as Scotland's premier garden, the Royal Botanic Garden Edinburgh is one of the city's most popular tourist attractions. The garden, which was first opened in 1670 as a small physic (medicinal) garden near Holyrood House, was designed by two doctors, Andrew Balfour and Robert Sibbald. It was moved to its present location during the 1820s and expanded to cover an area of 31 hectares (78 acres). Today, the garden contains a unique collection of plants from around the world, housed in the world-famous *Rock Garden*, the *Pringle Chinese Collection* and the *Glasshouse Experience.* Visitors can also see the *Woodland Gardens & Arboretum* and the *Winter Garden*, as well as enjoy spectacular views across the city of Edinburgh.

Contact Address

Royal Botanic Garden Edinburgh, 20A Inverleith Row, Edinburgh, EH3 5LR, UK
Tel: (0131) 552 7171. Fax: (0131) 248 2901.
E-mail: info@rbge.org.uk
Website: www.rbge.org.uk

Transportation

Air: Edinburgh Airport. **Rail:** Train: Waverley Station. **Road:** Bus: 7A, 8, 9, 19, 23, 27, 37 or 29 to the East Gate entrance; bus 20A to Inverleith Row. Car: M8 to Edinburgh (from Glasgow); A696 and A68 or A1 (from Newcastle-Upon-Tyne). Then B901 (from Edinburgh city centre).

Opening Times

Daily 0930-1600 (Jan); daily 0930-1700 (Feb); daily 0930-1800 (Mar); daily 0930-1900 (Apr-Aug); daily 0930-1800 (Sep); daily 0930-1700 (Oct); daily 0930-1600 (Nov-Dec). Closed 25 Dec and 1 Jan.

Admission Fees

Free, although donations are welcome.

The Water Garden, Royal Botanic Garden Edinburgh

Royal Botanic Garden Edinburgh

Royal Museum and Museum of Scotland

The *Royal Museum* and the *Museum of Scotland* are located on the same site in Edinburgh city centre. The Royal Museum, which has 36 galleries and is well known for its impressive Main Hall, houses an international collection of artistic, archaeological, scientific and industrial exhibits, ranging from Japanese art through to natural history. The Museum of Scotland, which opened in a striking new building in 1998, designed by Benson & Forsyth, has over 10,000 artefacts detailing the country's history from its geological formation and earliest inhabitants up to the 20th century. Many of Scotland's finest regional treasures are on display, including a communal drinking cup (the *Bute Mazer*), made after the Scots beat the English during the Battle of Bannockburn in 1314, and jewellery, coins and medals which once belonged to Mary Queen of Scots. There are also fine views of Edinburgh Castle from the museum's rooftop, which is accessible to the public.

Contact Address

Royal Museum, Chambers Street, Edinburgh, EH1 1JF, UK
Tel: (0131) 247 4219. Fax: (0131) 220 4819.
Website: www.nms.ac.uk
Museum of Scotland, Chambers Street, Edinburgh, EH1 1JF, UK
Tel: (0131) 247 4422. Fax: (0131) 220 4819.
Website: www.nms.ac.uk

Transportation

Air: Edinburgh Airport. **Rail:** Train: Waverley Station. **Road:** Bus: 2, 23, 27, 28/28A or 40. Car: M8 to Edinburgh (from Glasgow); A696 and A68 or A1 (from Newcastle-Upon-Tyne). Chambers Street is located just off the A7 South Bridge in central Edinburgh.

Opening Times

Mon and Wed-Sat 1000-1700, Tues 1000-2000, Sun and Bank Holidays 1200-1700. Closed 25 Dec.

Admission Fees

Free

Scotch Whisky Heritage Centre and Royal Mile

In 1723, Daniel Defoe claimed that the *Royal Mile* was 'the largest, longest and finest street in the World'. This historic street in Edinburgh's Old Town, which leads from *Edinburgh Castle* to the *Palace of Holyrood House*, is actually one mile and 107 yards

Corel

Plaque on the Royal Mile

long, and encorporates many of Edinburgh's finest attractions. Visitors can tour the *Scotch Whisky Heritage Centre*, situated at the top of the Royal Mile, which allows them to see how whisky is made and is believed to have a resident ghost. The *Camera Obscura* at the top end of the Royal Mile, is also one of Edinburgh's top attractions, where visitors can see a panoramic view of the city reflected onto a white table. *Tron Kirk* is located at the junction of North Bridge and the Royal Mile and is a traditional place for partygoers to gather and hear the bells toll, ringing in the new year at midnight on Hogmany (31st December). The long list of other attractions on the Royal Mile include: *Higland Tolbooth Kirk, Ramsay Garden, Writers' Museum, Brodie's Close, Parliament Square, John Knox's House, Museum of Childhood, Netherbow Port, Huntly House, Canongate Kirk, Abbey Lairds, Gladstone's Land, Queen Mary's Bath House* and *St Giles' Cathedral.*

Contact Address

Edinburgh and Lothians Tourist Board, 3 Princes Street, Edinburgh, EH2 2QP, UK
Tel: (0131) 473 3800. Fax: (0131) 463 3881.
E-mail: esic@eltb.org
Website: www.edinburgh.org
Scotch Whisky Heritage Centre, 354 Castlehill, The Royal Mile, Edinburgh, EH1 2NE, UK
Tel: (0131) 220 0441. Fax: (0131) 220 6288.
E-mail: info@whisky-heritage.co.uk
Website: www.whisky-heritage.co.uk

Transportation

Air: Edinburgh Airport. **Rail:** Train: Waverley Station. **Road:** Bus: 23, 27, 41 or 46. Car: M8 to Edinburgh (from Glasgow); A696 and A68 or A1 (from Newcastle-Upon-Tyne). The Royal Mile is located in Edinburgh city centre, just off the A7 North Bridge.

Opening Times

Scotch Whisky Heritage Centre: Daily 1000-1745 (Oct-Apr); daily 0930-1800 (May-Sep). Closed 25 Dec. *Royal Mile*: Daily 24 hours. Opening times to other attractions on the Royal Mile vary and visitors are advised to contact Edinburgh and Lothians Tourist Board (see **Contact Address** above) for further information.

Admission Fees

Scotch Whisky Heritage Centre: £6.50 (adult), £3.25 (child). *Royal Mile*: Free. Prices for entry to other attractions on the Royal Mile vary and visitors are advised to contact Edinburgh and Lothians Tourist Board (see **Contact Address** above) for further information.

Stirling Castle

The medieval *Stirling Castle*, which is perhaps the finest in Scotland, sits on a rocky outcrop, looking down upon some of the most famous battlefields in Scotland's history. These include *Stirling Bridge*, where William Wallace defeated the English in 1297 during the War of Independence, and *Bannockburn*, where Robert the Bruce was triumphant over King Edward II's troops in 1314. Historians are unclear as to the castle's exact date of construction, although it is believed to have been built between 1370 and 1750. Stirling also has famous associations with Mary Queen of Scots, who lived here during her childhood and was crowned in the *Chapel Royal* in 1543. Today, visitors can still see the outstanding architecture, including the 15th-century *Great Hall*, King James V's Renaissance *Royal Palace* and King James VI's Chapel Royal, where Prince Henry was also christened in 1594. There are many other attractions in or near Stirling, which include *Argyll's Lodging*, the *Wallace Monument*, the *Smith Art Gallery & Museum, Alloa Tower* and *Bannockburn*.

Contact Address

Stirling Castle, Castle Wynd, Stirling, FK8 1EJ, UK
Tel: (01786) 450 000. Fax: (01786) 464 678.
Website: www.historic-scotland.gov.uk

Transportation

Air: Glasgow International Airport. **Rail:** Stirling Station. **Road:** Car: M9 (from Edinburgh); A80 and M9 (from Glasgow).

Opening Times

Daily 0930-1700 (Oct-Mar); daily 0930-1800 (Apr-Sep).

Admission Fees

Stirling Castle and *Argyll's Lodging*: £6.50 (adult), £2 (child). Concessions available.

Wales

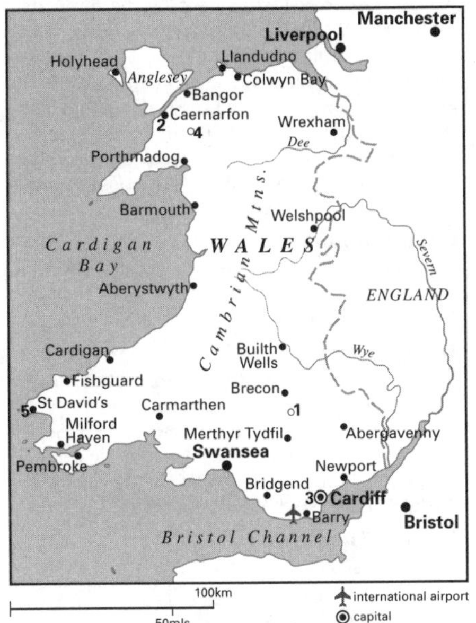

1	Brecon Beacons National Park
2	Caernarfon Castle
3	Museum of Welsh Life
4	Snowdonia National Park
5	St David's Cathedral

Tourist Information

Bwrdd Croeso Cymru (Wales Tourist Board)
10th Floor, Brunel House, 2 Fitzalan Road, Cardiff CF24 0UY, UK
Tel: (02920) 499 909. Fax: (02920) 485 031.
E-mail: info@tourism.wales.gov.uk
Website: www.visitwales.com

Brecon Beacons National Park

The *Brecon Beacons National Park* is one of Wales's most beautiful outdoor areas. Situated amongst hills and mountains, the park covers an area of 1344 sq km (519 sq miles) and stretches from the Welsh/English border to Lladeilo. The park includes the *Black Mountains*, the *Brecon Beacons* and *Fforest Fawr*, as well as moorland, forests, valleys, waterfalls, lakes, caves and gorges. *Brecon Cathedral*, in the town of Brecon, and *Hay-on-Wye*, with its annual book fair and many bookshops, are also popular tourist attractions. There are also numerous castles in the park, including *Trecastle, Tretower, Bronllys* and *Morlais*. The *Brecon Beacons Mountain Centre*, which is located 9km (5.5 miles) southwest of Brecon, provides visitors with information on the park and offers a fine view of the surrounding area, including *Pen y Fan* and *Corn Du* peaks. Visitors can also take the *Brecon Mountain Railway*, which runs from near Merthyr Tydfil up into the park, and gives spectacular views across Wales.

Contact Address

Brecon Beacons National Park, 7 Glamorgan Street, Brecon, Powys, LD3 7DP, UK
Tel: (01874) 624 437. Fax: (01874) 622 574.
E-mail: enquiries@breconsbeacons.org
Website: www.breconbeacons.org

Transportation

Air: Cardiff International Airport. **Rail:** Train: Merthyr Tydfil Station or Abergavenny Station. **Road:** Bus: A bus runs to the park between May-Sep (from towns in South Wales). Coach: National Express operates services to the park (from Cardiff, Newport and Swansea). Car: M4 and A470 (from Bristol); M5, M50 and A40 (from Birmingham).

Opening Times

Daily 0930-1630 (Nov-Feb); daily 0930-1700 (Mar-Jun); daily 0930-1800 (Jul-Aug); daily 0930-1700 (Sep-Oct). Closed 25 Dec.

Admission Fees

Free.

P ✕ 🧺 ♿

Brecon Beacons National Park

Corel

Caernarfon Castle

Begun in 1283 by King Edward I, *Caernarfon Castle* is one of Europe's great medieval castles, set on a peninsula overlooking the Menai Straits that divide North Wales from the island of Anglesey. The design of the castle, with its high walls marked with arrow slits and its angular towers, is said to have been inspired by the great city of Constantinople (now Istanbul), the former imperial power base of Rome. The castle was built when Edward conquered Wales in 1284 and was intended not only as a military fortress, but also as a royal palace and the English administrative centre of the area. The dual purpose of the castle was demonstrated by the fact that he also founded a town and market within its walls. The future Edward II, son of Edward I, was the first English Prince of Wales, and to this day the ruling British monarch may confer the title of Prince of Wales upon their eldest son. Prince Charles' investiture as the 21st Prince of Wales took place at the castle in 1969. Today, visitors can enjoy informative exhibitions and displays at the castle and walk around the ramparts for fine views over the town and the Menai Straits.

Contact Address

Caernarfon Castle, Castle Ditch, Caernarfon, Gwynedd LL55 2AY, UK
Tel: (01286) 677 617. Fax: (01286) 677 617.
E-mail: cadw@wales.gov.uk
Website: www.cadw.wales.gov.uk

Transportation

Air: Manchester Airport. **Rail:** Train: Bangor Station. **Road:** Car: M56, then A55 (from Manchester); M6, then A55 (from Birmingham or London); M62, then M56, then A55 (from Leeds); A1, then M62, then M56, then A55 (from York, Newcastle or Scotland); M5, then M6, then A55 (from Bristol and southwest England).

Opening Times

Daily 0930-1730 (Sep/Oct-late May); daily 0930-1800 (late May-Sep/Oct).

Admission Fees

£4.20 (adult), £3.20 (child 5-15), free (child under 5). Concessions and family pass available.

Museum of Welsh Life

The *Museum of Welsh Life*, which is located on the outskirts of Cardiff, offers visitors an insight into how life in Wales used to be. Opened in July 1948, this open-air museum explains Wales's history over the past 500 years and allows visitors to imagine how rural life would have been over the centuries. The museum is set in 40 hectares (100 acres) of parkland, on the estate of the Elizabethan mansion, St Fagans Castle, a 16th-century manor house, which was donated to the people of Wales in 1947 by the Earl of Plymouth. Today, St Fagans, which has been refurbished in the style of a late-Victorian Welsh mansion, houses an exhibition on Welsh life through the ages. Other impressive buildings at the site which have all been magnificently built to recreate Welsh life, include a chapel, a village store, several 19th-century farmhouses and a Victorian schoolhouse.

Contact Address

Museum of Welsh Life, St Fagans, Cardiff, CF5 6XB, UK
Tel: (029) 2057 3500. Website: www.nmgw.ac.uk

Transportation

Air: Cardiff International Airport. **Rail:** Train: Cardiff Central Station. **Road:** Bus: 32 to St Fagans (from Stand B1 at Cardiff Central Bus Station; 56 from opposite Cardiff Castle). Car: The museum is signposted from junction 33 of the M4 motorway and can be accessed from the A4232.

Opening Times

Daily 1000-1700.

Admission Fees

£4.50 (adult), free (child) (Nov-Apr); £5.50 (adult), free (child) (Apr-Oct).

Snowdonia National Park

Founded in 1951, *Snowdonia National Park*, known in Welsh as *Parc Cenedlaethol Eryri*, covers 2180 sq km (840 sq miles) of wild and unspoilt countryside in the western corner of North Wales. Mountain peaks, river valleys and lakes contrast with the 37km (23 miles) of craggy coastline and provide a natural habitat for many species of wildlife, some of which, such as the Snowdon Lily and Rainbow Beetle, are unique to Snowdonia. Much of the dramatic mountainous landscape is the result of millions of years of erosion, with the hanging valleys, moraines and glacial lakes having been formed over 10,000 years ago, during the Great Ice Age. The highest peak is *Mount Snowdon*, which at 1085m (3559ft) is also the highest mountain in Wales. The park's natural attractions have made it a popular place with outdoor enthusiasts, who come to the lakes, mountains and beaches to walk, climb and enjoy watersports. Another way to take in the park's scenery is to ride the *Ffestiniog Narrow Gauge Railway*; steam trains run from *Porthmadog* in the east to *Blaenau Ffestiniog* in the west, stopping off at various beauty spots, such as *Tan y Bwlch* which has excellent views over *Llyn Mair*, one of Snowdonia's most beautiful lakes. History has also made its mark on Snowdonia in the form of man-made constructions, ranging from the castles built by the Welsh princes and Edward I's 13th-century fortress, *Harlech Castle*, to farmworkers' cottages and early Christian churches. There are also many cultural events in the park, focusing on Welsh language and traditions which are very much kept alive in this part of Wales. Visitors to the park in summer months should look out for *eisteddfodou*, which are Welsh cultural festivals featuring choral music, Celtic dancing and readings of poetry and folk tales, and are held in many towns and villages.

Contact Address

Snowdonia National Park Authority, National Park Office, Penrhyndeudraeth, Gwynedd LL48 6LF, UK
Tel: (01766) 770 274. Fax: (01766) 771 211.
E-mail: parc@snowdonia-npa.gov.uk
Website: www.eryri-npa.gov.uk

Transportation

Air: Manchester Airport. **Rail:** Train: Llandudno Junction Station, Blaenau Ffestiniog Station or Penrhyndeudraeth Station. **Road:** Car: M56, then A55 (from Manchester); M6, then A55 (from Birmingham or London); M62, then M56, then A55 (from Leeds); A1, then M62, then M56, then A55 (from York, Newcastle or Scotland); M5, then M6, then A55 (from Bristol and southwest England). The A55 is the coastal road running along the North Wales coast through the park; the A487 also runs through the park from Caernarfon to Ffestiniog.

Opening Times

Harlech Castle: Mon-Sat 0930-1600, Sun 1100-1600 (29 Oct-31 Mar); daily 0930-1700 (1 Apr-26 May); daily 0930-1800 (27 May-30 Sep); daily 0930-1700 (1-31 Oct). *Snowdonia National Park*: Daily 24 hours.

Admission Fees

Harlech Castle: £3 (adult), £2 (child 5-15), free (child under 5). Concessions and family pass available. *Snowdonia National Park*: Free.

St David's Cathedral

The tiny city of St David's, Britain's smallest city with a population of just 1500, is dominated by its cathedral. St David, the patron saint of Wales, was one of the earliest Celtic missionaries who sought to convert the barbaric tribes of western Europe to Christianity. He founded a monastery on the site where the cathedral now stands in AD 589. After Pope Calixtus canonised David (or *Dewi* as he is known in Welsh) in 1120, the site became a major place of pilgrimage. In terms of securing remission for sins and a place in heaven, two pilgrimage journeys to St David's were reputed to be equal to one journey to Rome, and three journeys equal to one journey to Jerusalem, the most holy city. Bishop Bernard dedicated the cathedral in 1131 and construction work began in 1181. The oldest surviving section of the cathedral is the nave, built in Transitional Norman style with an Irish oak ceiling supported by five rounded arches. Each arch is carved with a different pattern. In the south transept there are some fine Celtic carvings on the Abraham Stone, the gravestone of the sons of Bishop Abraham who was killed by Vikings in 1080. Other sections of the cathedral, such as *Holy Trinity Chapel* and the choir, were added in the 15th and 16th centuries. The *Lady Chapel* was restored in 1901 after the original 16th-century ceiling collapsed. Every May and June, the cathedral hosts the St David's Cathedral Festival, featuring nine days of classical music performances.

Contact Address

St David's Cathedral, St David's, Pembrokeshire SA62 6RH, UK
Tel: (01437) 720 199. Fax: (01766) 721 885.
Website: www.stdavidscathedral.org.uk

Transportation

Air: Cardiff International Airport. **Rail:** Train: Haverfordwest Station. **Road:** Car: A487 (from Fishguard or Haverfordwest); M4, then A40, then A487 (from Cardiff or London).

Opening Times

Mon-Sat 0830-1730, Sun 0800-1800. Closed to visitors during services Sun 0800, 0930 and 1115, and at certain other times.

Admission Fees

Free.

United States of America

Arizona

1	Grand Canyon National Park

Tourist Information

Arizona Office of Tourism
2702 North Third Street, Suite 4015, Phoenix, AZ 85004, USA
Tel: (602) 230 7733. Fax: (602) 240 5475.
E-mail: travel-info@azot.com.
Website: www.arizonaguide.com

Arizona Office of Tourism
Ringway House, Bell Road, Basingstoke, Hants RG24 8FB, UK
Tel: (01256) 316 555 *or* 316 568 (trade enquiries only). Fax: (01256) 316 523.
E-mail: azsquire@msn.com
Website: www.arizonaguide.com

Grand Canyon National Park

One of the seven natural wonders of the world, the *Grand Canyon* is a stunning geological formation that is synonymous for many with the majestic desert landscape of America's west. The canyon flows (in terms of river miles) for 365km (227 miles), and reaches a vertical depth of 1829m (6000ft) and a width of 29km (18 miles). Visitors can take in the breathtaking view from the rim and make prolonged explorations within the canyon, on jeep trips, horseriding safaris, hiking tours or by plane. Other activities available within the park include whitewater rafting, cross-country skiing, snowshoeing and fishing. The Grand Canyon is divided into three geographically separated areas: the *South Rim*, the *North Rim* and the *Inner Canyon*. There are three visitor centres in the Grand Canyon National Park. The *Canyon View Information Plaza*, located at the

Grand Canyon National Park

Corel

Corel

Grand Canyon National Park

South Rim, offers daily talks and exhibitions on the Canyon as well as information on activities on offer in the area. The *Desert View Information Center*, also located at the South Rim, provides orientation guides and literature on the park's history and facilities. Lastly, the *North Rim Visitor Center*, located at the North Rim, offers visitors talks and exhibits from May to October. All three visitor centres offer restroom facilities; those who wish to stay overnight in the park can choose from a variety of lodges, log cabins and campsites, although there is no youth hostel. Shops, a post office and a bank are located at Market Plaza in Grand Canyon Village at the South Rim. The North Rim Campground has a small shop selling camping supplies.

Contact Address

Grand Canyon National Park, PO Box 129, Grand Canyon, Arizona, AZ 86023, USA
Tel: (520) 638 7888. Fax: (520) 638 7797.
E-mail: GRCA_Superintendent@nps.gov
Website: www.thecanyon.com *or*
www.nps.gov/grca

Transportation

Air: Las Vegas McCarran International Airport, Phoenix Sky Harbor International Airport or Grand Canyon Airport (domestic flights). **Rail:** Train: Services from Williams. **Road:** Coach: Services from Phoenix. Bus: Services from Williams and Flagstaff. Car: I-40 (from Barstow, Albuquerque, Little Rock, Oklahoma City, Nashville, Memphis and Raleigh to Williams or Flagstaff), then US Hwy-64 (from Williams to Grand Canyon Village, South Rim); US Hwy-180 (from Flagstaff to Grand Canyon Village, South Rim); US Hwy-67 (from North Rim to Grand Canyon Village, South Rim).

Opening Times

South Rim: Daily 24 hours. *North Rim*: Daily 24 hours (mid-May to mid-Oct, weather permitting); daylight hours only (mid-Oct to mid-May). *Canyon View Information Plaza*: Daily 0800-1800. *Desert View Information Center*: Daily 0900-1700. *North Rim Visitor Center*: Daily 0800-1800 (12 May-15 Oct).

Admission Fees

Vehicle: U$20. Pedestrian/cyclist: US$10. Entrance valid for 7 days. *Visitor Centers*: Free.

California

1 Alcatraz
2 Death Valley National Park
3 Disneyland Resort
4 Golden Gate Bridge
5 Hollywood Walk of Fame
6 Pier 39, Fisherman's Wharf
7 San Diego Zoo
8 Universal Studios Hollywood
9 Venice Beach
10 Yosemite National Park

Tourist Information

California Tourism

801 K Street, Suite 1600, Sacramento, CA 95814, USA
Tel: (916) 322 2881 *or* (800) 862 2543 (toll free USA and Canada only).
Fax: (916) 322 3402.
E-mail: caltour@commerce.ca.gov
Website: www.gocalif.ca.gov

California Tourism

Fourth Floor, High Holborn House, 52-54 High Holborn, London WC1V 6RB, UK
Tel: (020) 7405 4746 *or* 7242 3131.
Fax: (020) 7242 2838.
E-mail: supereps@compuserve.com

Alcatraz

Alcatraz, which is also known as *'the Rock'*, is the notorious American super-prison located on *Alcatraz Island*, a remote rocky outcrop in San Francisco Bay. The prison was used between 1934 and 1963, and designed to remove kidnappers, racketeers and predatory criminals far from the outside world. It was home to some very illustrious alumni, including famous gangsters Al Capone, George 'Machine Gun' Kelly and Robert 'The Birdman' Stroud. Between 1969 and 1971, the island was taken over by Native Americans, when, under the leadership of Richard Oakes, they tried to lay claim to it for themselves. Today, the island is a venue for tourists rather than criminals, although a few former prisoners and guards can be heard on the prison's audio tour of the famous *Cell House*. Excellent views of San Francisco can be enjoyed from this world-famous island, which has featured in many Hollywood films, including 'The Birdman of Alcatraz', 'The Rock' and 'Escape from Alcatraz'.

Contact Address

National Park Service, Alcatraz Island, Golden Gate National Recreation Area, Fort Mason, Building 201, San Francisco, CA 94123, USA
Tel: (415) 705 1044 *or* (415) 705 5555 (reservations).
E-mail: goga_alcatraz@nps.gov
Website: www.nps.gov/alcatraz

The lighthouse and warden's house ruins, Alcatraz

Jay Blakesberg, National Park Service

Transportation

Air: San Francisco International Airport. **Water:** Ferry: The only access to Alcatraz Island is by Blue and Gold Fleet Ferry from Pier 41, Fisherman's Wharf, San Francisco.

Opening Times

Daily 0930-1630 (winter); daily 0930-1830 (summer).

Admission Fees

US$14.50 (adult and child 12-18), US$9.25 (child aged 5-11). Concessions available. Price includes ferry access, audio tour and telephone booking fee.

Death Valley National Park

Although only a national park since 1994, *Death Valley* has long been prized for its unique wildlife and austere desert beauty. Today, the park covers 13,500 sq km (5212 sq miles), the majority of which is wilderness. Although there are occasional winter storms, Death Valley's summers are notorious for temperatures in excess of 48°C (120°F). Despite this, the park attracts many visitors who come to see wildflowers, snow-covered peaks, sand dunes and abandoned mines. One of the most famous sites in Death Valley is *Badwater*, a salty pool which lies 86m (282ft) below sea level – it is said to be the lowest point in the western hemisphere and is often represented as the classic picture postcard view of the park. From the pool, there are spectacular views of Death Valley's mountains, including *Dante's Peak*, which reaches to 1670m (5479ft), as well as the surrounding desert.

Contact Address

Death Valley National Park, PO Box 579, Death Valley, CA 92328, USA
Tel: (760) 786 2331. Fax: (760) 786 3283.
E-mail: DEVA_Superintendent@nps.gov
Website: www.nps.gov/deva

Transportation

Air: Las Vegas McCarran International Airport, Furnace Creek Airport (domestic flights). **Road:** Car: Hwy-190 (runs through the park from east to west); Hwy-95 (from Las Vegas); I-15 (from Montana, Idaho, California or Utah).

Opening Times

Visitor Centre: Daily 0800-1800.

Admission Fees

Vehicle: US$10. Pedestrian: US$5. Entrance valid for 7 days.

Disneyland® Resort

Opened on 17 July 1955 in a 160-acre (65-hectare) orange grove in Anaheim California, *Disneyland® Resort* claims to be the 'happiest place on earth'. The park, which was conceived by Walt Disney in 1948, was originally to be called Mickey Mouse Park and was built as a place where adults could recapture their youth and enjoy a great day out with their children. Today, the park is one of America's most famous attractions and undoubtedly California's most visited theme park. There are eight 'lands' in total: *Main Street USA, Tomorrowland, Frontierland, Fantasyland, Adventureland, Critter Country, Mickey's Toontown* and *New Orleans Square*. Some of the most popular of the 60 rides available include the *Haunted Mansion, Space Mountain* and *Indiana Jones Adventure*. There are also regular shows, including *Fantasmic!*, which stars the legendary Mickey Mouse himself, and the *Parade of Stars* where guests have the opportunity to meet other famous Disney characters, such as Donald Duck and Goofy.

Contact Address

Disneyland Resort, PO Box 3232, 1313 South Harbor Boulevard, Anaheim, CA 92803, USA
Tel: (714) 781 4565 (recorded information) *or* 781 7290 (operator). Fax: (714) 781 1341.
Website: www.disney.go.com

Transportation

Air: Los Angeles International Airport. **Rail:** Metro Bus: 460. **Road:** Bus: There are shuttle buses from the majority of hotels in the vicinity of the park. Car: I-5, Disneyland Drive exit (from the north); I-5, Katella Avenue exit (from the south); Fwy-22, Harbor Boulevard exit (from the east or the west).

Opening Times

Daily 0800-2400. Times may vary according to the day of the week or the season. Guests are advised to telephone the park recorded information line before their visit.

Admission Fees

One-day pass: US$43 (adult), US$33 (child). Two, three and four-day passes available.

Golden Gate Bridge

Completed in 1937, San Francisco's best-known landmark, the *Golden Gate Bridge*, stretches 1966m (6500ft) across San Francisco Bay, connecting the city with Oakland Bay and the Northern Counties. The elegant suspension towers reach a height of 227m (746ft) and the clearance over the channel below is 67m (220ft). For those who wish to walk the 2.7km

(1.7 miles) across the bridge, access is from the Joseph B Strauss statue. To the left of the statue a cross section of one of the cables displays a list of the essential statistics of this feat of engineering, and the gardens behind offer excellent views. Other viewing areas are located at the north and south ends of the pedestrians' east sidewalk. *Fort Point*, located south of the bridge, is a military defence, constructed between 1853 and 1861 to protect San Francisco Bay from hostile attack. It was also occupied by US federal troops during the American Civil War (1861-65), but the last troops were withdrawn in 1886 and Fort Point was later used as the operational base for the construction of the Golden Gate Bridge. Nowadays, visitors can explore the fort itself, as well as learn about the history of the American Civil War and the construction of the Golden Gate Bridge through displays and video presentations in the *Fort Point Bookstore Visitor Center*.

Contact Address

Golden Gate Bridge, PO Box 9000, Presidio Station, San Francisco, CA 94112, USA
Tel: (415) 921 5858. Fax: (415) 457 2892.
Website: www.goldengatebridge.org

Transportation

Air: San Francisco International Airport. **Rail:** Train: Caltrain Station. **Road:** Bus: Golden Gate Transit bus stop or Muni bus stop. Car: Hwy-101 (from Oregon, Washington State, North California or Los Angeles).

Opening Times

Golden Gate Bridge Roadway: Daily 24 hours. Bicycle access: Mon-Fri 0500-1530 and 2100-0500, Sat and Sun 2100-0500 (east sidewalk); Mon-Fri 1530-2100, Sat and Sun 0500-2100 (west sidewalk). Pedestrian access: Daily 0500-2100 (east sidewalk). *Fort Point*: Thurs-Mon 1000-1700. Closed 1 Jan, 22 Nov and 25 Dec. *Fort Point Bookstore*: Daily 1000-1630. Closed 1 Jan, 22 Nov and 25 Dec.

Admission Fees

Golden Gate Bridge: US$3 (southbound toll per car). *Fort Point*: Free.

Hollywood Walk of Fame

In 1958, the *Hollywood Walk of Fame* was envisioned as a means of enshrining the memory of the Hollywood greats, with the first star being laid for the actress Joanne Woodward on 9 February 1960. Today, it is the defining emblem of Los Angeles and one of its most popular tourist attractions. Two hectares (five acres) of bronze stars, embedded in pink and charcoal terrazzo squares, honour famous luminaries from the world of cinema, including Elvis Presley, John Travolta, Elizabeth Taylor and Frank Sinatra. The Walk of Fame takes visitors on a tour of Hollywood's entertainment industry, passing in front of the famous *Mann's Chinese Theatre*, where stars have literally made their mark, with their hand- and footprints. Visitors to Hollywood will undoubtedly also want to see the famous *Hollywood Sign*. Standing some 15m (50ft) tall and 137m (450ft) wide, this internationally renowned sign, which is located in the Hollywood Hills, was erected in 1923 by a property developer who wanted to advertise new homes in the area. It is one of the most photographed structures in the world, symbolising for many people all the glitz of the Hollywood film industry.

Contact Address

Hollywood Chamber of Commerce, 7018 Hollywood Boulevard, Hollywood, CA 90028, USA
Tel: (323) 469 8311. Fax: (323) 469 2805.
E-mail: stargirl@hollywoodcoc.org
Website: www.hollywoodchamber.net

Transportation

Air: Los Angeles International Airport. **Rail:** Metrorail: Redline Station. **Road:** Bus: 26, 156, 163, 180, 181, 210, 212, 217, 310 or 426. Car: I-5 to Los Angeles (from Seattle in the north and San Diego in the south); Pacific Coast Highway (State Hwy-1) (from Santa Barbara and San Francisco); I-10 (from Phoenix); I-15 (from Las Vegas and Salt Lake City); I-40 (from Oklahoma City and Memphis).

Opening Times

Daily 24 hours.

Admission Fees

Free.

Pier 39, Fisherman's Wharf

Claiming to be the most visited tourist attraction in the USA, *Fisherman's Wharf* is a bustling area located on San Francisco's waterfront. Developed solely to attract tourists, the area was once a working fishing port. Today, visitors throng the piers along Fisherman's Wharf, to buy souvenirs, eat in bay-side restaurants and visit the numerous attractions located along Embarcadero. *Pier 39* is one of 29 piers located on the waterfront, and is San Francisco's number one attraction. It hosts daily street performances and is home to many attractions, including the *Wax Museum, Underwater World* and *Turbo Ride*, and to world-famous resident sea lions, which crowd onto pontoons and bask in the midday sun. Visitors can also take sightseeing boats from Pier 39 and from neighbouring *Pier 41*, and enjoy fabulous views of the bay area and *Alcatraz* island. Other attractions at Fisherman's Wharf include the *Cannery*, which houses 30 speciality shops and *Ghirardelli Square* shopping centre, which is a former chocolate factory.

Contact Address

Fisherman's Wharf Merchants Association, 1873 Market Street, #3, San Francisco, CA 94103, USA
Tel: (415) 626 7070. Fax: (415) 626 4651.
E-mail: cbaccari13@aol.com
Website: www.fishermanswharf.org
Pier 39, PO Box 193730, San Francisco, CA 94119, USA
Tel: (415) 705 5500. Fax: (415) 981 8808.
Website: www.pier39.com

Transportation

Air: San Francisco International Airport. **Rail:** Muni: Streetcar on the F-line to Beach Street. Cable Car: Bay Street on the Powell–Mason line. **Road:** Car: Hwy-101 North to Hwy-80 East (exit 4th Street), then along Bryant Street to Embarcadero (from the South Bay). Hwy-101 South across the Golden Gate Bridge (Lombard Street exit), then until Van Ness Avenue and Bay Street, which turns into Embarcadero (from the North Bay); I-80 West across the Bay Bridge (Harrison/Embarcadero exit), then right at Harrison Street and continue to Embarcadero (from the East Bay).

Opening Times

Ghirardelli Square: Sun-Thurs 1000-1800, Fri-Sat 1000-2100 (winter); Mon-Sat 1000-2100, Sun 1000-1800 (summer). *Wax Museum*: Mon-Fri 0900-2300; Sat and Sun 0900-2400. Attractions on *Pier 39*: Sun-Thurs 1100-1900, Fri and Sat 1000-2000 (Jan and Feb); Sun-Thurs 1000-2000, Fri and Sat 1000-2100 (Mar-24 May); Sun-Thurs 1000-2100, Fri and Sat 1000-2200 (25 May-3 Sep); Sun-Thurs 1000-2000, Fri and Sat 1000-2100 (2 Sep-28 Oct); Sun-Thurs 1100-1900, Fri and Sat 1000-2000 (29 Oct-Dec).

Admission Fees

Pier 39: Free. *Wax Museum*: US$12.95 (adult), US$6.95 (child). *Turbo Ride*: US$8 (adult), US$5 (child). *Underwater World*: US$12.95 (adult), US$6.50 (child). *Cinemax Theatre*: US$7.50 (adult), US$4.50 (child). *Ghiradelli Square*: Free.

San Diego Zoo

San Diego Zoo is undoubtedly the city of San Diego's most famous attraction. Located in the beautiful *Balboa Park*, just northeast of the city centre, the zoo is considered to be one of the most impressive in the world with the largest collection of animals, birds and reptiles in North America. The 40.5-hectare (100-acre) zoo was originally opened by Dr Harry Wegeforth in 1916. He opened it using animals left over from the Panama-California International Exposition in 1915, a public display of live animals in Balboa Park. Today, the San Diego Zoo houses more than 4000 animals from 800 different species and also has a large collection of more than 6500 species of plants. Balboa Park itself is home to one of the largest groups of museums in the United States, including the *Museum of Man, San Diego Museum of Art*, the *Museum of San Diego History*, the *National History Museum* and the *Aerospace Museum*; the park, which was first cultivated by a local woman, Kate Sessions, in 1898, contains many gardens, trees and colonial-style Spanish buildings. There are around 15,000 trees in the park, including palms, pines and eucalyptus, the most famous tree in the park is the Moreton Bay fig, located near the National History Museum and planted in around 1915. Highlights include the *Alcazar Garden* which was modelled on the gardens found at Alcazar Castle in Seville (Spain), with many ornate fountains and tiles, the *Botanical Building* which houses around 2100 tropical plants, the *Desert Garden* with 1300 varieties of desert plants and the *Old Cactus Garden* with hundreds of varieties of large cactus.

Contact Address

San Diego Zoo, PO Box 120551, San Diego, CA 92112, USA
Tel: (619) 234 3153. Fax: (619) 718 3021.
Website: www.sandiegozoo.org

Transportation

Air: San Diego International Airport. **Road:** Bus: 20, 20C, 210, 810, 820, 850, 860 or 980. Car: State Road 163, north exit, then Zoo/Museums exit (from I-5 in the north); State Road 163 south to the Park Boulevard/I-5, south exit (from I-15); Pershing exit

San Diego Zoo

to Florida Drive north, then left at Zoo Place (from I-5 in the south); State Road 163 south to Park Boulevard/I-5 south exit (from I-8 in the east); towards central San Diego until 12th Avenue, then right on 12th Avenue and then north (from Route 94). The zoo entrance is located off Park Boulevard at Zoo Place.

Opening Times

Daily 0900-1800 (winter, last admission 1600); daily 0900-2200 (summer, last admission 2100).

Admission Fees

US$18 (adult), US$8 (child 3-11).

Universal Studios Hollywood

Universal Studios Hollywood is reputedly the world's largest film studio and theme park, and one of the most popular tourist attractions in Los Angeles. The park opened to the public in 1964, allowing the public to see behind the scenes of the film world. The site's origins can be traced back to 1912, however, when Carl Laemmle opened the *Universal Film Manufacturing Company* on a converted chicken ranch in Universal City. Today, a visit to the park, which attracts around 35,000 visitors per day, begins with an exciting behind-the-scenes tram tour of famous film sets, with a simulated earthquake, a collapsing bridge, and several surprise attacks from key Hollywood film characters, such as the shark 'Jaws' and the famous giant gorilla 'King Kong'. The park features the latest in state-of-the-art video and audio technology, and uses impressive special effects and stunt shows to entertain visitors. It also provides musical entertainment and a variety of thrill rides, such as *Back to the Future, ET Adventure* and *Jurassic Park – The Ride.* Guests can also see TV shows being filmed for free by obtaining tickets from the Audiences Unlimited Ticket Booth, which is located next to the *Wild, Wild, Wild West Stunt Show*. Universal Studios has other theme parks around the world, including *Universal Studios Port Aventura Spain, Universal Studios Japan, Universal Studios Experience Beijing* and *Universal Orlando.*

Contact Address

Universal Studios Hollywood, 100 Universal City Plaza, Universal City, CA 91608, USA
Tel: (818) 622 3801.
Website: www.universalstudios.com

Transportation

Air: Los Angeles International Airport or Burbank Airport. Airport buses operate from Los Angeles International Airport to Universal Studios Hollywood. **Rail:** Metro: Universal City (Red Line). **Road:** Bus: The Metropolitan Transportation Authority operates buses from the Los Angeles area. There is also a free shuttle bus from hotels in Anaheim on presentation of a Universal Studios Hollywood ticket. Car: Just off Hwy-101 (Hollywood) Freeway, north of downtown Los Angeles (Universal Center Drive or Lankershim Blvd exit).

Opening Times

Mon-Fri 0900-1800, Sat-Sun 0900-1900 (winter); daily 0800-2200 (summer). Opening times vary according to season and guests are advised to check with the park before their visit.

Admission Fees

US$43 (adult), US$32 (child).

Venice Beach

Originally developed in 1905 by Abbot Kinney, an ex-cigarette manufacturer who relocated to Los Angeles, the area around Ballona Creek was intended to attract Los Angeles's urban populace to live by the ocean. Based on the canals in Venice, the developers hoped to create a European/Bohemian atmosphere by the sea. Today, the area around *Venice Boardwalk*, which is locally-known as *Venice Beach*, attracts thousands of Angelenos and tourists every week who come to soak up the party atmosphere. Venice Boardwalk is also known as the *Ocean Front Walk*, and is home to hundreds of street performers, including jugglers, palm readers, buskers, snake charmers, fire-eaters, cyclists and roller skaters. *Muscle Beach*, which is situated close by, is just as famous for its legendary weightlifters who work out daily in the sun.

Contact Address

Los Angeles Convention & Visitors Bureau, 633 West 5th Street, Suite 6000, Los Angeles, CA 90071, USA
Tel: (213) 624 7300. Fax: (213) 624 9746.
Website: www.lacvb.com

Transportation

Air: Los Angeles International Airport. **Road:** Bus: Metro Bus 33. Car: I-10 (from central Los Angeles); Fwy-405 or Pacific Coast Hwy-1 (from Los Angeles International Airport or San Francisco), then Fwy-90 via Marina Del Rey to Venice Beach.

Opening Times

Daily 24 hours.

Admission Fees

Free.

Yosemite National Park

Designated a national park in 1890, *Yosemite National Park* stretches along California's eastern flank and covers almost 3108 sq kilometres (1200 sq miles) of alpine meadows, rivers, lakes, cliffs and waterfalls in the central Sierra Nevada mountain range. The park is well known for its giant sequoia trees, particularly in *Mariposa Grove* where some of the trees are over 3000 years old and reach 80m (219ft) in height. Until 1969, when the tree fell during a heavy storm, it was possible to drive through the 3.4-metre (11.2-foot) tunnel carved through the trunk of the famous Wawona Tunnel Tree. Other scenic highlights include *Yosemite Falls*, which cascade 739m (2425ft) into the valley below and *Glacier Point*, which offers spectacular views of the park, particularly in late summer and autumn. The area is also home to abundant wildlife and provides a natural habitat for no less than 247 species of bird, 80 species of mammal – including black bears, squirrels and chipmunks – and 24 species of amphibian and reptile. Visitors can stay at lodges and campsites situated around the park and enjoy activities such as hiking, fishing, climbing, horseriding and cross-country skiing.

Contact Address

Yosemite National Park, PO Box 577, Yosemite, CA 95389, USA
Tel: (209) 372 0200. Fax: (209) 372 0220.
E-mail: yose_web_manager@nps.gov
Website: www.nps.gov/yose

Transportation

Air: Fresno Yosemite International Airport. **Rail:** Train: Merced Amtrak Station. **Road:** Car: Hwy-120 (from the west or the east); I-395 (from the northeast or the southeast); Hwy-41 (from the south); Hwy-140 (from the southwest).

Opening Times

Daily 24 hours. Roads to Glacier Point and Mariposa Grove closed Oct/Nov-May/Jun due to snow conditions.

Admission Fees

Vehicle: US$20. Pedestrian/cyclist: US$10. Entrance is valid for 7 days.

Winter in Yosemite National Park

Corel

Florida

1 Everglades National Park
2 Kennedy Space Center Visitor Complex
3 SeaWorld Adventure Park Florida
4 Universal Orlando
5 Walt Disney World Resort

Tourist Information

Visit Florida
PO Box 1100, Tallahassee, FL 32302, USA
Tel: (850) 488 5607. Fax: (850) 224 2938.
Website: www.flausa.com

Visit Florida
Roebuck House, First Floor Mezzanine, Palace Street, London SW1E 5BA, UK
Tel: (020) 7630 6602 *or* (09001) 600 555 (24-hour information hotline; calls cost 60p per minute).
Fax: (020) 7630 7703.
E-mail: visitfloridauk@flausa.com

Everglades National Park

Florida's *Everglades* make up the largest sub-tropical wilderness on the United States mainland and were designated a national park in 1947. Both temperate and tropical plant communities are represented in the park's 610,684 hectares (1,509,000 acres), including cypress swamps, pinelands and sawgrass prairies. *Florida Bay*, the largest body of water within the park, covering 2072 sq km (800 sq miles), is home to fish, shellfish, coral and sponges. The park is particularly well known for its abundant birdlife. During the dry season, from November to May, between 5000 and 10,000 wading birds, such as heron and storks, flock to the freshwater and estuarine wetlands in the park to feed in the drying marshes. In total, no less than 347 species of bird can be seen in the Everglades, including the Great Blue heron, Roseate spoonbill, Snow goose and two endangered species, the red-cokaded woodpecker and the wood stork. Other endangered species protected in the park are the Green turtle, the Key Largo Cotton mouse, the American crocodile and the Schaus swallowtail butterfly. The park's five visitor centres provide information on the flora and fauna in the Everglades, as well as details of various park trails. Hiking and canoeing trails start at *Flamingo Visitor Center, Gulf Coast Visitor Center* and *Shark Valley Visitor Center*. Shark Valley Visitor Center also hires out bicycles and visitors can take a narrated tram ride or a boat tour of the park.

Contact Address

Everglades National Park, 40001 State Road 9336, Homestead, FL 33034, USA
Tel: (305) 242 7700. Website: www.nps.gov/ever

Transportation

Air: Miami International Airport or Southwest Florida International Airport (Fort Myers). **Rail:** Train: Miami Amtrak Station. **Road:** Car: Route 821 (Florida Turnpike), then US Hwy-1, then Palm Drive, then signs to the park (to *Main Entrance* and *Flamingo Visitor Center* from Miami, Florida Keys and the north); Route 821 (Florida Turnpike), then US Hwy-41 to signs for Shark Valley (to *Shark Valley* from Miami, Florida Keys and the north); US Hwy-41 (to *Shark Valley* from Naples); US Hwy-41, then US Hwy-29 to Everglades City, then signs to the visitor centre (from Miami to *Gulf Coast Visitor Center*); US Hwy-41, then US Hwy-29 (from Naples to *Gulf Coast Visitor Center*).

Opening Times

Main Entrance: Daily 24 hours. *Flamingo Visitor Center*: Daily 0730-1700 (Nov-Apr). *Gulf Coast Visitor Center*: Daily 0730-1700 (Nov-Apr); daily 0830-1700 (May-Oct). *Shark Valley Visitor Center*: Daily 0830-1715.

Admission Fees

Gulf Coast Entrance: Free. Main Entrance: US$10 (per vehicle), US$5 (adult), free (child under 17). *Shark Valley Entrance*: US$8 (per vehicle), US$4 (adult), free (child under 17).

Kennedy Space Center Visitor Complex

Visitors to the *Kennedy Space Center Visitor Complex* at Cape Canaveral in Florida find a mix of space-age technology and nature. The attraction is primarily known as the home of the *Space Shuttle*, where spectacular launches can be viewed from a safe distance. The centre has been pioneering space exploration since the success of the Apollo lunar programme in the late 1960s. Visitors can also tour the *Apollo/Saturn Visitor Center* to see an actual Saturn V moon rocket, which stands a staggering 111m (363ft) high, and experience *Astronout Encounter*, an interactive show hosted by real astronauts. Other facilities include a *Rocket Garden* and an *I-MAX* cinema. The Kennedy Space Center's location on *Merritt Island National Wildlife Refuge*, home to bald eagles, alligators, otters and sea turtles, means that visitors can also enjoy wildlife walks or drives and learn about the animals that inhabit the area.

Contact Address

Kennedy Space Center Visitor Complex, Delaware North Park Services, Mail Code DNPS, Kennedy Space Center, FL 32899, USA
Tel: (321) 452 2121. Fax: (321) 452 3043.
Website: www.kennedyspacecenter.com

Transportation

Air: Melbourne International Airport, Orlando International Airport, Orlando Sanford Airport, Miami International Airport or Fort Lauderdale Hollywood International Airport. **Road:** Coach: Services from Orlando. Car: I-95 (from New York, Jacksonville, Miami, Fort Lauderdale, Richmond, Baltimore or Washington DC); US-1 (from Maine and the northeast).

Kennedy Space Center

Kennedy Space Center

Opening Times

Daily 0900-2000.

Admission Fees

US$24 (adult), US$15.90 (child 3-11), free (child under 3).

P ✕ Shop ♿

SeaWorld Adventure Park Florida

SeaWorld Adventure Park, located just outside Orlando, is the most popular marine theme park in the world. It has attracted over 80 million visitors since opening in 1978 and offers rides, shows and various other ocean-themed attractions. The site covers an area of 494 hectares (200 acres) and aims to educate visitors as well as entertain. *Terrors of the Deep* is an underwater ride past live sharks, eels, pufferfish and lionfish from the safe environment of an acrylic tunnel, whilst braver visitors can experience *Atlantis*, an 18 metre-high (60 foot) roller coaster ride through a large-scale version of the mythical underwater city. Shows include the *Cirque de la Mer* (Circus of the Sea), featuring athletes, acrobats, singers and dancers together with comedy based on South American folklore. Children will particularly enjoy games such as *Shamu's Happy Harbor*, where they can explore a tropical paradise incorporating ball pools, slides, water mazes and tunnels. One of the highlights for visitors of all ages is the chance to meet hundreds of marine animals, including dolphins, walrus, otters, penguins and polar bears.

Contact Address

SeaWorld of Florida, 7007 SeaWorld Drive, Orlando, FL 32821, USA
Tel: (800) 327 2424 (toll free USA and Canada only).
Website: www.seaworld.com

Transportation

Air: Orlando International Airport. **Rail:** Train: Orlando Amtrak Station. **Road:** Car: I-4 (from Orlando or Tampa).

Opening Times

Daily 0900-1900 (1 Jan-25 May); daily 0900-2200 (26 May-12 Aug); daily 0900-2100 (13-31 Aug); daily 0900-1900 (4 Sep-25 Dec); daily 0900-2200 (26-30 Dec); 0900-0100 (31 Dec). Times may vary according to the day of the week. Visitors are advised to telephone the park or visit the SeaWorld website for exact opening times.

Admission Fees

One-day ticket: US$47.95 (adult and child over 9), US$38.95 (child 3-9), free (child under 3). Other passes available, including multi-passes which give access to SeaWorld Adventure Park, Universal Orlando and other Florida attractions.

Universal Orlando

Universal Orlando, which opened in 1990, covers more than 162 hectares (400 acres) and includes modern TV- and movie-making facilities alongside its ever-popular recreational activities. The latter consists of three parks. *Universal Studios* features rides and attractions based on films produced at Universal Film Studios, such as 'Men in Black' and 'Back to the Future'. *Universal Studios Islands of Adventure* is a technologically advanced theme park with many rides, such as 'Duelling Dragons', two rollercoasters which intertwine as they race at speeds of up to 97kmph (60mph). *Universal CityWalk*, an evening and night-time entertainment complex, features restaurants, nightclubs, state-of-the-art cinemas, street theatre, shopping, live concerts and festivals. Universal Studios also has many rides suitable for younger children, such as the interactive *ET Adventure*, part-designed by Steven Spielberg himself.

Contact Address

Universal Orlando, 1000 Universal Studios Plaza, Orlando, FL 32819, USA
Tel: (407) 363 8000 (general information) *or* (800) 711 0080 (tickets).
Website: www.universalstudios.com

Transportation

Air: Orlando International Airport. **Rail:** Train: Orlando Amtrak Station. **Road:** Bus: 21, 24, 37, 40 or 43. Car: I-95, then I-4 (from New York, Jacksonville, Miami, Fort Lauderdale, Richmond, Baltimore or Washington DC or Orlando International airports).

Opening Times

Daily 0900-1900.

Admission Fees

One-day pass to one park: US$48 (adult or child over 9), US$39 (child 3-9), free (child under 3). Two-day combined pass: US$98.95 (adult or child over 9), US$76.95 (child 3-9), free (child under 3). Three-day combined pass: US$104.95 (adult or child over 9), US$91.95 (child 3-9), free (child under 3).

Walt Disney World® Resort

The world's largest theme park, *Walt Disney World® Resort* covers a space twice the size of Manhattan, delivering the Disney promise of magical escapism and thrilling rides. It is divided into four theme parks, alongside numerous water parks, restaurants, theatres and hotels. The best-known of the theme parks is the *Magic Kingdom*, which provides traditional Disney rides and attractions and allows visitors to meet their favourite Disney characters. *Disney's Animal Kingdom* is an animal park, where visitors can learn about the animal kingdom, enjoy shows such as the 'Festival of the Lion King', and go on an animated jungle trek or African safari. *Disney-MGM Studios* is a Hollywood-inspired theme park featuring rides, shows and tours of Hollywood sets, both real sets and reconstructions, including a children's playground adventure based on the film 'Honey, I Shrunk the Kids'. *Epcot* is a science-based park which explores the earth's natural phenomena and the human anatomy, as well as taking visitors on virtual trips around countries such as China and France (in *World Showcase*) and offering a glimpse into the technology of the future (in *Future World*).

Contact Address

Walt Disney World Resort, PO Box 10040, Lake Buena Vista, FL 32830, USA
Tel: (407) 824 2222 *or* 934 7639 (tickets).
Website: www.disneyworld.com

Transportation

Air: Orlando International Airport. **Road:** Car: I-95, then I-4 (from New York, Jacksonville, Miami, Fort Lauderdale, Richmond, Baltimore or Washington, DC); I-4 to Osceola Parkway West (exit 3) (from Orlando International Airport).

Opening Times

Disney Animal Kingdom: Daily 0900-1800 (opening times extended to 2400 depending on season). *Disney-MGM Studios*: Daily 0900-1900 (opening times extended to 2200 depending on season). *Epcot* (*World Showcase*): Daily 1100-2100 (opening times extended to 2200 depending on season). *Epcot* (*Future World*): Daily 0900-2100 (opening times extended to 2200 depending on season). *Magic Kingdom*: Daily 0900-1800 (opening times extended to 2400 depending on season).

Admission Fees

One-day, one-park pass: US$48 (adult), US$38 (child 3-9), free (child under 3). Concessions and other passes available.

Hawaii

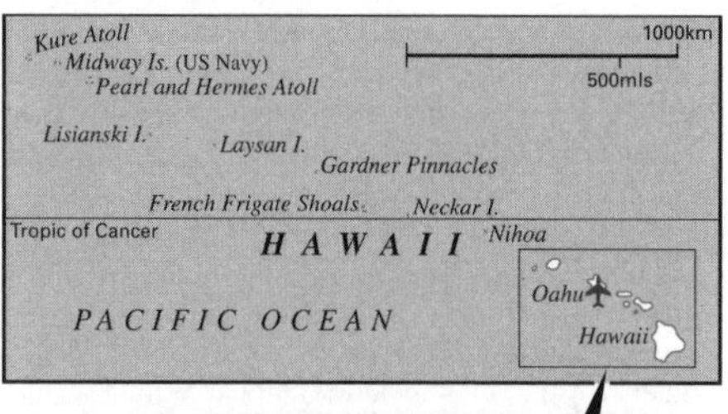

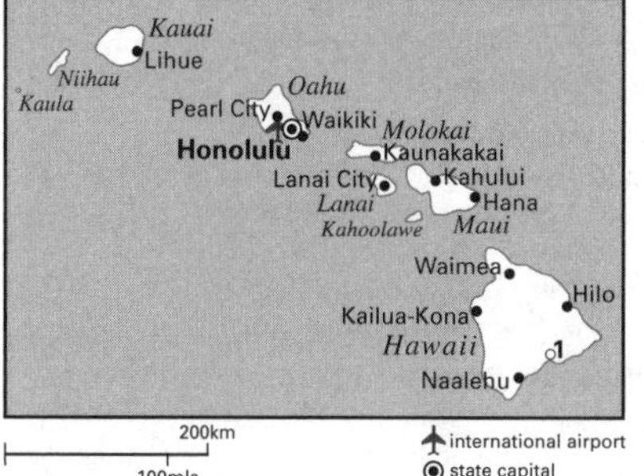

1 Hawaii Volcanoes National Park

Tourist Information

Hawaii Tourism Authority
Hawaii Convention Centre, 1801 Kalakaua Avenue, Honolulu, HI 96815, USA
Tel: (808) 973 2255. Fax: (808) 973 2253.
Website: www.hawaii.gov/tourism

Hawaii Visitors & Convention Bureau
2270 Kalakaua Avenue, Eighth Floor, Honolulu, HI 96815, USA
Tel: (808) 923 1811. Fax: (808) 922 8991.
E-mail: infooff@hvcb.org
Website: www.gohawaii.com

Hawaii Visitors & Convention Bureau
PO Box 208, Sunbury-on-Thames, Middlesex, TW16 5RJ, UK
Tel: (020) 8941 8166 (trade enquiries) *or* 8941 4009 (consumer enquiries). Fax: (020) 8941 4001.
E-mail: xcd16@dial.pipex.com
Website: www.gohawaii.com

Hawaii Volcanoes National Park

Hawaii Volcanoes National Park is located on the *Big Island of Hawaii*, which is 800,000 years old. Established in 1916, the park spans 878 sq kilometres (339 sq miles) and ranges from sea level to the top of *Mauna Loa*, the world's tallest volcano at 4169m (13,677ft) high. The result of 70 million years of volcanic activity is on display, encompassing the creation of Hawaii out of the ocean to the evolution of its complex and unique ecosystems. Many rare species of plant have flourished in the volcanic landscape, indeed over 90 per cent of the park's flora and fauna, including 10,000 species of insects and spiders, is unique to Hawaii. Hiking trails are a popular way of seeing the wildlife and also the dramatic lava fields and steam vents surrounding *Kilauea*, the world's most active volcano.

Contact Address

Park Administration, PO Box 52, Hawaii Volcanoes National Park, HI 96718, USA
Tel: (808) 985 6000. Fax: (808) 985 6004.
E-mail: norrie_judd@nps.gov
Website: www.nps.gov/havo

Transportation

Air: Honolulu International Airport, Hilo Airport (domestic flights). **Road:** Bus: Services from Hilo. Car: Hwy-11 (from Hilo).

Opening Times

Daily 24 hours.

Admission Fees

Vehicle: US$10. Pedestrian/cyclist: US$5. Entrance valid for 7 days.

Hawaii Volcanoes National Park

Hawaii Visitors & Convention Bureau

Illinois

1 Sears Tower

Tourist Information

Illinois Bureau of Tourism

James R Thompson Center, Suite 3-400, 100 West Randolph Street, Chicago, IL 60601, USA
Tel: (312) 814 4732 *or* (800) 226 6632 (toll free USA and Canada only). Fax: (312) 814 6175.
E-mail: tourism@commerce.state.il.us
Website: www.enjoyillinois.com

Illinois Bureau of Tourism (UK Office)

c/o Global Enterprise Marketing, 15 Nonsuch Estate, Kiln Lane, Epsom, Surrey, KT17 1DH, UK
Tel: (01372) 729 140 (trade enquiries) *or* (01372) 726 928 (consumer enquiries).
Fax: (01372) 726 298.

Sears Tower

Soaring 475m (1450ft) into the air above the 'Windy City' of Chicago, *Sears Tower*, opened in 1973 after a three-year building project, was the world's tallest building until it was overtaken by Kuala Lumpur's *Petronas Towers* in 1996. It was designed by Chicago architects Skidmore, Owing and Merrill and consists of 110 floors of black aluminium and bronze-tinted glass. The lift takes visitors up to the Skydeck on the 103rd floor in just seven seconds for spectacular views that can stretch as far as 80km (50 miles) to the surrounding states of Michigan, Illinois, Wisconsin and Indiana on a clear day. Although the tower is a working office building – it is owned by real estate and property management company TrizecHahn – there are various visitor attractions and entertainment facilities on the Skydeck. Attractions include interactive multimedia displays showcasing Chicago's history, music, literature and sport, with special knee-high versions for children, and several restaurants.

Contact Address

Sears Tower Skydeck, Sears Tower, 233 S Wacker Drive, Chicago, IL 60606, USA
Tel: (312) 875 9696. Fax: (312) 906 1118.
E-mail: skydeckinfo@trizechahn.com
Website: www.sears-tower.com

Transportation

Air: Chicago O'Hare International Airport or Midway Airport (domestic flights). **Rail:** Train: Chicago Union Station. Underground: Quincy Station. **Road:** Car: I-80 (from San Francisco or New York); I-90 (from Seattle or Indianapolis); I-55 (from St Louis or New Orleans). Entrance to the car park is on Jackson Boulevard.

Opening Times

Daily 0900-2300.

Admission Fees

US$9.50 (adult), US$6.75 (child 3-11), free (child under 3). Concessions available.

P

Sears Tower

Corel

Louisiana

1 New Orleans' French Quarter

Tourist Information

Louisiana Office of Tourism
Department of Culture, Recreation and Tourism, PO Box 94291, Capitol Station, Baton Rouge, LA 70804, USA
Tel: (225) 342 8100 *or* (800) 227 4386 (toll free USA and Canada only). Fax: (225) 342 8390.
E-mail: free.info@crt.state.la.us
Website: www.crt.state.la.us/crt/tourism.htm *or* www.louisianatravel.com

Louisiana Office of Tourism
33 Market Place, Hitchin, Herts SG5 1DY, UK
Tel: (01462) 458 696. Fax: (01462) 455 391.
E-mail 10047.657@compuserve.com

New Orleans' French Quarter

New Orleans' French Quarter covers a grid of 98 square blocks stretching back from the *Mississippi River* in downtown New Orleans. It was known to the French, who colonised the state of Louisiana in 1718, as *Vieux Carré*, or Old Square, and contains some superb examples of 18th- and 19th-century architecture. It was in fact the Spanish, who gained control of Louisiana in 1762, who constructed many of the buildings there now, with their arches, fanlights and filigreed wrought-iron balconies, after most of the original French buildings were destroyed by fire in the late 18th century. The focal point of the French Quarter is *Jackson Square*, regarded by many as the loveliest square in America, with its Louis XIV-style garden landscaping and symmetrical architecture. It is home to several monuments and churches including *St Louis Cathedral*, the oldest cathedral in the USA, dedicated in 1794, and the *Cabildo*, which was the meeting place of the Spanish council in colonial times, and is now home to a museum of Louisiana history. *Bourbon Street* is popular for its many jazz clubs and bars, including the historic tavern, *Lafitte's Blacksmith Shop* at No 941, where there is live piano entertainment every evening at 2000. In February each year, the French Quarter plays host to the city's colourful *Mardi Gras* celebrations, one of the world's most famous carnivals, with music, dancing, food, floats and parades.

Contact Address

New Orleans Metropolitan Convention and Visitors Bureau, 1520 Sugar Bowl Drive, New Orleans, LA 70112, USA
Tel: (504) 566 5011.
E-mail: tourism@neworleanscvb.com
Website: www.neworleanscvb.com

Transportation

Air: New Orleans International Airport. **Rail:** Train: New Orleans Union Passenger Terminal. Tram: Riverfront Streetcar. **Road:** Car: I-10 (from Houston, Los Angeles or Jacksonville); I-55 (from Memphis, Chicago or St Louis); I-59 (from Birmingham or Chattanooga).

Opening Times

Cabildo: Tues-Sun 0900-1700. Closed public holidays. *Lafitte's Blacksmith Shop*: Daily 1130-late. *St Louis Cathedral*: Mon-Sat 0730-1800, Sun 1330-1800.

Admission Fees

Cabildo: US$5 (adult), US$4 (child 12-18), free (child under 12). *Lafitte's Blacksmith Shop*: Free. *St Louis Cathedral*: Free.

Massachusetts

1 Freedom Trail

Tourist Information

Massachusetts Office of Travel & Tourism
State Transportation Building, 10 Park Plaza, Suite 4510, Boston, MA 02116, USA
Tel: (617) 973 8500 *or* (800) 227 MASS (toll free USA and Canada only). Fax: (617) 973 8525.
E-mail: vacationinfo@state.ma.us
Website: www.massvacation.com

Massachusetts Office of Travel & Tourism
c/o First Public Relations, Molasses House, Clove Hitch Quay, Plantation Wharf, York Place, London SW11 3TN, UK
Tel: (020) 7978 7429. Fax: (020) 7924 3134.
Website: www.massvacation.com

Freedom Trail

The *Freedom Trail* consists of a four-kilometre (2.5-mile) walking tour of historic Boston and Charlestown, encompassing 16 sites and structures of historical significance to both the city and the nation. Highlights include the *USS Constitution*, the world's oldest commissioned warship still afloat, which was used in battle against France and Britain, in particular during the War of 1812. Visitors can tour *Paul Revere House*, the one-time home of the quintessential 'American Patriot', who was a key figure in the Boston Tea Party and fought for American independence. Also open to the public is the *Old State House*, built in 1713, which was once the seat of the British government in Boston, and the 18th-century *Old South Meeting House*, where protesters gathered to challenge British rulers in the years leading up to the American

First Public Relations

Old State House

Revolution. The trail also takes in the golden-domed *State House*, situated in the charming Beacon Hill district of the city; and the *Granary Burying Ground*, where famous Declaration of Independence signers Samuel Adams, Robert Treat Paine and John Hancock are buried. The trail begins at *Boston Common* in the centre of the city.

Contact Address

Freedom Trail Foundation, 3 School Street, Boston, MA 02108, USA
Tel: (617) 227 8800. Fax: (617) 227 2498.
E-mail: ftfoffice@aol.com
Website: www.thefreedomtrail.org

Transportation

Air: Boston Logan International Airport. **Rail:** Train: South Station. Underground: Park Street. **Road:** Bus: Services to South Station. Car: I-90, the Massachusetts Turnpike (from Chicago, Seattle, Cleveland, New York City and Philadelphia); I-93 (from north Massachusetts and New Hampshire).

Opening Times

Most sites: Daily 1000-1600 (winter); daily 0930-1700 (summer), although there are some exceptions.

Admission Fees

Old South Meeting House: US$3 (adult), US$1 (child 12-18), free (child under 12). Concessions available. *Old State House*: US$3 (adult), US$1 (child 12-18), free (child under 12). *Paul Revere House*: US$2.50 (adult), US$1 (child 12-18), free (child under 12). All other sites: Free.

Minnesota

1 Mall of America

Tourist Information

Minnesota Office of Tourism
Suite 100, 121 Seventh Place East, St Paul, MN 55101, USA
Tel: (651) 296 5029.
E-mail: explore@state.mn.us
Website: www.exploreminnesota.com

Mall of America

The *Mall of America*, opened in 1992, is the world's largest undercover shopping centre, covering 32 hectares (78 acres) of land just outside Bloomington. The site was previously occupied by Minnesota's football and baseball teams, the Vikings and the Twins, who had their Met Stadium there until 1982, when they moved to the Metrodome in downtown Minneapolis. It now houses over 520 shops, including American giants such as *Macy's, Bloomingdale's, Nordstrom* and *Sears*, and attracts more visitors each year than *Disney World® Resort*, the *Grand Canyon* and *Graceland* combined. In addition to the shops, there are 14 cinema screens, eight nightclubs, and no less than 49 restaurants, including the Rainforest Café, complete with all the sights and sounds of the Amazon, as well as a host of other attractions. *Camp Snoopy* is a three-hectare (seven-acre) indoor theme park, featuring roller coasters, a ferris wheel and 26 other rides. At *Underwater Adventure*, a huge aquarium, visitors come face to face with 300,000 sea creatures, whilst the *Lego® Imagination Center* contains Lego models and thousands of Lego bricks for children to play with.

Contact Address

Mall of America Management, 60 East Broadway, Bloomington, MN 55425, USA
Tel: (952) 883 8800.

Transportation

Air: Minneapolis-St Paul International Airport. **Rail:** Train: Merced Amtrak Station. **Road:** Bus: 80 (from Minneapolis), 54 (from St Paul) or services from Minneapolis-St Paul International Airport. Car: I-94, then I-494 (from the east); I-35, then I-35W, then I-94 (from the north or south); I-94, then I-494, then Hwy-77 (from the west).

Opening Times

Mon-Sat 1000-2130, Sun 1100-1900. Closed 31 Mar, 22 Nov and 25 Dec.

Admission Fees

Camp Snoopy: Prices vary according to the attraction; visitors should contact Mall of America for more details. *Lego Imagination Center*: Free. *Underwater Adventure* (all-day wristband): US$13.95 (adult), US$11.95 (child 13-17), US$7.95 (child 3-12), free (child under 3).

Mall of America

Minnesota Office of Tourism

Nevada

1	Hoover Dam
2	Las Vegas Strip

Tourist Information

Nevada Commission on Tourism
401 North Carson Street, Carson City, NV 89701, USA
Tel: (775) 687 4322 *or* (800) 237 0774 (toll free USA and Canada only). Fax: (775) 687 6779.
E-mail: ncot@travelnevada.com
Website: www.travelnevada.com

Nevada Commission on Tourism
c/o Cellet Travel Services Ltd, Brook House, 47 High Street, Henley-in-Arden, Warks B95 5AA, UK
Tel: (01564) 794 999. Fax: (01564) 795 333.

Hoover Dam

Completed in 1935, after five years of intensive construction, the *Hoover Dam* is a modern engineering marvel. It stretches 380m (1247ft) across the Colorado River, holding in *Lake Mead* the equivalent volume of two years' worth of the river's flow. Thousands of workers were involved in the project, which provided much needed employment during the Great Depression, although tragically 96 men died in industrial accidents during its construction. The dam contains 2,486,250 cubic metres (3,250,000 cubic yards) of concrete, and functions primarily as a power generator, supplying electricity to Nevada as well as nearby California and Arizona. Visitor tours examine the construction of the dam and explore its hydroelectric generating facilities, whilst the *Hoover Dam Visitor Center* features displays on the engineering process and the operation of the dam.

Contact Address

DOI Bureau of Reclamation, Visitor Services, PO Box 60400, Boulder City, NV 89006, USA
Tel: (702) 294 3524. Fax: (702) 597 9685.
E-mail: lcdweb@lc.usbr.gov
Website: www.hooverdam.usbr.gov

Transportation

Air: Las Vegas McCarran International Airport.
Road: Coach: Chartered services from Las Vegas. Car: US Hwy-93 (from Las Vegas).

Opening Times

Daily 0800-1745.

Admission Fees

Hoover Dam Visitor Center: US$4 (adult), free (child under 7). *Tour* (including Visitor Center exhibitions): US$10 (adult), US$3 (child 7-16), free (child under 7). Concessions available.

Las Vegas Strip

The *Strip* in Las Vegas (officially known as Las Vegas Boulevard) is, perhaps, the defining symbol of American excess in the name of money. Every year, millions of people descend upon the city, the vast majority of whom come with the sole intention of gambling. In 2000, almost 36 million visitors came to Las Vegas, gaming revenue in the city totalled US$6.1 billion, with the average visitor spending US$665 per trip. Nevada is the only state in the USA where gambling is legal, and nowhere is this more evident than on the Las Vegas Strip, where there are more slot machines and roulette wheels than anywhere else in the world. Here, massive neon casino-hotel complexes vie for supremacy in an ongoing competition to be the biggest and the best. In order to attract trade, many of them have turned into brightly-lit mini-theme parks, open 24 hours a day. The *Luxor*, a 36-storey bronze and glass pyramid themed on Ancient Egypt, shoots the most powerful artificial light beam ever created from its apex, whilst *Paris Las Vegas* has a reconstruction of the *Eiffel Tower*, offering fantastic views of Las Vegas Valley. Other legendary casinos include *Caesar's Palace,* with its full-size replica of Caravaggio's 'David', and the *MGM Grand Hotel and Theme Park*, which is entered through the mouth of the world-famous MGM lion. The whole place is a non-stop cabaret of glitz and extravagance, with nightly performances in all the big hotels, featuring dancing girls, stand-up comedians and live music to keep the punters entertained. Famous performers over the years have included Frank Sinatra who performed here for over 40 years, and Elvis Presley, who married Priscilla Presley here in 1967 and made his famous comeback at the International Hotel in 1969. The city is also famous as a place to get hitched, with around 200,000 couples visiting Las Vegas every year to get married. Ceremonies range from the kitsch, complete with Elvis impersonator in the *Graceland Wedding Chapel* to ultra-quick drive-in weddings at the *Little White Chapel*, open 24 hours a day. If all this is not enough, there are also numerous museums including *Madame Tussaud's Wax Museum*, *Guinness World of Records Museum*, the *Elvis-A-Rama Museum* and the *Liberace Museum.*

Contact Address

Las Vegas Convention and Visitors Authority, 3150 Paradise Road, Las Vegas, NV 89109, USA
Tel: (702) 892 0711. Fax: (702) 892 7692.
Website: www.lasvegas24hours.com

Transportation

Air: Las Vegas McCarran International Airport. **Road:** Bus: 113, 301, 302 or 303. Car: I-15 into the centre of Las Vegas, then Spring Mountain Road, Desert Inn Road or Flamingo Road to join Las Vegas Boulevard (from the north or south).

Opening Times

Daily 24 hours.

Admission Fees

Free.

P ✗ 🛒 ♿

Las Vegas Strip

Las Vegas News Bureau

New York State

1 Central Park
2 Empire State Building
3 Greenwich Village
4 Metropolitan Museum of Art
5 Niagara Falls
6 Statue of Liberty
7 Times Square

Tourist Information

New York State Division of Tourism
PO Box 2603, Albany, NY 12220, USA
Tel: (518) 474 4116 *or* (800) 225 5697 (toll free USA, Canada and US External Territories).
Fax: (518) 486 6416.
E-mail: iloveny@empire.state.ny.us
Website: www.iloveny.state.ny.us

New York State Department of Economic Development (Tourism Division)
Media House, 4 Stratford Place, London, W1N 18T, UK
Tel: (020) 7629 2720. Fax: (020) 7629 2758.
E-mail: info@nyseurope.com
Website: www.empire.state.ny.us

Central Park

Completed in 1873, *Central Park* was designed to provide New York with 341 hectares (843 acres) of rural paradise in what was, at the time, the out-of-the-way northern reaches of Manhattan. Now, located almost in the dead centre of New York due to urban expansion, Central Park is very much an integral part of the city's landscape. Apart from being a refreshing area of greenery in the middle of a very dense and busy city, Central Park has a cultural side, with public programmes offered by the Central Park Conservancy, as well as a small zoo, a dairy, fountains and an ice-skating rink. The park, which was designed by Frederick Law Olmsted and Calvert Vaux, has featured in many Hollywood films, including 'When Harry Met Sally', 'Ghostbusters' and 'Wall Street', and is also home to statues of famous people (real and fictional), including Ludwig Van Beethoven, Alice in Wonderland, Hans Christian Anderson and Robert Burns. It is also home to the Strawberry Fields Memorial, dedicated to the late John Lennon who was shot dead in the city on 8 December 1980. Every year on the anniversary of his death thousands of fans gather in the park to pay their respects to the former Beatles singer. Today, it is a colourful recreational area, attracting joggers, rollerbladers and buskers every day, as well as thousands of tourists who come to see the most famous urban park in the USA.

Contact Address

Central Park Conservancy, Eighth Floor, 14 East 60th Street, New York, NY 10022, USA
Tel: (212) 310 6600.
E-mail: contact@centralparknyc.org
Website: www.centralparknyc.org

Transportation

Air: New York La Guardia International Airport or New York John F Kennedy International Airport. **Rail:** Train: Grand Central Station. Underground: Fifth Avenue or 59th Street Columbus Circle. **Road:** Bus: Services to Fifth Avenue or 59th Street Columbus Circle. Car: I-95 (from Boston, Washington DC, Newark, Providence, Philadelphia, Baltimore,

Winter in Central Park

Corel

Richmond, Miami); I-80 (from San Francisco, Salt Lake City, Iowa City, Cleveland, Chicago or Rutherford).

Opening Times

Park: Daily dawn-dusk. *Dairy*: Tues-Sun 1000-1600 (winter); daily 1000-1700 (summer).

Admission Fees

Park and *Dairy*: Free.

Empire State Building

Completed in 1931 during the Great Depression at a cost of US$40,948,900, the *Empire State Building* is an enduring symbol of New York City and the USA. It was built during an era of skyscraper wars, and at 443.2m (1454 ft) tall, the Empire State Building defeated the world's then tallest building and fellow Art Deco gem, the nearby *Chrysler Building*. The developers, Empire State Inc, initially struggled to find any tenants for the gigantic office block, due to its size, although it was eventually leased to various companies and is currently owned by a company called Hemsley Spears (business tycoon Donald Trump owns the land on which it sits). Visitors can visit the two observatories, one on the 86th floor and one on the 102nd (top) floor for spectacular views over the Big Apple. There is also a virtual-reality movie theatre with *Skyride*. Famous visitors to the Empire State Building include the British Queen Elizabeth II, football star Pele, former Russian President Nikita Krushchev and Cuban dictator Fidel Castro. The tower has also featured in numerous films, such as 'An Affair to Remember', 'When Harry Met Sally', 'King Kong', 'Independence Day', 'Taxi Driver' and 'Sleepless in Seattle'.

Contact Address

Empire State Building, 350 Fifth Avenue, New York, NY 10118, USA
Tel: (212) 736 3100 *or* 279 4927 (*Skyride*).
Fax: (212) 947 1360.
E-mail: info@esbnyc.com
Website: www.esbnyc.com

Transportation

Air: New York La Guardia International Airport or New York John F Kennedy International Airport. **Rail:** Train: Grand Central Station. Underground: 34th Street. **Road:** Bus: 5, 6, 7 or 8 to 34th Street or 34th Street Crosstown services to 34th Street and Fifth Street. Coach: Port Authority Bus Terminal. Car: I-95 (from Boston, Washington DC, Newark, Providence, Philadelphia, Baltimore, Richmond or Miami); I-80 (from San Francisco, Salt Lake City, Iowa City, Cleveland, Chicago or Rutherford).

Opening Times

Daily 0930-2400.

Admission Fees

US$9 (adult), US$4 (child 5-11), free (child under 5). Concessions available.

Greenwich Village

Greenwich Village is one of the liveliest and trendiest districts of New York City. Originally a tobacco plantation located towards the tip of *Manhattan Island*, it was given its name by British naval commander, Sir Peter Warren who purchased a farm there in the early 18th century. It was not until New York's yellow fever outbreak in 1822 that people began to move here to escape the disease-ridden conditions of the city, and Greenwich quickly flourished, as banks and businesses sprang up alongside the elegant houses of their wealthy owners. By the turn of the last century, New York's richest residents had begun to move to more fashionable areas of town, such as *Fifth Avenue*. This exodus meant that the houses were populated by struggling artists and writers, who spent their time in the Village's many bars and coffee houses, discussing political ideals. Greenwich thus gained its reputation as New York's Bohemian, anti-establishment quarter, as well as a centre for women's liberation. The Village also gained a reputation as the focus of the gay rights movement after the infamous Stonewall Riots that followed the police raid on the Stonewall Inn, a gay bar in Greenwich Village, in 1969. The area's reputation as a Bohemian melting pot has stuck, despite the fact that it has once again become home to the city's well-heeled professionals since the sharp rise in property prices during the 1980s economic boom forced writers and artists out. Visitors still come to Greenwich Village to explore its history and experience New York's 'alternative' scene. Some particularly fine examples of 19th-century townhouses can be seen in *Washington Square*, where writers Edith Wharton and Henry James once lived; other features of the square are Stanford White's *Triumphal Arch*, built in 1892 in honour of George Washington's inauguration as president, and a park, popular with sunbathers and rollerbladers. *Christopher Street*, which runs through the centre of the district, is the hub of New York's gay scene, whilst *Greenwich Avenue* is a good place to shop, with plenty of bookstores and second-hand clothes shops. Greenwich Village also has a thriving nightlife, with many of its lively cafés and bars staying open later than those elsewhere in Manhattan.

Contact Address

New York City & Company (Convention & Visitors Bureau), 810 Seventh Avenue, Third Floor, New York, NY 10019, USA
Tel: (212) 484 1200 *or* 484 1222. Fax: (212) 397 1931.
E-mail: nytourism@nycvisit.com
Website: www.greenwich-village.com

Transportation

Air: New York La Guardia International Airport or New York John F Kennedy International Airport. **Rail:** Train: Grand Central Station. Underground: Christopher Street or West 4 Street–Washington Square. **Road:** Bus: M5, M6 or M8. Coach: Port Authority Bus Terminal. Car: I-95 (from Boston, Washington DC, Newark, Providence, Philadelphia, Baltimore, Richmond or Miami); I-80 (from San Francisco, Salt Lake City, Iowa City, Cleveland, Chicago or Rutherford).

Opening Times

Daily 24 hours.

Admission Fees

Free.

Metropolitan Museum of Art

With a diverse collection embracing over two million works of art, the *Metropolitan Museum of Art* ranks as one of the world's great museums. Visitors could literally spend days taking in works from the USA, Europe, China, the Far East and Africa, as well as the Classical (including Greek and Roman) and Islamic (including Moroccan and Central Asian) worlds. The museum houses particularly impressive collections of work by Monet, Cézanne, Vermeer and Giovanni Battista Tiepolo. The modern art section comprises paintings by a wide variety of artists including Modigliani, Picasso, Braque and Charles Rennie Mackintosh. As would be expected, there are also fine displays of American art, from colonial times to the present day; these include pieces of decorative art, such as ceramics and Tiffany glass. *The Cloisters* is a separate branch of the museum, located in Ford Tryon Park in north Manhattan overlooking the Hudson River, and is considered to be one of the greatest collections of Medieval art in the world. Its design is modelled on elements of French Medieval cloisters and monastic sites in the south of France and, as well as gardens laid out and planted according to Medieval documents, it contains over 5000 works of European art, including tapestries and stained-glass windows.

Contact Address

Metropolitan Museum of Art, 1000 Fifth Avenue, New York, NY 10028, USA
Tel: (212) 535 7710. Website: www.metmuseum.org

Transportation

Air: New York La Guardia International Airport or New York John F Kennedy International Airport. **Rail:** Train: Grand Central Station. Underground: 77th Street or 86th Street or Fifth Avenue. **Road:** Bus: M1, M2, M3 or M4 to 82nd Street or Fifth Avenue. Car: I-95 (from Boston, Washington DC, Newark, Providence, Philadelphia, Baltimore, Richmond or Miami); I-80 (from San Francisco, Salt Lake City, Iowa City, Cleveland, Chicago or Rutherford).

Opening Times

Tues-Thurs 0930-1715, Fri and Sat 0930-2100, Sun 0930-1715. Entrance includes a visit to *The Cloisters* on the same day.

Admission Fees

US$10 (adult, suggested donation), US$5 (child 12-18, suggested donation), free (child under 12).

Niagara Falls

Niagara Falls is one of the most popular tourist destinations in North America, made up of two separate parts, *Horseshoe Falls*, on the Canadian side and *American Falls* on the US side. Although not the highest waterfall in the world (that record goes to the *Angel Falls* in Venezuela), they move a staggering volume of 168,000 cubic metres (219,600 cubic yards) of water per minute over a drop of 51m (167ft), making them one of the natural wonders of the world. In the past, people have attempted numerous daring stunts here, including walking a tightrope across the falls and dropping over the edge in a barrel. The first men to organise a tourist stunt at the Falls were William Forsyth, John Brown and Parkhurst Whitney who sent an old schooner filled with animals over the Horseshoe Falls in 1827; of all the animals on board only the goose survived. Just two years later, the first human stunt was carried out by Sam Patch who dived from a height of 26m (85ft). The most famous daredevil was the Frenchman Jean Francois Gravelot (known as The Great Blondin) who crossed the Niagara Falls on a tightrope in 1859 and lived to tell the tale. The town surrounding Niagara Falls, a celebrated North American honeymoon destination, offers a wealth of visitor activities including a casino, as well as land and boat tours of the falls.

Contact Address

Niagara Falls Convention and Visitors Bureau, 310 Fourth Street, Niagara Falls, NY 14303, USA

Tel: (716) 285 2400. Fax: (716) 285 0809.
E-mail: nfcvb@nfcvb.com
Website: www.nfcvb.com

Transportation

Air: Buffalo Niagara Airport or Pearson International Airport (Toronto). **Rail:** Train: Amtrack Station. **Road:** Bus: Transportation Centre. Car: Queen Elizabeth Way (QEW) towards Niagara, then Hwy-420 to Niagara Falls (from Toronto).

Opening Times

Daily 24 hours.

Admission Fees

Free.

Statue of Liberty

A gift to the USA from France in 1886 to celebrate the 100th anniversary of American independence, the *Statue of Liberty* greeted millions of immigrants during the 19th century who came to America to seek a better life. Enjoying a fine position in New York Harbour, this world-famous statue, which was originally called *Liberty Enlightening the World*, has become a defining American symbol of freedom and democracy. This 45m (151ft) statue of a woman holding a torch aloft, was designed by the French sculptor Frédéric-Auguste Bartholdi, and was modelled on the Colossus of Rhodes. Today, visitors to the monument can make the 22-storey climb to the statue's crown, or take a lift to the Pedestal observation deck, which offers excellent views of New York. Nearby Ellis Island, part of the Statue of Liberty National Monument, houses a museum devoted to the history of immigration.

Contact Address

Statue of Liberty National Monument and Ellis Island, Liberty Island, New York, NY 10004, USA
Tel: (212) 363 3200. Fax: (212) 363 6304.
E-mail: stli_interpretation@nps.gov
Website: www.nps.gov/stli

Transportation

Air: New York La Guardia International Airport or New York John F Kennedy International Airport. **Water:** Ferry: The Statue of Liberty/Ellis Island Ferry departs from Battery Park (New York City) and Liberty State Park (Jersey City, New Jersey). Road: Car: Battery Park can be reached from West Side Highway South or FDR Drive South; Liberty State Park can be reached from Jersey Turnpike (exit 14B).

Opening Times

Daily 0900-1715, although this may vary seasonally. Closed 25 Dec.

Admission Fees

Return ferry trip including access to island/statue: US$8 (adult), US$3 (child). Concessions available.

Times Square

Located just north of 42nd Street, *Times Square* has long been associated with theatre and nightlife and all the excitement and glitz of New York City. There is no better way to discover the Big Apple than by going to see a show in a Broadway theatre, located just off Times Square; the area is home to 45 theatres, around 30 hotels, cinemas, shops, restaurants and bars. Often referred to as New York's 'Crossroads of the World', the city's theatre district is alight with neon signs and giant TV screens. Always buzzing with energy, it is an ideal place to experience the atmosphere of life on New York's busy streets. Attracting approximately 27 million tourists every year, a visit to Times Square can be a daunting experience to first time visitors due to the constant stream of traffic and huge crowds. The square is, however, an excellent place to spend New Year's Eve when up to a million people gather to join in the festivities.

Contact Address

Times Square Business Improvement District, 1560 Broadway, Suite 800, NY 10036, USA
Tel: (212) 768 1560. Fax: (212) 768 0233.
E-mail: questions@timessquarebid.org
Website: www.timessquarebid.org

Transportation

Air: New York John F Kennedy International Airport. **Rail:** Underground: 11 subway lines go to Times Square. **Road:** Bus: Port Authority Bus Terminal is nearby on Eighth Avenue; buses stop here from the airport and from New Jersey. Five city bus lines serve the area around Times Square.

Opening Times

Times Square Visitors Center: Daily 0800-2000. *Times Square*: Daily 24 hours.

Admission Fees

Free.

Ohio

1	Rock and Roll Hall of Fame

Tourist Information

Ohio Division of Travel & Tourism

29th Floor, 77 High Street South, Columbus, OH 43215, USA

Tel: (614) 466 8844 *or* (800) 282 5393 (toll free USA and Canada only). Fax: (614) 466 6744.

E-mail: askohiotourism@calltech.com

Website: www.ohiotourism.com

Rock and Roll Hall of Fame

The *Rock and Roll Hall of Fame* celebrates the American pop-cultural institution of rock music by honouring its most popular and influential performers, producers, songwriters and disc jockeys. The phrase 'rock and roll' was coined by the Cleveland disc jockey Alan Freed in 1951, so it somehow seems fitting that Cleveland should have been chosen as the home of this attraction. Opened in 1995 and designed by the renowned Chinese architect I M Pei, the building is a 13,935 sq m (150,000 sq ft) modern structure with bold designs

Ohio Division of Travel & Tourism

Rock and Roll Hall of Fame

and a dramatic location on the shores of Lake Erie. Pei was also responsible for the addition of the great glass pyramids to the *Louvre* in Paris between 1983 and 1989. The museum features a *Hall of Fame* exhibit, which includes a computerised juke-box containing nearly every song by performers featured, their signatures etched in glass, film exhibits and displays of artefacts. Exhibitions cover seven rock genres – rockabilly, punk, grunge, psychedelia, R&B, hip-hop and Motown – and tend to focus on key figures from the world of rock and pop, including the Beatles, Elvis Presley and the Rolling Stones.

Contact Address

Rock and Roll Hall of Fame, 1 Key Plaza, Cleveland, OH 44114, USA

Tel: (888) 764 7625. Fax: (216) 781 1326.

E-mail: tmesek@rockhall.org

Website: www.rockhall.com

Transportation

Air: Cleveland Hopkins International Airport. **Water:** Waterfront Rapid: North Coast Harbour Station. **Rail:** Rapid: Downtown to Public Square. **Road:** Bus: Downtown to Public Square. Car: I-71 (from Columbus and Cincinnati); I-77 (from Akron); I-90 (from Toledo and Ashatabula). Then, towards central Cleveland (East 9th Street exit).

Opening Times

Mon-Tues and Thurs-Sun 1000-1730, Wed 1000-2100 (Sep-May); Mon-Tues, Thurs-Fri and Sun 1000-1730, Wed and Sat 1000-2100 (Jun-Sep).

Admission Fees

US$15 (adult), US$11.50 (child aged 9-11 and OAP), free (child under 8 if accompanied by one adult).

Pennsylvania

1 Independence National Historic Park

Tourist Information

Philadelphia Convention and Visitors Bureau
1515 Market Street, Suite 2020, Philadelphia, PA 19102, USA
Tel: (215) 636 3300. Fax: (215) 636 3327.
E-mail: info@pcvb.org
Website: www.pcvb.org

Office of Tourism and Marketing
Department of Community and Economic Development, Commonwealth of Pennsylvania, Fourth Floor, Commonwealth Keystone Building, Harrisburg, PA 17120, USA
Tel: (717) 787 5453 *or* (800) 237 4363 (toll free USA and Canada only).
Fax: (717) 787 0687.
E-mail: RA-travel@state.pa.us
Website: www.experiencepa.com

Pennsylvania Tourism
Molasses House, Clove Hitch Quay, Plantation Wharf, London SW11 3TN, UK
Tel: (020) 7738 9422. Fax: (020) 7924 3171.
E-mail: penn@destination-marketing.co.uk
Website: www.experiencepa.com

Independence National Historic Park

Independence National Historical Park contains important monuments that reflect key events in the history of America. Most significant is *Independence Hall*, considered the birthplace of the United States – where both the Declaration of Independence and the US Constitution were signed in 1776 and 1787 respectively. Nearby, the famous *Liberty Bell* is a hugely popular symbol of American freedom, as it was sounded at the first public reading of the Declaration of Independence; it was given its current name in the 19th century by the abolitionists who sought to end slavery. The park also reflects the period between 1790 and 1800, when Philadelphia was the capital of America, as it contains the home of the US Supreme Court (*Old City Hall*) and the meeting place of the US Congress (*Congress Hall*) during that time. A good starting point is the Visitor Center, where a short film entitled *Independence*, introducing the park's monuments, is shown.

Contact Address

Independence National Historic Park Visitor Center, 313 Walnut Street, Philadelphia, PA 19106, USA
Tel: (215) 597 8974 (visitor information) *or* 597 8787 (headquarters). Fax: (215) 597 0042.
Website: www.nps.gov/inde

Transportation

Air: Philadelphia International Airport. **Rail:** Train: 30th Street Station. Underground: Market Street Station. **Road:** Bus: 76. Coach: Greyhound Terminal. Car: I-95 (from New York, Boston or Washington DC); I-76 (from the east or the west); US Hwy-30 (from the north).

Opening Times

All monuments: Daily 0900-1700.

Admission Fees

All monuments: Free.

Liberty Bell

Pennsylvania Tourism

South Dakota

1 Mount Rushmore National Memorial

Tourist Information

South Dakota Department of Tourism
711 East Wells Avenue, c/o 500 East Capitol Avenue, Pierre, SD 57501, USA
Tel: (605) 773 3301 *or* (800) 732 5682.
Fax: (605) 773 3256.
E-mail: sdinfo@.state.sd.us
Website: www.travelsd.com

Rocky Mountain International
PO Box 13652, London SW5 0ZR, UK
Tel: (020) 7835 0928. Fax: (020) 7244 0828.
Website: www.RMI-realamerica.com

Mount Rushmore National Memorial

Mount Rushmore National Memorial is one of the USA's most renowned national monuments. The site in South Dakota is home to 18m-tall (60ft) faces of four US presidents, George Washington, Thomas Jefferson, Theodore Roosevelt and Abraham Lincoln, perched 152m (465ft) in the air. These giant faces are carved into solid rock and stand as a gateway to America's majestic west. Originally called *The Shrine of Democracy*, the idea to build a monument of this size was conceived by the historian Duane Robinson and the sculptor Gutzon Borglum in 1923. Work began on the monument, which is surrounded by the *Black Hills National Forest*, in 1927, taking over 14 years of carving and fundraising to complete. Today, the memorial is an internationally-recognised symbol of the first 150 years of America's history and the part the four presidents played in founding it. The memorial hosts many exhibits, walks and lectures during the summer months.

South Dakota Department of Tourism

Mount Rushmore National Memorial

Contact Address

Mount Rushmore National Memorial, PO Box 268, Keystone, SD 57751, USA
Tel: (605) 574 2523 *or* 574 3171 (recorded information).
Fax: (605) 574 2307.
E-mail: jim_popovich@nps.gov
Website: www.nps.gov/moru

Transportation

Air: Rapid City Regional Airport. **Road:** Car: Hwy-16 and Hwy-244 (from Rapid City).

Opening Times

Monument: Daily 24 hours. *Visitor Centre*: Daily 0800-1800 (winter); daily 0800-2000 (summer). Closed 25 Dec.

Admission Fees

Free.

Tennessee

1 Graceland
2 Grand Ole Opry

Tourist Information

Tennessee Department of Tourism Development
320 Sixth Avenue North, Rachel Jackson Building, Fifth Floor, Nashville, TN 37243, USA
Tel: (615) 741 2159 *or* (800) 836 6200 (toll free USA and Canada only). Fax: (615) 741 7225.
E-mail: tourdev@mail.state.tn.us
Website: www.tnvacation.com

Tennessee Tourism
Lofthouse Enterprises, Coach House Mews, r/o 99 Bancroft, Hitchin, Herts SG5 1NQ, UK
Tel: (01462) 440 007. Fax: (01462) 440 783.
E-mail: tennessee@david-nicholson.com
Website: www.deep-south-usa.com/tenn.html

Graceland

Graceland is America's monument to one of its favourite musicians and icons, Elvis Presley. The 'King' bought the colonial-style mansion in 1957 and lived there until his death in 1977, when distraught fans flocked to the site to pay their respects. The house has been open to the public since 1982, becoming a shrine to his music and his legacy. At the site, which is located 16km (10 miles) from Memphis, visitors can enter the rooms where the star and his family lived, tour Elvis' jet planes, shop at *Graceland Plaza* or stay at the *Heartbreak Hotel.* Highlights for die-hard fans include the *Trophy Building*, where many of his awards are displayed alongside personal momentoes, and the *Meditation Garden* where Elvis was buried.

Contact Address

Graceland, PO Box 16508, Memphis, TN 38186, USA
Tel: (901) 332 3322. Fax: (901) 332 1636.
E-mail: graceland@icom.com
Website: www.elvis-presley.com

Transportation

Air: Memphis International Airport. **Rail:** Train: Memphis Central Station. **Road:** Bus: 13. Car: I-55 (exit 5-B) (from St Louis, Chicago or New Orleans); I-240 (from Memphis International Airport).

Opening Times

Mon-Sat 0900-1700, Sun 1000-1600. Closed Tues (Nov-Feb).

Admission Fees

Mansion Tour: US$12. *Platinum Tour*: US$22. Concessions available.

Grand Ole Opry

Grand Ole Opry is the world's longest running live radio show, and an American institution. It was first broadcast as a weekly barn dance show on 28 November 1925, at a time when the radio was fast growing in popularity. The show's first performer was Uncle Jimmy Thompson, a fiddler with a repertoire of over 1000 tunes, and it was presented by George D Hay. In the early days, the show used to follow a classical music programme, and the radio announcer joked that the Grand Opera that listeners had just heard would be followed by performances of 'Grand Ole Opry' – Hay adopted this impromptu name and it stuck. The show soon became so popular that thousands of fans were flocking to see it performed live. After a succession of venues, including the excellent acoustics of the Ryman Theater from 1943 until 1974, it finally settled in the specially designed 4400-seater Grand Ole Opry House in Nashville in 1974, from where it has been broadcast ever since, on Tuesday afternoons and Friday and Saturday evenings. Over the years the cast has included many hundreds of members, such as Patsy Cline, Ira Louvin and Hank Snow, who perform country and western music every weekend in Nashville, America's 'Music City'.

Contact Address

Grand Ole Opry, 2802 Opryland Drive, Nashville, TN 37214, USA
Tel: (615) 889 3060. Website: www.opry.com

Transportation

Air: Nashville Airport. **Rail:** Train: Memphis Amtrak Station. **Road:** Car: Hwy-40 (from Knoxville or Memphis); Hwy-65 (from Louisville or Birmingham); Hwy-24 (from Chattanooga or Paducah).

Opening Times

Tues 1500 (12 Jun-14 Aug only), Fri 1930 (all year), Sat 1830 and 2130 (all year).

Admission Fees

US$25 (adult), US$15 (child).

Texas

1	Sixth Floor Museum

Tourist Information

Texas Department of Economic Development, Tourism Division
1700 North Congress, Suite 200, PO Box 12728, Austin, TX 78711, USA
Tel: (512) 462 9191 *or* (800) 888 8839 (toll free USA and Canada only).
Fax: (512) 936 0088. Website: www.traveltex.com

State of Texas Tourism Office
c/o First Public Relations, Molasses House, Clove Hitch Quay, Plantation Wharf, London SW11 3TN, UK
Tel: (020) 7978 5233. Fax: (020) 7924 3134.

Sixth Floor Museum

The *Texas School Book Depository* was a rather ordinary building in downtown Dallas until the infamous assassination of US President John F Kennedy on 22 November 1963 as he travelled in an open limousine through Dallas on a pre-election visit. Lee Harvey Oswald, the 24-year-old Dallas citizen who was accused of the crime, and was himself shot dead by nightclub owner Jack Ruby just two days later, had a filing job at the depository. The deadly shot was fired from the sixth floor of the building, which is now the *Sixth Floor Museum* documenting both the assassination itself and the life and times of JFK. Visitors can immerse themselves in the events of the fateful day, with a minute-by-minute account of the action as well as recordings of news broadcasts and even material showing mourning vigils in India and Germany. Other exhibitions focus on the four investigations into the crime, the legacy of Kennedy's administration, and the various theories on who carried out the assassination. The corner staircase where the rifle was found, and down which the assassin is thought to have escaped, has been reconstructed according to official police photographs. There are views from the building over *Dealey Plaza*, where the President was shot, with a commentary to help visitors visualise the assassination. Background information to the shooting is provided through displays on the 1960s political, cultural and social movements, and visitors can add their own comments to memorial books which are kept as part of the museum archives.

Contact Address

Sixth Floor Museum at Dealey Plaza, 411 Elm Street, Dallas, TX 75202, USA
Tel: (214) 747 6660. Fax: (214) 747 6662.
E-mail: jfk@jfk.org
Website: www.jfk.org

Transportation

Air: Dallas-Fort Worth International Airport, Dallas Love Field Airport (domestic flights). **Rail:** Train: Union Station. DART (Light Rail System): West End Station or Union Station. **Road:** DART Trolleybus: Route 706 to Union Station or West End Station. Car: I-35 (from the north or south); I-30 (from the east or west); I-80 (from the east); I-175 or I-45 (from the southeast); I-67 (from the southwest).

Opening Times

Daily 0900-1800. Closed 25 Dec.

Admission Fees

Admission only: US$7 (adult), US$6 (child 6-18), US$3 (child under 6). Admission with audio tour: US$10 (adult), US$9 (child 6-18), US$3 (child under 6).

Washington, DC

1 Lincoln Memorial
2 Smithsonian Institution
3 White House

Tourist Information

Washington, DC Convention & Visitors Association
1212 New York Avenue, Suite 600, NW, Washington, DC 20005, USA
Tel: (202) 789 7000. Fax: (202) 789 7037.
Website: www.washington.org

Washington, DC Convention & Visitors Association
c/o Representation Plus, 11 Blades Court, 121 Deodar Road, London SW15 2NU, UK
Tel: (020) 8877 4521. Fax: (020) 8874 4219.
E-mail: name@representationplus.co.uk.
Website: www.washington.org

Lincoln Memorial

Modelled upon a Doric temple, the *Lincoln Memorial* is a tribute to President Abraham Lincoln and the nation he fought to preserve during the Civil War (1861-1865), the nation's bloodiest conflict. Enclosed by a colonnade and complimented by a reflecting pool in front, a large statue of President Lincoln, sculpted by Daniel Chester French, sits in solemn thought, grasping the arms of his throne-like chair. The monument has the Gettysburg Address inscribed on its southern wall and a mural painted by Jules Guerin above it, showing the angel of truth liberating a slave. As a symbol of freedom and racial harmony, the Lincoln Memorial was the site of Martin Luther King's 'I Have a Dream' speech in August 1963.

Contact Address

The National Mall, Washington, DC 20024 *or* National Capital Parks-Central, 900 Ohio Drive, Washington, DC 20242, USA
Tel: (202) 426 6841. Fax: (202) 426 1844.
E-mail: National_Mall@nps.gov
Website: www.nps.gov/linc

Transportation

Air: Washington Dulles International Airport, Washington Ronald Reagan National Airport. **Rail:** Train: Union Station. Underground: Foggy Bottom. **Road:** Bus: 21st Street and Constitution Avenue. Car: I-66 or I-395, then Independence Avenue SW (from the south); I-495, New York Avenue, Rock Creek Parkway, George Washington Memorial Parkway and Cabinet John Parkway (from the north).

Opening Times

Daily 0800-2345.

Admission Fees

Free.

Smithsonian Institution

The *Smithsonian Institution*, which was set up in 1846 with money left to the USA by the English scientist James Smithson, is made up of 14 museums, the most famous of which is the *National Air and Space Museum*. Opened in 1976, the National Air and Space Museum celebrates the history and evolution of air and space technology. Documenting both historical and technical achievements, virtually all aircraft and spacecraft on display were actually flown or used as backup vehicles to replace the original if out of service. Exhibits include the Wright Brothers' 1903 *Flyer*, Charles Lindbergh's *Spirit of St Louis*, and moon rock collected by the Apollo astronauts (Neil Armstrong and Buzz Aldrin) from the lunar surface, when they touched down on 20 July 1969. Other museums include the *National Museum of African Art, National Museum of American History, National Museum of Natural History, National Museum of the American Indian, National Portrait Gallery, National Postal Museum, National Zoological Park* and the *Smithsonian American Art Museum*. The

National Portrait Gallery, which has a unique collection of portraits of famous Americans from politics, sport, the stage and screen, as well as official portraits of US presidents, is closed for renovation and is not expected to re-open until 2004.

Contact Address

Smithsonian Information Center, SI Building, Room 153, Washington, DC 20560, USA
Tel: (202) 357 2700. E-mail: info@info.si.edu
Website: www.si.edu

Transportation

Air: Washington Dulles International Airport, Washington Ronald Reagan National Airport. **Rail:** Train: Union Station. Metrorail: Smithsonian. **Road:** Car: I-66 (from Virginia); I-50 (from Annapolis in Maryland); I-95 (from Baltimore, Richmond, Philadelphia and New York); I-270 (from Maryland).

Opening Times

Museums: Daily 1000-1730. Closed 25 Dec. *Smithsonian Information Center*: Daily 0900-1730.

Admission Fees

Free.

White House

The *White House* is where the President of the United States of America lives and carries out official duties as Head of State. It is the most famous building in Washington, DC and was built between 1792 and 1800 by the Irish-born architect James Hoban. Although commissioned during President George Washington's lifetime, the first residents of the White House were President John Adams and his wife, Abigail, who moved into the house in 1800. The building has had a colourful past. It burned down during the War of 1812 (which is often called America's second War of Independence) between America and Great Britain which lasted until the end of 1814, and was rebuilt in 1815, only to endure (and survive) another fire in the West Wing in 1929, under the presidency of Harry S Truman. Today, members of the public can visit the interior of the White House; tours are very popular, however and in peak period, from the third Tuesday in March to the end of August, visitors have to obtain free tickets dispensed by the *White House Visitors Center*. The tour takes visitors around certain permitted areas of the White House, including the *Vermeil Room and Library*, as well as other rooms which play host to official governmental functions.

Contact Address

President's Park, 100 Ohio Drive SW, Washington, DC 20242, USA *or*
White House Visitor Center, 1450 Pennsylvania Avenue NW, Room 1894, Washington, DC 20230, USA
Tel: (202) 208 1631 *or* 456 7041. Fax: (202) 208 1643.
E-mail: whho_white_houseliaison@nps.gov
Website: www.nps.gov/whho

Transportation

Air: Washington Dulles International Airport, Washington Ronald Reagan National Airport. **Rail:** Train: Union Station. Metrorail: Federal Triangle or Metro Center. **Road:** Bus: Metrobus Federal Triangle or Metro Center. Car: I-66 (from Virginia); I-50 (from Annapolis in Maryland); I-95 (from Baltimore, Richmond, Philadelphia and New York); I-270 (from Maryland).

Opening Times

White House Tours: Tues-Sat 1000-1200. May close for official events. *Visitor Center*: Daily 0730-1600.

Admission Fees

Free.

Smithsonian Institution

Corel

Washington State

1	Space Needle

Tourist Information

Seattle/King County Convention & Visitors Bureau
520 Pike Street, Suite 1300, Seattle, WA 98101, USA
Tel: (206) 461 5800 *or* 461 5840. Fax: (206) 461 5855 *or* 461 8304.
E-mail: visinfo@seeseattle.org
Website: www.seeseattle.org

Washington State Tourism Office
PO Box 42500, Olympia, WA 98504, USA
Tel: (360) 725 5051 *or* (800) 544 1800 (toll free USA and Canada only). Fax: (360) 753 4470.
E-mail: info@tourism.wa.gov
Website: www.tourism.wa.gov

Washington State Information Office
c/o First Public Relations, Molasses House, Clove Hitch Quay, Plantation Wharf, London SW11 3TN, UK
Tel: (020) 7978 5233. Fax: (020) 7924 3134.

Space Needle

Standing at 185 metres (605ft) high, Seattle's most famous building is a great place from which to enjoy outstanding 360-degree views across the city and the whole of Washington State, including the Cascade and Olympic mountain ranges, Puget Sound and Mount Rainier. The *Space Needle* is the most recognised landmark in Seattle, and visitors can also eat in its famous revolving restaurant. Designed by Edward E Carlson and completed in 1961 for US$4.5 million, the top of this Space Age tower can be reached in just 43 seconds by a futuristic glass lift. The tower is located at the *Seattle Center*, a 30-hectare (74 acre) site built for the 1962 World Fair, which is also home to the *Pacific Science Center*, offering laser and hologram exhibits, the *Boeing IMAX Theater* and the *Children's Museum*.

Contact Address

Space Needle, 219 Fourth Avenue North, Seattle, WA 98109, USA
Tel: (206) 905 2200 *or* (206) 905 2100.
Fax: (206) 905 2107.
E-mail: groups@speedneedle.com
Website: www.spaceneedle.com.

Transportation

Air: Seattle International Airport. **Road:** Monorail: A monorail service operates from Westlake Center and stops near the Space Needle. **Road:** Coach: Coaches set down on Broad Street, west of Fifth Avenue. Bus: 1, 2, 3, 4, 8, 13, 15, 16, 18, 19, 24 or 33. Car: The Space Needle is located in the central area of Seattle, just off I-5 (from Portland or San Francisco).

Opening Times

Sun-Thurs 0900-2300, Fri-Sat 0900-2400.

Admission Fees

US$11 (adult), US$5 (child 5-12).

P ✕ 🧺 ♿

Space Needle

Seattle/King County Convention & Visitors Bureau

Wyoming

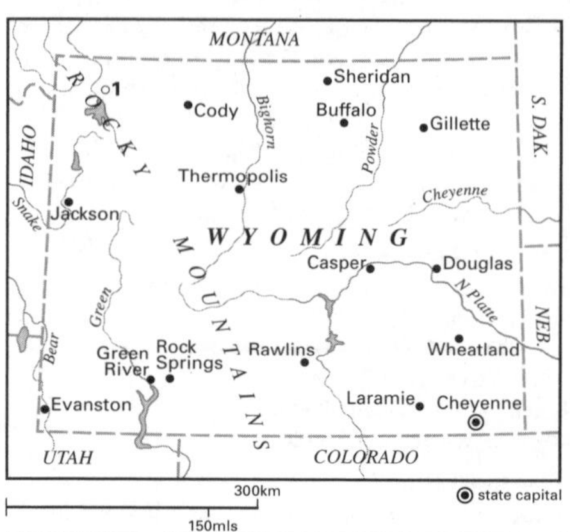

1 Yellowstone National Park

Tourist Information

Wyoming Business Council – Tourism Office
I-25 at College Drive, Cheyenne, Wyoming, WY 82002, USA
Tel: (307) 777 7777 *or* (800) 225 5996 (toll free USA and Canada only).
Fax: (307) 777 6094.
E-mail: tourism@missc.state.wy.us
Website: www.wyomingtourism.org

Rocky Mountains International
PO Box 13652, London SW5 0ZR, UK
Tel: (020) 7835 0928 *or* 7244 0828.
Fax: (020) 7242 2838.
Website: www.RMI-realamerica.com

Yellowstone National Park

Established in 1872, *Yellowstone National Park* is the first and oldest national park in the world. Renowned for its geothermal phenomena, the park has more geysers and hot springs than the rest of the world combined. The mineral waters of *Mammoth Hot Springs* in the northwest of the park, have long been attracting visitors seeking a natural cure for various ailments. Other natural attractions include the *Grand Canyon of the Yellowstone River* (not to be confused with the *Grand Canyon* in Arizona), fossil forests and *Yellowstone Lake*. Natural wildlife, such as bears, wolves, elk, bison and trout, abound and can often be seen from the road. Evidence of human activity in the park dating back as far as 12,000 years has also been found and visitors can learn more about the area's history at the *Albright Visitor Center Museum*. The *Canyon Visitor Center* also features displays on the culture and wildlife of Yellowstone. Visitors who wish to stay overnight in the park can take advantage of the many inns, lodges and campsites located within the park boundaries.

Contact Address

Yellowstone National Park Visitor Information Services, PO Box 168, Yellowstone National Park, WY 82190, USA
Tel: (307) 344 7381. Fax: (307) 344 2005.
E-mail: yell_visitor_services@nps.gov
Website: www.nps.gov/yell

Transportation

Air: Denver International Airport, Cody Airport (domestic flights), Jackson Airport (domestic flights), Bozeman Airport (domestic flights), Billings Airport (domestic flights), Idaho Falls Airport (domestic flights) or West Yellowstone Airport (open Jun-early Sep) (domestic flights). **Road:** Bus: Services to West Yellowstone (from Bozeman); summer services to West Yellowstone (from Idaho). Car: I-90, then US Hwy-89 (from the east or the west); I-25, then US Hwy-89 (from the north and the south).

Opening Times

Daily 24 hours to wheeled vehicles. Many entrances operate seasonally. *Albright Visitor Center*: Daily 0800-1900. *Canyon Visitor Center*: Daily 0800-1900.

Admission Fees

Vehicle: US$20. Snowmobile/motorcycle: US$15. Pedestrian/cyclist: US$10. Entrance valid for 7 days. *Albright Visitor Center*: Free. *Canyon Visitor Center*: Free.

Yellowstone National Park

Corel

Venezuela

Angel Falls

1 Salto Ángel (Angel Falls)

Tourist Information

Corporación de Turismo de Venezuela (Venezuela Tourism Board)
Avenida v. Lecuna, Parque Central, Torre Oeste, Piso 37, Caracas, Venezuela
Tel: (02) 507 8831. Fax: (02) 573 8983.
E-mail: corporpturismo@latino.hov.ve

Embassy of the Republic of Venezuela
1 Cromwell Road, London SW7 2HW, UK
Tel: (020) 7584 4206 *or* 7584 4207.
Fax: (020) 7589 8887.
E-mail: venezlon@venezlon.demon.co.uk
Website: www.venezlon.demon.co.uk

Salto Ángel (Angel Falls)

At 988m (3212ft), *Angel Falls* is the tallest waterfall in the world. To many it is also the most stunning, with water spilling into a freefall of nearly one kilometre (0.6 miles) before tumbling into a pool. Double rainbows can often be seen in the spray-drenched air above. Located in *Canaima National Park*, 600km (373 miles) south of Ciudad Bolívar and 50km (30 miles) southeast of Canaima village, the waterfall was made public to the wider world in 1937 by American pilot Jimmie Angel, who was searching for gold in the area. Angel Falls used to be a holy site for the Incas, and is still sacred to the local Venezuelan tribes today. Tours to the falls can be arranged from the nearest town, Ciudad Bolívar, by boat or plane. Each mode of transport offers visitors a different perspective of the falls – the plane circles several times overhead, whilst the boat trip offers visitors a chance to see the spectacle at a more leisurely pace from below.

Contact Address

For more information on Angel Falls, contact Corporación de Turismo de Venezuela (see **Tourist Information** above).

Transportation

Air: Caracas Simon Bolivar International Airport or Ciudad Bolívar Airport to Canaima Airport; then private tour operator's plane or boat. **Water:** Boat: Motorised canoe services from Ciudad Bolívar (Jun-Dec). **Road:** Bus: Services from Caracas or Ciudad Bolívar. Car: El Dorado–Santa Elena de Uairén Road, then La Ciudadela Road (from Caracas or Ciudad Bolívar).

Opening Times

Daily 24 hours.

Admission Fees

Bs5000.

P ✕ ♿

Vietnam

1 Cu Chi Diadao (Cu Chi Tunnels)
2 Hué Cung Vua (Hué Imperial Palace)

Tourist Information

Vietnam Tourism
30A Ly Thuong Kiet, Hanoi, Vietnam
Tel: (04) 825 7532. Fax: (04) 825 7583 *or* 826 4322.
E-mail: vntourism2@hn.vnn.vn
Website: www.vn-tourism.com

Embassy of the Socialist Republic of Vietnam
12 Victoria Road, London W8 5RD, UK
Tel: (020) 7937 1912. Fax: (020) 7937 6108.

Cu Chi Diadao (Cu Chi Tunnels)

The *Cu Chi Tunnels* is an underground network which was excavated by the Vietnamese and used by the Viet Cong during both the French-Indochina War (1946-1954) and the Vietnam War (1955-1975). Situated near Ho Chi Minh City, the tunnels took around 25 years to construct and were finished in the 1960s. Stretching for over 200km (124 miles) and connecting numerous villages in the provinces, the tunnels once housed mini-hospitals, store rooms and factories, and were used as living quarters by both Vietnamese fighters and local villagers. During the French-Indochina war, Vietnam struggled to gain independence from France, whilst during the Vietnam war, the United States and South Vietnamese fought to prevent communists in North Vietnam from uniting with South Vietnam under communist rule. The Americans feared this would lead to the spread of communism in Asia and as a result, launched a military attack on the Viet Cong during the 1960s. The tunnels stand today as a symbol of the struggle by the Vietnamese people on one of the most famous battlegrounds of the Vietnam War. Cu Chi district was heavily bombed during the two wars and was particularly targeted at night, forcing residents to live in underground tunnels. Today, visitors to the site can experience life underground during their tour of the tunnels and imagine what life would have been like for the Vietnamese. They can also gain a better understanding of one of history's most atrocious wars, which saw 458,000 Americans soldiers killed and more than 303,000 wounded. Between 185,000 and 225,000 South Vietnamese were also killed during the war and between 500,000 and 570,000 were wounded; in addition, approximately 900,000 North Vietnamese and Viet Cong were killed, along with over one million North and South Vietnamese civilians.

Contact Address

For more information on Cu Chi Tunnels, contact Vietnam Tourism (see **Tourist Information** above).

Transportation

Air: Tan Son Nhat International Airport. **Road:** Coach: Daily coach trips are organised by private tour operators (from Ho Chi Minh City). Car: 30km (19 miles) northwest of Ho Chi Minh City.

Opening Times

Daily 0700-1700.

Admission Fees

VND65,000.

Hué Cung Vua (Hué Imperial Palace)

Hué was the political, cultural and religious capital of unified Vietnam between 1802 and 1945 when the Nguyen Emperors ruled the country. Today, the imperial city is home to many important sites, the most famous of which is the *Imperial Palace* (or *Citadel*). The palace is situated on the north banks of the Perfume River which winds its way through the city, and covers an area of five sq km (1.9 sq miles). The Citadel was built in a Vauban style (after the French military architect who built the citadel in Besançon, France during the 17th century) by Emperor Gia Long in 1805 and completed in 1832 by King Minh Mang. Surrounded by a wall and a moat, the Citadel can be entered via one of ten gates, the most famous of which is the ornately decorated *Ngo Mon* (Noon) Gate which was built in 1834, through which the Emperor used to pass to reach his quarters. The citadel contains the *Nine Holy Cannons* that used to defend the palace, the *Imperial Enclosure* where the Emperor carried out his official business, the *Palace of Supreme Harmony* and the *Hall of the Mandarins*. It was also home to the *Purple Forbidden Palace* which was reserved for use by the Emperor himself; this was almost entirely destroyed during the Vietnam War, however. Today the whole city, which was officially recognised as a UNESCO World Heritage Site in 1993, remains an important cultural and religious centre, housing many other historic monuments and attractions, including eight Royal Tombs located outside Hué which house the remains of the Nguyen Emperors. The most famous of these tombs is *Lang Gia Long* (Gia Long's Tomb) constructed in 1814, the tomb of the Emperor responsible for building Hué's famous Citadel.

Contact Address

Vietnam Tourism, 18 Le Loi, Hué, Vietnam
Tel: (054) 828 316. Fax: (054) 821 090.
E-mail: vntourismhue@dng.vnn.vn.
Website: www.vn-tourism.com

Transportation

Air: Phu Bia Airport. **Rail:** Train: Reunification Express train to Hanoi (from Ho Chi Minh City). **Road:** Bus: Dong Ba Bus Station. Coach: Private tour operators organise trips to Hué (from Ho Chi Minh City). Car: Coast road north (from Ho Chi Minh City), then the Bui Thi Xuan road, the Le Loi road and Phu Xuan Bridge.

Opening Times

Citadel: Daily 0700-1630.

Admission Fees

Citadel: D55,000 (adult), D27,500 (child under 8).

Hué Cung Vua

Vietnam Tourism

Yemen

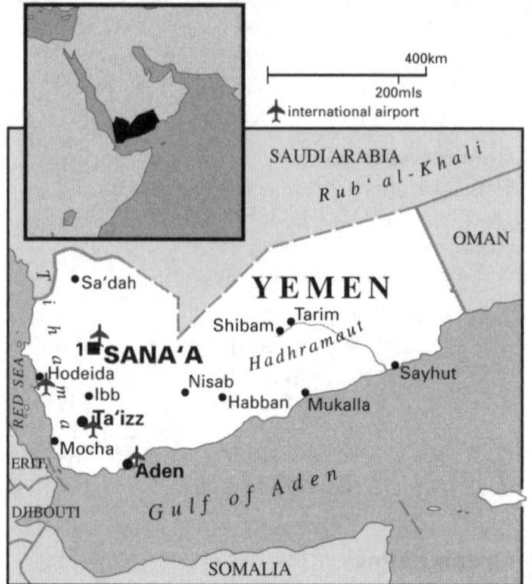

1 al-Medina al-qadima, Sana'a-fi Sana'a (Old City of Sana'a)

Tourist Information

General Authority of Tourism, Yemen
PO Box 129, Sana'a, Republic of Yemen
Tel: (01) 252 319. Fax: (01) 252 316.
E-mail: mkt@yenet.com
Website: www.yenet.com/tourism
Embassy of the Republic of Yemen
57 Cromwell Road, London SW7 2ED, UK
Tel: (020) 7584 6607. Fax: (020) 7589 3350.

al-Medina al-qadima, Sana'a-fi Sana'a (Old City of Sana'a)

The UNESCO-preserved site of the *Old City of Sana'a* is the largest preserved old city in the Arab world. Sana'a, which translates from Arabic as 'fortified place', has been the political capital of Yemen since the unification of the Yemen Arab Republic and the People's Democratic Republic of Yemen in 1990. It is one of the oldest continuously inhabited cities in the world, and according to Yemeni legend was founded by Shem, one of the three sons of Noah, possibly as early as the second century BC. Once an Arabian centre for Christians and Jews, the city was converted to Islam in AD 632. Apart from brief periods of Ottoman control – in the 16th century and between 1872 and 1940 – members of the Zaydi dynasty thereafter ruled Sana'a more or less continuously until 1962, when it became the capital of the newly founded Yemen Arab Republic. Surrounded by ancient clay walls which stand six to nine metres (20-30ft) high, the old city is a wonderland of over 100 mosques, 12 hammams (baths) and 6500 houses. Most of the buildings date back to the seventh and eighth centuries BC when the city achieved prominence as an important centre for Islam, and was constructed from dark basalt stone and brick. Many of the houses look rather like ancient skyscrapers – reaching several storeys high and topped with flat roofs, they are decorated with elaborate friezes and intricately carved windows. One of the most popular attractions is the 1000-year-old *Suq al-Milh* (Salt Market), where it is possible to buy not only salt but also bread, spices, raisins, cotton, copper, pottery, silverware, antiques, and a host of other goods. The seventh century *al-Jami'al-Kabir* (Great Mosque) is one of the oldest in the Muslim world and its Persian-style minarets pierce the city's skyline. The *Liberty Gate*, formerly known as Bab al-Yaman (Yemen Gate) until the 1962 revolution, is one of the many points of entry through the city walls and is over 700 years old. The *National Museum* consists of three floors of displays and exhibitions, including ancient Yemeni writings, coins, jewellery and traditional costume.

Contact Address

For more information of the Old City of Sana'a, contact the General Authority of Tourism, Yemen (see **Tourist Information** above).

Transportation

Air: Sana'a International Airport. **Road:** Car: Hodeida Way (from Hodeida); Aden Way (from Aden); Ta'izz Way (from Ta'izz); Marib Way (from Marib); Sa'dah Way (from Sa'dah).

Opening Times

al-Jami'al-Kabir: Daily dawn-dusk. Closed at prayer times. *National Museum*: Sat-Thurs 0900-1430. *Suq al-Milh*: Daily 0600-2200.

Admission Fees

al-Jami'al-Kabir: Free. *National Museum*: YR130. *Suq al-Milh*: Free.

Zambia

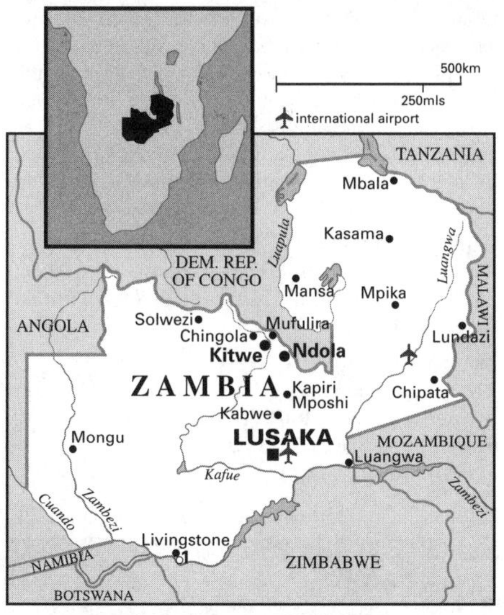

1 Victoria Falls

Tourist Information

Zambia National Tourist Board
PO Box 30017, Lusaka, Zambia
Tel: (01) 229 087. Fax: (01) 225 174.
E-mail: zntb@zamnet.zm
Website: www.zambiatourism.com *or* www.africa-insites.com/zambia

Zambia National Tourist Board
2 Palace Gate, London W8 5NG, UK
Tel: (020) 7589 6343/4. Fax: (020) 7225 3221

Victoria Falls

Made known to the wider world by the famous British explorer Dr David Livingstone in 1855, the *Victoria Falls*, which form a natural border between Zimbabwe and Zambia, are one of Africa's best-known natural wonders and one of the world's most impressive waterfalls. The falls, which Livingstone named after Queen Victoria, were known to native Kololo tribes in the 18th century as *Mosi-oa-Tunya,* meaning 'the smoke that thunders', and the spray that they generate can be seen for miles around. The cascade is formed as the calm, two-kilometre-wide (1.2 miles) *Zambezi River* spills out of a flat basalt lip and plunges into the gorge below. At their highest, the Victoria Falls drop a distance of 108m (345ft), almost twice as far as the *Niagara Falls.* As much as 546,000,000 cubic metres (713,725,490 cubic yards) per minute plummet over the edge at the height of the flood season. Viewing the falls from the Zambia side means that visitors can follow a path that goes right up to the falling water. An alternative view can be had from the *Boiling Pot,* right in the depths of the gorge at the bottom of the falls. The 111-metre high (364-foot) *Victoria Falls Bridge,* commissioned by British statesman Cecil Rhodes in 1900 as a railway crossing, is now a popular place for bungee jumping, and can be crossed by foot for excellent views of the falls and the winding blue-green waters of the Zambezi River. It is also possible to see an aerial view of the falls from a Micro-light or fixed-wing plane. The area around the falls is a prime game-viewing location.

Contact Address

For more information on Victoria Falls, contact the Zambia National Tourist Board (see **Tourist Information** above).

Transportation

Air: Lusaka International Airport, Harare International Airport or Livingstone Airport (domestic flights). **Rail:** Livingstone Station. **Road:** Coach: Services from Lusaka. Car: Victoria Falls border road (from Zimbabwe); from the south on Mosi-oa-Tunya Road (from Livingstone).

Opening Times

Daily 0600-1800.

Admission Fees

Non-residents: US$10 (adult), US$5 (child 4-12), free (child under 4). Residents: K2000 (adult), K1000 (child 4-12), free (child under 4).

Zimbabwe

1 Great Zimbabwe
2 Victoria Falls

Tourist Information

Zimbabwe Tourism Authority (ZTA)
PO Box CY286, Causeway, Harare, Zimbabwe
Tel: (04) 758 730 *or* 758 734 *or* 758 712.
Fax: (04) 758 828.
E-mail: info@ztazim.co.zw
Website: www.tourismzimbabwe.co.zw
Zimbabwe Tourism Office
Zimbabwe House, 429 Strand, London WC2R OJR, UK
Tel: (020) 7240 6169. Fax: (020) 7240 5465

Great Zimbabwe

Great Zimbabwe was a large iron-age settlement that existed from the 13th to 15th centuries and lent its name to modern-day Zimbabwe, which derives from a Shona word meaning 'house of stone'. The *Great Enclosure*, with its 250m (820ft) wide and 11m (36ft) high perimeter wall, is the largest single ancient structure south of the Sahara Desert, whilst the *Hill Complex* rises 79m (260ft) above the surrounding area on a steep, granite hill. For many years, the origins of Great Zimbabwe and its inhabitants were the subject of much debate; various claims for it were made by different groups of white colonisers following its discovery in the 1870s, who raided it for its many treasures and gold. However, archaeologists have proved that it is actually an authentic native African site, developed by a long-dead civilisation advanced enough to trade with people as far away as China.

Contact Address

For more information on Great Zimbabwe, contact Zimbabwe Tourism Authority (see **Tourist Information** above).

Transportation

Air: Harare International Airport, Masvingo Airport (domestic flights). **Rail:** Train: Masvingo Station. **Road:** Bus: Services to Morgenster Mission which is one kilometre (0.6 miles) from Great Zimbabwe

Mask used in dancing, Victoria Falls

Corel

Corel

Great Enclosure, Great Zimbabwe

(from Masvingo). Coach: Services to Great Zimbabwe (from Harare and Bulawayo). Car: Beitbridge Road south (from Masvingo).

Opening Times

Daily 0900-1700.

Admission Fees

Non-residents: US$10 (adult), US$5 (child 4-12), free (child under 4). Residents: Z$30 (adult), Z$15 (child).

Victoria Falls

Made known to the wider world by the famous British explorer Dr David Livingstone in 1855, the *Victoria Falls*, which form a natural border between Zimbabwe and Zambia, are one of Africa's best-known natural wonders and one of the world's most impressive waterfalls. The Falls, which Livingstone named after Queen Victoria, were known to native Kololo tribes in the 18th century as *Mosi-oa-Tunya*, meaning 'the smoke that thunders', and the spray that they generate can be seen for miles around. The cascade is formed as the calm, two-kilometre wide (1.2 mile) *Zambezi River* spills out of a flat basalt lip and plunges into the gorge below. At their highest, the Victoria Falls drop a distance of 108m (345ft), almost twice as far as the *Niagara Falls*. As much as 546,000,000 cubic metres (713,725,490 cubic yards) per minute plummet over the edge at the height of the flood season. The 111-metre high (364-foot) *Victoria Falls Bridge*, commissioned by British statesman Cecil Rhodes in 1900 as a railway crossing, is now a popular place for bungee jumping, and can be crossed by foot for excellent views of the falls and the winding blue-green waters of the Zambezi River. It is also possible to see an aerial view of the falls from a Micro-light or fixed-wing plane. The area around the falls is a prime game-viewing location.

Contact Address

For more information on Victoria Falls, contact Zimbabwe Tourism Authority (see **Tourist Information** above).

Transportation

Air: Lusaka International Airport, Harare International Airport or Victoria Falls Airport (domestic flights). **Rail:** Train: Victoria Falls Station. **Road:** Bus: Services to Victoria Falls Bus Station. Car: Bulawayo–Livingstone (Zambia) Highway; main road to Kazangula (from Botswana).

Opening Times

Daily 0800-1700.

Admission Fees

Non-residents: US$20 (adult), US$10 (child 6-11), free (child under 6). Residents: Z$50 (adult and child over 6), free (child under 6).

Calendar of Events

January

Australia Day	Australia
Australian Open	Australia
Brussels on Ice	Belgium
Burns' Night	United Kingdom
Celtic Connections	United Kingdom
Hogmanay	United Kingdom
Krakow Christmas Crib Contest	Poland
London Parade	United Kingdom
Mummers Parade	United States of America
Munich Carnival	Germany
National Western Stock Show & Rodeo	United States of America
New Year	Russian Federation
New Year's Eve	Brazil
Perth International Arts Festival	Australia
Sydney Festival	Australia
Thorri Feast	Iceland
Three Kings Parade	Spain

February

Berlin International Film Festival	Germany
Chinese New Year	United Kingdom
Dubai Shopping Festival	United Arab Emirates
Hong Kong Arts Festival	People's Republic of China
Krakow Christmas Crib Contest	Poland
Lisbon Carnival	Portugal
Madrid Carnival	Spain
Mardi Gras	United States of America
Munich Carnival	Germany
Perth International Arts Festival	Australia
Rio de Janeiro Carnival	Brazil
Sydney Gay and Lesbian Mardi Gras	Australia
Thorri Feast	Iceland
Toronto Winterfest	Canada
Venice Carnival	Italy

March

Budapest Spring Festival	Hungary
Daily Mail Ideal Home Show	United Kingdom
Dubai World Cup	United Arab Emirates
Explosion of the Cart	Italy
Festival of the Historic Centre	Mexico
Hong Kong Arts Festival	People's Republic of China
International Motor Show	Switzerland
Rio de Janeiro Carnival	Brazil
Singapore Food Festival	Singapore
St Patrick's Day Parade	United States of America

St Patrick's Festival	Ireland
Sydney Gay and Lesbian Mardi Gras	Australia
Ueno Cherry Blossom Festival	Japan
Venice Biennial	Italy

April

Boston Marathon	United States of America
Budapest Spring Festival	Hungary
Daily Mail Ideal Home Show	United Kingdom
Edinburgh International Science Festival	United Kingdom
Flora London Marathon	United Kingdom
Hong Kong International Film Festival	People's Republic of China
Lisbon Half Marathon	Portugal
Queen's Day	The Netherlands
Rand Easter Show	South Africa
Royal Easter Show	New Zealand
Singapore Food Festival	Singapore
Singapore International Film Festival	Singapore
Songkran Festival	Thailand
Ueno Cherry Blossom Festival	Japan
Venice Biennial	Italy
Zurich Spring Festival	Switzerland

May

Atlanta Jazz Festival	United States of America
Bergen International Festival	Norway
Bergen Night Jazz Festival	Norway
Cannes Film Festival	France
Cape Gourmet Festival	South Africa
Chelsea Flower Show	United Kingdom
Festimad Alternative Music Festival	Spain
French Tennis Open (Roland Garros)	France
Heineken Green Energy Festival	Ireland
National Windmill and Pumping Station Day	The Netherlands
Prague International Marathon	Czech Republic
Rand Easter Show	South Africa
San Isidro Festival	Spain
Sanja Festival	Japan
Vancouver International Children's Festival	Canada
Venice Biennial	Italy
Vienna Festival	Austria

June

Barcelona Summer Festival (GREC)	Spain
Bergen International Festival	Norway
Bergen Night Jazz Festival	Norway
Bloomsday Festival	Ireland
Carnival of the Cultures	Germany
Christopher Street Day	Germany
City Foundation Day	Germany

Festival of Music	France
French Tennis Open (Roland Garros)	France
Grant Park Music Festival	United States of America
Historical Soccer Tournament	Italy
Holland Festival	The Netherlands
Jewish Culture Festival	Poland
Lisbon Festivities	Portugal
Montréal International Jazz Festival	Canada
Queen's Birthday Parade – Trooping the Colour	United Kingdom
Roskilde Festival	Denmark
Royal Highland Show	United Kingdom
San Isidro Festival	Spain
Swedish National Day	Sweden
Vancouver International Children's Festival	Canada
Venice Biennial	Italy
Vienna Festival	Austria
Vienna Music Film Festival	Austria
Warsaw Mozart Festival	Poland
Wimbledon Championships	United Kingdom
Zurich Festival	Switzerland

July

Arrival of the Tour de France	France
Athens Festival	Greece
Avignon Festival	France
Barcelona Summer Festival (GREC)	Spain
Bastille Day	France
Calgary Stampede	Canada
Cardiff Festival	United Kingdom
Copenhagen Jazz Festival	Denmark
Geneva Festival	Switzerland
Grant Park Music Festival	United States of America
Havana Carnival	Cuba
Independence Day	United States of America
Istanbul Jazz Festival	Turkey
Jewish Culture Festival	Poland
Krakow International Street Theatre Festival	Poland
Light Nights	Iceland
Love Parade	Germany
Montréal International Jazz Festival	Canada
Ommegang Royal Pageant	Belgium
Rockwave Festival	Greece
Roman Summer	Italy
Roskilde Festival	Denmark
Summer Arts Festival	France
Tokyo Fireworks Festival	Japan
Venice Biennial	Italy
Vienna Music Film Festival	Austria
Warsaw Mozart Festival	Poland
Wimbledon Championships	United Kingdom

Zurich Festival	Switzerland

August

Amsterdam Gay Pride	The Netherlands
Avignon Festival	France
Cardiff Festival	United Kingdom
Copenhagen International Ballet Festival	Denmark
Edinburgh Fringe Festival	United Kingdom
Edinburgh International Festival	United Kingdom
Edinburgh Military Tattoo	United Kingdom
Elvis Week	United States of America
Geneva Festival	Switzerland
Grant Park Music Festival	United States of America
Havana Carnival	Cuba
Helsinki Festival	Finland
Jaffa Nights	Israel
Light Nights	Iceland
Queen's Birthday Celebrations	Thailand
Roman Summer	Italy
Summer Arts Festival	France
Swiss National Day	Switzerland
Venice Biennial	Italy
Venice International Film Festival	Italy
Vienna Music Film Festival	Austria
Western Union Notting Hill Carnival	United Kingdom

September

Athens Festival	Greece
Autumn Festival	France
Avignon Festival	France
Berlin Marathon	Germany
Côtes du Rhône Grape Harvest	France
Dublin Fringe Festival	Ireland
Edinburgh International Festival	United Kingdom
Helsinki Festival	Finland
Istanbul Biennial	Turkey
Moscow International Peace Marathon	Russian Federation
October Festival	Germany
Our Lady of Mercy Festival	Spain
Prague Autumn International Music Festival	Czech Republic
Roman Summer	Italy
Stockholm Beer & Whisky Festival	Sweden
Venice Biennial	Italy
Venice International Film Festival	Italy
Vienna Music Film Festival	Austria

October

Autumn Festival	France
Budapest Autumn Festival	Hungary
Diwali	India

Dublin Fringe Festival	Ireland
Frankfurt Marathon	Germany
International Festival of Authors	Canada
Istanbul Biennial	Turkey
Lord of Miracles	Peru
Madrid Autumn Festival	Spain
Melbourne Festival	Australia
October Festival	Germany
Prague Autumn International Music Festival	Czech Republic
Rome Jazz Festival	Italy
Venice Biennial	Italy

November

Athens Marathon	Greece
Autumn Festival	France
Budapest Autumn Festival	Hungary
Ellerslie Flower Show	New Zealand
International Festival of Advent & Christmas Music	Czech Republic
International Film Festival of Wales	United Kingdom
Istanbul Biennial	Turkey
Lord Mayor's Show	United Kingdom
Macy's Thanksgiving Day Parade	United States of America
Madrid Autumn Festival	Spain
Magic of Advent in Vienna	Austria
Melbourne Festival	Australia
Rome Jazz Festival	Italy
Stockholm International Film Festival	Sweden
Strasbourg Christmas Market	France
Venice Biennial	Italy

December

Autumn Festival	France
Boston Tea Party Re-enactment	United States of America
Brussels on Ice	Belgium
Christmas Market	Germany
Christmas Mass in St Peter's Basilica	Italy
European Christmas Market	Belgium
Festival of Lights	France
Hogmanay	United Kingdom
International Festival of Advent & Christmas Music	Czech Republic
Krakow Christmas Crib Contest	Poland
Magic Night	Portugal
Magic of Advent in Vienna	Austria
New Year	Russian Federation
New Year's Eve	Brazil
New Year's Eve Gala and Ball at the Opera	Hungary
Rome Jazz Festival	Italy
Strasbourg Christmas Market	France

Australia

Melbourne

Tourist Information

Tourism Victoria
GPO Box 2219T, 55 Swanston Street, Melbourne, VIC 3001, Australia
Tel: (03) 9653 9777. Fax: (03) 9653 9733.
E-mail: tourvic@dsd.vic.gov.au
Website: www.visitvictoria.com

• January

Australian Open

The *Australian Open*, which is Australia's main tennis tournament, forms part of the Grand Slam competition, which also encorporates the *Wimbledon Championships*, the *United States Open* and the *French Open*. The American player Jennifer Capriati took the women's singles title in 2001, with Andre Agassi (also from the USA) winning the men's singles title. A total of 543,843 people attended the event. The first tennis tournament in Australia was held in Warehouseman's Cricket Ground in Melbourne in 1905, when the Australian Rodney Heath won the men's singles title. The first woman to win the women's single title was another Australian, Margaret Molesworth, in 1922. Over the years, the tournament has been played across Australia, however in 1972 it was decided to hold the tournament permanently in Melbourne. The event has grown in popularity and as a result, moved to a bigger venue at Flinders Park in 1988, with the name changing to Melbourne Park in 1996.

Event Organiser
Australian Open, Private Bag 6060, Richmond, South Victoria, VIC 3121, Australia
Tel: (03) 9286 1355. Fax: (03) 9654 5897.
E-mail: ausopen@tennisaustralia.com.au
Website: www.ausopen.org

Venue
Melbourne Park.

Transport
Air: Melbourne Airport. **Rail:** Train: Richmond, Flinders Street or Jolimont stations. Tram: Yarra Trams Route 70 (from the City to Wattle Park). There is also a shuttle service to Flinders and Spencer Street which runs between Melbourne Park and the City during the tournament. **Road:** Car: Melbourne Park is located on Bateman Avenue; there is, however, no public parking during the tournament and visitors are advised to use public transport. Taxi: Taxi rank in Swan Street, opposite Olympic Park.

• October-November

Melbourne Festival

Melbourne Festival is one of the most important arts festivals in Australia with performances from the worlds of dance, theatre, music, opera, visual arts and film. The event runs for 17 days each October and November and was first held in 1986, when it was headed by the composer Gian Carlo Menotti, responsible for the Spoleto Festival series, also held in Italy and the USA. The festival in Australia was originally known as the *Melbourne Spoleto Festival*, but changed its name to the *Melbourne International Festival of the Arts* in 1990 and to Melbourne Festival in 1997. In 2001, the festival will see performances by the Kirov Opera and for the first time in Australia, the St Petersburg Opera; the conductor Valery Gergiev will oversee performances of Richard Strauss' 'Salome' and Prokofiev's 'The Fiery Angel'.

Event Organiser
Melbourne Festival, PO Box 10, Flinders Lane, Melbourne, VIC 8009, Australia
Tel: (03) 9662 4242. Fax: (03) 9663 4141.
E-mail: contact.us@melbournefestival.com.au
Website: www.melbournefestival.com.au

Venue
Theatres, cinemas and cathedrals in and around Melbourne.

Transport
Air: Melbourne Airport. **Rail:** Train: Spencer Street Station. **Road:** Coach: Greyhound Pioneer runs services to the Melbourne Transit Centre (from across Australia). Car: Western Highway (from Adelaide); Hume Highway (from Sydney).

Perth

Tourist Information

Events Corp (Western Australian Tourism Commission)
First Floor, 16 St Georges Terrace, Perth, WA 6000, Australia
Tel: (08) 9270 3311. Fax: (08) 9270 3399.
E-mail: events@tourism.wa.gov.au
Website: www.eventscorp.com.au

• January-February

Perth International Arts Festival

Perth International Arts Festival is one of the highlights of Perth's cultural events calendar. Every year, the whole city comes alive with national, international and aboriginal dance, music and visual art performances. Highlights in 2001 included performances by the Perth Theatre Company and the Merce Cunningham Dance Company, as well as concerts from the WA Symphony Orchestra. This internationally-acclaimed festival has won the Western Australian Tourism Award for Best Major Festival and Special Event on three occasions (1996, 1998 and 1999) and is the longest-running and biggest international arts festival in the Southern Hemisphere.

Event Organiser

Perth International Arts Festival, University of Western Australia, Nedlands, Western Australia, WA 6907, Australia
Tel: (08) 9380 8634. Fax: (08) 9380 8555.
E-mail: info@perthfestival.com.au
Website: www.perthfestival.com.au

Venue

Various venues across Perth.

Transport

Air: Perth International Airport. **Rail:** Train: Perth Station or East Perth Terminal. **Road:** Coach: Greyhound and Westrail operate services to the East Perth Terminal (from across Australia). Car: Great Eastern Highway (from Fremantle and Kalgoorlie-Boulder); Wanneroo Road (from Geraldton); Southwestern Highway (from Bunbury); Albany Highway (from Albany).

Sydney

Tourist Information

Sydney Visitor Centre
106 George Street, The Rocks, Sydney, NSW 2000, Australia
Tel: (02) 9255 1788 *or* 132 077. Fax: (02) 9931 1490.
E-mail: visitmail@tourism.nsw.gov.au
Website: www.tourism.nsw.gov.au

• January

Australia Day

Australia was formally colonised by the British First Fleet, which arrived at Sydney Cove, led by Captain Arthur Phillip, on 26 January 1788. By the early 19th century there are records of celebratory events being held to mark the occasion, including formal dinners, bonfires and the consumption of large amounts of alcohol. The first official national celebrations were held on 26 January 1818, the 30th anniversary of formal colonisation, when a salute of 30 guns was fired from Dawes Point, followed by a ball at Government House. Since then, the celebrations have expanded to encompass the whole nation, although Sydney remains the focal point. In the last few decades, the more formal, imperialistic *Australia Day* celebrations, such as the military parades and the re-enactment of the First Fleet landing, have been replaced with more light-hearted events recognising Australia's cultural heritage and multicultural population. Typical Sydney celebrations are many and varied, and range from free access to the city's museums to citywide galas, parades, concerts and street theatre. *Hyde Park* is the focus for family events, featuring music, wine tasting, face painting and children's entertainment, whilst The Rocks play host to jazz and blues concerts and puppet shows. The grand finale is the *Australia Day Fireworks Spectacular* which takes place at Cockle Bay, Darling Harbour at 2100.

Event Organiser

Australia Day Council of New South Wales, PO Box R1193, Royal Exchange, Sydney NSW 1225, Australia
Tel: (02) 8274 2044. Fax: (02) 8274 2055.
E-mail: melrosk@adc.nsw.gov.au
Website: www.adc.nsw.gov.au

Venue

Various locations across Sydney.

Transport

Air: Sydney Kingsford Smith International Airport. **Rail:** Train: Sydney Central Station. Cityrail: Circular Quay (to The Rocks), Town Hall (to Darling Harbour), St James (to Hyde Park), Martin Place (to Hyde Park). **Road:** Car: Hume Highway or Princes Highway (from Melbourne); Pacific Highway (from Brisbane).

Sydney Festival

The *Sydney Festival* has been a leading light in the Australian and international arts scene for over 25 years. Every year over 2 million spectators flock to venues as diverse as the *Sydney Opera House*, the *Royal Botanic Gardens* and the *Museum of Sydney* to enjoy hundreds of performances of theatre, jazz, classical music, dance, opera, cinema and puppet shows. There are also visual art exhibitions, complemented by events ranging from guided tours of Sydney's corporate art collections to lectures by visiting artists. Past performers at the Sydney Festival have included Nederlands Dans Theater, the Russian Philharmonic Orchestra and the Catalan theatre group Els Comediants, famous for its performances at the opening of the 1992 Barcelona Olympic Games. The Sydney Festival lasts for three weeks and incorporates elements of the city's *Australia Day* celebrations, such as the free concerts in *Hyde Park* and the fireworks display in *Darling Harbour* on 26 January.

Event Organiser

Sydney Festival, 36-38 Young Street, Sydney, NSW 2000, Australia
Tel: (02) 8248 6500. Fax: (02) 8248 6599.
E-mail: mail@sydneyfestival.org.au
Website: www.sydneyfestival.org.au

Venue

Various venues across Sydney.

Transport

Air: Sydney Kingsford Smith International Airport. **Rail:** Train: Sydney Central Station. Cityrail: Circular Quay (to Museum of Sydney, Sydney Opera House or Royal Botanic Gardens); Town Hall (to Darling Harbour); St

James (to Hyde Park or Royal Botanic Gardens); Martin Place (to Hyde Park or Royal Botanic Gardens). **Road:** Car: Hume Highway or Princes Highway (from Melbourne); Pacific Highway (from Brisbane).

• February-March

Sydney Gay and Lesbian Mardi Gras

Sydney Gay and Lesbian Mardi Gras began in 1978 as a parade down the city's Oxford Street to mark *International Gay Solidarity Day* (in commemoration of the famous Stonewall Riots in New York's Greenwich Village). The Mardi Gras name was adopted the following year and the event steadily grew in size and status during the 1980s and 1990s to become the largest gay carnival in the world, lasting for three weeks and attracting hundreds of thousands of revellers. Over 150 gay and lesbian community groups spend months creating the colourful floats and outrageous costumes for the Oxford Street parade on the final Saturday. Concerts, art exhibitions and theatre performances, all showcasing gay and lesbian talent and highlighting issues relating to sexuality, are held throughout the three weeks.

Event Organiser

Sydney Gay and Lesbian Mardi Gras, 21-23 Erskineville Road, Erskineville 2042, NSW 2043, Australia
Tel: (02) 9557 4332.
E-mail: mardigras@mardigras.com.au
Website: www.mardigras.com.au

Venue

Various venues across Sydney.

Transport

Air: Sydney Kingsford Smith International Airport. **Rail:** Train: Sydney Central Station. **Road:** Bus: 380 or 382 to Oxford Street (from Circular Quay). Car: Hume Highway or Princes Highway (from Melbourne); Pacific Highway (from Brisbane).

Austria

Vienna

Tourist Information

Wien Tourismus (Vienna Tourist Board)
Obere Augartenstrasse 40, 1025 Vienna, Austria
Tel: (01) 2111 4222. Fax: (01) 216 8492.
E-mail: wtv@info.wien.at
Website: www.info.wien.at *or*
www.vienna-tourism.at

Need more information on Austria?
Consult the *World Travel Guide*

• May-June

Vienna Festival

The *Vienna Festival* comprises performances of dance, music and theatre, as well as displays of visual art. The festival is renowned for its thought-provoking programmes: in 2001, the music theatre programme focused on the topic of xenophobia and foreignness and included the Chinese opera 'Mudan Ting' (The Peony Pavilion) by Tang Xianzu. It also featured Luigi Nono's opera 'Intolleranza', which looks at the existential struggle of the individual in a socially and culturally foreign environment. Other acclaimed past performances have included Peter Brook's 'Tragedy of Hamlet', which looks at Shakespeare's work in a new light by encompassing many different cultures and continents, and a production of the South African drama 'Le Costume', by Can Themba, which tells the story of a group of artists seeking refuge from apartheid in a district of Johannesburg. Musicians from around the world, including the Arnold Schoenberg Choir and the Vienna Symphony Orchestra, open the festival with a free concert in the *Rathausplatz* (Town Hall Square).

Event Organiser

Wiener Festwochen (Vienna Festival Office), Lehárgasse 11/1/1/6, 1060 Vienna, Austria
Tel: (01) 589 220. Fax: (01) 589 2249.
E-mail: festwochen@festwochen.at
Website: www.festwochen.at

Venue

Various venues across Vienna.

Transport

Air: Vienna International Airport. **Rail:** Train: Westbahnhof Station. Underground: Rathaus (to Rathausplatz). **Road:** Car: A1 (from Linz, Salzburg and Western Europe); A2 (from Graz, Klagenfurt or Italy); A4 (from Bratislava or Budapest); A22 (from Prague).

• June-September

Vienna Music Film Festival

This highly popular film festival, which was first held in 1991, brings the very best in music cinema to Vienna each summer. The open-air programme includes dance, music and opera films, many of which are shown in Austria for the first time at the festival, and every year there are new innovations as well as old favourites. The 2000 edition featured music by J S Bach, Leonard Bernstein and Kurt Weill; S4C Wales presented six well-known opera arias on screen using the latest in animation technology and there was also a screening of 'Swan Lake'. Recent festivals have also seen the introduction of an even bigger screen with improved audiovisual quality. Films begin at dusk (around 2100) every evening. Many food stalls are set up around the auditorium as part of the festival to enable filmgoers and passers-by to enjoy mouthwatering dishes from around the world.

Event Organiser

Stadt Wien Marketing Service GmbH, Kolingasse 11/13, 1090 Vienna, Austria
Tel: (01) 3198 2000. Fax: (01) 3198 20082.
E-mail: info@wien2000.at
Website: www.wien-event.at

Venue

Rathausplatz (Town Hall Square).

Transport

Air: Vienna International Airport. **Rail:** Train: Westbahnhof Station. Underground: Rathaus (to Rathausplatz). **Road:** Car: A1 (from Linz, Salzburg and Western Europe); A2 (from Graz, Klagenfurt or Italy); A4 (from Bratislava or Budapest); A22 (from Prague).

• November-December

Magic of Advent in Vienna

Vienna's Christmas market, held each year in front of the town hall, is the perfect way to stock up on presents and soak up the festive atmosphere. There are over 140 stalls to browse and plenty to eat and drink, including candied fruit, candyfloss, maroni (roasted chestnuts) and the traditional Austrian winter warmer, *Glühwein* (mulled wine). Children will enjoy the Christmas workshop in the Volkshalle (assembly hall) of the town hall, where they can bake Christmas cookies and make their own gifts, or try out the latest games. There is an exhibition on Christmas traditions in other European countries, as well as a life-size nativity scene, and every Sunday during Advent, choirs from around the world sing Christmas carols inside the town hall. In the park next to the town halls there are pony rides and a merry-go-round to enjoy. All the attractions are open 0900-1900 Monday-Sunday until 23 December and 0900-1700 on 24 December.

Event Organiser

Wienwerbepool-City Marketing, Breitenfurter Strasse 513, 1230 Vienna, Austria
Tel: (01) 888 9933. Fax: (01) 889 8707.
Website: www.christkindlmarkt.at

Venue

Town Hall Square (Rathausplatz).

Transport

Air: Vienna International Airport. **Rail:** Train: Westbahnhof Station. Underground: Rathaus. **Road:** Car: A1 (from Linz, Salzburg and Western Europe); A2 (from Graz, Klagenfurt or Italy); A4 (from Bratislava or Budapest); A22 (from Prague).

Belgium

Brussels

Tourist Information

Tourist Information Brussels (TIB)
Hôtel de Ville, Grande-Place, 1000 Brussels, Belgium
Tel: (02) 513 8940. Fax: (02) 514 4538.
E-mail: tourism.brussels@tib.be

• December-January

Brussels on Ice

The *Grand' Place* has been the social and economic heart of Brussels since the Middle Ages and is flanked by lavish Gothic and Renaissance buildings which once served as guildhouses and now house museums, coffee shops and restaurants. It is turned into a giant ice rink over the Christmas period, allowing visitors and locals to skate in a magical open-air setting to the sounds of festive music.

Event Organiser

VO Communication, 342 chaussée d'Alsemberg, 1190 Brussels, Belgium
Tel: (02) 346 5949. Fax: (02) 346 3074.
E-mail: info@vocommunication.com
Website: www.vocommunication.com

Venue

Grand' Place.

Transport

Air: Brussels International Airport. **Rail:** Train: Bruxelles-Central, Bruxelles-Midi or Bruxelles-Nord stations. Underground: De Brouckère or Gare Centrale/Centraal Station. Tram: 23, 52, 55, 56 or 81 to Bourse. **Road:** Car: E19 (from Antwerp); E40 (from Ghent); E17 (from Ostend).

• July

Ommegang Royal Pageant

Ommegang is a colourful reconstruction of the pageant held in 1549 in honour of Emperor Charles V, his son Don Philip and his sisters Eleanor of Austria and Mary of Hungary. Although the festival was essentially a religious event in Medieval Brussels, today's Ommegang celebrations are resolutely secular. The action starts in the *Grand' Place* in the centre of Brussels as the royal guests, some of whom are descended from those present in 1549, take their places and the crossbow men surround the statue of *Notre Dame du Sablon*, their patron saint. Once the peasant dancers and performers have led the way, the Emperor walks the streets past the Gothic and Renaissance façades of the old guildhouses surrounded by horses, dogs, flagbearers, ladies-in-waiting and a falconry train. The costumes, which are lavish reproductions of the originals, can be up to 6m

(23 feet) in height and the whole event has all the pomp and circumstance of the original pageant. The parade leaves the Sablon statue in the Grand' Place at 2050 and parades through rue Lebeau and other streets until it reaches rue Charles Buls.

Event Organiser

Ommegang-Brussels, rue des Tanneurs 180, 1000 Brussels, Belgium
Tel: (02) 512 1961. Fax: (02) 502 6835 *or* 548 0444 (to book tickets).
E-mail: info@ommegang-brussels.be
Website: www.ommegang-brussels.be

Venue

Sablon statue (Grand' Place) at 2050, then parades through rue Lebeau, rue Marché aux Herbes, rue Tabora, rue Midi, rue Lombard, rue Etuve and rue Charles Buls.

Transport

Air: Brussels International Airport. **Rail:** Train: Bruxelles-Central, Bruxelles-Midi or Bruxelles-Nord stations. Underground: De Brouckère or Gare Centrale/Centraal Station. Tram: 23, 52, 55, 56 or 81 to Bourse. **Road:** Car: E19 (from Antwerp); E40 (from Ghent); E17 (from Ostend).

• December

European Christmas Market

The *Grand' Place* has been Brussels's main square since the Middle Ages. For one week in December each year, the square has a very special atmosphere and a truly European flavour with the arrival of the Christmas market. There are hundreds of stalls to browse, with gift ideas from many countries. The culinary choices are endless – visitors can feast on Italian *panettone* (Christmas cake) or German speciality sausage, whilst enjoying any number of variations on mulled wine: Scandinavian *glögg*, Austrian *Glühwein* or French *vin chaud*. Alternatively, there are numerous varieties of Belgian beer available at the many bars surrounding the Grand' Place. There is also entertainment from choirs from around Europe who perform traditional festive songs. The market is open 1100-1900 Monday to Thursday and 1100-2100 Friday to Sunday.

Event Organiser

For more information on the European Christmas Market, contact Tourist Information Brussels (see **Tourist Information** above).

Venue

Grand' Place.

Transport

Air: Brussels International Airport. **Rail:** Train: Bruxelles-Central, Bruxelles-Midi or Bruxelles-Nord stations. Underground: De Brouckère or Gare Centrale/Centraal Station. Tram: 23, 52, 55, 56 or 81 to Bourse. **Road:** Car: E19 (from Antwerp); E40 (from Ghent); E17 (from Ostend).

Brazil

Rio de Janeiro

Tourist Information

Empresa de Turismo do Município do Rio de Janeiro SA (RioTur, City of Rio de Janeiro Tourism Authority)
Rua da Assembléia, 10-9º andar, 20119, Centro, Rio de Janeiro, Brazil
Tel: (021) 217 7575. Fax: (021) 531 1872.
E-mail: riotur.riotur@pcrj.rio.gov.br
Website: www.riodejaneiro-turismo.com.br

• December-January

New Year's Eve

Rio de Janeiro is said to be one of the most exciting and happening places in the world at New Year (known locally as *Reveillon*). Hundreds of thousands of people gather on the city's beaches every year on 31 December to watch the giant firework display at midnight and to dance the night away. The main festivities take place on Copacabana Beach, with live music and DJ sets continuing through the night. There are also events in major hotels in the city, as well as in the many bars and restaurants. The dancing and partying goes on into the small hours, with many people staying up all night to drink a champagne breakfast at dawn.

Event Organiser

For more information on New Year's Eve, contact RioTur (see **Tourist Information** above).

Venue

The main focus is Copacabana Beach.

Transport

Air: Rio de Janeiro International Airport. **Rail:** Train: Estacao D Pedra II or Estacao Barao de Maua stations. **Road:** Coach: Novo Rio Rodoviaria Coach Station. Car: BR116 (from Sao Paulo); BR040 (from Brasilia).

• February-March

Rio de Janeiro Carnival

Rio de Janeiro Carnival is one of the biggest festivals in the world, attracting hundreds of thousands of tourists and locals every year who come to participate in this incredibly lively event. Carnival is undoubtedly the biggest cultural event in Rio and an annual orgy of over-the-top fun and frivolity. The event originates from the Easter revelry tradition that took place in Portugal in the 15th century. Its date varies from year to year, usually ranging from late February to early March. It starts officially on a Saturday and goes through to the following Wednesday (*quarta-feira de cinza* – Ash Wednesday). There are many events across the city, including street parades, carnival balls and the samba school parade.

Event Organiser

For more information on Rio de Janeiro Carnival, contact RioTur (see **Tourist Information** above).

Venue

Various venues across Rio de Janeiro.

Transport

Air: Rio de Janeiro International Airport. **Rail:** Train: Estacao D Pedra II or Estacao Barao de Maua stations. **Road:** Coach: Novo Rio Rodoviaria Coach Station. Car: BR116 (from Sao Paulo); BR040 (from Brasilia).

Canada

Calgary

Tourist Information

Calgary Convention & Visitors Bureau
Suite 200, 238 11th Avenue, SE Calgary, AB T2G 0X8, Canada
Tel: (403) 263 8510. Fax: (403) 262 3809.
E-mail: destination@visitor.calgary.ab.ca
Website: www.tourismcalgary.com

• July

Calgary Stampede

Calgary Stampede is one of the world's biggest celebrations of the cowboy way of life and attracted 1,218,851 visitors in 2000. The event lasts for ten days in July and includes an annual rodeo, with bull riding, bareback bronco riding and wild horse racing, as well as various stage performances, chuckwagon (chariot) races, agriculture and livestock displays and live music on the Coke Stage. This annual event dates back to 1886 and has grown to become an enormous celebration of all things related to being a cowboy. Highlights in 2000 included the Heavy Horse Show performance and the World Championship for Marching Show Bands.

Event Organiser

Calgary Stampede, PO Box 1060, Station M, Calgary, AB T2P 2K8, Canada
Tel: (800) 661 1260 (toll free USA and Canada only).
E-mail: sales@calgarystampede.com
Website: www.calgary-stampede.com

Venue

Stampede Park, Calgary.

Transport

Air: Calgary International Airport. **Rail:** Train: C-train routes 201 to Brentwood in the north (from Anderson Road in the south) or 202 to Tenth Street in the west (from Whitehorn in the east). **Road:** Car: The Trans-Canada highway, Hwy-1, becomes 16th Avenue as it passes through Calgary (from Banff, Kamloops and Vancouver to the west and Medicine Hat and Regina to the east). Hwy-2 runs through the city centre, where it becomes Macleod Trail (from Lethbridge to the south and Edmonton to the north).

Montréal

Tourist Information

Centre Infotouriste (Tourisme Montréal) (Montréal Tourist Information)
1001 rue du Square-Dorchester, Montréal H3B 1G2, Canada
Tel: (514) 873 2015. Fax: (514) 864 3838.
E-mail: info@tourisme.gouv.qc.ca
Website: www.tourisme-montreal.org

• June-July

Montréal International Jazz Festival

The 23rd *Montréal International Jazz Festival* will be held in the city in 2002. The first jazz festival was held in Montréal in 1980 and attracted 12,000 spectators. Today, the event is one of the biggest jazz festivals in the world, attracting around 100,000 spectators every year to see over 120 concerts, ranging from traditional jazz through to blues and reggae. Top performers in 2001 included Michael Brecker, Oscar Peterson, Roy Hargrove, George Benson and John McLaughlin.

Event Organiser

Montréal International Jazz Festival, 822 Sherbrooke Street East, Montréal, Quebec H2L 1K4, Canada
Tel: (514) 523 3378. Fax: (514) 525 8033.
E-mail: commentaires_jazz@equipespectra.ca
Website: www.Montréaljazzfest.com

Venue

Concert halls and cafés across Montréal.

Transport

Air: Montréal Dorval International Airport. **Rail**: Train: Gare Centrale (Central Station). **Road:** Car: Hwy-20 and Hwy-40 (the Trans-Canada Highway) (from Québec City to the east and Toronto (via Hwy-401) and Ottawa (via Hwy-417) from the west); US Interstate 87 (from New York City) becomes Hwy-15 at the border, south of Montréal.

Toronto

Tourist Information

Tourism Toronto
Suite 590, 207 Queens Quay West, Toronto, ON M5J 1A7, Canada
Tel: (416) 203 2600. Fax: (416) 203 6753 *or* (800) 363 1990 (toll free USA and Canada only).

E-mail: toronto@torcvb.com
Website: www.toronto.com

• February

Toronto Winterfest

Every February, Toronto organises three days of family entertainment aimed at banishing the winter blues. Events are held both indoors and outside, and include circus acts, storytelling, musical concerts, theatre productions, ice-skating shows, dance and cultural exhibitions. There are creative hands-on activities for both children and adults at the Civic Centre and the Toronto Public Library Auditorium, including colouring contests, baking cookies, origami and pyjama parties. In Mel Lastman Square in the centre of Toronto, there are daily parades featuring street entertainers. A giant ice sculpture is exhibited at the top of the square throughout the *Winterfest*. Nathan Phillips Square plays host to steel bands, food festivals, acrobat displays and virtual reality games.

Event Organiser

Toronto City Hall, 100 Queen Street, Ninth Floor East Tower M5H 2N2, Toronto, Canada
Tel: (416) 395 0490. Fax: (416) 395 0278.
E-mail: Spevmktg@city.toronto.on.ca
Website: www.city.toronto.on.ca/special_events/winterfest

Venue

Various venues across Toronto.

Transport

Air: Toronto Lester B Pearson International Airport. **Rail:** Train: Union Station. Underground: North Yorke Centre (to Mel Lastman Square or Civic Centre); Queen Station (to Nathan Phillips Square); Bloor (to Toronto Public Library). **Road:** Car: Hwy-401 (from London, Windsor or Montréal); Queen Elizabeth Expressway (from Niagara Falls or Hamilton).

• October

International Festival of Authors

Toronto's *International Festival of Authors* is a literary treat for both adults and children. Every year, writers of poetry, fiction, drama and biography converge on the city's Harbourfront Centre to give readings, lectures, talks and seminars and to chat with audiences. The festival invites both new writers and international celebrities – the line-up for the 21st edition in 2000 included J K Rowling, Joanna Trollope, Candace Bushnell, Margaret Atwood, Maeve Binchy, Carlos Fuentes, Susan Sontag and Blake Morrison.

Event Organiser

Harbourfront Reading Series, 235 Queens Quay West, M5J 2G8 Toronto, Canada
Tel: (416) 973 4000. Fax: (416) 954 0366.
Website: www.city.toronto.on.ca/special_events/winterfest

Venue

Various venues across Toronto.

Transport

Air: Toronto Lester B Pearson International Airport. **Rail:** Train: Union Station. Tram: 510 (from Union Station). **Road:** Car: Hwy-401 (from London, Windsor or Montréal); Queen Elizabeth Expressway (from Niagara Falls or Hamilton).

Vancouver

Tourist Information

Tourism Vancouver – Tourist Information Centre
Waterfront Centre, Plaza Level, 200 Burrard Street, Vancouver, BC V6C 3L6, Canada
Tel: (604) 683 2000. Fax: (604) 682 6839.
Website: www.tourismvancouver.com

• May-June

Vancouver International Children's Festival

Vancouver International Children's Festival was first held in 1977 to entertain, educate and inspire children and young people from Vancouver and the surrounding area. It comprises seven days of activities and events in Vanier Park, a scenic setting on Vancouver's waterfront. Every year, artists come from across Canada and around the world to entertain visitors through performances of theatre, circus, puppetry, jazz and pop music. There are colourful daily parades, as well as interactive exhibitions and a variety of hands-on activities such as kite-making, music sessions, exotic crafts, stilt-walking workshops, pottery classes and imaginative games for younger children. Special performances are staged for older children and young people, encouraging them to think about the world they live in and their place in society, whilst younger children can play in a giant sandbox full of toys.

Event Organiser

Festival Communications, 317A Cambie Street, Vancouver, BC V6B 2N4, Canada
Tel: (604) 220 9118. Fax: (604) 687 7167.
E-mail: kdm@festcom.com
Website: www.vancouverchildrensfestival.com

Venue

Vanier Park.

Transport

Air: Vancouver International Airport. **Water:** Ferry: False Creek services (from Granville Island, Aquatic Centre or Science World along the waterfront). **Rail:** Train: Pacific Central Station. **Road:** Bus: 22 (to Cornwall and Cypress streets). Car: Trans-Canada Hwy-

1 (from Calgary, Toronto or Montréal); I-5 (from Seattle); Hwy-99 (from Whistler).

People's Republic of China

Hong Kong

Tourist Information

Hong Kong Tourism Board
9-11th Floor, Citicorp Centre, 18 Whitfield Road, North Point, Hong Kong, People's Republic of China
Tel: 2807 6543. Fax: 2806 0303.
E-mail: info@discoverhongkong.com
Website: www.discoverhongkong.com

• February-March

Hong Kong Arts Festival

Hong Kong Arts Festival is one of the most important cultural events in Southeast Asia. The festival, which is the leading arts event in Hong Kong, features numerous performances from international stars of theatre, opera, art, dance and classical and popular music. Highlights in 2001 included performances by the legendary Russian dancer Mikhail Baryshnikov, the French-born cellist Yo-Yo Ma and the Greek singer Nana Miskouri. Every year, artists from around the world flock into Hong Kong to take part in this internationally-renowned event.

Event Organiser
Hong Kong Arts Festival Society Ltd, 12/F Hong Kong Arts Centre, 2 Harbour Road, Wanchai, Hong Kong, People's Republic of China
Tel: 2824 3555. Fax: 2824 3798.
E-mail: afgen@hkaf.org
Website: www.hk.artsfestival.org

Venue
Various venues across Hong Kong including Hong Kong Cultural Centre, Hong Kong City Hall, Hong Kong Academy for the Performing Arts (HKAPA), Hong Kong Arts Centre, Sha Tin Town Hall, Tsuen Wan Town Hall, Tuen Mun Town Hall and Kwai Tsing Theatre.

Transport
Air: Hong Kong International Airport. **Rail:** Train: Hong Kong Station. **Road:** Bus: HKAPA can be reached on First Buses 781, M21, 720 or 722, or on City Buses 29R or 70; City Hall can be reached on Kowloon Bus 603, City Buses 1, 3B, 6, 47A, 61, 70 or 788 or on First Buses 2, 13, 15, 88, M590 or 720.

• April

Hong Kong International Film Festival

Hong Kong International Film Festival, which was first held in 1977, is an enormous annual event in Hong Kong's calendar. In 2000, during the 24th film festival, 232 films were screened in the city, including film premieres from Japan, Iran and China. The festival is a non-competitive event which comprises of four main areas: Asian Cinema, Hong Kong Panorama, World Cinema and Special Section Contributed by Hong Kong Film Archive. In 2000, 145,330 people attended the festival to watch 340 screenings, a substantial increase on the 18,624 people who attended the first film festival in Hong Kong in 1977.

Event Organiser
Leisure and Cultural Services Department, Head Film Programmes Office, Level 7, Administration Building, Hong Kong Cultural Centre, 10 Salisbury Road, Tsimshatsui, Hong Kong, People's Republic of China
Tel: 2734 2903. Fax: 2366 5206.
E-mail: hkiff@hkiff.org.hk
Website: www.hkiff.org.hk

Venue
Various cinemas across Hong Kong.

Transport
Air: Hong Kong International Airport. **Rail:** Train: Hong Kong Station. **Road:** Car: The most accessible places to drive to are Lantua Island, Macau and Guangzhou; from here visitors must take a ferry trip to get to Hong Kong.

Cuba

Havana

Tourist Information

Ministerio de Turismo (Ministry of Tourism)
Calle 19, No 710, Entre Paseo y A, Vedado, Havana, Cuba
Tel: (07) 330 545. Fax: (07) 334 086.
E-mail: promo@mintur.mit.cma.net
Website: www.cubatravel.cu

• July-August

Havana Carnival

The Cuban capital is well known for its party spirit, and carnival time, which has been reinstated after the hardships suffered by the communist country since the collapse of the USSR, promises particularly colourful celebrations as the Cuban holiday period begins in earnest. The festivities begin on a Friday night in late July with a gun salute fired from the San Pedro de la

Cabana fortress. The event then continues every weekend until mid-August, with shows, dancing, fireworks, floats and parades, food and drink all accompanied by traditional Cuban rhythms and Latino pop. Each Havana neighbourhood spends months designing costumes and floats for its own parties and parades, whilst the *Malecón* (seafront) is the venue for fairs and concerts.

Event Organiser

For more information on the Havana Carnival, contact the Ministry of Tourism (see **Tourist Information** above).

Venue

Malecón (seafront) and across Havana.

Transport

Air: José Marti International Airport. **Rail:** Train: Central, Egido y Arsenal Station. **Road:** Bus: *Guaguas* and *camellos*, which are Havana buses, run to all areas of Havana. Car: Via Blanca (from Varadero); Autopista (from Ciego de Avila or Pinar del Rio); Carreterra Central (runs across Cuba from east to west, passing through Havana). Taxi: This is the best way to reach locations around Havana.

Czech Republic

Prague

Tourist Information

Pražské informační služby (Prague Information Service – PIS)
Betlemske namesti 2, 116 98 Prague 1, Czech Republic
Tel: (02) 264 022. Fax: (02) 264 023.
E-mail: tourinfo@pis.cz
Website: www.pis.cz

• May

Prague International Marathon

Prague International Marathon was first held in 1995, with 980 runners taking part in the main event and 10,000 runners taking part in a non-competitive race covering 4.8km (3 miles). More than 3000 runners take part in the marathon every year, with a further 13,000 and 12,000 respectively taking part in a City Run and Family Run. This year, the 2001 marathon was won by Andrew Sambu of Tanzania (men's) and Maura Viceconte of Italy (women's). Spectators line the historic streets of Prague during the event, cheering on the competitors. There are also concerts and street entertainment, with music including jazz, classical, blues, reggae and rock and roll. The marathon starts at 0900 in Pařížská Street and finishes in Old Town Square.

Event Organiser

Prague International Marathon, Záhoranského 3, 120 00 Prague 2, Czech Republic
Tel: (02) 2491 9209. Fax: (02) 2492 3355.
E-mail: marathon@pim.cz
Website: www.pim.cz

Venue

Streets of Prague, passing over Charles Bridge.

Transport

Air: Prague Ruzyně International Airport. **Rail:** Train: Hlavní nádraží Station (Prague Station). Underground: Staromestká. **Road:** Coach: Praha-Florenc Coach Station or Želivského coach park. Car: E55 (from Dresden or Berlin, Germany); E67 (from Warsaw or Wroclaw, Poland); E50 (from Paris).

• September-October

Prague Autumn International Music Festival

Prague Autumn International Music Festival, which takes place in Prague every year, is one of the most important classical music events in Eastern Europe. The city is famous for its orchestras and boasts two of the finest in the world: Prague Philharmonic Orchestra and Prague Symphony Orchestra. Highlights of the festival in 2000 included the Rossini Gala, performed by Prague Philharmonic Orchestra, the Gala Mozart, performed by Mozarteum Orchester Salzburg and Mozart in Concert, performed by the Prague Chamber Orchestra. In 2001, the world-renowned Moscow Philharmonic Orchestra will tour Europe as part of the festival and will also perform in Warsaw (Poland), Bratislava (Slovak Republic), Villach (Austria), Meran and Verona (Italy), Besançon (France) and Zagreb (Croatia) in September, before performing in Prague at the beginning of October. Many of the festival's events take place in Dvorak Hall in Rudolfinum, which is home to Prague Philharmonic Orchestra, and overlooks the River Vltava. Located next to the famous *Mánesuv Bridge*, the venue is regarded by many to be one of the most beautiful concert venues in Eastern Europe.

Event Organiser

Prague Autumn Musical Management, Příbenická St 20, 13000 Prague 3, Czech Republic
Tel: (02) 627 8740 *or* 627 8742. Fax: (02) 627 8642.
E-mail: festivals@pragueautumn.cz *or* tickets@pragueautumn.cz
Website: www.pragueautumn.cz

Venue

Concert halls in Prague, including Dvorak Hall in Rudolfinum, Smetana Hall in the Municipal House, State Opera Prague, St Simon and Judas Church, Lucerna and Grand Hotel Pupp Karlovy Vary.

Transport

Air: Prague Ruzyně International Airport. **Rail:** Train: Hlavní nádraží Station (Prague Station). Underground: Staromestská or Námesti Republiky. **Road:** Bus: 207 (Starometská). Car: E55 (from Dresden or Berlin,

Germany); E67 (from Warsaw or Wroclaw, Poland); E50 (from Paris, France). Visitors should note that the historic centre of Prague is pedestrianised.

• November-December

International Festival of Advent & Christmas Music

The *International Festival of Advent & Christmas Music*, which was first held in Prague eleven years ago, begins on the first weekend during Advent. During the festival, there are performances by various amateur choirs, including entries to the competition from women's choirs, men's choirs, small mixed chamber choirs, large mixed choirs and children's choirs. The choirs perform Advent and Christmas music of their choice, either a capella or with instrumental accompaniment. The competition is judged by experts in the field, both from the Czech Republic and abroad. Winners are judged on their choice of compositions and programme structure, technical level of interpretation and general artistic impression. At the end of the competition, there is singing in the *Old Town Square*, where Christmas and Advent songs are sung. There is also a competition to win the Petr Eben Prize; entrants perform a composition which has been written especially for the occasion by Petr Eben himself, who is one of the main judges.

Event Organiser

Or Fea AS, Dlouhá 10, Prague 1 110 00, Czech Republic
Tel: (02) 232 1949. Fax: (02) 232 7862.
E-mail: orfea@orfea.cz
Website: www.orfea.cz

Venue

Old Town Square in the centre of Prague.

Transport

Air: Prague Ruzyně International Airport. **Rail:** Train: Hlavní nádraží Station (Prague Station). Underground: Staromestká. **Road:** Coach: Praha-Florenc Coach Station or Želivského coach park. Car: E55 (from Dresden or Berlin, Germany); E67 (from Warsaw or Wroclaw, Poland); E50 (from Paris, France). Visitors should note that the historic centre of Prague is pedestrianised.

Denmark

Copenhagen

Tourist Information

Wonderful Copenhagen Tourist Information
Gl Kongevej 1, 1610 Copenhagen V, Denmark
Tel: 7022 2442. Fax: 7022 2452.
E-mail: woco@woco.dk
Website: www.woco.dk

• June-July

Roskilde Festival

Roskilde Festival, which is one of the biggest rock and pop music festivals in Europe, celebrated its 31st birthday in 2001. The festival began in 1971, when it featured approximately 20 bands. Today, as many as 170 bands perform at the event on a total of seven stages, watched by around 70,000 spectators. Highlights in 2001 included performances from Bob Dylan, Beck, P J Harvey, Queens of the Stone Age, Robbie Williams and Neil Young, whilst recent performers at the festival have included Blondie, David Bowie, Blur, REM, Primal Scream and Monster Magnet. Any profit made by the festival organisers is donated to support humanitarian, cultural and non-profit making initiatives.

Event Organiser

Roskilde Festival, Havsteensvej 11, 4000 Roskilde, Denmark
Tel: 4636 6613. Fax: 4632 1499.
E-mail: bigbox@roskilde-festival.dk
Website: www.roskilde-festival.dk

Venue

Roskilde Festival ground, which is 35km (20 miles) from Copenhagen city centre.

Transport

Air: Copenhagen Airport. **Rail:** Train: Trains to the festival's own train station which is located in the middle of the festival grounds (from Roskilde Station). **Road:** Bus: Services to the festival grounds (from Roskilde Station).

• July

Copenhagen Jazz Festival

Copenhagen Jazz Festival sees around 600 concerts by Danish and international jazz artists in the city. Many concerts are performed in the city's most historic streets and squares, as well as along the banks of the canals. Clubs and small cafés in the city play host to a varied programme, ranging from New Orleans jazz and swing to experimental music. 'Giant Jazz', which is held in the old Circus Building, is one of the main events of the festival. There are also concerts at the Tivoli Gardens which attract a large audience. As well as top performances from artists such as Keith Jarret and Sonny Rollins, there are also street parades every day, concerts and workshops for children, and other events such as midnight concerts at the National Museum. In 2000, more than 300 musicians performed during the festival, with around 100,000 people enjoying the music and other events in the city.

Event Organiser

Copenhagen Jazz Festival, Nytorv 3, 1450 Copenhagen, Denmark
Tel: 3393 2013. Fax: 3393 2024.

E-mail: info@jazzfestival.dk
Website: www.jazzfestival.dk

Venue

Various venues in Copenhagen, including Copenhagen JazzHouse, Circus Building and Tivoli Gardens.

Transport

Air: Copenhagen Airport. **Rail:** Train: Copenhagen Central Station. S-Bahn: Services to København H Station. **Road:** Bus: Bus 250 to Town Hall Square (from the airport). Car: E47 (from Rodby). Signs to the city centre and the Town Hall.

• August

Copenhagen International Ballet Festival

The 11th *Copenhagen International Ballet Festival* will be held in Frederiksberg, just outside Copenhagen, in August 2001. This summer festival features both classic and new performances from the Copenhagen International Ballet Group, which was founded by Danish ballet dancer Alexander Kølpin. The group consists of principals and members from the New York City Ballet, Ballet Béjart, Lyon Opera Ballet, Royal Danish Ballet, Momix and Hamburg Ballet. The ballets are staged in beautiful outdoor settings, including the courtyard of the *Royal Veterinary and Agricultural University*, where audiences can watch performances under the night sky.

Event Organiser

Copenhagen International Ballet, Stranezejen 451, 2938 Klanpenborg, Denmark
Tel: 3963 4900 or 3325 2107. Fax: 3963 0512.
E-mail: ak@xproduction.com
Website: www.xproduction.com

Venue

Various outdoor venues in Frederiksberg.

Transport

Air: Copenhagen Airport. **Rail:** Train: Copenhagen Central Station. **Road:** Car: E47 to Copenhagen (from Rodby), then E20 to Frederiksberg.

• August-September

Helsinki Festival

Helsinki Festival is a giant performing arts festival, which is held during three weeks in August and September every year. In 2000, more than 300,000 visitors attended the festival to see the extensive programme of orchestral and chamber music, opera, dance, theatre, jazz, rock, art exhibitions and film. The festival opened with a performance of James Joyce's 'Ulysses' in 2000 and saw the 'Three is a Crowd' dance performance by three choreographers. There were also various classical music concerts, dance, circus and theatre events, and numerous exhibitions across the city. The festival reaches its climax with the 'Night of the Arts', when art galleries, museums and bookshops open their doors, free of charge, into the small hours. A marquee called 'Villa' is erected on the shore of Töölönlahti Bay and during 'Art goes Kapakka (AGK)' evenings, an urban mini-festival which has been held in Helsinki five times, theatre, music, poetry and songs are performed in restaurants and bars around the city. Visitors can also try local food during the 'Piazza of Tastes' in the Senate Square, when tents are erected, offering a range of menus, with music playing in the background.

Event Organiser

Helsinki Festival, The Lasipalatsi, Mannerheimintie 22-24, 00100 Helsinki, Finland
Tel: (09) 6126 5100. Fax: (09) 6126 5161.
E-mail: info@helsinkifestival.fi
Website: www.helsinkifestival.fi

Venue

Various venues, including Aurora Park, Finlandia Hall, The Alexander Theatre, Helsinki City Theatre, Senate Square, Huvila Festival Tent, The Savoy Theatre, Kunsthalle Helsinki, Cinema Orion, Bio Rex, Atemeum Hall and Temppeliaukio Church.

Transport

Air: Helsinki-Vantaa Airport. **Rail:** Train: Helsinki Station. **Road:** Car: E18 to Helsinki (from Turku); E12 (from Vaasa); E75 (from Rovaniemi).

Finland

Helsinki

Tourist Information

Helsingin kaupungin matkailu – ja kongressitoimisto (Helsinki City Tourist & Convention Bureau)
Pohjoisesplanadi 19, 00100 Helsinki, Finland
Tel: (09) 169 3757. Fax: (09) 169 3839.
E-mail: tourist.info@hel.fi
Website: www.hel.fi/tourism

France

Avignon

Tourist Information

Office de Tourisme d'Avignon (Avignon Tourist Board)
41 cours Jean Jaurès, 84000 Avignon, France
Tel: (04) 3274 3274. Fax: (04) 9082 9503.
E-mail: information@ot-avignon.fr
Website: www.avignon-tourisme.com

• July-September

Avignon Festival

The *Avignon Festival* began in 1947 when French actor and director Jean Vilar staged three works that were previously unknown to the French public in the *Palais des Papes* (Popes' Palace) in the historic centre of the city. Since then the festival has become a major cultural event, attracting thousands of visitors and performers from all corners of the globe. The emphasis is on experimental theatre and presenting new theatrical works to the public, many of which then go on tour in France and abroad. Dance and musical theatre also feature in the programme. Avignon is worth visiting at this time of year just for the atmosphere created by the festival – colourful and bizarre parades wind their way through the crowds in the Place du Palais and fire eaters and jugglers entertain visitors and locals in the streets from morning until night. A parallel event called the *Festival Off* allows performers to set up stage wherever they can find space (with permission from the city council), providing an alternative theatre scene.

Event Organiser

Festival d'Avignon, 8 bis rue de Mons, 84000 Avignon, France
Tel: (04) 9027 6656. Fax: (04) 9027 6684.
E-mail: info-doc@festival-avignon.com
Website: info-doc@festival-avignon.com

Venue

Various venues across Avignon.

Transport

Air: Marseille-Provence Airport, Avignon-Caumont Airport or Nîmes-Arles-Camargue Airport. **Rail:** Train: Avignon Station (high-speed TGV services from Paris Gare de Lyon, Montpellier, Lyon and Barcelona, Spain). **Road:** Coach: Services to the coach station on Avenue St Roch. Car: A7 or A9 (from Lyon, Marseille and Nîmes).

• September

Côtes du Rhône Grape Harvest

Avignon is the capital of the Côtes du Rhône, one of the most well-known French wine-producing regions. The wine is harvested at the beginning of September and visitors and locals can taste the results at the many stalls in the square in front of one of the city's most spectacular buildings, the *Palais des Papes* (Popes' Palace). Entertainment is provided around the city as folk groups, jugglers and actors perform for the crowds, and at 1700 the Bacchic confraternities (wine guilds or organisations) parade through the streets in costume, followed by floats bearing barrels of wine. There are also parachutists, films, concerts, shows and exhibitions of painting and crafts to accompany the bacchanalian festivities.

Event Organiser

Compagnons du Ban des Vendanges, Hôtel de Ville, 84045 Avignon, France
Tel: (04) 9016 0032.

Venue

Palais des Papes and various locations across Avignon.

Transport

Air: Marseille-Provence Airport, Avignon-Caumont Airport or Nîmes-Arles-Camargue Airport. **Rail:** Train: Avignon Station (high-speed TGV services from Paris Gare de Lyon, Montpellier, Barcelona and Lyon). **Road:** Coach: Services to the coach station on Avenue St Roch. Car: A7 or A9 (from Lyon, Marseille and Nîmes).

Cannes

Tourist Information

SEMAC (Cannes Tourist Board)
Palais des Festivals, La Croisette, BP 272, 06403 Cannes, France
Tel: (04) 9339 2453. Fax: (04) 9299 8423.
E-mail: semoftou@palais-festivals-cannes
Website: www.cannes-on-line.com

• May

Cannes Film Festival

In 1939, the French government chose Cannes as a suitably sunny and enchanting location for its international film festival. Initially it was merely a chance for wealthy tourists to attend the many parties organised in the luxury villas of Cannes and in the hotels and palaces along La Croisette (the main boulevard), and all films shown at the festival received a prize. Nowadays, an award at Cannes can set actors, producers and directors on the path to fame and fortune, as the festival is one of the premier events in the cultural calendar and the annual rendez-vous of the international film industry. Only film professionals and journalists may attend the actual festival; however, the original air of glamour and prestige is still felt in Cannes during the two weeks, and for many it is a chance to spot the many stars and millionaires who pose in restaurants and along the expensive private beaches of La Croisette.

Event Organiser

Cannes Film Festival, 99 boulevard Malesherbes, 75008 Paris, France
Tel: (01) 4561 6608. Fax: (01) 4561 9761.
E-mail: festival@festival-cannes.fr
Website: www.festival-cannes.fr

Venue

Palais des Festivals et des Congrès.

Transport

Air: Nice-Côte d'Azur International Airport. **Rail:** Train: Cannes Ville Station. **Road:** Bus: 8 (runs along boulevard de la Croisette and stops at Palais-Croisette for the Palais des Festivals) or 7 (from Cannes Ville Station to La Croisette). Car: A8 (from Paris or Nice).

Lyon

Tourist Information

Office du Tourisme et des Congrès du Grand Lyon (Lyon Convention and Visitors Bureau)
Place Bellecour, BP 2254, 69214 Lyon cedex 02, France
Tel: (04) 7277 6969. Fax: (04) 7842 0432.
E-mail: lyoncvb@lyon-france.com
Website: www.lyon-france.com

• December

Festival of Lights

The *Festival of Lights* takes place every year in Lyon, when residents hang lights from their balconies and place candles in their windows, lighting up the city with a thousand lights. The locals congregate in the streets to admire the spectacle on 8 December, which is a religious celebration dating back to 1852 honouring the statue of the Virgin Mary on *Fourvière Hill.* The festival is one of Lyon's most popular and traditional events. During the festivities, there are also a number of music performances throughout the city which is dominated by the *Fourvière Basilica.* During the Franco-Prussian war, Catholics in Lyon promised to build a giant church on Fourvière Hill in honour of the Virgin Mary, if she spared the city from the Prussian enemy. The city was spared and so the church was built in 1896.

Event Organiser

For more information on the Festival of Lights, contact Lyon Convention and Visitors Bureau (see **Tourist Information** above).

Venue

Fourvière Hill and various venues across Lyon.

Transport

Air: Lyon-Saint Exupéry Airport. **Rail:** Underground: Fourvière. **Road:** Car: A6 (from Paris); A7 (from Marseille); A43 (from Geneva, Switzerland); A48 (from Grenoble, Switzerland).

Paris

Tourist Information

L'Office de Tourisme et des Congrès de Paris (Central Tourist Office)
127 avenue des Champs-Elysées, 75008 Paris, France
Tel: (08) 3668 3112. Fax: (01) 4952 5300.
E-mail: info@paris-touristoffice.com
Website: www.paris-touristoffice.com

• May-June

French Tennis Open (Roland Garros)

Tennis first came across the Channel to France at the end of the 19th century and was a popular pursuit among the French upper classes. Various clubs were formed, such as the Racing Club de France and the Stade Français; the first national competition was held in 1891, with the ladies competition following in 1897. Since then, *Roland Garros* (named after a French engineer and fighter pilot shot down during World War I) has become increasingly more commercial. This is one of the grand slam championships and the hall of fame includes most of the big names in the sport – the 2001 singles winners were American Jennifer Capriati, ranked fourth in the world, and Brazilian Gustavo Kuerten, who is currently the world's top player. The international prestige of this tournament and its importance to world tennis, particularly in the run-up to Wimbledon a few weeks later, create an exciting atmosphere.

Event Organiser

Fédération Française de Tennis, 2 avenue Gordon Bennett, 75016 Paris, France
Tel: (01) 4743 4800. Fax: (01) 4743 0494.
Website: www.frenchopen.org

Venue

Roland Garros stadium (Stade Roland Garros) on the edge of the Bois de Boulogne.

Transport

Air: Paris Roissy-Charles de Gaulle Airport or Paris Orly Airport. **Rail:** Train: Paris Gare du Nord (Eurostar). Underground: Porte d'Auteuil. **Road:** Bus: 22, 32, 52, 62, 72, 241 or PC1. Car: A1 (from Lille); A16 (from Boulogne); E60 (from Brussels, Belgium); A62, then A20, A71 and A10 (from Toulouse); A3 (from Roissy-Charles de Gaulle Airport); A4 (from Strasbourg); A6 (from Lyon and Marseille); A13 (from Caen). Access to the car parks is from the Boulevard Périphérique (Porte de Saint-Cloud exit).

• June

Festival of Music

The *Festival of Music* (*Fête de la Musique*) is a nationwide event, although most major concerts take place in Paris;

the city's huge variety of venues makes it an excellent place to catch a performance of virtually anything from classical to reggae. The main events take place in Place de la Bastille in the fourth *arrondissement* (district), the Hôtel des Invalides in the seventh, Place de la République in the third and Parc de la Villette in the 19th. Just wandering the streets is probably the best way to enjoy this festival however, as there is music everywhere – even the *métro* stations have bands playing, as do parks, street corners, churches, cafés and museums.

Event Organiser

ADCEP (Association pour le développement de la création, études et projets), 30 rue René Boulanger, 75010 Paris, France
Tel: (01) 4003 9470. Fax: (01) 4206 6606.
E-mail: adcep@wanadoo.fr
Website: www.fetedelamusique.culture.fr

Venue

Various venues across Paris.

Transport

Air: Paris Roissy-Charles de Gaulle Airport or Paris Orly Airport. **Rail:** Train: Paris Gare du Nord (Eurostar). **Road:** Car: A1 (from Lille); A16 (from Boulogne); E60 (from Brussels, Belgium); A62, then A20, A71 and A10 (from Toulouse); A3 (from Roissy-Charles de Gaulle Airport); A4 (from Strasbourg); A6 (from Lyon and Marseille); A13 (from Caen).

• July

Arrival of the Tour de France

The *Tour de France* is widely acknowledged as the world's toughest cycling competition. Started in 1903 by Henri Desgrange, a French cyclist and journalist, the race covers both flat and mountainous terrain and travels through different regions every year in 20 stages. The 20 teams each consist of nine cyclists and the famous yellow jersey is awarded to the cyclist who has the lowest cumulative time for the race at the end of each day. The route changes slightly each year; 2001 features an eastern bias, with the Tour starting at Dunkerque before heading briefly into Belgium, on through Alsace and the Jura mountains and down to the Alps. The cyclists are then flown to Perpignan where the arduous stretches through the Pyrénées begin, before the route heads north again through central France to the Loire Valley and finally to the finishing line in Paris. Thousands of spectators, including film stars and celebrities, line the Champs-Elysées to see the winners speed towards the end of their three-week journey. The end often turns into a nerve-wracking sprint, followed by the cracking open of champagne and huge celebrations.

Event Organiser

La Société du Tour de France, 2 rue Rouget de Lisle, 92130 Issy-Les-Moulineaux, France
Tel: (01) 4133 1500.
E-mail: mail@letour.fr
Website: www.letour.fr

Venue

Champs-Elysées.

Transport

Air: Paris Roissy-Charles de Gaulle Airport or Paris Orly Airport. **Rail:** Train: Paris Gare du Nord (Eurostar). Underground: Charles-de-Gaulle-Étoile, Georges V or Franklin D Roosevelt. RER: Charles-de-Gaulle-Etoile. **Road:** Bus: 22, 30, 31, 52, 73, 92 or Balabus. Car: A1 (from Lille); A16 (from Boulogne); E60 (from Brussels, Belgium); A62, then A20, A71 and A10 (from Toulouse); A3 (from Roissy-Charles de Gaulle Airport); A4 (from Strasbourg); A6 (from Lyon and Marseille); A13 (from Caen). Visitors should note that traffic is severely disrupted by the Arrival of the Tour de France, and it is therefore advisable to avoid travelling by road.

Bastille Day

Towards the close of the 18th century, disenchantment with Louis XVI's monarchy, the aristocracy and the church had spread across France and was expressed, increasingly, in acts of civil unrest. On 14 July 1789, several hundred ordinary Parisians marched to the Bastille prison, killed the governor and triggered the revolution that signalled the end of the monarchy in France with the pronouncement of *liberté, egalité, fraternité* (freedom, equality and brotherhood). To this day, the storming of the Bastille is commemorated across France as the *Fête de la Bastille*. The biggest celebrations are on the Champs-Elysées, with around 6000 people marching down the tree-lined avenue accompanied by military bands playing rousing music. At night there is a huge fireworks display over the city, as well as special entertainment and singing in bars and cafés throughout Paris. This is a national holiday in France, and the sense of pride that the French still feel for their republic is particularly evident on this day.

Event Organiser

For more information on Bastille Day, contact the Central Tourist Office (see **Tourist Information** above).

Venue

Champs-Elysées and various locations across Paris.

Transport

Air: Paris Roissy-Charles de Gaulle Airport or Paris Orly Airport. **Rail:** Train: Paris Gare du Nord (Eurostar). Underground: Charles-de-Gaulle-Étoile, Georges V or Franklin D Roosevelt. RER: Charles-de-Gaulle-Etoile. **Road:** Bus: 22, 30, 31, 52, 73, 92 or Balabus. Car: A1 (from Lille), A16 (from Boulogne), E60 (from Brussels, Belgium), A62, then A20, A71 and A10 (from Toulouse), A3 (from Roissy-Charles de Gaulle Airport), A4 (from Strasbourg), A6 (from Lyon and Marseille), A13 (from Caen). Visitors should note that traffic is severely disrupted by the Bastille Day celebrations, and it is therefore advisable to avoid travelling by road.

• July-August

Summer Arts Festival

For one month each summer the *Summer Arts Festival* (*Quartier d'Été*) transforms the streets of Paris into a huge open-air venue for the performing arts. Lovers of opera, jazz, theatre, classical music, circus, film and dance will all find something to entertain them – there are over 90 different events with a focus on several different countries each year. Venues range from cinemas in the bohemian Latin Quarter to the elegance of the *Jardin des Tuileries*. Parisians traditionally escape the capital for their summer holiday at this time of year, leaving more space for visitors to enjoy the show.

Event Organiser

Festival Paris Quartier d'Été, 5 rue Boudereau, 75009 Paris, France
Tel: (01) 494 9800. Fax: (01) 4494 9801.
E-mail: paris@quartierdete.com
Website: www.quartierdete.com

Venue

Various locations across Paris.

Transport

Air: Paris Roissy-Charles de Gaulle Airport or Paris Orly Airport. **Rail:** Train: Paris Gare du Nord (Eurostar). **Road:** Car: A1 (from Lille); A16 (from Boulogne); E60 (from Brussels, Belgium); A62, then A20, A71 and A10 (from Toulouse); A3 (from Roissy-Charles de Gaulle Airport); A4 (from Strasbourg); A6 (from Lyon and Marseille); A13 (from Caen).

• September-December

Autumn Festival

The Paris *Autumn Festival* (*Festival d'Automne*) presents a cultural mélange of literature, film, poetry and theatre from around the world. Each year a different country provides the focus – in 2000 it was Iran, and events included readings of Persian poetry, meetings with Iranian writers and artists, and performances of traditional Persian music. Other past events include Peter Brook's adaptation of 'Hamlet' and a staging of Boccaccio's Medieval 'Decameron' tales.

Event Organiser

Festival d'Automne, 16 rue de Rivoli, 75001 Paris, France
Tel: (01) 5345 1700. Fax: (01) 5345 1701.
Website: www.festival-automne.com

Venue

Various venues across Paris.

Transport

Air: Paris Roissy-Charles de Gaulle Airport or Paris Orly Airport. **Rail:** Train: Paris Gare du Nord (Eurostar). **Road:** Car: A1 (from Lille); A16 (from Boulogne); E60 (from Brussels, Belgium); A62, then A20, A71 and A10 (from Toulouse); A3 (from Roissy-Charles de Gaulle Airport); A4 (from Strasbourg); A6 (from Lyon and Marseille); A13 (from Caen).

Strasbourg

Tourist Information

Office de Tourisme de Strasbourg (Central Tourist Office)
17 place de la Cathédrale, 67082 Strasbourg, France
Tel: (03) 8852 2828. Fax: (03) 8852 2829.
E-mail: otsr@strasbourg.com
Website: www.strasbourg.com

• November-December

Strasbourg Christmas Market

Strasbourg Christmas Market is the biggest of its kind in France, and one of the most famous in Europe. It was first held in 1570 and is known in the local Alsatian dialect as *Christkindelsmärik*. There are hundreds of stalls selling gingerbread, spicy sausages, *vin chaud* (mulled wine), crafts and Christmas decorations around the beautiful Cathédrale Notre-Dame and along Place Broglie. A fir tree from the Vosges mountains is erected in Place Kléber in the heart of the city. There are over 50 concerts and shows, providing musical accompaniment, and there is also an ice rink and a Christmas trail, where visitors can discover local crafts and traditions and the history of the festive season in Alsace. Children will enjoy 'chocolate cruises', which are boat rides through the city with entertainment and sweets.

Event Organiser

For more information on the Strasbourg Christmas Market, contact the Central Tourist Office (see **Tourist Information** above).

Venue

Place de la Cathédrale and various locations across Strasbourg.

Transport

Air: Euro-Airport Basel-Mulhouse-Freiburg. **Rail:** Train: Strasbourg Station. Tram: Homme de Fer or Langstrosse/Grande Rue. **Road:** Bus: Services to Homme de Fer or Langstrasse/Grande Rue. Car: A4 (from Paris); A8 (from Stuttgart, Germany or Munich, Germany); A35 (from Mulhouse or Karlsruhe, Germany).

Germany

Berlin

Tourist Information

Berlin Tourismus Marketing GmbH (Berlin Tourist Office)
Am Karlsbad 11, 10785 Berlin, Germany
Tel: (030) 264 7480. Fax: (030) 2500 2424.
E-mail: information@btm.de
Website: www.btm.de

• February

Berlin International Film Festival

The 52nd *Berlin International Film Festival* will be held in the city in February 2002. The festival was founded in 1951 as the result of an American Cold War initiative and quickly grew to become a well-established and important cultural event both in Berlin and worldwide. Film directors including Ingmar Bergman, Roman Polanski, Jean-Luc Godard and François Truffaut have all enjoyed considerable success with their films at the festival. It features an international competition, numerous film screenings, the Forum of Young Cinema and a children's film festival.

Event Organiser

Internationale Filmfestspiele, Potsdamerstrasse 5, 10785 Berlin, Germany
Tel: (030) 259 200. Fax: (030) 2592 0299.
E-mail: info@berlinale.de
Website: www.berlinale.de

Venue

Various cinemas across Berlin, including Berlinale Palast (Stella Musical Theater), Zoo Palast, Royal Palast, CinemaxX Potsdamer Platz, CineStar Potsdamer Platz, International, Delphi und Filmtheater am FriedrichshaininemaxX, Grand Hotel Hyatt and debis Atrium.

Transport

Air: Berlin Tegel Airport. **Rail:** Train: S-Bahn trains serve the whole of Berlin. Underground: U-Bahn trains operate across Berlin. **Road:** Car: A24 (from Hamburg); A2 (from Hanover); A9 (from Leipzig and Munich); A13 (from Dresden); A12 (from the Polish border).

• June

Carnival of the Cultures

Carnival of the Cultures is a four-day street festival celebrating Berlin's cultural diversity and its ethnic communities. The carnival was established in 1996 and has grown to become one of the most important cultural events in Berlin. This huge annual street party sees around 4000 performers, jugglers, musicians, dancers and DJs parade through the city's streets. The highlight of the weekend is the giant Whitsum street parade, when 110 groups and 4200 participants from around 70 countries dance through the streets of the Kreuzberg district. There is also a giant programme of events during the festivities, with approximately 750 artists playing on four giant stages, and a children's party in *Goerlitzer Park*. International food, drinks and handicrafts are on sale at over 200 stalls during the four days, giving visitors the chance to sample international cuisine. Around half a million people attended the festival in 2000, with approximately 1.1 million visitors attending the sixth Carnival of the Cultures in 2001.

Event Organiser

Werkstatt der Kulturen, Wissmannstrasse 32, 12049 Berlin, Germany
Tel: (030) 622 4232. Fax: (030) 622 3519.
E-mail: info@karneval-berlin.de
Website: www.karneval-berlin.de

Venue

Various streets in Berlin, including Blucherplatz, Zossenerstrasse, Blucherstrasse and Gneisenaustrasse.

Transport

Air: Berlin Tegel Airport. **Rail:** Underground: Lines U1, 6 or 15 to Hallesches Tor or lines U6 or 7 to Mehringdamm. **Road:** Bus: 240, 241 or 341. **Road:** Car: A24 (from Hamburg); A2 (from Hanover); A9 (from Leipzig and Munich); A13 (from Dresden); A12 (from the Polish border).

Christopher Street Day

Christoper Street Day is an enormous outdoor gay and lesbian party, which has been held every June in Berlin since 1979. Every year around 400,000 visitors join in the festivities, which rival gay and lesbian festivals in London, Amsterdam and San Francisco. The motto for the celebrations in 2001 was 'Berlin stands up against the right!', with festivalgoers uniting to show their opposition to right-wing politics in Europe, which try to stamp out minority groups such as gays and lesbians. There is a rally which starts at 1000, followed by a huge parade which sets off from Kurfürstendamm at 1300, passing by *Postdamer Platz* and *Brandenburg Tor*. In 2000, the parade finished at Siegessäule with a giant party and live music from the German-based band, Terra Brasilis, and from DJs Mo and Solaris, as well as a performance of the musical 'The Hunchback of Notre Dame'. Every year, there is a gigantic firework display at the end of the night, which brings the festivities to a spectacular close.

Event Organiser

Berliner CSD eV, Geschäftsführung, Michael Schmidt, Fuggerstrasse 7, 10777 Berlin, Germany
Tel: (0177) 277 3176.
E-mail: info@csd-berlin.de
Website: www.csd-berlin.de

Venue

Various outdoor venues across Berlin, with parades setting off from Kurfürstendamm in the city centre.

Transport

Air: Berlin Tegel Airport. **Rail:** Underground: U9 or U15 to Kurfürstendamm. **Road:** Car: A24 (from Hamburg); A2 (from Hanover); A9 (from Leipzig and Munich); A13 (from Dresden); A12 (from the Polish border).

• July

Love Parade

The annual *Love Parade* takes place in Berlin in July. The festivities start at 1400 when around 50 'lovetrucks' and 250 DJs set off on a giant parade from both *Ernst-Reuter-Platz* and *Brandenburg Tor* to Siegessäule, promoting the 'one world, one Love Parade' idea. Once they reach Siegessäule they turn around before setting off again on the big rally of the day at 1900. The first Love Parade took place on Berlin's Kurfürstendamm in 1989, when German DJ Dr Motte promoted an acid house party in the streets of Berlin to promote love and peace, and respect and understanding between nations; the event attracted 150 partygoers. The Berlin Love Parade has since grown into one of the biggest street parties in the Western world, with well over one million people attending the parade every year to watch the floats parade along the Strasse des 17 Juni, past some of Germany's most important monuments.

Event Organiser

Berlin Love Parade GmbH, Alexander Platz, 5, 10178 Berlin, Germany
Tel: (030) 284 620. Fax: (030) 284 6222.
E-mail: infopool@loveparade.net
Website: www.loveparade.com

Venue

Berlin city centre, starting at the Golden Angel monument in the middle of the Tiergarden and continuing down to Brandenburger Tor.

Transport

Air: Berlin Tegel Airport. **Rail:** Train: For Brandenburg Tor, S-Bahn S3, S5, S7, S9 or S75 to Friedrichstrasse Station. Underground: For Ernst-Reuter-Platz, U-Bahn 2 or 12 to Ernst-Reuter-Platz Station. **Road:** Car: A24 (from Hamburg); A2 (from Hanover); A9 (from Leipzig and Munich); A13 (from Dresden); A12 (from the Polish border).

• September

Berlin Marathon

The *Berlin Marathon* is an annual event which first took place on 13 October 1974, with 284 runners from four nations starting the race. In 2000, 27,017 runners from over 85 countries took part in the event. Simon Biwott (from Kenya), who actually entered the race as a pacemaker, won the men's event, whilst Kazumi Matsuo (from Japan) won the women's race. The race starts in Strasse des 17 Juni, at the *Charlottenburg Tor*, near *Ernst-Reuter Square* and ends in Kurfürstendamm. The participants run through ten districts of Berlin: Charlottenburg, Tiergarten, Mitte, Friedrichshain, Kreuzberg, Neukölln, Schöneberg, Steglitz, Zehlendorf and Wilmersdorf, passing the *Brandenburg Gate*, the *Victory Column*, the *State Opera*, *Berlin Cathedral* and the *Botanical Gardens*. Over 60 bands and one million spectators line the streets to cheer on participants and create a truly exciting atmosphere.

Event Organiser

Berlin Marathon, Sigmaringerstrasse 11, 10713 Berlin, Germany
Tel: (030) 8642 1431. Fax: (030) 8642 1434.
E-mail: info@berlin-marathon.com
Website: www.berlin-marathon.com

Venue

Streets of Berlin, starting at Charlottenburg Tor and ending at Kurfürstendamm.

Transport

Air: Berlin Tegel Airport. **Rail:** Train: S-Bahn S5 or S75 to Charlottenburg (start). Underground: U9 or U15 to Kurfürstendamm (finish). **Road:** Car: A24 (from Hamburg); A2 (from Hanover); A9 (from Leipzig and Munich); A13 (from Dresden); A12 (from the Polish border).

Frankfurt

Tourist Information

Tourismus+Congress GmbH Frankfurt am Main (Frankfurt Tourist & Congress Board)
Kaiserstrasse 56, 60329 Frankfurt/Main, Germany
Tel: (069) 2123 8800. Fax: (069) 2123 7880.
E-mail: info@tcf.frankfurt.de
Website: www.frankfurt.de

• October

Frankfurt Marathon

The 20th *Frankfurt Marathon* will take place on the last Sunday in October in the centre of the city. The marathon, which was first held in 1981, is the oldest city marathon in Germany, leading through the city centre, on to the west of the city and back through Sachsenhausen to the finish at the *Frankfurt Trade Fair Centre*. As well as the annual 42.2km (26.2 miles) marathon, there is also a 4.2km (2.6 miles) mini marathon for children and a breakfast run. The latter starts at *Frankfurt Römer*, one of the main sights in Frankfurt, and leads 5km (3.1 miles) through the city centre to the city's fairground. Visitors and spectators can also take part in a pasta party, a marathon breakfast and marathon buffet. In addition to this, there is a sportswear and sports equipment exhibition, a presentation ceremony and various course parties.

Event Organiser

Euro Marathon Frankfurt GmbH, 60135 Frankfurt am Main, Germany

Tel: (069) 9717 6330. Fax: (069) 9717 6555.
E-mail: euromarathon@malekigroup.com
Website: www.euro-marathon.de

Venue

Starts and finishes at the Frankfurt Trade Fair Centre, in the centre of Frankfurt.

Transport

Air: Frankfurt Airport. **Rail:** Train: S-Bahn S3, S4, S5 or S6 to Messe Station. **Road:** Bus: 33, 34 or 50. There is also a free shuttle service to the start and finish of the marathon at the Frankfurt Trade Fair Centre.

Munich

Tourist Information

Fremdenverkehrsamt München (Munich Tourist Office)
Sendlingerstrasse 1, 80331 Munich, Germany
Tel: (089) 233 0300. Fax: (089) 2333 0233.
E-mail: tourismus@ems.muenchen.de
Website: www.muenchen-tourist.de

• January-February

Munich Carnival

Munich Carnival (or *Fasching* as it is known in Germany) is held every year in the city, with major celebrations taking place during Germany's carnival period; this is known as the 'Fifth Season' or the 'Season of Fools', when Germans let their hair down before Lent. The first Fasching Ball was held in Munich in 1829 and was soon followed by many more masquerades and balls. Their popularity led to the establishment of a Munich carnival society in 1839 to organise annual events, marking the beginning of Fasching as it is known today. Every year, partygoers can choose from thousands of parties, balls and other festivities, which take place in the city, ranging from fancy-dress parties through to black-tie affairs. The climax of the carnival, *München Harrisch* (Mad Munich) costume parade, takes place on the Sunday before Shrove Tuesday, with revellers partying in the streets and passing through the crowds on floats. Thousands of dancers and musicians congregate in *Marienplatz* after the parade to fill the city's beer halls. Fasching is also celebrated in other parts of Germany, such as Mainz and Düsseldorf, although Munich's Fasching lasts the longest and is the most famous.

Event Organiser

For more information on the Munich Carnival, contact the Munich Tourist Office (see **Tourist Information** above).

Venue

Various dance halls in hotels and breweries in Munich.

Transport

Air: Munich International Airport. **Rail:** Train: S-Bahn to Marienplatz. Underground: U-Bahn U3, U4, U5 or U6 to Marienplatz. **Road:** Bus: 52. Car: A9 (from Berlin via Würzburg and Nuremberg); A92 (from Passau); A96 (from Lindau); A8 (from Salzburg, Austria).

• June

City Foundation Day

City Foundation Day is held every year to celebrate the founding of Munich, which took place on 14 June 1158 by the German prince, Henry the Lion, who also held the titles Duke of Saxony (1142-1180) and Duke of Bavaria (1156-1180). Every year, in commemoration, the locals drink beer and eat vast quantities of sausages during this giant street party. The festivities are accompanied by music from local bands and street performances. The event is held betweeen *Marienplatz* and *Odeonsplatz* in Munich's city centre. Many attractions, such as the *Neues Rathaus* (New Town Hall), built in the 19th century, *Altes Rathaus* (Old Town Hall), which houses a delightful toy museum, and *Frauenkirche* – Munich's cathedral, are located nearby and are well worth a visit whilst in the city.

Event Organiser

For more information on the City Foundation Day, contact the Munich Tourist Office (see **Tourist Information** above).

Venue

Between Marienplatz and Odeonsplatz in Munich city centre.

Transport

Air: Munich International Airport. **Rail:** Train: S-Bahn to Marienplatz. Underground: U-Bahn to Marienplatz. **Road:** Car: A9 (from Berlin via Würzburg and Nuremberg); A92 (from Passau); A96 (from Lindau); A8 (from Salzburg, Austria).

• September-October

October Festival

The Munich *October Festival* (or *Oktoberfest* as it is known in Germany) starts at the end of September and is one of the world's biggest public festivals. The event began in 1810 to celebrate the marriage of King Joseph Maximiliam of Bavaria to Princess Theresa of Saxony. The event was such a huge success that it has taken place ever since. In 2001, Munich will celebrate its 168th Oktoberfest, with more than six million partygoers expected to drink around five million litres of beer. Events include the *Grand Entry of the Oktoberfest Landlords and Breweries*, the *Costume and Riflemen's Procession*, performances by Oompah bands, dancing and a giant funfair at the foot of the *Bavaria Statue*. The festivities take place in beer tents in the Theresienwiese district (a district named after Princess Theresa of Saxony).

Event Organiser

For more information on the October Festival, contact the Munich Tourist Office (see **Tourist Information** above).

Venue

Theresienwiese District.

Transport

Air: Munich International Airport. **Rail:** Underground: U-Bahn U4 or U5 to Theresienwiese. **Road:** Car: A9 (from Berlin via Würzburg and Nuremberg); A92 (from Passau); A96 (from Lindau); A8 (from Salzburg, Austria).

• December

Christmas Market

Every year, thousands of people crowd into Marienplatz to watch the Lord Mayor open the *Christmas Market* (known as *Weihnachtsmarkt* in German). This event occurs at 1700 on the Saturday before the first day of Advent, when the mayor switches on the Christmas lights on a 30m-high (98ft) Christmas tree. The market's origins can be traced back to Nicholas Market, which started in 1310, with people shopping in Nenhauserstrasse, buying toys for Christmas. In 1597, the market moved location; changing its name to Christmas Market in 1805. Since 1972, the market has taken place in Marienplatz in the centre of Munich. Every year, gifts are on sale at more than 140 market stalls. Craftsmen can also be seen at work, making gifts such as Christmas baubles and candles. There is also a *Crib Market*, based on the Nativity Crib in the Town Hall Courtyard. Folk music is played at 1730 every evening and Santa Claus greets children in the square on 5 and 6 December.

Event Organiser

For more information on the Christmas Market, contact the Munich Tourist Office (see **Tourist Information** above).

Venue

Marienplatz in Munich city centre.

Transport

Air: Munich International Airport. **Rail:** Train: S-Bahn to Marienplatz. Underground: U-Bahn to Marienplatz. **Road:** Car: A9 (from Berlin via Würzburg and Nuremberg); A92 (from Passau); A96 (from Lindau); A8 (from Salzburg, Austria).

Greece

Athens

Tourist Information

Ellinikos Organismos Tourismou (Hellenic Tourism Organisation)
Amerikis 2B, 105 64 Athens, Greece
Tel: (01) 327 1300. Fax: (01) 322 4148.
E-mail: info@gnto.gr
Website: www.areianet.gr

• July

Rockwave Festival

This is Greece's major rock music event, featuring performances by groups from around the world. The festival first took place in 1998 and has attracted many big name bands since then, including Moby, Pulp, Prodigy, Blur, Garbage, Patti Smith and The Fun Lovin' Criminals. As with any event of this size (in 1999 the festival drew 55,000 people), there are other activities to entertain the crowd, such as bungee jumping, skate-boading, simulators, acrobats and even a troupe of British stilt-walkers. There are also merchandise stalls and food and drink available, and festivalgoers can take time out to relax in the park.

Event Organiser

Didi Music, 3 Eptanisou Street – 2 Pipinou Street, 11257 Athens, Greece
Tel: (01) 821 7095. Fax: (01) 882 0817.
E-mail: didi@otonet.gr
Website: www.didimusic.gr

Venue

Varies annually. Contact the Hellenic Tourism Organisation for more details.

Transport

Air: Athens International Airport. **Rail:** Train: Larissa or Pelopónnisos stations. Underground: Monastiraki or Theseion. **Road:** Car: PATHE motorway (from Patra, Evloni or Thessaloniki). Taxi: Services from across Athens. Taxi is the easiest way of getting around Athens.

• July & September

Athens Festival

In AD 161 the Roman ruler Herodes Atticus commissioned the *Odeon* amphitheatre at the foot of the *Acropolis* in memory of his wife, Rigilla. Decorated in marble and seating 5000 spectators, this beautiful auditorium has been used to stage performances since ancient times, when musicians, actors, poets and dancers performed to gain the favour of the gods. Since 1955, the Odeon has provided a splendid setting for the *Athens Festival*, an international celebration of theatre, music, dance and literature. Highlights of the festival in 2001 include performances by the State Orchestras of Athens and Istanbul, the State Theatre of Northern Greece's rendition of 'Plutus' by Aristophanes, and Schumann's 'Manfred Overture', conducted by Angelo Cavalaro with the Music Ensemble of Greek National Television. The starry night sky above the amphitheatre provides the perfect backdrop for a magical evening's entertainment. Anyone wishing to try a more unusual performance might like to watch a poetry reading or avant-garde musical recital at the *Pnyx*, at the entrance to the Acropolis.

Event Organiser

Athens Festival, Athens Festival Box Office, 4 Stadiou Street, Athens, Greece
Tel: (01) 928 2900. Fax: (01) 928 2932.

Venue

Odeon of Herodes Atticus (at the foot of the Acropolis).

Transport

Air: Athens International Airport. **Rail:** Train: Larissa or Pelopónnisos stations. Underground: Monastiraki or Theseion. **Road:** Bus: 230 or 231 to Dionisiou Areopagitou (from Amalias Avenue). Car: PATHE motorway (from Patra, Evloni or Thessaloniki). Taxi: Services from across Athens. Taxi is the easiest way of getting around Athens.

• November

Athens Marathon

Almost every major city in the world has its own marathon, but only Athens can claim to have the original. The event is so called after the legendary 40.2km (25 mile) journey undertaken by the messenger, Phiedippes, when he brought news of the Athenian victory over the Persians at the *Marathon* battlefield in 490 BC. The first marathon event took place at the 1896 Olympic Games in Athens and the winner was a Greek, Spyridon Louis. Today, runners must follow in the footsteps of Phiedippes, to complete a route over 42.2km (26 miles 385 yards) between the ancient battlefield in the village of Marathon and the historic *Olympic Stadium* in the centre of Athens. The standard distance for a marathon event was set in 1924, when the British Olympic Committee decided that the route for the London Games should lead from *Windsor Castle* to the royal box in the *London Olympic Stadium*.

Event Organiser

SEGAS, 137 Syngrou Avenue, 171 21 N Smirni, Athens, Greece
Tel: (01) 935 1888. Fax: (01) 935 8594.
E-mail: segas-gr@otenet.gr
Website: www.athensmarathon.com

Venue

Starts at the village of Marathon and ends at the Olympic Stadium.

Transport

Air: Athens International Airport. **Rail:** Train: Larissa or Pelopónnisos stations. **Road:** Bus: 2, 4, 11 or 12. Car: PATHE motorway (from Patra, Evloni or Thessaloniki). Taxi: Services from across Athens. Taxi is the easiest way of getting around Athens.

Need more information on Greece?
Consult the
World Travel Guide

Hungary

Budapest

Tourist Information

Budapesti Turisztikai Hivatal (Tourism Office of Budapest)
1364 Budapest PF 215, 1052 Budapest, Hungary
Tel: (01) 266 0479. Fax: (01) 266 7477.
E-mail: info@budtour.hu
Website: www.budapestinfo.hu

• March-April

Budapest Spring Festival

Although classical music predominates, the *Budapest Spring Festival* encompasses music for most tastes, as well as cinematic and theatrical events. It is the largest cultural festival in Hungary and has a growing reputation abroad. Performances take place in beautiful locations around the city, and in 2001 ranged from open-air events such as the *Celebration of Spring* parade, featuring mummers, stilt-walkers and puppeteers, to Wagner's 'Tristan und Isolde', staged in the lavish surroundings of the Hungarian State Opera House. Other past opera performances have included Puccini's 'La Bohème', Bartòk's 'The Miraculous Mandarin', 'Il Trovatore' by Verdi and Leoncavallo's 'I Pagliacci', complete with circus acts. There is a vast array of other classical concerts, ranging from piano recitals and string quartets to evenings of French Baroque music. Those interested in discovering traditional Hungarian culture can enjoy performances by the 100-member Budapest Gypsy Orchestra. Jazz, films, exhibitions and children's activities are also on offer each year.

Event Organiser

Budapest Festival Centre (Budapest Fesztiválközpont KHT), Rákóczi út 65, 1081 Budapest, Hungary
Tel: (01) 210 8301. Fax: (01) 210 5906.
E-mail: email@fesztivalvaros.hu
Website: www.festivalcity.hu

Venue

Various locations across Budapest.

Transport

Air: Budapest Ferihegy Airport. **Rail:** Train: Eastern, Western or Southern stations. **Road:** Car: A4, then M1 (from Vienna, Austria); M1 (from Győr); E65, then E60 (from Prague, Czech Republic, Brno, Czech Republic or Bratislava, Slovak Republic).

• October-November

Budapest Autumn Festival

The *Budapest Autumn Festival* is an experimental arts festival aiming to highlight new forms within the contemporary arts scene. Variety is the key – visitors can explore almost any genre, from high-brow literary readings and classical orchestral concerts to fun circus acts and eclectic art exhibitions. Children can join in play workshops and there are coffee shop concerts where live music can be enjoyed alongside the mouthwatering Budapest tradition of coffee and cakes. Hungarian folk dancing, jazz, film premieres, clown shows and literary sightseeing tours are also on offer. The theme for 2001 is 'Railway Stations'.

Event Organiser

Budapest Festival Centre (Budapest Fesztiválközpont KHT), Rákóczi út 65, 1081 Budapest, Hungary
Tel: (01) 210 8301. Fax: (01) 210 5906.
E-mail: budfest@elender.hu
Website: www.fesztivalvaros.hu

Venue

Various locations across Budapest.

Transport

Air: Budapest Ferihegy Airport. **Rail:** Train: Eastern, Western or Southern stations. **Road:** Car: A4, then M1 (from Vienna, Austria); M1 (from Győr); E65, then E60 (from Prague, Czech Republic, Brno, Czech Republic or Bratislava, Slovak Republic).

• December

New Year's Eve Gala and Ball at the Opera

This ball has taken place every year for the past decade in the opulent surroundings of the Hungarian State Opera House in central Budapest and is open to everyone. The Opera House was built in Italian neo-Renaissance style to designs by Miklós Ybl and was first opened in 1884. It was reopened on its 100th birthday in September 1984 after undergoing extensive restoration to return it to its former glory. Those who take part in the New Year's Eve festivities can expect to be richly entertained, with a gala concert of music and dance performed by the resident Opera House ensemble, Hungarian food and drink served on the stage and in the box areas, and old-style Viennese ballroom dancing. For those who prefer something more contemporary, there is a piano bar and disco.

Event Organiser

Organisational Department of the Opera House, 24 Andrássy Street, VI Budapest 1061, Hungary
Tel: (01) 332 7914. Fax: (01) 311 9017.
Website: www.opera.hu

Venue

Hungarian State Opera House.

Transport

Air: Budapest Ferihegy Airport. **Rail:** Train: Eastern, Western or Southern stations. Underground: Opera. **Road:** Car: A4, then M1 (from Vienna, Austria); M1 (from Győr); E65, then E60 (from Prague, Czech Republic, Brno, Czech Republic or Bratislava, Slovak Republic).

Iceland

Reykjavik

Tourist Information

Islenska Tourist Board (Icelandic Tourist Board)
Laekjargata 3, 101 Reykjavik, Iceland
Tel: 535 5500. Fax: 535 5501.
E-mail: info@icetourist.is
Website: www.icetourist.is

• January-February

Thorri Feast

Thorri is the Icelandic name for the fourth month of winter. Every year in February, Icelanders continue the ancient Viking tradition of celebrating the end of winter and the coming of spring with dancing, singing and huge feasts. The tradition all but disappeared with the advent of Christianity, but was revived in 1873 during Iceland's struggle for independence from Denmark. Traditional delicacies include *slatur* (a type of black pudding), *svith* (boiled sheep's head), *hakarl* (rotten shark meat) and *hrutspungar* (ram's testicles). For the less adventurous there are other specialities on offer, such as various kinds of bread, *lundabaggar* (lamb meatballs), *hardfiskur* (dried fish with butter) and *skyr* (curds and fresh blueberries). Restaurants in Reykjavik offer their own *Thorri Feasts*, usually as a buffet to allow guests to sample as many dishes as they can manage.

Event Organiser

For more information on the Thorri Feast, contact the Icelandic Tourist Board (see **Tourist Information** above).

Venue

Various locations across Reykjavik.

Transport

Air: Keflavik International Airport. **Road:** Car: Hwy-1 (from all coastal towns in Iceland, including Akureyri, Höfn and Isafjördur).

• July-August

Light Nights

In the 12th century, *sagnaskemmtun* (saga entertainment) was a popular way of spending evenings on Icelandic farms. Stories were passed on from generation to generation and many have been recorded in writing, although the identity of many of the authors remains a mystery. The sagas are based on legends, historical events, secular fiction and the lives of the saints, and tell the story of everyday people in a bid to give Icelanders an awareness of themselves and the society around them through the tales of their forbears. The saga remains an important cultural tradition in Iceland and every year since 1970 actress Kristín Magnús has presented a selection in English in Reykjavik. The audience is taken on a two-hour journey through several centuries of Icelandic history with storytelling, slides, folksongs and chants. This is a unique theatrical and cultural experience, and performances are held every Thursday, Friday and Saturday at 2100.

Event Organiser

The Travelling Theatre, Baldursgata 37, 101 Reykjavik, Iceland
Tel: 551 9181 (summer months only). Fax: 551 5015.
E-mail: travelling-theatre@simnet.is

Venue

Tjarnarbíó Theatre (next to the City Hall).

Transport

Air: Keflavik International Airport. **Road:** Bus: 1, 2, 3, 4, 5, 6, 7, 110, 112 or 115 (towards Lækjatorg). Car: Hwy-1 (from all coastal towns in Iceland, including Akureyri, Höfn and Isafjördur).

India

Delhi

Tourist Information

Government of India Tourist Office
88 Janpath, New Delhi 110011, India
Tel: (011) 332 0005. Fax: (011) 332 0342.
E-mail: newdelhi@tourisminindia.com
Website: www.tourisminindia.com

• October

Diwali

Diwali is one of the most well-known Hindu festivals and is celebrated throughout India. According to Hindu legend, King Dashratha wished for his son Rama, born to his wife Queen Kaushalaya, to be the heir to his throne. Another of his wives, Queen Keykayee, used the two wishes granted to her by her husband to send Rama into exile for 14 years so that her son, Bharat, would be the future king instead. Rama is believed to have spent his years in exile in the southern tip of the Indian sub-continent killing the king of demons before returning to rule over his kingdom of Ayodhya. Diwali thus symbolises the victory of good over evil and the lifting of spiritual darkness. The Sanskrit name, 'Deepavali', is derived from two words – 'deepa', meaning 'light' and 'avali', meaning 'row', thus 'row of lights'. Diwali is commonly referred to as the 'festival of lights', and many Indians place small oil lamps, or *diyas*, outside their homes, while candles light up the city centres to welcome Lakshmi, the goddess of wealth and prosperity. Firecrackers are also burned and Hindu families hold huge feasts in their homes. Sweets are traditionally given as presents and Delhi stages its own festivities at *Lal Quila* (Red Fort) with fireworks and a funfair.

Event Organiser

For more information on Diwali, contact the Government of India Tourist Office (see **Tourist Information** above).

Venue

Various locations across Delhi with the main focus at Lal Quila (Red Fort).

Transport

Air: Indira Gandhi International Airport. **Rail:** Train: New Delhi or Old Delhi stations. **Road:** Car: Grand Trunk Road (from Amritsar); Mathura Road (from Agra); N2 (from Calcutta); Gurgaon Road (from Jaipur).

Ireland

Dublin

Tourist Information

Dublin Tourism
Tourism Centre, Suffolk Street, Dublin 2, Ireland
Tel: (01) 605 7700. Fax: (01) 605 7757.
E-mail: information@dublintourism.ie
Website: www.visitdublin.com

• March

St Patrick's Festival

St Patrick's Festival takes place in Dublin every year to remember St Patrick, who is the Patron Saint of Ireland. St Patrick was born around AD 387 and died on 17 March AD 461. He was the second bishop of Ireland and was most famous for using the shamrock to show how the Father, Son and Holy Ghost can exist as separate parts of the same body, leading to the shamrock becoming the national emblem. Patrick is also believed to have given a sermon that drove all snakes from Ireland. To commemorate his life, there is a parade through Dublin city centre on 17 March, as well as a giant carnival and celebrations during the four days of festivities. The parade begins at 1100 at *Christ Church Cathedral* and ends in O'Connell Street. St Patrick's Day, on 17 March, is a bank holiday in Ireland, when the Lord Mayor of Dublin is driven through the streets in a horse-drawn carriage and is cheered on by spectators. Other events include the *Fanfare Celebration* of marching bands and the *St Patrick's Eve Night Parade* on 16 March, the *Ceili Mor Celebration* of Irish dance on 17 March and *The Big Day Out* on 19 March. The Big Day Out consists of more than 100 events, including street theatre, magic shows, comedy shows, puppet shows and parades. The festivities end with a giant fireworks display on 19 March. St Patrick's Day celebrations take place around the world, with many major cities, including New York, Boston and Chicago, hosting their own Irish celebrations.

Event Organiser

St Patrick's Day Festival Office, St Stephens Green House, Earlsfort Terrace, Dublin 2, Ireland
Tel: (01) 676 3205. Fax: (01) 676 3208.
E-mail: info@stpatricksday.ie
Website: www.stpartricksday.ie

Venue

Various locations across Dublin, centred around Christ Church Cathedral and O'Connell Street.

Transport

Air: Dublin Airport. **Road:** Bus: For Christ Church Cathedral, 78A (Aston Quay) or 50 (Eden Quay). **Road:** Car: N2 (from Monaghan); M1, A1 and N1 (from Belfast); N9, M9, M7 and N7 (from Waterford); N11 (from the port of Dún Laoghaire).

• May

Heineken Green Energy Festival

The sixth annual *Heineken Green Energy Festival* took place in May 2001, with both unsigned and international bands playing in venues across the city. In 2000, more than 50,000 people attended the festival to see acts including Bryan Ferry, The Charlatans, The Cranberries and Tracy Chapman. Previous years' bands have included UB40, Texas, Jesus & Mary Chain, Beck, Happy Mondays and The Beautiful South. Big names play at *Dublin Castle*, the *Olympia Theatre* and *Temple Bar Music Centre*. As well as performances from well-known international artists, unsigned groups also play gigs in Dublin and compete in the festival's band challenge.

Event Organiser

For more information on Heineken Green Energy Festival, contact Ticketmaster (tel: (0870) 534 4444 (Ticketmaster, UK) *or* (01) 456 9569 (Ticketmaster, Ireland) or visit the Heineken Green Energy Festival website (website: www.heinekengreenenergy.com).

Venue

Various locations across Dublin, including Temple Bar Music Centre, Dublin Castle and Olympia Theatre.

Transport

Air: Dublin Airport. **Rail:** Train: Connolly or Heuston stations. **Road:** Bus: 44, 47 or 86. **Road:** Car: N2 (from Monaghan); M1, A1 and N1 (from Belfast); N9, M9, M7 and N7 (from Waterford); N11 (from the port of Dún Laoghaire).

• June

Bloomsday Festival

The *Bloomsday Festival* celebrates the life of James Joyce, who was born in 1882 and died in 1941. James Joyce is one of Ireland's most famous writers, responsible for works that include 'Ulysses' and 'Portrait of the Artist as a Young Man'. Events include a re-enactment of Paddy Dignam's funeral in Ulysses, walking tours around Dublin and various talks on James Joyce, Ulysses and Bloomsday. The actual Bloomsday celebration takes place on 16 June, starting with the *Guinness Bloomsday Breakfast* which consists of 'eating with relish the inner organs of beasts and fowls', washed down with the 'foaming ebon ale', and listening to readings from the book of the day. The event is named Bloomsday after Leopold Bloom, the main character in 'Ulysses', and takes place on this day as the book was set on 16 June 1904. The annual *Bloomsday Lecture & Walking Tour* also takes place on 16 June, with talks by Ken Monaghan, Cultural Director of the Centre and nephew of James Joyce, and a walking tour through the city, with characters from 'Ulysses' popping up along the way. Other events include the Riverrun which celebrates the River Liffey and the women in Joyce's books and involves a bus trip to the mouth of the river and Howth Head, rounded off with readings and refreshments in the *Bloody Steam Pub*.

Event Organiser

The James Joyce Centre, 35 North Great George's Street, Dublin 1, Ireland
Tel: (01) 878 8547. Fax: (01) 878 8488.
E-mail: jamesjoyce@adnet.ie
Website: www.jamesjoyce.ie

Venue

Various locations across Dublin, including North Great George's Street, Westland Row train station, Temple Bar, National Library and the James Joyce Centre.

Transport

Air: Dublin Airport. **Rail:** Train: Tara Street or Connolly stations. **Road:** Bus: 3, 10, 11, 13, 16, 19, 22 or 123 to the northern end of O'Connell Street and then signposts from the Parnell Monument. **Road:** Car: N2 (from Monaghan); M1, A1 and N1 (from Belfast); N9, M9, M7 and N7 (from Waterford); N11 (from the port of Dún Laoghaire).

• September-October

Dublin Fringe Festival

Dublin Fringe Festival first took place in 1995 and now takes place every year at the end of September. The festival, which lasts for three weeks, encorporates the best of theatre, dance, comedy and visual arts. Performances in 2000 included Ben Street's 'A Good One is a Dead One', which also showed at the *Edinburgh Fringe Festival*, and starred

Fergal McElherron, who won the 1999 Dublin Fringe Theatre Best Actor Award for his performance in Owen McCafferty's 'Mojo Mickybo'. Other highlights in 2000 included a theatrical adaptation of 'The Countrywoman', written by the Irish writer Paul Smith in 1961, and Phillip Owen's 'Homer', a collection of dramatic and comic tales.

Event Organiser

Dublin Fringe Festival, 5 Aston Quay, Dublin 2, Ireland
Tel: (01) 872 9016. Fax: (01) 872 9138.
E-mail: fringe@eircom.net
Website: www.fringefest.com

Venue

20 locations in Dublin, including Civic Theatre, Samuel Beckett Theatre, Temple Bar Square and The Crypt at Dublin Castle.

Transport

Air: Dublin Airport. **Rail:** Train: Connolly or Heuston stations. **Road:** Car: N2 (from Monaghan); M1, A1 and N1 (from Belfast); N9, M9, M7 and N7 (from Waterford); N11 (from the port of Dún Laoghaire).

Israel

Tel Aviv

Tourist Information

Tel Aviv-Jaffa Tourist Information Office
New Central Bus Station, Sixth Floor, Room 6108, Tel Aviv, Israel
Tel: (03) 639 5660. Fax: (03) 639 5659.
Website: www.infotour.co.il

• August

Jaffa Nights

Jaffa Nights is held annually in the city of Tel Aviv during mid-August. Lasting for four days, it comprises over 70 music, theatre, dance and art exhibitions, and is Israel's largest street-staged event. In the evenings, the streets of the Old Jaffa area are closed to traffic, during which time the streets come alive with music and dance performed on stages erected in the city's various squares and alleys. Tens of thousands of visitors attend the festival every year.

Event Organiser

Tel Aviv Municipality, Events Department, Tel Aviv 64162, Israel
Tel: (03) 521 8264. Fax: (03) 521 8852.

Venue

Old Jaffa area of Tel Aviv.

Transport

Air: Ben-Gurion International Airport. **Train:** Rail: Tel Aviv Central Station. **Road:** Coach: Egged Bus Company provides services to Tel Aviv (from Jerusalem, Haifa, Beersheva and Ashdod). Car: Ayalon Highway (from the north, via Haifa and Netanya).

Italy

Florence

Tourist Information

Azienda di Promozione Turistica di Firenze (Florence Tourist Board)
Via Cavour 1r, 50129 Florence, Italy
Tel: (055) 290 832. Fax: (055) 276 0383.
E-mail: infoturismo@provincia.fi.it
Website: www.firenze.turismo.toscana.it

• March

Explosion of the Cart

The origins of this ritual, which is known as the *Scoppio del Carro* in Italian, go back to the time of the first Christian crusade to seize control of the Holy City of Jerusalem from the Muslims in 1095. A valiant soldier called Pazzino dei Pazzi fought bravely against the enemy and was the first to scale the walls of Jerusalem, where he raised the Christian flag. For this he was rewarded with some stones from the Holy Tomb. The hero took these with him to Florence to be used by the bishop to light the fire in the cathedral on Easter morning; this fire was then distributed to every Florentine citizen. The Pazzi family then began to build a cart (or *Brindellone*, as it is called in Italian), which has been burned at this annual event for many centuries. On Easter Sunday, starting at 0950, two separate processions transport the stones and the cart (which is led by oxen) from the *Chiesa dei Santi Apostoli* (the Church of the Holy Apostles) throughout the city to the *Piazza del Duomo* (Cathedral Square), where they meet. A special Easter mass then takes place inside the cathedral. During the Gloria (the second element of Catholic mass) at 1100, a rocket, in the form of a dove, which is connected to the car, is set alight. This in turn causes the cart, which is loaded with fireworks, to explode in a mass of colour and light, watched by hundreds of spectators. According to tradition, if the ceremony goes smoothly Florence will have good harvests and a prosperous year.

Event Organiser

For more information on the Explosion of the Cart, contact the Florence Tourist Board (see **Tourist Information** above).

Venue

Piazza del Duomo in central Florence.

Transport

Air: Amerigo Vespucci Airport (Florence) or Galileo Galilei Airport (Pisa). **Rail:** Train: Firenze Santa Maria

Novella Station (Florence). **Road:** Bus: 14, 23 or 71 (from Santa Maria Novella to Piazza del Duomo). Car: A1 (from Milan, Bologna, Rome or Naples); A11 (from Pisa, Lucca, Prato or Siena).

• June

Historical Soccer Tournament

Costumed football matches (now known as *Calcio Storico Fiorentino* in Italian) have long been played in the Piazza Santa Croce in the historic heart of Florence. The origins of the game date back at least to Roman times, with the moves involved in the game being similar to the battle order of the Roman army. It was not until centuries later that football migrated north to England and evolved into the modern game known today. The game was characterised by fights and locked battles for possession of the ball, all of which were meant to strengthen both the body and the mind of the civilians and soldiers who played. Famous players included members of prestigious Renaissance families such as Lorenzo de' Medici and Vincenzo Gonzaga. Matches were played at Carnival time and throughout the year until the end of the 18th century; the tradition was revived in 1930, the 400th anniversary of the siege of Florence, as a means of celebrating the city's resilience in the face of adversity through the centuries. Nowadays, three matches are held on the city's patron saint's day in June and players wear Medieval costumes representing the four districts of the city: white for Santo Spirito, blue for Santa Croce, red for Santa Maria Novella and green for San Giovanni. The backdrop to this colourful spectacle is the celebrated Franciscan church of Santa Croce.

Event Organiser

Calcio Storico Fiorentino – Segretaria, Piazzetta di Parte Guelfa 1, 50123 Florence, Italy
Tel: (055) 295 409 *or* 239 8828. Fax: (055) 276 8401.
E-mail: feste.tradizioni.fiorentine@comune.it
Website: www.globe.it/caf/info.html

Venue

Piazza Santa Croce in central Florence.

Transport

Air: Amerigo Vespucci Airport (Florence), Galileo Galilei Airport (Pisa). **Rail:** Train: Firenze Santa Maria Novella Station (Florence). Road: Bus: 14 or 23. Car: A1 (from Milan, Bologna, Rome or Naples); A11 (from Pisa, Lucca, Prato or Siena).

Rome

Tourist Information

Azienda di Promozione Turistica di Roma (Rome Tourist Office)
Via Parigi 11, 00185 Rome, Italy
Tel: (06) 4889 9253. Fax: (06) 4889 9250.
Website: www.romaturismo.com

• July-September

Roman Summer

Rome's summer arts festival (*Estate Romana* in Italian) is a three-month extravaganza encompassing all manner of events. Balmy summer evenings can be spent watching some of the many Italian and foreign films showing at the open-air cinema in *Piazza Vittorio*, or enjoying a live classical music concert in one of the city's parks. The programme for 2000 featured a huge variety of performances, including Alan Ayckbourn's play 'Confusion', concerts given by Beatles tribute bands from around the globe, an exhibition of Christian art in Bulgaria and a celebration of Latin American culture through dance, music, and food and drink. The Italians are renowned for their love of children, and younger visitors will find plenty of distractions to amuse them, from sports competitions to games and cartoons; parents who accompany them can learn Latin American dancing or surf the Internet.

Event Organiser

For more information on the Roman Summer, contact the Rome Tourist Office (see **Tourist Information** above).

Venue

Various locations across Rome.

Transport

Air: Rome Leonardo de Vinci Airport (Fiumicino) or Rome Ciampino Airport. **Water:** Ferry: Civitavecchia port, from where there are services to central Rome. **Rail:** Train: Roma Termini, Roma Tiburtina, Roma Ostiense or Roma Trastevere stations. **Road:** Car: A12 (from the west); A24 (from the east); SS7 (from Ciampino Airport).

• October-December

Rome Jazz Festival

Throughout its 25-year history, the *Rome Jazz Festival* has featured many prominent artists, including the Steve Lacy Quartet, Cuban jazz player Gonzalo Rubalcaba, guitarist John McLaughlin and the Brad Mehldau Trio. Venues range from *Big Mama*, Rome's premier blues club, which has earned the nickname 'Home of the Blues in Rome', to *Auditorium del Massimo*, an historic cultural institute now housed in the city's ultra-modern EUR business district. Jazz and Latin American music have long been popular in Italy's capital and this festival brings together the best of both.

Event Organiser

Rome Jazz Festival, Via Salaria 292, 00199 Rome, Italy
Tel: (06) 5630 9574. Fax: (06) 5630 5015.
E-mail: m.ciampa@romajazzfestival.it
Website: www.romajazzfestival.it

Venue

Various venues across Rome.

Transport

Air: Rome Leonardo de Vinci Airport (Fiumicino) or Rome Ciampino Airport. **Water:** Ferry: Civitavecchia port, from where there are services to central Rome. **Rail:** Train: Roma Termini, Roma Tiburtina, Roma Ostiense or Roma Trastevere stations. Underground: EUR Palasport (to Auditorium del Massimo). **Road:** Bus: 75 or 170 (to Big Mama from Roma Termini Station). Car: A12 (from the west); A24 (from the east); SS7 (from Ciampino Airport).

• December

Christmas Mass in St Peter's Basilica

One of the most moving ways to celebrate Christ's birthday is by attending this mass in the second largest church in the Christian world. Work on the *Basilica di San Pietro*, or St Peter's Basilica (so named as it is said to stand on the burial site of St Peter), was begun in 1506 during the time of Pope Julius II, and completed in 1615 under Pope Paul V. Artists and architects involved in its design and construction include famous Renaissance names such as Raphael, Bramante and Michelangelo. The fruits of their labour are awe-inspiring, with the huge interior filled with works of Renaissance and Baroque art, among them Michelangelo's 'Pietà'. Visitors who wish to join the crowds for this special occasion must book in advance by contacting the Prefettura della Casa Pontificia and stating the number of tickets they require.

Event Organiser

Prefettura della Casa Pontificia, 00120 Vatican City, Italy
Tel: (06) 6988 3114. Fax: (06) 6988 5863.
Website: www.vatican.va

Venue

Basilica di San Pietro (St Peter's Basilica).

Transport

Air: Rome Leonardo de Vinci Airport (Fiumicino) or Rome Ciampino Airport. **Water:** Ferry: Civitavecchia port, from where there are services to central Rome. **Rail:** Train: Roma Termini, Roma Tiburtina, Roma Ostiense or Roma Trastevere stations. Underground: Ottaviano-San Pietro. **Road:** Car: A12 (from the west); A24 (from the east); SS7 (from Ciampino Airport).

Venice

Tourist Information

Azienda di Promozione Turistica (Venice Tourist Board)
Calle dell'Ascensione 71C, Venice, Italy
Tel: (041) 529 8711. Fax: (041) 523 0399.
E-mail: info@turismovenezia.it
Website: www.turismovenezia.it

• February

Venice Carnival

The wearing of masks has been a Venetian tradition since the 13th century. It was particularly popular with gamblers as a means of disguising their identity from their creditors, although the law stated that masks were not allowed during religious festivals, including Lent. They were, however, permitted from San Stefano's Day (26 December) until Shrove Tuesday and this period, the *Carnevale* (as it is known in Italian), saw huge celebrations across the city, with masked balls in the *palazzi* lining the Grand Canal and bullfights and cart-racing in the streets. Nowadays, although it does not start until February, *Venice Carnival* is one of the most famous in Europe and the age-old traditions continue to thrive. Visitors to the city can see actors and ordinary Venetians posing in opulent costumes around *Piazza San Marco* (St Mark's Square), and there are still masked balls in the historic buildings, or *palazzi*, along the canals; tickets for the *Golden Night Ball* in the Palazzo Ca' Zenobio on the last night of the carnival cost about L520,000 (£170) and, as for all balls, guests must arrive in costume. A cheaper option is to enjoy the long-standing tradition of hot chocolate and cakes in one of the city's many cafés, or listen to one of the concerts that take place during the event. Many visitors are content just to mix with the crowds and take in the festive atmosphere. On the first day of the carnival, the *Festa delle Marie* (Festival of the Brides) takes place – seven young women, representing seven brides who were kidnapped and robbed by pirates in AD 948, travel from *San Pietro di Castello* to St Mark's Square where dancing and street entertainment follow. The real climax of the carnival is the last Saturday, when thousand of people flock to the city; many of the balls take place on this night and there are concerts in St Mark's Square.

Event Organiser

Comitato per il Carnevale di Venezia Consortium, Piazzale Roma, Santa Croce 473, 30133 Venice, Italy
Tel: (041) 717 065. Fax: (041) 722 285.
E-mail: info@guestinvenice.com
Website: www.guestinvenice.com

Venue

Various locations across Venice with the focus on St Mark's Square.

Transport

Air: Marco Polo Airport (Venice). **Water:** Waterbus (*Vaporetto*): 1 or 82 (from Piazzale Roma to San Zaccaria for St Mark's Square). **Rail:** Train: Venezia Santa Lucia or Mestre stations. **Road:** Car: A4 (from Padua, Milan or Turin); A13, then A4 (from Bologna); A1, then A13, then A4 (from Florence, Rome or Naples). From Mestre, follow signs for *centro* (centre) to Piazzale Roma, where car parking is available. Transportation is then by ferry to the historic city centre.

• March-November

Venice Biennial

The *Venice Biennial* is a major cultural institution endorsed by the Italian Parliament. It was founded in 1895 with the aim of promoting contemporary art and culture to a wider audience by setting up permanent workshops and projects. Every two years, the *Biennale* (as it is known in Italian) presents a varied programme of art exhibitions, dance, music, cinema and theatre in the city, attracting worldwide interest and often provoking controversy. Past exhibitors have included Benetton designer Oliviero Toscani and American artist Robert Rauschenberg. The 49th International Art Exhibition, directed by Harald Szeemann in 2001 features work by artists from around the world at the Castello Gardens (Giardini di Castello) and the Venice Arsenal (Arsenale di Venezia). The seventh International Architecture Exhibition takes place from the 18 June to the 29 October. The dance element of the festival (June, July and September) includes pieces choreographed by artists from Egypt, Turkey and Morocco, amongst others. The Biennial also incorporates the *Festival of Music* (May and September), the *International Film Festival* and the *International Theatre Festival* (March, May, July and September).

Event Organiser

Venice Biennale Cultural Corporation, Ca' Giustinian, San Marco 1364/a, 30124 Venice, Italy
Tel: (041) 521 8711. Fax: (041) 523 6374.
E-mail: segregen@labiennale.com
Website: www.labiennale.org

Venue

Various venues across Venice.

Transport

Air: Marco Polo Airport (Venice). **Water:** Waterbus (*Vaporetto*): 1 or 82 (from Piazzale Roma to San Zaccaria for St Mark's Square). **Rail:** Train: Venezia Santa Lucia or Mestre stations. **Road:** Car: A4 (from Padua, Milan or Turin); A13, then A4 (from Bologna); A1, then A13, then A4 (from Florence, Rome or Naples). From Mestre, follow signs for *centro* (centre) to Piazzale Roma, where car parking is available. Transportation is then by ferry to the historic city centre.

• August-September

Venice International Film Festival

The *Venice International Film Festival* was founded in 1932 by Mussolini in a bid to demonstrate Italy's increasing global importance and it is still the second most important film festival in the world, after Cannes. In 2000, over 2000 journalists attended the festival, and almost half of these were from outside Italy. The main action takes place on the *Lido*, where directors and film stars mingle with the world's press and compete for the prizes, the most prestigious award being the Golden Lion, which was won in 2000 by Iranian director Jafar Panahi for his film 'Dayereh' (The Circle). Films are open to the public and screened in the *Palazzo del Cinema* on Lungomare Marconi and at the *Astra* on Via Corfu; tickets can either be bought on the door or purchased a day in advance from VeLa ticket agency at Calle dei Fuseri or at Piazzale Roma between 0830-1830.

Event Organiser

Venice Biennale Cultural Corporation, Ca' Giustinian, San Marco 1364/a, 30124 Venice, Italy
Tel: (041) 521 8711. Fax: (041) 523 6374.
E-mail: segregen@labiennale.com
Website: www.labiennale.org

Venue

The main focus is the Venice Lido.

Transport

Air: Marco Polo Airport (Venice). **Water:** Waterbus (*Vaporetto*): 51, 52, 61 or 82 (from Piazzale Roma). **Rail:** Train: Venezia Santa Lucia or Mestre stations. **Road:** Car: A4 (from Padua, Milan or Turin); A13, then A4 (from Bologna); A1, then A13, then A4 (from Florence, Rome or Naples). From Mestre, follow signs for *centro* (centre) to Piazzale Roma, where car parking is available. Transportation is then by ferry to the Lido.

Japan

Tokyo

Tourist Information

Tokyo Tourist Information Center (TIC)
Tokyo International Forum, 3-5-1 Marunouchi, Chiyoda-ku, Tokyo, Japan
Tel: (03) 5221 9084. Fax: (03) 5221 9083.
Website: www.tcvb.or.jp

• March-April

Ueno Cherry Blossom Festival

Every year thousands of people gather in *Ueno Park* in Tokyo to see over 1300 beautiful cherry blossom trees come into bloom. Cherry blossoms (or *sakura* in Japanese) are the national flower in Japan and are believed to represent beauty, as well as signifying the end of winter and the beginning of spring. During the annual *Ueno Cherry Blossom Festival*, Ueno Park is lit by lanterns every evening. People hold various parties to admire the cherry blossoms and also gather in *Sumida Park* along the Sumida River to see even more cherry blossom trees bloom.

Event Organiser

For more information on the Ueno Cherry Blossom Festival, contact the Tokyo Tourist Information Center (see **Tourist Information** above).

Venue
Ueno Park, Tokyo.

Transport
Air: New Tokyo Narita International Airport or Haneda Airport (domestic flights). **Rail:** Train: Tokyo Station. Underground: Ueno Station. **Road:** Car: Tomei-Meishin Expressway (from Kobe); Chuo Expressway (from Nagano and Nagoya).

• May

Sanja Festival

First held more than 200 years ago, *Sanja Festival* is one of Tokyo's biggest festivals when the city's residents carry *Mikoshi* (mini-shrines) through the crowded streets surrounding the *Asakusa Shrine*. The shrine (*Asakusa-jinja* in Japanese) was founded during the 17th century and is housed in the grounds of the famous *Senso-ji Temple* in Tokyo. It is dedicated to the two fishermen who discovered the Kannon statuette, which is also housed in the Senso-ji Temple, whilst fishing in the Sumida River. Today, the festival sees around two million people gather in Tokyo to watch the festivities, which include annual music performances, and to carry around one hundred shrines through the city to honour the famous shrine.

Event Organiser
For more information on the Sanja Festival, contact Tokyo Tourist Information Center (see **Tourist Information** above).

Venue
The streets of Asakusa, surrounding the Asakusa Shrine in Sensoji Temple.

Transport
Air: New Tokyo Narita International Airport or Haneda Airport (domestic flights). **Rail:** Train: Tokyo Station. Underground: Asakusa. **Road:** Bus: Asakusa Bus Stop. Car: Tomei-Meishin Expressway (from Kobe); Chuo Expressway (from Nagano and Nagoya).

• July

Tokyo Fireworks Festival

Tokyo Fireworks Festival, which is known as *Sumida-gawa Hanabi Taikai* in Japanese, was first held in the city in 1733 by Shogun Yoshimune who organised the display to pay respects to those who had died during a famine in 1732. It has since grown to become firmly established as Tokyo's main summer fireworks event. Around 20,000 *hanabi* (flower-fires) light up the night skies and up to one million people line the streets and river banks to watch the displays. The event is usually held on the last Saturday in July every year.

Event Organiser
For more information on the Tokyo Fireworks Festival, contact the Tokyo Tourist Information Center (see **Tourist Information** above).

Venue
Along the banks of the Sumida River.

Transport
Air: New Tokyo Narita International Airport or Haneda Airport (domestic flights). **Rail:** Train: Tokyo Station. Underground: Asakusa. **Road:** Car: Tomei-Meishin Expressway (from Kobe); Chuo Expressway (from Nagano and Nagoya).

Mexico

Mexico City

Tourist Information
Oficina de Turismo de la Ciudad de México (Mexico City Tourist Office)
Londres Amberes, Colnia Juarez, Zona Rosa, 06600 Mexico City, Mexico
Tel: (05) 525 9380.
E-mail: Mitdf001@netservice.com.mx
Website: www.mexicocity.gob.mx

• March

Festival of the Historic Centre

The *Festival del Centro Histórico* (as it is known in Spanish), first held in 1985 to promote Mexico City's old quarter, is a three-week festival celebrating the best in Mexican and international culture. It has become increasingly popular and in 2000 attracted unprecedented audiences of 950,000. A wide variety of events are held in churches, cloisters, squares and concert halls around the historic centre, ranging from performances of theatre, dance and opera to food and drink tastings and children's activities. There are also film screenings, art exhibitions, cultural seminars and guided tours of the historic centre, with themes such as 'Prehispanic times' and 'Jewish Life'.

Event Organiser
Festival del Centro Histórico de la Ciudad de México AC, Avenida Benjamin Franklin 176, Col Escandón, Mexico DF, 11800 Mexico
Tel: (0525) 277 9757. Fax: (0525) 272 2936.
E-mail: festival@mail.infolatina.com.mx
Website: www.festival.org.mx

Venue
Various locations across Mexico City.

Transport
Air: Mexico City International Airport. **Rail:** Train: Buenavista Station. **Road:** Car: Route 57/57D (from Querétaro, San Luis Potosí or Monterrey); Route 150D (from Veracruz or Puebla); Route 15/15D (from Toluca or Guadalajara). Route 95D (from Cuernavaca or Acapulco).

The Netherlands

Amsterdam

Tourist Information

VVV Amsterdam Kantoor Stationsplein (Amsterdam Tourist Office)
Stationsplein 10, 1012 AB Amsterdam, The Netherlands
Tel: (020) 551 2525. Fax: (020) 625 2869.
E-mail: info@amsterdamtourist.nl
Website: www.visitamsterdam.nl

• April

Queen's Day

On *Queen's Day* (which is known as *Koninginnedag* in Dutch), Amsterdamers take part in a giant street party to celebrate the Queen's birthday. Every year on 30 April, people take to the streets to join in the festivities on what has been a national holiday since the end of World War II. The festivities kick off around 1800 on 29 April and last well into the small hours of the next day. People consume large amounts of alcohol and dress up in orange clothes, as the Queen is from the House of Orange; some of them even paint their faces orange in order to join in the celebrations. Queen's Day actually takes place on the Queen Mother's (Juliana) birthday as Queen Beatrix's birthday is 31 January and considered too cold for any festivities. On 30 April, people also attempt to sell their unwanted household items in the street when the city turns into a giant flea market. There is a chance to pick up a real bargain, although much of the merchandise could easily be classed as junk. Amsterdam becomes extremely crowded on Queen's Day, particularly if it is sunny, and visitors are advised to get there early.

Event Organiser
Rijks Voorlichtings Dienst (RVD), Debennenhof 20, 20001 The Hague, The Netherlands
Tel: (070) 356 4000. Fax: (070) 363 3214.
E-mail: info@koninginnedag.nl
Website: www.koninginnedag.nl

Venue
Various locations across Amsterdam and Holland.

Transport
Air: Amsterdam Airport Schiphol. **Rail:** Train: Amsterdam Centraal Station. **Road:** Car: E19 (from the airport and The Hague); A2 (from Utrecht); A6 and A7 (from Groningen).

• May

National Windmill and Pumping Station Day

National Windmill and Pumping Station Day is organised every year on the second Saturday in May. Approximately 650 watermills and windmills across Holland open their doors free of charge to visitors. Many windmills also put on exhibitions and demonstrations to explain a miller's work to the general public. Mills which take part in the event can be recognised easily as they have large blue banners on display and they also all turn their sails. There are over 1000 windmills in Holland, although there are only four working windmills in Amsterdam itself. Windmills in Amsterdam include De Rieker, on the banks of the Amstel, two windmills on Haarlemmerweg (1200 Roe and De Bleom), De Gooyer, 1100 Roe and d'Admiraal.

Event Organiser
De Hollandsche Molen, Zeeburgerdijk 139, 1095 AA, Amsterdam, The Netherlands
Tel: (020) 623 8703. Fax: (020) 638 3319.
E-mail: dhm@molens.nl
Website: www.molens.nl

Venue
Windmills across Amsterdam and Holland.

Transport
Air: Amsterdam Airport Schiphol. **Rail:** Train: Amsterdam Centraal Station. **Road:** Car: E19 (from the airport and The Hague); A2 (from Utrecht); A6 and A7 (from Groningen).

• June

Holland Festival

The *Holland Festival* takes place in Amsterdam every June and focuses on the performing arts, including opera, theatre, music and dance. In 2000, the 53rd festival attracted 118,000 visitors, with more than 50,000 attending the popular *Amsterdam Roots Festival* in the city. In total, there were 42 productions and 104 performances, appealing to all ages and tastes. Highlights in 2000 included concerts paying tribute to legendary musician Frank Zappa and dance performances choreographed by Sasha Waltz of Germany. There were also numerous theatre performances by groups from across Europe, the USA, South Africa and New Zealand.

Event Organiser
Stichting Holland Festival, Kleine Gartmanplantsoen 21, 1017 RP, Amsterdam, The Netherlands
Tel: (020) 530 7110. Fax: (020) 530 7119.
E-mail: info@hollandfestival.nl
Website: www.hollandfestival.nl

Venue
Across Amsterdam, in various theatres and concert halls, including the Paradiso, Theater Bellevue and the festival centre, Stadsschouwburg. There are also events around Leidesplein.

Transport
Air: Amsterdam Airport Schiphol. **Rail:** Train: Amsterdam Centraal Station. **Road:** Car: E19 (from the airport and The Hague); A2 (from Utrecht); A6 and A7 (from Groningen).

• August

Amsterdam Gay Pride

Amsterdam Gay Pride is one of Europe's largest gay and lesbian events and takes place in the city in the middle of summer. There is an enormous *Canal Parade*, when the city's gay and lesbian community takes to the canals in boats, wearing fancy dress and playing music. There are also numerous sport and cultural events throughout the city, as well as huge weekend parties. In 2000, *Amsterdam Sport 2000* saw 1000 participants competing in events including swimming, football and wrestling. Also in 2000, there was an *Open Air Film Festival* at Nieuwmarkt and gay-themed performances in many of the city's theatres.

Event Organiser

Siep de Haan, Lange Niezel 7, Amsterdam, NH 1012 GS, The Netherlands
Tel: (020) 620 8807. Fax: (020) 662 7572.
E-mail: guide@gayamsterdam.com
Website: www.gayamsterdam.net/pride

Venue

Various locations across Amsterdam city centre, including festivities on the canals.

Transport

Air: Amsterdam Airport Schiphol. **Rail:** Train: Amsterdam Centraal Station. **Road:** Car: E19 (from the airport and The Hague); A2 (from Utrecht); A6 and A7 (from Groningen).

New Zealand

Auckland

Tourist Information

Tourism Auckland

PO Box 5561, Wellesley Street, Auckland, New Zealand
Tel: (09) 979 7070. Fax: (09) 970 7080.
E-mail: citysails@aucklandnz.com
Website: www.aucklandnz.com

• April

Royal Easter Show

The first *Royal Easter Show* was held in 1843 by the newly-formed Auckland Agricultural and Horticultural Society to promote the advantages the town could offer to prospective settlers. It has grown from its origins as a small livestock show to incorporate sporting events, family entertainment, animal shows and commercial exhibits, attracting thousands of visitors throughout the ten days. There are equine events such as showjumping and dressage, displays of rare sheep breeds, a 'New Zealand's Strongest Man' competition, junior sporting championships including basketball and karate, craft demonstrations and exhibits featuring ceramics, photography, Chinese art and painting by mouth and foot. Various stalls are situated in the Commercial Exhibit Halls, and feature food and wine, home improvements and information and technology. Musicians, acrobats and theatre groups travel from as far afield as England to entertain the crowds, and there is also a special children's theatre, a children's art workshop and the opportunity for visitors to try their hand at milking cattle or shearing sheep.

Event Organiser

Auckland Show Grounds, PO Box 26014 Auckland, New Zealand
Tel: (09) 638 9969. Fax: (09) 630 3350.
E-mail: kevin@akl-showgrounds.org.nz
Website: www.royaleastershow.co.nz

Venue

Auckland Showgrounds.

Transport

Air: Auckland International Airport. **Rail:** Train: Auckland Station. **Road:** Bus: Services to Otahuhu (from the city centre Britomart Bus Terminal). Car: SH1 (from Warkworth, Bay of Islands, Hamilton or Rotorua). Visitors should take the Manukau exit and follow Royal Easter Show signs to Great South Road.

• November

Ellerslie Flower Show

Every summer, Auckland's 64-hectare (160-acre) *Regional Botanic Gardens* host the largest gardening and outdoor show in the Southern Hemisphere, the *Ellerslie Flower Show*. Some 65,000 visitors come from New Zealand and around the world to enjoy floral displays, plant stalls, fruit and vegetable markets, musical concerts, food and drink and garden sculptures by top New Zealand artists, situated around the lake. Gardening enthusiasts can pick up tips from lectures and demonstrations and, on the last Sunday, materials used in the exhibits, such as paving stones and exotic flowers, are sold off to the public.

Event Organiser

Ellerslie Flower Show, PO Box 6855 Wellesley Street, Auckland, New Zealand
Tel: (09) 309 7875. Fax: (09) 307 6840.
E-mail: mail@ellersliefIowershow.co.nz
Website: www.ellersliefIowershow.co.nz

Venue

Auckland Regional Botanic Gardens.

Transport

Air: Auckland International Airport. **Rail:** Train: Auckland Station. **Road:** Bus: Services to Drury, Papakura or Pukehohe (from central Auckland). Car: SH1 (from Warkworth, Bay of Islands, Hamilton or Rotorua). Visitors should take the Manukau exit and follow Ellerslie Flower Show signs to Everglade Drive or Great South Road, where car parking is available.

Norway

Bergen

Tourist Information

Turistinformasjonen
(Bergen Tourist Information)
Vågsallmenningen 1, 5014 Bergen, Norway
Tel: (055) 321 480. Fax: (055) 321 464.
E-mail: info@visitBergen.com
Website: www.visitBergen.com

• May-June

Bergen International Festival

Bergen International Festival features numerous music, ballet and theatre performances and is the largest event of its kind in Norway and one of the premier international performing arts festivals in Europe. In 2000, dance highlights included the Paul Taylor Dance Company and Carte Blanche, whilst theatre highlights included the first Bergen performances of Henrik Ibsen's drama 'Emperor and Galilean'. The festival's extensive music programme focuses primarily on Norwegian music. There are regular performances by the highly-acclaimed Bergen Philharmonic Orchestra, performing work by the composer Edvard Grieg, as well as appearances from the violinist Ole Bull and the composer Arne Nordheim.

Event Organiser

Bergen International Festival, Box 183 Sentrum, 5084 Bergen, Norway
Tel: (055) 210 630. Fax: (055) 210 640.
E-mail: henning.malsnes@fib.no
Website: www.fib.no

Venue

Various venues in the Bergen area, including the Grieg Hall, the Hakon Hall, the Masonic Lodge and the houses of three local composers: Edvard Grieg, Ole Bull and Harald Sæverud.

Transport

Air: Bergen Airport. **Rail:** Train: Bergen Station. **Road:** Car: E16 (from Voss); E18, E16 and E39 (from Oslo).

Bergen Night Jazz Festival

Bergen Night Jazz Festival (known as *Nattjazz* in Norway) takes place every year and is one of the longest jazz festivals in Northern Europe, lasting for almost two weeks. The festival plays host to a wide range of performances, ranging from traditional jazz to world music, rock, folk, bebop, hard pop, jazz rock, fusion and funk. The majority of events take place in venues at the *Kulturhuset USF* (*United Sardines Factory*), which can hold approximately 1600 people; they include Røkeriet USF, Sardinen USF and Scene USF. Previous artists have included John Scofield Quartet, Cesaria Evora, Kari Bremnes, Gli Impossibli and Anneli Drecker.

Event Organiser

Natt Jazz, PO Box 1957, Nordnes 5817 Bergen, Norway
Tel: (055) 307 250. Fax: (055) 307 260.
E-mail: nattjazz@nattjazz.no
Website: www.nattjazz.no

Venue

Held in an area reserved for the festival, as well as at other venues in the city. The festival area is an old sardines factory, called Kulturhuset USF, which is now used for concerts, exhibitions, theatre and cinema.

Transport

Air: Bergen Airport. **Rail:** Train: Bergen Station. **Road:** On foot: Kulturhuset USF is located on Sergels torg square in the centre of the city and can be reached easily on foot from the city centre. Car: E16 (from Voss); E18, E16 and E39 (from Oslo).

Peru

Lima

Tourist Information

PromPeru
Edificio Mitince, Calle Uno, 13th and 14th Floor, San Isidro, Lima, Peru
Tel: (01) 224 3125. Fax: (01) 224 3323.
E-mail: infoperu@promperu.gob.pe
Website: www.peruonline.net

• October

Lord of Miracles

The *Lord of Miracles* festival is the most important cultural event in Lima's calendar and the largest religious procession in the Americas. Hundreds of purple-clad worshippers carry an image of a black Christ through the city's streets every day during the festival to the sound of chanting and church bells. The image has hung in Lima's Church and Convent of the Nazarenes since it was painted in 1665. It is known as *Neustro Señor de los Milagros* (Our Lord of Miracles) since it survived several earthquakes remarkably intact. Concerts and firework displays also form part of the celebrations, which are followed throughout November by Lima's bullfighting season at the 200-year-old *Plaza de Acho*, the oldest arena in the Americas.

Event Organiser

For more information on the Lord of Miracles, contact PromPeru (see **Tourist Information** above).

Venue

Various locations across Lima.

Transport

Air: Jorge Chavez International Airport (Lima). **Road:** Car: Pan-American Highway (from Arequipa, Trujillo, Talara or coastal cities in Chile and Ecuador).

Poland

Krakow

Tourist Information

Centrum Informacji Turystycznej (Tourist Information Centre)
ulica Pawia 8, 31-154 Krakow, Poland
Tel: (012) 422 6091. Fax: (012) 422 0471.
Website: www.krakow.pl

• December-February

Krakow Christmas Crib Contest

The *szopki* (nativity crib) is very much a part of the Polish Christmas tradition. The first ever crib was made by Jan Velita in Italy on the instruction of St Francis of Assisi three years before his death in 1225. From its simple origins, the idea was taken up by the rich merchants and noblemen who commissioned artists to create ever more elaborate versions. Krakow cribs, which can be up to 1.8m (6ft) tall, maintain this tradition and are modelled on local buildings with their Gothic towers, Baroque onion domes and Renaissance façades. The city's first crib contest was held in 1937 and the event is organised annually by the Krakow Ethnography Museum. All entries, made by both professional craftsmen and amateurs, are put on show at the *Adam Mickiewicz Monument* in the Old Market for several days, and are then taken to the *Ethnography Museum* where they are judged; the prizewinners are announced in early December. The most exquisite and beautifully crafted cribs are then displayed in the museum for the next two months.

Event Organiser

Museum of History (Muzeum Historyczne), Rynek Gÿówny 35, Krakow, Poland
Tel: (012) 422 9922.

Venue

Plac Wolnica (Wolnica Square) and Muzeum Etnograficzne (Museum of Ethnography).

Transport

Air: Krakow-Balice John Paul II International Airport. **Rail:** Train: Krakow Station. Tram: 10 (from Main Market Square). **Road:** Coach: Services from Lviv (Ukraine), Prague (Czech Republic) and Vienna (Austria) to Dworzec PKS (Central Bus Station). Car: E77 (from Warsaw or Gdansk); E40 (from Lviv, Ukraine or Dresden, Germany).

• June-July

Jewish Culture Festival

For centuries the *Kazimierz* district of Krakow provided a haven for persecuted Jews in Europe. Professional, middle-class Jews contributed much to Polish cultural life, particularly in the fields of music and literature, and Jews were free to worship and set up their own organisations and societies. Steven Spielberg's film 'Schindler's List' famously depicts the destruction of Kazimierz during World War II, when Jewish businesses and institutions were razed to the ground and the Jews were deported from the ghetto to the concentration camps, where they were tortured and murdered. Now, some 50 years on, Kazimierz is once again a thriving centre for Jewish culture, and the last 12 years have seen the *Jewish Culture Festival* grow to become an internationally-recognised event. The streets, theatres and synagogues of Krakow host a range of events incuding film, dance, theatre, the visual arts, lectures and music, with the Jerusalem Jazz band, the Klezmatics and Double Edge Theatre all having performed at the festival in the past. Workshops enable visitors to learn about Jewish traditions such as paper cutting, Hebrew calligraphy, dance and cookery; the workshops are led by instructors who earn a living from such skills. This is a particuarly poignant and triumphal celebration of Jewish culture and a chance for visitors to Krakow to learn more about the rich heritage of this remarkable people.

Event Organiser

Jewish Culture Festival Society, Graffiti Film Centre, sw Gertrudy 5, Krakow, Poland
Tel: (012) 431 1535. Fax: (012) 431 2573.
E-mail: office@jewishfestival.art.pl
Website: www.jewishfestival.pl

Venue

Various locations across Kazimierz.

Transport

Air: Krakow-Balice John Paul II International Airport. **Rail:** Train: Krakow Station. Tram: 13, 19 or 10 (from Krakow Station or Main Market Square). **Road:** Coach: Services from Lviv (Ukraine), Prague (Czech Republic) and Vienna (Austria) to Dworzec PKS (Central Bus Station). Car: E77 (from Warsaw or Gdansk); E40 (from Lviv, Ukraine or Dresden, Germany).

• July

Krakow International Street Theatre Festival

Krakow's main market square, *Rynek Glówny,* is the biggest Medieval square in Europe and every July it is the venue for the city's street theatre festival. Theatre groups from around Europe entertain the crowds each evening against the backdrop of period houses and pavement cafés. The programme for 2001 included shows from France, Poland and Ukraine, with several experimental theatre groups taking part. Performances take place between 1800 and 2200 each day.

Event Organiser

Teatr KTO, ulica Gzymsików 8, 30-015, Krakow, Poland
Tel: (012) 623 7300. Fax: (012) 633 8947.
E-mail: teatrkto@kki.net.pl *or* info@tcatr-kto.art.pl

Venue

Rynek Glówny in Krakow's Old Town.

Transport

Air: Krakow-Balice John Paul II International Airport. **Rail:** Train: Krakow Station. Tram: 10 (from Krakow Station). **Road:** Coach: Services from Lviv (Ukraine), Prague (Czech Republic) or Vienna (Austria) to Dworzec PKS (Central Bus Station). Car: E77 (from Warsaw or Gdansk); E40 (from Lviv, Ukraine or Dresden, Germany).

Warsaw

Tourist Information

Centrum Informacji Turystycznej (Tourist Information Centre)
Aleja Jerezolimsie 54, Warsaw, Poland
Tel: (022) 635 1881. Fax: (022) 831 0464.
E-mail: info@warsawtour.pl
Website: www.warsawtour.pl

• June-July

Warsaw Mozart Festival

Warsaw Mozart Festival began in 1991, when all 24 of the great composer's stage pieces were performed, and is the largest festival of its kind in the world. Mozart enthusiasts are able to hear oratorio, chamber, symphony and stage pieces in the Warsaw Chamber Opera Theatre. Mozart's connections with Warsaw date back to 1783, when 'Die Entführung aus dem Serail' ('Abduction from the Seraglio') was performed by the German theatre troupe Gottlieb Lorenz. The programme for 2001 once again offered music lovers the chance to see all of Mozart's operas, including 'The Magic Flute', 'The Marriage of Figaro' and 'Così Fan Tutte'.

Event Organiser

Warsaw Chamber Opera, Aleja Solidarnosci 76B, Warsaw, Poland
Tel: (022) 831 2240 *or* 621 9383.
E-mail: tickets@wok.pol.pl

Venue

Warsaw Chamber Opera Theatre, Solidarnosci Avenue (near Bankowy Square).

Transport

Air: Warsaw (Okecie) International Airport. **Rail:** Train: Warsaw Central Station. Tram: 17, 29 or 33. **Road:** Bus: 148 (to Zoliborz from Warsaw Central Station). Car: E30 (from Lodz, Poznan, Belarus or Berlin, Germany); E77 (from Krakow or Gdansk); E67 (from Wroclaw).

Portugal

Lisbon

Tourist Information

Associação Turismo de Lisboa (Lisbon Tourist Association)
Apartado 3326, 1301 Lisbon, Portugal
Tel: (021) 346 3314. Fax: (021) 031 2899.
E-mail: atl@atl-turismolisboa.pt
Website: www.atl-turismolisboa.pt

• February

Lisbon Carnival

Carnival signals the end of winter and the beginning of Lent and is celebrated in Lisbon with colourful costume parades and copious amounts of food and drink. In recent years, the Portuguese festivities have taken on a Latin American flavour and many Brazilian TV stars cross the Atlantic to join in the fun. The best place to go to watch the celebrations is the *Parque das Naçoes*.

Event Organiser

Câmara Municipal de Lisboa (Lisbon City Council), Avenida 5 de Octubro, 283 8º, 1600-035 Lisbon, Portugal
Tel: (021) 793 4702. Fax: (021) 793 4628.
E-mail: turismo@netpub.cm-lisboa.pt

Venue

Parque das Naçoes and across various locations across Lisbon.

Transport

Air: Lisbon International Airport. **Rail:** Train: Santa Apolónia, Rossio, Barreiro or Cais do Sodré stations. Tram: Estação do Oriente. **Road:** Bus: Services to Estação do Oriente (Eastern Station). Car: A1 (from Porto); A5 (from Cascais); E1 (from Faro).

• April

Lisbon Half Marathon

The *Lisbon Half Marathon* is watched with particular interest by those in the athletic field as it determines the world's top long distance runners before the major marathons in Boston and London later in the month. The 2001 winner, South African Hendrick Ramaala, won over US$100,000 after he completed the notoriously fast course of 21km (13.1 miles) in 60 minutes and 26 seconds. There is a party atmosphere in the streets, with live music playing. In addition, free ice cream and gifts are provided by the race sponsors at the finish line.

Event Organiser

Maratona Clube de Portugal, Bàrro Francisco Sà Caraeiro, Av. João Freitas Branco 10, Caxias, 2780 Paço de Arcos, Portugal
Tel: (021) 441 3182. Fax: (021) 441 3073.
Website: www.maratona-clube-portugal.pt

Venue

Starts at the 25 April suspension bridge across the River Tejo and finishes at the Mosteiro dos Jeronemos in Belém via the city centre.

Transport

Air: Lisbon International Airport. **Rail:** Train: Santa Apolónia, Rossio, Barreiro or Cais do Sodré stations. Tram: 15 or 17 (to Belém). Underground: Belém. **Road:** Bus: 27, 28, 29, 43 or 49 (to Belém). Car: A1 (from Porto); A5 (from Cascais); E1 (from Faro).

• June

Lisbon Festivities

Lisbon celebrates its patron saint (St Anthony) in a three-week spectacular of street parties, fireworks and entertainment known as the *Festas de Lisboa* in Portuguese. The *Marchas Populares* in mid-June are a chance to see thousands of people from the different neighbourhoods of the city march down the Avenida da Liberdade, displaying colourful costumes and banners that have taken many months to create. The festivities continue long into the night, with music, dancing and sardine barbecues. The best place to go to join one of these parties, or *arraiais*, is the *Alfama* district of the city. Throughout the whole three-week period, both visitors and locals can enjoy theatre, circus, mime and all kinds of music, from pop and ethnic to classical and jazz, in Lisbon's many squares.

Event Organiser

Equipamentos dos Bairros Històricos de Lisboa EM, rua de Campo de Ourique, 120, 1250 Lisbon, Portugal
Tel: (021) 383 9130. Fax: (021) 383 9139.
E-mail: festas@aeiou.pt
Website: www.ebahl.com

Venue

Alfama district and various locations across Lisbon.

Transport

Air: Lisbon International Airport. **Rail:** Train: Santa Apolónia, Rossio, Barreiro or Cais do Sodré stations. **Road:** Car: A1 (from Porto); A5 (from Cascais); E1 (from Faro). Taxi: Taxi is the best way to reach Alfama.

• December

Magic Night

Magic Night (*Noite Mágica* in Portuguese) aims to create a New Year's Eve party with a difference. There is a ten-minute firework display over the *River Tejo*, which is choreographed to a specially-created musical soundtrack featuring Portuguese bands past and present. Once the show is over, there is a Latin American disco and live music also in the area along the river into the early hours of New Year's Day. Many hotels in Lisbon also organise their own events featuring food, wine and live entertainment. The *Casino Estoril* (Estoril Casino), located 18km (11 miles) outside Lisbon, hosts various shows and an outdoor party.

Event Organiser

Câmara Municipal de Lisboa (Lisbon City Council), avenida 5 de Outubro, no 293-80, 1600 Lisbon, Portugal
Tel: (021) 793 4702. Fax: (021) 793 4628.
E-mail: turismo@netpub.cm-lisboa.pt

Venue

Along the River Tejo between Parque das Nações and the district of Algés.

Transport

Air: Lisbon International Airport. **Rail:** Train: Santa Apolónia, Rossio, Barreiro or Cais do Sodré stations. Tram: 15 or 17. Underground: Belém. **Road:** Bus: 27, 28, 29, 43 or 49. Car: A1 (from Porto); A5 (from Cascais); E1 (from Faro).

Russian Federation

Moscow

Tourist Information

Ministerstvo Turisma (Ministry of Tourism)
18 ul. Kazakova, 103064 Moscow, Russian Federation
Tel: (095) 207 7117 *or* 207 3891. Fax: (095) 263 0761.

• December-January

New Year

On 31 December every year, revellers party in the streets of Moscow to see in the *New Year*. Traditionally Moscovites used to celebrate New Year's Eve (which is known as *Noivy God* in Russian) at home before taking to the streets after midnight to visit friends and neighbours and drink vast amounts of alcohol until the early hours. Increasingly, more and more people gather in Red Square to hear the stroke of midnight from the Kremlin, and to drink champagne in the city centre. Many people also dress in fancy dress, either as 'Grandfather Frost' or the 'Snow Maiden', as they go about the city wishing a happy new year to fellow revellers.

Event Organiser

For more information on New Year, contact the Ministry of Tourism (see **Tourist Information** above).

Venue

Red Square and across the city.

Transport

Air: Moscow Sheremetyevo International Airport. **Rail:** Train: Kiev Station. Underground: Kitay-Gorod. **Road:** Bus: 2 or 33 to Okhotny ryad. Car: M1 (from Minsk); M2 (from Kiev); M7 (from Nizhny Novgorod); M9 (from Riga); M10 (from St Petersburg). Then, Moskovskaya Koltsevaya Avtomobilnaya Doroga (Moscow ring road) to the city centre.

• September

Moscow International Peace Marathon

The 21st *International Peace Marathon* will take place in Moscow in September 2001. The event takes place through the streets of Moscow, starting at 1100 at Red Square in front of St Basil's Cathedral. The course runs along the Moscow River, past many of the city's finest historic monuments, including the Kremlin, the Cathedral of Christ the Saviour and the Peter the Great Monument in Gorky Park. The event finishes in front of the Rossya Hotel, near St Basil's Cathedral. On the day before the marathon, there is a *Marathon Expo* conference for runners and a lottery draw. In the evening, there is a pasta party at the Golden Hill restaurant in the Rossya Hotel, with musical performances from folk bands.

Event Organiser

For more information on Moscow International Peace Marathon, contact the Ministry of Tourism (see **Tourist Information** above).

Venue

Starts at Red Square through the streets of Moscow, and finishes at the Rossya Hotel, near St Basil's Cathedral.

Transport

Air: Moscow Sheremetyevo International Airport. **Rail:** Train: Kiev Station. Underground: Kitay-Gorod. **Road:** Bus: 2 or 33 to Okhotny ryad. Car: M1 (from Minsk); M2 (from Kiev); M7 (from Nizhny Novgorod); M9 (from Riga); M10 (from St Petersburg). Then, Moskovskaya Koltsevaya Avtomobilnaya Doroga (Moscow ring road) to the city centre.

Singapore

Singapore

Tourist Information

Singapore Tourism Board

Tourism Court, 1 Orchard Spring Lane, Singapore 247729

Tel: (65) 736 6622. Fax: (65) 736 9423.

E-mail: stb_sog@stb.gov.sg

Website: www.newasia-singapore.com

• March-April

Singapore Food Festival

First held in 1994, *Singapore Food Festival* is a giant culinary event that allows visitors to taste food from around the world. During the month-long event, visitors can sample culinary delights from as far afield as Italy, Turkey and Japan, as well as taste the best of Chinese and Asian cuisine. They can also take part in food tours and wander through the streets of Singapore, which are filled with the aromatic smells of different dishes. In 2001, the theme of the eighth Singapore Food Festival was 'Feast Your Senses'. The festival kicks off with a three-day opening celebration which is a carnival of food and entertainment, featuring live music, as well as food and drink from around the world.

Event Organiser

Singapore Tourism Board, Events Marketing Division, Tourism Court, 1 Orchard Spring Lane, Singapore 247729

Tel: 323 5150.

E-mail: sff@eventspeople.com

Website: www.singaporefoodfestival.com.sg

Venue

Various locations across Singapore.

Transport

Air: Singapore Changi Airport. **Rail:** Train: Singapore Station. **Road:** Car: Singapore can be reached from the one kilometre-long causeway, which links the northern district of Woodlands with Malaysia's Johor Bahru.

• April

Singapore International Film Festival

Singapore International Film Festival is one of the most important celebrations of Asian cinema in the world, with more than 300 films from over 40 countries shown in Singapore during the event. In 2001, the 14th international film festival focused on a tribute to the Filipino director, Mario O'Hara, and on showing documentaries from around the world in the special 'Stranger than Fiction – the Documentary Film' programme. The festival opened with Sergei Eisestein's 1938 classic, 'Alesander Nevsky', accompanied by the Singapore Symphony Orchestra. It also looked back over 100 years of cinema and payed tribute to Harun Farockis and Chris Marker, as well as looking at films by Georges Méliès and the Lumière brothers. The festival was first held in 1987 to allow film enthusiasts to view films which would not normally be given a mainstream release. The festival also awards Silver Screen Awards which were introduced in 1991 and are given to the best Asian film, as well as to the best actor, actress and director.

Event Organiser

Film Festival Pte Ltd, 45A Keong Saik Road, Singapore 089149
Tel: 738 7567. Fax: 738 7578.
E-mail: filmfest@pacific.net.sg
Website: www.filmfest.org.sg

Venue

Golden Village (GV) cinemas in the city, such as Golden Village Grand, as well as the Goethe Institut and Alliance Française de Singapour.

Transport

Air: Singapore Changi Airport. **Rail:** Train: Singapore Station. **Road:** Car: Singapore can be reached from the one kilometre-long causeway, which links the northern district of Woodlands with Malaysia's Johor Bahru.

South Africa

Cape Town

Tourist Information

Cape Town Tourism
PO Box 1403, Cape Town 8000, South Africa
Tel: (021) 426 4260. Fax: (021) 426 4266.
E-mail: info@cape-town.org
Website: www.cape-town.org

• May

Cape Gourmet Festival

Every May, Cape Town plays host to two weeks of events celebrating the indulgent world of food and wine. The central focus is the Good Food and Wine Show on the last weekend of the festival, with culinary demonstrations and masterclasses, wine-tasting sessions, stalls selling olive oil, cheeses and local wines and appearances by celebrity chefs. Chefs come from around the world to exchange ideas and prepare gastronomic delights in the city's restaurants, and a whole host of hotels and eating establishments organize their own special menus and events, from international food-tasting evenings to jazz concerts.

Event Organiser

Cape Gourmet Festival, Suite 80, Roeland Square, Roeland Street, Cape Town, Western Cape, South Africa 8001
Tel: (021) 465 0069. Fax: (021) 465 8901.
E-mail: info@capegourmet.co.za
Website: www.capegourmet.co.za

Venue

Good Hope Centre (Good Food and Wine Show) and various venues across Cape Town.

Transport

Air: Cape Town International Airport. **Rail:** Train: Cape Town Station. **Road:** Car: N1 (from Johannesburg); N7 (from the west coast and Namibia); N2 (from the Garden Route and Overberg).

Johannesburg

Tourist Information

Tourism Johannesburg
Upper Shopping Level, Village Walk Shopping Centre, corner of Rivonia Road and Maud Street, Rosebank, Johannesburg, South Africa
Tel: (011) 784 1354. Fax: (011) 883 4035.
E-mail: marketing@tourismjohannesburg.co.za
Website: www.tourismjohannesburg.co.za

• April-May

Rand Easter Show

The *Rand Easter Show* is one of the biggest exhibitions in Southern Africa, attracting around half a million visitors in 2000. The show has developed from its origins as an agricultural event in 1894, when it was hosted by Witwatersrand Agricultural Society, to become a giant consumer fair and entertainment show. As well as merchandise on display from almost 600 South African exhibitors and over 100 foreign exhibitors from nine different countries, the show also features live music, as well as sporting events and an amusement park. Highlights in 2001 included the *5FM Easter Rock Festival*, featuring the best of South African rock music, *Kyknet Rapport Musiekfees Afrikaans* music event, a football tournament featuring celebrities, a strongman championships and *South African Gladiators*. There was also an animal carnival in 2001 which included Bobtail dog jumping and camel appearances.

Event Organiser

Kagiso Exhibitions Pty Ltd, Private Bag X 383, Cresta, 2118, South Africa
Tel: (011) 670 2000. Fax: (011) 679 5729.
E-mail: randshow@kagisoexpo.co.za
Website: www.randshow.co.za

Venue

Expo Centre, which is located in the Nasrec area of Johannesburg.

Transport

Air: Johannesburg International Airport. **Rail:** Train: Trains stop at the grounds (from Park Station). **Road:** Car: N1 (from Cape Town); N3 (from Harrismith, Pietermaritzberg and Durban); N2 (between Durban and Cape Town); N4 Trans-Kalahari Highway (from Zeerust, Botswana and Namibia); N4 Maputo Corridor (from Witbank, Middleberg and Nelspruit).

Spain

Barcelona

Tourist Information

Turisme de Barcelona (Barcelona Tourist Office)
Plaça de Catalunya 17-S, 08002 Barcelona
Tel: (093) 238 4000. Fax: (093) 238 4010.
Website: www.bcn.es

• January

Three Kings Parade

The story of the Three Kings is recorded in the Bible, in St Matthew's Gospel, and tells of three wise men who travelled from the east to Bethlehem to present gifts of gold, frankincense and myrrh to the infant Jesus. Epiphany, as Twelfth Night (5 January) is known in the Christian church, commemorates the journey of the Three Kings and is widely celebrated throughout Europe. At the end of each year, Catalan children post their wish lists to the Three Kings in special boxes in stores around Barcelona. On the night of 5 January, they then place a shoe on the balcony of their house for the Three Kings to fill with sweets, as well as a bucket of water and food for the camels. Every 5 January, for the *Cabalgata de los Reyes Magos*, or *Three Kings Parade*, the Three Kings arrive at the harbour at *Moll de Fusta* with their entourage and sacks full of presents, and are greeted by city officials and excited children before going about their annual duties. The kings arrive at 1800 in the harbour and it is advisable to arrive as early as possible to get the best view. The men who represent the three kings are chosen from among Barcelona's citizens; Melchior and Caspar are elected by members of the city's council, while Balthazar has been represented by the same person for over 40 years. Toy and sweet stalls are set up in the streets from the beginning of the New Year to Twelfth Night; the most popular are those on Gran Vía which sell candy miniatures of food.

Event Organiser

For more information on the Three Kings Parade, contact Barcelona Tourist Office (see **Tourist Information** above).

Venue

The stalls are mainly located along Gran Vía; the Three Kings arrive at the harbour.

Transport

Air: Barcelona Airport. **Rail:** Train: Central-Sants Station. Underground: Tetuan or Monumental (to Gran Vía); Drassanes or Barceloneta (to harbour). **Road:** Car: A7 (from Alicante, Perpignan, France or Montpellier, France); A2 (from Zaragoza); NII-E90, then A2 (from Madrid).

• June-July

Barcelona Summer Festival (GREC)

The *Teatre Grec* amphitheatre, built into the mountainside at *Montjuic*, is the birthplace of the *Barcelona Summer Festival* (popularly known as GREC), which started when a group of disillusioned actors and directors got together to produce a small fringe theatre festival in 1976. It has since grown to become the biggest and most popular festival in Barcelona. Every summer for around six weeks, tourists and locals are treated to a huge variety of events, from theatre, dance and cinema to classical music, rock and circus. The venues are just as varied, with Gothic chapels, vast modern theatres and concert halls all hosting events. At the open-air *Picornell* swimming pool it is even possible to watch a film whilst relaxing in the water.

Event Organiser

GREC, Palau de la Virreina, La Rambla 99, 08002 Barcelona, Spain
Tel: (093) 301 7775 *or* 479 9920 (tickets).
Fax: (093) 301 6100.
E-mail: infoicub@mail.bcn.es
Website: www.grec.bcn.es

Venue

Various venues across Barcelona.

Transport

Air: Barcelona Airport. **Rail:** Train: Central-Sants Station. **Road:** Car: A7 (from Alicante, Perpignan, France or Montpellier, France); A2 (from Zaragoza); NII-E90, then A2 (from Madrid).

• September

Our Lady of Mercy Festival

According to legend, *La Mercé* (Our Lady of Mercy, or the Virgin Mary) once saved Barcelona from a plague of locusts, and thus became the patron saint of the city. A wide range of activities takes place during the festival, such as musical concerts and theatre performances in outdoor theatres, food and wine fairs, and sports activities. The main events are a huge fireworks display, the *Dance of the Giants* and the *Correfac*, when demons, dragons and other devilish creatures run amock through the streets of the city's old quarter, throwing firecrackers.

Event Organiser

For more information on the Our Lady of Mercy Festival, contact Barcelona Tourist Office (see **Tourist Information** above).

Venue

Various locations across Barcelona.

Transport

Air: Barcelona Airport. **Rail:** Train: Central-Sants Station. **Road:** Car: A7 (from Alicante, Perpignan,

France or Montpellier, France); A2 (from Zaragoza); NII-E90, then A2 (from Madrid).

Madrid

Tourist Information

Oficina Municipal de Turismo (City Tourist Office)
Plaza Mayor 3, 28012 Madrid, Spain
Tel: (091) 588 1636. Fax: (091) 366 5477.
Website: www.tourspain.es

• February

Madrid Carnival

In February each year, before the beginning of Lent, a week of festivities brightens up the streets of the Spanish capital as the centuries old tradition of *Carnaval* (Carnival) comes to town. There is a procession of carriages and a costumed parade through the streets of Madrid with a fancy dress competition adding to the fun. The party ends with a peculiar ritual known as *El Entierro de la Sardina* (the Burial of the Sardine). This ritual involves people in black cloaks and top hats following a coffin that contains an effigy of a sardine, which is then buried at the 18th-century hermitage of *San Antonio de la Florida* near the city centre. However, the mood is not entirely sombre as the procession stops at *tavernas* on the way for a drink or two.

Event Organiser

For more information on the Madrid Carnival, contact the City Tourist Office (see **Tourist Information** above).

Venue

Calle de Cádiz, San Antonio de Florida and various locations across Madrid.

Transport

Air: Madrid Barajas Airport. **Rail:** Train: Chamartín or Atocha stations. **Road:** Car: NI (from Irún, Burgos or Biarritz, France); NIII (from Zaragoza or Barcelona); NIII (from Valencia or Alicante); NIV (from Seville); NV (from Badajoz or Lisbon, Portugal); N401 (from Toledo).

• May

Festimad Alternative Music Festival

Visitors to *Festimad* can catch the latest in the alternative music scene in a beautiful 350 sq metres (325 sq ft) of parkland. The two days of events that have been held each summer since 1995 attract some 20,000 spectators who come to be entertained by a whole host of rock and indie bands, DJs and other performers – concerts in the past have featured groups such as Metallica, Deftones, Limp Bizkit and the Black Crowes. The site is turned into a music village with facilities including bars, restaurants, a supermarket and showers for those who wish to camp.

Event Organiser

Festimad, Gran Vía 68, 5E 28013 Madrid, Spain
Tel: (091) 547 2385. Fax: (091) 541 3513.
Website: www.festimad.es

Venue

El Soto de Móstoles, which is located 20km (12.4 miles) from central Madrid.

Transport

Air: Madrid Barajas Airport. **Rail:** Train: Chamartín or Atocha stations. Underground: El Soto (the festival site can then be accessed on foot). **Road:** Bus: 522 (from Príncipe Pío underground station in central Madrid). Car: NI (from Irún, Burgos or Biarritz, France); NIII (from Zaragoza or Barcelona); NIII (from Valencia or Alicante); NIV (from Seville); NV (from Badajoz or Lisbon, Portugal); N401 (from Toledo). From central Madrid, access to festival car parks is from exit 18 of the NV motorway.

• May-June

San Isidro Festival

San Isidro is the patron saint of Madrid and every year, from mid-May to mid-June, festivities take place throughout the city in celebration; these festivities are known as the *Fiestas de San Isidro* in Spanish. According to tradition, all those from Madrid must make a pilgrimage to the shrine on the banks of the River Manzanares on the spot where the saint is said to have miraculously caused a spring to open up from the ground. Traditional dress is worn and specialities such as *barquillos* (rolled wafers), *buñuelos* (fritters) and *rosquillas* (doughnuts) are sold throughout the city. The famous *taurina* (bullfighting fair) is part of the Fiestas and fights take place every day at the historic *Plaza Monumental Las Ventas* bull ring.

Event Organiser

Plaza Monumental Las Ventas, Calle Acalá 237, 28000 Madrid, Spain
Tel: (091) 726 4800. Fax: (091) 361 1607.
Website: www.las-ventas.com

Venue

Various locations across Madrid.

Transport

Air: Madrid Barajas Airport. **Rail:** Train: Chamartín or Atocha stations. Underground: Ventas (to Plaza Monumental Las Ventas). **Road:** Car: NI (from Irún, Burgos or Biarritz, France); NIII (from Zaragoza or Barcelona); NIII (from Valencia or Alicante); NIV (from Seville); NV (from Badajoz or Lisbon, Portugal); N401 (from Toledo).

• October-November

Madrid Autumn Festival

This festival brings a huge variety of cultural performances to Madrid and encompasses theatre, jazz, musical theatre, dance, literature and art. The 27th year of the festival in 2000 featured such diverse offerings as a musical entitled 'Spinach! Spinach!', a Spanish production of Beckett's 'Waiting for Godot', flamenco dancing and performances by the Nederlands Dans Theater and the Merce Cunningham Dance Company. Groups come from as far afield as Cuba, India and the USA to take part, and the festival offers a welcome diversion for *Madrileños* and visitors alike as the nights grow darker and the weather colder.

Event Organiser

Comunidad de Madrid – Consejería de Cultura (Culture Department of Madrid City Council), Plaza de España 8, 28000 Madrid, Spain
Tel: (091) 580 2505.
Website: www.comadrid.es

Venue

Various locations across Madrid.

Transport

Air: Madrid Barajas Airport. **Rail:** Train: Chamartín or Atocha stations. **Road:** Car: NI (from Irún, Burgos or Biarritz, France); NIII (from Zaragoza or Barcelona); NIII (from Valencia or Alicante); NIV (from Seville); NV (from Badajoz or Lisbon, Portugal); N401 (from Toledo).

Sweden

Stockholm

Tourist Information

Stockholm Information Service

Hamngatan 27, Kungsträdgården, 10393 Stockholm, Sweden
Tel: (08) 789 2490. Fax: (08) 789 2491.
E-mail: info@stoinfo.se
Website: www.stockholmtown.com

• June

Swedish National Day

Every year on 6 June, Skansen Open-air Museum in the heart of Stockholm hosts the *Swedish National Day* celebrations. The event is attended by the Swedish Royal family: King Carl XVI Gustaf, Queen Silvia, Crown Princess Victoria, Prince Carl Philip and Princess Madeleine. King Carl XVI Gustaf is the 74th King of Sweden who came to the throne in 1973. On this patriotic day, when Swedes remember their heritage, highlights include songs, speeches and flag-waving. The festivities are transmitted live on Swedish national television, allowing an even wider audience to see the day's events.

Event Organiser

Stiftelsen Skansen, Post Box 27807, 115 93 Stockholm, Sweden
Tel: (08) 442 8000 *or* 578 9005. Fax: (08) 442 8280.
E-mail: info@skansen.se
Website: www.skansen.se

Venue

Skansen Open-air Museum in Stockholm city centre.

Transport

Air: Stockholm Arlanda Airport. **Rail:** Train: Stockholm Central Station. Tram: From Norrmalmstorg to Skansen. **Road:** Bus: 44 or 47 from the city centre. Car: E18, E20 or E6 (from Oslo); E4 (from Malmö). Skansen is clearly signposted from Stockholm city centre.

• September

Stockholm Beer & Whisky Festival

The tenth *Stockholm Beer & Whisky Festival* will take place in Stockholm in September 2001. The festival, which began in 1992, is the leading festival for beer, cider and whisky in Scandinavia. Approximately 500 different varieties of beer are available for the public to sample and vote for in an awards ceremony, with a further 100 varieties of whisky and cider also on offer. Every year, more than 150,000 visitors attend the festival to taste different varieties of beer, whisky and cider. Highlights of the event include beer tastings, tutorings and the annual beer awards. Awards are given to the best fresh beer, best blond lager, best porter, best ale and best Swedish beer.

Event Organiser

Stockholm Öl & Vin AB, Karlavägen 75B, 114 49 Stockholm, Sweden
Tel: (08) 662 9494. Fax: (08) 662 9455.
E-mail: marianne.wallberg@stockholmbeer.se
Website: www.stockholmbeer.se

Venue

Nacka Strand in Stockholm.

Transport

Air: Stockholm Arlanda Airport. **Road:** Bus: 150, 404, 443, 475 or 830. Car: E18, E20 or E6 (from Oslo); E4 (from Malmö).

• November

Stockholm International Film Festival

The 12th *Stockholm International Film Festival*, which is one of the most important film festivals in Northern Europe, will take place in the city in November 2001. The festival, which was set up in 1990 by two Swedish film enthusiasts, is attended by more than 70,000 people every year who view some 150 films on offer.

Many entries are received from directors making their first, second or third film, as well as from directors of short films. The festival also focuses on different regions and screens films ranging from American independent films through to Asian cinema. Many famous names have attended the festival in previous years, including Dennis Hopper and Quentin Tarrantino. In 2000, a lifetime achievement award went to Lauren Bacall.

Event Organiser

Stockholm International Film Festival, PO Box 3136, 103 62 Stockholm, Sweden
Tel: (08) 677 5000. Fax: (08) 20 0590.
E-mail: info@cinema.se
Website: www.filmfestivalen.se

Venue

Various cinemas in Stockholm.

Transport

Air: Stockholm Arlanda Airport. **Rail:** Train: Stockholm Central Station. **Road:** Car: E18, E20 or E6 (from Oslo); E4 (from Malmö).

Switzerland

Geneva

Tourist Information

Genève Tourisme (Geneva Tourism)
Rue du Mont-Blanc 18, PO Box 1602, 1211 Geneva 1, Switzerland
Tel: (022) 909 7070. Fax: (022) 909 7075.
E-mail: info@geneva-tourism.ch
Website: www.geneva-tourism.ch

• March

International Motor Show

The *International Motor Show* takes place in Geneva every March. In 2000, during the 70th show, 714,000 visitors were in attendance from 87 different countries to see some of the world's newest and most innovative cars. Leading car manufacturers, including BMW, Audi, Ferrari, Ford, Jaguar, Mercedes-Benz and Porsche, are all present at the fair, eager to show off their new cars to the world. In 2000, the BMW M3 Coupé, Ford Galaxy and Rolls Royce Park Ward were all given their world premieres. Around 900 makes of car are exhibited, from 35 different countries, by 275 exhibitors. Cars are exhibited in numerous sectors, which include cars, fun cars, converted cars, special bodywork, equipment, accessories and components for cars, garage equipment and electric vehicles.

Event Organiser

ORGEXPO, Foundation for the promotion and organization of exhibitions and conferences – PO Box 112, 1218 Grand-Saconnex, Geneva, Switzerland
Tel: (022) 761 1111. Fax: (022) 798 0100.
E-mail: info@palexpo.ch
Website: www.salon-auto.ch

Venue

PalExpo Exhibition Centre in Geneva.

Transport

Air: Geneva International Airport. **Rail:** Train: Cornavin Station to Geneva Airport Station, which is 300m (328 yards) from PalExpo Hall 7. **Road:** Bus: Special buses run from Geneva city centre during the exhibition. Car: PalExpo is well signposted from Geneva; alternatively, Route de Meyrin (from the motorway towards Lausanne), then signs for Palais des Expositions or PalExpo.

• July-August

Geneva Festival

The *Geneva Festival* begins at the end of July and is one of Switzerland's biggest parties, with street parades, floats, techno parties and theatre performances. There are also various performances by folk groups and live concerts featuring international stars, as well as numerous operatic shows. Children are kept entertained by a giant clown parade, as well as a funfair on children's day at the end of July. Food from around the world is also on sale at street stalls during the festivities. More than 1,500,000 visitors attended the festivities in 2000 to join in this great outdoor party, which also includes spectacular firework displays over Lake Geneva.

Event Organiser

For more information on the Geneva Festival, contact Geneva Tourism (see **Tourist Information** above).

Venue

In and around Geneva harbour, Parc des Eaux-Vives, Théatre de Verdure and Grand Casino de Genève.

Transport

Air: Geneva International Airport. **Rail:** Train: Cornavin Station. **Road:** Car: N1 (from Lausanne).

• August

Swiss National Day

Swiss National Day takes place on 1 August every year to celebrate the union of three former Swiss states, Uri, Schwyz and Unterwalden on this date in 1921. Every year, Geneva holds celebrations, which include fireworks at the *Mur des Réformateurs*, a traditional bonfire and dancing after dark in the streets. On this day, which has been a national holiday since 1993, the Swiss drink large amounts of wine and eat local sausages cooked on barbecues. There are also plenty of speeches and a rendition of the national anthem. Other celebrations take place at the *Parc des Bastions* in Geneva's Old Town. In villages throughout Switzerland, the locals also join in the festivities to celebrate their national day, with children lighting coloured lanterns and parents dancing around the bonfire.

Event Organiser

For more information on Swiss National Day, contact Geneva Tourism (see **Tourist Information** above).

Venue

Mur des Réformateurs and the Parc des Bastions in Geneva. Celebrations also take place across Switzerland.

Transport

Air: Geneva International Airport. **Rail:** Train: Cornavin Station. Underground: Place Neuve Station. **Road:** Bus: 3 or 5 to Mur des Réformateurs. Car: N1 (from Lausanne).

Zurich

Tourist Information

Zürich Tourismus (Zurich Tourist Office)
Bahnhofbrücke 1, 8023 Zurich, Switzerland
Tel: (01) 215 4000. Fax: (01) 215 4044.
E-mail: information@zurichtourism.ch
Website: www.zurichtourism.ch

• April

Zurich Spring Festival

Zurich Spring Festival, which is known locally as *Sechseläuten*, celebrates the end of the cold winter weather and the start of spring. The festival begins with a children's parade on 22 April, with more than 2000 children taking part. This is followed by the main events on 23 April, when members of various guilds (or societies) eat a midday meal at their respective Guildhouses, before taking part in the *Parade of the Guilds* at 1515. Thousands of spectators line the streets of the city's Old Town to watch more than 7000 participants parade through the city. The highlight of the festival, the *Burning of the Böögg*, begins on the stroke of 1800 on 23 April. At the moment the bells of St Peter signal an end to winter in the city, a giant Böögg bonfire (in the shape of a snowman, representing the figure, Old Man Winter) is lit on Sechseläuten Field.

Event Organiser

Zentralkomitee der Zünfte, Herr Pit Wyss, Gumpenwiesenstrasse 13, 8157 Dielsdorf, Switzerland
Tel: (01) 853 1777. Fax: (01) 853 4150.
Website: www.sechselaeuten.ch

Venue

Sechseläutenwiese (Sechseläuten field) at Bellevue.

Transport

Air: Zurich Airport. **Rail:** Tram: Opernhaus or Bellevue Tram to Sechseläutenwiese, which is in front of Zurich's opera house. **Road:** Car: A1 (from Geneva).

• June-July

Zurich Festival

Every summer, Zurich's three main arts institutions – the Opera, the Tonhalle (concert hall) and the Kunsthalle (art gallery) – join forces to transform the city into a hive of cultural activity, with high-quality performances of opera, jazz, classical music, theatre, cinema and ballet, alongside exhibitions of art and literature. Highlights of 2000 included Alban Berg's 'Lulu' which, like the original 1937 production, was staged at the Zurich Opera House, and the Zurich Ballet's performance of Prokofiev's 'Cinderella'. The city's chapels and churches host smaller concerts.

Event Organiser

Zürcher Festpiele, Falkenstr 1, 8008 Zürich, Switzerland
Tel: (01) 269 9090. Fax: (01) 260 7025.
Website: www.zuercher-festspiele.ch

Venue

The Opera House, the Kunsthalle, the Tonhalle, and various other venues across Zurich.

Transport

Air: Zurich Airport. **Rail:** Train: Zurich Station. Tram: Opernhaus or Bellevue (to Opera House). **Road:** Car: A1 (from Geneva).

Thailand

Bangkok

Tourist Information

Kan Tong Teow Hang Prated Thai (Tourism Authority of Thailand)
Le Concorde Building, Tenth Floor, 202 Ratchadaphisek Road, Bangkok 10310, Thailand
Tel: (02) 694 1222. Fax: (02) 694 1220.
E-mail: center@tat.or.th
Website: www.tat.or.th

• April

Songkran Festival

Songkran, meaning 'to pass' or 'to relocate', heralds the arrival of the Thai New Year (when the sun exits Pisces and enters Aries), which is celebrated throughout the country. Bangkok festivities are centred on *Sanam Luang* (Royal Palace Ground), close to *Phra Barom Maha Rajcha Wang* (Royal Grand Palace), where an image of the Buddha is worshipped and bathed by religious elders and devotees; *Wat Phra Kaeo* (Temple of the Emerald Buddha) is another important site where worshippers gather during Songkran to receive blessings from elders. Water fights take place throughout the city, in particular in the old commercial district of *Bang Lamphu*. There are concerts and other forms of cultural entertainment on offer along the Khao San Road, where a *Miss Songkran* beauty pageant is also held.

Event Organiser

For more information on Songkran, contact the Tourism Authority of Thailand (see **Tourist Information** above).

Venue

Various locations across Bangkok.

Transport

Air: Bangkok International Airport. **Rail:** Train: Hualampong Station. **Road:** Car: NH4 (from Hua Hin); NH3 (from Pattaya); NH32 or NH177 (from Phitsanulok).

• August

Queen's Birthday Celebrations

Thailand's present queen, Queen Sirikit, was born M R Sirikit Kitiyakara on 12 August 1932. She enjoys a great deal of popularity in the country due to her humanitarian approach and the projects she has established to revive traditional arts and crafts. Every year, Thais celebrate her birthday by erecting portraits decorated with flowers on Ratchadamnoen Avenue near the Phra Barom Maha Rajcha Wang (Royal Grand Palace). The palace itself is festooned with coloured lights and other decorations, as are many other public buildings and private homes.

Event Organiser

For more information on the Queen's Birthday Celebrations, contact the Tourism Authority of Thailand (see **Tourist Information** above).

Venue

Various locations across Bangkok.

Transport

Air: Bangkok International Airport. **Rail:** Train: Hualampong Station. **Road:** Car: NH4 (from Hua Hin); NH3 (from Pattaya); NH32 or NH177 (from Phitsanulok). Taxi: Taxis or *tuk tuks* (three-wheeled taxis) are the best way to get around Bangkok.

Turkey

Istanbul

Tourist Information

Turizm Danisma Burosu (Tourist Information)
Sultanahmet Square, Istanbul, Turkey
Tel: (0212) 518 1802.
Website: www.turkey.org

• July

Istanbul Jazz Festival

The *Istanbul Jazz Festival* began life as an integral part of the *International Istanbul Music Festival* in 1986, and became a festival in its own right in 1994. For two weeks every July, the vibrant music venues and clubs of Istanbul's *Taksim* district, on the Asian side of the *Bosphorus*, play host to a variety of concerts that attract over 100,000 visitors each year. Jazz obviously features most prominently on the programme, past performers having included Dizzy Gillespie, Miles Davis and the Modern Jazz Quartet, but other musical genres, such as blues, reggae, pop, electronica, rock and World Music are also represented. Bryan Adams, Björk, Suzanne Vega and Keith Jarrett have all played at the Istanbul Jazz Festival, making it one of Europe's top music events.

Event Organiser

Istanbul Foundation for Culture and Arts, Istiklal Cadesi, Luvr Apt No 146 Beyoglu, Istanbul, Turkey
Tel: (0212) 293 3133. Fax: (0212) 249 5667.
E-mail: jazz.fest@istfest-tr.org
Website: www.istfest.org

Venue

Taksim district of Istanbul.

Transport

Air: Istanbul Atatürk Airport or Istanbul Sabiha Gökçen International Airport. **Rail:** Train: Sirkeci or Haydapasa stations. Tram: Taksim. **Road:** Bus: Services to Taksim Square. Car: E-80 or D-100 (from Edirne).

• September-November

Istanbul Biennial

The first *Istanbul Biennial* was organised in 1987 by the Istanbul Foundation for Culture and the Arts, and every two years presents a showcase of international contemporary art. The works of art are displayed in a variety of venues across the city, which have in past years included the beautiful *Topkapi Palace* gardens, the historic *Yerebatan Cisterns*, Ottoman warehouses and even Istanbul Atatürk Airport. The sixth Istanbul Biennial in 1999 was staged at a difficult time, during the aftermath of the terrible earthquake that shook the city, but still managed to attract work by 56 artists from 32 countries, that was viewed by 40,000 visitors. Exhibitors at the festival included British Turner Prize winners Gillian Wearing and Gavin Turk. The seventh edition in autumn 2001 bears the title 'Fugue from Ego for the Next Emergence' and looks at a move away from the selfish individuality of the 20th century towards a collective consciousness, intelligence and co-existence.

Event Organiser

International Istanbul Biennial, Istiklal Cadesi, Luvr Apt No 146 Beyoglu, Istanbul, Turkey
Tel: (0212) 293 3133. Fax: (0212) 249 5667.
E-mail: ist.biennial@istfest-tr.org

Website: www.istfest.org

Venue

Various venues across Istanbul.

Transport

Air: Istanbul Atatürk Airport or Istanbul Sabiha Gökçen International Airport. **Rail:** Train: Sirkeci or Haydapasa stations. **Road:** Bus: Car: E-80 or D-100 (from Edirne).

United Arab Emirates

Dubai

Tourist Information

Department of Tourism and Commerce Marketing (DCTM) Welcome Bureau
Beni Yas Square, Deira, Dubai, UAE
Tel: (04) 228 5000. Fax: (04) 228 0011.
Website: www.dubaitourism.co.ae

• February

Dubai Shopping Festival

Dubai has established itself in recent years as a mecca for duty-free shopping, and every March, visitors to the glittering Arab city can find even more bargains. The *Dubai Shopping Festival* features special discounts on a whole host of goods, from Rolls Royce cars to perfumes and jewellery, in shops across the city. In addition, visitors have the opportunity to win hundreds of prizes in shopping malls and department stores. There is also a Global Village, with pavilions selling goods from countries including Bangladesh, Vietnam and the Czech Republic. Once the purse is empty, there are many events and shows on offer, such as street theatre, fireworks and fashion shows.

Event Organiser

Dubai Shopping Festival Secretariat, PO Box 25425, Dubai, UAE
Tel: (04) 223 5444. Fax: (04) 223 5888.
E-mail: dsf@mydsf.com

Venue

Various venues across Dubai.

Transport

Air: Dubai International Airport. **Road:** Coach: Services to Gold Souk Bus Station or Al-Ghubaiba Bus Station. Car: Route 77 (from Jebel Ali); Route 88 (from Sharjah); Route 44 (from Wajajah); Route 66 (from Al Ain); Route 11 (from Abu Dhabi).

• March

Dubai World Cup

The *Dubai World Cup*, held in late March each year, is one of the most glamorous events in the sporting calendar, and certainly the richest. The two-kilometre (1.3-mile) sand and dirt track is floodlit for the thousands of spectators who come to watch the thoroughbred horses and their jockeys compete for the US$3.6 million prize. Unsurprisingly, the race attracts some of the best in the field and is closely watched by all involved in the sport. The 2001 Dubai World Cup was won by Jerry Bailey of the USA on Captain Steve, with Japan, France and the UAE taking second, third and fourth places.

Event Organiser

Dubai World Cup, Suite 213, City Tower 1, PO Box 1178, Dubai, UAE
Tel: (04) 332 2277. Fax: (04) 332 2288.
E-mail: dwc@dubaiworldcup.com
Website: www.dubaiworldcup.com

Venue

Nad Al Sheba Race Track.

Transport

Air: Dubai International Airport. **Road:** Coach: Services to Gold Souk Bus Station or Al-Ghubaiba Bus Station. Car: Route 77 (from Jebel Ali); Route 88 (from Sharjah); Route 44 (from Wajajah); Route 66 (from Al Ain); Route 11 (from Abu Dhabi).

United Kingdom

Cardiff

Tourist Information

Cardiff Visitors Centre
16 Wood St, Cardiff CF10 1ES, UK
Tel: (029) 2022 7281. Fax: (029) 2023 9162.
E-mail: enquiries@cardifftic.co.uk
Website: www.cardiffmarketing.co.uk

• July-August

Cardiff Festival

The *Cardiff Festival* takes place in Wales's capital city during July and August. This giant outdoor event attracts hundreds of thousands of people every year to its various free events. The three-week festival features the best in street theatre, live music and comedy in numerous events which take place across the city. The festivities kick off with *Celtic Food & Drink* in Cardiff Bay's Oval Basin. There are various concerts from the Welsh Proms, and the city's streets around Queen Street are brought to life with *Fiesta Nights*, which sees street performances from international artists. Queen Street is also the scene of more celebrations at the end of July when the *International Street Festival* brings the best of street theatre to the city. Also at the end of July, there is a *Children's Festival* in the grounds of Cardiff Castle, and *Admiral Comedy Antics* in the Sherman Theatre. One of the most popular events during the festival is

MAS Carnival on 28 July in Oval Basin, when around 400 partygoers, including stilt walkers, dancers and samba bands, join in the celebrations. The festival comes to a climax at the beginning of August, with the free, open-air *Big Weekend*, which attracts more than 750,000 visitors. Highlights of the weekend festival include a free music festival, free entry to the National Museum's exhibitions, the Lord Mayor's Parade, a giant funfair and a dance party.

Event Organiser

Cardiff County Council, County Hall, Atlantic Wharf, Cardiff CF10 4UW, UK
Tel: (029) 2087 3690 (festival information hotline). Fax: (029) 2087 3209.
Website: www.cardiff-info.com

Venue

Various locations across the city. The festival ends in the city's Civic Centre with the Big Weekend.

Transport

Air: Cardiff International Airport. **Rail:** Train: Cardiff Central Station. **Road:** Car: M4 (from London, Reading, Swindon, Bath, Bristol and Swansea).

• November

International Film Festival of Wales

The 13th *International Film Festival of Wales* will take place in Cardiff in November 2001. During the event, more than 100 short, feature-length and animated films will be screened in various venues across the capital. The festival attracts thousands of visitors every year, including members of the public, industry professionals and film enthusiasts, and there are many film premieres during the event. Highlights in 2000 included the opening-night premiere of 'A Beautiful Mistake' directed by Mark Evans of Wales; the film looks at collaborations between John Cale and some of Wales's biggest musical talents, including Catatonia and Super Furry Animals. Other premieres in 2000 included Karl Francis' 'One of the Hollywood Ten', a political drama set in the 1950s during the McCarthy era, starring Jeff Goldblum, as well as a screening of Martin Duffy's 'The Testimony of Taliesin Jones'. On the Sunday, there was a tribute to Desmond Llewelyn, who played Q for 36 years in the James Bond films before his death in 1999. It featured a documentary on one of Wales's best loved actors and an insight into the actor by biographer Sandy Hernu, as well as secrets on Q gadgets. Llewelyn's last Bond movie, 'The World is Not Enough', was also screened at the festival in 2000.

Event Organiser

International Film Festival of Wales, Market House, Market Road, Cardiff CF5 1QE, UK
Tel: (029) 2040 6220. Fax: (029) 2023 3751.
E-mail: enq@iffw.co.uk
Website: www.iffw.co.uk

Venue

Various cinemas and other venues across Cardiff, including Chapter Canton, Chapter Globe and UCI cinemas.

Transport

Air: Cardiff International Airport. **Rail:** Train: Cardiff Central Station. **Road:** Car: M4 (from London, Reading, Swindon, Bath, Bristol and Swansea).

Edinburgh

Tourist Information

Edinburgh and Lothians Tourist Board
3 Princes Street, Edinburgh EH2 2QP, UK
Tel: (0131) 473 3800. Fax: (0131) 473 3881.
E-mail: esic@eltb.org
Website: www.edinburgh.org

• December-January

Hogmanay

Edinburgh is undoubtedly one of the most exciting cities in the world to be at New Year, with celebrations taking place throughout the city over a five-day period. Traditional *Hogmanay* celebrations in Scotland date back to 1560 when the Protestant Reformation meant that many religious events, including Christmas, were banned. This meant that the Scots focused on celebrating non-Catholic days, such as New Year, as these were spared a religious ban. Edinburgh's Homanay celebrations began in 1992 when the Summit in the City and the European Union Heads of State Conference were held in the city. The festival has grown to be one of the world's largest New Year celebrations, attracting over half a million visitors, with performances from over 400 artists in around 60 venues. Edinburgh's Hogmanay mixes tradition with modern performances and appeals to all age groups. Highlights include the *Concert in the Gardens*, the *New Year Revels*, the *Winter Wonderland* ice rink in West Princess Street Gardens and the *Candlelit Concert* in the Cathedral. On 31 December 2000, the highly-acclaimed American artist, Moby, performed in Edinburgh Castle, New Year Revels took place at the Assembly Rooms, Bjorn Again played at the Concert in the Gardens and the *Royal Bank of Scotland Street Party* was held. Fireworks are let off around the city every year at midnight to celebrate Hogmanay.

Event Organiser

Edinburgh's Hogmanay Box Office, The Hub, Castle Hill, Royal Mile, Edinburgh EH1 2NE, UK
Tel: (09069) 150 150 (information; calls cost £1 per minute) *or* (0131) 473 2000. Fax: (0131) 473 2002.
E-mail: boxoffice@eif.co.uk
Website: www.edinburghshogmanay.org

Venue

Various locations across Edinburgh, with the main festivities taking place in the area around Princes Street and Edinburgh Castle.

Transport

Air: Edinburgh International Airport. **Rail:** Train: Waverley or Haymarket stations. **Road:** Car: M8 to Edinburgh (from Glasgow); A696 and A68 or A1 (from Newcastle-Upon-Tyne).

• January

Burns' Night

Every year, Scotsmen and women around the world gather to eat a traditional Burns' Supper to celebrate the life and works of the great Scottish poet, Robert Burns. He was born on 25 January 1759 and died on 21 July 1796. The National Bard of Scotland is most famous for poems which include 'To a Haggis', 'To a Daisy', 'Halloween' and 'To a Mouse'. He is also famous for writing the traditional New Year's Song, 'Old Langs Syne', as well as 'Scots Wha Hae', 'A Red, Red Rose' and 'Comin' Through the Rye'. On his birthday, people around Scotland remember his life and celebrate Scottish culture by eating a traditional meal of tatties (potatoes), neeps (turnip) and haggis (a mutton, oatmeal and onion mix, cooked in a sheep's stomach bag) and by consuming large quantities of Scotch whisky. It is customary to hear 'To a Haggis' recited during the celebrations; this famous poem is read by the evening's host. As he reads the line 'an cut you up wi' ready slight', he cuts open the haggis and the meal begins. *Burns' Night* celebrations range from formal gatherings, where Burn's most well-known poems are recited, to informal parties, where drunken revellers sing his most famous songs.

Event Organiser

For more information on Burns' Night, contact the Edinburgh and Lothians Tourist Board (see **Tourist Information** above).

Venue

Various venues, restaurants and bars across Scotland.

Transport

Air: Edinburgh International Airport or Glasgow International Airport. **Rail:** Train: Waverley Station (Edinburgh) or Glasgow Central Station (Glasgow). **Road:** Car: M8 (from Glasgow); A696 and A68 or A1 (from Newcastle-Upon-Tyne).

• April

Edinburgh International Science Festival

The 12th *Edinburgh International Science Festival* took place on 7-17 April 2001. The festival celebrates all aspects of science and technology, and has a wide appeal to all age groups. Visitors can take part in many interesting events, including lying on a bed of nails and floating in the Dead Sea Loch. Every year, approximately 175,000 visitors enjoy shows, workshops, exhibitions, talks and tours across Edinburgh. At the beginning of the 1990s, there were around 100 events at the festival, which attracted approximately 60,000 visitors. Today, there are around 300 events, attracting visitors from the UK and across Europe.

Event Organiser

Edinburgh International Science Festival, 8 Lochend Road, Edinburgh EH6 8BR, UK
Tel: (0131) 530 2001. Fax: (0131) 530 2002.
E-mail: esf@scifest.demon.co.uk
Website: www.go-edinburgh.co.uk/science

Venue

Various venues, including many of Edinburgh's art galleries.

Transport

Air: Edinburgh International Airport. **Rail:** Train: Waverley or Haymarket stations. **Road:** Car: M8 to Edinburgh (from Glasgow); A696 and A68 or A1 (from Newcastle-Upon-Tyne).

• June

Royal Highland Show

The *Royal Highland Show* takes place every year in June, just outside Edinburgh. The show attracts approximately 160,000 visitors who come to see over 5000 livestock and 2000 exhibitors. The highlights of the show are the displays of cattle, sheep and horses, as well as the *Food From Scotland* exhibition, which is the largest display of Scottish food and drink in the world. There is also a giant flower display, a crafts show and one of the largest displays of agricultural machinery in the UK.

Event Organiser

Royal Highland & Agricultural Society of Scotland, Royal Highland Centre, Ingliston, Edinburgh EH28 8NF, UK
Tel: (0131) 335 6200. Fax: (0131) 333 5236.
E-mail: info@rhass.org.uk
Website: www.rhass.org.uk

Venue

Royal Highland Centre, outside Edinburgh.

Transport

Air: Edinburgh International Airport. There is a free bus service to the show (from the airport). **Rail:** Train: Waverley Station. **Road:** Bus: 98 (from Waverley Bridge, via Princes Street and Haymarket), 39 (from St Andrew Square, via George Street, the West End and Haymarket Station), Citylink bus which stops on the main A8 road in Ingliston (from Glasgow) or Fife Scottish X58 bus (from St Andrews, via Glenrothes, Cowdenbeath and Dunfermline). Car: M9 or M90 (from the north); M8 (junction 2) (from Glasgow); A8 via Gogar Roundabout (from the east and south).

Need more information
on the United Kingdom?
Consult the *World Travel Guide*

• August

Edinburgh Fringe Festival

The *Edinburgh Fringe Festival* is held in August every year in parallel with the *Edinburgh International Festival.* The first Edinburgh Fringe Festival was held in 1947; it has since grown to become the world's largest arts festival. In 1947, eight theatre groups turned up uninvited to the Edinburgh International Festival, but were unable to perform at the event. Finding themselves on the 'fringe' of the event, they found alternative venues at which to perform. The Fringe Festival has continued every year and has developed into an enormous festival where amateur and unknown artists are able to perform. The festival sees many performances in unconventional locations in the city by any artist who is prepared to hire a venue for the night. In 2000, more than 650 groups performed a total of 1350 shows during the festival. Some well-known artists also appeared in 2000, including David Soul who once played Hutch in the popular TV show, 'Starsky and Hutch'.

Event Organiser

The Fringe Office, 180 High Street, Edinburgh EH1 1QS, UK
Tel: (0131) 226 5257. Fax: (0131) 220 4205.
E-mail: admin@edfringe.com
Website: www.edfringe.com

Venue

Various venues in Edinburgh city centre, including Holyrood Park, La Belle Angele, George Square Theatre, Randolph Studio and Edinburgh College of Art.

Transport

Air: Edinburgh International Airport. **Rail:** Train: Waverley Station (Edinburgh). **Road:** Car: M8 to Edinburgh (from Glasgow); A696 and A68 or A1 (from Newcastle-Upon-Tyne).

Edinburgh Military Tattoo

The *Edinburgh Military Tattoo* is a well-established, world-renowned event, attracting visitors from around the globe. The Tattoo was first performed in 1950 as the Scottish Army's contribution to the *Edinburgh International Festival.* The word 'tattoo' comes from the cry used by innkeepers in the Low Countries in the 17th and 18th centuries to signal closing time. Every year, hundreds of performers from more than 30 countries, including India, the USA, Norway, Australia and Pakistan, take part in this event, which is watched by an audience of 200,000. The Tattoo is also shown on television in around 30 countries to an annual television audience of 100 million. The event sees international musical performances, theatre and dance, as well as marching by the Army in the spectacular grounds of Edinburgh Castle. Other highlights include the sounds of the Massed Pipes and Drums, music from the Massed Military Bands, the Guards of His Majesty The King of Norway and a Highland Dance display. At the end of each day's events, a lone piper plays a haunting lament on the castle's ramparts, before all the day's performers march off the *Esplanade* to the sounds of the famous pipe melody 'The Black Bear'.

Event Organiser

Edinburgh Military Tattoo, The Tattoo Office, 32 Market Street, Edinburgh EH1 1QB, UK
Tel: (0131) 225 1188. Fax: (0131) 225 8627.
E-mail: edintattoo@edintattoo.co.uk
Website: www.edinburgh-tattoo.co.uk

Venue

Castle Esplanade, Edinburgh Castle.

Transport

Air: Edinburgh International Airport. **Rail:** Train: Waverley Station. **Road:** Car: M8 to Edinburgh (from Glasgow); A696 and A68 or A1 (from Newcastle-Upon-Tyne).

• August-September

Edinburgh International Festival

The 55th *Edinburgh International Festival* will take place in the city in 2001 and promises once again to provide its audience with impressive arts performances, ranging from theatrical productions through to opera, dance and music. Every year, this giant festival attracts visitors from all over the globe to see many of the world's greatest artists perform at this renowned festival. The first Edinburgh International Festival took place in 1947 to celebrate the end of World War II. In 2001, conductors including Donald Runnicles, William Christie, Sir Charles Mackerras and Paavo Berglund will also appear, as will orchestras, including the Leipzig Gewandhaus, the Boston Symphony Orchestra and the St Petersburg Philharmonic. In 2000, there were 182 performances from over 2500 performers, including 763 from Scotland, 418 from the USA, 122 from Hungary and 120 from the Czech Republic.

Event Organiser

Edinburgh International Festival, The Hub, Castlehill, Edinburgh EH1 2NE, UK
Tel: (0131) 473 2001 (bookings) *or* 473 2099 (administration). Fax: (0131) 473 2003.
E-mail: eif@eif.co.uk
Website: www.eif.co.uk

Venue

Various venues across Edinburgh, including Usher Hall, Festival Theatre and The Hub.

Transport

Air: Edinburgh International Airport. **Rail:** Train: Waverley or Haymarket stations. **Road:** Car: M8 to Edinburgh (from Glasgow); A696 and A68 or A1 (from Newcastle-Upon-Tyne).

Glasgow

Tourist Information

Greater Glasgow & Clyde Valley Tourist Board
11 George Street, Glasgow G2 1DY, UK
Tel: (0141) 566 4056. Fax: (0141) 204 4772.
E-mail: corporate@seeglasgow.com
Website: www.seeglasgow.com

• January

Celtic Connections

Celtic Connections is a celebration of traditional and contemporary Celtic music and culture from Scotland, Ireland and Brittany, as well as other Celtic places around the world. The event takes place across Glasgow during January. The festival first took place seven years ago and has rapidly grown to become an important international event. In 1999, over 65,000 people attended at least one event and the festival received the award of 'Best International Festival 1998/99' from the French Festival Association in Paris. In 2000, Celtic Connections' performers included Dick Gaughan, Wolfstone, Dougie MacLean and Sileas (featuring founding members Patsy Seddon and Mary McMaster) who all appeared on the opening night of the first festival. The festival also features the best names in Celtic music and literature (including the band, RunRig and the poet, Seamus Heaney and the folk musician, Liam O'Flynn). Previous performers have included Arlo Guthrie, Kathy Mattea, Carlos Nunez, La Bottine Souriante, Anuna, Phil Cunningham, Brian Kennedy, Alasdair Fraser and Skyedance. In 2000, the celebrations also included readings by literary figures in Waterstone's bookshop in Glasgow, including Edwin Morgan, poet laureate, and Christopher Brookmyre who wrote 'Quite Ugly One Morning'.

Event Organiser

Glasgow Royal Concert Hall, 2 Sauchiehall Street, Glasgow G2 3NY, UK
Tel: (0141) 353 8050 (information line) *or* 287 5511 (booking line). Fax: (0141) 353 8006.
E-mail: grch@grch.com
Website: www.grch.com

Venue

Twenty venues in Glasgow, including the Piping Centre, Old Fruitmarket, Tron, Glasgow Cathedral, St Aloysius Church, St Mary's Cathedral and the Central Hotel; many events take place in Glasgow Royal Concert Hall.

Transport

Air: Glasgow International Airport. **Rail:** Train: Glasgow Central Station. **Road:** Car: M8 (from Edinburgh); M74 and A74 (from Carlisle).

London

Tourist Information

London Tourist Board & Convention Bureau
Glen House, Stag Place, Victoria, London SW1E 5LT, UK
Tel: (020) 7932 2000. Fax: (020) 7932 0222.
E-mail: enquiries@londontouristboard.co.uk
Website: www.londontown.com

• January

London Parade

The 16th *London Parade* will take place in central London on 1 January 2002. During this giant, free party, spectacular marching bands parade through the streets, along with thousands of cheerleaders, clowns and vintage cars. The parade first took place in the city in 1987, when a few hundred performers from the USA and the UK paraded through London's streets to celebrate the New Year. The event was first called the *Lord Mayor of Westminster's Big Parade*, but was renamed the London Parade in 1994, by which time thousands of professional cheerleaders from the USA had joined the procession. Today, the parade features almost 10,000 participants from all over the world and attracts around one million spectators who line the streets of central London to watch the show. Every year, the event raises large amounts of money for charity. The parade sets off from Parliament Square at 1200 and continues for 3.5km (2.2 miles) through the streets of central London, finishing in Berkeley Square, off Piccadilly and Regent Street.

Event Organiser

London Parade, Research House, Fraser Road, Greenford, Middlesex UB6 7AQ, UK
Tel: (020) 8566 8586. Fax: (020) 8566 8494.
E-mail: tickets@londonparade.co.uk
Website: www.londonparade.co.uk

Venue

Central London, beginning in Parliament Square and finishing in Berkeley Square.

Transport

Air: London Heathrow Airport. **Rail:** Train: London Charing Cross Station. Underground: Westminster (start); Piccadilly Circus (Piccadilly or Bakerloo lines) or Green Park (Jubilee, Piccadilly or Victoria lines) (finish). **Road:** Bus: 6, 9, 11, 13, 14, 15, 19, 22, 23, 28, 91, 77A or 176 to the Strand and Piccadilly Circus areas. Car: M4 (from Bristol); M1 (from Leeds, Sheffield and Nottingham); M3 (from Southampton); M23 (from Brighton); M40 (from Oxford).

• February

Chinese New Year

Chinese New Year festivities take place every year in London's Chinatown, which is located in the Soho district of the city. The festival, which is known as *Spring Festival* in its native country, is the oldest and most important festival in China. The Chinese New Year takes place on a different date every year as the Chinese calendar is based on lunar and solar movements. A leap month is added in every couple of years, thus changing the date of the New Year, which takes place on the first day of the new moon every year. The Chinese use twelve animals to represent a twelve-year cycle, with a different animal representing each Chinese Year; 2001 is the Year of the Snake; whilst 2002 will be the Year of the Horse. In London, New Year festivities take place in Gerrard Street, between Soho and Leicester Square, and also spread into nearby *Covent Garden*. There are numerous parades during the festivities, as well as music, Chinese opera, kung fu, and lion and dragon dances. There are also many food stalls in the area selling traditional Chinese cuisine, as well as around 60 Chinese restaurants located in Soho.

Event Organiser

For more information on Chinese New Year, contact the London Tourist Board & Convention Bureau (see **Tourist Information** above).

Venue

Gerrard Street, between Leicester Square and Soho.

Transport

Air: London Heathrow Airport. **Rail:** Train: London Victoria Station. Underground: Leicester Square (Piccadilly and Northern lines) or Piccadilly Circus (Piccadilly and Bakerloo lines). **Road:** Bus: 3, 6, 9, 11, 14, 19, 24, 29, 38 or 176. Car: M4 (from Bristol); M1 (from Leeds, Sheffield and Nottingham); M3 (from Southampton); M23 (from Brighton); M40 (from Oxford).

• March-April

Daily Mail Ideal Home Show

The *Daily Mail Ideal Home Show* is a major event in the UK calendar, taking place every year in London's Earls Court. The show, which began in 1908, attracts thousands of keen homemakers every year, who are drawn to see inspirational homes from both the past and future. One of the most famous features of the show is the *House of the Future* display which sees leading designers give their impressions of the shape of things to come. Homes from previous decades are also on display and attract huge crowds of people. A key attraction in 2001 was the *London Electricity Lighthouse*, which was converted into a fantastic family home.

Event Organiser

Daily Mail Ideal Home Show, Dmg World Media, Equitable House, Lyon Road, Harrow, Middlesex HA1 2EW, UK
Tel: (020) 8515 2000. Fax: (020) 8515 2086.
E-mail: sarahlewer@uk.dmgworldmedia.com
Website: www.idealhomeshow.co.uk

Venue

Earls Court Exhibition Centre, SW5, London.

Transport

Air: London Heathrow Airport. **Rail:** Train: West Brompton Station (from Clapham Junction). Underground: Earls Court (District or Piccadilly lines) or West Brompton (District Line). **Road:** Bus: 74, 328, C1, C3, N31 or 190. Car: A4 West Cromwell Road (from both central and west London).

• April

Flora London Marathon

The *Flora London Marathon* is a 42.2km (26.2 miles) race, which first took place on 29 March 1981. Around 7750 runners took part in the first London Marathon, with approximately 6250 completing the race successfully, compared to 31,542 runners completing the race in 2001. The event takes place around the streets of central London, starting in Greenwich Park and ending in the Mall. Runners pass many major London sites, including the Cutty Sark, Canary Wharf, the Tower of London, Buckingham Palace and Big Ben. More than 30,000 competitors take part in this annual event every year, including top athletes from around the world, as well as thousands of fun runners. The majority of amateur competitors also raise money for charity and many of them take part in fancy dress. Spectators line the streets, joining in the festivities and cheering on the runners, in what has become one of London's biggest street parties.

Event Organiser

Flora London Marathon, Suite 3, Waterloo Court, 10 Theed Street, London SE1 8ST, UK
Tel: (020) 7620 4117. Fax: (020) 7620 4208.
E-mail: zoek@london-marathon.co.uk
Website: www.london-marathon.co.uk

Venue

Central London, starting in Greenwich Park and ending in the Mall.

Transport

Air: London Heathrow Airport. **Rail:** Train: Greenwich, Maze Hill or Blackheath stations (start), Charing Cross Station (finish). Docklands Light Railway: Cutty Sark or Greenwich (start) (from Bank). Underground: Charing Cross (Bakerloo or Northern lines), Green Park (Jubilee, Piccadilly or Victoria lines) or St James's Park (District or Circle lines) (finish). **Road:** Car: M25, M11, A406 towards East London, A13 and then Blackwell Tunnel (from Cambridge); M25 and A2 to Greenwich (from Canterbury); A202, A2209, A200 and A2211 (from Victoria in central London) (to the start).

• May

Chelsea Flower Show

The *Chelsea Flower Show* is one of the most famous

garden displays in Europe. Every year, visitors from all over the world flock to London to see this spectacular event which was first held in 1913. Displays range from modern sculptured displays through to wild, untamed gardens. In 2001, the biggest show garden ever designed was displayed, along with gardens based on themes, including a Japanese garden. Also new were two new floral pavilions in the showground, which provided extra space for displays. The show also has a *Lifelong Learning in the Garden* feature, explaining how gardens grow, and Royal Horticultural Society experts are on hand to offer advice about gardening to visitors.

Event Organiser

Royal Horticultural Society, 80 Vincent Square, London SW1P 2PE, UK
Tel: (020) 7649 1885. Fax: (020) 7233 9525.
E-mail: info@rhs.org.uk
Website: www.rhs.org.uk

Venue

Showgrounds at the Royal Hospital, Chelsea.

Transport

Air: London Heathrow Airport. **Rail:** Train: Victoria Station. Underground: Sloane Square (District or Circle lines). **Road:** Bus: 11, 19, 22, 137, 211, 239 or C1. Car: M4 (from Reading and Bristol); M3 (from Southampton).

• June

Queen's Birthday Parade – Trooping the Colour

Trooping the Colour takes place every year in central London to celebrate the Queen's birthday. The ceremony takes place on *Horse Guards Parade* in Whitehall and is watched by thousands of spectators, as well as invited guests and members of the Royal Family. Queen Elizabeth II was actually born on 21 April, although her birthday is officially celebrated in summer. Troops from the Household Division parade down the ranks, escorting regimental colour, before giving the Queen a royal salute at *Buckingham Palace.* A musical 'troop' is also performed, prior to the Queen carrying out an inspection of the troops. The word 'trooping' can be dated back to the origins of the ceremony in the early 18th century, when the colours of the battalion were carried (or trooped) down the ranks on parade to the soldiers. The parade has been a celebration of the Sovereign's official birthday since 1748, although the Sovereign has officially only taken part in the ceremony since the time of Edward VII's reign.

Event Organiser

Household Divisions Headquarters, Horse Guards, Whitehall, London SW1A 2AX, UK
Tel: (020) 7414 2479. Fax: (020) 7414 2259.
Website: www.royal.gov.uk/today/trooping

Venue

Horse Guards Parade, London SW1.

Transport

Air: London Heathrow Airport. **Rail:** Train: London Charing Cross Station. Underground: Charing Cross (Bakerloo or Northern lines) or Westminster (District, Circle or Jubilee lines). **Road:** Car: M4 (from Bristol); M1 (from Leeds, Sheffield and Nottingham); M3 (from Southampton); M23 (from Brighton); M40 (from Oxford).

• June-July

Wimbledon Championships

The *Wimbledon Championships* is an internationally-renowned tennis tournament, which attracts leading tennis professionals from around the world. The first *Lawn Tennis Championships* was held at The All England Croquet and Lawn Tennis Club in 1877, with the introduction of the Men's Singles which was won by Englishman Spencer Gore. The first Ladies' Singles event was held in 1884 and was won by Englishwoman Maud Watson; the Men's Doubles was also started in the same year. Every year the event is attended by thousands of spectators, as well as by members of the British Royal Family. Traditionally the event is plagued by rain, with play called off due to the weather; it is also traditional to eat strawberries and drink champagne. The winner of the championships in 2001 was the Croatian, Goran Ivanisevic, who defeated the Australian, Pat Rafter, whilst in the Ladies' Singles, the American, Venus Williams, beat Belgian player, Justine Henin. The youngest man to win the championships was Boris Becker of Germany in 1985, who at 17 was also the first German to win the title. The youngest female to win the title was Martina Hingis of Switzerland, who was just 15 years old when she won the Ladies' Singles event in 1996.

Event Organiser

The All England Lawn Tennis & Croquet Club, Church Road, Wimbledon, London SW19 5AE, UK
Tel: (020) 8944 1066. Fax: (020) 8947 8752.
E-mail: internet@aeltc.com
Website: www.wimbledon.org

Venue

All England Lawn Tennis & Croquet Club Grounds, Wimbledon, SW19.

Transport

Air: London Heathrow Airport. **Rail:** Train: Wimbledon Station (from Waterloo Station). Underground: Southfields (District Line). **Road:** Bus: Shuttle buses from Southfields Station, Victoria Station and Marble Arch. Car: A3 and A219 (from Kingston-Upon-Thames); A232, A217 and A219 (from Croydon).

• August

Western Union Notting Hill Carnival

The *Western Union Notting Hill Carnival* takes place

every year in West London. The first Notting Hill Carnival took place in 1964, when Caribbean immigrants introduced the Carnival to London to unite the inhabitants of the area, which had suffered racial tensions. The event has grown from its origins as a small procession of people in costume carrying steel drums to an enormous multicultural festival which is attended by more than two million people every year. There are five disciplines to the carnival; these are Mas, Steelband, Calypso, Soca and static sound systems. There is a procession of costumes, soca and steel bands along a 4.8km (3 miles) route and 40 licensed static sound systems, playing different types of music, including jazz, soul, funk and reggae. Hundreds of street stalls sell food from around the globe, as well as numerous arts and crafts. There are two live stages, featuring local bands and international artists, which have in the past included Eddie Grant, Jamiroquai, Wyclef Jean, Burning Spear and Finley Quaye. The motto of the carnival is 'Every Spectator is a participant – Carnival is for all who dare to participate'.

Event Organiser

The Notting Hill Carnival Trust, 332 Ladbroke Grove, London W10 5AH, UK
Tel: (020) 8964 0544. Fax: (020) 8964 0545.
E-mail: harwoodandco@btinternet.com

Venue

Streets around Ladbroke Grove and Notting Hill.

Transport

Air: London Heathrow Airport. **Rail:** Train: London Victoria Station. Underground: Westbourne Park (Hammersmith & City Line), Notting Hill Gate (Central, District or Circle lines) or Latimer Road (Hammersmith & City Line). Ladbroke Grove (Hammersmith & City Line) is usually closed during the weekend and other underground stations close if they become overcrowded. **Road:** Bus: 7, 12, 18, 23, 27, 28, 31, 36, 52, 70, 94, 295, 316 or 328. Road: A40 (from central London). Visitors are, however, advised to leave their car at home as parking is impossible in the vicinity of the carnival.

• November

Lord Mayor's Show

The *Lord Mayor's Show* takes place in the City of London every year when the Lord Mayor of London parades through the streets as a show of allegiance to the Crown. The position of Lord Mayor of London was created by King John in 1215, as a way of showing thanks to the City for its support. The City is an area around the Bank of England covering 1.6 sq km (one sq mile) which was developed by the Romans and is today the financial heart of the capital. The Lord Mayor (not to be confused with the new title Mayor of London) was originally selected by the people of London in 1215, making this one of the first elected posts in the world. Every year the Lord Mayor must swear loyalty to the Crown in person; the show is a celebration which evolved from his journey. 2001 will be the 675th full show, and the 785th time a Mayor has been presented to the Crown. On the day of the show, the procession leaves the Guildhall at 1105, walking past key London attractions and financial buildings around the city, including St Paul's Cathedral and the Bank of England. The Lord Mayor himself joins the procession at Mansion House at 1155. The parade arrives at the Royal Courts of Justice at 1225, where the Lord Mayor must swear allegiance to the Crown. At 1325 they set off on the return journey, arriving back at Mansion House at 1430. At 1700, fireworks are launched by the Lord Mayor over the River Thames, bringing a spectacular end to the day's festivities. In 2000, the show involved over 6500 participants, 67 floats from organisations across the country, 200 horses, 20 bands and 20 carriages, making a 4km (2.5 miles) procession of 126 participating groups.

Event Organiser

Lord Mayor's Show, PO Box 270, Guildhall, London EC2P 2EJ, UK
Tel: (020) 7332 1456. Fax: (020) 7332 3540.
E-mail: pageantmaster@lord-mayors-show.org.uk
Website: www.lordmayorsshow.org

Venue

Central London parade route between Mansion House and Aldwych.

Transport

Air: London Heathrow Airport or London City Airport. **Rail:** Train: London Blackfriars or London Bridge stations. Underground: St Paul's (Central Line), Mansion House (District or Circle lines), Bank (Central, District, Circle or Northern lines) or Blackfriars (District or Circles lines). **Road:** Car: M4 (from Bristol); M1 (from Leeds, Sheffield and Nottingham); M3 (from Southampton); M23 (from Brighton); M40 (from Oxford).

United States of America

Atlanta

Tourist Information

Atlanta Convention & Visitors Bureau
Suite 100, 233 Peachtree Street NE, Atlanta, GA 30303, USA
Tel: (404) 521 6600. Fax: (404) 577 3293.
E-mail: acvb@acvb.com
Website: www.acvb.com

• May

Atlanta Jazz Festival

Atlanta Jazz Festival is a ten-day music event featuring many of the world's great jazz legends, as well as rising international stars. The festival, which has been running for over 23 years and is the largest free jazz festival in the USA, sees around 100 entertainers perform every year during the *Free Weekend Concert Series* in Piedmont Park. There are also concerts in various other parks across Atlanta, as well as night performances in local bars and clubs. A wide selection of food is on sale in Piedmont Park and a large arts and crafts market is held during the festival. In 2001, during the 24th festival, highlights included the singer Dee Dee Bridgewater, the pianist Bob James and the trumpet player Terence Blanchard.

Event Organiser

Atlanta Jazz Festival, City Hall East, Fifth Floor, 675 Ponce de Leon Avenue, Atlanta, GA 30308, USA
Tel: (404) 817 6851.
E-mail: karen@fountainheadadv.com
Website: www.atlantafestivals.com

Venue

Piedmont Park and various other venues in Atlanta.

Transport

Air: Hartsfield Atlanta International Airport. **Rail:** Train: Brookwood Station. **Road:** Car: I-20 (from Birmingham, Dallas, Augusta and Columbia); I-75 (from Florida and Michigan); I-85 (from Montgomery, Charlotte and Virginia).

Boston

Tourist Information

Greater Boston Convention & Visitors Bureau
2 Copley Place, Suite 105, Boston, MA 02116, USA
Tel: (617) 536 4100. Fax: (617) 424 7664.
E-mail: visitus@bostonusa.com
Website: www.bostonusa.com

• April

Boston Marathon

The *Boston Marathon* is the world's oldest annually contested marathon and was first held in 1897 by the Boston Athletic Association, who were inspired by the revival of the marathon event at the 1896 Olympic Games in Athens. The winner of the 1897 marathon was John J McDermott of New York, who completed the 39.4-kilometre (24.5-mile) route from Boston's Irvington Oval to Metcalf's Mill in Ashland in 2 hours, 55 minutes and 10 seconds to earn his place in marathon history. The standard distance of 42.2km (26 miles 385 yards) for a marathon event was set in 1924, when the British Olympic Committee decided that the route for the London Games should lead from Windsor Castle to the royal box in the London Olympic Stadium. Despite the increased distance, the race has speeded up since 1897 and Korean Lee Bong-Ju won the 105th marathon in 2001, which attracted 15,606 runners, in 2 hours, 9 minutes and 43 seconds. Kenyan Catherine Ndereba won the women's race in 2 hours, 23 minutes and 53 seconds. The men's wheelchair marathon was won by Ernst Van Dyk from South Africa, with Switzerland's Louise Sauvage the champion in the women's event. The Boston Marathon is held on Patriot's Day, the third Monday in April and a Massachusetts public holiday, which gives the event a party atmosphere. The liveliest places with the best views for spectators are at Boston College or Beacon Street before the race ends at Boylston Street.

Event Organiser

Boston Athletic Association, 1 Ash Street, Hopkinton, MA 01748, USA
Tel: (508) 435 6905. Fax: (508) 435 6590.
E-mail: mile27@baa.org
Website: www.bostonmarathon.org

Venue

The marathon starts at Irvington Oval and finishes at Metcalf's Mill, Ashland passing through the streets of central Boston.

Transport

Air: Boston Logan International Airport. **Rail:** Train: South or Back Bay stations. Underground: Boston College or Cleveland Circle. **Road:** Car: I-90 Massachusetts Turnpike (from Chicago, Seattle, Cleveland, New York City and Philadelphia); I-93 (from north Massachusetts and New Hampshire).

• December

Boston Tea Party Re-enactment

On the night of 16 December 1773, a group of American patriots, called the Sons of Freedom, disguised themselves as Mohawk Indians and boarded three tea clippers – Eleanor, the Dartmouth and the Beaver – belonging to the ailing British East India Company. They then threw the cargo into the waters of Boston Harbour in protest at the taxes levied upon tea and other goods by the British colonists and the perceived monopoly granted to the East India Company by the British Parliament. Every year, visitors to Boston can see a re-enactment, performed by the Massachusetts Council of Minutemen and Militia, of what is generally considered to be the single most important event leading up to the American Revolution. The events start with a recreation of the town meeting in the city's South Meeting House where the Tea Party was planned. From there, the band of actors, accompanied by cheers from the assembled crowd, proceed down Congress Street to Beaver II, the replica of one of the original East India Company ships that now serves as a permanent Tea Party Museum, where they ceremonially throw tea chests into the water.

Event Organiser

Boston Tea Party Ship and Museum, 2 Copley Place, Suite 105, Boston, MA 02116, USA
Tel: (617) 338 1773. Fax: (617) 338 1974.

E-mail: teapartyship@historictours.com
Website: www.bostonteapartyship.com

Venue

Various locations in central Boston, focusing on the South Meeting House and Boston Tea Party Ship.

Transport

Air: Boston Logan International Airport. **Rail:** Train: South or Back Bay stations. Underground: South Station. **Road:** Car: I-90 Massachusetts Turnpike (from Chicago, Seattle, Cleveland, New York City and Philadelphia); I-93 (from north Massachusetts and New Hampshire).

Chicago

Tourist Information

Chicago Office of Tourism
78 East Washington Boulevard, Chicago IL 60602, USA
Tel: (312) 744 2400 *or* (0800) 487 2446.
Fax: (312) 744 2359.
E-mail: tourism@cityofchicago.org
Website: www.ci.chi.il.us/culturalaffairs/tourism

• March

St Patrick's Day Parade

Chicago is well known for its parades, and the city's large Irish population means that the *St Patrick's Day Parade* is one of the biggest and the best. The parade, which features 50 floats decorated with huge shamrocks and leprechauns, over 30 bands, some 2000 Irish step dancers in traditional costume and even Irish dog and horse breeds, begins at 1200 at Balbo Drive and ends at Monroe Street at around 1700. Irish celebrities (who included author Maeve Binchy and Miss Ireland, Yvonne Ellard in 2001) can also be seen in the parade. Other activities, which last well into the evening, include Celtic dancing in churches, and pipe bands by the Chicago River, which in 2001 was dyed green in honour of the celebrations.

Event Organiser

St Patrick's Day Parade Committee, 1340 West Washington Boulevard, Chicago IL 60607, USA
Tel: (312) 942 9188. Fax: (312) 421 1010.
E-mail: chicagostpatsparade@worldnet.att.net
Website: www.chicagostpatsparade.com

Venue

Balbo Drive to Monroe Street.

Transport

Air: Chicago O'Hare International Airport or Midway Airport (domestic flights). **Rail:** Train: Chicago Union Station. Underground: Balbo. **Road:** Car: I-80 (from San Francisco or New York); I-90 (from Seattle or Indianapolis); I-55 (from St Louis or New Orleans). Entrance to the car park is on Jackson Boulevard.

• June-August

Grant Park Music Festival

Grant Park Music Festival was founded by the Chicago Park District in 1935. The concept grew from a desire to allow Chicagoans of all backgrounds to enjoy live classical music and for professional live musicians, who were suffering due to the rise in popularity of recorded music, to gain secure employment. Today, the festival is the only free, municipally funded, outdoor classical music festival in the USA, and continues to offer an excellent opportunity to enjoy symphonic concerts in a beautiful open-air setting in the heart of the 'Windy City'. Over 40 performances are held for two months each year, mainly at the Petrillo Music Shell (named after James C Petrillo, the former president of the Chicago Federation of Musicians who convinced the park authorities to hold the event on an annual basis) on the Lake Michigan side of Grant Park, but also in churches and community centres around Chicago. The Grant Park Orchestra and Chorus and Chicago Children's Choir perform a variety of concerts most Wednesdays and Sundays, including opera, folk music, classical music made popular by films, songs from musicals and jazz. Composers featured include Beethoven, Strauss, Rachmaninoff, Sibelius, Rodrigo, Verdi and Britten.

Event Organiser

Chicago Park District Press Office, 425 East McFetridge Drive, Two East, Chicago IL 60605, USA
Tel: (312) 747 2623. Fax: (312) 747 6064.
Website: www.grantparkmusicfestival.com

Venue

Grant Park.

Transport

Air: Chicago O'Hare International Airport or Midway Airport (domestic flights). **Rail:** Train: Chicago Union Station. Underground: Jackson. **Road:** Car: I-80 (from San Francisco or New York); I-90 (from Seattle or Indianapolis); I-55 (from St Louis or New Orleans). Entrance to the car park is on Jackson Boulevard.

Denver

Tourist Information

Denver Metro Convention & Visitors Bureau
1555 California Street, Suite 300, Denver, CO 80202, USA
Tel: (303) 892 1112 *or* (800) 233 6837 (toll free USA and Canada only). Fax: (303) 892 1636.
E-mail: corr@dmcvb.org
Website: www.denver.org

• January

National Western Stock Show & Rodeo

Denver's *National Western Stock Show & Rodeo* attracts over 400,000 cowboys every year and is the largest festival in Colorado. It was first held in 1907 in a tent; it has since grown, however, to become a huge annual event which attracted more than 630,000 visitors in 2000. The show, which will be held for the 96th time in 2002, aims to preserve the western lifestyle through a giant agricultural festival, which includes livestock displays and an annual horse show. Every year, there are events for all the family, including the *Indoor Rodeo of the Year* event and *The Super Bowl of Cattle Shows*, when cattle are judged to win the *National Western Grand Champion* prize.

Event Organiser

National Western Stock Show, 4655 Humboldt Street, Denver, CO 80216, USA
Tel: (303) 297 1166. Fax: (303) 292 1708.
E-mail: nwss@nationalwestern.com
Website: www.nationalwestern.com

Venue

National Western Complex, off I-25 and I-70.

Transport

Air: Denver International Airport. **Rail:** Train: Union Station. **Road:** Car: I-25 (from Billings and El Paso); I-70 to Brighton Boulevard (exit 275), then north to the venue (from Pittsburgh and St George).

Memphis

Tourist Information

Memphis Convention & Visitors Bureau
47 Union Avenue, Memphis, TN 38103, USA
Tel: (901) 543 5300. Fax: (901) 543 5335.
E-mail: vic1@mcvb.org
Website: www.memphistravel.com

• August

Elvis Week

Elvis Week, which takes place in Memphis every August, is a celebration of the music and life of the late Elvis Presley. Every year, fans of the singing legend gather in Memphis to take part in this major event and pay homage to the star. During the week-long festival, there are many concerts and individual events around Memphis. There are also events at Elvis's former home, *Graceland*, the highlight of which is the *Candlelight Vigil* on 15 August, the anniversary of his death in 1977, where fans have the chance to pay their respects to 'The King'.

Event Organiser

Elvis Presley Enterprises Inc, PO Box 16508, 3734 Elvis Presley Boulevard, Memphis, TN 38186, USA
Tel: (901) 332 3322 *or* (800) 238 2000 (toll free USA and Canada only). Website: www.elvis-presley.com

Venue

The main festivities take place at Graceland, the former home of Elvis.

Transport

Air: New Orleans International Airport. **Rail:** Train: Memphis Central Station. **Road:** Bus: A free shuttle bus departs from Elvis Presley's Memphis (a downtown restaurant) daily from 1130 onwards. Car: I-55 (exit 5-B) (from Memphis city centre).

New Orleans

Tourist Information

New Orleans Metropolitan Convention & Visitors Bureau Inc
1520 Sugar Bowl Drive, New Orleans, LA 70112, USA
Tel: (504) 566 5011. Fax: (504) 566 5021.
Website: www.neworleanscvb.com

• February

Mardi Gras

Mardi Gras, which was first held in New Orleans in 1837, is today a giant celebration, with elaborately decorated floats, marching bands, parades, parties and lots of live music. The day itself, Mardi Gras (or *Fat Tuesday*), fell on Tuesday 27 February in 2001; it takes place on a different date each year, although it always ends on Mardi Gras day (46 days before Easter) with enormous parades through the streets. Every year, hundreds of thousands of visitors descend upon the city to join in the festivities, which also include private masked balls. Many partygoers dress up in fancy dress costumes during Mardi Gras, often wearing the official festival colours – purple, green and gold. These colours, which represent justice, faith and power respectively, were chosen by the King of the Carnival (known as Rex today) in 1872. This started a carnival tradition and every year a King and Queen is chosen to ride on the largest float, dressed in flamboyant costumes.

Event Organiser

For more information on Mardi Gras, contact New Orleans Metropolitan Convention & Visitors Bureau Inc (see **Tourist Information** above).

Venue

New Orleans Convention Centre and various venues across the city.

Transport

Air: New Orleans International Airport. **Rail:** Train: New Orleans Station. **Road:** Coach: Greyhound buses arrive at the Union Passenger Terminal (from Baton Rouge, Lafayette, Memphis and Mobile). Car: I-10 (from Houston, Los Angeles, Mobile and Jacksonville); I-55 (from Memphis, St Louis and Chicago); I-59 (from Birmingham and Chattanooga).

New York

Tourist Information

NYC & Company
810 Seventh Avenue, between 52nd and 53nd Streets, New York NY 10019, USA
Tel: (212) 484 1222. Fax: (212) 246 6310.
Website: www.nycvisit.com

• November

Macy's Thanksgiving Day Parade

Macy's Thanksgiving Day Parade is one of the Big Apple's most dynamic and colourful events. Its origins can be traced back to the 1920s when the city's European immigrant population decided to celebrate the American *Thanksgiving Day* holiday (which celebrates the harvest) with the sort of festivities they had known in their homelands. Hundreds of immigrant workers marched from 145 Street to 34th Street in costume, accompanied by floats, live animals on loan from Central Park Zoo and music bands. The parade attracted over 250,000 spectators and the Thanksgiving Day Parade quickly became a New York institution. Trademark giant balloons of cartoon characters were introduced for the first time in 1927, with Felix the Cat. The only interruption to the tradition came during World War II, but the festivities were soon revived and are now as popular as ever, with millions of people lining the streets from 0900-1200 to see the balloons, floats, marching bands and clowns and enjoy the holiday atmosphere.

Event Organiser

For more information on Macy's Thanksgiving Day Parade, contact NYC and Company (see **Tourist Information** above).

Venue

West 77th Street and Central Park West to Macy's Department Store, 34th Street and 6th Avenue.

Transport

Air: New York La Guardia International Airport or New York John F Kennedy International Airport. **Rail:** Train: Grand Central Station. Underground: West 81st Street (for West 77th Street) or 34th Street (for Macy's). **Road:** Bus: M10 (to West 77th Street). Coach: Port Authority Bus Terminal. Car: I-95 (from Boston, Washington DC, Newark, Providence, Philadelphia, Baltimore, Richmond or Miami); I-80 (from San Francisco, Salt Lake City, Iowa City, Cleveland, Chicago or Rutherford).

Philadelphia

Tourist Information

Philadelphia Visitors Center
Love Park, 1515 Market Street, Philadelphia, PA 19103, USA
Tel: (215) 636 1666.
E-mail: ccvg@phillyvisitor.com
Website: www.phillyvisitor.com

• January

Mummers Parade

Philadelphias's extravagant *Mummers Parade* heralds the New Year and, like *Macy's Thanksgiving Day Parade* in New York, can trace its origins back to customs and traditions brought over from Europe by the city's immigrant workers. Mummers plays were performed at Christmas time by troupes of actors in towns and villages in Medieval England and told the story of a dead warrior brought back to life by a doctor, loosely based on the story of St George and the Dragon. 'Momerie' was also a popular form of winter entertainment in Europe from the 13th to the 16th century, where groups of masked performers would enter houses to dance or play dice, and the German word for mask, 'Mumme' is thought to derive from this practice. The earliest known Philadelphia mummers band was the Chain Gang, formed in the 1840s and other bands soon formed in other parts of the city. In 1876 these bands of mummers staged their own individual parades, and marched to *Independence Hall* in the heart of the city; it was not until 1901, however, that the first official Mummers Parade was organised. Today's Parade lasts for 11 hours, and the city's various troupes of mummers start their lively march down Market Street or Broad Street at around 0800. There are four divisions: 'Comics' (clowns who impersonate public figures); 'Fancies' (fancy dress costumes developed around a given theme); 'String Bands' (combining fancy dress and music); and 'Fancy Brigades' (mummer troupes who give indoor performances at City Hall and Philadelphia Convention Center). There are prizes for the best costumes and music, awarded by a panel of judges, guaranteeing high standards and plenty of imagination.

Event Organiser

For more information on the Mummers Parade, contact the Philadelphia Visitors Center (see **Tourist Information** above).

Venue

Fifth & Market Street to City Hall.

Transport

Air: Philadelphia International Airport. **Rail:** Train: 30th Street Station. Underground: 5th & Market Street, 15th Street or City Hall. **Road:** Bus: 76. Coach: Greyhound Terminal. Car: I-95 (from New York, Boston or Washington DC); I-76 (from the east or the west); US Hwy-30 (from the north).

• July

Independence Day

Philadelphia, founded by Quaker William Penn in 1682, is regarded as the birthplace of the United States. It was here that the Declaration of Independence was signed in 1776 and the city also served as the country's first capital from 1790-1800. It is therefore fitting that the city's *Independence Day* celebrations should be some of the most impressive and significant in the USA, starting with the presentation of the Liberty Medal in *Independence Hall* where the Declaration was first adopted on 4 July 1776 (but not signed until 8 July). The Liberty Medal is presented to foreign or US citizens who have advanced the cause of freedom; past recipients include Polish trade unionist, Solidarity leader and former president Lech Walesa and former South African president and freedom fighter Nelson Mandela. The commemoration of the importance of this day in American history continues, when at 1300 a group of descendants of the signatories of the Declaration attend a simple ceremony at the Liberty Bell. After this, the fun begins, in the form of parades, concerts and picnics, as Philadelphia celebrates its place in American history and indulges in proud displays of patriotism. A fireworks display over the Delaware River lights up the evening sky to provide a magnificent finale.

Event Organiser

For more information on Independence Day, contact the Philadelphia Visitors Center (see **Tourist Information** above).

Venue

Independence Hall and various locations across Philadelphia.

Transport

Air: Philadelphia International Airport. **Rail:** Train: 30th Street Station. Underground: Fifth Street. **Road:** Coach: Greyhound Terminal. Car: I-95 (from New York, Boston or Washington DC); I-76 (from the east or the west); US Hwy-30 (from the north).

Index

Indexer's Note: A term in **bold** indicates that a main entry is given. (E) after a country or city denotes an entry in the Events section.

A

B

C

D

E

F

H

M

Q

R

S

T

U

V

W

X

Y

Z